INTERNATIONAL MANAGEMENT

A Cultural Approach

INTERNATIONAL MANAGEMENT

A Cultural Approach

CARL RODRIGUES

Montclair State University

WEST PUBLISHING COMPANY

MINNEAPOLIS/ST. PAUL   NEW YORK   LOS ANGELES   SAN FRANCISCO

Production Credits
Copyeditor: Sheryl Rose
Text Designer: Rebecca Lemna
Artwork: Precision Graphics
Part and Chapter Opener Illustration: Opusculum
Geographicum, from The Bettman Archive
Composition: Carlisle Communications
Indexer: Teresa Casey
Cover Designer: Sara Day
Cover Image: Colored Globe Abstract, by Walter Bibikow,
from the Image Bank.

WEST'S COMMITMENT TO THE ENVIRONMENT
In 1906, West Publishing Company began recycling materials left over from the production
of books. This began a tradition of efficient and responsible use of resources. Today, 100%
of our legal bound volumes are printed on acid-free, recycled paper consisting of 50% new
paper pulp and 50% paper that has undergone a de-inking process. We also use vegetable-
based inks to print all of our books. West recycles nearly 22,650,000 pounds of scrap paper
annually—the equivalent of 187,500 trees. Since the 1960s, West has devised ways to capture and recycle waste inks, solvents, oils, and vapors created in the printing process. We
also recycle plastics of all kinds, wood, glass, corrugated cardboard, and batteries, and have
eliminated the use of polystyrene book packaging. We at West are proud of the longevity and
the scope of our commitment to the environment.

West pocket parts and advance sheets are printed on recyclable paper and can be collected and recycled with newspapers. Staples do not have to be removed. Bound volumes can
be recycled after removing the cover.

Production, Prepress, Printing and Binding by West Publishing Company.

TEXT IS PRINTED ON 10% POST
CONSUMER RECYCLED PAPER

Printed with Printwise ∞
Environmentally Advanced Water Washable Ink

British Library Cataloguing-in-Publication Data. A catalogue
record for this book is available from the British Library.

Library of Congress Cataloging in Publication Data

Rodrigues, Carl Alberto.
    International management : a cultural approach / Carl Alberto
Rodrigues.
        p.   cm.
    Includes index.
    ISBN 0-314-06741-8 (hardcover : alk. paper)
    1. International business enterprises--Management--Social aspects.
2. Strategic planning--Social aspects.   3. Intercultural
communication.   I. Title.
HD62.4.R645   996   95-42063
658'.049--dc20   CIP

03 02 01 00 99 98 97 96   8 7 6 5 4 3 2 1 0

To Nailin Bu

CONTENTS IN BRIEF

CONTENTS

7   EFFECTIVE INTERNATIONAL HUMAN RESOURCE MANAGEMENT 217

Part   Five

CROSS-CULTURAL COMMUNICATION AND NEGOTIATIONS   265

8   CROSS-CULTURAL COMMUNICATION   267

9   CROSS-CULTURAL BUSINESS PRACTICES AND NEGOTIATIONS   301

Part Ten
INTEGRATIVE CASES

PREFACE

TO THE STUDENT

Text Objective

The purpose of *International Management: A Cultural Approach* is to teach, in a comprehensive, "user friendly" style, the managerial process (planning, organizing, staffing, coordinating, and controlling) in a global context to upper undergraduate and MBA students who will take a course on international management. Ideally, students who enroll in this course will have completed a generic management course, such as Introduction to Management, or Principles of Management, or Management Process, or Organizational Behavior.

In the past, in some nations, the United States for example, most business enterprises were able to maintain a steady growth rate or at least survive in their home-country market. However, since costs have steadily increased in those nations and foreign competitors with lower costs have rapidly emerged, many of those businesses lost that market stability and have been or are now being forced to compete in the international market arena. And, as technologies continue to transfer across countries, businesses in more and more nations are becoming active and competitive participants in the global economy. These developments will continue to generate not only new global competitors, but new business opportunities in foreign markets as well. This means that more and more firms will have to, or choose to, become involved in international business. It also means that more and more companies will need managers with the ability to apply the managerial process across countries and cultures with differing characteristics. A good starting point toward the development of such managers is at the college/university level (and even at the pre-college level). Thus, there is a need for a college/university text of this nature. This text was written because such a book is scarce.

Text Organization

The text describes how varying national cultures affect the application of the managerial process. For example:

◆ Individuals in some cultures commit to plans more readily than individuals in others.

- Strategies are affected by the varying cross-cultural preference for products and services and marketing techniques.
- People in some cultures require more organizational structure than people in others.
- Executives sent abroad to manage a firm's foreign subsidiary adapt more readily in some cultures than in others. And many executives have great difficulty adapting in any foreign culture.
- Individuals in some cultures want to participate more in the decision-making process and have a lower tolerance for authoritarian managers than individuals in other cultures.
- The business practices and negotiation styles that work in one culture usually do not succeed in another culture.
- Most nations have their own unique language, both verbal and nonverbal, which affects the application of the communication process across cultures.
- Employee motivation and work values vary from country to country. Thus, the motivational technique that works at home does not necessarily work in a foreign culture.
- Managers in some cultures want more control over an international corporation's local subsidiary than managers in other cultures.
- The practice of business ethics is affected by the country's culture, as is a corporation's social responsibility.

Chapters 1 and 2 give an overview of how culture and other country factors, such as the legal, political/government, economic, and technological systems, affect the managerial process. Chapters 3 and 4 discuss strategies for internationalizing business operations. Chapter 5 presents various international organizational structures. Chapters 6 and 7 discuss options for staffing international operations and training and developing global managers. Chapters 8 and 9 discuss cross-cultural communication, business practices and negotiations. Chapters 10 and 11 discuss cross-cultural decision making, leadership, and motivation. Chapter 12 discusses controlling global organizations. Chapter 13 discusses cross-cultural business ethics and corporate social responsibility. And Chapter 14 presents some of the managerial challenges executives may face in the future in managing global business enterprises, especially the difficulties of applying total quality management (TQM) across cultures.

TO THE INSTRUCTOR

Text Flexibility

Some of the chapters in *International Management: A Cross-Cultural Approach* can be adapted to an instructor's preference for sequencing of topics. For example, some instructors may prefer to cover certain topics, such as cross-cultural business ethics and corporate social responsibility (Chapter 13), or cross-cultural human resources management (Chapters 6 and 7) earlier in the course. Some instructors may prefer to cover international organizational structures (Chapter 5) and international controls (Chapter 12) sequentially. And some instructors may see fit to cover parts of chapters out of sequence.

Pedagogy

The text provides the following pedagogy features.

Practical Chapter Opening Quotes

Each chapter begins with a practical international management opening quote intended to whet students' appetite for the material contained in the chapter.

Objectives of the Chapter

After the practical opening quote, all chapters present a brief background of the substance of the chapter and its objectives.

Practical Perspectives and Anecdotes

All chapters contain numerous practical perspectives inserted in toned form. (One practical perspective in Chapter 7 and two in Chapter 9 are long, and are thus presented as appendices at the end of the chapter.) The chapters also contain short practical anecdotes throughout the body. The aim of these practical perspectives and anecdotes is to help students understand the theoretical aspects of the chapter.

Figures, Tables, and Graphs

To make reading the chapters more interesting, many of the processes, concepts, and theories are presented in figure or table or graphic form. For classroom discussion, these can generally be displayed via overhead transparencies (or via some other more advanced means).

Key Terms, Questions and Exercises, Assignment, and Case Studies

At the end of each chapter there is a set of key terms, questions and exercises, an assignment, and case studies. All of these tie to the body of the chapter, and help students develop an integrative understanding of the essence of the chapter.

Textbook Integrative Cases

Seven textbook integrative cases are presented after the final chapter (Chapter 14). These are to be assigned just before the end of the semester, after students have completed the key terms, questions and exercises, assignment, and case studies in all chapters.

Glossary, Name and Subject Index

A glossary section and a name and subject index is contained at the end of the text.

The Supplement Package For Instructors

An *Instructor's Manual and Text Bank* provides lecture assistance. The manual includes the purpose of each chapter, teaching notes, the answers to the questions and exercises and to the chapter integrative cases. It also includes the purpose of the seven text integrative cases, how they should be used, the questions which should be posed to students, and the answers. The Test Bank part of the manual includes multiple-choice, true-false, and suggested essay questions, and the answers.

Acknowledgments

Sheila A. Adams
University of North Carolina at Wilmington

Douglas Allen
University of Denver

Richard Baldwin
Cedarville College

B. R. Baliga
Wake Forest University

Charles Byles
Virginia Commonwealth University

Warnock Davies
Golden Gate University

Raffaele DeVito
Emporia State University

Richard E. Dutton
University of South Florida

David Flynn
Hofstra University

George Gore
University of Cincinnati

Sara L. Keck
Pace University

Franz T. Lohrke
Louisiana State University

Robert C. Losik
New Hampshire College

Ray Montagno
Ball State University

Francine Newth
Providence College

Steven K. Paulson
University of North Florida

Joseph A. Petrick
Wright State University

S. Benjamin Prasad
Central Michigan University

Abdul Rasheed
University of Texas at Arlington

John A. C. Stanbury
Indiana University at Kokomo

Rajib N. Sanyal
Trenton State College

Gregory K. Stephens
Texas Christian University

C. Richard Scott
Metropolitan State College of Denver

Arthur Whatley
New Mexico State University

A deep debt of gratitude is owed to the reviewers for their expert assistance. Each comment and suggestion was thoroughly evaluated and served to improve the final product. To each of the above reviewers, I give my sincerest thanks.

I especially wish to thank Nailin Bu, my colleague and friend at Queen's University, Canada, for providing me numerous materials which were very useful in the development of the text, as well as for her willingness to help whenever I needed it. I also wish to thank Sharon Adams Poore, editor at West Publishing Company, for her belief in this project and her contribution of many ideas which helped improve the text, and especially for the extraordinary skillful way she managed this project. My thanks also go to Brad Smith, the initial editor, for his belief in this project. Many thanks also go to Paul O'Neill who put all the pieces of the puzzle together and produced the book on schedule, to Sheryl Rose for her superb copyediting, and to Carol Yanisch for her expert marketing of the book. Finally, I wish to thank the entire team at West Publishing Company for a job well done.

I

INTRODUCTION TO INTERNATIONAL MANAGEMENT

The term *management* is defined in many Western, especially U.S., textbooks as the process of completing activities efficiently with and through other individuals. The process consists of the functions or main activities engaged in by managers, usually labeled planning, organizing, staffing, coordinating (leading and motivating), and controlling. The management process is affected by the organization's home country environment, which includes the shareholders, creditors, customers, employees, government, and community, as well as technological, demographic, and geographic factors. *International management* is applied by managers of enterprises that attain their goals and objectives across unique multicultural, multinational boundaries. These business enterprises are generally referred to as international corporations, multinational corporations (MNCs), or global corporations—these are discussed in Chapter 1. This means that the process is affected by the environment where the organization is based, as well as by the unique culture and other distinct environmental factors (for example, a country's legal and political systems) existing in the country or countries where it conducts its business activities. Chapter 1 discusses the impact of culture on the managerial process, and Chapter 2 describes other factors that have an impact on international management.

Chapter One

The International Management Process: *An Overview*

> *"Most people think that culture is manners, food, dress, arts, and crafts," says Clifford Clarke, president of IRI International, a Redwood City, California, consulting company. "They don't realize that how you motivate a guy is culturally determined. Every managerial task is culturally determined."*[1]

Objectives of the Chapter

Since the environment differs across countries, the managerial approach that works in one country does not necessarily work in another. This suggests that, to manage effectively across cultures, managers require skills beyond those required to manage in the home country. For example, managers would know that in the U.S. it is the individual that counts. In Japan, it is the group. Things get done not by nonconforming lone rangers, but by group consensus. The consensus is possible only through cultivation of relationships. Relationships help define the essence of Japanese society, including the conduct of business. The objectives of this chapter, therefore, are to:

1. Describe culture.
2. Briefly describe the impact of culture on international planning, international organization, international staffing, international coordinating, and international controlling.

3. Describe the skills international/global managers require.
4. Discuss why it is important to study international management.

PRACTICAL PERSPECTIVE 1–1

Managing Cultural Diversity in Asia

Cultural elements can affect business behavior in Asia in several ways. Western companies may find differences occur in areas such as commitment to the organization; work ethic; the drive to achieve and succeed; acceptance of responsibility; the relationship with seniors; the way in which subordinates are motivated; or handling discipline and control. The Confucian cultures hold a secret to success [*the author cites Gordon Redding, a professor at Hong Kong University*].

From the huge monolithic networks of Japan (Keiretsu) and Korea (Chaebol) to the small family-owned businesses of overseas Chinese that dominate Taiwan, Hong Kong, and Southeast Asia "patterns replicate like successful recipes," he [Professor Redding] says. The common denominator is paternalism. It is difficult to generalize, but it has been argued that the hierarchical, vertical, familial, highly status-differentiated structures that permeate Asia show marked contrast with the more egalitarian, horizontal institutions of the West.

Social relationships tend to be more authoritarian, paternalistic, and personal in Asia, nurturing autocratic or unilateral decision-making processes and interpersonal relationships that are based on collectivism and group welfare. Corresponding parameters in the West include more consultative decision making but an emphasis on individualism, self-interest, and impersonal or aggressive relations. Words such as loyalty, trust, and cooperation enjoy high rating in motivating and controlling Asian employees, against competency and individual performance in the West.

Western multinationals planning to gear up their businesses in Asia may have to adapt their corporate cultures to embrace elements more familiar to Asian businesses. This could include profit sharing, a highly disciplined structure, a more humanistic corporate culture, increased nonindividualistic reward, a greater sense of corporate pride, or a stronger cementing-in of workers by use of fringe benefits.

Source: Excerpted from Lyn Tattum, "Managing Cultural Diversity in Asia," *Chemical Week*, February 3, 1993, p. 14.

THE INTERNATIONAL MANAGEMENT PROCESS

The **international management process** is heavily affected by the culture (as well as other factors) of the country where enterprises pursue their goals and objectives. (For an illustration of how culture affects the international management process in Asia, read Practical Perspective 1–1 "Managing Cultural Diversity in Asia.")

Culture

Culture comprises an entire set of social norms and responses that condition people's behavior; it is acquired and inculcated, a set of rules and behavior patterns that an individual learns but does not inherit at birth.[2] It enables people to make sense of their world, and it is foreign only to those outside. Knowledge of the concept of culture is imperative for understanding human behavior throughout the world, including one's own country. Fundamentally, groups of individuals develop a social environment as an adaptation to their physical environment, and they pass down their customs, practices, and traditions from generation to generation.[3]

For a brief illustration of how cultures differ across countries, see Practical Perspective 1–2, "Different Cultures, Different Meanings." For an

---

P R A C T I C A L   P E R S P E C T I V E   1–2

Different Cultures, Different Meanings

Never touch the head of a Thai or pass an object over it, as the head is considered sacred in Thailand. Likewise, never point the bottoms of the feet in the direction of another person in Thailand or cross your legs while sitting, especially in the presence of an older person. Avoid using triangular shapes in Hong Kong, Korea, or Taiwan, as a triangle is considered a negative shape in those countries. Remember that the number 7 is considered bad luck in Kenya, good luck in Czechoslovakia [now Czech Republic and Slovakia Republic], and has magical connotations in Benin. Red is a positive color in Denmark, but represents witchcraft and death in many African countries. A nod means "no" in Bulgaria, and shaking the head side-to-side means "yes."

Source: Excerpted from M. Katharine Glover, "Do's and Taboos: Cultural Aspects of International Business," *Business America*, August 13, 1990, p. 2.

illustration of how culture affects international business practices, read Practical Perspective 1–3, "Culture in the Arab World."

Culture in the Arab World

Most managers in the U.S. and other Western countries say that culture consists of beliefs, values, ways of thinking, and language. But most Arab managers—like their Japanese counterparts—think of culture as history, tradition, and a way of life. Clearly, culture is a behavioral norm that a group of people have agreed upon in order to survive. These norms vary by time and place, and are constantly adapted to the changing environment.

Within each culture, there are many subcultures of which we are simultaneously a member. An Egyptian-born executive of a Cairo computer company belongs to the subcultures of Egypt, his company, his sales department, product group, family, and so forth. Every sort of normal, day-to-day business activity is affected by these cultural differences—including personal introductions, meetings, presentations, training, motivation, and written communication.

One way of looking at culture is to consider what values are most important:

competition, formality, group harmony, risk-taking, or authority. Among Americans, emphasis is usually placed on independence, competition, and individual success. In the Arab world, however, primacy is given to family security, compromise, and personal reputation. Let's consider a few situations in which dramatic differences in behavior can generate conflict, or at least misunderstanding:

An American attending a business conference is likely to introduce himself to an Arab businessman, then quickly walk off to talk to other Arab executives, declining invitations to have some coffee during the break. The American doesn't have enough time for more than a brief chat with anyone; his objective is to make as many contacts as possible. The Arab businessmen are put off by this behavior because Arabs place a high value on building personal relationships; they want to get to know someone fairly well before discussing business matters. . . . Like the Japanese, Arabs hold a much longer-term view of time; they don't shun spending months or years building personal relationships and trust. . . .

Friction is likely to occur when there is disagreement in the workplace, since Arabs take a very different view of how to manage conflict than do Americans. If an American worker disagrees with his manager, he is most likely to discuss the matter directly with his manager. This is because Americans value social equality and believe that frank discussion can solve many difficult problems. In the Arab countries, however, an employee who has a disagreement with

his or her immediate supervisor (American or otherwise) may well decide to appeal to a higher authority— the manager's boss. If the immediate supervisor is American, this surprise can generate even greater ill will.

Even the "simple" subject of physical distance can create misunderstandings. An Arab executive may well stand closer to you than would an American or Japanese. While this is a way of expressing personal warmth and hospitality, most Westerners—and Japanese—will retreat, because they feel their comfort zone of personal space has been invaded.

Source: Excerpted from Farid Elashmawi, "Managing Culture in the Arab World," *Trade & Culture* (September–October 1994): 48–49. Farid Elashmawi, Ph.D., a native of Cairo, Egypt, is president of Tech-Trans/Global Success, a consultancy that specializes in issues of global cultural diversity. Copyright 1994, Trade and Culture Inc. Reprinted with permission. All rights reserved.

How Culture Is Learned

According to the well-known anthropologist Edward T. Hall, culture is learned through formal, informal, and technical means.

In **formal learning,** "formal activities are taught by precept and admonition. The adult mentor molds the young according to patterns he [or she] himself [herself] has never questioned."[4]

In **informal learning,** "the principal agent is a model used for imitations. Whole clusters of related activities are learned at a time, in many cases without the knowledge that they are being learned at all or that there are patterns or rules governing them."[5]

Technical learning, in its pure form, "is close to being a one-way street. It is usually transmitted in explicit terms from the teacher to the student, either orally or in writing."[6]

Sources of Cultural Learning

Sources of cultural learning include the family, educational institutions, and religion.

The Family

The most fundamental unit to the development of culture is the family.[7] The construction of family households varies among cultures. For example, in America, the family has been a fairly independent unit. However, in many cultures, such as that of Italy, the family unit is made up of the mother, father, children, grandparents, aunts, and uncles.

Educational Institutions

Another fundamental source of cultural development is educational institutions, which differ from society to society. Some societies, such as Germany, heavily emphasize organized, structured forms of learning stressing logic, while others, including Great Britain and America, take a more abstract, conceptual approach.[8]

Religion

Different societies develop different **religions,** which are the major causes of cultural differences in many societies. Basically, religious systems "provide a means of motivation and meaning beyond the material aspects of life."[9] For example, the United States, to a great extent, reflects the Protestant work ethic. Protestantism, as does Catholicism, derives from Christianity. On the other hand, many Asian cultures, such as Japan and China, are heavily influenced by Buddhism, and the practical aspects of Confucianism (it should be noted that, as will be discussed below, Confucianism is not a religion; it is a practical philosophy).

There are many religions throughout the world, but four dominate: Christianity, Islam, Hinduism, and Buddhism.

Christianity. Most Christians live in Europe and the Americas, but Christianity is growing rapidly in Africa. The major symbol of Christianity, which emerged from Judaism, is Jesus Christ. As is Judaism, Christianity is a monotheistic (belief in one god) religion. The two major Christian organizations are the Roman Catholic Church and the Eastern Orthodox Church. The Roman Catholic Church is dominant in Southern Europe and Latin America, and the Eastern Orthodox Church is dominant in numerous countries, including Greece and Russia.

The Reformation in the 16th century led to a split in the Catholic Church and to the formation of Protestantism by Martin Luther. Subsequently, numerous denominations, including Baptist, Methodist, and Calvinist, emerged under the umbrella of Protestantism. The famous

German sociologist, Max Weber, once noted that in Western Europe "business leaders and owners of capital, as well as the higher grades of skilled labor, and even more the higher technically trained personnel of modern enterprises, are overwhelmingly Protestant".[10]

Islam.   Islam, which dates back to about 600 A.D., was started by the Prophet Muhammad. Those who adhere to Islam are referred to as Muslims. Muslim is the major religion in many African and Middle Eastern countries, and in some parts of China, Malaysia, and some other Far East countries. Islam has some roots in both Judaism and Christianity—it accepts Jesus Christ as one of God's prophets. The major principles of Islam (similar to Judaism and Christianity) are: honor and respect parents, respect the rights of others, be generous but do not squander, avoid killing when no justifiable cause is present, do not commit adultery, be just and equitable with others, have a pure heart and mind, safeguard the possessions of orphans, and be humble and nonpretentious.[11] Religion is paramount in all aspects of Muslims' lives—for example, Muslim ritual necessitates prayer five times a day, and women dress in a certain way and must be subordinate to men.

Hinduism.   Hinduism is dominant in the Indian subcontinent, where it began about 4,000 years ago. Hindus adhere to the belief that there exists a moral force in society that requires the acceptance of certain responsibilities, referred to as dharma. They believe in reincarnation and karma—the spiritual progression of each individual's soul. One's karma is affected by the way he or she lives, and it determines the challenges the individual will be confronted with in his or her next life. Hindus believe that by making their soul more perfect in each new life, they can eventually attain nirvana—a state of total spiritual perfection that makes reincarnation no longer necessary. They also believe that nirvana is attained through a lifestyle of material and physical self-denial—by devoting one's life to spiritual, rather than material attainment.

Buddhism.   Buddhism also has roots in India. It was founded about 600 B.C. by Siddhartha Gautama. Gautama, who later became known as Buddha ("the awakened one"), was an Indian prince who renounced his wealth to pursue an austere lifestyle and spiritual perfection. He believed he achieved nirvana, but decided to stay on earth to teach his followers. According to Buddhism, misery and suffering derives from people's desires for pleasure. These desires can be repressed by following the Noble Eightfold Path: right views, right intention, right speech, right action, right livelihood, right effort, right awareness, and right concentration. Hinduism supports the caste systems, Buddhism does not. And Buddhism does not advocate the type of extreme ascetic behavior that is encouraged by Hinduism. Most of the world's followers of Buddhism reside in central and southeast Asia, China, Korea, and Japan.

The Effects of Religion on International Management.   It is apparent that religion is closely associated with the development of cultural values, and that it affects people's day-to-day activities, such as a business' opening and closing times, employees' days off, ceremonies, work habits, and foods. For example, most businesses in Christian-dominated societies close on Christmas Day and during the week before Christmas Day, because of festivities; output slows down enormously. And Muslim ritual requires prayer five times a day; thus, work is often interrupted. Managers of international corporations must therefore be sensitive to employees' religious needs and corporate policies must be flexible and accommodating to the varying needs existing throughout the globe—otherwise there may be high employee absenteeism and many disappearances from work to satisfy these needs.

Religion also affects international management with respect to employee motivation. For example, the principles of Hinduism and Buddhism do not focus on the practice of working to accumulate wealth; Hindus value spiritual achievements more than they value material achievements.

The Impact of Culture on International Planning

Basically, planning entails defining the organization's mission and establishing goals and objectives and an overall strategy to achieve them. It means being more proactive than reactive. Instead of just responding to a situation, planning allows an organization to create and influence its environment, to exert some degree of control over its destiny. International planning is affected by the various ideas on which normative cultural concepts are based, including the master-of-destiny versus the fatalistic viewpoint, and the never-ending quest for improvement viewpoint.[12]

The **master-of-destiny** viewpoint is prominent in numerous cultures, including America. Individuals holding this viewpoint believe that they can substantially influence the future, that they can control their destiny, and that through work they can make things happen. Planning in such cultures is feasible because individuals are willing to work to achieve objectives.

In contrast, in many societies, including numerous Middle East cultures, the **fatalistic** viewpoint is part of the cultural fabric. Individuals influenced by this viewpoint believe that they cannot control their destiny; that God has predetermined their existence and willed what they are to do during their lives. International managers are therefore likely to encounter more difficulty in obtaining a commitment to their plans in fatalistic cultures than they would in master-of-destiny cultures.

Furthermore, some societies, such as those of Native Americans, are dominated by **anti-planning** beliefs. Antiplanners believe that "any attempt to lay out specific and 'rational' plans is either foolish or dangerous or downright evil. The correct approach is to live in them [existing systems], react in terms of one's experience, and not to try to change them by means of some grandiose scheme or mathematical model."[13] Implementing managerial plans in these cultures is therefore difficult.

The international planning function is also affected by the concept of **never-ending quest for improvement.** Managers in some cultures, such as America, adhere to this view: a belief that change is normal and necessary, and that no aspects of an enterprise are above improvement. Organizations' current practices, therefore, are constantly evaluated in hopes that improvements can be made. In contrast, in many other cultures, managers' power arises not from change, but from the maintenance of stability in the status quo. These managers will interpret a suggestion for improvement as a threat and an implication that they have failed.[14] Planned change may be difficult to implement in these cultures as well.

The Impact of Culture on International Organizing

Organizing involves designing an organizational structure that best enables the enterprise to attain its goals and objectives. This includes determining what tasks need to be done, by whom, how tasks should be grouped, who is responsible for what, and how authority should be delegated. Organizing across countries is affected by the cultural views held by the society, such as the cultural viewpoint of the independent enterprise as an instrument of social action.

The concept of **independent enterprise as an instrument of social action** is widely accepted in some cultures, such as America. Here a corporation is viewed as an entity that has rules and a continuous existence, a separate and important social institution that must be protected and developed. As a result, individuals develop strong feelings of obligation to serve the company, and the enterprise can take priority over their personal preferences and social obligations, including family, friends, and other activities. American managers, for example, assume that each member of the organization will give primary effort to carrying out assigned tasks in the interests of the firm, that they will be loyal and conforming to the enterprise's managerial systems. In contrast, individuals in many cultures, including some South American cultures, consider personal relationships more important than the enterprise.[15] The organizing approach applied in the two cultures would thus be different—for example, there is likely to be less delegation of authority in the personal relationships culture than in the independent enterprise culture.

The Impact of Culture on International Staffing

Staffing means finding, training, and developing the people necessary to accomplish the tasks. It is obvious from the previous discussion that the cultural views held by a society have an enormous impact on international staffing strategies and policies. One cultural viewpoint is the concept of personnel selection based on merit.

That **personnel selection is based on merit** is a managerial view dominant in some cultures, including the United States. Managers holding this view select or promote the best qualified people for jobs and keep them as long as their performance standards meet the firm's expectations. In contrast, in many cultures, including some South American cultures, friends and family are considered more important than the enterprise's vitality; organizations expand to accommodate the maximum number of friends and relatives. Individuals who are not members of the family or the circle of friends may therefore be less motivated to work hard or may work harder to make themselves indispensable, and family members may not work as hard since their jobs are guaranteed.[16]

The staffing function is also affected by individuals' view of wealth. In most cultures, wealth is generally considered desirable, and the prospect of tangible gains serves as a substantial motivator. However, the practice in some cultures is to work only until one earns a desired amount of money and then not return to work until the money has been spent.[17]

The Impact of Culture on International Coordinating

Coordinating refers to the function of directing the people in the organization, including inspiring, appealing to individual motivations, communicating, and resolving conflicts. In their leading role, some managers make all the decisions, and some managers allow their subordinates to make decisions. Culture also affects this managerial function. For example, the wide sharing in decision making cultural viewpoint has an impact on the coordination of organizations across cultures.

In some cultures, such as America, managers adhere to the viewpoint of **wide sharing in decision making.** They believe that personnel in an organization need the responsibility of making decisions for ongoing development, and they give employees the opportunity to grow and to prove their ability, decentralizing decision making as they grow. On the other hand, managers in many cultures, such as France, believe that only a few people in the organization have the right to make decisions, and they offer no such opportunities; they centralize decision making.[18]

Culture also impairs international communication. As was suggested earlier, societies possess unique social norms and responses that condition their members' behavior. The behavior includes the tendency to block out practices that are not congruent with one's own cultural beliefs. As a result, many groups tend to reject prospective change, and dissimilar groups tend to misjudge one another. When an individual from one group interacts with an individual from another group, there is the tendency to make certain assumptions about the precepts, judgments, and thought processes of the other person. When these assumptions are inaccurate, misunderstanding and miscommunication occur.[19]

This means that international managers must be aware of countries' local practices with respect to leadership style and communication approaches

and adapt accordingly to them. For example, an international manager from
a culture in which employee participation or consultation in decision making is the norm would not do well applying the same practice in cultures in
which employees expect authoritarian leadership, and vice versa. And an
international manager who is frank in communicating with people because
it is a valued practice in his or her culture (America, for example) would not
be respected by people in a culture in which frankness is unacceptable and
modesty is valued (Japan, for instance). Also, in some cultures (America, for
example), an individual feels uneasy when the person with whom he or she
is communicating becomes silent (pauses to think). Americans find silence
clumsy and like to plug any conversational pauses, and they measure people
who respond directly as being trustworthy. On the other hand, the Japanese
distrust a person who responds directly; they value a person who pauses
(becomes silent) to give careful thought to a question before responding.[20]

The Impact of Culture on International Controlling

Controlling is the act of evaluating performance; it is monitoring the results
of the goals and objectives previously established and implemented, including measuring individual and organizational performance and taking corrective action when required. Establishing controlling mechanisms across
countries is also affected by the cultural views held by the society's members, such as making decisions based on objective analysis.

A belief in **making decisions based on objective analysis** is widely held
by managers in numerous cultures, including the American culture.
Managers who practice this belief make decisions based on accurate and
relevant information, and they are prompt in reporting accurate data to all
levels in the organization. On the other hand, in many cultures managers
do not place much value on factual and rational support for decisions, and
the reporting of details is unimportant. These decision makers do not seek
out facts; they often rely on emotional and mystical considerations, rather
than on objective analysis; and when they are asked to explain the rationale
for their decisions, they will interpret the question as a lack of respect and
confidence in their judgment.[21] The international manager has to address
this problem when establishing controls.

Hofstede's Cultural Dimensions Model

Currently one of the most popular theories addressing the impact of culture
on the management process is that developed by Geert Hofstede, a researcher
from the Netherlands.[22] He proposed a paradigm to study the impact of
national culture on individual behavior and examined the values and beliefs
of 116,000 IBM employees based in forty nations throughout the world
(he subsequently conducted the study in ten other countries). Hofstede
developed a typology consisting of four national, cultural dimensions by
which a society can be classified: **power distance, uncertainty avoidance,**

individualism, and **masculinity.** The characteristics of these cultural dimensions are depicted in Figures 1–1, 1–2, 1–3, and 1–4. Figures 1–5 and 1–6

◆   **FIGURE 1–1**   **The Power Distance Dimension**

Small Power Distance	Large Power Distance
Inequality in society should be minimized.	There should be an order of inequality in this world in which everybody has a rightful place; high and low are protected by this order.
All people should be independent.	A few people should be independent; most should be dependent.
Hierarchy means inequality of the roles, established for convenience.	Hierarchy means existential inequality.
Superiors consider subordinates to be "people like me."	Superiors consider subordinates to be a different kind of people.
Superiors are accessible.	Superiors are inaccessible.
The use of power should be legitimate and is subject to the judgment as to whether it is good or evil.	Power is a basic fact of society that antedates good or evil. Its legitimacy is irrelevant.
All should have equal rights.	Power-holders are entitled to privileges.
Those in power should try to look less powerful than they are.	Those in power should try to look as powerful as possible.
The system is to blame.	The underdog is to blame.
The way to change a social system is to redistribute power.	The way to change a social system is to dethrone those in power.
People at various power levels feel less threatened and more prepared to trust people.	Other people are a potential threat to one's power and can rarely be trusted.
Latent harmony exists between the powerful and the powerless.	Latent conflict exists between the powerful and the powerless.
Cooperation among the powerless can be based on solidarity.	Cooperation among the powerless is difficult to attain because of their low-faith-in-people norm.

Source: Geert Hofstede, "Motivation, Leadership, and Organization: Do American Theories Apply Abroad?" *Organizational Dynamics* (Summer 1980): 46. Copyright © Geert Hofstede. Reprinted with permission.

The Uncertainty Avoidance Dimension   FIGURE 1–2 ◆

Weak Uncertainty Avoidance	Strong Uncertainty Avoidance
The uncertainty inherent in life is more easily accepted and each day is taken as it comes.	The uncertainty inherent in life is felt as a continuous threat that must be fought.
Ease and lower stress are experienced.	Higher anxiety and stress are experienced.
Time is free.	Time is money.
Hard work, as such, is not a virtue.	There is an inner urge to work hard.
Aggressive behavior is frowned upon.	Aggressive behavior of self and others is accepted.
Less showing of emotions is preferred.	More showing of emotions is preferred.
Conflict and competition can be contained on the level of fair play and can be used constructively.	Conflict and competition can unleash aggression and should therefore be avoided.
More acceptance of dissent is entailed.	A strong need for consensus is involved.
Deviation is not considered threatening; greater tolerance is shown.	Deviant persons and ideas are dangerous; intolerance holds sway.
The ambience is one of less nationalism.	Nationalism is pervasive.
More positive feelings toward younger people are seen.	Younger people are suspect.
There is more willingness to take risks in life.	There is great concern with security in life.
The accent is on relativism, empiricism.	The search is for ultimate, absolute truths and values.
There should be as few rules as possible.	There is a need for written rules and regulations.
If rules cannot be kept, we should change them.	If rules cannot be kept, we are sinners and should repent.
Belief is placed in generalists and common sense.	Belief is placed in experts and their knowledge.
The authorities are there to serve the citizens.	Ordinary citizens are incompetent compared with the authorities.

Source: Geert Hofstede, "Motivation, Leadership, and Organization: Do American Theories Apply Abroad?" *Organizational Dynamics* (Summer 1980): 47. Copyright © Geert Hofstede. Reprinted with permission.

show Hofstede's classification of the fifty countries and three regions on a range of moderate-to-low or moderate-to-high for each dimension. Exhibit 1:1 shows the index and the ranking for the fifty countries and three regions.

These cultural dimensions have an impact on international management in many ways (as will be demonstrated throughout the book). For example, people in large power distance cultures prefer stronger leadership than do people in small power distance cultures, and people in strong uncertainty avoidance cultures take fewer risks than individuals in weak uncertainty

◆ FIGURE 1–3   The Individualism Dimension

Collectivist	Individualist
In society, people are born into extended families or clans who protect them in exchange for loyalty.	In society, everybody is supposed to take care of himself/herself and his/her immediate family.
"We" consciousness holds sway.	"I" consciousness holds sway.
Identity is based on the social system.	Identity is based in the individual.
There is emotional dependence of the individual on organizations and institutions.	There is emotional independence of the individual from organizations or institutions.
The involvement with organizations is moral.	The involvement with organizations is calculative.
The emphasis is on belonging to organizations; membership is the ideal.	The emphasis is on individual initiative and achievement; leadership is ideal.
Private life is invaded by organizations and clans to which one belongs; opinions are predetermined.	Everybody has the right to a private life and opinion.
Expertise, order, duty, and security are provided by the organization or clan.	Autonomy, variety, pleasure, and individual financial security are sought in the system.
Friendships are predetermined by stable social relationships, but there is need for prestige within these relationships.	The need is for specific friendships.
Belief is placed in group decisions.	Belief is placed in individual decisions.
Value standards differ for in-groups and out-groups (particularism).	Value standards should apply to all (universalism).

Source: Geert Hofstede, "Motivation, Leadership, and Organization: Do American Theories Apply Abroad?" *Organizational Dynamics* (Summer 1980): 48. Copyright © Geert Hofstede. Reprinted with permission.

| The Masculine Dimension | FIGURE 1–4 ◆ |

Feminine	Masculine
Men needn't be assertive, but can also assume nurturing roles.	Men should be assertive. Women should be nurturing.
Sex roles in society are more fluid.	Sex roles in society are clearly differentiated.
There should be equality between the sexes.	Men should dominate in society.
Quality of life is important.	Performance is what counts.
You work in order to live.	You live in order to work.
People and environment are important.	Money and things are important.
Interdependence is the ideal.	Independence is the ideal.
One sympathizes with the unfortunate.	One admires the successful achiever.
Small and slow are beautiful.	Big and fast are beautiful.
Unisex and androgyny are ideal.	Ostentatious manliness ("machismo") is appreciated.

Source: Geert Hofstede, "Motivation, Leadership, and Organization: Do American Theories Apply Abroad?" *Organizational Dynamics* (Summer 1980): 49. Copyright © Geert Hofstede. Reprinted with permission.

Country Abbreviations For Figures 1–5 and 1–6

ARA	Arab countries (Egypt, Lebanon, Libya, Kuwait, Iraq, Saudi Arabia, U.A.E.)	GBR	Great Britain	PAN	Panama
		GER	Germany	PER	Peru
		GRE	Greece	PHI	Philippines
		GUA	Guatemala	POR	Portugal
ARG	Argentina	HOK	Hong Kong	SAF	South Africa
AUL	Australia	IDO	Indonesia	SAL	Salvador
AUT	Austria	IND	India	SIN	Singapore
BEL	Belgium	IRA	Iran	SPA	Spain
BRA	Brazil	IRE	Ireland	SWE	Sweden
CAN	Canada	ISR	Israel	SWI	Switzerland
CHL	Chile	ITA	Italy	TAI	Taiwan
COL	Columbia	JAM	Jamaica	THA	Thailand
COS	Costa Rica	JPN	Japan	TUR	Turkey
DEN	Denmark	KOR	South Korea	URU	Uruguay
EAF	East Africa (Kenya, Ethiopia, Zambia)	MAL	Malaysia	USA	United States
		MEX	Mexico	VEN	Venezuela
		NET	Netherlands	WAF	West Africa (Nigeria, Ghana, Sierra Leone)
EQA	Equador	NOR	Norway		
FIN	Finland	NZL	New Zealand	YUG	Yugoslavia
FRA	France	PAK	Pakistan		

◆ FIGURE 1–5   **Power Distance and Individualism (Collectivism) Measures for Fifty Countries and Three Regions**

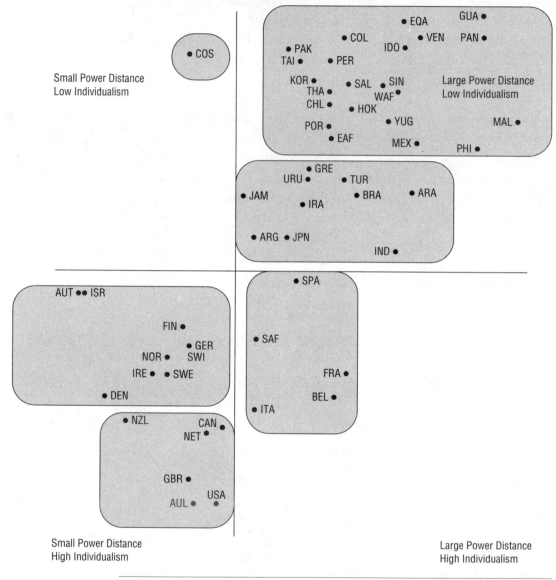

Source: Geert Hofstede, "The Cultural Relativity of the Quality of Life Concept," *Academy of Management Review* 9, no. 3 (1984): 391, 392. Reprinted with permission by the Academy of Management.

Masculinity and Uncertainty Avoidance Measures for Fifty Countries and Three Regions

FIGURE 1–6 ◆

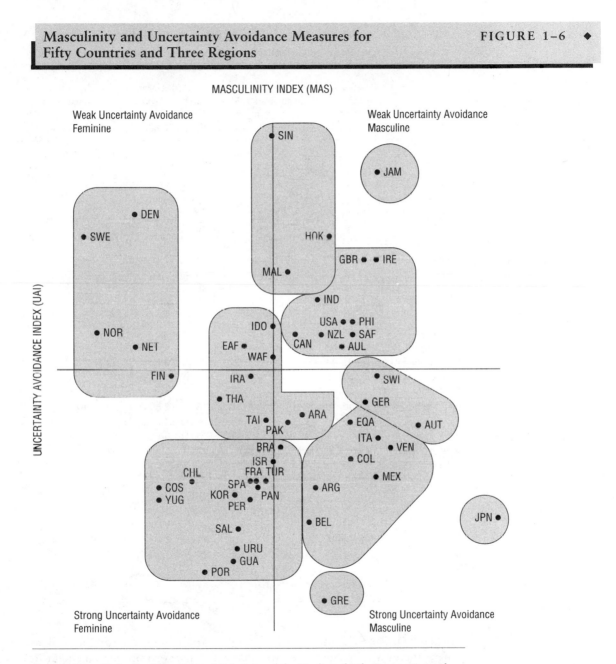

Source: Geert Hofstede, "The Cultural Relativity of the Quality of Life Concept," *Academy of Management Review* 9, no. 3 (1984): 393. Reprinted with permission by the Academy of Management.

◆ **EXHIBIT 1:1**   **Scores on Five Dimensions for Fifty Countries and Three Regions in IBM's International Employee Attitude Survey**

Country	Power Distance		Individualism		Masculinity		Uncertainty Avoidance		Confucian Dynamism	
	Index	Rank	Index	Rank	Index	Rank	Index	Rank	Index	Rank
Argentina	49	35–36	46	22–23	56	20–21	86	10–15		
Australia	36	41	90	2	61	16	51	37	31	11–12
Austria	11	53	55	18	79	2	10	24–25		
Belgium	65	20	75	8	54	22	94	5–6		
Brazil	69	14	38	26–27	49	27	76	21–22	65	5
Canada	39	39	80	4–5	52	24	48	41–42	23	17
Chile	63	24–25	23	38	28	16	80	10–15		
Columbia	67	17	13	49	64	11–12	80	20		
Costa Rica	35	42–44	15	46	21	48–49	86	10–15		
Denmark	18	51	74	9	16	50	23	51		
Equador	78	8–9	8	52	63	13–14	67	28		
Finland	33	46	63	17	26	47	59	31–32		
France	68	15–16	71	10–11	43	35–36	86	10–15		
Germany (F R)	35	42–44	67	15	66	9–10	65	29	31	11–12
Great Britain	35	42–44	89	3	66	9–10	35	47–48	25	15–16
Greece	60	27–28	35	30	57	18–19	112	1		
Guatemala	95	2–3	6	53	37	43	101	3		
Hong Kong	68	15–16	24	37	57	18–19	29	49–50	96	1
Indonesia	78	8–9	14	47–48	46	30–31	48	41–42		
India	77	10–11	48	21	56	20–21	40	45	61	6
Iran	58	19–20	41	24	43	35–36	59	31–32		
Ireland	28	49	70	12	68	7–8	35	47–48		
Israel	13	52	54	19	47	29	81	19		
Italy	50	34	76	7	70	4–5	75	23		
Jamaica	45	37	39	25	68	7–8	13	52		
Japan	54	33	46	22–23	95	1	92	7	80	3
Korea (S)	60	27–28	18	43	39	41	85	16–17	75	4
Malaysia	104	1	26	36	50	25–26	36	46		
Mexico	81	5–6	30	32	69	6	82	18		
Netherlands	38	40	80	4–5	14	51	53	35	44	9

avoidance cultures. This would affect international coordinating and planning functions. For instance, the current buzzword in management is empowerment—higher levels transferring responsibilities to lower levels. However, people in large power distance and strong uncertainty avoidance cultures may not be able to cope with the increased responsibility that empowerment brings.

Country	Power Distance		Individualism		Masculinity		Uncertainty Avoidance		Confucian Dynamism	
	Index	Rank	Index	Rank	Index	Rank	Index	Rank	Index	Rank
Norway	31	47–48	69	13	8	52	50	38		
New Zealand	22	50	79	6	58	17	49	39–40	30	13
Pakistan	55	32	14	47–48	50	25–26	70	24–25	0	20
Panama	95	2–3	11	51	44	34	86	10–15		
Peru	64	21–23	16	45	42	37–38	87	9		
Philippines	94	4	32	31	64	11–12	44	44	19	18
Portugal	63	24–25	27	33–35	31	45	104	2		
South Africa	49	36–37	65	16	63	13–14	49	39–40		
Salvador	66	18–19	19	42	40	40	94	5–6		
Singapore	74	13	20	39–41	48	28	8	53	48	8
Spain	57	31	51	20	42	37–38	86	10–15		
Sweden	31	47–48	71	10–11	5	52	29	49–50	33	10
Switzerland	34	45	68	14	70	4–5	58	33		
Taiwan	58	29–30	17	44	45	32–33	69	26	87	2
Thailand	64	21–23	20	39–41	34	44	64	30	56	7
Turkey	66	18–19	37	28	45	31–33	85	16–17		
Uruguay	61	26	36	29	38	42	100	4		
United States	40	38	91	1	62	15	46	43	29	14
Venezuela	81	5–6	12	50	73	3	76	21–22		
Yugoslavia	76	12	27	33–35	21	48–49	88	8		
Regions:										
East Africa	64	21–23	27	33–35	41	39	52	36	25	15–16
West Africa	77	10–11	20	39–41	46	30–31	54	34	16	19
Arab Ctrs.	80	7	38	26–27	53	23	68	27		

The distance between the lowest- and the highest-scoring country is about 100 points.
Rank Numbers: 1=Highest; 53=Lowest (For Confucian Dynamism: 20=Lowest)

The Confucian Dimension

Subsequent to his study that identified the cultural dimensions of power distance, individualism, masculinity, and uncertainty avoidance, Geert Hofstede, in collaboration with Michael Bond, a professor and researcher currently at the Chinese University of Hong Kong, identified an additional cultural dimension by which nations can be classified, the *Confucian*

Dynamism. This fifth dimension was identified through a questionnaire (labelled the Chinese Value Survey) developed on the basis of traditional Confucian values which are believed to influence East Asian countries (including the People's Republic of China, South Korea, Japan, Hong Kong, and Singapore).[23]

This survey included twenty-two countries. Eighteen of these countries and two regions were included in Hofstede's earlier study. The scores for Confucian Dynamism for the eighteen countries and two regions are listed in the last column of Exhibit 1:1. As shown, Hong Kong, with an index score of 96, ranked number one on the Confucian Dynamism dimension, and Pakistan, with an index score of zero, ranked number twenty. As Exhibit 1:1 also depicts, East Asian countries measure high on the Confucian dimension, while non-East Asian countries, with the exception of Brazil, tend to measure low.

Confucianism.   Confucianism is not a religion, but a system of practical ethics; it is based on a set of pragmatic rules for daily life derived from experience. The key tenet of **Confucian** teachings is that unequal relationships between people create stability in society. The five basic relationships are ruler–subject, father–son, older brother–younger brother, husband–wife, and older friend–younger friend. The junior owes the senior respect, and the senior owes the junior protection and consideration. The prototype for all social institutions is the family. A person is mainly a member of a family, as opposed to being just an individual.

Harmony in the family must be preserved, and harmony is the maintenance of one's *face*, that is, one's dignity, self-respect, and prestige. Treating others as one would like to be treated oneself is virtuous behavior. *Virtue* with respect to one's tasks consists of attempting to obtain skills and education, working hard, not spending more than necessary, being patient, and persevering. It should be noted that individuals may have inner thoughts that differ from the group's norms and values; however, individuals may not act on those thoughts, because group harmony and not shaming the group is of paramount importance.[24] (For an illustration on how Confucianism affects international management, refer again to Practical Perspective 1–1.)

Other Factors That Affect the Management Process

Besides culture, different societies also develop distinct economic and technological systems by which they produce and distribute goods and wealth; distinct political systems, such as tribal, democratic, or communistic systems;[25] and distinct legal systems. Societies also develop distinct written, verbal, and nonverbal means of communication, and are at differing stages of economic development. These factors affect international management in many ways. For example, differences in language make cross-country business negotiations difficult to conduct. And the stage of the country's economic development affects product/service strategies. For instance, economically poor countries usually cannot afford the expensive products manufactured in economically richer countries. The quality of the product may have to be reduced to make it affordable in poorer countries. Or the enterprise may have to move manufacturing to a country where labor is cheaper as a means of making the product affordable in poorer countries. These factors will be discussed more thoroughly in Chapter 2 and in subsequent chapters.

GLOBAL MANAGEMENT: A FUTURE PERSPECTIVE

Because more and more nations are developing economically, interdependence among countries is increasing, the competition confronting firms is intensifying, and the opportunities for business growth and expansion are increasing. The increased interdependence, the intensified competition, and the increased opportunities means that more and more **domestic enterprises** (those whose revenues derive totally from sales in their home markets) will develop strategies to internationalize their operations. It also means that those enterprises whose current revenues from international business is only a small percentage of their total revenues will develop strategies to increase and restructure their international business operations.

For example, an American business enterprise may currently obtain 100 percent of its revenues from its home market operations, or it may obtain 90 percent, for instance, from sales at home and 10 percent from sales in foreign markets. But when more competitive firms (perhaps because they have access to cheaper labor) from foreign countries penetrate its home market and it loses market share, to survive, it must either "get out of the old business" and get into a new one, or look for new customers in foreign markets, or transfer manufacturing operations to a foreign site where labor is cheaper (this will be discussed more thoroughly in Chapter 3). Practical Perspective 1–4 presents a brief description of the internationalization of MTV. Below are some other examples of the globalization of business enterprises:

- The sequel to *Gone with the Wind*, published by Warner Books in 1991, was released simultaneously in 40 countries.[26]
- New technologies in state-of-the-art Ford Motor Company plants are set up in Mexico.[27]
- Five of the six giant corporations that dominate the U.S. music industry are foreign. Warner Music is the American one. Bertelsmann now owns the RCA label; Sony, CBS Records, Columbia Pictures, and Radio City Music Hall; Matsushita, MCA. Bertelsmann owns Bantam, Doubleday, and Dell book publishers.[28]

♦ Mattel now produces black, Hispanic and Asian Barbie dolls for the world market.[29]

♦ The number-one baker of Girl Scout cookies in the United States is President Enterprises, a Taiwanese company.[30]

♦ The major-league baseball, that most American of icons, is made exclusively in Costa Rica.[31]

PRACTICAL   PERSPECTIVE   1–4

MTV: Music Television Goes Abroad

On August 1, 1981, MTV: Music Television became the first 24-hour rock music video network in the United States with a start-up base of 1.5 million subscribers. Today, MTV, which is owned by Viacom International Inc., has more than 55 million subscribers on over 7700 cable affiliates. It has appeal to the consciousness of 12–34-year-olds with such programming as "Unplugged" and "Liquid TV," and launches and revitalizes the careers of many musical artists. Since 1981, MTV: Music Television has become MTV Networks, adding Nickelodeon/ Nick at Nite, entertainment for kids, and VH-1: Video Hits One, a video channel for graduates of MTV.

Being aware of the huge opportunity for growth in the international marketplace and the advantages of establishing a strong, early position in foreign markets, led MTV Networks to expand its programming efforts overseas. Using the universal language of music, MTV moved forth in expanding its influence on pop culture by becoming the first global network when it entered into a licensing agreement in 1984 with Japan's Asahi Broadcast Company to broadcast on a limited basis in Japan. Subsequently, it became MTV Japan. Since then, MTV has expanded into Europe (MTV Europe), Australia (MTV Australia), Brazil (MTV Brazil), Asia (MTV Asia), and MTV International. These global affiliates reach more than 200 million households in over 70 countries. MTV's philosophy is "Think locally, act globally." Each affiliate adheres to the style of MTV, but supports local tastes and talent—the majority of programming is unique to each network.

Source: Adapted from "I Want My MTV," *Viacomments* (June 1992): 4; "MTV Fact Sheet," September 1991; "VH-1 Fact Sheet," August 1991; "VH-1 Fact Sheet," September 1991; "MTV Links for Japan Channel," *Billboard*, August 29, 1992; "MTV: Music Television Global Fact Sheet," May 1992.

- ◆ Freightliner, of Portland, Oregon, America's largest manufacturer of heavy-duty trucks, is owned by Germany's Daimler-Benz, maker of the Mercedes-Benz.[32]
- ◆ Kellogg, of Battle Creek, Michigan, sells over 50 percent of the cold cereal consumed outside the United States.[33]
- ◆ In 1992, Honda exported 55,000 of its Ohio-made cars to eighteen countries, Japan included. By 1996, Honda will produce *all* its Civic and Accord cars in Ohio.[34]

These are just a few examples that help demonstrate the increasing trend of companies investing more and more in foreign countries. Figure 1–7 shows the direct investment made by foreign institutions in the United States and the direct investment made by United States institutions in foreign countries. As Figure 1–7 depicts, from 1980 to 1992, the investment grew immensely, especially foreign direct investment in the United States.

Direct Foreign Investments   FIGURE 1–7 ◆

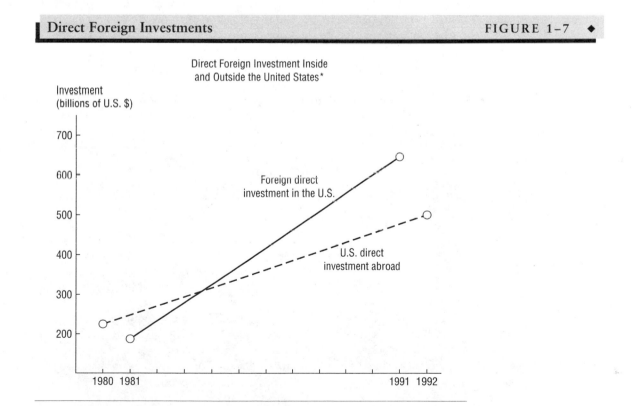

Source: U.S. Bureau of the Census, American Almanac 1994–1995: Statistical Abstract of the United States, pp. 809, 811.

Global Corporations

Another increasing trend is the emergence of the global corporation. (Refer to Practical Perspective 1–5.) Enterprises involved in international business are usually referred to as international corporations, multinational corporations (MNCs), or global corporations. Some people use the **international corporation** label to mean firms that export their products to other countries and the **multinational corporation** label to mean companies that establish subsidiaries in foreign countries. Other people use the two labels interchangeably; both labels refer to companies that have expanded their business activities beyond their home-country market. These enterprises are therefore, for example, Japanese or American or German or Dutch companies that do business in multinations—usually their own and at least one other. There appears to be, however, a clear difference between the global corporation label and the other two labels.

Global corporations view themselves as "world corporations" (sometimes referred to as *stateless corporations*); they view the world as their marketplace. In other words, these corporations do not promote any overall national label; instead, they integrate themselves into the environment in which they happen to be doing business. For example, Honda, a Japanese global corporation, established operations in the United States. Through the media, Honda has tried to convince the American public that it is, in reality, an American company—not a Japanese company. Other global corporations include Bertelsmann, Coca-Cola, Ford, Citicorp, and Asea Brown Boveri.

Another distinct difference is that global corporations, because of their size, scope, and power, are able to make decisions with little regard to national boundaries, and they are able to move factories and laboratories

PRACTICAL PERSPECTIVE 1–5

The Stateless Corporation

Percy Barnevik, the Swedish chief executive of Asea Brown Boveri, heads to his British Aerospace 128 jet for a quick hop to Rome. . . . Barnevik's enterprise is at the forefront of one of the most significant business and economic trends of the late 20th century. As cross-border trade and investment flows reach new heights, big global companies are effectively making decisions with little regard to national boundaries. Though few companies are totally untethered from their home countries, the trend toward a form of "stateless" corporation is unmistakable. The European, American, and Japanese giants heading in this direction are learning how to juggle multiple identities and multiple loyalties. Worried by the emergence of regional trading blocs in Europe, North America and East Asia, these world corporations are developing chameleon-like abilities to resemble insiders no matter where they operate. At the same time, they move factories and labs "around the world without particular reference to national borders," says Unisys Corp. Chairman W. Michael Blumenthal. World corporations represent a dramatic evolution from the U.S. multinational alternately feared and courted since the 1960s.

These giants treated foreign operations as distant appendages for producing products designed and engineered back home. The chain of command and nationality of the company were clear. Not today. With the U.S. no longer dominating the world economy or holding a monopoly on innovation, new technologies, capital, and talents flow in many different directions. The most sophisticated manufacturing companies are making breakthroughs in foreign labs, seeking to place shares with foreign investors and putting foreigners on the fast track to the top. A wave of mergers, acquisitions, and strategic alliances has further clouded the question of national control. . . .

Today, dozens of America's top manufacturing names, including IBM, Gillette, Xerox, Dow Chemical, and Hewlett-Packard sell more of their products outside the U.S. than they do at home, and U.S.-service companies are close behind. . . . The trend is even more pronounced in terms of profits. In the past three years Coke made more money in both the Pacific and Western Europe than it did in the U.S. Nearly 70% of General Motors Corp.'s 1989 profits were from non-U.S. operations. As companies begin to reap half or more of their sales and earnings from abroad, they are blending into the foreign landscape to win acceptance and avoid political hassles. . . . At the same time, foreign-based multinationals are arriving on American shores in greater strength than ever before, a result of their spending $200 billion over the past four years on acquisitions and new plants. Sweden's ABB, the Netherlands' Philips, France's Thomson, and Japan's Fujitsu are waging campaigns to be identified as American companies that employ Americans, transfer technology, and help the U.S. trade balance and overall economic health. . . .

around the world freely. On the other hand, MNCs make decisions with much regard to national boundaries. Some observers believe that the power of global corporations transcends the power of national governments. Some observers also believe that global corporations are forming even more powerful strategic alliances in response to the threats presented by the emergence of regional trading blocks in Europe, North America, and East Asia.[35]

Although these corporations view themselves as stateless, at this time most of them still maintain their corporate headquarters in the nation where they were first established—Honda is headquartered in Japan and Citicorp is headquartered in the United States. Thus, realistically, these corporations still maintain their original nationality. Therefore, whether an international business enterprise is an international corporation, an MNC, or a global corporation is a matter of perception and definition. For the most part, this book uses the three labels interchangeably.

Characteristics of the Global Manager

These trends mean that more and more business firms must now develop managers with global management capabilities. (Refer to Practical Perspective 1–6.) The managerial skills that are effective in managing enterprises at home will not be effective in managing enterprises across the globe. What type of skills do **global managers** need? According to Ed Dunn,

PRACTICAL PERSPECTIVE 1-6

The Rise of the Mega Managers

A growing number of U.S. companies now recognize the importance of taking a global view—and of grooming candidates for top management posts to become global managers. One executive recruiter calls them "megamanagers" or "supermanagers." Their view of the big picture doesn't end at the Atlantic or Pacific coast. . . . In the future, megamanagers will be cultivated by design—through experience and classroom training. . . . There are compelling reasons why

American firms should be thinking in global terms, targeting the global marketplace. For one, television and other media have helped to create a globally standardized consumer demand. For another, companies can improve processes and products by drawing on talents from different cultures and traditions.

But executing global strategies will call for people who know how to do business not only in the U.S., but also throughout the world. What's needed are "nothing less than megamanagers," asserts Lester Korn, chairman of Korn/Ferry International, a Los Angeles–based executive recruiting firm. . . . Clearly, the next generation of successful chief executives will have to sharpen their strategic leadership skills. "Leadership that is capable of directing the forces must have a thorough understanding of the world marketplace and world economics," asserts Mr. Korn. Then we must use that understanding to shape the future. . . . The coming generation of megamanagers must also understand and learn to deal with: the continuing trend of international mergers and huge joint ventures; the importance of creating products for worldwide consumption; how to structure and manage organizations with multiple headquarters locations—perhaps in Los Angeles, Beijing, and Frankfurt; the continuing rise of manufacturing in "non-industrial" countries; the role of advanced telecommunications.

"Telecommunications tools will dramatically alter how the megamanager does business," says Mr. Korn. The tools exist today, but relatively few executives have mastered them. "Telecommunications in the office will have at least as profound an impact on the next 15 years as the computer has had on the last 15 years," he predicts. Another important criterion will be executives' ability to commu-

nicate on a worldwide stage. "They must be able to get their points across clearly and persuasively to their many and diverse constituencies," say Mr. Korn, "and I am not sure rising executives always take this seriously enough." As you might expect, not all of today's global corporations are managed alike. Nor do they all follow the same formula for grooming supermanagers of the future.

IBM Corp., for example takes a "top down" approach—that is, it is managed globally from its headquarters in Armonk, N.Y. "IBM has evolved an effective blend of delegating appropriate tasks and responsibilities to area managers, while at the same time maintaining certain standards and beliefs that everyone around the globe adheres to," says Thomas Horton, president of the American Management Assn., New York, who spent 27 years with IBM. Although IBM does rotate management personnel between foreign countries and the U.S., for the most part its overseas operations are headed by foreign nationals. General Electric, a more diversified firm, has had a policy of rotating personnel at the functional level of each of its 20-odd key businesses—to develop managers with a cosmopolitan view. Most of its businesses operate worldwide. At higher corporate levels GE makes sure that top managers who lack international experience get it—

through assignments, transfers, or training.

Over the last seven years, General Motors has formalized its approach to grooming people who have the potential to become global managers. Company policy specifies that domestic and foreign managers be developed through a variety of movements between functions, between divisions, and from divisions to central staff. But stints overseas are not mandatory. A manager can turn down an overseas assignment if he feels it is not in his best interests or his family's. "We think it's a mistake to force somebody to go overseas," says William MacKinnon, vice president for personnel administration and development. Nevertheless—overseas experience is considered important. And most of GM's seven top officers have spent some time abroad.

Likewise, Ford Motor Co. has transferred senior executives to foreign posts to broaden their horizons. After a stint as vice president of Ford's tractor opera-

tions, Mervyn Manning was sent to Australia in 1984 to head Ford Asia-Pacific Inc. And Harold Poling, Ford's president, previously served as chairman of Ford of Europe, maintaining an office in London. . . . Managers destined for foreign shores obviously need some kind of preparation. And the types of training programs they're exposed to can also be useful in helping U.S.-bound managers develop global insights.

Honeywell Inc., Minneapolis, has developed one of the most comprehensive internal classroom programs focusing on international operations. Entitled "Managing in a Worldwide Environment," the program is designed for middle managers, directors, and vice presidents. It runs for four days and covers corporate global organizational structure, cross-cultural management issues, foreign-exchange management, and global strategy formulation. In addition, the company offers a number of other seminars on international topics.

Source: Excerpted from Lad Kuzela, "The Rise of the Mega Managers," *Industry Week*, November 27, 1986, pp. 38–40. Copyright © Penton Publishing Inc., Cleveland, Ohio. Reprinted with permission.

corporate vice president of Whirlpool Corporation, "The top 21st-century manager should have multi-environment, multi-country, multi-functional, multi-company, multi-industry experience."[36]

Cecil G. Howard, a consultant and professor of management at Howard University, Washington, D.C., has proposed that the twenty-first-century global managers will possess multidimensional skills and knowledge. He grouped the skills and knowledge into two categories: core skills and augmented skills. These are depicted in Figure 1–8. According to Professor Howard, the core skills are a must for the expatriate manager to succeed in the

Characteristics of the Twenty-First-Century Expatriate Manager	FIGURE 1–8 ◆

Core Skills	Managerial Implications
Multidimensional perspective	Extensive multiproduct, multiindustry, multifunctional, multicompany, multicountry, and multienvironment experience.
Proficiency in line management	Track record in successfully operating a strategic business unit(s) and/or a series of major overseas projects.
Prudent decision-making skills	Competence and proven track record in making the right strategic decisions.
Resourcefulness	Skillful in getting himself or herself known and accepted in the host country's political hierarchy.
Cultural sensitivity	Quick and easy adaptability into the foreign culture. An individual with as much cultural mix, diversity, and experience as possible.
Ability as a team builder	Effective people skills in dealing with a variety of cultures, races, nationalities, genders, religions. Also sensitive to cultural differences.
Physical fitness & mental maturity	Endurance for the rigorous demands of an overseas assignment.

Augmented Skills	Managerial Implications
Computer literacy	Comfortable exchanging strategic information electronically.
Prudent negotiating skills	Proven track record in conducting successful strategic business negotiations in multicultural environment.
Ability as a change agent	Proven track record in successfully initiating and implementing strategic organizational changes.
Visionary skills	Quick to recognize and respond to strategic business opportunities and potential political and economic upheavals in the host country.
Effective delegatory skills	Proven track record in participative management style and ability to delegate.

Source: Cecil G. Howard, "Profile of the 21st-Century Expatriate Manager," *HR Magazine*, June 1992, p. 96. Reprinted with the permission of HRM Magazine, published by the Society for Human Resource Management, Alexandria, VA. All rights reserved.

foreign assignment, but the augmented skills help facilitate managing in the foreign country.[37]

WHY STUDY INTERNATIONAL MANAGEMENT?

The discussion above shows that the transfer of business activities across nations is growing at a rapid rate. Furthermore, the recent collapse of communism in the Soviet Union and Eastern Europe, the emergence of market economies in Latin America and Asia, and emerging democracy in Africa has led to placing a nation's economic destiny in the hands of its people. To set the stage for economic boom, these countries are making themselves attractive places for foreign enterprises to invest. This means that in the years ahead, the globalization of business activities is likely to increase enormously and global competition is likely to intensify even more than in recent years. It also means that, in order to remain competitive in the glob-

---

◆   **TABLE 1–1   Survey Overall Ranking and Rating of Skills**

Ranking	Skills	Overall Rating
1.	International marketing	3.27
2.	Import/export procedures	3.16
3.	International management	2.93
4.	Cross-cultural communication	2.68
5.	International finance	2.67
6.	Foreign language	2.51
7.	World geography	2.41
8.	Liberal arts/general cross-cultural perspective	2.30
9.	International economics	2.25
10.	International government/politics	2.18
11.	Liberal arts/focused cross-cultural perspective	2.17
12.	International personnel & human resources mgmt.	2.05
13.	International legal systems	2.01
14.	World religions	1.42

4.00 = Very important	2.00 = Somewhat important
3.00 = Important	1.00 = Unimportant

Source: Carl A. Rodrigues and Eileen Kaplan, "Executive Perceptions of International Skills Needed By MNEs and College Course Offerings: Do They Match?" *Issues in International Business,* 5, no. 1 (Spring 1989), p. 17. Reprinted with permission.

al marketplace, firms must employ people who possess international business skills (refer again to Practical Perspective 1–7).

To determine the importance of fourteen international skills managers require to be effective in conducting business across countries and cultures, a questionnaire was prepared during fall 1987 and mailed to the members of the World Trade Association of New Jersey and the New Jersey World Trade Council.[38] Table 1–1 presents the overall ranking and ratings of the fourteen skills. As Table 1–1 depicts, the top five rated skills were international marketing, import/export procedures, international management, cross-cultural communication, and international finance, respectively. However, as Table 1–2 and Table 1–3 show, the respondents from firms with foreign sales of 26 percent and above of total sales and those from firms producing abroad rated international management skills a very close second to international marketing skills. Firms that produce abroad and

| Ratings by Respondents in Firms with Foreign Sales of 26% and Above of Total Sales ($n = 18$) | | | TABLE 1–2 ◆ | |

Ranking	Skills	Rating ($n = 18$)	Overall Rating	Overall Ranking
1.	International marketing	3.39	3.27	1
2.	International management	3.12	2.93	3
3.	Import/export	2.88	3.16	2
4.	Cross-cultural communication	2.67	2.68	4
5.	International finance	2.53	2.67	5
6.	Foreign language	2.50	2.51	6
7.	World geography	2.35	2.41	7
8.	International government/politics	2.29	2.18	10
9.	International economics	2.24	2.25	9
10.	International personnel & human resources mgmt.	2.24	2.05	12
11.	International legal systems	2.00	2.01	13
12.	Liberal arts/general	1.94	2.30	8
13.	Liberal arts/focused	1.82	2.17	11
14.	World religions	1.38	1.42	14

4.00 = Very Important   2.00 = Somewhat Important
3.00 = Important   1.00 = Unimportant

Source: Carl A. Rodrigues, "A Survey to Ascertain the Importance of Various International Human Resources Skills Needed by Enterprises Operating in the Global Economy," paper presented at the National Conference of the Academy of International Business, San Diego, CA, October 1988.

◆   TABLE 1–3   **Ratings by Respondents in Firms Producing Abroad**

Ranking	Skills	Rating ($n = 18$)	Overall Rating	Overall Ranking
1.	International marketing	3.50	3.27	1
2.	International management	3.28	2.93	3
3.	Import/export	3.00	3.16	2
4.	International finance	2.82	2.67	5
5.	Cross-cultural communication	2.67	2.68	4
6.	World geography	2.44	2.41	7
7.	Foreign language	2.39	2.51	6
8.	International economics	2.33	2.25	9
9.	International government/politics	2.22	2.18	10
10.	Liberal arts/focused	2.22	2.17	11
11.	International legal systems	2.22	2.01	13
12.	Liberal arts/general	2.11	2.30	8
13.	International personnel & human resources mgmt.	1.94	2.05	12
14.	World religions	1.47	1.42	14

4.00 = Very important	2.00 = Somewhat important
3.00 = Important	1.00 = Unimportant

Source: Carl A. Rodrigues, "A Survey to Ascertain the Importance of Various International Human Resources Skills Needed by Enterprises Operating in the Global Economy."

firms with 26 percent and above in foreign sales therefore find international marketing and international management skills to be the most important. Thus, college graduates who possess strong knowledge of international management will be of value to business and other kinds of organizations.

SUMMARY

A major thrust of this chapter was to point out that the managerial approach that works in one country may be ineffective in another. This is because the managerial process is affected by unique national factors, including culture and religion. Some cultures view change positively; others view it negatively. Organizations are viewed in some cultures as entities to be protected and developed; in many cultures, they are viewed simply as a place to socialize. In some cultures, employees are selected and promoted on the basis of merit; in others, promotion is on the basis of friendship and family affiliations. Managers in some cultures make decisions participatively; in many cultures, decisions are made authoritatively. Organizational controls in some cultures are based on objective data and information; in others, they are based on subjective means. People in some cultures, such as weak uncertainty avoidance cultures, take higher risks than people in other cultures, such as strong uncertainty avoidance cultures.

Another major thrust was to point out that, because business opportunities in foreign nations are increasing rapidly, and because enterprises from foreign countries are increasingly presenting threats to many businesses, more and more domestic firms will enter the international business arena, and more and more firms will become global corporations. This suggests that in the future more and more managers with the ability to manage in multinational, multicultural environments will be required. The study of international management is thus becoming increasingly more important.

Key Terms

1. The international management process

2. Culture

3. Formal, informal, and technical cultural learning

4. Religion

5. The concepts of decisions based on objective analysis; independent enterprise as an instrument of social action; master of destiny; fatalistic; never-ending quest for improvement; personnel selec-

tion based on merit; wide sharing of decision making

6. Antiplanning

7. The cultural dimensions of power distance; uncertainty avoidance; individualism; masculinity; and Confucianism

8. Domestic enterprises

9. International corporations, multinational corporations, and global corporations

10. The global manager

Discussion Questions and Exercises

1. Differentiate between management and international management.
2. What is culture? How is it learned? What are the sources of learning it?
3. Discuss how the cultural viewpoints of decisions based on objective analysis; independent enterprise as an instrument of social action; master of destiny; fatalistic; never-ending quest for improvement; personnel selection based on merit; and wide sharing of decision making affect international planning, international organization, international staffing, international coordinating, and international controlling.
4. How does religion affect international management?
5. You are the personnel director of an American international corporation. You are interviewing an American executive for assignment in the firm's

subsidiary in Japan. You noticed that the executive is quite frank and direct in communication. What would you advise the executive to do?

6. How do the large power distance and strong uncertainty avoidance cultural dimensions affect international management?

7. What is Confucianism? What is the key tenet of Confucianism? What are the five basic relationships of Confucianism? In Confucianism, what does virtue mean?

8. Besides culture, what are some of the other factors that affect international management?

9. What are some of the characteristics of the effective global manager?

10. Differentiate between the international corporation, the multinational corporation, and the global corporation.

11. Why is it important to train global managers?

12. You are the cross-cultural trainer for an American global corporation. You are preparing a group of American executives for assignment in China. What would you point out to these executives?

13. Why is it important to study international management?

Assignment

Go to the library. Peruse business periodicals, such as *The Wall Street Journal, Business Week,* and *Fortune.* Select an article that discusses an international management topic and prepare a short summary to be shared with your peers.

Toward an International Management Style

CASE 1–1

Source: Excerpted from Martha H. Peak, "Developing an International Style of Management," *Management Review,* February 1991, p. 32.

When a flutist in Japanese dress appeared at the opening ceremony, it made it clear to the attendees at the first Global Conference on Management Innovation, held in Tokyo in November 1990, that they were in for something different. This was made further clear when the president of NEC Corp., Tadahiro Sekimoto, put forth his management philosophy and NEC corporate motto as such: "Feel the wind on your shoulders . . . Smell the wind. Keenly sense the strength and direction of the confronting wind."

The conference, which was jointly sponsored by the American Management Association (AMA), Management Centre Europe (AMA's European affiliate), and the Japan Management Association (JMA), was attended by more than 1,000 top managers from 44 countries. The conference, which is scheduled to be held annually, aims to serve as a forum for senior level managers to develop an international management style that can be applied effectively in all countries. As Tatsuki Mikami, JMA's vice chairman, pointed out, "Music and the arts have no national borders. Why should management?"

QUESTIONS

1. What do you think is meant by the term "international management style"?
2. Based on what you learned in this chapter, do you believe the conference's objective is attainable? Why?
3. Discuss your view of the analogy: "Music and the arts have no national borders. Why should management?"

Managing in the Constantly Changing Global Environment

CASE 12

Source: Excerpted from "Decentralization for Competitive Advantage," *Across the Board,* 31 (January 1994): 24–25. Copyright © 1994, Conference Board Inc., New York. All rights reserved. Used by permission of publisher.

How do we manage in this constantly changing global and regional environment? Change is certainly not new. But I [*Paul Allaire, CEO of Xerox Corp.*] think there are two aspects of change that are different and worth focusing on. First is the speed of change. It is clearly faster and, in my view, it is accelerating. And that acceleration is going to continue. The second difference is that change is much less predictable. And in addition to global and regional issues, there are a number of other changes that complicate our jobs of managing global enterprises in this environment. I'll just mention a couple of those.

The first is our traditional sources of competitive advantage are now short-lived. Capital is becoming a global commodity moving very easily across borders. Technology also is being very quickly dispersed. And in almost all of the markets in which we operate, we're also finding very fine skills that previously existed only in the developed countries, generally our home markets. . . .

So, the question is: How do we manage in this new environment? Rather than trying to give you a prescription, let me briefly tell you about some principles that Xerox has used to change our corporation in order to manage in this new environment that we foresee continuing at least through the 90s and into the 21st century.

The first principle in which I believe very strongly is that the old command-and-control system of management will no longer work. It is too slow and cumbersome, our environment is too complex, and our customers are too demanding. As we move away from this command-and-control approach, we must focus on speed. Our organizations must have the capability of making decisions much more quickly, and, more importantly, implementing those decisions much more quickly. So what we are trying to do is to maintain the advantages of a large global enterprise and still have the speed of a small local company.

Another key principle around which we've organized is empowerment: pushing responsibility and accountability down to the people who really have the knowledge—first, to do what is right for the customer, and second, to bring capabilities to the customer in a value-added manner. This includes allowing the individuals down in the organizations to define the management process that they will use to best achieve that.

QUESTIONS

1. CEO Allaire's ideas certainly have substance. However, there are bound to be cultural barriers. Discuss some of the barriers culture may present.
2. What are technological changes which have taken place in the past few decades that have helped improve international organizations' capability of making decisions more quickly than was the case prior to these changes?
3. How is the implementation of empowerment programs hindered by culture? Give some examples.

Notes

1. "American Culture Is Often a Puzzle for Foreign Managers in the U.S.," *The Wall Street Journal,* February 12, 1986, p. 34.

2. A. L. Roeber and C. Kluckhorn, "Culture: A Critical Review of Concepts and Definitions," *Papers of the Peabody Museum of American Archaeology and Ethnology* (Cambridge, MA: Harvard University, 1952), no. 1.

3. P. H. Harris and R. T. Moran, *Managing Cultural Differences* (Houston, TX: Gulf Publishing, 1979).

4. E. T. Hall, *The Silent Language* (Garden City, NY: Anchor Press/Doubleday, 1973), p. 68.

5. Ibid., p. 69.

6. Ibid., p. 71.

7. Harris and Moran, *Managing Cultural Differences.*

8. Ibid.

9. Ibid., p. 63.

10. Max Weber, *The Protestant Ethic and the Spirit of Capitalism* (New York: Scribner's Sons, 1958, originally 1904–1905).

11. S. M. Abbasi, K. W. Hollman, and J. H. Murray, "Islamic Economics: Foundations and Practices," *International Journal of Social Economics,* 16, no. 5 (1990), pp. 5–17.

12. A descriptive discussion of these concepts appears in W. H. Newman, C. E. Summer, and E. K. Warren, *The Process of Management* (Englewood Cliffs, NJ: Prentice-Hall, 1977).

13. C. West Churchman, *The System Approach* (New York: Dell Books, 1968), p. 14.

14. Newman, Summer, and Warren, *Process of Management.*

15. Ibid.

16. Ibid.

17. R. N. Farmer and B. M. Richman, *Comparative Management and Economic Progress* (Homewood, IL: Richard D. Irwin, 1965), pp. 177–189.

18. Newman, Summer, and Warren, *Process of Management.*

19. Harris and Moran, *Managing Cultural Differences,* p. 63.

20. "Go Along and Get Along," *The Economist,* November 24, 1990, p. 76.

21. Newman, Summer, and Warren, *Process of Management.*

22. Geert Hofstede, "The Cultural Relativity of the Quality of Life Concept," *Academy of Management Review* 9, no. 3 (1984): 389–398; and Geert Hofstede, "Motivation, Leadership, and Organization: Do American Theories Apply Abroad?" *Organizational Dynamics* (Summer 1980): 42–63.

23. G. Hofstede and M. Bond, "The Confucius Connection: From Cultural Roots to Economic Growth," *Organizational Dynamics* (Spring 1988): 5–21.

24. Ibid.

25. Ibid.

26. Cited in Robert Mamis, "Who's in Control of the New World Order," *Profiles* (February 1994): 50.

27. Ibid.

28. Ibid., p. 51.

29. Ibid., p. 53.

30. See Rhonda Richards, "Famous Amos Goes to Taiwan," *USA Today*, September 18, 1992, p. 1B.

31. Mark Starr, "Kiss That Baby Goodbye," *Newsweek*, May 10, 1993, p. 72.

32. See Dori Jones Yang, "How Freightliner Put the Pedal on the Metal," *Business Week*, September 6, 1993, p. 86.

33. Gary Belsky, "The 12 Best Investments in the World Today," *Money* 22 (April 1993): 102–110.

34. Alex Taylor III, "The Dangers of Running Too Lean," *Fortune*, June 14, 1993, pp. 113–116; and Warren Brown, "The Humbling of Honda," *The Washington Post National Weekly Edition*, October 11–17, 1993, p. 18.

35. See Richard J. Barnet and John Cavanagh, *Global Dreams* (New York: Simon & Schuster, 1994); and W. J. Holstein et al., "The Stateless Corporation," *Business Week*, May 14, 1990, pp. 98–106.

36. Cecil G. Howard, "Profile of the 21st-Century Expatriate Manager," *HR Magazine*, June 1992, p. 96.

37. Ibid.

38. Carl A. Rodrigues, "A Survey to Ascertain the Importance of Various International Human Resources Skills Needed by Enterprises Operating in the Global Economy," (paper presented at the National Conference of the Academy of International Business, San Diego, CA, October 1988).

Chapter Two

The Global Environment

Every company is looking to reduce its costs, raise its market share or generate more value for the money it spends. When contemplating a project, you can't afford to look only at your home market. Instead, you evaluate the whole world. You look at what countries offer in terms of infrastructure, tax structure, intellectual property protection, technical capabilities and markets, and you evaluate the trade-offs.
—Robert Ackerman, an advisor to Mitsubishi International[1]

Objectives of the Chapter

Effective managers are constantly aware of the changes taking place at home and throughout the globe; they scan their environment on an ongoing basis, and when they detect opportunities and/or threats, they transform their organization to seize the opportunities and/or combat the threats.[2] This means that, to make effective decisions, managers must gather information from their **domestic** (home country) **environment,** as well as from the international and foreign environments. The objectives of this chapter are therefore to:

1. Briefly discuss the nature of the firm's home country environment.
2. Describe the international environment, such as groupings of nations that have an impact on international business—the European Union, for example.
3. Discuss the nature of countries' cultural, economic, legal and political, competitive, trade barriers, exchange rates, and labor relations environments.
4. Point out some sources of this information.

THE DOMESTIC ENVIRONMENT

At the domestic (home country) level, international business enterprises are affected by numerous factors, including the political, competitive, economic, legal and governmental climate.

Domestic Political Climate

International managers must remain informed about the political climate in their home country; based on the information, they must ascertain whether the climate can now or in the future have an impact on their enterprises' industry. For example, for economic and other reasons, interest groups sometimes persuade their government to attach tariffs (a tax) or place quotas (a number limit) on certain imports. Tariffs can have a direct, as well as an indirect, effect on businesses. For illustration purposes, suppose that the managers of a corporation manufacturing tractors in country X are considering exporting to country Y; that companies in country Y export wheat to country X; and that wheat growers at home (country X) are attempting to persuade their government to apply a quota or a tariff to wheat imports. It is possible that if a tariff or a quota is imposed, country Y's wheat exporters, in retaliation, might persuade their government to attach a tariff or quota on tractor imports (as history shows, one tariff usually begets another). The tariff or quota would affect the tractor exporters' business.

International business managers thus need to be thoroughly familiar with nations' tariffs and quotas practices. In the United States, an aid is *The National Trade Estimate Report on Foreign Trade Barriers,* generated by the Office of the U.S. Trade Representatives (U.S.T.R.), which had a new purpose bestowed upon it by the 1988 Trade Act. The act requires the U.S.T.R. to submit the report to Congress by the end of April and point out the trade barriers that cost the U.S. the most exports. Recalcitrants will be open to retaliatory tariffs or bans.[3] (For illustration purposes, read Practical Perspective 2–1.)

Domestic Competitive Climate

Managers also need information about domestic competitors' objectives. Domestic competitors may be developing similar strategies to penetrate foreign markets, and they may be introducing a newer product that would give them a competitive edge. Or they may be planning to manufacture their products in a foreign country where labor is cheaper, which would also give them a competitive edge. This would have an impact on the enterprise's promotional, product, pricing, and place (channels of distribution) strategies (discussed in Chapter 4).

Domestic Economic Climate

Information is also needed about the domestic economic climate. If it is deteriorating, the government may place constraints on foreign investments in order to strengthen the domestic economy. On the other hand, if a firm's sales are declining because the local economy is in recession and there are no governmental constraints, entering prosperous foreign countries may be a viable survival strategy. (This will be discussed more thoroughly in Chapter 3.)

Domestic Legal System and Government Policies

Managers must be thoroughly familiar with their home country's legal system and government policies. For security and for political reasons, governments sometimes prohibit the export of certain technologies. For example, managers of several American high-tech industries, such as machine tools, telecommunications, and supercomputers, have complained about contradictions in U.S. government policies. They claim that while the government helped them develop technology for military reasons, it used the same national security concerns to impose export controls on high technology, hence keeping America's most dynamic corporations from competing in global commercial markets. Machine tool manufacturers, for instance, were deterred from exporting advanced machines for producing soda cans to Hungary. U.S. West was prohibited from assisting the former U.S.S.R. lay modern optical fiber cable. And Cray Research Corporation, a maker of supercomputers subsidized by the military, has had difficulty getting government clearance to sell products in India and Brazil.[4]

PRACTICAL PERSPECTIVE 2-1

One Tariff Begets Another

Brazil [as of 1989] requires foreign video-cassette distributors to buy Brazilian film rights, copy the films, and market them. Movie theaters must set aside 140 days a year for domestic films, and foreign distributors have to turn 3.4% of their gross receipts to Brazilian film makers. . . . Last October [1988] the U.S. struck back at Brazil by imposing 100% tariffs on some $40 million in Brazilian exports.

Source: Excerpted from Rahul Jacob, "Export Barriers the U.S. Hates the Most," *Fortune*, February 27, 1989, p. 89.

THE INTERNATIONAL ENVIRONMENT

Managers must remain informed about the **international environment,** which consists of groupings of nations (such as the European Union), of worldwide bodies (such as the World Bank), and of organizations of nations by industry agreements (such as OPEC—the Organization of Petroleum Exporting Nations). It seems as if the consolidation of nations into free trade blocks is going to continue (for illustration purposes, read Practical Perspective 2–2). Such organizations also have an impact on firms' international strategies. For example, the economic unification of the European Union (EU) will have a strong impact on international business. The unification, which officially took place on December 31, 1992, is the result of the Single European Act of July 1, 1987. The act aims to commit twelve member EU nations to an economically standardized/harmonized single market of about 320 million people—which is expected to be the industrialized world's largest single market.[5] The twelve nations are Belgium, Denmark, France, Germany, Great Britain, Greece, Ireland, Italy, Luxembourg, Netherlands, Portugal, and Spain, and in January 1995, Sweden, Finland, and Austria also became members. This change will generate many opportunities and threats for external firms, both small and large.

Opportunities Presented by the EU

The harmonization aims to replace the existing patchwork of standards, which vary from country to country, region to region within countries, and even city to city within regions. This means that external firms can realize greater profits, because they will need to produce only one version of a product as opposed to their current practice of producing dozens. Furthermore, the EU intends to establish mutual recognition among member countries. Under the mutual recognition directive, goods and services legitimately produced in one member country can be marketed without hindrance anywhere in the EU.[6] This also helps firms attain greater economies of scale, as they will no longer need to make expensive modifications and prepare the 100 or so customs forms now required to meet different EU regulations.[7]

The EU also aims to establish the means for capital, including cash and bank transfers, to move freely between member countries. This, too, is likely to provide new opportunities to many external firms, as will the EU's deregulation of transportation. Previously, trucks entering one EU country could make only one stop in the nation. Now trucks will be permitted to make several stops and will not be required to stop for border checks.[8] This will decrease transportation costs and make transportation more efficient. For example, U.S.'s Federal Express, which is likely to benefit from this change, has been purchasing companies in the EU that hold national trucking licenses.[9]

The EU also has proposed a directive permitting cross-border transmission of television signals. This will enable firms to advertise more efficiently. As a result, many new cable and satellite stations have already been started. 3M Corporation, for example, is taking a pan-European approach to advertising and expects to reach a vast audience at far less cost.[10] The EU also is committed to fair competition. The cartels that monopolize certain EU industries are to be dismantled to provide competition and opportunities to new businesses.[11]

Threats Presented by the EU

The objective of the EU unification is to make its members' firms more competitive in the global marketplace, not to offer external enterprises a large market to exploit. This threatens many external firms. For example, some external firms that plan to start operating in the EU fear that they will not have direct contact with the EU's standard-setting body. To combat this, some American companies already in the EU are trying to secure fair treatment in tenders for public contracts and to avert being handicapped when the EU sets product and safety standards. In order to have input, IBM has been attempting to join JESSI, a government-backed European research project on semiconductors.[12]

PRACTICAL PERSPECTIVE 2–2

Toward Free Trade Blocks

The world will consolidate into three free trade blocks. By 1992 the 12 nations of the European Community will—they hope— have knit themselves into a sort of United States with free flow of goods and services and harmonious tax and regulatory policies. . . . Meanwhile, the U.S., building on last year's [1990] free trade treaty with Canada, will make similar agreements with Mexico, Colombia, Ecuador and Bolivia and, quite possibly, with Brazil and Argentina—thereby creating an American block. . . . The third block will encompass the Pacific—Japan, Hong Kong, Singapore, Taiwan, South Korea, and . . . North Korea . . . says Robert Lawrence of the Brookings Institute. . . . Block dealing with block . . . could be easier than nation dealing with nation.

Source: Excerpted from Susan Lee, "Are We Building New Berlin Walls?" *Forbes,* January 7, 1991, p. 86.

External companies also fear that a "Fortress Europe," which allows protectionism and preferential treatment, may evolve. For example, the EU has indicated that it may continue imposing quantitative restrictions on some imported products—such as automobiles—to enable EU companies to adjust to their internal market. Its directive on telecommunications proposes that bids must be rejected unless 50 percent or more of their value is derived from EU sources, and that EU companies be preferred even when the 50 percent condition is met. Furthermore, the harmonization of the EU is expected to lead to the fall of prices across Europe.[13] This is likely to provide threats to many external firms who depend on the prices they are currently charging in the EU but may have to lower them to compete with EU enterprises.

It should be noted that the North American Free Trade Agreement (NAFTA), a union consisting of Canada, Mexico, and the United States, presents opportunities and threats similar to those presented by the European Union.

THE FOREIGN ENVIRONMENT

Foreign (individual nations') **environmental** factors can have a dramatic impact on international business. The factors include the cultural environment, the economic environment, the legal and political environment, the competition, trade barriers, fluctuating monetary exchange rates, and labor relations. These factors differ in many respects from country to country, and in some cases from region to region within each nation. In order to develop an effective strategic plan for doing business in a foreign country, enterprises' managers must first become thoroughly familiar with the foreign factors and how they differ from their home country factors.[14] And they must make the necessary adaptations—otherwise, failure is almost inevitable. The ensuing sections briefly explain the above factors.

CULTURE

Basically, culture is the total of humankind's knowledge, beliefs, arts, morals, laws, customs, and other capabilities and habits adapted by individuals as members of society.[15] As it was pointed out in Chapter 1, societies throughout the globe develop differing cultures. In order to develop an effective international business strategy, the critical aspects of culture must be identified. (As an illustration of how culture affects international strategies, read Practical Perspective 2–3.) Practical Perspective 2–4 suggests that Japanese international business managers tend to make greater efforts to learn foreign cultures than do U.S. international managers.

The **cultural environment,** as demonstrated in Chapter 1, affects the international management process. It also dictates what a product or service should look like or be able to do, what people will consume, as well as promotional strategies. For example, the British like dry cakes with their tea; Americans, on the other hand, tend to favor fancy, iced cakes. United Airlines entered the Pacific market. During the inauguration of its concierge services for first-class passengers from Hong Kong, each concierge proudly wore a white carnation. This was not well received by the Chinese, for whom the white carnation is a symbol of death.[16]

Culture also affects how business and negotiations are conducted across cultures. For example, in many cultures, for instance, in Mexico and most of South America, personal relationships must be established before business negotiations can begin. Furthermore, culture affects a country's human resources management practices. For example, in China, employees expect their enterprise to watch out for their welfare, ranging from the provision of pay and bonuses, to housing, health care, child education, meal services, and recreation. Chinese managers are expected to become involved in their employees' personal family matters. And, although divorce is rare in China,

---

PRACTICAL PERSPECTIVE   2–3

The Case of the Sacred Ground

A civil engineer in a U.S. construction firm was given the responsibility of selecting a site for, designing, and constructing a fish-processing plant in a West African nation. The engineer identified viable sites on the basis of availability of reliable power, closeness to transportation means and to the river which accesses fishing boats from the Atlantic Ocean, nearness to major markets, and the availability of housing and human resources.

Following the analysis of the viable sites, the optimum site was selected. Just before obtaining bids from contractors for site preparation, the engineer happened to learn that the site was located on ground considered by local people to be sacred—where their gods resided. The local people on whom the engineer was counting on to "man" the operation would thus not work there. The engineer therefore chose another site.

Source: Excerpted from H. W. Lane and J. J. DiStefano, *International Management Behavior,* 2d ed. (Boston: PWS-Kent, 1992), p. 27. Reproduced with permission of South-Western College Publishing. Copyright © 1992, PWS-Kent. All rights reserved.

when a couple divorce, the enterprise is often expected to provide housing for the departing spouse.

As it was also pointed out in Chapter 1, closely related to culture is religion. The religious aspects of culture are of great importance in consumption patterns. For example, Judaism and Islam prohibit the consumption of pork. In essence, religion influences people's habits, the products they buy, and their perception of life. Sex in advertising, for example, which is widely used in the United States, may not be acceptable in some cultures as a result of religious beliefs; it may be viewed as immoral or demeaning. And some religions have a negative view of profits earned by investors who do not work for the business.

ECONOMIC ENVIRONMENT

Economics is the way people manage their material wealth and the results of their management. The **economic environment** includes the production of goods and services, their distribution and consumption, means of exchange, and income derived from them. In the search for new markets, international business managers will find that nations differ in their stage of economic development. A nation's stage of economic development will have a dramatic effect on the types of products and services needed, the price, the promotional strategies, and the distribution system. It will also have a dramatic effect on the type of financial concessions a foreign government is willing to make to attract technologies that will aid the country in its economic development efforts. Nations in an earlier stage of development tend to subsidize foreign investments more than countries in a later stage of development. (For illustration purposes, read Practical Perspective 2–5.)

Nations' Technological Needs as They Develop

Walt W. Rostow, a professor in the U.S., developed a theory that can aid managers in assessing a foreign country's technological needs.[17] The theory concludes that societies pass through **five stages of economic development,** described in Figure 2–1. In general, the goods and services required by a country in an earlier stage of economic development are different from the goods and services required in a later stage. For example, residents in a country where electricity is scarce would have little use for electric refrigerators. A **less-developed country** may need to import industrial machinery and equipment to explore its raw materials and to produce agricultural

P R A C T I C A L   P E R S P E C T I V E   2–5

Singer's Internationalization Strategy

The Singer Company developed itself into an international enterprise, conducting business in more than 30 countries, including the U.S., soon after it was founded in Europe in the late 1800s by Sir Isaac Singer. The firm primarily produced sewing machines. Early this century, Singer applied techniques for assessing entry into foreign markets which are widely applied by many corporations today. It analyzed foreign country variables, such as geography, labor costs, economic environment, financial stability, market support for the product, export potential, and the country's repatriation of profits policies. Singer considered foreign government subsidies, such as tax breaks and land and factories provided for free or at reduced rates, important factors in deciding whether or not to start operations in a foreign nation. Foreign governments were willing to make many concessions to Singer because they needed the technology for economic development reasons. Singer thus became a pioneer in entering markets in less-developed countries and developed excellent skills in negotiating foreign government subsidies.

Source: Excerpted from an unpublished term paper by M.B.A. student William Werner for the course "Issues in International Management," Montclair State University, spring 1992.

products, as well as specialized construction equipment in order to develop a transportation system.[18] It may need management consulting, accounting systems, and training and development services. These services are needed because nations seldom possess the systems and skilled personnel required to manage the new technologies.

When a country begins to process its raw materials and resources for export, the demand may be for other kinds of machinery and industrialized goods. Entering the stage in which investment and manufacturing become a leading growth sector, a country may need products necessary to operate entire manufacturing facilities. When the country becomes fairly well industrialized, producing capital and consumer goods such as machinery, automobiles, and refrigerators, it may need more specialized and heavy capital equipment not yet manufactured there. For example, a country producing automobiles may need more modern equipment, such as wheel alignment indicators. In the fifth stage, a country reaches complete industrialization and usually assumes world leadership in the production of a variety of

---

◆ **FIGURE 2–1   The Stages of Economic Development of Nations**

Stage One	In the first stage, agriculture usually comprises the largest part of the country's resources. The society operates on past societal precepts, technology is essentially static, occupations are passed down from one generation to the next, and the social and economic systems remain essentially closed to change.
Stage Two	In the second stage, government and entrepreneurs establish the preconditions for take-off. The government must be dedicated to modernization and must be willing to spend public monies on education and infrastructure to service industry (roads, communication, electricity, etc.). A leading sector, such as agriculture, mining, petroleum, etc., is essential.
Stage Three	In stage three, take-off begins. Investment rises; manufacturing becomes a leading growth sector; political, social, and institutional structures are transformed to help maintain a steady rate of growth. This period lasts 20 to 30 years.
Stage Four	Stage four is the drive to maturity. The most advanced technology available is used. This period lasts about 60 years.
Stage Five	In stage five, high mass consumption occurs. Emphasis is given to consumer durables and services which allow the majority of a country's population to attain a relatively high standard of living.

Source: Excerpted from Walt W. Rostow, *The Stages of Economic Development* (New York: Cambridge University Press, 1971).

goods. Even though a country may be totally industrialized, a demand for goods from another country still exists, because highly industrialized countries tend to specialize in the production of certain goods. For example, U.S. enterprises are highly skilled in producing communications and sophisticated computer technologies, and Japanese enterprises are highly skilled in producing process technologies.

It should be noted that Rostow's theory has received several criticisms. First, in practice the stages are not clearly distinguishable from each other. Second, they do not display characteristics that can be tested empirically. Third, the characteristics that tend to cause movement from one stage to another are not identifiable. Fourth, the time periods Rostow suggests do not apply to all industrialized nations. And fifth, the model is more applicable to some nations than others.[19] Nevertheless, the theory can be useful as a concept or framework for strategic analysis. For example, the theory tells the international manager that people in countries in an earlier stage of development may possess a different perspective from those in countries in a later stage with respect to the aesthetic values of a product/service and preference for managerial styles. For instance, people in less-developed countries may place relatively little value on electric toothbrushes, and they may not value participative management as much as do people in the more developed nations.

LEGAL AND POLITICAL SYSTEMS

A nation's legal and political systems have an enormous impact on international business management. As Joseph Conner, chairman of Price Waterhouse World Firm, has indicated, "Multinational corporations start by looking at the stability of government, the legal structure regarding expropriation and how strongly private property is protected, and they look at how easy it is to move capital in and out of the country."[20]

Legal Systems

Laws vary widely in the world's societies. The following are some common issues of the **legal environment** that must be given special attention when planning to transact business in a foreign country:

1. Rules of competition on (a) collusion, (b) discrimination against certain buyers, (c) promotional methods, (d) variable pricing, and (e) exclusive territory agreements
2. Retail price maintenance laws
3. Cancellation of distributor or wholesaler agreements
4. Product quality regulations and controls
5. Packaging laws

6. Warranty and after-sales exposure
7. Price controls, limitations on markups or markdowns
8. Patents, trademarks, and copyright laws and practices[21]

Labor laws, foreign investment, and contract enforcement must also be given special attention.

Labor Laws

Wages may be low in a nation, but its legal authority may require that high fringe benefits be given to workers, such as profit sharing, health and dental, and retirement benefits. **Labor laws** in many countries provide extensive security for workers and make it extremely expensive to terminate an employee. For example, China has a 100 percent employment policy. Many companies in China are therefore overstaffed.

Foreign Investment

Many countries' laws often dictate that **foreign investments** in their nation must be in the form of a joint venture with local partners, and that the local partners must be majority owners. For example, in the past, IBM's policy was that their foreign subsidiaries had to be wholly owned (100 percent ownership). IBM became confronted with a problem when many countries' governments began to mandate joint ventures with local partners. For instance, IBM was operating in India on a wholly owned basis. The Indian government subsequently issued a mandate requiring that foreign investments in India be on a joint-venture basis, with the local partners owning 70 percent. Not wanting to take on partners, IBM elected to pull its operations out of India.

Also, the legal systems in some countries mandate that top management of foreign-owned enterprises must consist of locals. This can lead to problems when capable managers are not available in the foreign country. For example, when Russia began to shift from a communistic to a market-like economy in the mid-1980s and began to draw foreign investments, its laws required that top management of foreign-owned enterprises be Russian. However, since Russians lacked experience in managing market-like enterprises, they were not very effective. By the late 1980s, the Russian government repealed the law, allowing foreigners to manage foreign-owned operations.

Contract Enforcement

Contract enforcement can sometimes be a problem. For example, if there is a default in a contract entered into by firms from different nations, which nation's law is applied? Usually, the contract stipulates whose law is applied in the event of default. However, some countries' legal systems mandate that the laws of the nation where the contract was signed shall be applied.

Other legal systems mandate that the laws of the country where the contract was executed shall be applied.

Political Systems

Awareness of the foreign country's political thinking and activities is absolutely essential. Before investing in a foreign country, a manager must learn about the country's type of government and what effect it could have on business operations. Is the **political system** primarily a democracy, dictatorship, monarchy, a socialist or communist system, or does it seem to be moving in any of these directions? The **political environment,** if it is extreme or headed toward extremes, would greatly influence an investment decision. If a country's radical party is likely to be dominant, investment may be too risky. International companies have had their foreign subsidiaries confiscated when a radical political party in the country suddenly assumed power. Extreme social and economic turbulence are sometimes omens that foreshadow the emergence of extremist parties.

Types of Political Systems

Some nations, such as the U.S. and Britain, function with a two-party system. Change from one party to another does not cause great changes in the business realm. Some countries, such as Germany and France, are not dominated by any one party; theirs is a multiparty system, and the government may be controlled by a coalition of parties. Some countries, such as Mexico, have a multiparty system, but only the candidates of one party have a real chance of being elected and controlling the government. This one-party control provides some degree of stability in Mexico's governmental policies. The most extreme type is the one-party political system, such as in the former U.S.S.R., where opposition is repressed. The one-party system can, however, also provide stability.

Regardless of the political system, firms can generally do business in any nation and with any party as long as there is stability in policy. For example, some American firms, such as Pepsi-Cola, conducted business effectively in the former U.S.S.R. If policies change gradually, as they do in most nations, the firm has time to adjust its business strategies accordingly. The danger occurs when a country's dominant party makes radical changes in its policy. In this case, the firm would not have sufficient time to adapt, thus placing it in a difficult situation.

Government Policies

Extreme social and economic conditions may sometimes force a political party into radical policy changes. Generally, however, **government policies** change gradually; governments implement new policies to attract the foreign investments needed by the nation to attain its economic development objectives. William Stoever, a professor of international business at Seton Hall University, has developed a schema linking the stages of a country's economic development described in Rostow's theory to the country's policy changes toward foreign investment.[22] This model can be helpful to international managers in predicting and understanding a nation's policy changes.

According to Professor Stoever, countries at stage one of development are usually unattractive to foreign investment, though government subsidies may attract some "show" factories. Stage two countries tend to attract low-technology investments; they attract labor-intensive technology for assembling or producing for the local market, or for assembling for export. In moving to stage three, Professor Stoever proposes, policy makers begin to be more selective in the type of investments they import, and their policies aim to take over part or full ownership of foreign-owned facilities. In order to move to stage four, the country's economy must strengthen and diversify to the point where it can rely more on market mechanisms. The country's policies are therefore those that guide the nation to a "free market" system. The more productive capabilities now existing in these countries make it an attractive investment for multinational corporations, and firms are usually more willing to supply their advanced technologies to these countries.

The Government's Attitude Toward the Product

International business managers also need to learn about the foreign **government's attitude toward investment and products.** Some investments and products are more politically vulnerable than others. Some receive favorable consideration by a nation, such as lower tariffs and higher quotas, while others receive unfavorable impositions. Product vulnerability is influenced by political philosophies, economic variations, and cultural differences. By obtaining accurate answers to the questions in Figure 2–2, an international manager may discover whether a product will face a favorable or a hostile environment. Generally, a firm may expect to receive favorable consideration if its product/service contributes toward the achievement of the import nation's goals, and it will receive unfavorable attention when, in view of the nation's current needs, the product/service is nonessential. Figure 2–3 presents a framework that helps international firms improve the political considerations they will receive in a foreign country.

As a case illustration, Honda Motor Company of Japan applies a strategy of localizing profits and production.[23] Honda reinvests as much of its profits as possible in the local market. It regards itself as a local company and aims to prosper together with the host nation. For example, in 1959 Honda established a wholly owned marketing subsidiary, American Honda, in California with a capital investment of $250,000. As of 1990, this sum has grown to $200 million, achieved through reinvestment of American Honda's profits. Honda has invested in the construction and expansion of motorcycle, automobile, and engine manufacturing plants in Ohio and Canada. Relative to localization of production, Honda does not merely make profits by exporting completed products to a foreign market; it produces where major markets exist, therefore contributing to the development of the host country and achieving mutual prosperity. For example, in 1990, Honda produced about 470,000 automobiles in its North American plants, in 1994 it produced about 520,000, and it plans to produce 610,000 in 1995—an indication that Honda continues to invest locally *(Source:* Honda Motor Corp. Ltd. Annual Report [March 31, 1995]: 13).

Scarce Foreign Exchange

International managers must understand the dynamics of hard versus soft currencies. **Hard currencies** are those readily accepted as payment in international business transactions. The currencies of most of the industrialized nations, such as Japan, the U.S., Germany, France, and Britain, are hard currencies. The currencies of most less-developed countries, and of countries with government-controlled economies (Russia and China, for example), are generally classified as **soft currencies.** These are normally not accepted as payment in international business transactions.

The government of countries whose money is classified as soft currency usually accumulates hard currencies. These countries' government uses the hard currencies to pay for foreign goods and services which in their view are needed to accomplish national goals. If the product or service is viewed as being needed, the government may authorize payment in hard currency; if not, the government usually will not authorize such payment. (Figure 2–2 aids the international manager in assessing the situation.) Payment in hard currency usually must be negotiated with authorized government officials. If the officials do not authorize payment in hard currency, international managers who have decided to do business in the country must seek alternative ways, such as barter trade; payment is made in goods or services that can be sold for a profit in another market. For example, the U.S.'s Pepsi Cola sells its product to Russia for vodka, which it sells in other markets for a profit.

Political Risk Insurance

Many industrial nations offer some form of political risk insurance when investments are made in foreign countries. The U.S., for example, provides coverage through the Overseas Private Investment Corporation (OPIC). OPIC insures new investments in qualified projects, in less developed but friendly countries, against losses owing to certain political risks. OPIC is authorized to provide insurance against three specific types of risks:

1. Inability to convert into dollars currencies received by the investor as profits of earnings or return on the original investment.

◆   FIGURE 2-2   A Process for Assessing the Political Vulnerability of a Product

1. Is the availability of the product ever going to be subject to political debate? (Sugar, salt, gasoline, public utilities, medicines, foodstuffs)
2. Do other industries depend upon the production of the product? (Cement, power machine tools, construction machinery, steel)
3. Is the product considered socially or economically essential? (Key drugs, laboratory equipment, medicines)
4. Is the product essential to agricultural industries? (Farm tools and machinery, crops, fertilizers, seed)
5. Does the product affect national defense capabilities?
6. Does the product require important components that are available from local sources? (Labor, skills, materials)
7. Is there local competition or potential local competition from manufacturers in the near future? (Small, low investment manufacturing)
8. Does the product relate to channels of mass communication media? (Newsprint, radio equipment)
9. Is the product primarily a service?
10. Does the use of this product or its design depend upon legal requirements?
11. Is the product potentially dangerous to the user? (Explosives, drugs)
12. Does the product induce a net drain on scarce foreign exchange?

Source: Adopted from Richard D. Robinson, "The Challenge of the Underdeveloped National Market," *The Journal of Marketing* (October 1961): 24–25. Used with permission of publisher. © 1961 American Marketing Association, Chicago, IL. All rights reserved.

2. Loss of investments resulting from expropriation, nationalization, or confiscation by action of a foreign government.
3. Loss due to war, revolution, civil strife, or insurrection. Civil strife, which is optional, would encompass damage resulting from politically motivated violent acts, including terrorism and sabotage.[24]

Expropriation is the seizure by a government of foreign-owned assets. This does not violate international law if it is followed by prompt, adequate, and effective compensation.

Nationalization occurs when a government takes over private property. Reasonable compensation is usually paid by the government.

Confiscation occurs when a government seizes foreign-owned assets and does not make prompt, effective, and adequate compensation.

COMPETITION

Throughout the twentieth century, most nations have tried to avoid competition. The major exception has been the United States. However, as the

| How to Make Friends in Foreign Countries | FIGURE 2–3   ◆ |

Remember that:

1. The company is a guest in the country and its managers should act accordingly.

2. The profits of an enterprise do not belong solely to the company—the local "national" employees and the economy of the purchasing country should also benefit.

3. It is not wise to try to win over new customers by trying to completely "Americanize" them.

4. Although English is an accepted language overseas, a fluency in the language of the international customer goes further in making sales and cementing good public relations.

5. The international company should try to contribute to the host country's economy and culture with worthwhile public projects.

6. It should train its executives, and their families, to act appropriately overseas.

7. It is best not to conduct business from headquarters but to staff foreign offices with competent foreign nationals and supervise the operation from headquarters.

Source: Adapted from "Making Friends and Customers in Foreign Lands," *Printer's Ink,* June 3, 1960, p. 59.

world heads toward a single marketplace, a more aggressive international **competitive environment** seems to be evolving. (As a case illustration, read Practical Perspective 2–6.) Japanese culture considers competition a wasteful practice, but the Japanese behave very competitively in the global arena. Numerous factors restrict international competition, including cartels, bribery, economic conditions, government-owned enterprises, and a short-range versus a long-range managerial orientation.

Cartels

Cartels, which consist of groups of private business agreements to set prices, share markets, and control production (OPEC is a prime example), restrict competition. In Japan, *keiretsu* links (giant industrial groups linked by cross-ownership, such as Mitsubishi or Sumitomo), bidding cartels, and old-boy networks present external firms with formidable obstacles that Japanese corporations do not face in some markets, such as the U.S. market.[25]

Bribery

Bribery as a means of obtaining a competitive edge is an accepted business practice in some nations. The U.S. Foreign Corrupt Practices Act of 1977 makes it illegal for U.S. business people to engage in bribery in any country, even if it is an accepted practice there. Many U.S. business people have complained that this law has made their firms less competitive, because competitors from other nations are not bound by such laws. Numerous U.S. business people, however, have said that the law has not impeded their competitive position, and that what really makes some U.S. firms less competitive in the international arena is the high-cost, low-quality products they are trying to market. (This will be discussed more thoroughly in Chapter 13.)

Economic Conditions

Competition is also affected by a nation's economic conditions. During difficult economic times, many governments apply protectionist policies, such as tariffs and quotas, to restrict or diminish foreign competition.

Government-Owned Enterprises

Competition is further weakened by government-owned enterprises competing with private firms. Governments do not necessarily have to realize profits and therefore can afford to cut prices. These government-owned enterprises can also get cheaper financing, can easily win government contracts, and, with government assistance, can even hold down wages in their country. Government-owned firms thus have a competitive advantage over private enterprises. The Japanese, for example, through the Ministry of International Trade and Industry (MITI), target certain industries, help them reduce the risk of developing new technologies, and assist them in achieving large-scale production to reduce costs. These practices enable Japanese firms to compete more effectively in international markets.[26] By conducting research, which is made available to businesses for commercialization, the U.S. government also aids firms in reducing risk and in obtaining a competitive edge. The NASA program, for example, has generated many ideas that were subsequently commercialized by business entrepreneurs. Furthermore, the U.S. government awards grants to less-developed nations to aid them in their development objectives. Some of these grants stipulate that certain goods and services necessary to carry out the program must be procured from U.S.-based enterprises. Such practices also restrict competition.

Long-Range versus Short-Range Orientation

Firms holding a short-range managerial orientation (for example, many U.S. firms) often find it difficult to compete with firms holding a long-range managerial orientation (for example, many Japanese firms). For instance, one of Japan's top computer manufacturers won a contract over a U.S. firm to design a computer system in Hiroshima by bidding $1. Its strategy was to give away the design job in order to gain the inside advantage for the city's equipment purchase. This exemplifies a common Japanese strategy of forgoing short-range profits for long-term profits. Japanese firms project

PRACTICAL   PERSPECTIVE   2–6

The U.S. Textile Industry is Losing to Foreign Competitors

The day of reckoning is at hand for the $55 billion [U.S.] textile industry. Its largest customer, the apparel industry, is rapidly disintegrating. Garment imports have doubled since 1980, to $20 billion a year. . . . Textile makers are trying to fight back with more automation, better controls, and an $11 million "Buy American" advertising campaign. But unless the dollar suddenly plummets against foreign currencies, the industry faces hundreds of new plant closings and the loss of hundreds of thousands more jobs. Some 250 textile mills have been closed since 1980. . . . Some 110,000 jobs have vanished. . . . There's little indication that the past decade's 12% annual growth in textile/apparel imports will slow soon. At this pace, imports will have 80% of the U.S. market by 1990. By then, predicts Data Resources Inc., imports may have cut U.S. textile/apparel employment by half, to 915,000—and eliminated 943,000 more jobs in related industries. . . . How can [U.S.] textile and apparel makers survive? The two industries and their unions, the Amalgamated Clothing & Textile Workers and the International Ladies' Garment Workers, have several strategies. One is to slow imports. . . . The companies and the unions are lobbying Congress for a law to limit textile imports from major Asian producers to 1% growth a year.

that once they have established a business relationship, they will obtain lifetime orders. Firms that cannot wait for possible profits down the road will therefore encounter difficulties in competing with Japanese companies.

It should be noted that some Japanese MNCs have been accused of "dumping," which, under GATT (the General Agreement on Tariffs and Trade), is illegal. (GATT will be discussed further in the "Trade Barriers" section.) **Dumping** is practiced when an MNC sells a product in a foreign market at a price lower than the one it sells the product for in its own market and/or at below production cost. The intent of dumping is to sell the product at a price much lower than the competitors' price, thus putting the competition out of business. Once the competition is out of the way, the

MNC raises the price. These accusations are debatable and Japanese managers refute them. Many international business managers and scholars view managers of Japanese MNCs not as "dumpers," but as effective customer- and quality-oriented strategists.

A Theory That Aids in Predicting Foreign Competition

Raymond Vernon and Louis T. Wells, Jr., professors at Harvard Business School, developed a theory labeled the **International Product Life Cycle (IPLC)**, which can be used to assess which products are in danger of international competition.[27] According to this theory, many products pass through four phases.

Phase One

As a result of competition, large market size, strong market expertise, and openness to innovation in the society, firms in advanced countries, through research and development (R&D), create new products. In this phase, for reasons which will be discussed in Chapter 3, many firms eventually sell the product in foreign markets. In this century, U.S. firms have been the leaders in this phase.

Phase Two

Demand in some of these foreign markets grows large enough to justify local production, and many firms make direct investment in manufacturing facilities in those markets. (For changes in direct foreign investment in recent years, see Figure 1–7 in Chapter 1.) Eventually, locals in some of the overseas market learn the manufacturing process and gain control of domestic production. The original manufacturers' sales thus begin to decline.

Phase Three

Some of the early foreign producers become experienced in marketing and manufacturing the product, and their costs lessen. As their markets become saturated, they look for customers in foreign markets. For example, in the 1960s Japan and West Germany (now Germany) began competing with U.S. firms in many industries, including the automobile industry. Japan, for instance, had only one industrial corporation in the top 50 of the world's largest industrial corporations in 1970; by 1980 it had six.[28] As of 1993, Japan had 128 companies on *Fortune*'s Global 500 list; the U.S. had 161; Great Britain, 40; Germany, 32; and France, 30. U.S. firms held 10 of the 15 major industries in 1960; the number was reduced to 9 in 1970, and to three in 1980.[29] At this point, according to the IPLC theory, foreign producers are competing in the original producer's foreign markets. The original producers' sales continue declining.

Phase Four

Production to meet the wants of both domestic and foreign consumers may be large enough to allow the foreign manufacturers to reach economies of scale similar to those of the original producers. Since foreign producers began later, they possess newer plants, which may result in a cost advantage. At this point, the original manufacturers' exports dwindle, and sales in their domestic market by the foreign producers accelerate. Such competition may become so severe that the original manufacturers close production completely. For example, in the late 1960s, there were as many as eighteen American television set manufacturers; today most brands (e.g., RCA, G.E., Magnavox) are made by Japanese and European companies.[30] German steel, Japanese radios and automobiles compete with U.S. industries in the domestic market. A great many of the automobiles sold in the U.S. market are imported from Japan. By 1979, the Japanese, unchallenged, were flooding the American market with videocassette recorders.[31] (For a case illustration of the U.S. textile/apparel industry, read Practical Perspective 2–6, and for the automobile industry, read Practical Perspective 2–7.)

The U.S. television, steel, and automobile industries are cases that help substantiate the IPLC theory. These industries seem to be in phase four, and to remain "alive," they have tried to push the U.S. government to take protective measures;[32] that is, through tariffs and quotas (discussed in the next section), the government keeps out or limits foreign competition (refer again to Practical Perspective 2–6). It should be noted that it is not a necessary condition that the original producers go out of business. They often, as indicated above, make direct investment in foreign markets to enjoy the same advantages foreign producers enjoy. The large increases in U.S. direct foreign investment and the huge U.S. trade deficits in recent years indicate that many U.S. firms are doing this. Many U.S. firms are producing goods in foreign markets and shipping them back to the U.S. domestic market.

TRADE BARRIERS

In an effort to limit or restrict competition, nations often take protective measures by imposing **trade barriers**. (As an illustration, read Practical Perspective 2–8.) Some of the reasons for protectionist activities include:

- ◆ Protection of an infant industry
- ◆ Protection of the home market
- ◆ The need to keep money at home
- ◆ The encouragement of capital accumulation
- ◆ Maintenance of the standard of living and real wages
- ◆ Conservation of natural resources
- ◆ Industrialization of a low-wage nation

PRACTICAL PERSPECTIVE 2–7

The U.S. Auto Industry is Sliding

By moving from exporting cars to the U.S. to building them in the American heartland, the Japanese are steadily taking over the American car industry. . . . Japanese companies captured a record 26% of U.S. auto sales last year [1989]. By the mid-1990s, their combined share could top one-third of the market and exceed that of General Motors Corporation. . . . Next fall [1990], Chrysler Corp. will close its third U.S. assembly plant—out of nine—in less than two years. In part because of them, Chrysler in the fourth period [1989] suffered a giant $664 million loss, its worse ever. . . .

Yesterday GM reported a 50% decline for the period, and Ford said its quarterly sank 73%. . . . By the year 2000, predicts John Casesa of the Wertheim Schroder & Co. investment firm, Japan's gain in the U.S. and Europe will give its auto makers 40% of global sales, up from 28% today. He estimates that Detroit's share will drop to 28% from 35%. In a market free of trade restraints, the securities analyst adds, "the Japanese auto industry would overtake the U.S. in about five years and assume undisputed leadership by the end of the century. The new Big Three would be Toyota, Nissan, and Honda."

Source: Excerpted from Paul Ingrassia, "Auto Industry in U.S. Is Sliding Relentlessly Into Japanese Hands," *The Wall Street Journal*, February 16, 1990. A1, A6.

- ◆ Maintenance of employment and reduction of unemployment
- ◆ National defense
- ◆ Increase of business size
- ◆ Retaliation and bargaining[33]

Tariffs and Quotas

Tariffs and quotas are often employed by governments to restrict trade. **Tariffs** are a form of tax imposed on incoming products. **Quotas** specify the number of foreign units allowed to enter the country. The tax added to the incoming products will increase prices on imported goods, thus reducing competition for domestic manufacturers. Quotas also tend to reduce competition and increase the price domestic manufactures charge their home-country customers. For example, for a period of three years in the early 1980s, Japanese car manufacturers could export only an established num-

P R A C T I C A L   P E R S P E C T I V E   2–8

Japan's Trade Barriers

Does Japan tilt its economic playing field against the rest of the world? The question is crucial, for despite years of pressure to open the world's No. 2 economy to foreign goods and investment, Japan has amassed an unheard-of-trade surplus now soaring above $100 billion a year. If Japan's policies and business culture really do deny foreign companies a fighting chance, what can be done to set the balance right? Unless it is corrected, governments around the world, including the U.S. president elected in November [1992], are sure to feel rising protectionist demands.

Source: Excerpted from Edmund Faltermayer, "Does Japan Play Fair," *Fortune,* September 7, 1992, p. 38.

ber of cars to the U.S. per year. The quota was established by the Japanese government—which was encouraged by the U.S. government. This measure was taken so that U.S. car manufacturers could earn higher profits, which they would use to invest in retooling strategies. General Motors, for instance, diversified into other manufacturing fields, such as robotics and artificial intelligence.

Tariffs tend to:

◆ *Increase:* inflationary pressures, special interests' privileges, government control and political considerations in economic matters, and the number of tariffs—tariffs beget other tariffs. (As an illustration, refer again to Practical Perspective 2–1.)

◆ *Weaken:* balance of payment positions, supply and demand patterns, and international understanding—they can start trade wars.

◆ *Restrict:* manufacturers' supply sources, choices available to consumers, and competition.[34]

GATT

The imposition of tariffs have in the past been governed (although not very effectively) by **GATT**—the 124-nation General Agreement on Tariffs and Trade. GATT provided the conditions under which a nation could impose tariffs—for example, a nation could impose a tariff to protect its infant industry. GATT also prohibited a nation from imposing tariffs on selected countries; that is, if the tariff was legally imposed, it had to be applicable to all nations. There is a current (1995) movement among nations to make GATT a more forceful regulatory organization. A new organization, the World Trade Organization (WTO) has been established to replace the old GATT organization. The new organization, if implemented, will slash tariffs by an average of 38 percent worldwide; and for some products, such as beer, tariffs are eliminated altogether. The World Trade Organization, based in Geneva, will also settle trade disputes.

Monetary Barriers

Monetary barriers are another form of protection imposed by governments. Using this approach, the government creates a trade barrier by imposing exchange restrictions. Three methods used are blocked currency, differential exchange rate, and governmental approval requirements. *Blocked currency* is a method used for cutting off all importing above a certain level. In using this approach, a government refuses to redeem national currencies in the world financial marketplace for specified imports or above specified amounts on certain imports. With *differential exchange rates,* a government encourages the importation of certain goods and discourages the importation of others. The government accomplishes this by requiring the importer to pay a higher amount of domestic currency for the foreign currency needed to pay for the imported product being discouraged and a lower amount for the foreign currency needed to pay for the imported product being encouraged. Using *governmental approval requirements* for securing foreign exchange, a government can create a barrier by not approving the acquisition of foreign exchange needed by importers for the purchase of specific foreign products.

Nontariff Protection

Nontariff barriers are used by many governments. Using this approach, a government can discourage imports by creating administrative barriers, such as by making importing a complex, frustrating, and expensive process. Japan is a prime example. Because of administrative barriers, many foreign firms refuse to export to Japan. There are also cultural barriers. For example, Americans with an individualistic cultural perspective (discussed in Chapter 1) often do not transact business well in Japan's collectivistic culture. In other words, Americans' "spirit of competitiveness" culture does not integrate well into the Japanese "spirit of cooperation" culture, and many Americans would thus have difficulty when attempting to penetrate Japan's market.

Consequences of Trade Barriers

The added costs that result from the trade barriers have an impact on a product's price, as well as on the channels of distribution. The higher the tariffs, the higher the costs, and therefore the higher the prices. To avoid tariffs, instead of exporting, a firm may decide to manufacture or at least assemble the product in the foreign market. Many countries have a much higher tariff rate on products brought in assembled than on products brought in unassembled because assembling the products locally helps create jobs, which in turn helps the nation's economy. On the other hand, the exporting country will encounter loss of jobs. Furthermore, tariffs keep out competition. Lack of competition leads to higher prices being charged to consumers. For example, in 1989, Japan's virtual ban on rice imports was costing Japanese consumers an estimated $28 billion a year. The U.S. Rice Millers' Association claimed that "if even 10 percent of the Japanese market were opened to imports, the resulting lower prices would have saved the Japanese $6 billion annually."[35]

FLUCTUATING EXCHANGE RATES

Countries' **currency exchange rates,** just like the selling value of a company's stock, can fluctuate up and down. For example, one U.S. dollar can equal 100 Japanese yen today, and change to 95 yen or to 105 yen next month. Fluctuations can be "dirty" or "clean." *Dirty fluctuations* are the result of a government, for economic and/or other reasons, adjusting the exchange rate up or down. *Clean fluctuations* are the result of supply and demand, just like a company's stock. If there is an abundance of a nation's currency for sale in international financial markets, its sale value is likely to decline, and if it is scarce and there is a demand for it, it is likely to appreciate.

The fluctuation can have an enormous impact on international business transactions. And the impact can be positive or negative depending on the direction of the fluctuation. International business managers must thus be skilled, or employ skilled people, in this area. The case of Laker Airways serves as a good example of what can happen to an international enterprise when exchange rates fluctuate and its managers had not taken into account that possibility.

Laker Airways, a British firm, was gravely affected by fluctuating exchange and interest rates and by fixed prices.[36] In 1980, Fred Laker borrowed $240 million from banks in the U.S. to finance its growing fleet of airplanes. At the time it seemed like a strong transaction because British interest rates were far above the U.S. levels. Laker sold advance tickets to British travellers with fares fixed in British pounds. Subsequently, U.S. interest rates rose and the value of the U.S. dollar also began rising rapidly. The fares had been fixed late in 1980 when one British pound equalled U.S. $2.40. Laker's U.S. bank loans had to be repaid in dollars in August 1981 when one British pound equalled U.S. $1.93.

When Laker borrowed the $240 million, it was the equivalent of 100 million British pounds (240 million divided by $2.40). When the loans were to be paid, however, Laker had to pay back approximately 124 million British pounds ($240 million divided by $1.93). In other words, to purchase the 240 million U.S. dollars it owed the U.S. banks, Laker Airways now had to spend 124 million British pounds, which is far more than the 100 million it would have spent had the exchange rate remained stable. Since Laker had sold tickets at a fixed rate, it could not adjust its prices to compensate for the change in the exchange rates. As a result of this and the refusal of the banks to postpone payment or grant more loans, Laker went bankrupt in early 1982.

Of course, if the fluctuation had gone the other way, Laker Airways would have realized unexpected profits. Although there are businesses that realize profits solely by buying and selling foreign currencies, like Laker Airways, most companies are in the business of realizing profits from sales of goods and/or services—not from buying and selling foreign currencies. As a result, such businesses often attempt to protect against negative fluctuations by contracting for a fixed exchange rate; by contracting for payment with a nation's currency that has a history of being relatively stable, for example, the U.S. dollar; or by contracting for a choice of payment by one of several nations' currencies, for instance, German marks, British pounds, French francs (whichever is the most advantageous at the time of payment is selected).

LABOR RELATIONS

Labor relations, also referred to as *industrial relations,* has been defined as the "totality of the interactions between an organization's management and organized labor."[37] The term **international labor relations** can be misleading when applied within the context of the MNC. *Webster's New Collegiate Dictionary* defines "international" as: "1. of, relating to, or constituting a group or association having members in two or more nations. 2. affecting or involving two or more nations. 3. of or relating to one whose activities extend across national boundaries." Even though some labor unions contain the word "international" in their title, they are not really international. This is because their domain does not really cut across multiple nations. International labor relations in the context of the MNC thus means management interacting with organized labor units in each country. It should be noted, however, that in the early 1980s some American unions began seeking transnational bargaining and standardization of labor conditions among MNC operations.[38]

Furthermore, it is difficult to compare labor (or industrial) relations systems and behavior across nations. For example, *collective bargaining* in the U.S. means negotiations between the firm's management and the labor union local, but in Germany and Sweden it means negotiations between an employer's organization and a trade union at the industry level. Also, the objective of collective bargaining is viewed differently across nations. For example, in the U.S. it is viewed mostly in economic terms, but in Europe it is viewed as a form of "class struggle." And workers' actions also differ across countries. For instance, dissatisfied workers in U.S. unionized firms may disrupt output as a way of protesting, but in Japan, dissatisfied workers may protest during their work breaks, thus not disrupting output.

Differences in Labor Relations Across Nations

Labor relations across nations have their roots in two fundamental ideological themes: the *pluralist/systems approach* and the *class approach.*[39] ***The pluralist/systems approach,*** which is the prevalent ideology in, for example, the United States and the United Kingdom, tends to focus on procedural and institutional methods in labor relations problem solving. ***The class (Marxist) approach*** places greater emphasis on politics, political action, and tensions between employers and employees than it does on procedures and practices related to labor relations. This type of system is dominant in Italy. Japan melds the two approaches. Different societies have thus developed their labor relations systems differently. It should be noted that governments also play an increasingly significant role in collective bargaining. In "varying ways, countries have developed income policies, or wage and price guidelines, for the purpose of controlling the outcomes of the collective bargaining process."[40]

Labor Unions' Impact on MNCs' Strategies

Labor unions affect MNCs' strategies in three ways: by influencing wage levels; by limiting MNCs' employment level variation; and by preventing MNCs from integrating their operations globally.[41]

Influencing Wage Levels

Unions can influence wages to a cost level that puts MNCs at a disadvantage. This makes them less competitive.

Limiting Employment Level Variation

Redundancy legislation in many nations often specifies that enterprises must compensate involuntarily terminated employees on the basis of a specified formula, such as one week's pay for each year of service, and in some countries it may even be more. For example, if an employer in Mexico decides to terminate an employee who has been with the company for six months, the employee could create a back pay issue of as much as an additional six weeks, plus prorated vacation and bonuses.[42] Labor unions influence this process by lobbying for such legislation.

Hindering Global Integration

As Chapter 4 will discuss, many MNCs rationalize production and pricing across a number of nations to optimize their investments. Powerful unions, however, can force MNCs not to undertake such activities or force them to make suboptimal investments in their nation.

SOURCES OF INFORMATION

The above discussion of the global environment suggest that effective international business managers require an abundance of information. How is the information obtained? Information can be obtained through primary research and/or secondary research. **Primary research** is carried out to obtain first-hand information about the environment. Generally only larger, wealthier corporations can afford to gather primary information, and only a few can afford to establish information sources around the globe. General Electric Corporation, for example, a huge multinational corporation, has established its own global scanning system. Less wealthy enterprises usually depend on information obtained through secondary research, which is less costly. Basically, **secondary research** means obtaining information that was gathered through primary research by other organizations. There are many sources of secondary data. Some of these include:

- ◆ *Corporations.* Some large multinational enterprises, such as General Electric, and banks, such as Citicorp, gather primary information. These corporations make much of the information available to other organizations.
- ◆ *Governments.* Many governments have established agencies to gather and compile information to aid managers in making international business decisions. For instance, the United States Department of Commerce has established agencies that gather information relative to worldwide economic, social, political, and technological developments. This information is available at nominal cost.
- ◆ *The United Nations.* The U.N. also gathers and disseminates an abundance of information about global economic, political, social, and technological developments.
- ◆ *International organizations.* Organizations such as the Organization for Economic Cooperation and Development, the European Union, the Pan American Union, the World Bank, and the Inter-national Monetary Fund gather and compile information that is useful in international business decisions.
- ◆ *Chambers of commerce and trade organizations.* National and international chambers of commerce and foreign trade associations also gather and disseminate useful information.

- ◆ *Research universities.* Many professors at universities conduct empirical research relevant to global economic, social, political, and technological developments. Their findings are made available in published practical (and academic) journals, books, and professional conference papers.
- ◆ *Business periodicals.* There is an abundance of business periodicals. In the U.S., to mention just a few, there are *The Wall Street Journal, Business Week, Fortune, Business International,* and *Business America.*

Caveat

Before they use information, managers first must analyze carefully its sources and its age. They must obtain answers to the following questions:

- ◆ Who collected the information? Would there be any reason for deliberately misrepresenting the facts? (National pride and politics sometimes persuade the gatherers of information to inflate or deflate the data. For example, around election time politicians like to create optimism or establish a positive image of their past performance; they sometimes do this by manipulating economic data.)
- ◆ For what purpose were the data collected?
- ◆ How were they collected (methodology)?
- ◆ Are the data internally consistent and logical in light of known data sources or market factors?[43]

The age of data must also be considered. Information about nations now changes very rapidly. For example, not too long ago, the idea of a McDonald's in Paris, France, was absurd. They are popular there now. Also, many countries are rapidly growing economically. The national totals of income and income distribution are therefore quickly invalidated. And, while primary and secondary data are of vital importance to international managers for decision-making purposes, it is also very important that they make on-site visits to intuitively assess the situation before they make a final decision.

SUMMARY

The major thrust of this chapter was that managers of effective international businesses must be aware of the changes taking place in their home country and throughout the globe. At home, they remain informed about changes that can affect their organization, including legal, political, economic, and competitive changes. They also remain informed about changes taking place in international organizations, such as the European Union, and in individual foreign nations. When the changes present opportunities and/or threats, managers develop strategies to seize the opportunities and/or combat the threats. These managers also recognize that different countries present different cultural, economic, legal, political, competitive, trade barriers, monetary exchange, and labor relations environments. When they develop international strategies, these managers consider the differing factors and make the necessary adaptations. Therefore, effective international business managers do their "homework"; they gather the information needed to make effective decisions.

Key Terms

1. Domestic environment
2. International environment
3. Foreign environment
4. Cultural environment
5. Economic, legal, and political environments
6. Competitive environment
7. Trade barriers; tariffs and quotas
8. Currency exchange rates
9. International labor relations
10. The five stages of economic development
11. A less-developed country
12. Labor laws; foreign investment; contract enforcement
13. Political systems; government policies
14. Cartels, *keiretsu*
15. Government's attitudes toward products/services
16. The international product life cycle (IPLC)
17. Hard and soft currencies
18. Nontariff barriers
19. GATT/WTO
20. Monetary barriers
21. Expropriation, nationalization, and confiscation
22. Primary and secondary research
23. Dumping

Discussion Questions and Exercises

1. Discuss how the domestic environment affects international business strategies.
2. What is meant by the term *international environment*? How does the international environment affect international business strategies?
3. What is meant by the term *foreign environment*?
4. How does culture affect international business?
5. You are an international business consultant who has been employed by a domestic company involved in selling beef and pork products. The firm wants to expand its business activities into foreign markets. What would be the primary advice you would give your client?
6. How does a nation's economic environment affect international business?

7. The theory of the stages of economic development has been criticized. What are the criticisms? Notwithstanding the criticisms, how is the theory useful to international business managers?

8. How do labor laws, foreign investment laws, and contract enforcement laws affect international business management?

9. Political systems differ from country to country. A nation's political system should not be a factor in an international corporation's decision on whether or not to do business there. Do you agree or disagree with this statement? Why?

10. How can an international firm reduce its political vulnerability?

11. You are an international business consultant employed by a domestic firm seeking to conduct business in a less-developed country. The chapter discusses hard and soft currencies. In this context, what advice would you give your client?

12. How do cartels, bribery practices, the state of a nation's economic conditions, government-owned enterprises, and a long-range versus a short-range managerial orientation affect competition?

13. Discuss the international product life cycle (IPLC) theory. How is it useful to international business managers?

14. Discuss the reasons for a nation's protectionist activities (tariffs and quotas).

15. What is nontariff protection?

16. What are the negative aspects of tariffs?

17. What is the role of GATT in international business?

18. What are monetary barriers?

19. How do fluctuating monetary exchange rates affect international business?

20. What are "clean" and "dirty" exchange fluctuations?

21. Discuss how labor relations differ across nations.

22. How do labor relations affect international business strategies?

23. You are an international consultant employed by a firm seeking to establish a subsidiary in China. What would you tell your client to expect?

24. Discuss the major sources of information available to international managers.

25. What are the major concerns about information?

Assignment

Interview a student or an acquaintance who is from another country. Ask him or her to describe the ways some of the factors discussed in this chapter differ between his or her country and your country.

C A S E   2–1

Source: Excerpted from
ASY, "Wholly Foreign
Owned Enterprises," *The
China Business Review*
(January–February
1990): 32–33. Reprinted
with the permission of
The China Business
Forum, The U.S.–China
Business Council,
Washington, D.C.

Protecting the Pepsi Taste

When PepsiCo Corp. was obliged to begin producing concentrate within China for its Chinese bottling plants, the company decided a wholly owned venture would be the only viable option. Only a WFOE [wholly foreign-owned enterprise] could adequately protect patented soft-drink formulas—but Chinese central government officials drove a hard bargain before approving the project.

While PepsiCo chose the WFOE option to protect formulas, there was another compelling reason for opening a new plant—pressure from the Chinese government to reduce imports of soft-drink concentrates. The company currently imports concentrates and sells them in hard currency to four joint-venture bottling plants—producing Pepsi Cola, 7 Up, and Mirinda orange—in which it has equity stakes of up to 15–20 percent. PepsiCo balances foreign exchange through various countertrade and production ventures, such as its joint venture with McCormick & Co. Inc. in Shanghai, which processes spices sourced in China and sells them to the United States. Even though PepsiCo was not a net user of foreign exchange, China expressed dissatisfaction with the use of scarce hard currency to buy soft-drink concentrate. China views soda as a luxury item and refuses to let PepsiCo open any new bottling facilities before localizing concentrate production. Thus, PepsiCo agreed it would produce concentrate within China, selling in renminbi (RMB) to domestic factories and exporting part of the production—expected to average 20–50 percent—to bottling plants in Asia to balance foreign exchange. "This puts the monkey on our back to balance our foreign-exchange requirements," says Peter M. R. Kendall, regional vice president for PepsiCo/North Asia. PepsiCo hopes eventually to source most of the citrus extracts, essential oils, caramel, and other ingredients within China, but finding suppliers that meet international standards is expected to be a problem. Negotiations for the 20-year, $10 million venture began in 1988, and construction is expected to be completed in June 1990.

"WHAT'S IN IT FOR CHINA?"

PepsiCo chose the WFOE site in the Huangpu Economic and Technological Development Zone (ETDZ), about 20 miles from the center of Guangzhou. Near Hong Kong, the site offers proximity to shipping lines and convenience for expatriate staff. Perhaps more important, PepsiCo had developed good working relationships with local Guangzhou and Guangdong authorities through its bottling plants in Guangzhou and Shenzhen, and that local support proved important in selling the project in Beijing. As "very visible signs of foreign presence," soft drink production ventures must receive central approval regardless of the size of investment, says Kendall. Huangpu ETDZ authorities acted, in effect, as consultants to PepsiCo in shepherding the project through the approval process involving the central Ministry of Light Industry (MLI), MOFERT [the Ministry of Foreign Economic Relations and Trade], and the State Planning Commission.

MLI proved to be the toughest sell. "The ministry was saying, 'What's in it for China?' " Kendall says. "They put pressure on PepsiCo to give a better deal," in part by initially refusing permission for a WFOE that would sell its products domestically on grounds that WFOEs must produce exclusively for export.

In order to win WFOE approval and demonstrate their long-term commitment to China, PepsiCo agreed to build a neighboring joint-venture plant in partnership with the Chinese soda giant Asia Soft Drinks, which will produce concentrate for new, local soft-drink brands and a product-development lab and training facility to help China develop high-quality soft drinks. The two facilities, which will together employ around 40 people (the same number as planned to staff the WFOE), will also provide training in water treatment, packaging, and the development of new flavors.

Government authorities stipulated that the joint-venture plant use the most modern equipment and made specific demands about staffing, management, expatriate compensation, and training. At the WFOE, however, PepsiCo will have a free hand in staffing and compensation. In the later stages of negotiation, government authorities concerned themselves only with holding PepsiCo to a capital-commitment schedule and negotiating foreign-exchange arrangements. Authorities have promised PepsiCo the WFOE plant will receive "high-technology enterprise" status, providing lower land-use fees and possibly some reduction in taxes. Under Chinese law, PepsiCo will not receive notification of its legal status until the plant's opening in fall 1990.

SODA MARKET GOING FLAT

Construction was already underway at the WFOE plant in June 1989, when political upheaval devastated China's tourist trade. Not only are tourists avoiding China, but the domestic austerity campaign has reduced spending power and helped discourage official banquets, which formerly provided much business to companies selling international-name beverages. In addition, tightening restrictions on the import and production of aluminum cans has had severe impact on PepsiCo's domestic can business, which accounted for 20 percent of total volume. With plastic-bottle (PET) sales also reduced by austerity, the plants have seen a rising volume of returnable-bottle sales, necessitating a bigger truck fleet and glass investment by PepsiCo and associated bottlers. And while before austerity PepsiCo's joint venture plants made some of their sales in foreign-exchange certificates (FEC), now sales are almost exclusively in RMB.

Since its initial feasibility study for the WFOE, PepsiCo has lowered sales projections by about 20 percent and is keeping a cautious eye on China's political situation. However, in China's enormous market, PepsiCo believes that even severe constrictions in the short term leave ample room for sales. One sign of encouragement may be the strong support PepsiCo has continued to receive from local Guangzhou officials, despite attempts by Beijing to curtail Guangdong's authority over foreign investment. PepsiCo is confident China will continue to support its sales, Kendall says. "A bottle of Pepsi produced in the PRC is almost entirely a Chinese product. It contributes to the country's economic development."

QUESTIONS

1. Based on what you have learned in this chapter, do you believe PepsiCo's managers effectively analyzed China's environment? Why?
2. Based on what you have learned in the chapter, discuss the problems China's systems present for foreign companies planning to invest in China.
3. What did PepsiCo do to establish a more positive relationship with the Chinese government?
4. What draws foreign investors to China?

The Competitive Edge

CASE 2–2

Source: Excerpted from Roderick MacLeod, *China, Inc.: How to Do Business with the Chinese* (Toronto: Bantam Books, 1988), p. 32. Copyright © by Roderick MacLeod. Used by permission of Bantam Books, a division of Bantam Doubleday Dell Publishing Group, Inc.

The Belgian unit of ITT negotiated a large contract to set up a factory to make and sell modern telephone sets. The plan called for importing while Chinese technicians were trained, then assembling the imported components while more technology was transferred, and finally making everything in China. The training and other technology-transfer costs were an investment that, spread over the cost of the projected minimum of half a million sets, could easily be recovered while still selling the sets at a reasonable price. The agreement guaranteed foreign exchange convertibility of the earnings so that the investment could be recovered. All went well until the time came to start selling the sets in large quantities in China. It turned out that equivalent imported Japanese sets were available, and since the Japanese company had no technology-transfer costs, the price was low enough to preempt the market.

QUESTIONS

1. Based on what you learned in this chapter, where did the Belgian unit of ITT go wrong?

Notes

1. Cited by Stephen Kindel, "Staying Competitive in a Shrinking World," *FinancialWorld* 160, no. 21 (October 15, 1991): 22.

2. E. J. Miller and A. K. Rice, *Systems of Organization* (London: Tavistock, 1967).

3. Rahul Jacob, "Export Barriers the U.S. Hates Most," *Fortune,* February 27, 1989, p. 88.

4. R. Kuttner, "Facing Up to Industrial Policy," *The New York Times Magazine,* April 19, 1992, pp. 22, 26, 27, 42.

5. *Europe in the 1990s* (State of New Jersey Department of Commerce and Economic Development, KPMG Peat Marwick, 1990).

6. R. E. Gut, "The Impact of the European Community's 1992 Project," *Vital Speeches of the Day,* November 1988, pp. 34–37.

7. *Europe in the 1990s.*

8. R. Straetz, "U.S. Exporters Should Find the Benefits of Europe 1992: Program Will Outweigh Problems," *Business America,* May 1989, pp. 10–11.

9. L. C. White, "Bold Strategies for a Brave New Market: Federal Express," *Business Month,* August 1989, pp. 32–34.

10. T. Murray, "Bold Strategies for a Brave New Market: 3M," *Business Month,* August 1989, pp. 35–37.

11. *Europe in the 1990s.*

12. "American Firms in Europe," *The Economist* 311 (May 13, 1989): 70–71.

13. Ibid.

14. P. R. Cateora and J. M Hess, *International Marketing,* 4th ed. (Homewood, Il: Richard D. Irwin, 1979), p. 262.

15. P. H. Harris and R. T. Moran, *Managing Cultural Differences* (Houston, TX: Gulf Publishing Co., 1979).

16. J. R. Zeeman, "Service—The Cutting Edge of Global Competition: What United Airlines Is Learning in the Pacific" (remarks before the annual meeting of the Academy of International Business, Chicago, November 14, 1987).

17. W. W. Rostow, *The Stages of Economic Development* (New York: Cambridge University Press, 1971).

18. This discussion draws on Cateora and Hess, *International Marketing,* pp. 263–266.

19. W. A. Stoever, "The Stages of Developing Country Policy Toward Foreign Investment," *The Columbia Journal of World Business,* 20(3) (Fall 1985): 6–8.

20. Cited by Kindel, "Staying Competitive," pp. 22–24.

21. "151 Checklists—Decision Making in International Operations," *Business International,* 1974, p. 84.

22. Stoever, "The Stages of Developing Country Policy."

23. This case illustration draws from Hideo Sugiura, "How Honda Localizes Its Global Strategy," *Sloan Management Review* 32(1) (Fall 1990): 77–82.

24. Overseas Private Investment Corporation, *Investment Insurance Handbook,* p. 4, cited in M. C. Schnitzer, M. L. Liebrenz, and K. W. Kubin, *International Business* (Cincinnati, OH: South-Western Publishing Co., 1985), p. 253.

25. Edmund Faltermayer, "Does Japan Play Fair?" *Fortune,* September 7, 1992, p. 41.

26. Lionel H. Olmer, "Japan Trip Report: Japan's Drive for Technological Preeminence Challenges U.S.," *Business America,* January 24, 1983, pp. 6–10.

27. R. Vernon and L. T. Wells, Jr., *Manager in the International Economy* (Englewood Cliffs, NJ: Prentice-Hall, 1976).

28. U.S. Congress, Office of Technology Assessment, *U.S. Industrial Competitiveness: A Comparison of Steel, Electronics, and Automobiles* (Washington, DC: U.S. Government Printing Office, 1981), pp. 11–17.

29. M. A. Hitt, R. E. Hoskisson, and J. S. Harrison, "Strategic Competitiveness in the 1990s: Challenges and Opportunities," *Academy of Management Executive* 5(2) (May 1991): 8.

30. Ibid., p. 1.

31. C. Christopher, *The Japanese Mind* (New York: Linden Press, 1983).

32. See R. B. Reich, *The Next American Frontier* (New York: Times Books, 1983).

33. Cateora and Hess, *International Marketing,* p. 63.

34. Ibid., p. 64.

35. Rahul Jacob, "Export Barriers the U.S. Hates the Most," p. 88.

36. The information on Laker Airways is drawn from Frederick Gluck, "Global Competition in the 1980's," *Journal of Business Strategy* (Spring 1983): 223–27.

37. Jay Shafriz, *Directory of Personnel Management and Labor Relations* (Oak Park, IL: Moore Publishing Co., 1980), p. 188.

38. Roy B. Helfgott, "American Unions and Multinational Companies: A Case of Misplaced Emphasis," *Columbia Journal of World Business* 18, no. 2 (1983): 81–86.

39. The source of this discussion is Peter Doeringer, *Industrial Relations in International Perspective* (New York: Holmes and Meier Publishers, 1981).

40. Albert Blum, *International Handbook of Industrial Relations Contemporary Developments and Research* (Westport, CT: Greenwood Press, 1981), p. 674.

41. This discussion draws from P. J. Dowling and R. S. Schuler, *International Dimensions of Human Resource Management* (Boston: PWS-Kent Publishing 1990), pp. 145–147.

42. Jeff Stinson, "Maquiladoras Challenge Human Resources," *Personnel Journal* (November 1989): 92.

43. Cateora and Hess, *International Marketing*, p. 255.

II

THE INTERNATIONAL PLANNING PROCESS

Planning means monitoring the enterprise's external environment to ascertain where there are business opportunities and/or threats and to become familiar with the internal aspects of the organization, including knowledge of its resources and business strengths. When opportunities and/or threats are presented by the external environment, planning involves preparing a strategy to mobilize the firm's resources and strengths to seize the opportunities or combat the threats. The global environment was discussed in Chapter 2. The reasons why firms establish strategy to penetrate the international business arena, as well as the types of international strategies and objectives, are discussed in Chapter 3. International product/service, place/entry, price, and promotion strategies are discussed in Chapter 4.

Chapter Three

International Strategy

Today, dozens of America's top manufacturing names, including IBM, Gillette, Xerox, Dow Chemical, and Hewlett-Packard sell more of their products outside the U.S. than they do at home, and U.S.-service companies are close behind. . . . The trend is even more pronounced in terms of profits. In the past three years Coke made more money in both the Pacific and Western Europe than it did in the U.S. Nearly 70% of General Motors Corp.'s 1989 profits were from non-U.S. operations.[1]

Objectives of the Chapter

The changes taking place throughout the globe are creating many opportunities and/or threats for business enterprises. These opportunities and/or threats will lure many domestic enterprises into the international business arena; they will entice those firms that rely only slightly on revenues derived from international business into expanding and relying more on their international operations. This means that more and more corporations will have to develop strategies and establish objectives to internationalize their domestic business operations or to expand their current international business operations. The objectives of this chapter are therefore to:

1. Discuss the opportunities and threats that cause firms to internationalize their operations.
2. Discuss the strategic approaches used by international corporations.
3. Discuss the internal factors managers must understand before they attempt to internationalize their enterprises' business operations.
4. Discuss international strategic and tactical objectives.
5. Discuss the areas in which international objectives should be established.

WHY FIRMS INTERNATIONALIZE THEIR OPERATIONS

Historically, domestic enterprises have **internationalized their business operations** either to seize **opportunities** or to deal with **threats**, or both.[2] For example, as it was pointed out in Chapter 2, the European Union (EU) current efforts to become more unified are expected to present both opportunities and threats for non-EU business enterprises. Practical Perspective 3–1 lists some of the corporations that have developed strategies to seize the opportunities and/or combat the threats anticipated to be presented by the EU unification. The ensuing sections discuss the opportunities and threats that cause domestic enterprises to internationalize their operations.

Opportunity Reasons

The opportunity reasons for internationalizing operations include greater profits, appearance of new markets, faster growth in new markets, obtaining new products for the domestic market, and globalization of financial markets.

Greater Profits

Many domestic firms have internationalized their operations because their managers saw the opportunity to earn greater profits by charging higher prices in a higher per capita income foreign country where a high demand for the product or service existed, or where there was less competition. Enterprises have also internationalized their operations because their managers determined that they could earn higher profits by attaining greater *economies of scale* with the foreign expansion. Additionally, many enterprises have been able to earn greater profits by producing in a country where labor was cheaper and/or where materials cost less than at home.

Selling the Product at Higher Prices.   Companies in many countries, especially in less-developed countries, can often sell their products at a higher price in the more advanced countries. For example, in China one can purchase a bottle of Tsingtao beer for about U.S. $0.20. The same bottle of beer sells for about U.S. $1.15 in the United States.

For illustration purposes, suppose the following scenario exists. A company's annual domestic market share is 110,000 units, its sales price per unit is $100, its variable costs per unit amount to $70, and its fixed costs total $3 million annually. This enterprise's before-tax earnings would be $300,000, computed as follows:

PRACTICAL PERSPECTIVE 3–1

Examples of Firms That Have Reacted to the EC's Unification Aims

The popular press reports many cases of external firms acting to take advantage of the opportunities and/or to combat the threats presented by the EC-92. The Whirlpool Corporation has entered into a $2 billion joint venture in order to penetrate the European appliance market. The International Paper Company has made a $350 million bid for a French paper maker. Shearson Lehman Hutton Inc. has expanded its investment banking offices in Milan and Madrid. Coca-Cola has started construction of one of the world's largest canning plants in France and has revamped its organizational chart to put greater emphasis on the EC. Citicorp, already the most prominent non-European bank in Europe, has purchased banks in Belgium, Italy, and Spain.

AT&T has built a $220 million semiconductor plant in Spain. Connecticut Mutual has set up a Luxembourg-based company, CM Transnational, to sell life insurance. American International Group is restructuring its $500 million European property and casualty insurance operations. AIG is merging most of its operations into one new company, UNAT Europe, replacing 13 different national companies. The U.S.-based Scott Paper Company has started planning for EC-92, because it expects to benefit from simplified border restrictions and the deregulation of trucking, grocery distribution, and retailing. Federal Express has established regional counsels in Belgium and the United Kingdom in order to stay close to EC political developments at all times. To adapt to the anticipated fierce competition in the EC, 3M has formed European Management Action Teams consisting of representatives from management, R&D, sales and marketing, and finance. These teams aim to integrate individual units' business plans and blend them into a Europe-wide strategy in order to compete on a pan-European basis.

Source: Adapted from S. Greenhouse, "U.S. Corporations Expand in Europe for '92 Prospects," *The New York Times*, March 13, 1989, pp. 1, 6; R. W. King, S. J. Dryden, and J. Kapstein, "Who Is That Knocking on Foreign Doors? U.S. Insurance Salesmen," *Business Week*, March 6, 1989, pp. 84–85; H. Lampert, "Bold Strategies for a Brave New Market: Scott Paper Company," *Business Month*, August 1989, pp. 39–41; L. C. White, "Bold Strategies for a Brave New Market: Federal Express," *Business Month*, August 1989, pp. 32–34; T. Murray, "Bold New Strategies for a Brave New Market: 3M," *Business Month*, August 1989, pp. 35–37.

Number of units sold	110,000
Profit margin per unit ($100 − $70)	$30
Net income before fixed costs and taxes	$3,300,000
Fixed costs	$3,000,000
Earnings before taxes	$300,000

Assume the firm determined that if it exported to a certain foreign market it could increase the unit sales price there to $110; that the foreign market share would be 20,000 units; and that it would incur additional costs of $20 per unit to modify those units to fit the specific market's needs and to ship them overseas. In this situation the company would earn, before taxes, an additional $400,000, computed as follows:

Additional units sold	20,000
Before tax profit margin ($110 − $70 − $20)	$20
Additional earnings before taxes	$400,000

Greater Economies of Scale.   To demonstrate the case where the firm can obtain larger profits by attaining greater economies of scale, assume the company determined that, due to market and/or other conditions (such as foreign government restrictions), it could not increase the price to $110 as illustrated above, that it could sell the unit in the foreign market only for the same $100 domestic price. In this situation, due to the attainment of greater economies of scale, the company would still realize an additional $200,000 before tax earnings, computed as follows:

Additional units sold	20,000
Profit margin ($100 − $70 − $20)	$10
Additional earnings before taxes	$200,000

Cheaper Labor and/or Materials.   The cost of labor and materials varies among countries. Table 3–1 presents a comparison of the hourly compensation for workers in manufacturing in some countries (of course, currently the numbers are likely to be higher). And many less-developed nations, to attract foreign investments, have developed a **capable workforce.** The cheaper costs and the capable workforce in a country will sometimes enable foreign firms to realize greater profits if they transfer their manufacturing operations there.

To illustrate the instance where **cheaper labor and/or cheaper materials** in foreign markets contribute to greater profits, suppose the corporation determined that if it established operations in a foreign country it would incur an additional $800,000 in fixed costs; that the variable costs for the units produced abroad would be reduced by 50 percent to $35 per unit; and

Comparative Hourly Compensation (in U.S. dollars) for Workers in Manufacturing	TABLE 3–1 ◆

Country	Hourly Compensation	Year
Britain	$19.42	1991
China	0.26	1990
Germany	22.17	1991
India	0.39	1986
Ireland	11.90	1991
Jamaica	1.61	1990
Japan	14.41	1991
Mexico	2.17	1991
Singapore	4.38	1991
Thailand	0.68	1990
U.S.	15.45	1991

Source: Excerpted from Brian O'Reilly, "Your New Global Work Force," *Fortune,* December 14, 1992, p. 58. Copyright © 1992, Time, Inc., New York. All rights reserved. Reprinted with permission.

that the $20 per unit exporting costs would be reduced to $2. In this scenario, the firm would earn, before tax, an additional $460,000, computed as follows:

Additional units sold	20,000
Before tax profit margin ($100 − $35 − $2)	$63
Earnings before fixed costs/taxes	$1,260,000
Less additional fixed costs	$800,000
Additional earnings before taxes	$460,000

Appearance of New Markets

Population expansion, income growth, and technological advancements around the globe have created **new markets** and demands, and thus new business opportunities. Many domestic firms have internationalized their operations to meet those new demands. For example, Motorola Inc. reorganized its operations to tap into the huge market for chips used by Japanese companies to manufacture consumer goods.[3] Xircom, Inc., which manufactures pocket-size adapters for portable notebook computers, targeted the European Union (EU) in 1991 because of the increased popularity of portable computers there. They expect even greater success when the

EU completes its market integration process.[4] Kobs & Draft, a U.S. direct marketer, has been expanding into foreign markets at a rapid pace because common U.S. technologies are now reaching the rest of the world, therefore creating a demand for its services.[5] Automobile executives throughout the globe are drooling at the vision of hundreds of millions of potential drivers in China. For example, W. Wayne Booker, Ford Motor Co.'s executive vice-president for international operations, has indicated that his No. 1 priority for the 1990s is China.[6]

Faster Growth in New Markets

Many domestic organizations have a strong growth orientation. These firms often enter foreign markets because they can grow at a faster rate there than they can in the established domestic market. For instance, Asian and European computer markets are stronger than the U.S. market, partly because they lag behind the U.S. in computer installations. This enables U.S. computer companies to grow much faster in Asia and Europe than at home. As an example, in 1989, Intel Corporation's European sales were growing twice as fast as they were in the U.S. market.[7] Fusion Systems Corp. of Maryland, which makes sophisticated industrial equipment, began penetrating foreign markets in 1975. At that time, Fusion had 15 employees and $450,000 in annual sales; in 1989, it had 320 employees and $33 million in sales—35 percent from overseas—and for the past five years (1985 to 1990) has grown at the rate of 25 percent.[8]

Obtaining New Products for the Domestic Market

Many individuals from the home market travel abroad and sometimes develop a desire for a new product which they would like to have available in their home market. For example, English ales, German beers, and French wines sell well in the U.S. market. Domestic enterprises therefore internationalize their operations to obtain products for domestic consumers. If they do not, their competitors will.

Globalization of Financial Systems

In recent decades, there has been an expansion in the ways by which international business can be financed. This growth in **financial options** has been the catalyst for the expansion of international business. These new tools include the International Monetary Fund, created in 1945 by the United Nations to encourage and aid world trade, and the World Bank, created by the United Nations for the purpose of encouraging the extension of loans to less-developed countries. Banks such as Citicorp, Dai-IchiKangyo Bank, and Bank Nationale de Paris have grown into international organizations that draw on a variety of investors from many parts of the world.[9]

Threat Reasons

The threat reasons for internationalizing operations include protection from declining demand in the home market, acquisition of raw materials, acquisition of managerial know-how and capital, protection of the home market, and protection from imports.

Protection from Declining Demand in Home Market

Demand for a firm's product or service may be low in the home market due to recessionary conditions, a saturated market, or a declining product life cycle. Many firms have been able to hedge against recessions at home and to maintain their growth by expanding into foreign markets. For example, in the late 1980s, many U.S. technology corporations found themselves headed for a slump in domestic sales. To offset the slump, many of these companies entered the European and Asian markets. For instance, the market for chips in the U.S. went flat in the 1980s, but U.S. firms such as International CMOS Technology Inc. and Microsoft Corp. have done well as a result of booming sales in Europe and Asia. Microsoft's senior vice president for international operations, Jeremy Butler, has said that a firm with overseas sales has a much better chance of surviving because it does not put all its eggs in one basket.[10]

By 1989, several U.S. semiconductor-equipment makers, such as Perkin Elmer Corp., were dropping out of the business. Applied Materials Inc., however, was doing 40 percent of its sales in Japan. Applied Materials is doing well now, in part because it got its foot in the door early; it established its own subsidiaries in Japan in the 1970s. It has gained experience in dealing with Japanese customers, therefore eliminating dependency on Japanese representatives, third parties that increase costs.[11]

Because the American market is saturated, dozens of U.S. insurance companies, including Prudential, Equitable Life, and Connecticut Mutual Life, have been aggressively penetrating new global markets.[12] Philip Morris Co. realized that the domestic cigarette market would shrink because of Americans' evolving health consciousness. It thus expanded into foreign markets.[13] Even though Anheuser-Busch, the beer brewing company, controls 43 percent of the U.S. beer market, its domestic sales growth is slowing dramatically. Analyst Emanuel Goldman of Paine-Webber Inc. estimated that Busch's profits would grow less than 1 percent in 1993 to $1 billion, as sales rose by a mere 2 percent, to $11.6 billion. "That's forcing the brewer to tap into thirstier regions abroad."[14]

To illustrate this aspect mathematically, assume the same conditions used to demonstrate the attainment of greater profits. Suppose that the company's market share declined from 110,000 units annually to 104,000. If this happened, the enterprise's before-taxes earnings would decline from $300,000 to $120,000, computed as follows:

Number of units sold	104,000
Profit margin	$30
Income before fixed costs and taxes	$3,120,000
Fixed costs	$3,000,000
Earnings before taxes	$120,000

If the corporation internationalized its operations, as illustrated in the greater profits discussion above, it could maintain its profit margin or even increase it.

Acquisition of Raw Materials

Many domestic manufacturers depend on and import raw materials available in foreign countries. To be assured of the necessary raw materials, numerous enterprises have set up operations overseas. For example, rubber, which is required by numerous U.S. manufacturers, is not available in continental America. It must therefore be acquired from other countries—those in Southeast Asia, for instance.

Acquisition of Managerial Know-How and Capital

Enterprises sometimes must go abroad to obtain the **managerial know-how and capital** that they lack but need to improve their operations. For example, in recent years, there has been a booming demand for travel in Russia. The Russian airline, Aeroflot, was one of the least efficient airlines in the world. To deal with this problem, the Russian carrier's management shopped around for Western partners who could bring the managerial know-how and capital it needed to meet its expansion demands.[15]

Protection of Home Market

Many firms have internationalized their operations to protect their home market. For example, a firm services a domestic manufacturer which, for its own reasons, decides to set up subsidiary operations abroad. The service enterprise would be wise to follow and provide the services required by the manufacturer's foreign subsidiaries. Otherwise, an aggressive competitor, which gets its "foot in the door" through the manufacturer's foreign subsidiary, may soon take over the service activities in the domestic market as well.

Protection from Imports

Foreign competitors often hold an advantage over domestic firms because they have access to cheaper labor and/or materials in a foreign country. To remain competitive, domestic firms must often transfer their production activities to a foreign country to obtain the same cost advantages the foreign competitors enjoy. For example, many of the parts used to manufacture U.S.-produced automobiles are actually manufactured abroad. Practical Perspective 3–2 presents the case of Applied Digital Data Services, which transferred its manufacturing operations from the U.S. abroad because its chief competitors who had already gone abroad had access to much cheaper material costs.

PRACTICAL PERSPECTIVE 3–2

Applied Digital Data Services Transfers Manufacturing Abroad

Applied Digital Data Services (ADDS), a wholly owned subsidiary of NCR Corp., produces terminals for both its parent company and for other computer OEMs. Founded in 1969 and acquired by NCR in 1981, the firm puts heavy emphasis on a flexible assembly operation that offers quick response—and reliable just-in-time (JIT) delivery—to its customers. The "flex" system was devised as part of ADDS' overall strategy for achieving competitive advantage in returning to U.S. soil. Not many years ago, however, that notion might have seemed a bit paradoxical. In the early 1980's, the company found itself at a distinct cost disadvantage with respect to its chief competitors. Most of them had already shifted manufacturing operations to the Far East—which today dominates many of the core technologies for producing TV and display-terminal components.

It wasn't so much a question of labor costs. "The thing that defeated us in those days was material costs," says David G. Laws, president and CEO of ADDS. "We were buying materials in the U.S. at U.S. prices; and our competitors were buying materials—and consuming them—in the Far East at Far Eastern prices. We found that we were paying in excess of a 30% premium for parts compared to our competitors. And we couldn't crack that problem." So in 1985 ADDS made the difficult decision to shut down its assembly operation in Hauppauge, N.Y. and have its product built by an offshore contract manufacturer that would be able to take advantage of Far Eastern component prices. In some respects, it was a smart decision. The immediate impact was a 23% reduction in product cost—even after adding shipping costs back to the U.S. (More than half of ADDS' business volume is with U.S.-based customers.)

Source: Excerpted from John Sheridan, "ADDS Finds 'There's No Place Like Home'," *Industry Week,* June 17, 1991, pp. 12–13. Reprint with permission from *Industry Week.* Copyright © Penton Publishing, Inc., Cleveland, Ohio.

Why Do Firms Internationalize?

It is not always clear whether firms' internationalization strategies are to seize opportunities or to combat threats. For example, a few years ago PepsiCo's management recognized that its U.S. markets were mature and that it was unlikely to realize profits attempting to capture market share in cola drinks from the formidable Coca-Cola Co. To deal with the situation, PepsiCo's management developed a strategy to cash in on changing eating and drinking habits in the rapidly industrializing parts of the world.[16] Was PepsiCo's strategy stimulated by the threatening situation in its home market or by its desire to seize the new opportunities that arose in foreign markets? In other words, if there had been no threats in its home market, would PepsiCo's management still have developed a strategy to seize the new opportunities in the foreign markets?

THE INTERNAL AUDIT

As suggested above, environmental changes, which are detected through an **external audit** of the global environment (covered in Chapter 2), often require that firms develop international strategies. To help them develop effective international strategies, along with total familiarity with the external environment, managers must examine their enterprises' internal conditions; they must conduct an **internal audit** to become familiar with the company's internal situation. Knowledge of their firm's internal factors will help its managers develop wise strategies for penetrating a foreign market or for coping with environmental changes. Basically, managers need to determine how much money the firm has access to, including cash on hand, borrowing power, and ability to sell stock, which can be used to finance the strategy; the nature of its physical assets; its personnel capabilities; and its strengths.

Foreign Sources of Finance

Even if an enterprise has access to the funds required to finance the expansion, managers should inquire about the availability of financial assistance in the foreign market. The governments of many foreign countries make special concessions to foreign firms that bring them the technologies they believe will aid their nations' development efforts. For example, the government of Morocco was actively seeking foreign investment in its tourist sector. To attract investment, it offered several incentives, such as the possibility of 100 percent foreign ownership, tax exemptions of up to ten years, depending on the location of investment, and the availability of long-term, low-interest financing.[17] (As another illustration, read Practical Perspective 3–3.)

PRACTICAL PERSPECTIVE 3–3

Bangkok's Strategies to Draw Foreign Investments

Bangkok, famed for its tourist attractions and warm hospitality, is now attracting more business people than sightseers. . . . Thailand wavers on the brink of becoming an important international business hub, and opportunity knocks for those who understand this country's native culture and its business and economic climate. . . . One of the reasons why many multinationals have decided to do business in Thailand is that the Thai government is favorable to foreign trade. . . . Thai government development policies, stated under the Sixth Five-Year Development Plan (1987–92), restrict the public sector to a supporting, coordinating, and advisory role, while fostering activity and growth in the private sector.

The Office of the Board of Investments (OBI) encourages development in key industrial segments such as telecommunications, building supplies, medical supplies, and electronics and other technologies by offering privileges and incentives for business that support governmental policy. . . . Encouragement is offered in a number of forms, including holidays or reductions in corporate income taxes, exemptions or reductions on import duty, and exclusion of dividends from taxation. . . . The Thai government also offers guarantees against price controls, state competition, nationalization, the formation of state monopolies, or the granting of special privileges to government agencies or enterprises.

Source: Excerpted from Bill Bruce, "Thailand: The Next NIC?" *The International Executive,* November–December 1990, pp. 35–37. Copyright © 1990. John Wiley & Sons, Inc., New York. All rights reserved. Reprinted by permission of publisher.

Nature of the Firm's Physical Assets and Personnel Competencies

Managers also need to obtain information about the enterprise's physical assets and their current state. Is there idle manufacturing capacity capable of producing the product for the foreign market? Or are new manufacturing means needed? Furthermore, managers must obtain information about their firm's **personnel competencies** in relation to the company's international strategy. Does the enterprise have the personnel capable of producing for the foreign market(s)? Does it have the personnel capable of managing the international operations? Again, the governments of many foreign countries will help foreign firms finance machinery and factories, and will provide trained personnel, or assist them in training personnel, as a means of attracting the technologies to aid in accomplishing the nation's developmental objectives.

The firm's internal conditions also affect how it enters a foreign market. Two fundamental approaches to conducting business in a foreign market are by exporting to it or by manufacturing in it. Exporting involves manufacturing at home and shipping the goods to the foreign market. Exporting generally requires less investment than manufacturing abroad. If the firm is cash-short, has idle equipment, and its personnel is not highly competent in international business, the firm may prefer to export. However, by producing abroad, the company can often save on transportation, labor, and materials costs, as well as on tariffs. Therefore, if an enterprise has adequate cash to invest, has international managerial know-how, the foreign demand justifies the investment, and the foreign environment is conducive to the investment, it may want to produce abroad.

Lead from Strength

The internal audit should also include an assessment of the enterprise's strengths. A business should always "**lead from strength**"; that is, it should focus on doing what it can do better than its competitors. For example, a firm's strength may be engineering and design. Instead of manufacturing, it may be more efficient for the firm to farm it out to a company whose strength is manufacturing. For instance, Apple vice president Al Eisenstat said that "If I can loop off one area of activity and say, 'Gee, I can join with such and such company,' then I can focus my resources on what I do best."[18] Firms such as Apple, Nike, and IBM's PCs have established themselves as design, engineering, and marketing companies, farming out much of their manufacturing to those who are able to do it cheaper and better. Maatschappij Van Berkel's Patent N.V., a Dutch-based multinational supplier of weighing and food processing equipment, met competitive cost pressures by outsourcing its manufacturing and engineering activities and transforming itself into a sales and service company.[19]

Furthermore, a firm may be strong in production, but weak in conducting foreign business. This firm may therefore have to form a **joint venture** or enter into a **strategic alliance** with an enterprise that is strong in conducting foreign business. (Joint ventures and strategic alliances will be discussed more thoroughly in Chapter 4.) Basically, organizations enter into joint ventures or strategic alliances to share costs and risks, to gain additional technical and market knowledge, to complement each other, to serve an international market, to strengthen themselves against other competitors, and to develop industry standards together.[20] As Jack Welch of GE put it, "tomorrow's organization will be boundaryless. It will work with outsiders as closely as if they were insiders."[21] Managers should be aware, however, that joint ventures and strategic alliances can backfire, especially when one of the partners becomes stronger by learning more than the other(s). The stronger partner may break up the alliance and go on its own, which may harm the weaker partner. (For an illustration, read Practical Perspective 3–4, the case of Schwinn Bicycle Co.)

PRACTICAL PERSPECTIVE 3–4

Bury Thy Teacher

In October, Chicago's 97 year-old Schwinn Bicycle Co., the grand name in American bicycles, filed for bankruptcy. On the other side of the world, Antony Lo took a breather from promoting his high-priced mountain bikes at the Tokyo International Cycle Show to deliver an eloquent eulogy for Schwinn, the company that Lo helped bury. "Without Schwinn, we never would have grown to where we are today," said Lo, the polished president of Taiwan's Giant Manufacturing Co., now the world's largest bike exporter. "We learned many basic things from them: quality, value, service." Down in Hong Kong, in his office in a converted factory near the colony's mammoth container port, Jerome Sze, the managing director and a large shareholder of Shenzhen, China's publicly traded China Bicycles Co., also pays his respects to the American company that helped him grow. "Schwinn," says Sze, "helped to promote our products in the U.S."

. . . [The] great American company lost its way and, through management blunders, created powerful competitors that ultimately did it in. Says Scott Montgomery, president of Cannondale Japan, a wholly owned unit of the successful Georgetown, Conn. high-end bike company: "After Schwinn built them up (Giant and China Bicycles), they ate Schwinn." . . . Schwinn's fortunes began to unravel in the 1980s. In the 1970s Schwinn still had a strong ten-speed business; this was based on its powerful retail distribution network and brand name. But in the 1980s the market shifted to mountain bikes, now 60% of the entire market, and to exotic bikes for adult enthusiasts, built of lightweight materials such as aluminum and carbon fibre. Once the innovator, Schwinn became the market follower. It never led with innovation in mountain bikes. Says J.C. McCullagh, editor and publisher of *Bicycling*, the industry's leading trade publication: "Schwinn had the best bike engineers in the country but it lost its edge because its management didn't respond quickly enough." Schwinn had grown flabby in other areas. Until recently, for example, it hadn't bothered to develop much of a presence in overseas markets, a deficiency because specialty bikes—not unlike cars—are global, fast-changing products.

Going overseas in the 1970s, Schwinn was more concerned with moving production out of the U.S. than with selling abroad. "Schwinn was obsessed with cutting costs," says Cannondale Japan's Montgomery, "instead of innovation." Schwinn began its foreign campaign by sourcing many of its bicycles from Japan. By 1978 the expanding Taiwanese bike industry was already beating Japanese producers on price. Again Schwinn was forced to react. This time it did so by importing a small quantity of Taiwanese-made Giant bikes, on which Schwinn slapped its nameplate. Then, in 1981, another nail in the coffin: The workers went on strike at Schwinn's main factory in Chicago. Management panicked. Instead of negotiating a settlement, Schwinn closed the plant and sent its engineers and equipment to Giant's factory in Taichung, a port city in western Taiwan. Recalls Giant's Antony Lo: "Schwinn thought that if the strike went on a long time, it would kill Schwinn dealers. They asked for our help in increasing capacity quickly."

As part of its new partnership with Giant, Schwinn handed over everything—technology, engineer-ing, volume—that Giant needed to become a dominant bikemaker. In return, Schwinn imported the bikes and marketed them in the U.S. under the Schwinn name. Says an executive of a U.S. competitor. "Schwinn gave the franchise to Giant on a silver platter." (Schwinn declined to be interviewed for this story.) By 1984 the Taiwanese tail was wagging the American dog. Giant was shipping 700,000 bicycles a year to Schwinn under the Schwinn nameplate, fully 70% of Schwinn's and Giant's sales. According to the U.S. competitor, Schwinn could have driven a much harder bargain in Taiwan. "If Schwinn had gone to any bicycle maker in Taiwan and told them they would give them 700,000 units, they could easily have gotten a 50% share of the company," he says. But privately owned Giant refused to sell any equity to Schwinn, and Schwinn declined to press the point.

As a result, the Americans had no control over Giant's strategy. They could not, for instance, later prevent Giant from using the knowledge gained about specialty bike dealers to launch its own brand name in the U.S. Which is what the Taiwanese did. Armed with Schwinn's technical specifications but able to produce at lower prices, Giant introduced its own brand-name bikes in Europe in 1986 and in the U.S. in 1987. No copycat, Giant later improved upon Schwinn's technology. By 1990, for example, it had become the world's largest manufacturer of carbon fibre frame bikes. Its best selling bikes retail for $400 to $600, more than Schwinn's popular models. The clever student quickly stole business from its old American teacher. "Giant bought market share in the U.S. by telling dealers, its bikes were the same as Schwinn's, but 10% to 15% cheaper," says Ash Jaising, president of the independent Boston-based Bicycle Market Research Institute. To build its U.S. distribution, Giant hired several former Schwinn executives. . . .

Dazed by Giant's aggressive brand-name push, Schwinn tried to protect itself by forging a new alliance, this time with Jerome Sze's China Bicycle Co. It began buying CBC's bikes and selling them under the Schwinn name. This time Schwinn demanded and got some equity in the venture with CBC, buying a 33% stake in 1987 (since diluted to 18% after CBC went public on the fledgling Shenzhen stock exchange early this year [1992]). Until Schwinn went into business with China Bicycles, CBC's main business in the U.S. was supplying commodity house-brand bikes to Sears and other mass merchandisers from its low-cost factory in Shenzhen, in the heart of southern China's capitalist revolution. . . . But Schwinn taught CBC about the U.S. specialty dealer market, raised the Chinese factory's quality standards and lent it credibility. "CBC came light-years in a short period of time because of a lot of technology transfer from Schwinn," says Bicycling's McCullagh. Sze subsequently used all the knowledge he gleaned from Schwinn to help bolster his business supplying bicycles to the European operations of bike companies such as Scott and France's MBK (owned by Japan's Yamaha).

Burned once by Giant, Schwinn tried to dissuade China Bicycles from developing its own brand-name business in the U.S. But that didn't stop Sze. In 1990, despite Schwinn's opposition, Sze and his Shenzhen partner together acquired a medium-size U.S. bicycle importer and distributor, which owned the Diamond Back name. That gave CBC its own U.S. brand name and distribution channels. Diamond Back competes directly with Schwinn and is particularly strong on the West Coast. With Giant, China Bicycles and other competitors taking big bites out of its market share, Schwinn was finally forced to file for bankruptcy in October. It still imports bikes from its two former students and sells them under the Schwinn name. But production of its own bikes in the U.S. is down to under 10,000 units a year, sold under the Paramount name of high-priced racing bikes.

Source: Excerpted from Andrew Tanzer, "Bury Thy Teacher," *Forbes*, December 21, 1992, pp. 90–95. Reprinted by permission of *Forbes* magazine. Copyright © Forbes, Inc., 1992.

It should be noted that foreign countries' environments generally have an effect on a firm's strengths and weaknesses. For example, an organization may possess a strong ability to distribute a product in one nation because it is capable of dealing with that country's distribution laws and practices. At the same time it may possess a weak capability to distribute in another country because it lacks the ability to deal with that nation's distribution laws and practices. For instance, international business transactions are either in cash or in barter trade (to be discussed in Chapter 4). Many enterprises have experience in cash transactions, but not in barter trade transactions. In the latter case, if the enterprise wishes to penetrate a foreign market where barter trade is required, it may have to form a partnership with a firm that has experience in barter trade.

Also, an enterprise may possess the ability to differentiate a product to fit the needs of a specific country's culture, and at the same time lack the ability to differentiate to fit another country's cultural needs. U.S. car manufacturers, for example, have historically possessed the capability of differentiating their automobiles to fit the needs of many countries, but not the needs of some countries, such as England, where the steering wheel is located on the right-hand side of the automobile. In this case, if a U.S. car manufacturer wanted to penetrate the British car market, it might have to form a partnership with a car manufacturer that had the capability of producing cars with the steering wheel on the right-hand side.

TYPES OF INTERNATIONAL STRATEGIES

International firms typically develop their core strategy for the home country first. Subsequently, they internationalize their core strategy through international expansion of activities and through adaptation. Eventually, they globalize their strategy by integrating operations across nations.[22] These steps translate into three distinct types of strategies applied by international enterprises: ethnocentric, multidomestic, and global.

Ethnocentric Strategy

Following World War II, U.S. enterprises operated mainly from an **ethnocentric** perspective. These companies produced unique goods and services, which they offered primarily to the domestic market. The lack of international competition offset their need to be sensitive to cultural differences. When these firms exported goods, they did not alter them for foreign consumption—the costs of alterations for cultural differences were assumed by the foreign buyers. In effect, this type of company has one strategy for all markets.

Multidomestic Strategy

The **multidomestic firm** (discussed as an MNC in Chapter 1) has a different strategy for each of its foreign markets. In this type of strategy, "a company's management tries to operate effectively across a series of worldwide positions with diverse product requirements, growth rates, competitive environments and political risks. The company prefers that local managers do what is necessary to succeed in R&D, production, marketing, and distribution, but holds them responsible for results."[23] In essence, this type of corporation competes with local competitors on a market-by-market basis. A multitude of American corporations use this strategy, for example, Procter & Gamble in household products, Honeywell in controls, Alcoa in aluminum, and General Foods in consumer goods. Practical Perspective 3–5 presents Aldus' international localization strategy.

PRACTICAL PERSPECTIVE 3–5

Aldus International Strategy

At Aldus, entering foreign markets was not a strategy pursued after its products had been successfully marketed in the U.S. Aldus President Paul Brainerd set out from the beginning to build products that could be quickly adapted to local markets. . . . Aldus, established in 1984, currently [1990] employs about five hundred people and grossed nearly $80 million in 1988. The firm's major product is a computer program known as PageMaker that allows individuals to design, edit, and produce printed documents using microcomputer systems available to most businesses. The firm's potential market includes both businesses that generate documents and the publishing industry itself. . . .

The first U.S. version of Aldus PageMaker was shipped in July 1985. But even before the end of 1984, Brainerd had made a trip to Europe to set up channels of distribution. He was determined to introduce Aldus products almost simultaneously in the U.S. and Europe. But the firm was small and had very little capital at the time. (An initial public offering of common stock would raise approximately $30 million in June 1987.) "We had to build a step-by-step progression of just what we could afford to do at any given point in the development of the company," Brainerd says. So Aldus developed a strategy to penetrate foreign markets quickly and at minimal cost. . . . The first phase of the plan was to engineer PageMaker in such a way that the computer program could be readily and quickly adapted to different national markets. "Localization" is the term employed by Aldus executives.

Since PageMaker and similar programs are oriented to text and
design considerations, the same
program can hardly be sold in different countries. Software must be
modified to conform to local languages and design idioms. . . .

Localization projects have
ranged from international English
(distinct from American usage) to
European languages with their different hyphenation requirements,
to Asian languages with thousands
of characters as well as vertical

headlines and right to left orientation . . . . Although PageMaker
was designed to be adopted to foreign requirements, the capital constraints remained. Brainerd
describes the Aldus solution: "We
worked out a strategy where the
distributors who wished to carry
our products would essentially do
the work for us. They would front
end the investment for localization,
and we would pay them back on a
per-unit basis as they sold the software."

Global Strategy

The **global corporation** (discussed in Chapter 1) uses all of its resources against its competition in a very integrated fashion. All of its foreign sub-sidiaries and divisions are highly interdependent in both operations and strategy. As an expert said:

> In a global business, management competes worldwide against a small number of other multinationals in the world market. Strategy is centralized, and various aspects of operations are decentralized or centralized as economics and effec-tiveness dictate. The company seeks to respond to particular local market needs, while avoiding a compromise of efficiency of the overall global system.[24]

Therefore, whereas in a multidomestic strategy the managers in each country react to competition without considering what is taking place in other countries, in a global strategy, competitive moves are integrated across nations. The same kind of move is made in different countries at the same time or in a systematic fashion. For example, a competitor is attacked in one nation in order to exhaust its resources for another country, or a competitive attack in one nation is countered in a different country—for instance, the counterattack in a competitor's home market as a parry to an attack on one's home market.[25] As an illustration, read Practical Perspective 3–6, the case of Goodyear.

Numerous MNCs are applying the global strategy, including IBM in computers, Caterpillar in large construction equipment, Timex, Seiko, and

PRACTICAL PERSPECTIVE 3-6

Goodyear's Think and Act Globally Philosophy

In the early 1970s, France's Group Michelin shocked America's leading tire makers—particularly Goodyear Tire & Rubber Co.—by invading the U.S. market. Goodyear, which was serving French and other European markets before Michelin ever existed, viewed the very presence of the French upstart in the U.S. as a frontal attack. The Akron-based company responded immediately. But it didn't limit its retaliation to the U.S., where only a small fraction of Michelin's business was concentrated. Instead, Goodyear attacked in Europe—the source of most of the French tire maker's profits. Goodyear's counter assault didn't bring Michelin's expansion plans to an halt, but it did slow its penetration into the U.S. considerably. Michelin was forced to divert its financial resources to defend its home-front market. Today [1986], Goodyear remains the No. 1 tire builder in the U.S.—and in the world. . . . Ever since that marketplace attack/counterattack, Goodyear has insisted that all of its managers and employees, domestic and foreign, think and manage "globally" without regard to national borders.

Source: Excerpted from Lad Kuzela, "The Rise of the Mega Managers," *Industry Week*, November 27, 1986, p. 37.

Citizen in watches, and General Electric, Siemens, and Mitsubishi in heavy electrical equipment. The reasons why this strategy can work include "growing similarity of what citizens of different countries want to buy; the reduction of tariff and nontariff barriers; technology investments that are becoming too expensive to amortize in one market only; and competitors that are globalizing the rules of the game."[26] Whirlpool, which was mainly a North American corporation, now applies a global strategy. It manufactures in eleven nations with facilities in the U.S., Europe, and Latin America, and markets products in more than 120 locations as diverse as Thailand, Hungary, and Argentina.[27] Practical Perspective 3–7 describes Whirlpool's global strategy.

Advantages and Disadvantages of the Global Strategy

Outlined below are the advantages and disadvantages of the global strategy.[28] The advantages of the global strategy would negate the disadvantages of the multidomestic strategy, and the disadvantages of the global strategy

PRACTICAL PERSPECTIVE   3-7

Whirlpool's Views on Global Strategy

The only way to gain lasting competitive advantage is to leverage your capabilities around the world so that the company as a whole is greater than the sum of its parts. Being an international company—selling globally, having global brands or operations in different countries—isn't enough. In fact, most international manufacturers aren't truly global. They're what I [Whirlpool CEO David R. Whitwan] call flag planters. They may have acquired or established businesses all over the world, but their regional and national divisions still operate as autonomous entities. In this day and age, you can't run a business that way and expect to gain a long-range competitive advantage.

To me, "competitive advantage" means having the best technologies and processes for designing, manufacturing, selling, and servicing your products at the lowest possible costs. Our vision at Whirlpool is to integrate our geographical businesses wherever possible, so that our most advanced expertise in any given area—whether it's refrigeration technology, financial reporting systems, or distribution strategy—isn't confined to one location or division. We want to be able to take the best capabilities we have and leverage them in all our operations worldwide.

In the major-appliance industry, both the size of our products and varying consumer preferences require us to have regional manufacturing centers. But even though the features, dimensions, and configurations of machines like refrigerators, washing machines, and ovens vary from market to market, much of the technology and manufacturing processes involved are similar. In other words, while a company may need plants in Europe, the United States, Latin America, and Asia to make products that meet the special needs of local markets, it's still possible and desirable for those plants to share the best available product technologies and manufacturing processes. . . . [Before you can develop common technologies and processes] you must create an organization whose people are adept at exchanging ideas, processes, and systems across borders, people who are absolutely free of the "not-invented-here" syndrome, people who are constantly working together to identify the best global opportunities and the biggest global problems facing the organization. If you're going to ask people to work together in pursuing global ends across organizational and geographic boundaries, you have to give them a vision of what they're striving to achieve, as well as a unifying philosophy to guide their efforts.

That's why we've worked so hard at Whirlpool to define and communicate our vision, objectives, and the market philosophy that represents our unifying focus. Our vision is to be one company worldwide. Our overarching objective is to drive this company to world-class performance in terms of delivering shareholder value. . . . Our market philosophy suggests that the only way to deliver this value over a long term is by focusing on the customer. Only prolonged, intensive effort to understand and respond to genuine customer needs can lead to the breakthrough products and services that earn long-term customer loyalty. . . .

Before 1987, we didn't see the potential power our existing capabilities could give us in the global market because we had been limiting our definition of the appliance market to the United States. Obviously, this also limited our definition of the industry itself and the opportunity it offered. Our eight months of analysis turned up a great deal of evidence that, over time, our industry could become global, whether we chose to become global or not. With that said, we had three choices. We could ignore the inevitable—a decision that would have condemned Whirlpool to a slow death. We could wait for globalization to begin and then try to react, which would have put us in the catch-up mode, technologically and organizationally. Or we could control our own destiny and try to shape the very nature of globalization in our industry. In short, we could force our competition to respond to us.

Before we began making moves on the global stage, Electrolux was out in front of us. It had bought White Consolidated and had acquired several appliance makers in Europe. But Electrolux appeared to be taking advantage of individual opportunities rather than following a coordinated plan. After our Philips acquisition, we also saw General Electric take some opportunities steps. Today, however, Whirlpool is the front-runner when it comes to implementing a pan-European strategy and leveraging global resources. By expanding our strategic horizon, not just our geographic reach, we've been able to build global management capability that provides us with what we feel is a distinct competitive advantage. Clearly, this should enable us to improve returns to our shareholders significantly.

Source: Reprinted by permission of *Harvard Business Review.* An excerpted from Regina Fazio Maruca, "The Right Way to Go Global: An Interview with Whirlpool CEO David Whitwan," *Harvard Business Review* (March–April 1994): 136–139. Copyright © 1994 by the President and Fellows of Harvard College; all rights reserved.

of the multidomestic strategy, and the disadvantages of the global strategy would be negated by the advantages of the multidomestic strategy.

Advantages (*Multidomestic strategy does not provide these advantages*)

- By pooling production or other activities for two or more nations, a firm can increase the benefits derived from economies of scale.
- A company can cut costs by moving manufacturing or other activities to low-cost countries.
- A firm that is able to switch production among different nations can reduce costs by increasing its bargaining power over suppliers, workers, and host governments.
- By focusing on a smaller number of products and programs than under a multidomestic strategy, a corporation is able to improve both product and program quality.
- Worldwide availability, serviceability, and recognition can increase preference through reinforcement.
- The company is provided with more points from which to attack and counterattack competition.

Disadvantages (*Multidomestic strategy can reduce these disadvantages*)

- Through increased coordination, reporting requirements, and added staff, substantial management costs can be incurred.
- Overcentralization can harm local motivation and morale, therefore reducing the firm's effectiveness.
- Standardization can result in a product that does not totally satisfy any customers.
- Incurring costs and revenues in multiple countries increases currency.
- Integrated competitive moves can lead to the sacrificing of revenues, profits, or competitive positions in individual countries—especially when the subsidiary in one country is told to attack a global competitor in order to convey a signal or divert that competitor's resources from another nation.

INTERNATIONAL STRATEGIC AND TACTICAL OBJECTIVES

Organizations generally establish two kinds of measurable objectives: strategic and tactical. **Strategic objectives**, which are guided by the enterprise's mission or purpose and deal with long-term issues, associate the enterprise to its external environment and provide management with a basis for comparing performance with that of its competitors and in relation to environmental demands. (Refer again to the Whirlpool case, Practical Perspective 3–7.) Examples of strategic objectives include: to increase sales, to increase market share, to increase profits, and to lower prices by becoming an international firm. **Tactical objectives**, which are guided by the enterprise's strategic objectives and deal with shorter term issues, identify the key result areas in which specific performance is essential for the success of the enterprise, and aim to attain internal efficiency. They identify specifically how, for example, to lower costs, to lower prices, to increase output, to capture a larger portion of the market, and to penetrate an international market.

Areas in Which Objectives Should Be Established

Professor Peter Drucker, the globally known management authority, has indicated that objectives should be established in at least eight areas of organizational performance: market standing, innovations, productivity, physical and financial resources, profitability, manager performance and responsibility, worker performance and attitude, and social responsibility.[29]

Market Standing

In general, *market standing* objectives measure performance relating to products/service, markets, distribution, and customer service. In an international context, a firm's strategic objective may be to increase market share by entering foreign markets. Tactical objectives established to enter foreign markets may include refocusing advertising, product/service, and pricing to fit each foreign market's environment. Performance measures must therefore be developed for each foreign market. Overall, international firms need to measure performance relating to worldwide, region, and country sales volume.

Innovations

A strategic *innovation* objective may be to lead the industry in introducing new products; a tactical objective may be to spend a specific percentage of revenues from sales for research and development (R&D). Innovation objectives are based on a clear vision of where a firm wants to be ten, fifteen, twenty years from now. R&D may aim at innovation of patentable products and/or production technology—U.S. firms tend to focus on the former and Japanese firms on the latter. It is generally believed that the global and competitive battles of the 1990s will be won by enterprises that are able to get out of the traditional and declining product markets by building and dominating basically new markets. Many believe that Japanese firms' **production technology superiority** coupled with the fact that they are rapidly catching up to the U.S. in the ability to innovate in new products will put them at a competitive advantage in the global market (read Practical Perspective 3–8). Managers must also establish tactical objectives concerning the redesigning of products/services to fit the needs of each specific foreign market their firms wish to penetrate. And they must develop strategies related to the type of technology to be transferred abroad.

PRACTICAL PERSPECTIVE 3–8

Other Nations Catching Up to the U.S. in Creativity

The U.S. still spends the most on research and development by far. But the rest of the world is spending more and more, unleashing a flood of creative energy. . . . It was inevitable, of course that other countries should catch up. "Simple statistics tell you that the U.S. can never again monopolize science and technology, no matter how hard it tries," says Simon Ramo, co-founder of TRW Inc. "Today, we've got somewhat less than half of the world population of technical PhDs, so we can realistically expect to generate close to half of all new innovations." As education levels rise throughout the world, the U.S. will lose its PhD edge. "Tomorrow, we'll have much less than half," Ramo adds. . . .

For the Japanese, already the masters of manufacturing, making a mark in original science is the goal. "Given the financial resources they can bring to bear," says C. Kumar N. Patel, executive director of materials-science research at AT&T Bell Laboratories, "they will be giving us a real run for our money in 5 or 10 years." Sony Corp., for example, now devotes up to 25% of its R&D to precompetitive research. No U.S. company spends half that percentage. West Germany and other nations of

Northern Europe are coming from the other direction. Building on a rich scientific heritage, they are focusing on innovation—becoming more receptive to new inventions and moving them quickly to market. . . .

Both Europe and Japan can afford these measures because their private and public coffers are flush, thanks in part to policies that preserved the wealth-generating potential of such manufacturing industries as consumer electronics and machine tools. That also gives them the means to buy American talent in the hunt for ideas. At leading research labs in the U.S. such as SRI International, PA Consulting Group, and Battelle Memorial Institute, most research is now funded by overseas companies, mainly Japanese. . . . The Japanese have always been willing to invest in risky long-term projects, because of a sense that they're on the same team. "We know we can trust each other—we share this common culture," says Junichi Shimada, senior manager at Japan's Electrotechnical Laboratory (ETL), an arm of the Ministry of International Trade and Industry (MITI).

On the other hand, he concedes, this sameness extracts a toll: Potential whiz-kid scientists are culturally discouraged from expressing their creativity. In the U.S. "geniuses aren't so shy" about challenging authority, he adds, "and that's why the major new ideas always come from the U.S." To tap that well of innovation, several Japanese companies are sprinkling research centers throughout the U.S. In 1986, the local subsidiary of Otsuka Pharmaceuticals, Oncomembrane Inc., created Biomembrane Institute, a nonprofit operation in Seattle. Hitachi Chemical Co. has a $20 million research facility at the University of California at Irvine. And last year, NEC Corp. opened a $25 million artificial intelligence lab in Princeton, N.J. All told, Japanese industry has close to 200 R&D bases on foreign soil, employing nearly 4,500 researchers.

In 1987, says Shoichi Saba, former president of Toshiba Corp., Japan's overseas R&D expenditures topped $300 million. That figure is bound to surge as the Japanese turn their attention to Europe's united market, now just around the corner.

European and Japanese companies also are picking American brains by buying whole companies or minority positions, much to the dismay of some U.S. legislators. One recent headline-grabber was Swiss drugmaker Hoffmann-La Roche Inc.'s $2.1 billion acquisition of 60% of Genentech Inc., the company that launched the biotechnology revolution. Far more prevalent are smaller investments that attract less attention. Three months ago, Silicon Graphics Inc. agreed to part with a 5% stake in return for $35 million from Japanese steelmaker NKK Corp. It was a tough decision for James H. Clark, chairman of the maker of graphics work stations. But SGI needed to round up the money to develop its next-generation system, and Clark couldn't find a competitive deal at home. "Every promising small company is going to be forced to seek capital overseas," he predicts, because Wall Street's short-term mind-set puts so low a value on long-term investment.

Classification of Technology.   The term *technology* has been defined as machinery, blueprints, process designs, equipment, products, patents, licenses, trademarks, and other techniques such as marketing and advertising, accounting, personnel management, and general management.[30] It should be noted that old technology in the home market may sometimes be innovative technology in a foreign market. Technology has been classified as hard and soft, proprietary and nonproprietary, bundled and unbundled, and front-end and obsolete technology.[31]

Hard technology includes hard goods, blueprints, technical specifications, and knowledge and assistance necessary for the efficient use of such hardware. *Soft technology* includes management, marketing, financial organization, and administrative techniques. *Proprietary technology* is technology that is owned by particular individuals or organizations. *Nonproprietary technology* includes knowledge that can be imitated or reproduced by observation or reverse engineering without infringement on proprietary rights. **Reverse engineering** means learning to reproduce technology by taking it apart to determine how it works and then copying it. *Bundled technology* is controlled technology which the owner is willing to transfer as part of a package. The owner maintains an ownership interest in the overseas affiliate using the technology. *Unbundled technology* is technology that is transferred independent of the supplier's total package of resources. *Front-end technology* is the most advanced technology available. *Obsolete technology* is usually older technology.

Export Older or Advanced Technology?   Historically, some less-developed countries (LDCs) have sought to import **advanced technologies** from developed countries and others have pursued the importation of **older technology**. A survey has addressed the question of whether LDCs should import the most advanced technology available or older technology that may be obsolete in the developed countries.[32] Some international executives feel that LDCs with low capital and an abundance of labor should import older technology. They believe that many LDCs in this situation lack the infrastructure, both material and in human resources, "to support, feed, operate and gainfully exploit advanced technology."[33] Other international executives suggest that LDCs should import technology that promotes employment, that is, they should import labor-intensive older technology, especially in those countries where unemployment and underemployment is a severe problem.

A number of executives disagree. They feel that in most situations, LDCs should import the most advanced technology available. One reason for this perspective is that in the long range, older technology produces inferior products and the country thus becomes less competitive in world markets. Another reason is that, regardless of social effects on employment, the most modern technology will contribute more to a country's national income. It is also felt that if countries import the obsolete technology of advanced countries, they will always remain LDCs. Some international executives feel that the sophistication of technology should be based on the destination of the product. If the product manufactured by the imported technology is for local consumption, then older technology would be more appropriate; if, however, the product produced is for exporting, advanced technology would work better.[34] Another view is that the approach a country uses is contingent upon such factors as its economic situation, its leaders, and its people. For example, an oil-rich LDC may be able to afford the acquisition of advanced technology. On the other hand, a very poor LDC may be better off importing older, labor-intensive technology, which is often obsolete in the advanced countries and thus less costly. Some leaders have greater ability than others in implementing new technologies, and people in some cultures are more open to innovation than people in others.

Tactical objectives relative to the type of technology—old or new—a firm transfers are therefore influenced by nations' perceived needs, as well as by the extent the enterprise's management protects its intellectual property rights. High-technology industries are generally very concerned with intellectual property rights. The laws protecting such rights, however, vary considerably throughout the globe. It was estimated by the U.S. International Trade Commission that in 1984 infringement of intellectual property throughout the world cost $8 billion in lost U.S. sales. The loss could be even greater today. Further, it is alleged that U.S. enterprises have suffered from a "lack of rigorous and uniform international standards for intellectual property rights."[35] U.S. Senator John J. Rockefeller has communicated some concerns in this respect. He stated that: "Once the technology is developed and the resulting product is commercialized, it is vital that patent rights be protected. If a company cannot sell its products and recoup its development costs, the next product will not be developed."[36]

Productivity

Productivity is usually measured by the ratio of output to input, for example, ratio of output to labor costs, ratio of output to capital costs, ratio of value added to sales, and ratio of value added to profit. In an international context, the manager is concerned with the ratio of foreign to domestic production volume, and the economics of scale by means of international production integration. A strategic objective may be to reduce production costs. Tactical objectives based on this strategic objective may include replacing equipment, enhancing plant utilization rates, improving quality control, and transferring production overseas where labor and/or material costs are lower (refer again to Practical Perspective 3–2). Tactical objectives may also include the development of a system for forecasting, monitoring, and interpreting costs. Japan's cost-management system is much more sophisticated than America's. For example, U.S. enterprises developing a new product normally design it first and then compute the cost. If it is too much, the product is returned to the drawing board—or the firm accepts a lower profit. On the other hand, the Japanese begin with a target cost estimated on the price the market is likely to accept. Subsequently, they instruct designers and engineers to meet the target. (See Figure 3–1.) The Japanese system also encourages managers to be concerned less about a product's cost than about the

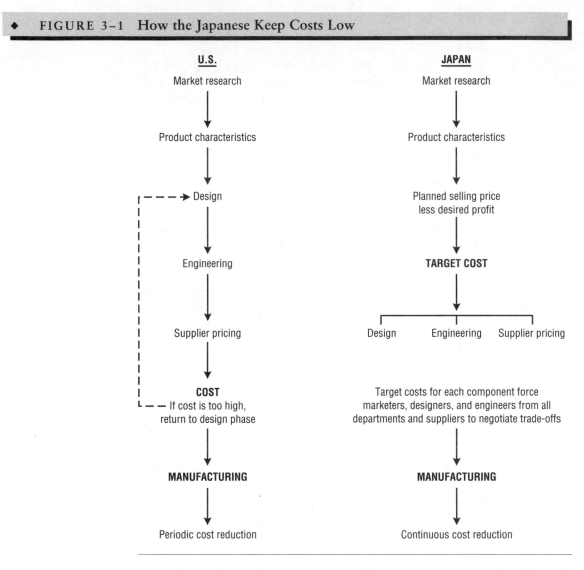

◆   FIGURE 3–1   How the Japanese Keep Costs Low

Source: Ford S. Worthy, "Japan's Smart Secret Weapon," *Fortune,* August 12, 1991, p. 73. Copyright © 1991 Time Inc., New York. All rights reserved. Reprinted by permission.

role it could play in gaining market share. This approach is a large reason Japanese firms often generate winning products the accountants would have killed in a U.S. firm.[37]

Physical and Financial Resources

Physical and financial measures include current ratio, working-capital turnover, the acid test ratio, debt to equity ratio, accounts receivable, and inventory turnover. In an international dimension, managers are concerned with how foreign affiliates are to be financed (for example, by retained earnings, franchising, borrowing, or forming joint ventures), with minimizing the tax burden globally, and with foreign exchange management that seeks to minimize losses from monetary exchange fluctuations.

Profitability

Profitability measures include the ratios of profits to sales, profits to total assets, and profits to net worth. A strategic objective may be to increase profits. Tactical objectives may be to reduce costs by consolidating functions, or, as discussed earlier in this chapter, by transferring operations overseas where costs and/or materials are lower.

Manager Performance and Responsibility

Managers' international performance and responsibility are based on their skills. A strategic objective may be to identify and upgrade critical areas of international management depth and succession. A tactical objective may be to establish programs aimed at developing managers with a **global outlook** (refer again to Chapter 1), at developing host country nationals for managerial positions, and to initiate programs aimed at preparing employees for foreign assignments. (This will be discussed more thoroughly in Chapters 6 and 7.)

Worker Performance and Attitude

A strategic objective to improve worker performance and attitude may be to maintain levels of employee satisfaction consistent with the firm's industry and with similar industries, since this is part of an organization's stability and durability. Tactical objectives in this aspect may include bonus plans, pay increases, and application of participative management. In an international context, equipment transfers to a foreign country, in comparison to transferring technical skills, is relatively easy. The problem is when there is a **shortage of trained personnel** in the country and/or workers do not maintain the proper attitude and are low producers. When this is the case, the firm must develop and implement training programs.

For example, after nearly a half a century of communism, China has recently began to shift to a market economy. The vastness of China's market potential and low labor costs makes it attractive for foreign corporations to invest there. Under the communist regime, a system evolved of paying employees the same whether they worked hard or not. Therefore, the skills and efficiency of China's workforce does not yet compare to those of the advanced nations' workforces. Thus, foreign corporations establishing subsidiaries in China may need to implement appropriate training programs. For instance, Motorola Inc. sponsors a technical university and provides hundreds of scholarships to support its new plant in China established to produce paging devices. Panasonic implemented a military-like boot camp for workers at its Beijing television tube plant. Xian-Jenssen Pharmaceutical Ltd., a China-U.S. joint venture, spends several thousand dollars to train each local employee; it offers in-house courses in sales, accounting, English, and computer usage.[38]

Other strategic objectives may be to control excessive absenteeism and lateness. It should be noted that individuals in some cultures object to too much control. They believe that it is none of the corporation's business as to why an employee is absent, and any attempt to control absenteeism is viewed as corporate exploitation of individuals. Therefore, rather than attempting to control absenteeism in some cultures, a flexible work system may sometimes be more appropriate.

Social Responsibility

A *social responsibility* objective would be to respond appropriately everywhere possible to societal expectations and environmental needs. For example, Canon Corporation's "spiritual" basis for its activities and the behavioral norms for employees are based on the following managerial philosophy:

> 1. To manufacture the best products in the world and thereby contribute to advancement of international development, and 2. To build an ideal corporation that will enjoy continuous prosperity.[39]

Corporate social responsibility is built into the Japanese system—more and more Japanese enterprises are giving a percentage of their profits to promote education, social welfare, and culture.

Furthermore, all businesses have the responsibility to correct the environmental problems they created in attaining their goals and objectives. Most nations are concerned with environmental problems and have laws mandating corrective and/or preventive action (in the U.S., the Environmental Protection Agency enforces these laws). Also, companies that employ child labor are viewed as socially irresponsible in many nations. International corporations must develop objectives in this respect, otherwise there can be negative consequences. (This topic will be discussed more thoroughly in Chapter 13.)

SUMMARY

This chapter has proposed that domestic business enterprises internationalize their operations in response to opportunities and threats generated by changes that have taken place in foreign markets. They develop international strategies to seize the opportunities or to combat the threats. To develop effective international strategies, managers must be totally familiar with the firm's external environment, as well as with its internal resources and capabilities. If a firm does not possess the ability to manage international operations, it may have to form a partnership with a firm that does. The chapter also described three types of international strategies: ethnocentric, multidomestic, and global, and it presented the advantages and disadvantages of the multidomestic and the global strategies. And it concluded that the international enterprise must establish strategic and tactical objectives in at least eight areas of organizational performance: market standing, innovations, productivity, physical and financial resources, profitability, manager performance and responsibility, worker performance and attitude, and social responsibility.

Key Terms

1. Internationalization of operations
2. Opportunities and threats
3. Capable workforce in foreign country
4. Cheaper labor and/or materials
5. Appearance of new markets
6. Globalization of financial systems; financial options
7. Declining demand in home market
8. Acquisition of managerial know-how and capital
9. External and internal audit
10. Foreign sources of finance
11. Personnel competencies
12. Lead from strength
13. Joint venture; strategic alliance
14. International strategies: ethnocentric, multidomestic, and global strategy
15. Competing locally
16. Competing worldwide
17. International strategic and tactical objectives
18. Production technology superiority
19. Classification of technology
20. Reverse engineering
21. Older and advanced technology
22. A global outlook
23. Shortage of trained personnel in foreign country
24. Corporate social responsibility

Discussion Questions and Exercises

1. Why do domestic enterprises internationalize their business operations?
2. You are an international management consultant hired by a firm that sells computers only in the U.S. market. The firm's growth rate has been steadily declining over the past few years. The firm's management

is seeking a solution to the problem. What would you advise the management to do? Why? Where?

3. How are greater profits realized in the global market?

4. Discuss the "globalization of financial systems" opportunity.

5. You are an international management consultant hired by a firm that manufactures and sells textiles in the U.S. Competition from Hong Kong is rapidly taking away the firm's market share. The firm's management is seeking a solution. What would you advise the management to do? Why? Where?

6. List some of the U.S. insurance companies that have internationalized their operations. Why did they do it?

7. You are an international management consultant hired by a domestic firm that has decided to internationalize its operations. An internal audit revealed that the firm has strong production capabilities but lacks personnel with international management capabilities. What would you advise the management to do?

8. Discuss some of the major ideas contained in Practical Perspectives 3–1 to 3–8.

9. Discuss the three types of international strategy.

10. What are the advantages and disadvantages of multidomestic strategy and global strategy?

11. Differentiate between international strategic and tactical objectives.

12. Briefly describe the areas in which international objectives should be established.

13. Describe the classification of technology.

14. You are an international management consultant hired by the government of a less-developed country wishing to begin industrializing. The country is relatively poor economically and has an abundance of untrained labor. The government needs your advice on establishing policy relating to technology imports. What advice would you give to the government?

15. Discuss the major concern of international corporations that transfer technology to a foreign country.

Assignment

Scan business periodicals. Select an article describing a company's international strategy. (The Practical Perspectives should help you in this respect.) Provide a brief summary of the major themes contained in the article for class discussion.

Levi's International Strategies

C A S E   3–1

Source: Excerpted from M. Shao, R. Neff, and J. Ryser, "For Levi's, a Flattering Fit Overseas," *Business Week,* November 5, 1990, pp. 76-77. Copyright © 1990, McGraw-Hill. All rights reserved. Used with permission.

As the U.S. denim jeans market continues to shrink, foreign sales are driving Levi's growth. In the nine months ended in August [1990], about 39% of the company's total revenues and 60% of its pretax profit before interest and corporate expenses came from abroad. . . . Ironically, it wasn't that long ago that Levi's stumbled around overseas like a clumsy American tourist. Back in 1984 and 1985, its international operations were losing money. A strong dollar clobbered foreign sales, and the designer-jeans craze made Levi's basic five-pocket model look rather declasse. . . . By the mid-1980's, Chief Executive Robert D. Haas recognized that Levi's was squandering its brand identity in jeans. So, he dumped the fashion businesses and focused anew on blue jeans, at home and abroad.

Then, in 1985, the great-great-grandnephew of company founder Levi Strauss, a Bavarian immigrant who sold canvas pants to California gold seekers, took Levi's private in a leveraged buyout. The restructuring paid off: Operating income hit $589 million in fiscal 1989, up 50% since 1986. Sales rose 31%, to $3.63 billion. . . . Since then, Levi's foreign ads have played up the company's American roots. An Indonesian television commercial shows Levi's-clad teenagers cruising around Dubuque, Iowa, in 1960s convertibles. In Japan James Dean serves as the centerpiece in virtually all Levi's advertising. And in most foreign ads for Levi's 501 buttonfly jeans, the dialogue usually is in English. Says John G. Johnson, president of VF International: "The positioning of the 501 has really set them apart." In more ways than one. Overseas, Levi's has cultivated a top-drawer image that would surprise most Americans, and the company is pricing accordingly. A pair of 501 jeans sells for $30 in the U.S. but fetches up to $63 in Tokyo and $88 in Paris.

To protect that tony image, Levi's eschews mass merchants and discounters abroad. Levi's snob appeal has meant lush profit margins. The company's international operation has the highest profit per unit of the company's seven operating divisions. Levi's garners gross margins of 45% on 501s sold outside the U.S., compared with less than 30% domestically, figures Bernard Duflos, chairman of the North American unit of London-based Pepe Clothing Inc., a jeans marketer. . . . To provide merchandise for its foreign subsidiaries, Levi's stitched together a global manufacturing network. With a mix of its own 11 sewing plants and contract manufacturers, Levi's can supply foreign customers from nearby factories. And by shortening shipping times, Levi's can react speedily to fads in denim shading. . . . Technology is also helping Levi's stay on top of global fashion trends. Through its Levi-Link system, retailers can transfer sales and inventory data from bar-coded clothing direct to Levi's computers. . . .

Levi's innovative approach overseas has allowed it to penetrate one of the world's toughest markets—Japan. The company set up its Japanese subsidiary in 1971. "That was a very important strategic decision—not to go the joint-venture or licensing route," says David E. Schmidt, a Canadian who runs Levi Strauss Japan, where only 4 out of 400 workers today are non-Japanese. "We brought over our own people and hired and trained Japanese." . . . Today, Levi's holds the No. 2 position in Japan behind domestic rival Edwin Co., up from No. 5 four years ago. Earnings for fiscal 1990 are expected to jump 38%, to $23.2 million, on $224 million in sales, a 30% gain. To gain a stronger local identity and raise cash, Levi's sold 15% of its Japanese subsidiary to the public in 1989. . . .

In Brazil, Levi's prospers by letting local managers call the shots on distribution. For instance, Levi's penetrated the huge, fragmented Brazilian market by launching a chain of 400 Levi's Only stores, some of them in tiny, rural towns. The stores now pull in 65% of Levi's $100 million-a-year Brazilian women sales. . . . Levi's also is sensitive to local tastes in Brazil, where it developed the Feminina line of jeans exclusively for women there. Brazilian women traditionally favor ultra tight jeans, and the curvaceous cut provides a better fit. What Levi's learns in one market can often be translated into another. Take the Dockers line of chino pants and casual wear. The name originated in Levi's Argentinean unit and was applied to a loosely cut pair of pants designed by Levi's Japanese subsidiary. The company's U.S. operations adopted both in 1986, and the line now generates $550 million a year in North American revenues.

QUESTIONS

1. Is Levi's seizing opportunities, or combating threats, or both? Explain your answer.
2. Did Levi's "lead from strength"? Explain.
3. Is Levi's strategy ethnocentric, multidomestic, or global, or a combination? Explain your answer.
4. Relative to "market standing," "innovation," "productivity," and "profitability," discuss Levi's' tactical objectives.

Notes

1. W. J. Holstein et al., "The Stateless Corporation," *Business Week*, May 14, 1990, p. 99.
2. Part of this discussion draws from S. Rose, "Why the Multinational Is Ebbing," *Fortune*, August 1977, pp. 111-120. Rose uses the labels "aggressive" and "defensive" reasons.
3. S. K. Yoder, "U.S. Technology Firms Go Global to Offset Weak Domestic Market," *The Wall Street Journal*, November 14, 1989 p. A1.
4. A. G. Holzinger, "Selling in the New Europe," *Nation's Business*, December 1991, p.18.
5. I. Teinowitz, "Kobs Looks to Growth Overseas," *Advertising Age*, February 27, 1989, p. 70.
6. J. B. Treece et al., "New Worlds to Conquer," *Business Week*, February 28, 1994, p. 50.

7. Yoder, "U.S. Technology Firms Go Global."

8. E. D. Welles, "Being There," *INC,* September 1990, p.143.

9. D. C. Shanks, "Strategic Planning for Global Competition," *Journal of Business Strategy* 5(3) (Winter 1985): 80.

10. S. K. Yoder, "U.S. Technology Firms Go Global."

11. Ibid.

12. K. H. Hammonds and J. Friedman, "Who's That Knocking on Foreign Doors? U.S. Insurance Salesmen," *Business Week,* Mar. 6, 1984, p. 8.

13. "Spain Puffs On," *Economist* 305, December 19, 1987, p. 47.

14. R. A. Melcher, J. Flynn, and R. Neff, "Anheuser-Busch Says Skoal, Salude, Prosit," *Business Week,* September 20, 1993, p. 76.

15. R. Brady, M. Maremont, and P. Galuszka, "Aeroflot Takes Off for Joint-Ventureland," *Business Week,* October 30, 1989, pp. 48–49.

16. Seth Lubove, "We Have a Big Pond to Play In," *Forbes,* September 13, 1993, p. 216.

17. Frank E. Bair, (Ed.) *International Marketing Handbook* 2nd Edition (Detroit: Michigan: Gale Research Company, 1985), p. 1582.

18. B. Dumaine, "The Bureaucracy Busters," *Fortune,* June 17, 1991, p. 46.

19. J. Dupuy, "Learning to Manage World-Class Strategy," *Management Review,* (October 1991): 40.

20. J. G. Wissema and L. Euser, "Successful Innovation Through Inter-Company Networks," *Long-Range Planning* 24 (December 1991): 33–39.

21. Dumaine, "The Bureaucracy Busters," p. 46.

22. Thomas Hout, Michael E. Porter, and Eileen Rudden, "How Global Companies Win Out," *Harvard Business Review* (September–October 1982): 103.

23. Ibid.

24. Ibid.

25. George S. Yip, "Global Strategy . . . in a World of Nations?" *Sloan Management Review* (Fall 1989): 29.

26. Ibid.

27. Regina Fazio Maruca, "The Right Way to Go Global: An Interview with Whirlpool CEO David Whitwan," *Harvard Business Review* (March–April 1994): 136.

28. George S. Yip, "Global Strategy . . . in a World of Nations?"

29. Peter Drucker, *The Practice of Management* (New York: Harper and Row, 1954).

30. J. R. Basch, Jr. and M. G. Duerr, *International Transfer of Technology: A Worldwide Survey of Executives* (New York: The Conference Board, Inc., 1975), p. 1.

31. S. H. Robock and K. Simmonds, *International Business and Multinational Enterprises* (Homewood, IL: Richard D. Irwin, Inc., 1983), p. 461.

32. Basch and Duerr, *International Transfer of Technology.*

33. Ibid., p. 8.

34. Ibid., pp. 10–11.

35. Masaaki Kotabe, "A Comparative Study of U.S. and Japanese Patent Systems," *Journal of International Business Studies* 23, no. 1 (First Quarter 1992): 148.

36. Ibid., p. 149.

37. Ford S. Worthy, "Japan's Smart Secret Weapon," *Fortune,* August 12, 1991, p. 72.

38. John R. Engen, "Getting Your Chinese Workforce Up to Speed," *International Business,* August 1994, p. 48.

39. Toshio Nakahara and Yutaka Isono, "Strategic Planning For Canon: The Crisis and the New Vision," *Long Range Planning* 25 (February 1992): 63.

Chapter Four

International Strategy:
The Four Ps

Brazilians are consuming more and more fast-food fare at equally fast-food rates. The market grew a whopping 40% last year [1992] alone, to more than $700 million. McDonald's, which had one store in the country in 1979, now has 111. Brazil is the eighth-largest market in the world for McDonald's. Pizza Hut, trying to cope with 22 stores that sell 50% more than the typical U.S store on an average day, intends to open 33 new stores in 1993. Burger King will buy its way into the market, with 84 stores of its own, by purchasing Bob's, Brazil's second-largest fast-food chain (after No. 1 McDonald's).[1]

Objectives of the Chapter

Because of changes taking place throughout the globe, to remain competitive and to increase their opportunities, domestic enterprises will need to develop strategies for entering the international business arena. Effective internationalization of business operations relies on managers' ability to develop international product/service, place/entry, price, and promotion strategies in light of the enterprise's external environment (discussed in Chapter 2), as well as in light of the firm's internal situation (discussed in Chapter 3). The objectives of this chapter are thus to discuss:

1. International product/service strategy.
2. International place/entry strategy.
3. International pricing strategy.
4. International promotion strategy.

PRODUCT/SERVICE STRATEGY

In developing **product/service strategy,** managers are typically concerned with what the product or service should look like and what it should be able to do. In conducting this assessment for foreign markets, managers must overcome the *self-reference criterion (SRC).* They must determine whether their product or service can be sold in standard form or if it must be customized to fit differing foreign market needs. They must understand that many products or services do not immediately sell well in foreign markets, but that they must undergo a diffusion process.

The Self-Reference Criterion (SRC)

Basically, the **self-reference criterion (SRC)** is the unconscious reference to one's own cultural values. This unconscious reference is the root of many international business problems.[2] Huge problems can occur when the SRC leads a manager to assume that a product or service that sells well in the home market will sell well in foreign markets. In many cases it does not because the needs for products and services differ among societies. Managers can eliminate the SRC by first defining the problem in terms of the home society's cultural traits, habits, and norms, and then redefining the problem, without value judgments, in terms of the foreign market's cultural traits, habits, and norms. The difference represents the cultural influence on the problem. The manager subsequently restates and solves the problem in the context of both cultures.

For example, Americans like moist, creamy cakes for dessert purchased already baked in grocery stores. However, attempting to market moist, creamy cakes in grocery stores in England may result in failure because the English generally like dry cakes that can be eaten with their fingers while having tea, and when the occasion calls for moist, creamy cakes, they like to bake their own. The problem to be solved would be to modify the production of the cakes to fit the English culture. As another example, Americans have in recent years developed a liking for commodious cupholders in their cars. Mercedes-Benz and BMW, the European car manufacturers, rejected the notion of installing cupholders in their socially prestigious automobiles. Now they are bowing to the American driver's wants; they are installing cupholders.[3] (As another example, read Practical Perspective 4–1, the case of Disney's expansion to France. Notice that Disney's management had to repackage some of the original Disney characters.)

It should be noted that the assessment may sometimes reveal that the firm's product or service, because of cultural or other factors, cannot be customized for a foreign market. For example, in the 1970s, Kentucky Fried Chicken (KFC), the popular U.S.-based fast-food chain, expanded its operations to Brazil. The expansion was a failure. A Brazilian marketing executive believes that KFC failed because Brazilians do not much care to eat

P R A C T I C A L   P E R S P E C T I V E   4–1

Disney Goes to France

A few years ago, an amazed Japanese girl asked an American visitor, "Is there really a Disneyland in America?" That should be music to the mouse ears of Euro Disneyland's management, beleaguered by charges that they are defiling the Frenchness of France. Ah, to convince the French that Mickey and Donald belong to Marne-la-Vallee as they do to Anaheim, Orlando and Tokyo. Sensitive to the charge that Euro Disneyland amounts to what theater director Ariane Mnouchkine, in a widely quoted assessment, called a "cultural Chernobyl," the company tried for months to persuade Europeans that, in the words of a Disney spokesperson, "It's not America, it's Disney." On opening day last month [April 1992], Disney's chairman Michael Eisner stressed, like a guest too eager to please, that the company had repackaged original European characters: the French Cinderella, the Italian Pinocchio, the German Snow White. More truculently, a Euro Disneyland spokesperson said: "Who are these Frenchmen, anyway? We offer them the dream of a lifetime and lots of jobs. They treat us like invaders."

Source: Excerpted from Todd Gitlin, "World Leaders: Mickey, et al.," *The New York Times,* Section 2, May 3, 1992, p. 1.

chicken outside of their homes.[4] KFC is, however, currently trying again. This time it is targeting only specific market groups—for example, Brazilians of Italian descent, who do like to eat chicken at restaurants and at home.

Customization versus Standardization

Fundamentally, there are three viable alternatives when entering a foreign market: (1) market the same product or service everywhere (**standardization**), (2) adapt the product or service for foreign markets (**customization**), and (3) develop a totally new product or service. By combining these three alternatives with promotional efforts, five different product strategies can be developed.[5]

1. **Standardize product/standardize message.** Using this strategy, a firm sells the same product and uses the same promotional appeals in all

markets. In other words, product and promotional appeals are globally standardized. Coca-Cola, Pepsi-Cola, Avon, and Maidenform follow this strategy.

2. **Standardize product/customize message.** Enterprises using this approach customize only the promotional message. For example, a bicycle may be sold in the U.S. market as a pleasure vehicle. In an economically poor country, however, the promotional message may have to be customized to stress economy; that is, the bicycle would be promoted as a means of relatively inexpensive basic transportation.

3. **Customize product/standardize message.** Using this strategy, the company customizes the product to meet the needs of the specific foreign market, but promotes the same use as it does in the domestic market. For example, electric sewing machines manufactured for the U.S. market would not sell well in a market where few residents have access to electricity. The manufacturer could, however, customize the machine to sell in that market by producing hand- or foot-cranked sewing machines. The hand-cranked machine would be promoted in the foreign market in the same way it is in the U.S. market—to sew clothes.

4. **Customize product/customize message.** Manufacturers applying this strategy customize the product to meet different use patterns in the foreign market and customize the promotional message attached to it as well. For example, bicycles in the U.S. are usually lightweight and are generally promoted for use in leisure activities. In many less-developed countries, however, because of rough roads, the need may be for a stronger bicycle, and the bicycle is often used as a major form of transportation. China is one example of a country where bicycles are heavyweight and are used as a major means of transportation.

5. **Different product.** Using this approach, rather than adapting an existing product, the manufacturer invests in the development of a totally new one to fit the needs of specific foreign markets. For example, Coca Cola's and Pepsi's diet sodas do not sell well in Asia and Europe because consumers there prefer the creamy sweetness of regular Coke or Pepsi and consider sugar-free sodas as drinks of diabetics and the obese, not of the young and vital. To deal with this problem, Pepsi designed a new diet cola, called Pepsi Max, specifically for these and other markets. Pepsi Max uses a sweetener that makes it close to the regular colas in taste.[6]

American marketing professor Theodore Levitt contends that in an era of global competition, the product strategy of successful firms is evolving from offering customized products (a multidomestic strategy) to offering globally standardized ones (a global strategy). Such a product strategy requires the development of universal products or products that require no more than a cosmetic change for adaptation to different local needs and use conditions.[7] Strategies 1 through 4 discussed above fit this mode (the global strategy). Strategy 5, however, can fit both the global and the multidomestic strategy modes. For example, Hollywood can make a film which, with some minor customization, such as dubbing in the local language, can be distributed globally, or it can make a film specifically for one market.

As it was discussed in Chapter 3, both the multidomestic and the global strategy approaches have advantages and disadvantages. The global strategy may be appropriate for some products and services and for some nations, but not for many products and services and countries. For example, Japan is a difficult market for many foreign companies—especially American companies—to penetrate because of **cultural barriers.** To penetrate Japan's market, most products and services require customization. For instance, when Kentucky Fried Chicken entered the Japanese market, it had to make adaptations to local taste buds, including taking the mashed potatoes and gravy off the menu and substituting french fries, and halving the sugar in the slaw recipe.[8] Furthermore, some products and services have global appeal only by age groups. For example, teenagers are the most global market of all age groups. Teenagers almost everywhere purchase a common gallery of products: Reebok sports shoes, Procter & Gamble Cover Girl makeup, Sega and Nintendo video games, Nikes, Macintosh computers, and Red Hot Chili Peppers music tapes and CDs.[9]

Subhash C. Jain, a professor of international marketing at the University of Connecticut, reviewed published sources to develop a framework for determining the extent of standardization feasible in a particular case. The determining factors in Professor Jain's framework are depicted in Figure 4–1.[10]

Diffusing Innovations

Not all products and services introduced in a foreign market will be immediately accepted by the prospective customers. Many products and services that are new to a market must go through the **diffusion process.** Basically, diffusion is "the process by which innovation is communicated through certain channels over time among members of a social system."[11] This means that the product or service is adopted by more and more members of the society gradually, over time. (As an illustration, read Practical Perspective 4–2. Note that Hunter Douglas Window Fashions has been diffusing its product in Japan for the past two-and-a-half years.) It also means that many companies introducing a new product or service often incur losses in the beginning years. This is because the company does not yet have the number of buyers required to cover the fixed costs of investment. In later years, however, after the product or service has been diffused, the enterprise should be able to earn enough money to recapture the early years' losses.

◆   **FIGURE 4-1   Factors That Help Determine Standardization or Customization**

◆ In general, standardization is more practical in markets that are economically alike.

◆ Standardization strategy is more effective if worldwide customers, not countries, are the basis of identifying the segment(s) to serve.

◆ The greater the similarity in the markets in terms of customer behavior and lifestyle, the higher the degree of standardization.

◆ The higher the cultural compatibility of the product across the host countries, the greater the degree of standardization.

◆ The greater the degree of similarity in a firm's competitive position in different markets, the higher the degree of standardization.

◆ Competing against the same adversaries, with similar share positions, in different countries leads to greater standardization than competing against purely local companies.

◆ Industrial and high technology products are more suitable for standardization than consumer products.

◆ Standardization is more appropriate when the home market positioning strategy is meaningful in the host market.

◆ The greater the difference in physical, political, and legal environments between home and host countries, the lower the degree of standardization.

◆ The more similar the marketing infrastructure in the home and host countries, the higher the degree of standardization.

◆ Companies in which key managers share a world view, as well as a common view of the critical tasks flowing from the strategy, are more effective in implementing a standardization strategy.

◆ The greater the strategic consensus among parent-subsidiary managers on key standardization issues, the more effective the implementation of standardization strategy.

◆ The greater the centralization of authority for setting policies and allocating resources, the more effective the implementation of standardization strategy.

Source: Adapted from Subhash C. Jain, "Standardization of International Marketing Strategy: Some Research Hypotheses," *Journal of Marketing*, 53 (January 1989): 70–79. Used with permission from publisher. Copyright © 1989 American Marketing Association, Chicago, IL. All rights reserved.

How Quickly Can a New Product/Service Be Diffused in a Culture?

The way people respond to a new product affects how quickly it is diffused. All new products and services can be categorized as to their varied degrees of newness, and the consumer reactions to each category affect the **quickness** or **slowness** of diffusion. Generally, the more disruptive the innovation

PRACTICAL PERSPECTIVE 4–2

Diffusing Window Coverings in Japan

Right now, Hunter Douglas and its line of window coverings are unknown in Japan. This will soon change, however. Recently, Hunter Douglas Window Fashions was established there. The new company is a 50-50 joint venture with Sekisui Jushi, a Japanese firm specializing in products for the home. The joint venture will assemble and market Hunter Douglas' full range of window coverings, with materials and components provided by the Hunter Douglas Group's worldwide operation, principally by its U.S. divisions. The company's entry into the Japanese mar-ket really started two-and-a-half years ago, when Jerry Fuchs, president of Hunter Douglas, the North American operation of the Dutch-based Hunter Douglas Group, made a trip to Japan to meet one of the company's suppliers. Fuchs discovered that peo-ple in the over-50 age group still preferred the traditional Japanese window coverings, such as the shoji screen. But Japanese in their 20s, 30s, and 40s were very interested in new Western ideas, and were anxious to see the interior design elements that are popular today in the United States.

Source: Excerpted from "A New Sales Opportunity: The Windows of Japan," *The International Executive* (January–February 1990): 27. Copyright © 1990 John Wiley & Sons, Inc., New York. All rights reserved. Reprinted with permission.

---

is, the longer the diffusion process will take. Innovations can be categorized as congruent, dynamically continuous, and discontinuous.[12]

Congruent Innovations. Congruent innovations do not disrupt established consumption patterns. Congruent innovation means introducing variety and quality or functional features, style, or perhaps a duplicate of an existing product. Introducing vegetable oil as a substitute for olive oil is an example of congruent innovation.

Continuous Innovations. Continuous innovation involves altering a product to enhance the satisfaction derived from its use. Menthol cigarettes, new model automobiles, and fluoride toothpaste are examples of continuous innovations. Continuous innovations have little disruptive influence on the culture's established consumption patterns.

Dynamically Continuous Innovations. Dynamically continuous innovation usually involves creating a new product or substantial altering an existing one to fulfill new needs created by changes in lifestyles or new expectations. Examples are frozen dinners, electric toothbrushes, and electric lawn mowers. These innovations are normally disruptive and therefore are resisted because the old patterns of consumption must be changed. Consumer behavior must be transformed if users are to recognize and accept the value of dynamically continuous innovations.

Discontinuous Innovations. Discontinuous innovation introduces an entirely new idea or behavior pattern. It means establishing fresh and untried consumption patterns. This would be the most disruptive innovation. An example is the introduction of a banking system into a traditional society where people tend to keep their money hidden at home or somewhere else.

Dualistic Technological Structures

Diffusion of new products or services is also affected by the technological structure of the country. A dualistic technological framework exists in the economies of most developing countries.[13] A **dualistic technological structure** refers to the simultaneous existence of a modern industrial sector and a sector involved in traditional agrarian and craft production. The modern sector involves large-scale, capital-intensive industries utilizing modern technologies and technically skilled labor to manufacture basic industrial goods such as energy, construction materials, and electrical and mechanical equipment. The traditional sector of many less developed economies is characterized by small-scale, labor-intensive industries using simple technologies with low capital investment and unskilled labor to produce agricultural and consumer products for domestic markets.

Managers should thus be aware that a developing nation may need advanced technologies in one sector and older technologies in another. They should also be aware that a developing nation may need both adaptive technological innovations and transformative technological innovations.[14] **Adaptive transformative innovations** are important to the modern industrial sector. They aim at modifying and adjusting modern technologies to the needs of domestic markets. An example of an adaptive technological innovation would be the introduction of a more modern tractor into an area where tractors are already in use. **Transformative technological innovations** are important to the traditional sector economically, socially, and culturally. An example of a transformative technological innovation would be the introduction of washing machines into a region where the laundry is being done manually, or the introduction of farming tractors into a region where horses and plows are being used.

PLACE/ENTRY STRATEGY

Managers of business enterprises must determine how their products or services will reach the consumer—the **place/entry strategy.** Distribution methods generally require variations from country to country, as well as within each country. Generally, the methods are shaped by the size of the market, by the scope and quality of the competition, by the available distribution channels, and by the firm's resources (as an illustration, read Practical Perspective 4–3, the case of Fusion Systems Corp.). Distribution methods are also shaped by the laws of the country (the laws of some countries require foreign companies to use local distribution systems) and by the firm's entry strategy.

Basically, manufacturing enterprises can enter a foreign country by:

1. Manufacturing the product at home and exporting it to the foreign country for distribution in the local market.
2. Manufacturing parts at home and exporting them to the foreign country for assembly, for distribution in the local market, and/or for export to other markets (including back to the home market).

PRACTICAL PERSPECTIVE 4–3

Fusion Systems Uses Local Distributor to Enter the Japanese Market

Fusion Systems Corp., a Rockville, Maryland company, makes sophisticated industrial equipment used to produce numerous goods, including optical fibers, automobile parts, graphic-arts printing plates, and semi-conductor chips. . . . Fusion has been in the Japanese market since 1975, four years after its founding by its president, Donald M. Shapiro, and four colleagues. . . . Because of its small size when it entered the Japanese market, Fusion lacked the resources to hire its own sales force there. It had to rely on a Japanese distributor. "We knew we couldn't just hire a trade house that would buy and resell our product," said David Harbourne, a Fusion vice president and manager of its core business. "We can always teach a distributor how to sell our product, but if it doesn't have strong service, we can't do much about that. Our philosophy at Fusion is to look for strong service organizations that have a lot of after-sales support."

Source: Excerpted from Edward O. Welles, "Being There," *Inc.*, September 1990, p. 143.

3. Manufacturing the product in the foreign country for distribution in the local market and/or for export to other markets (including back to the home market).

With respect to service enterprises:

1. Some, such as consulting companies, can provide the services from their home country or they can set up subsidiaries in the foreign country.
2. Some, such as insurance and banking companies, generally must establish subsidiaries in the foreign country.

The above suggests that, basically, firms enter a foreign market either by **exporting to it or setting up manufacturing facilities in it.** The ensuing sections describe various strategies enterprises use in exporting and manufacturing in foreign markets.

Exporting Strategy

When a firm decides to export, it must choose between indirect and direct exporting. Basically, **indirect exporting** involves using experienced middlemen to handle export functions and **direct exporting** involves assigning the export functions to employees of the company. In general, when a firm lacks personnel with exporting expertise, it usually prefers to start out using the indirect method, and after the enterprise has developed personnel with exporting expertise, and if it is more efficient, it develops its own export division.

Indirect Exporting

There are two basic types of middlemen: **agent middlemen** and **merchant middlemen.** The agent represents the principal directly and the merchant takes title to the goods. Agent middlemen include the export management company (EMC), the manufacturer's export agent (MEA), the broker, and buyers and selling groups. Merchant middlemen include export merchants and jobbers, export buyers and foreign importers, trading companies, and complementary marketers.

Middlemen may be located at home (**domestic middlemen**) or in the foreign country (**foreign middlemen**). Some firms prefer to deal with middlemen who are located in the foreign market. An advantage of using foreign middlemen is that they provide a channel that is closer to the customer than are domestic middlemen; that is, they provide personnel who are in constant contact with the foreign market. A disadvantage of using these middlemen is that the employing firm does not have the close contact it enjoys when dealing with a middleman located in the domestic market. Another disadvantage of using foreign middlemen is that language or communication barriers between the producer and the middlemen are more likely to develop than with the domestic middlemen. Elements that affect the indirect exporting strategy include the availability of middlemen, the cost of their services, the functions performed, and the extent of control the manufacturer can exert over the middlemen's activities.

Direct Exporting

To obtain greater control over their distribution systems and the volume of sales, firms often develop their own export organization. There are several approaches to establishing direct exporting means, among which are an international sales force, a sales branch, a sales subsidiary, and setting up a company's own distribution system.

International Sales Force.   An enterprise may establish an **international sales force** that travels abroad to sell the product. This may be the least expensive choice since the firm does not have to invest in any facilities abroad. This solution, however, would not give foreign customers immediate access to the firm's representatives, nor would the firm be able to effectively monitor foreign market changes.

Sales Branch.   A firm may choose to establish a **sales branch** in the foreign country. This approach requires investment in foreign facilities. It enables the firm to be closer to the market, however.

Sales Subsidiaries.   The manufacturer may also choose to establish a **sales subsidiary** abroad. A sales subsidiary differs from a sales branch in that it is an entirely separate entity, even though it is under the control of the company.

Set Up Own Distribution System.   If the foreign country's legal system permits it, a company can elect to set up a chain of wholly owned outlets, which may consist of retail shops.

Firms should not adhere to any one approach; they should be flexible and conform to the situation. The choice of approach depends on a number of factors. Some of them include:

1. The philosophy and the aims of the company.
2. The traditions of the target market.
3. The competition's behavior.
4. The existing and potential future size of the market.
5. Legal restrictions.
6. Usual patterns of distribution of the particular product(s).
7. Financial and staffing problems.[15]

It should be noted that, as mentioned above, a country's laws and regulations also have an impact on approach. For example, in Indonesia, only

Indonesian citizens and Indonesian companies may engage in any kind of distribution activity, including the importation of goods. In the Philippines, foreigners and foreign-controlled companies are not permitted to take part in any form of retailing.[16]

Direct or Indirect Exporting?

There are advantages as well disadvantages to both approaches. The advantages of the direct approach include:

1. The sales staff is more loyal than would be the sales staff of an intermediary.
2. The sales staff has greater knowledge of the product line of the firm than an outside vendor.
3. The sales staff can be trained by the parent company according to its individual sales methods.
4. Salaries of the sales staff can be set in accordance with the long-term goals of the firm instead of on a commission basis.
5. The sales staff can keep personal contact with the end users and retailers.
6. The manufacturer has a channel to receive feedback information on new marketing opportunities and trends that might not be available to a firm using sales intermediaries.
7. The manufacturer has a means of getting information about competitors, evaluating product acceptance, and gathering a multitude of useful information.
8. The sales branch or subsidiary can spend promotional money to advertise a new product, concentrating on building product acceptance in a wide region, which might not be the goal of the sales intermediary.[17]

The disadvantages of using the direct approach include:

1. It is usually very expensive to start. (Refer again to Practical Perspective 4–3.)
2. A large inventory is usually needed.
3. The establishment of a complex organization, including a warehousing network, an administrative organization, and a trained staff, is often required.[18]

Manufacturing in Foreign Country Strategy

After they have acquired experience in the international arena, many enterprises find it profitable to produce in foreign countries. Six of the most common approaches to foreign production are licensing, franchising, management contracting, equity-based joint ventures, non-equity-based contractual alliances, and wholly owned subsidiaries. Many companies sometimes use a mix. For example, in 1989, Kentucky Fried Chicken had outlets in 58 countries, and these international outlets generated almost half of KFC's $5 billion per year in sales. But KFC's success was especially notable with its 1,324 outlets in the Pacific Rim. KFC's director of public affairs, Richard Detwiller, said, "We operate all our outlets on a joint-venture or franchise basis, and the licenses are mostly held by local nationals."[19]

Licensing/Franchising

Licensing involves granting a foreign enterprise the use of a production process, the use of a trade name, or permission for the distribution of imported goods for a fee. Licenses allow for expansion without a great deal of capital investment or personnel commitment. However, supervising licenses may sometimes be a problem and, because of the partnership, profits may be lower. Nevertheless, overall, licensing can be profitable for many companies, especially those that are no longer producing the product at home and could lose their patent protection for lack of use.

In **franchising,** the contractor provides a standard package of products, systems, and management services; grants permission to use a certain product, including a special name or trademark; and often incorporates a special set of procedures for making the product. Under franchising agreements, the parent firm maintains a reasonable degree of control. The Disneyland located in Tokyo, Japan, is a franchise arrangement. Under the agreement, Walt Disney Productions is to receive 10 percent of every admission fee from the Tokyo park and 5 percent of the revenues from restaurants and shops.[20]

Numerous other companies have been entering the complex Japanese market via franchising or licensing arrangements, including 7-Eleven Stores, Stained Glass Overlay, Tiffany & Company, and Barney's of New York.[21] Practical Perspective 4–4 lists some of the other U.S. companies that have entered Japan via franchising/licensing.

Management Contracts

Using the **management contract** method, a firm provides managerial know-how in all or some functions to another organization, which produces under its trade name (a licensing arrangement) for a stated fee or a percentage share of the profits. This approach does not require much investment and it enables the parent firm to maintain control when the foreign government requires ownership or majority ownership of foreign investments by their own citizens. This approach is also used when a foreign nation's government nationalizes or takes over the industry, but needs the managerial know-how of the previous foreign owners to manage the enterprise. For a contracted fee, the previous owners manage the enterprise for the government.

Many U.S. Companies Enter Japan Through Franchising/Licensing

A slew of U.S. companies is quietly opening Japan's backdoor. Their key: franchising. On any day, 3,000 Japanese do their bench pressing at seven Nautilus Clubs around Tokyo. Elsewhere, 100 aerobic instructors offer lessons based on Jazzercise Co.'s system from California. Another 6,500 Japanese chomp into Domino's pizzas served by 54 licenses. Jazz lovers order a round before the evening set at Tokyo's version of the Blue Note, New York's famed nightclub. . . . Domino's Pizza Inc. sold a license for Domino's concept of a chain of delivery stores to K.K.Y. Higa Corp. Higa continues to pay Domino a small portion of sales, which were $43 million in 1988, in royalties each year. Nautilus USA exported equipment worth $14 million to Japanese clubs last year, although it received no royalties from Japanese licenses. Fortunate Life Centres Inc. in Charlottesville, Va., envisions its diet-related franchises cashing in on lifestyle changes among Japanese prompted by earlier American franchises. The company hopes to be selling concentrated diet food next March [1990] in 76 Japanese outlets and later opening weight-loss centers on the assumption that after all that fast food, dieting will be in order. . . . The department store Seibu now has a license to open Ralph Lauren stores in Japan.

Source: Excerpted from Ted Holden, "Who Says You Can't Break into Japan?" *Business Week*, October 16, 1989, p. 49.

Joint Ventures/Contractual Alliances

Many enterprises' entry strategy is via a joint venture or a contractual alliance. Many companies use a mix to attain the most efficient entry.

Joint Ventures.   Basically, a **joint venture** is an arrangement whereby a company joins in a partnership or a merger between one or more other companies. Some governments require that their citizens have majority ownership of foreign-owned firms located in their country. Advantages of joint ventures include: (a) it enables a firm to utilize the foreign partner's skills; (b) it enables a firm to gain access to the foreign partner's distribution system; and (c) it requires less capital investment than if the investment were wholly owned, therefore reducing the size of the risk. For example, Toys `Я´ Us Inc. planned to open 100 stores in Japan via joint ventures. Its strategy was to maintain 80 percent ownership. To compensate for its lack of understanding of Japan's real estate and cultural nuances, Toys `Я´ Us teamed up with McDonald's Co. Japan Ltd., whose management has experience in these matters.[22]

There are some disadvantages to this approach, however. First, profits must be shared with the partner, and second, because some nations require majority control by local people, the home company might lose managerial control—a management contract, however, can mitigate this problem. (For an illustration of how a company can lose control via partnership, refer back to Practical Perspective 3–4 in Chapter 3, the case of Schwinn Bicycle Co.)

Contractual Alliances.   Many joint ventures are in the form of a contractual alliance. (Practical Perspective 4–5 lists some of the companies that have taken this approach.) **Contractual alliances** are formed to share costs, to share risks, to gain additional market knowledge, to combine technical and market knowledge, to serve an international market, and to develop industry standards together.[23] These organizations attain greater efficiency by focusing on their

---

PRACTICAL PERSPECTIVE   4-5

Companies Look for Allies to Achieve Quality

Looking for allies is as much a part of the 1990s corporate Zeitgeist as achieving total quality, and the reason is clear: Even the biggest corporations need help in launching a new product or breaking a new market. Once proudly isolated and secretive giants like AT&T and IBM are embracing these partnerships. AT&T has links with many of the world's biggest telephone and electronics companies. IBM has created an alliance council of senior executives who meet monthly to keep track of more than 40 partnerships around the world. Boeing is the world's premier manufacturer of commercial jets but has still taken on three Japanese allies— the heavy industry divisions of Fuji, Mitsubishi, and Kowasaki— to make the new 777, a long-range, wide body plane set for delivery in 1995. Says Roland Smith, of British Aerospace, which got together with counterparts from France, Germany, and Spain to form aircraft manufacturer Airbus Industry: "A partnership is one of the cheapest ways to develop a global strategy."

Source: Excerpted from Jeremy Main, "Making Global Alliances Work," *Fortune*, December 17, 1990, p. 121.

strengths. That is, they do what they can do best ("lead from strength," as discussed in Chapter 3) and contract for other functions. For example, Nissan and Volkswagen have an arrangement whereby Nissan distributes Volkswagens in Japan and Volkswagen sells Nissan's four-wheel-drive cars in Europe.

In describing such an alliance, Professor Thomas G. Cummings used the label "transorganizational systems."[24] He described such systems as a group of two or more enterprises engaged in collective efforts to achieve goals they could not achieve by themselves. Riad Ajami, a professor at Ohio State University, proposed that such systems are characterized "by a shift from an equity-based investment . . . to that of a service-based organization providing technology know-how and other managerial services . . . ownership rests upon contractual arrangements rather than conventional ownership arrangements."[25] Professor Ajami listed fifteen examples of such collaborative ventures, including Toyota–General Motors, General Electric–Salelni (Italian construction firm), and MW Kellogg Co. of Houston–China Petrochemical International Corporation (SINOPEC).

Kenichi Ohmae, a management consultant for McKinsey, an international management consulting firm, described this type of arrangement as follows:

- There is no formal contract.
- There is no buying and selling of equity.
- There are few, if any, rigidly binding provisions.
- It is a loose, evolving kind of relationship.
- There are guidelines and expectations. But no one expects a precise, measured return on the initial commitment.
- Both partners bring to an alliance a faith that they will be stronger than either would be separately.
- Both believe that each has unique skills and functional abilities the other lacks.
- And both have to work diligently over time to make the union successful.[26]

Dr. Ohmae proposed that a non-equity-based alliance in many instances has advantages over the equity-based joint venture. He contended that when equity enters the picture, one becomes concerned with control and return on investment, and one cannot manage a global company through control—it demoralizes workers and managers. Furthermore, he contends that equity poisons the relationship, which can lead to the prevention of the development of intercompany management skills, which are crucial for success in today's global environment.[27]

There are certain problems in using this approach, however. Premature dissolution of agreement by a partner can create problems for the other partner(s). There is always the risk that a partner may not really be in it for the long term—for example, a British whisky company used a Japanese distributor until it felt it acquired sufficient experience to begin its own sales operations in Japan, and Japanese copier makers and automobile producers have done the same to their U.S. partners.[28] And the effectiveness of the approach depends on a solid relationship between partners. It may be a very lengthy and expensive process to find the right partner(s) and develop the required relationship.

Wholly Owned Subsidiaries

Using the strategy of a **wholly owned subsidiary,** the firm establishes an entity in a foreign country, paying all of the costs incurred. To establish a wholly owned foreign subsidiary, an enterprise may acquire an existing company in the foreign country or build one from scratch.

Advantages of the Wholly Owned Subsidiary:

1. The firm maintains total control and authority over the operation.
2. Profits need not be shared with anyone outside the company.
3. Since they do not need to consult a partner, firms have more flexibility to adapt faster to market demands and labor needs.
4. The enterprise is able to protect trade secrets.

Practical Perspective 4–6 lists some companies that have used the wholly owned strategy because of its advantages.

PRACTICAL PERSPECTIVE 4–6

The Wholly Owned Strategy Is Advantageous to Companies

In 1985, Minnesota Mining and Manufacturing Corp. established a wholly owned enterprise in Shanghai, People's Republic of China (PRC) to produce electrical tape, connectors, and electric splicing and terminating kits. The firm's officials said that the wholly owned enterprise would enable them to expand or reinvest as needed and would reduce response time to market changes. Motorola was [in 1990] negotiating a wholly owned plant in Tianjin, PRC that would produce equipment and components for the automotive and communications industries. According to a company spokesperson, it chose this option for operational flexibility. PepsiCo Inc. chose the wholly owned approach in the P.R.C. because of its need to protect trade mark concentrate formulas. Shanghai Hilton International chose the wholly owned method in the P.R.C. to gain a free hand in hiring and firing staff, determining compensation packages, and exercising discretion over other matters relating to the hotel's management.

Source: Excerpted from ASY, "Why Go Solo?" *The China Business Review* (January–February 1990): 31.

Disadvantages of the Wholly Owned Subsidiary:

1. The breeding of **"badwill"** because profits are not shared with local people.
2. Government officials in many countries tend to view wholly owned foreign investments in their nation unfavorably.
3. The risk is greater since it is totally company borne.

Within the past two decades or so, government officials in many countries have become uncomfortable with the situation in which much of their nation's industrial sector is controlled by foreigners. As a result, many governments have established policies mandating that the majority of control of foreign investments in their country must be in the hands of local citizens—although this trend currently seems to be declining. Practical Perspective 4–7 demonstrates the reluctance of governments to permit foreign corporations to establish wholly-owned subsidiaries in their countries.

Export or Manufacture Abroad?

Both approaches have advantages and disadvantages. The general advantages of investing in manufacturing facilities abroad, as opposed to exporting, include:

1. Capitalizing on low-cost labor.
2. Avoiding high import taxes.
3. Reducing transportation costs.
4. Gaining access to raw materials.
5. Developing **"goodwill"** in the foreign nation because direct investment may help in that nation's economic development.

The general disadvantages include:

1. Subsidiaries are far removed from the home country and are thus often difficult and expensive to control.
2. The risk of nationalization, confiscation, domestication, and expropriation exists to a greater degree than when using other methods.

Which strategy option, manufacture abroad or export, should a firm select? Naturally, the one that is the most efficient. And it is often most efficient for a company to manufacture in one country and export to another; that is, it is often most efficient to use a **mix**. Furthermore, firms sometimes shift back and forth from one strategy to another, as efficiency dictates.

For example, McIlhenny Company of Avery Island, Louisiana, the world's only maker of Tabasco pepper sauce, ships its product to Europe, where distributors get it onto grocery shelves. But McIlhenny did not always export its sauces abroad. The firm used to manufacture in England through a licensing agreement with a British company—a system that might be handy

PRACTICAL PERSPECTIVE 4–7

Wholly Foreign-Owned Enterprises in China

Of all the forms of foreign investments in China, wholly foreign-owned enterprises (WFOEs) have aroused the most controversy among Chinese. Many of China's policy makers find it hard to accept the idea of permitting foreign companies into socialist China to establish and operate businesses on their own. But other Chinese leaders have accepted WFOEs—just as earlier they accepted foreign majority controlled joint ventures—as long as the investment serves some of China's development priorities. . . . In 1986, when the National People's Congress adopted a WFOE law, policy makers passed up the chance to permanently set stringent requirements for WFOEs, stipulating instead that WFOEs "must be beneficial to the development of the Chinese national economy," must use "advanced technology and equipment," and "either all or a large portion of its products must be for export. . . ."

Three years later, detailed rules for implementation of the WFOE law have yet to emerge, suggesting that China's leadership remains divided on how to permit and, at the same time, control WFOEs. Recently, however, the Ministry of Foreign Economic Relations and Trade (MOFERT) completed a draft of WFOE implementing regulations for examination and approval by the State Council. Without a strong policy in support of WFOEs and clear-cut rules to facilitate their establishment, China has seen relatively few WFOEs develop. Before the 1986 law, only about 150 WFOEs were established, mostly in special economic zones. Even after the law's promulgation, WFOE contracts have lagged far behind other types of foreign investment. From 1979–88, only 594 WFOE contracts were signed, compared with contracts for 8,500 equity joint ventures and more than 6,770 cooperative joint ventures.

Source: Excerpted from ASY, "Why Go Solo?" *The China Business Review* (January–February 1990): 31.

after 1992, according to Carlos E. Malespin, vice president in charge of the company's international operations. "Although it's more profitable for us to use distributorship arrangements," says Malespin," we can fall back on our former strategy of licensing for manufacture in Europe if import tariffs are raised significantly after 1992."[29] (As of June 23, 1995, McIlhenny Company continues to export and has no plans to manufacture in Europe.)

PRICE STRATEGY

Operating in foreign markets brings new **price strategy** challenges, as there are new market variables to consider. For example, the attitudes of foreign governments are an important and serious problem that differs from one country to another. Sometimes foreign governments act as price arbiters. Therefore, effective price setting consists of much more than mechanically adding a standard markup to cost. Thus, international pricing strategy is much more complex than domestic pricing strategy.

International Pricing Strategy

International pricing strategy is made complex by monetary exchange factors, as well as by firms often being required to countertrade; that is, to trade by barter or a similar system (to be discussed more thoroughly later in the chapter). Pricing policy is also affected by the commercial practices of the country in which the firm is doing business, by the type of product to be merchandised, and by existing competitive conditions. In establishing pricing policy, some firms are influenced by the view that pricing is an active tool by which to accomplish their marketing objectives, and some are influenced by the belief that price is a static element in business decisions. Furthermore, some firms emphasize control over final prices and some over the net price received by the enterprise.

Pricing as an Active Tool

Utilizing the view that **pricing is an active tool,** the firm uses pricing to accomplish its objective relative to a target return from its overseas operations or to accomplish a target volume of market share. (For an illustration of pricing as an active tool strategy, read Practical Perspective 4–8, the case of Dell Computer Corp. in Japan.)

Pricing as a Static Element

If a firm follows the view that **pricing is a static element,** it will most likely be content to sell what it can overseas and consider it to be bonus value.

Pricing as an active tool is more closely allied with firms that make direct investment in the foreign country, whereas pricing as a static element is more closely allied with firms that export.

Control over Final Prices

To achieve a desired level of foreign market penetration, a firm must have the ability to control the end price. Enterprises with the desire to attain a high level of market penetration therefore attempt to obtain all possible **control over the final price.** These firms are more likely to view pricing as an active tool than as a static element.

PRACTICAL PERSPECTIVE 4–8

Dell Computer Corp. Wages Price War in Japan

Dell Computer Corp. escalated a personal computer price war in Japan by unveiling plans to sell six types of high-end PCs in Japan at prices 25% to 60% lower than those of its rivals. At a news conference in Dell's Tokyo offices, Chief Executive Officer Michael Dell outlined the company's plans to target corporate customers through "direct sales," the company's preferred euphemism for mail order, its main avenue for PC sales in the U.S. According to Mr. Dell, the company's "more efficient mode" will allow Dell to undercut its competitors' prices because the company can avoid paying the added costs of distribution. Dell's kickoff of its full-scale Japanese operations, foreshadowed for weeks by press leaks and speculation about the company's sales strategy, marks the latest move in aggressive U.S. marketing tactics into the once-placid world of Japanese PC sales.

Dell joins Compaq Computer Corp. and International Business Machines Corp., both which announced low-priced PCs for sale in Japan last fall [1992]. . . . The U.S. companies have set their eyes on the world's second largest market for personal computers, once ruled by NEC Corp. With an iron grip on its network of retail distributors and huge library of software, NEC has for years enjoyed a market share of more than 50% and the luxury of selling its computers at high prices. . . . Dell, the world's fifth largest PC maker, seems intent on pushing such competition even further. Officials at the news conference presented a price comparison of three Dell computers and machines from Compaq, IBM, and NEC with identical speed and memory and comparable hard-disk storage capacities. NEC's prices were as much as 60% higher than Dell's. Compaq's prices were generally closest to Dell's, at one point coming within 25%.

Source: Excerpted from David P. Hamilton, "Dell Computer Escalates Price War in Japan by Introducing Low-Cost PCs," *The Wall Street Journal*, January 22, 1993, p. 5.

Net Price Received

Firms using this approach do not attempt to control the price at which the product is finally sold. The enterprise's main concern is with the **net price it receives.** This type of firm most likely shares the view of pricing as a static element more than as an active tool.

Foreign National Pricing and International Pricing

Pricing for foreign markets is further complicated by managers' having to be concerned with two types of pricing: foreign national pricing and international pricing. Basically, the former is pricing for selling in another country and the latter is pricing in another country for export.

Foreign National Pricing

A firm's **foreign national pricing** is influenced by its international pricing strategy, discussed above, as well as by foreign governments. A government can influence its nation's prices by taking various actions. It can institute **national price controls.** These controls may encompass all products sold within the nation's borders or impose them on only specific products. Some governments influence prices on foreign imports by levying higher import duties or subsidizing local industries. Governments can also affect prices by applying legislation relative to labor costs. Higher labor costs means higher prices, and vice versa. A recent trend, however, among many nations is to open up their markets to price competition laws. Prices are likely to be lower in competitive environments. The product life cycle in a specific market also influences the price. If it is a new product and there is a demand for it, a higher price can often be charged. On the other hand, to achieve market penetration where the product is in a late life cycle stage, a firm may have to charge a lower price.

International Pricing

International pricing basically relates to the managerial decision of what to charge for goods produced in one nation and sold in another. A common practice of global corporations (discussed in Chapter 1) is intracorporate sales. In applying this practice, a global corporation attempts to rationalize production by requiring subsidiaries to specialize in the manufacture of some items while importing others. The subsidiaries' imports may consist of components assembled into the end product or they may be finished products imported to complement their product mix. This import-export practice among subsidiaries located in different countries enables the global corporation to control and transfer prices and to control the profits and losses of its subsidiaries. These corporations will realize no profits in a country where, for reasons discussed below, it is not beneficial to do so, and will realize them in a country where it is beneficial.

Avoiding a Country's High Tax Rate.   Both foreign and domestic governments are interested in profits and the role of transfer prices in their attainment. This is because of the consequences profits have on the amount of taxes paid. Because of the differences in tax structures among nations, global corporations can often obtain significant profits by instructing a subsidiary in a country that has a **high corporate tax rate** to sell the product at cost to another subsidiary in a country where taxes are lower. The profit is thereby earned in the country where taxes are lower.

Avoiding a Country's Currency Restrictions.   Transfer pricing may also be used to get around **currency restrictions.** For example, a nation suffering from a lack of foreign exchange may impose controls that limit the amount of profit that can be repatriated, that is, profits that can be transferred back to the corporation's home base. For instance, suppose nation X imposes controls on the amount of profits that can be repatriated, and that there is trade with country Y, which does not have such controls. The corporation at home could instruct the subsidiary in country X to sell its product to a subsidiary in country Y at cost. This would transfer X's profit to Y, from where the global corporation can repatriate profits.

Avoiding Currency Devaluations, Having to Reduce Prices, and Having to Increase Wages.   The international pricing approach could also be employed by global corporations when a foreign nation's **currency is devaluated,** when there is government pressure in the foreign country to **reduce prices** because of excessive profits, and when labor in the foreign country demands **higher wages** because of high profits earned.

Arms-Length Pricing.   Because of these manipulative practices, many governments insist on **arms-length pricing;** that is, the price charged to company affiliates must be the same as that paid by unrelated customers. For example, under section 482 of the U.S. Internal Revenue Code, U.S. tax authorities have the authority to reconstruct an intracorporate transfer price. When they suspect that low prices were set to avoid taxes, the tax authorities may recalculate the tax. It should be noted that many U.S. executives prefer the arms-length approach because it enables them to properly monitor and evaluate foreign managements.[30] They also tend to prefer it because the transfers can demoralize the management of the foreign subsidiaries that do not show positive results—they were transferred to another subsidiary.

Fluctuating Exchange Rates and Costs

Fluctuating exchange rates force periodic adjustments in price. For example, Zenith Electronics Corporation incorrectly estimated the fluctuating direction of the U.S. dollar when it hedged in forward exchange contracts, resulting in a $13 million loss in its 1989 second quarter, even though its sales grew.[31] The same principle applies to fluctuating costs, including costs of raw materials and supplies, inflation, and interest rates. When a firm enters into a long-term contract at a fixed rate, shifts can prove disastrous if the firm cannot adjust its prices in some way. The lesson is that in international pricing, a firm must develop strong international money management skills. (Refer again to the case of Laker Airways, the British firm discussed in Chapter 2, which went into bankruptcy because it did not manage well in this respect.)

Countertrade

The swapping of goods is a practice that has been around for thousands of years. A well-known swap deal occurred in 1626 when European settlers in America traded with America's aborigines $24 worth of cloth and trinkets for Manhattan Island [New York].[32]

Pricing strategies are further complicated by the fact that not all foreign transactions can be in cash. For example, sales to communist countries and to Third World countries with "soft currency," currency that is not readily accepted in international transactions, often take place in the form countertrade, which fundamentally means the buyer of a product pays the seller with another product that has the equivalent monetary value. The pricing problem derives from the difficulty of assessing the value of the product received in exchange. A miscalculation could lead to financial disaster. There are four basic types of countertrade transactions: barter, compensation, switch, and counterpurchase.[33]

Barter

Barter is an arrangement in which the exporter sells goods to a foreign importer without the exchange of cash. That is, specified goods are sold to the importer for other specified goods.

Compensation

Using the **compensation** procedure, the exporter sells technology and equipment to an importer in the foreign market. The importer pays the exporter with goods produced with the imported technology or equipment.

Switch

In the **switch** procedure, the exporter transfers the commitment to a third party who may be an end user of the product received by the exporter, or to a trading house employed to dispose of the product. An advantage here is that the third party can be highly effective in selling the product. A disadvantage is that the third party often seeks to obtain the product at a bargain price, therefore lessening profit and complicating negotiations.

Counterpurchase

Under a **counterpurchase** agreement, two parties agree to sell each other products or services with some balancing of values. The exporter sells goods, technology, or services to the foreign importer for cash, but agrees to purchase goods with the cash equivalent from the importer within a specified period—the goods are selected from a list that usually excludes those items produced by the technology being imported. An advantage of this approach is that the exporter has use of the cash for the specified period.

Exporters entering into countertrade agreements must often use a trading firm to market the goods they purchase. However, the goods purchased can often be distributed or used by a subsidiary of the exporter. For example, PepsiCo has been selling to Russia the concentrate for a drink to be bottled and sold in Russia. In return, PepsiCo has been paid with vodka, which it has distributed through a subsidiary. Often, exporters receive raw materials or parts that can be used in their production process.

In general, the major problem in countertrade is determining the value and the potential demand of the goods offered by the other firm, and it is time consuming. Firms, however, are motivated to participate in countertrade for various reasons, including to make sales in nonmarket nations and in many less-developed countries, and to adjust their accounting records to enable them to pay lower taxes and tariffs. This occurs when both parties underestimate the value of the goods.

PROMOTION STRATEGY

In general, problems related to international **promotion strategy** include the legal aspects of the country, tax considerations, language complexities, cultural diversity, media limitations, credibility of advertising, and degree of illiteracy. Some governments regulate advertising more closely than others. Laws in some nations restrict the amount of money that may be spent on advertising, the media utilized, the type of product advertised, the methods used in advertising, and the way in which the price is advertised. Some nations have special taxes on advertisements. Language translation, which will be discussed in Chapter 8, presents many barriers. For example, translation of semantic and idiomatic meanings across cultures are difficult to make, which presents huge impediments to communication.

Why International Promotional Strategies Fail

There are numerous reasons why international promotional strategies fail. The reasons include insufficient research, poor follow-up, narrow vision, overstandardization, and rigid implementation.[34]

Insufficient Research

Insufficient research prior to making international strategic decisions generally leads to failure. For example, Lego A/S, the Danish toy company, had improved its penetration in the American market by offering "bonus" packs and gift promotion. Encouraged by its success in the U.S., Lego decided to apply the same approaches, unaltered, to other markets, including Japan, where penetration had been lagging. The Japanese customers were not attracted to those tactics. A later investigation revealed that Japanese consumers viewed the promotions as wasteful, expensive, and not too appealing. The results were similar in other countries as well.

Overstandardization

Some commodities, such as Coca-Cola, have a global appeal. In this situation, the message to be communicated can be much the same throughout the world. Many products, however, do not have universal appeal.[35] The message to be communicated must therefore be tied to individual motivation; the promotional campaign, instead of being **overstandardized,** must reflect local tastes. The foreign environment thus has a significant effect on promotional strategy. Failure to adapt promotional strategy to the foreign environment inevitably creates difficulties. Managers therefore need to determine whether or not a promotional message is appropriate for the foreign culture, and if not, what adoptions must be made.

For example, the Marlboro cigarette advertisements, which contain a man projecting a strong Western masculine image, were unsuccessful in Hong Kong. Philip Morris subsequently changed its ad to reflect a Hong Kong–style man, still a virile cowboy, but younger, better dressed, and owning the truck and the land he is on.[36] Another example is a laundry detergent company's promotional campaign in the Middle East. The advertisement pictured soiled clothes on the left, a box of soap in the middle, and clean clothes on the right. Since many people in that part of the world read from right to left, many individuals interpreted the message to mean that the soap soiled the clothes.[37] And in the 1970s, Polaroid began selling its pathbreaking SX-70 camera in Europe. It used the same advertising strategy, such as TV commercials and print ads, that was successful to launch the product in the American market. Although the product itself had global appeal, the TV commercials featuring personalities well known in the U.S. did not. Testimonials by well known personalities did not stimulate European consumers' interest. Polaroid subsequently researched and adhered to European promotional practices that were known to work. (For further illustration, refer to Practical Perspective 4–9.)

Poor Follow-Up

Failure to monitor the promotional campaign for problems and solve them as they arise will contribute to failure. For instance, a U.S.-based computer company implemented a software house cooperation program in Europe to help penetrate the small- and medium-sized accounts market segment, where it was weak. The program needed a large change in sales force oper-

PRACTICAL   PERSPECTIVE   4–9

Advertising in Saudi Arabia Must Adhere to Local Customs

Saudi Arabia plays a key role in the Gulf Co-operation Council (GCC). . . . An understanding of advertising regulation in this gateway country thus becomes essential for marketers interested in the region. . . . As do many other developing countries, Saudi Arabia strongly adheres to local customs. Age-old traditions continue to be observed in dress, salutations, hospitality, and so forth. Although no laws specifically regulate the culture contents of ads, insensitivity may destroy credibility. A major tea company alienated Saudi customers after it aired a commercial that showed a Saudi host serving tea with his left hand to one of his guests. Moreover, the guest was shown wearing shoes while seated, which is considered disrespectful by traditional Saudies.

Source: Excerpted from M. Luqmani, Z. Quraeshi, and U. Yavas, "Advertising in Saudi Arabia: Content and Regulation," *The International Executive*, November–December 1989, pp. 35–38.

ation. The sales force, no longer in control of the hardware and software package, had to determine its content together with a software house that had access to the smaller accounts. The success of the new program depended on how effectively the sales force carried out its new assignments, as well as on central coordination and attention, which it never got. Lacking central coordination and **follow-up,** there was no communication channel for sharing and building on the experiences of subsidiaries.

Narrow Vision

An enterprise may centralize promotional strategic decision making or it may decentralize it to its local managers. Both approaches have pros and cons. The centralized approach can be effective by providing an overall global perspective, but it can be ineffective because decision making is not close to the market. The decentralized approach may be effective since decision making is close to the market; however, it may be ineffective because it does not provide a global perspective. (For an illustration, refer to Practical Perspective 4–10.) Firms that apply just one of the two approaches possess **narrow vision.**

For example, in the 1970s, the Anglo-Dutch company Unilever targeted its household cleaner, Domestos, for international expansion. Management

PRACTICAL PERSPECTIVE 4–10

Nestle's Decentralization of Promotion Proves Less Than Satisfactory

Nestle's experiences with *laissez-faire* in sales promotion are typical of the problems faced by many multinationals. In the early 1980s, management delegated to the local organizations many decisions that had traditionally been made or strongly influenced by the headquarters. Of all the marketing decisions, only branding and packaging were kept at the center. The rest, including consumer and trade promotions, became the domain of the company's country operations around the world. Although decentralization has helped enhance Nestle's performance internationally, it has been less than satisfactory in sales promotion.

The problem has to do with two developments over time: a worldwide shift in emphasis and budget allocation in favor of sales promotion and away from media advertising, and increasing reliance on price promotion to boost short-term local sales results, particularly in countries with a powerful trade and/or limited electronic media advertising. The outcome: reduced brand profitability, contradictory brand communication, and a serious potential for dilution of brand franchises with consumers. Today [1990] Nestle is trying to put some central direction back into its worldwide communication practices, including sales promotion. Management is painfully aware of the damage "brand management by calculators" and "commodity promotion" can do to its international brands and their long-term profitability. *Laissez-faire* in sales promotion is no longer considered a virtue at Nestle.

Source: Excerpted from K. Kashani and J. A. Quelch, "Can Sales Promotions Go Global?" *Business Horizons*, May–June 1990, pp. 37–43.

assigned development of a global "reference mix" to Britain, where the brand had been established. Several years and numerous market entries later, Unilever's top management was still waiting to repeat the success it attained in the British market. Failure was attributed to the lead market's insistence that their strategy be followed in other markets (centralization), but success to deviation from the lead market's strategy (decentralization). However, in the markets where there was deviation, the global theme also deviated. For instance, the theme for Domestos in West Germany was as an "all-purpose sanitary cleaner," and in Australia it was as a "bathroom plaque remover." To attain a balance between centralization and decentralization, Unilever's detergent unit subsequently established a multisubsidiary structure, the European Brand Group, to coordinate brands in Europe. The group consisted of executives from the central headquarters and from numerous large subsidiaries.

Rigid Implementation

High-level managers sometimes ignore local managers' reservations about **rigidly implementing** a standardized promotional program and force compliance, which usually leads to failure. This is so because local managers' reservations are often based on a solid understanding of local conditions. For example, Nestle launched an innovative cake-like chocolate bar in Europe. The British unit, however, refused to accept the product because of its knowledge that a soft bar would not appeal to British tastes. Forced adoption would therefore have resulted in failure.

Top management may also become inflexible to changing market conditions. For instance, Lego pioneered standardized marketing in its field and became a genuine global corporation by marketing its educational toys in the same way in more than 100 countries. However, Lego eventually encountered competition from look-alike and lower-priced rival products from Japan, the U.S., and other countries. Tyco, a leading competitor in the U.S., began placing its toys in plastic buckets that could be utilized for storage after play. Lego, however, used elegant see-through cartons standardized worldwide. American parents preferred the functional toys-in-a-bucket idea over cartons. Lego's U.S. managers sought permission from the central managers in Denmark to package Lego's toys in buckets. The central managers refused because they believed that the bucket could cheapen Lego's reputation for high quality, that it could change their reputation from innovator to follower, and that it deviated from the company's policy of standardization. Massive losses eventually led Lego to change and to develop its own innovative buckets.

Developing an Effective International Promotional Strategy

Basically, to develop an effective international promotional strategy, strategists must determine: (a) the promotional mix—the blend of advertising, personal selling, and sales promotions—needed for each market; (b) the extent of worldwide promotional standardization; (c) the most effective message; (d) the most effective medium; and (e) the necessary controls to aid in assessing whether or not the potential objectives are being met.[38]

SUMMARY

This chapter has proposed that when managers develop international product/service strategy, they must consider the SRC, which often leads one to assume that what sells at home will sell abroad in the same form—which usually is not true. Some products and services can be sold globally in standardized form, but most products and services must be customized to fit the varying needs of different societies. Managers must also consider that many products/services introduced into a society will not sell well right away; they must be diffused into the society over time.

The method of getting the product or service to foreign customers will vary from nation to nation. The fundamental approaches are exporting to it or manufacturing in it. Six approaches to manufacturing abroad were discussed: licensing, franchising, management contracts, joint ventures, contractual alliances, and wholly owned subsidiaries. The chapter also described how various factors influence international pricing strategy, such as the foreign government, monetary exchange, and the requirement for barter trade. Some international firms use pricing strategy to develop foreign markets; others are content to simply get some revenue from the foreign market. Some international firms use a transfer pricing approach to get around a country's high tax rate, currency restrictions, currency devaluations, and mandate to reduce prices and increase wages. Four types of barter trade were discussed: barter, compensation, switch, and counterpurchase.

Relative to promotion strategy, it was proposed that various factors influence international promotions, including the legal aspects of the country, language, and cultural diversity. Several reasons why international promotional strategies fail were discussed: insufficient research, poor follow-up, narrow vision, overcentralization, and rigid implementation.

Key Terms

1. Product/service, place/entry, price, and promotion strategies
2. Self-reference criterion
3. Standardization versus customization
4. Cultural barriers
5. The diffusion process
6. Quickness or slowness of diffusion
7. Dualistic technological structure
8. Adaptive transformative and transformative technological innovations
9. Exporting to and manufacturing abroad
10. Indirect and direct exporting
11. Domestic and foreign middlemen
12. Agent and merchant middlemen
13. International sales force
14. Foreign sales branch, foreign sales subsidiary, and company's own foreign distribution system

15. Firms should not adhere to any one approach

16. Licensing, franchising, management contracting, joint ventures, contractual alliances, and wholly owned subsidiaries

17. "Goodwill" and "badwill"

18. A mix of strategies

19. International pricing strategy

20. Pricing as an active tool and as a static element

21. Control over final prices and net price received

22. Foreign national and international pricing

23. National price controls

24. Getting around a country's high tax rate, currency restrictions, currency devaluations, and requirements to reduce prices and increase wages

25. Arms-length pricing

26. Barter, compensation, switch, and counterpurchase

27. Insufficient research, overstandardization of promotion, poor follow-up on promotion program, narrow vision, and rigid implementation of promotion program

Discussion Questions and Exercises

1. Why is it important that managers of international firms remain informed about their enterprises' external environment and internal situation?

2. You are the strategic planner for a domestic firm that produces soft drinks. Your firm's sales at home are stagnant. As a solution, you have decided to sell your product in Europe and Asia. What should your next step be?

3. Briefly discuss the five different product strategies.

4. Some writers on international strategy contend that the effectiveness of international businesses is relying more and more on the offering of standardized products (a global strategy). Do you agree or disagree? Why?

5. You are an international management consultant hired by a domestic company, which invented a unique product for its home market. The firm's management is now considering expansion into foreign markets and is currently considering the financial aspects of the transfer. With respect to revenues, what would you advise your client?

6. Discuss the dualistic technological structure.

7. A domestic firm, whose managerial personnel lack international business experience, is considering entering a foreign market. What would be its logical entry strategy? Why?

8. A domestic firm, whose managerial personnel have had considerable prior experience in international business in a similar industry, is

considering entering a foreign market. What would be its logical entry strategy? Why?

9. Differentiate between an international sales force, sales branch, sales subsidiary, and own distribution system. Discuss some of the factors that affect the approach taken.

10. Discuss some of the advantages and some of the disadvantages of direct exporting over indirect exporting.

11. Discuss the six strategic options to manufacturing abroad.

12. An international business has been exporting to a foreign market. The firm's product is well diffused in the market. Because of high local labor costs, rises in transportation costs, and increases in tariff costs, the firm has been incurring financial losses. The firm's management has decided that it is time to manufacture abroad. The management of the cash-short firm likes to be in control of total operations. Which of the six options to manufacture abroad do you believe is best suited for this firm? Why?

13. Discuss advantages and disadvantages of the wholly owned strategy.

14. Discuss advantages and disadvantages of manufacturing abroad over exporting.

15. Operating in foreign markets brings new pricing challenges. Discuss some of them.

16. Discuss the "pricing as an active tool," "pricing as a static element," "control over final prices," and "net price received" pricing strategies.

17. Differentiate between foreign national pricing and international pricing.

18. Why do international managers currently prefer arms-length pricing?

19. How do fluctuating exchange rates and costs affect pricing strategy?

20. Discuss the four approaches to countertrade. What is the major problem with countertrade?

21. Discuss the general problems related to international promotion strategy.

22. You are an international promotion consultant hired by a firm getting ready to develop a massive international promotion program. What advice would you give your client?

Assignment

Interview an international executive of an international business firm. Ask him/her to describe his/her enterprise's general international strategies. How did the firm enter the foreign arena? What were some of the factors that affected the strategy? Has the firm changed strategies? If not, does it plan to do so? Prepare a short report for class discussion.

Setting Up Shop Far from Home

C A S E   4–1

Source: Joanne Cleaver, "Small Firms, Global View: Setting Up Shop Far from Home," *Crains Chicago Business* 15(17) (April 27, 1992): pp. 63. Copyright 1992 by Crain Communications Inc. Reprinted by permission.

MDA Scientific Inc. had some tough decisions to make two years ago. The Lincolnshire-based manufacturer of gas detection gauges had been pursuing sales in Japan through a distributor, with lackluster results. "We had some sales reps, and we still do, but you always have the feeling that you're not as well represented by them as you could be by your own staff," relates Mark Sztelle, vice president of finance. A unit of Switzerland-based Zellweger Uster AG, the company had sales of roughly $35 million last year. As semiconductor manufacturing in Japan grew to a third of the world's production, MDA executives were increasingly convinced that they weren't getting their share of gauges installed in the production facilities. (The custom-made gauges monitor the escape of toxic gases during semiconductor production.) Like many Illinois companies of comparable size, MDA was convinced it had to boost its profile in foreign markets. Investing a substantial portion of the company's financial and human resources in a full-fledged satellite sales office, though, was a proposition fraught with unknowns.

Despite the risks, a few small-to-mid-sized Illinois companies like MDA are forging ahead with ambitious multi-national plans. Disregarding the traditional wisdom that would have them conquer the domestic market before tackling other countries, they consider their overseas offices important strategic footholds for growth in the next decade. But the effort is not always easy—and it's almost always expensive. MDA's solution was to jettison its Japanese distributor and establish a proprietary sales office staffed with a husband-and-wife engineer-and-chemist team who had been working at the Lincolnshire headquarters for a decade. The couple are both Japanese natives, so, in a wry twist of fate, they were sent as expatriates back to their own country. Just to keep even with the high cost of living in Japan, MDA doubled the salaries of its sales team. It also spent several hundred thousand dollars securing a lease on a cubbyhole office in Tokyo and leasing an apartment for the couple. Though MDA hasn't snared dozens of sales since the office opened two years ago, the sales team is making progress in ways that MDA hopes will lead soon to a crop of orders. "Market penetration is very slow. But they're developing relationships," says Mr. Sztelle.

Of course, few smaller companies are fortunate enough to have on staff foreign nationals with the precise combination of technical skills and sales savvy to head up a beachhead sales office. In fact, according to consultants and foreign trade advisers, $300 million in annual sales is the usual threshold at which a corporation has the resources to devote to establishing overseas sales or operations facilities. But as smaller companies become more aggressive in landing business abroad, that threshold is showing signs of downward movement. "Ten years ago, these (small Midwest manufacturers) would say, 'Oh, we're focusing on the U.S. market, and yeah, we do some exports.'

Now, that's totally reversed," says Roger Herod, vice president at the Chicago office of New York-based Organization Resource Counsellors, an international human resources consulting firm. "It's amazing to go to a company with $30 million to $40 million in sales and you walk into the president's office and there's a map of the world with pins where they have sales reps," he says.

The typical evolution of a company's foreign marketing presence starts with choosing a distributor to handle exported goods. If sales via the distributor are promising, the company may dispatch a headquarters employee to more fully develop a strategic sales plan with the distributor. The next logical step is to have the distributor handle back-room operations, such as warehousing and tariff work, while a fledgling sales force establishes itself. The final stage is establishment of a full contingent of sales and support staff, sometimes augmented by a small assembly or manufacturing facility. Many small companies find satisfactory long-term arrangements at some point on this continuum and never do feel compelled to set up a freestanding sales office. However, government officials and private consultants who advise companies on foreign trade say that a go-it-alone attitude is becoming more prevalent. "I think controlling the thing by yourself makes the most sense," says Jim Waddell, group vice president at Clarcor Inc., a $179-million Rockford-based firm whose filtration division has sales offices in England and Belgium. "My next preference would be a joint venture."

Sandy Renner, president of Export Resources Associates Inc., a Minneapolis-based export consulting firm with an office in Chicago, agrees that the sense of control that comes with directly operating an overseas office can be an important factor. "The more of a presence a company can actually have in the market, the more of the market they'll capture," she says. "The more people they will have (in the foreign market), the better ideas they'll have of how to adapt their products to the market, and more and better ideas of the local relevant technology. The whole concept of being on-site gives you more of a hands-on feeling for the market." The concept is not without risk, however. Problems with budding foreign operations hit smaller companies particularly hard when they're trying to break into an overseas market. According to Paul Neubelt, director of international services for the New York-based accounting and consulting firm BDO Seidman, thinly staffed smaller and mid-sized companies usually have to raid their own corporate ranks to staff a new overseas office, especially at first. That can cause tension at the home office as executives must juggle the responsibilities normally handled by the just-departed staffers. In addition, says Mr. Neubelt, the process of making technical modifications in products and gaining local approval for redesigned products can be tedious and arduous. "In Europe, there aren't too many products that you wouldn't have to make modifications for, even things like toys and clothes. In Canada, there aren't too many dissimilarities," he says.

Pay structures and terminology are other areas of misunderstanding. In Italy, for example, salaries are discussed in terms of net, or actual take-home, pay. The employer pays all taxes directly to the government. That caused confusion for Ted Broland, president of Rockford-based machine tool company W. A. Whitney Co., which has operated an Italian plant since 1968 and sales offices in Mexico City and Toronto since 1969. "In the area of compensation, I was a little naive," admits Mr. Broland. "I was comparing wage surveys, gross, with what we paid net, and we have some wages that got out of line. Over time, we got those back in line." Adds Organization Resource Counsellors' Mr. Herod, "With a small-to-mid-sized company, you have very limited staff. Human resource issues are the last to be addressed. (Executives) are so intent on setting up the sales offices that they don't worry about all the other issues, like taxes and compensation. They just want to get Joe on the plane." "The general disadvantage of having a salesman is that you have to be very careful with the contract," warns Leslie Stroh, publisher of the New York-based magazine *The Exporter*. "Some contracts are forever. In France, if a salesman develops a customer, it's his customer, not yours."

Such pitfalls are avoided through diligence and experience. If a smaller company views international expansion as crucial, it will adopt a long-term viewpoint that helps put early mistakes in perspective. Take, for example, DBA Products Co., a Lake Bluff-based manufacturer of bowling alley mechanisms. Though its annual sales are only in the $20-million range, 30% of those sales are made outside the United States. Twenty-five years ago, Chairman and CEO Remo Picchietti adopted a "get there first" overseas strategy. He starts wooing proprietors of small bowling alleys while the sport is still obscure in a particular country. "We went (to Europe, Japan, Australia and Korea) and invested time, money and effort and, of course, there wasn't a return at first. And we were there when the market exploded," he relates. Mr. Picchietti is in the process of carrying that long-term strategy to South America. He recently returned from conducting management programs for owner/operators in Brazil, Venezuela, Argentina and Chile. His steps will be to establish a distribution system and eventually a permanent sales and service office. "It takes commitment, and a lot of hand-holding and hand-shaking, and good meals and bad meals," says Mr. Picchietti. "You can't just send a fax over and say, 'Do you want to buy my product?' "

QUESTIONS

1. Many organizations' strategy is to first sell their product or service in their home market, then subsequently sell it in foreign markets. How is MDA Scientific Inc.'s strategy different?
2. Discuss MDA's entry strategy.
3. Why did MDA select that entry strategy?
4. Discuss MDA's product strategy.
5. Discuss MDA's price strategy.
6. Relative to promotion strategy, how did MDA boost its profile in foreign markets.

Notes

1. J. R. Whitaker Penteado, "Fast-Food Franchises Fight for Brazilian Aficionados," Used with permission of publisher from *Brandweek*, June 7, 1993, p. 20.

2. James E. Lee, "Cultural Analysis in Overseas Operations," *Harvard Business Review* (March–April 1966,) 106–114.

3. Martha T. Moore, "Meeting the Cupholder Challenge," *USA Today*, May 2, 1994, p. 1B.

4. Whitaker Penteado, "Fast-Food Franschises," p. 20.

5. Warren J. Keegan, "Multinational Product Planning: Strategic Alternatives," *Journal of Marketing* (January 1969): 58–62.

6. Laurie M. Grossman, "PepsiCo Plans Big Overseas Expansion in Diet Cola Wars with Its Pepsi Max," *The Wall Street Journal*, April 4, 1994, p. B6.

7. Theodore Levitt, "The Globalization of Markets," *Harvard Business Review* 61 (May-June 1983): 92–102.

8. Global Strategies, "The Colonel Comes to Japan," *The International Executive* (July–August 1989): 28–29.

9. Shawn Tully, "Teens: The Most Global Market of All," *Fortune*, May 16, 1994, p. 90.

10. Subhash C. Jain, "Standardization of International Marketing Strategy: Some Research Hypotheses," *Journal of Marketing* 53 (January 1989): 70–79.

11. Everett M. Rogers, *Diffusion of Innovations,* 3rd ed. (New York: The Free Press, 1983), p. 10.

12. The discussion of these categories draws from P. R. Cateora and J. M. Hess, *International Marketing* (Homewood, IL: Richard D. Irwin, 1979), p. 377.

13. This discussion draws from Paul Shrivastava, "Technological Innovation in Developing Countries," *The Columbia Journal of World Business* XIX, no. 4 (Winter 1984): 23–39.

14. Ibid, p. 26.

15. *Distribution in Asia/Pacific's Developing Markets* (Hong Kong: Business International Asia/Pacific Ltd., March 1978), pp. 1–3.

16. Ibid.

17. Ibid.

18. Ibid., pp. 3–4.

19. Global Strategies, "The Colonel Comes to Japan."

20. John Marcom, Jr., "Japan to Host World's 3rd Disneyland but Park May Run Short of Funds, Fans," *The Wall Street Journal*, November 17, 1982, p. 36.

21. Ted Holden, "Who Says You Can't Break into Japan?" *Business Week*, October 16, 1989, p. 49.

22. Ibid.

23. J. G. Wissema and L. Euser, "Successful Innovation Through Inter-Company Networks," *Long Range Planning,* 24 (December 1991), p. 35.

24. Thomas G. Cummings, "Transorganizational Development," in B. Staw and L.L. Cummings, eds., *Research in Organizational Behavior,* Vol. 6 (Greenwich, CT: JAI Press, 1984).

25. R. Ajami, "Designing Multinational Networks," in R. H. Kilmann and I. Kilmann, eds., *Making Organizations Competitive* (San Francisco: Jossey-Bass, 1991).

26. Kenichi Ohmae, "The Global Logic of Strategic Alliances," *Harvard Business Review* (March–April 1989): 151.

27. Ibid., pp. 147–149.

28. Ibid., p. 152.

29. Seth J. Margolis, "Middle Market Companies Prepare for '92," *The International Executive,* January–February 1990, p. 41.

30. J. Greene and M. Duerr, *International Transactions in the Multinational Firm* (New York: The Conference Board, 1970), p. 8.

31. Stephen Kreider Yoder, "U.S. Technology Firms Go Global to Offset Weak Domestic Market," *The Wall Street Journal*, November 14, 1989, p. A1.

32. Arley A. Howard and John A. Yeakel, "Who Wins in International Countertrade," *Financial Executive*, January-February 1990, p. 49.

33. This discussion draws from P. Maher, "The Countertrade Boom," *Business Marketing* (January 1984): 50–52; and "Countertrade Without Cash?" *Finance and Development* (December 1983): 14.

34. The following discussion is adopted from Kamran Kashiani, "Beware the Pitfalls of Global Marketing," *Harvard Business Review* (September–October 1989): 91–98.

35. "Global Messages for the Global Village Are Here," *Business World*, Autumn 1983, p. 51.

36. David A. Ricks, *Big Business Blunders: Mistakes in Multinational Marketing* (Homewood, Il: Dow Jones/Irwin, 1983), p. 52.

37. Ibid., p. 55.

38. Adapted from Cateora and Hess, *International Marketing*, p. 417.

Part Three

ORGANIZING INTERNATIONAL ENTERPRISES

Two key questions managers must answer when they decide to market their firms' products or services in the international arena are how they will handle their foreign business, and how they will structure their organization to conduct that business in the most efficient and effective manner. The success of an international enterprise depends on many crucial factors. One is its organizational structure. The structure is the organization's "skeleton;" it provides support and ties together disparate functions. Therefore, it is imperative that managers totally understand the structuring factors to be considered and the structuring problems to be overcome when attempting to expand into foreign markets. Chapter 5 discusses various international organizational structures.

Chapter 5
International
Organizational
Structures

Chapter Five

International Organizational Structures

Going global has recently meant transferring world headquarters of important business units abroad. Multinational corporations are making these moves, despite some significant risks, because they want to operate near key customers and tough rivals in fast-changing markets far from home. More businesses recognize that they cannot manage worldwide operations from a single location, and experts predict that maybe 50 percent of Fortune 500 companies will be making such moves in the next 10 years. Relocated companies hope to gain power by acquiring an image of "a global firm with a global reach." Companies also hope that these moves help to break down parochialism and groom global managers.[1]

Objectives of the Chapter

Organizational structures generally establish internal authority relationships, responsibility for work performance, and paths of communication and control required for a company to achieve its objectives. These structure are typically set up to blend the specialized expertise needed to facilitate decision making on a variety of short- and long-range problems. The development of structures should generally be planned and managed. The type of structure managers select should take into consideration the social and psychological aspects of the environment and personnel, and should be designed to achieve operational efficiency and control without inhibiting individual creativity and initiative. This task becomes much more complex when a domestic enterprise desires to internationalize its operations. This is because organizations' managers need to establish line authority and responsibility from top headquarters management to managers in a variety of foreign environments, and at the same time keep open the necessary lines of communication required to manage effectively and efficiently in all the diverse environments.[2] The objectives of this chapter are therefore to:

1. Describe the basic traditional international organizational structures.
2. Present the advantages and disadvantages of each structure.
3. Discuss contemporary thinking on the structuring of international organizations.

TRADITIONAL AND CONTEMPORARY INTERNATIONAL STRUCTURES

The three basic dimensions of an international business enterprise are technical or product needs, functional needs, and regional or environmental needs. *Technical or product needs* are specialized factors such as construction, operation, manufacturing, research and development, special knowledge, and experience. *Functional needs* are special knowledge of such functions as personnel, planning, purchasing, and finance. *Regional or environmental needs* are special knowledge of areas such as the foreign government, politics, trends, and economy. To attain maximum overall benefit, and to assure effective communication and develop the means to make effective decisions, the *international organizational structure* managers select must effectively integrate these three basic dimensions throughout the organization.[3]

An organization's **international structure** is usually based on one of seven traditional or contemporary models. The traditional models include the functional structure, international division, foreign subsidiary, product division, and regional structure. The contemporary models include the matrix organization, the non-equity-based contractual/strategic alliance, and the mixed (hybrid) structure. These are discussed in the ensuing sections.

The Functional Structure

Under the **functional structure,** the major functions are the focus. Product knowledge is centered in manufacturing, engineering, and marketing, and each is responsible for both domestic and international activities. Large international companies rarely use this structure at the corporate level, it is sometimes used in regions, divisions, and/or subsidiaries. The functional structure is traditionally European. It is typically used by smaller firms, and sometimes by larger firms with one major product and stable demand. Domestic firms whose internationalization strategy (discussed in Chapter 4) entails indirect exporting often use this structure.

A firm's low dependence on foreign sales and its staff's lack of international business experience often leads it to adopt this structure, as opposed to the international division structure (discussed next). A typical functional structure is illustrated in Figure 5–1. Note that the organizational chart in Figure 5–1 shows a manager of domestic operations and a manager of foreign operations for each function. However, these two roles are often carried out by one individual. Two people might be used when there is a large volume of international sales. But even then, the domestic manager may appoint an assistant manager to oversee international sales for him/her.

Advantages of the Functional Structure[4]

1. *Emphasis on functional expertise.* The key business tasks define work, and functional expertise is brought to bear on all aspects of the operation.
2. *Tight control.* This centralized functional approach permits a small staff to control the firm's operations. Top management has authority and operational responsibility.
3. *Prevents "We" versus "Them" conflicts.* The absence of secondary profit centers (there is no international division) prevents internal conflicts—the "we" versus the international division problem (discussed in the next section) is prevented.

Disadvantages of the Functional Structure

1. *Weak regional coordination.* Disputes between functional managers must often be resolved at the corporate level. The CEO is often asked to solve problems in areas in which he or she lacks expertise, such as international business.
2. *In firms with multiple product lines, it can lead to a top-heavy structure.* In multiproduct firms, functional managers need expertise in each product or a functional manager is needed for each product. The latter, which is often the case, would lead to a top-heavy structure, which would be expensive. For example, if the volume of international business is high, a domestic functional manager and a foreign functional manager may be needed (as shown in Figure 5–1).

The International Division

After they have acquired some international business experience through indirect exporting and their reliance on international business has increased somewhat, many companies internationalize their operations further by creating an export department. Typically, the aim of the export department is simply to handle shipment of existing domestic products to foreign markets. But when firms' foreign transactions subsequently increase, the export department is generally developed into an international division. *The international division* usually supervises exports, distribution agreements, for-

◆   FIGURE 5–1   **An Illustration of a Functional Structure**

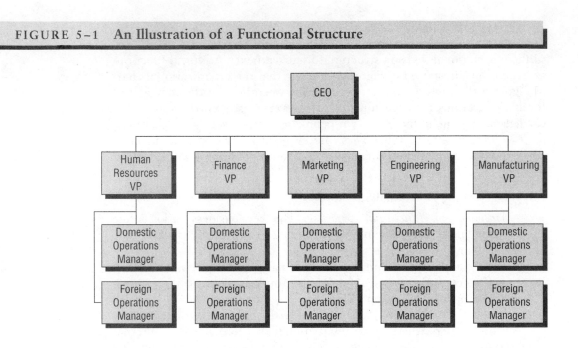

eign sales forces, foreign sales branches, and foreign sales subsidiaries. Staff members in the international division are selected on the basis of their general familiarity with corporate products, technology, and culture, combined with their ability to be "hands-on" managers who are culturally sensitive and adaptable to the constraints imposed by the foreign environmental factors (as discussed in Chapters 1 and 2).

In the **international division structure**, functional staffs, such as marketing, finance, and research and development, are typically established and an executive responsible for international operations is appointed. International businesses adopt this structure when they desire to have an expert responsible for managing each specialized function. Managing these functions across countries requires skills beyond those required for managing them in the home country. One of the earliest users of this type of structure was International Harvester.[5] Canon Corporation, before it became a multiproduct enterprise, also used this structure (read Practical Perspective 5–1).

The international division is generally given total authority and responsibility for the enterprise's foreign operations and activities. Historically, some smaller enterprises for whom an international division was not really necessary (an export department would have sufficed) have nevertheless adopted such a structure because they saw it being used by larger, successful enterprises.[6] A typical international division structure is illustrated in Figure 5–2.

PRACTICAL PERSPECTIVE 5–1

Canon Corporation

Since the adoption of diversification [becoming a multiproduct organization] policy in the company's [Canon Corporation] first long-range plan in 1962, the management has operated through a product divisional structure. In 1969, administrative departments were set up in each product group in order to pave the way for a divisionalized structure. By 1972 the Optical Products Group was divisionalized, and based on this experience, a corporate divisional structure came into effect in 1978. Canon then consisted of three divisions: the Camera Operation Group, the Business Machines Group and the Optical Products Group. The general manager of each division was delegated considerable power as the executive responsible for the consolidated profit of the relevant business. On the other hand, sales organizations such as Canon Sales Co. (Japan), Canon U.S.A., and Canon Europe N.V. began to assume a more important role as geographical divisions. At the same time, a Management Committee was formed to take responsibility for strategic decisions. The committee meets regularly once a week to discuss and decide strategic issues. Under the Management Committee, eight committees were set up to cover

the following areas: (1) Canon Global System, (2) Global Research and Development, (3) Global Production, (4) Global Marketing, (5) Legal Affairs, (6) International Trade Balance, (7) Environmental Issues, and (8) Cultural Activity Support.

In 1983, Canon consisted of two business groups and five divisions. Now, in 1991, the company has eight product groups and 21 product divisions. The Planning Department is responsible for: (1) developing long-range management plans, (2) formulating middle-range management plans, (3) serving as secretariat for the Management Committee, (4) analysis of the management structure, (5) control of subsidiary companies, (6) control of management information, (7) editing the company history, (8) the development of new business, (9) developing plans for improving the imbalance of trade, and (10) executing special assignments requested by top management. When implementing the full-scale divisional structure, special attention was given to: the establishment of strong divisions and a powerful headquarters; the balance between decentralization and integration; exploiting the benefits and minimizing the shortcomings of the conventional divisional system;

and building a divisionalized structure most suitable for [the] company. [Figure 5–7 on page 174 presents Canon's 1991 organizational chart.]

Source: Excerpted from T. Nakahara and Y. Isono, "Strategic Planning for Canon: The Crisis and the New Vision," *Long Range Planning* 25 (February 1992): 64. Copyright © 1982. All rights reserved. Used with kind permission from Elsevier Science Ltd., The Boulevard, Lanford Lane, Kidlington 0x51 GB.

◆   FIGURE 5–2   **An Illustration of an International Division Structure**

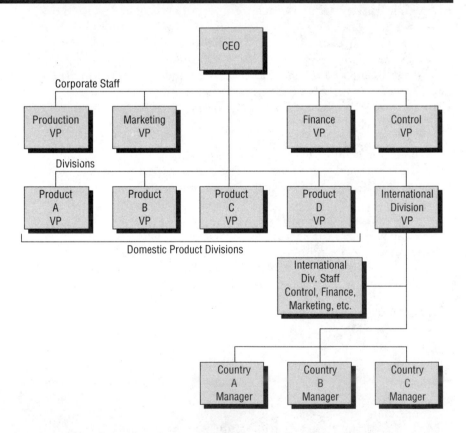

Advantages of the International Division[7]

1. *Focused international responsibility and authority.* Foreign operations are generally more complex than domestic operations and distant from the home base. An experienced executive whose sole responsibility and

authority is the international division is therefore more free to react to the needs of such areas than an executive whose responsibility and authority is for both domestic and international operations.

2. *International executive development.* Manager and employees in such a division are forced to develop expertise in international business and will subsequently be able to participate in, or direct, operations in foreign sites.

3. *The international operation has a single, strong voice in the company's strategy/policy-setting process.* Since heads of international division are usually totally responsible for profits and losses of the foreign operations, they will be forceful in acquiring the share of resources necessary to accomplish the firm's international goals. On the other hand, an executive in charge of both domestic and foreign operations may focus more on obtaining resources for domestic activities than for foreign operations.

4. *Company-wide view of international operations.* Managers in the international division are usually concerned with the success of all of the firm's products in foreign markets. These managers are therefore impartial in determining the best overall corporate strategy for international profits. On the other hand, managers of individual product lines made responsible for both domestic and foreign operations may be partial to their own international operations as opposed to the firm's overall international strategy.

5. *Top management is cognizant of consequences.* Due to the complexity of international business, many domestic executives focus mainly on their home-country operations and lose themselves in domestic issues, therefore ignoring global operations. By having an international division, top management is made cognizant of the consequences of their focused decisions on global operations.

Disadvantages of the International Division

1. *Bottleneck.* Managers of international divisions sometimes lack adequate product or technical expertise, and the physical separation between domestic and foreign operations often precludes enterprises from providing adequate technical support to international divisions. This causes bottlenecks.

2. *Exports slowdown.* Production divisions may not always adequately supply what the foreign division needs because they favor the domestic operations. Thus, foreign orders may go unfilled even if the profit potential is higher than for domestic orders. On the other hand, the heads of product divisions who are responsible for both domestic and foreign business may pay more attention to foreign operations when they see a higher profit potential than in the domestic market.

3. *Conflict between employees in the domestic division and the employees in the international division.* Organizational struggles between

domestic and foreign operations often occur. Because the international division cuts across all product areas, a "we-they" situation can occur.

4. *International versus other divisions.* In the "ideal" corporate organization, operating divisions should be equal in size and profit. In reality, however, the international division often becomes more profitable than the product divisions. When this occurs, the product divisions sometimes "gang up" to reduce the international division's powers.

5. Managers of international divisions are often made responsible for several disparate markets, such as South America, Europe, and Asia. This makes developing expertise difficult.

The Foreign Subsidiary Structure

Environmental changes, such as increased demand in foreign markets, or a foreign country's policies mandating it, or changing conditions in the home market, often force international corporations to cease exporting and to establish manufacturing facilities in the foreign markets—they establish subsidiaries in foreign countries. These firms thus restructure their organization; they change from an international division structure to a **foreign subsidiary structure**. Each foreign subsidiary is treated as an entity. Each reports directly to top management at headquarters. Coordination between product and service departments is carried out at the headquarters office. These firms therefore apply the multidomestic strategy (discussed in Chapter 3). Applying a multidomestic strategy, the headquarters' managers generally allow the subsidiaries to function as a loose federation with **local managers** possessing substantial autonomy, allowing them to respond quickly to local situations[8] (refer to Practical Perspective 5–2). A typical foreign subsidiary structure is illustrated in Figure 5–3.

Advantages of the Foreign Subsidiary Structure[9]

1. *Autonomy of affiliates.* The affiliate subsidiaries operate free of layers of management between them and top management. These independent affiliate companies are generally allowed to operate with not too much control from above, and can thus develop their own local identification (refer again to Practical Perspective 5–2).

2. *Direct top management involvement.* Problems beyond the affiliate's talents go to top management for response and resolution. This enables top management to reflect long-range corporate goals rather than parochial interests. Also, it forces top management to develop a stake in international business, and therefore develop knowledge in that area.

Disadvantages of the Foreign Subsidiary Structure

1. *Diffuseness of international responsibility.* There is no center for international operations responsibility. With so many groups report-

PRACTICAL PERSPECTIVE 5-2

Trust Local Managers

Think globally, act locally—it's easy to say but hard to do, especially the second part. The key is letting local managers make their own decisions, and if you wonder whether that works, check Bausch & Lomb. Its international sales have shot from 25% of the total in 1984, the year the company overhauled its overseas businesses, to 46% last year [1991]. Operating profit margins in its international businesses have more than doubled. The heart of Bausch & Lomb's new world order: liberating local managers. Until the big change, production and marketing policies had all come from headquarters in Rochester, New York. "Frankly, our foreign subsidiaries used to be treated as sales adjuncts to the U.S. division," says Ronald Zarella, senior vice president of the international division. "What we try to do today is set strategic goals and let local management take advantage of nuances in their market."

Source: Excerpted from Rahul Jacob, "Trust the Locals, Win Worldwide," *Fortune*, May 4, 1992, p. 76.

ing directly to the board, clarity and focus can be lost—although the board can delegate the responsibility to certain expert members.

2. *Potential unwieldiness.* Many items that could be resolved without board action, such as by experts, are often pushed to the board level—again, the board could delegate many responsibilities to expert members.

The Product Division Structure

Many corporations are diversified (multiproduct) and use the product division structure. Under the **product division structure**, each of the enterprises's product divisions has responsibility for the sale and profits of its product. Therefore, each division has its own functional, environmental, sales, and manufacturing responsibilities. When a product division decides to internationalize its operations, as in the case of one-product companies, it may first begin by indirect exporting, subsequently establishing its own export division, and then establishing foreign subsidiaries. This means that if sales in foreign markets by firms with numerous product divisions become substantial, these enterprises could end up operating numerous subsidiary companies in a single foreign territory. Ford Motors recently began

◆   **FIGURE 5–3   An Illustration of a Foreign Subsidiary Structure**

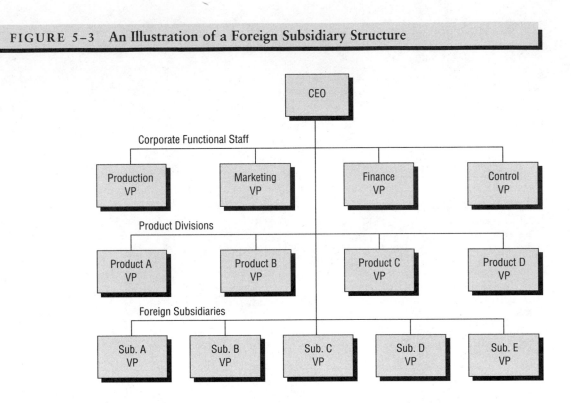

restructuring itself along the product line.[10] Canon Corporation used the product division structure when it became a multiproduct enterprise in 1962 (refer again to Practical Perspective 5–1). A typical product division structure is shown in Figure 5–4.

Advantages of the Product Division Structure[11]

1. *Product and technology emphasis.* Since both the domestic and international units report to the product division and compared to the whole, product divisions tend to be small, closer ties could result. Therefore, because of the common product benefit and the closer ties, products and technology can be easily transferred between the domestic and international units.

2. *Worldwide product planning.* Foreign and domestic plans can be more easily integrated in a product division than in an international division. A worldwide division perspective could therefore evolve.

3. *Conflict minimized.* The problem of substantiating the difference between international and domestic needs may be less difficult than when the international function is in the international division. Having both functions in the same division may lead to similar loyalties and the "we-they" conflict often caused by placing the international function in an international division may be mitigated.

An Illustration of a Product Division Structure   FIGURE 5–4 ◆

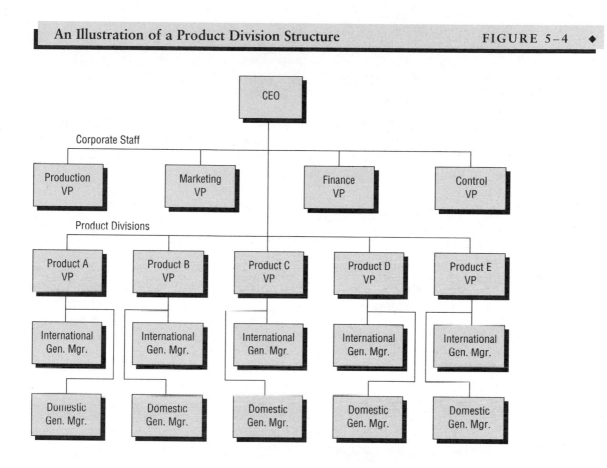

Disadvantages of the Product Division Structure

1. *Weakness in worldwide know-how.* Managers of individual product divisions may become knowledgeable in operating in certain markets, but worldwide knowledge is often impossible. For example, in the past, many managers of U.S, domestic enterprises that internationalized their operations have developed strong skills in the Canadian and European markets, but weaker skills in other parts of the world. This may result in weak performance in certain markets.

2. *Inherent weakness of multiproduct systems.* Managers of the overall corporate system may encounter conflicting international demands from the different product divisions. Since managers are part of the overall corporate system, they may not possess adequate abilities to handle such conflicting demands.

3. *Division managers often lack international skills.* International product managers are often selected on the basis of domestic performance and may therefore lack the required international skills. (This problem is addressed in Chapter 7.)

4. *Foreign coordination problems*. Managers of different product divisions operating in the same foreign country may not coordinate efforts to attain overall corporate efficiency because they are too busy looking out for each other's interests. For example, to cut costs, perhaps some support functions typically carried out in all product divisions, such as personnel and payroll, could be carried out by a single unit.

Canon Corporation has dealt with these disadvantages by developing a divisional structure at the corporate level as well. It has established a system consisting of eight product groups at the corporate level and twenty one product divisions (refer again to Practical Perspective 5–1).

The Regional Structure

Under the **regional structure**, regional heads are made responsible for specific territories, usually consisting of areas such as Europe, Asia, South America, North America, etc., and report directly to their C.E.O. or his/her designated executives at the headquarters. In general, firms with low technology and a high marketing orientation tend to use this structure. Firms whose foreign subsidiary or foreign product structure has become too large and too complex to manage from a single headquarters often restructure themselves using this form. This type of structure enables regional heads to keep abreast of, and provide for, the needs of their respective regional markets. Managers at **regional headquarters** are typically responsible for a range of activities, such as production for and marketing in their respective regions. Pharmaceutical, food, and oil companies tend to use this structure. (For further illustration, read Practical Perspective 5–3.) A typical regional structure is illustrated in Figure 5–5.

Advantages of the Regional Structure[12]

1. *Decentralization*. Authority and responsibility, and therefore performance accountability, is delegated directly to the regional office. The management tasks of planning and strategy are less complex than if the central headquarters held this responsibility. Also, management response time to environmental changes is shorter because the regional managers' knowledge about local conditions is stronger than the headquarters' managers'.
2. *Adaptation*. Regional managers are more capable of adapting to local needs than headquarters' managers because they are in closer touch with local changes and requirements.
3. *Single management units possess regional knowledge*. Regional managers develop local expertise because they are responsible for regional strategies and daily operations. Regional differences exist throughout the world. Inputs from knowledgeable regional managers can enable central headquarters' managers to effectively utilize these difference in developing and attaining overall corporate objectives.

PRACTICAL PERSPECTIVE 5–3

Moving International Headquarters Abroad

The limitations of a single "world" headquarters are not the stuff of theory but the lesson of painful experience. For years, a U.S.-based multinational addressed its markets in the Far East from its international division, which was located just down the road from its corporate headquarters. The head of Japanese operations had to make 20 pilgrimages a year to get approval first for his annual plans and later, when market conditions back home went through their inevitable fluctuations, for his revision of those plans. No one was happy. Worse, the inflexibility of these arrangements did nothing to stop a decline in Far East market share. It may even have accelerated the decline. Indeed, the only way the top manager in Japan could report acceptable numbers back home was to redefine who the competition was: with each report, more and more companies got removed from the denominator of the market share calculation. What seemed internally consistent was, inevitably, externally inconsistent. In effect, headquarters demanded that management in Japan remain faithful to previous plans rather than respond to the changing day-to-day realities of the marketplace.

The company finally recognized that this approach made no sense. At great cost, it moved its international headquarters from the United States to Tokyo, along with its key people. Now the head of Far East activities makes only a few trips a year to the States, and he has the freedom to solve local problems locally. It is not surprising that the division's performance has really turned around and its profits have soared—its global decision making it closer to its customers.

This new approach to regional headquarters is not an isolated discovery. In Japan, Yamaha, Sony, Honda, Omron, and Matsushita, among others, have decentralized responsibility for strategy and operations to each of the Triad markets, keeping only the corporate service and resource allocation functions at world headquarters. In fact, the real quantum jump in this direction comes when a company separates its domestic operations from its global headquarters, which can then sit at an equal managerial "distance" from each of the regional Triad headquarters. These companies have recognized that they cannot keep their ablest managers at home. They must send them where the critical action is. Decomposing the corporate center into several regional headquarters is fast becoming an essential part of almost every successful compa-

ny's transition to global competitor status.

Source: An excerpt from Kenichi Ohmae, "Planning for a Global Harvest," *Harvard Business Review* (July–August 1989): 137. Copyright © 1989 by the President and Fellows of Harvard College; all rights reserved. Reprinted by permission.

◆   FIGURE 5–5   **An Illustration of a Regional Structure**

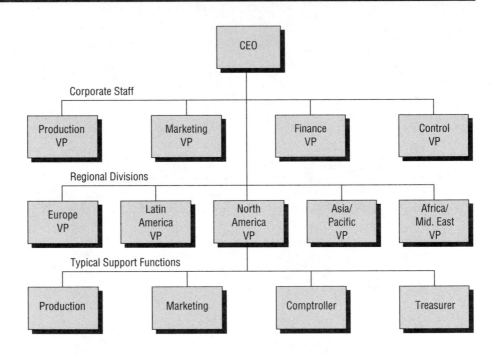

Disadvantages of the Regional Structure

1. *Weak worldwide product emphasis and technical knowledge.* Because technical knowledge is spread out, a global perspective on products is sometimes difficult to attain. And because the emphasis is usually on regional concerns, the formulation of worldwide strategy formulation can be difficult.
2. *Technology transfer barriers.* Employee loyalty is often focused on the region rather than on the overall organization, and managers in each region tend to claim things are different in their region.

Therefore, when headquarters' managers attempt to implement new technology on an overall corporate basis, it may not be readily accepted by the regionals.

3. *Policy barriers.* Inconsistent overall corporate management practices may evolve. This is especially so when central management tries to, or is persuaded to, satisfy specific regional needs.

4. *Costly application.* The typical support functions shown in Figure 5–5 exist in each regional division. Thus, there are costly duplication of efforts. Efficiency could result if these support functions were combined. But in this structure, functional product staff specialists tend to increase in numbers through the years.

5. *Weak communications.* Necessary information may not reach top management because of the regional managers' focus on regional performance. Overall corporate performance may therefore be weakened.

The Matrix Structure

The ideal global corporation, as defined by Carl Lindholm, former executive vice president of international operations at Motorola, is strongly decentralized. It allows local subsidiaries to develop products that fit into local markets. Yet at its core it is very centralized; it allows companies to coordinate activities across the globe and capitalize on synergies and economies of scale.[13] To accomplish this, many international businesses have adopted **matrix structures.**[14] Companies such as Nestle have adopted matrix organizations that allow for highly decentralized decision making and development while simultaneously maintaining a centralized corporate strategy and vision. (This idea will be discussed more thoroughly in Chapter 12.) Nestle, with 200,000 employees spread throughout 438 sites in 60 countries, "develops as much as can be decided locally," said Peter Brabeck, executive vice president. "But the interest of the corporation as a whole has priority."[15] Many firms that apply a global strategy (firms that rely heavily on foreign revenues and view themselves as global corporations) tend to use this structure.[16] For further illustration, refer again to Practical Perspective 5–1, and to Practical Perspective 5–4.

A typical matrix structure is shown in Figure 5–6. In general, managers from the functional side (e.g., Marketing, Africa) assign a staff to the product side (e.g., Product B). The staff leader is then responsible to both bosses. If conflicts arise, they are to be resolved between staff leaders if possible; then between general managers; then between vice presidents; and finally by the CEO, sometimes called the fulcrum. Figure 5–7 shows Canon's chart.

Advantages of the Matrix Structure[17]

1. Coordination and cooperation across subunits enable the firm to use its overall resources efficiently, and therefore to respond well to global competition in any market.

PRACTICAL PERSPECTIVE 5–4

The Asea Brown Boveri Group

The Asea Brown Boveri Group (ABB) is a global $30 billion company serving the electric power generation, transmission, and distribution industry, as well as industrial, environmental control, and mass transit markets. The ABB group is held by Asea Brown Boveri, Ltd. Its headquarters is in Zurich, Switzerland. ABB Ltd. was formed in 1987 with the merger of the Swedish electrical engineering firm Asea with the Swiss electrical manufacturing firm Brown Boveri. Each had been in existence for approximately 100 years. During 1988 and 1989, ABB acquired or took equity positions in more than 60 companies, necessitating an investment of $3.6 billion. All new acquisitions are restructured to streamline operations and flatten management layers before they are inserted into ABB's structure. Many of the companies were located outside of the old Asea's and Brown Boveri's traditional European market. The result was a group of companies under the ABB umbrella that covered almost all aspects of the core business areas of interest to ABB. Some of the businesses, such as several of the electrical installation service businesses, were very locally oriented. Some, such as the combined-cycle power plant business, were very

globally oriented. Most, however, fell somewhere in between those extremes.

ABB has 1,300 operating units in 140 countries with 215,000 employees located throughout the globe (e.g., 10,000 in India, 10,000 in South America). ABB's objective in building this group of companies was to gain a competitive advantage by increasing its economies of scale and creating local sourcing throughout all global markets. In order to achieve its objectives, ABB set out to create a new type of organizational structure. This organizational structure can be described as a loose matrix, designed to capitalize on global research and development power and economies of scale, while maintaining a local presence at the market level.

At the top of ABB's organizational structure is an executive committee headed by the CEO. The committee consists of eight members. Five nationalities are represented on the committee: Sweden, Switzerland, Germany, Luxembourg, and the United States. The members are physically located throughout the globe and meet every three weeks in a different country. The committee is responsible for devising the global strategy for the ABB Group and monitoring its performance. The entire headquarters operation consists of about 150 people, including executives who are responsible for coordinating such corporate functions as R&D, legal, and finance across all of ABB's business segments for the executive committee. The small number of headquarters' personnel is consistent with the corporate principle to flatten the organizational structure and empower the lower level profit centers. ABB believes that this improves communication and increases company involvement with the customer.

Underneath the executive committee is a matrix structure. Along one axis, the group is organized functionally by global business segments. There are seven segments: power plants, power transmission, power distribution, financial services, industry, transportation, and environmental control. Each segment is headed by an executive committee member. Business strategies for products and services are established on a global basis. Each segment is further broken down into business areas. Overall, there are 65 business areas. For example, business areas in the power plants business segment include gas turbine, fossil, nuclear; in power transmission, cables, transformers; in power distribution, LV systems, MV equipment; in financial services, leasing, insurance; in industry, drives; in transportation,

mass transit; and in environmental control, air pollution. Each business area has a manager who is responsible for development of the area on a global basis.

Along the next axis, ABB is organized by geographic regions—for example, Asia, Europe, North America, and Australia. In the regions there are 100 geographic companies, each managed by a CEO. The CEOs are responsible for attaining ABB's objectives and for dealing with local customers, governments, and other players in the markets assigned to them. In each geographic company there are several local companies—each with a CEO who is responsible for operating the local company as a profit center. As stated above, overall ABB has 1,300 local companies throughout the world. The local company presidents report to two bosses, the business area manager and the geographic company manager.

To illustrate ABB's two boss structure, as indicated above, ABB consists of eight business segments. The manager of the power transformer business area within the power transmission business segment, for example, is responsible for 25 companies in 16 countries. In each of the 16 countries, there is also a geographic manager who is also responsible for the local companies in those countries. The president of each local company must therefore report to both of them.

Corporate functions such as research and development also have a dual structure. For example, each business segment has a vice president of R&D. This person also reports to two bosses, the business segment executive and the executive vice president of R&D who is responsible for coordinating R&D efforts across all ABB business segments.

Source: Adapted from Charlene M. Solomon, "Transplanting Corporate Cultures Globally," *Personnel Journal* (October 1993): 89; Paul Kebnikov, "The Powerhouse," *Forbes,* September 2, 1991, pp. 46–50; Ted Agres, "Asea Brown Boveri—A Model for Global Management," *Research & Development Magazine,* December 1991, pp. 30–34; Carla Rapoport, "A Tough Swede Invades the U.S.," *Forbes,* June 29, 1992, pp. 76–79; J. Kapstein and S. Reed, "The Euro-Gospel According to Percy Barnevik," *Business Week,* July 23, 1990, pp. 64–66; William Taylor, "The Logic of Global Business: An Interview With ABB's Percy Barnevik," *Harvard Business Review* (March–April 1991): 91–105; *ABB Inc. 1991 Annual Review; Asea Brown Boveri 1990 Annual Report;* "Our Group," Asea Brown Boveri, internal communication.

2. Overall corporate global performance is highlighted.
3. Many internal conflicts are resolved at the lowest possible level, and those that cannot be resolved are pushed up.

Disadvantages of the Matrix Structure

1. Worldwide responsibility may be given to product managers with weak international experience. (This problem is addressed in Chapter 7.)
2. There is a tendency for the organization to create a mountain of paperwork.
3. The dual-boss, cross-communication system is expensive and complex.
4. Decisions sometimes must be made quickly. Quick decisions can be made by one person. In the matrix group decision-making process, decisions are usually made slowly.

Some international business enterprises have had an unhappy experience with the matrix structure. For example, in 1994, Digital Equipment announced that it was getting rid of its matrix system in a global restructuring that will cost $1 billion and 20,000 jobs. Dow Chemical has gone back to its conventional structure, with clear lines of responsibility given to geographic managers.[18]

Contractual Alliance Structures

As it was discussed in Chapter 4, many enterprises enter foreign markets via non-equity-based joint ventures, often referred to as contractual alliances

An Illustration of a Matrix Structure

FIGURE 5-6 ◆

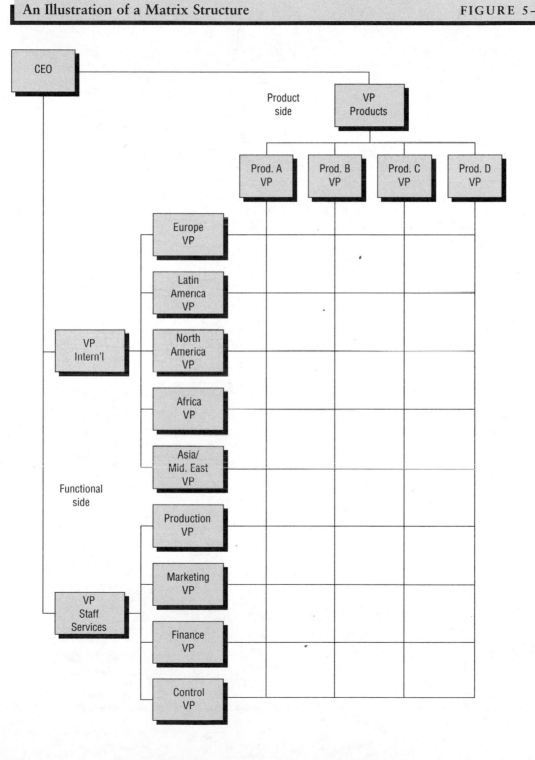

Cameras
- Photo Products — Camera Operations Planning & Management, Camera Design
- Still Video Camera — V Project
- Video Products
- Lens Products — Fukushima Plant

Business Machines Operations Planning & Management

Copying Machine Business
- Copying Machine 1 — Copying Machine Products Planning, Business Machines Technology Administration
- Copying Machine 2
- Copying Machine 3 — Copying Machine Quality Assurance, Toride Plant

Image Systems Business
- Image & Telecommunication Systems — Image Systems Design, Image Systems Quality Assurance
- Image Management Systems
- Image Peripherals — Peripherals Marketing

Peripherals
- Peripherals 1 — Peripheral Products Quality Assurance
- Peripherals 2

Computer & Information Systems
- Word Processor — Computer & Information Systems Design, Computer & Information Business Systems, Ami Plant Quality Assurance
- Computer & Systems
- Personal Information Products

Chemical Products
- Chemical Products Business 1 — Chemical Products Quality Assurance
- Chemical Products Business 2
- Cartridge Business

Optical Products
- Semiconductor Production Equipment
- Broadcast Equipment
- Medical Equipment

Board of Directors

Chairman / President

Executive Committee

Management Committees
- Global System
- Global Research and Development System
- Global Production System
- Global Marketing System
- Legal Affairs Coordination
- International Trade Balance Promotion
- Environment Preservation Assurance
- Social & Cultural Program Operators

- Statutory Auditor's Office
- Secretarial Office
- Internal Auditing Office
- Legal Affairs Coordination Div.
- China Div.
- NBU 1
- Social & Cultural Program Operations Center
- Corporate Strategy & Development
- Corporate Communications
- General Affairs
- Personnel & Organization
- Finance & Accounting
- Traffic & Distribution
- Planning & Marketing Center
- Quality Management
- Corporate Intellectual Property & Legal
- Production Management
- Research & Development
- Software Business Operations
- Component Business Operation

Source: Toshio Nakahara and Yutaka Isono, "Strategic Planning for Canon: The Crisis and the New Vision," *Long Range Planning* 25, (February 1992): 65. Copyright © 1982. All rights reserved. Used with kind permission from Elsevier Science Ltd., *The Boulevard*, Lanford Lane, Kidlington 0x51 GB.

and strategic alliances.[19] For example, one firm's strength may be production and another firm's is distribution. Instead of these two firms forming an equity-based joint venture to capitalize on each other's strengths, they form a non-equity-based **contractual alliance.** Thus, when the two firms no longer need each other, in theory, they simply break up the partnership. The advantage of this partnership arrangement is that when there is a break-up, there is no long, drawn-out fight for the division of assets—as often is the case when equity-based partnerships break up.

There are disadvantages to this approach, however. For instance, when one partner acquires the other partner's skills, and the reverse is not the case, the learned partner may leave the unlearned partner in a dubious situation—or the learned partner may easily take over the unlearned partner. Of course, this type of arrangement can only work when neither partner possess an ulterior motive—for example, "I'm really going into this arrangement to acquire the partner's skills, and once I have done so, I will break up the partnership." Furthermore, these arrangements are extremely difficult to manage on a global scale. For example, AT&T formed an alliance with Philips in Europe to swap technology for access to local markets. The alliance did not meet expectations, mostly because the companies failed to understand each other's strategic objectives.[20]

Networking

Somewhat similar to the contactual alliance arrangement is networking. Applying this approach, a corporation subcontracts its manufacturing function to other companies. For example, Nike, the American shoe maker, subcontracts the manufacture of its athletic shoes and clothing to forty separate locations, mostly in Asia.[21]

When an organization enters into such contactual alliances or network agreements, it must create a unit whose responsibility is to monitor the arrangement. For instance, IBM has created an alliance council of key executives who meet monthly to keep track of more than forty partnerships throughout the globe.[22]

The Mixed (Hybrid) Structure

The traditional and contemporary alternative structures described above are not independent entities that cannot co-exist within the same company. By **mixing** the structural types, the weaknesses of each type can be minimized. For example, companies with a worldwide product division structure can appoint regional coordinators who attempt to supply the concentrated environmental expertise that is usually absent in the product division structure. Similarly, companies with regional structures (either worldwide or within an international division) can set up positions for product coordinators. While such coordinator positions are not particularly new, giving them some real influence short of classical line authority is relatively new.[23] Furthermore, international organizations can centralize some functions, such as an accounting division that provides services for all worldwide subsidiaries, while other functions, such as marketing, remain decentralized.

A General Framework for Decision Making

The preceding discussion described several traditional and contemporary international organizational structures and presented the general advantages and disadvantages for each. The word "general" was used because what is advantageous and disadvantageous does not apply to all situations. For example, one of the disadvantages of the international division structure is conflict; the structure often creates organizational struggles between "we" (employees in the domestic divisions) and "they" (employees in the international division). In most cases it may be true that conflict causes harmful organizational disruptions, especially in organizations that rely on "team spirit" for effectiveness. But in some organizational situations, conflict can actually be advantageous, especially when it leads the groups to try to outperform each other. Thus, if the international division outperforms the domestic divisions, the latter may be stimulated to try to outperform the former, and so on. Therefore, the stated advantages and disadvantages are intended to serve as a general framework for decision making, not as a prescription. All situations must be examined separately, as different situations sometimes require different prescriptions.

FLAT STRUCTURES

Regardless of the structure used, it should be as **flat** as possible. That is, it should have fewer managerial layers than traditional hierarchical organizations. A flat structure is needed because a twelve-layer company cannot compete with a three-layer company. For example, a decade or so ago, General Motors, the U.S.-based car manufacturer, had an organizational structure consisting of about fifteen managerial levels. General Motors had a problem competing with Toyota, the Japanese car manufacturer, in part because Toyota's organizational structure contained only four managerial levels (this is in part because Japanese employees are not as motivated by the opportunity to climb up the hierarchy as are American employees). One reason why companies with tall structures are less competitive than firms with flat structures is that they have to pay more managers at more levels, thus increasing their costs.

Another reason is that an organization can only create an atmosphere of maximum creativity if it reduces hierarchical elements to the very minimum, and creates a corporate culture in which its vision, company philosophy, and strategies can be implemented by employees who think independently and take initiative.[24] Furthermore, as Henry Mintzberg, a well-known professor at McGill University in Canada, proposed in his explanation of *adhocracy*, many levels of administration restricts the organization's ability to adapt.[25]

The flatter structure means that managers have to communicate with more employees than do managers in tall structures. The ability to communicate with more subordinates has been made possible by the enormous advancements in communications technologies, which, as American management authority Peter F. Drucker noted, enables managers to communicate with a far wider span of individuals than was possible in the past.[26] Spans of control thus give way to spans of communication. For example, at Cypress Semiconductor, CEO T. J. Rodgers has a computer system that enables him to keep abreast of every employee (1,500) and team in his rapidly moving, decentralized, constantly changing organization.[27] The Asea Brown Boveri Group's structure is relatively flat (refer again to Practical Perspective 5–4).

ORGANIC VERSUS MECHANISTIC STRUCTURES

Another problem confronting international managers is determining how organic or how mechanistic the organizational structure should be. Basically, managers in *organic* structures allow employees considerable discretion in defining their roles and the organization's objectives.[28] In *mechanistic* organizations roles and objectives are clearly and rigidly outlined for employees—managers and subordinates are allowed little or no discretion.[29] Historically, large organizations have tended to adopt the mechanistic form and small organizations the organic form; mass-producing organizations have tended to adopt the mechanistic form and firms producing specialized products have tended to adopt the organic form. Thus, the form an organization adopts is determined by varying situational factors.

In making a determination as to which approach is appropriate for an organization functioning across nations, managers also need to consider national cultural factors. For example, organizational structures tend to be more mechanistic in *strong uncertainty avoidance* cultures (discussed in Chapter 1), such as France and Germany, than in *weak uncertainty avoidance* cultures, such as Great Britain, and organic structures tend to be more prevalent in the latter cultures than in the former. This concept of national cultural factors, as well as the situational approach discussed in the paragraph above, will be discussed thoroughly in Chapters 10 and 12. As it will be shown, national cultural factors provide international managers a starting point for decision analysis; but ultimately they must consider specific situations carefully. If one adheres to the national cultural factors model, subsidiaries in some nations will be more structured than subsidiaries in other nations; but if one adheres to the situational factors model, the same structure is applied in the same situation in all nations. As it will be demonstrated in Chapters 10 and 12, reconciling the national cultural factors model and situational factors model as determinants of the appropriate structure is a monumental task confronting all managers of international organizations.

ADAPTABLE MANAGEMENT

The international organizational structure adopted by a firm's management is influenced by many factors, including the firm's economic situation, the type of product or technology, managerial preference (organizational culture), the foreign country's cultural, economic, technological, and political conditions, the wide separation of operations, and the different foreign market characteristics, including the nature of competition. Therefore, organizational structures that work well for domestic operations are often not suitable for multinational operations. The structure is also influenced by the firm's level of experience in international business and its dependence on revenues from foreign markets. Table 5–1 presents the international organizational structures that might be appropriate for various levels of a firm's dependence on revenues generated from foreign sales.

Historically, when firms first ventured into foreign markets, and when both foreign sales and the diversity of products sold in the foreign country were limited, global companies generally managed their international operations through indirect exporting and subsequently through an international division. Companies that subsequently expanded their sales in foreign markets without significantly increasing foreign product diversity generally adopted the regional structure. Those enterprises that subsequently increased foreign product diversity tended to adopt the product division structure. Firms that increased both foreign sales and foreign product diversity tended to adopt the matrix structure.[30]

International business executives must be thoroughly familiar with the strengths and weaknesses of each organizational structure and be ready to switch from one form to another as a means of adapting to changing environments (including moving an important business unit's **headquarters** to foreign soil—as an illustration, read Practical Perspective 5–5 and refer to Table 5–2). The right structure must be matched to the right environment as both internal and external situations change. And the fit must attain a balance between organizational complexity and simplicity. Adopting an organizational structure too complex for its environmental demands can be as ineffective as adopting a structure too simplistic to operate in a turbulent environment.[31] Not adopting the right structure can be very costly—not only in the sense that it will be ineffective, but in the sense that reorganizing is very expensive. For example, AT&T indicated that global reorganization accounted for most of the $347 million it paid in fees to consultants in 1993.[32]

Dependence on Foreign Revenues and Organizational Structures

TABLE 5–1 ◆

Organization's Level of Dependence on Foreign Sales	Unit Responsible for Foreign Business	Potential International Organizational Structure
Very little	Middle person (indirect exporting)	The functional structure; contractual alliance
Somewhat	Export department	The functional structure; the international division; contractual alliance
Substantial	International division	The international structure; contractual alliance
Considerable	Foreign subsidiary	The subsidiary structure; the product structure
Very much	Foreign subsidiary/ regional headquarters	The regional structure; contractual alliance
Extensive	Foreign subsidiary/ central headquarters	The mixed (hybrid) structure; matrix

PRACTICAL PERSPECTIVE 5–5

Moving Headquarters of Business Units Abroad

Increasingly, going global means "move 'em out"—by transferring world headquarters of important business units abroad. [*Table 5–2* lists some of the MNCs that have made such a move.] In the process, many companies put a non-American in charge of the unit. And U.S. operations that once reported to Wilmington, Del., or Parsippany, N.J., now report to Tokyo—or the French Riviera. Multinational corpora- tions are making these shifts, risk- ing a loss of control, because they want to operate near key cus- tomers and tough rivals in fast- changing markets far from home. More big businesses "recognize that they can't rule the world from one single location" any longer, says Ingo Theuerkauf, an international management spe- cialist for consultants McKinsey & Co. In 10 years, Mr. Theuerkauf predicts, "we will see maybe 50% of Fortune 500 companies making [such] moves."

This fall [1992], American Telephone & Telegraph Co. moved the headquarters of its traditional corded-telephone business to France from Parsippany, N.J. It marked the first overseas move by a unit of AT&T, whose ranks of non-U.S. workers have jumped to 50,000 from 50 in 1984. The corded-telephone business had scant international sales until two years ago. Its approximately 2,000 employees around the globe now report to a Frenchman in Sophia Antipolis, a high-technology center near Nice on the Riviera. By 1995, several major AT&T units probably will have their headquarters outside the U.S., a spokesman says. Other examples abound. In August, Du Pont Co. announced the shift of its world-wide electronics operation from the U.S. to Tokyo, nearer its big base of Asian customers. Du Pont already manages its global agricultural-products operation plus parts of two other large businesses from Geneva.

Going the other direction, Hyundai Electronics Industries Co. in April moved its personal-computer division to San Jose, Calif., from Seoul, South Korea, so it could better compete in that industry's biggest market. International Business Machines Corp., Hewlett-Packard Co. and Germany's Siemens AG have taken similar steps since 1989 by moving units' global headquarters out of their home countries. "The name of the game is to get close to the customer and to understand the customer," says Jack Malloy, a Du Pont senior vice president. With the chemical giant growing fastest in non-U.S. markets, he says, "it wouldn't be surprising to see a couple more" units move their headquarters overseas.

Robert Bontempo, an assistant professor of international business at Columbia University, sees "a strategic competitive advantage" in uprooting operations from a parent's home country and basing them abroad. Relocated units often gain marketing power by acquiring the image of "a global firm with a global reach," he suggests. The strategy also helps to break down parochialism and to groom global managers, management experts say.

ORGANIZATION COMMUNICATION FLOW

Identifying the ideal international organizational structure is a huge challenge for the managers of any organization; and there may not even be an ideal structure. Nevertheless, regardless of which organizational structure a

| | Firms Ship Unit Headquarters Abroad | | | TABLE 5–2 ◆ |

Company	Home Country	New Location	Operation Shifted	Year Moved
AT&T	U.S.	France	Corded telephones	1992
DuPont	U.S.	Japan	Electronics	1992
Hyundai Electronics Industries	South Korea	U.S.	Personal computers	1992
IBM	U.S.	U.K.	Networking systems	1991
Siemens	Germany	U.K.	Air traffic management	1991
Siemens	Germany	U.S.	Ultrasound equipment	1991
DuPont	U.S.	Switzerland	Agricultural products and parts of fibers and polymers businesses	1991
Hewlett-Packard	U.S.	France	Desktop personal computers	1990
Siemens	Germany	U.S.	Nuclear medicine	1989
Cadbury Schweppes	U.K.	U.S.	Beverages	1987*
DuPont	U.S.	Swtizerland	Lycra business	1987

*Moved back to London in 1991.
Note: Every relocated operation had its headquarters in the same country as its parent company.

Source: Joann S. Lublin, "Firms Ship Unit Headquarters Abroad," *The Wall Street Journal,* December 9, 1992, p. B1. Reprinted by permission of *The Wall Street Journal.* Copyright © 1992 Dow Jones & Comany, Inc. All rights reserved worldwide.

firm adopts, a neat chart with neat boxes is useless unless **information and communications flow freely** to develop proper business decisions. The relationship of domestic, international, and senior corporate organization can be described by three general guidelines.[33]

1. The organization must be formulated in such a way that planning and decision making on every aspect of the firm's operations can be done by people with the breadth of functional, geographic, and/or product knowledge and responsibility necessary to develop the potential for a unified strategy.
2. The channels for the flow of important or recurring decisions and information should be as direct and as short as possible.

3. Individuals with expert international knowledge and competence in overcoming the obstacles to international communication should be readily available within the organization and be utilized wherever their capacities are needed.

This means that top management in all organizations must incorporate the following dimensions into their system:[34]

1. The structure must allow for the development and communication of clear corporate vision.
2. It must allow for the effective management of human resource tools to broaden individuals' perspectives and develop identification with corporate goals.
3. It must allow for the integration of individual thinking and activities into a broad corporate agenda.

SUMMARY

This chapter has discussed numerous international organizational structures, such as the international division and the matrix structure, adopted by international corporations, by multinational corporations, and by global corporations, and the advantages and disadvantages of each structure. Managers must be flexible regarding which structure to adopt for their organizations because different structures fit different environments, and environments change often. Regardless of which structure is adopted, it must allow information and communications to flow freely.

Key Terms

1. International organizational structures
2. Functional structure
3. International division structure
4. Foreign subsidiary structure
5. Product division structure
6. Regional structure
7. Matrix structure
8. Mixed (hybrid) structure
9. Flat structures
10. Contractual alliances
11. Local managers
12. Headquarters; regional headquarters
13. Information and communications must flow freely

Discussion Questions and Exercises

1. In the functional structure, who is usually responsible for the firm's international business activities?

2. When an international corporation establishes a single subunit to manage all of its international business activities, the firm is using which international organizational structure?

3. Briefly, discuss some advantages and disadvantages of the structure you gave as an answer to Question 2.

4. "Autonomy of affiliates" and "direct top management involvement" are advantages of which international organizational structure?

5. Which international structure is prone to "foreign coordination problems"?

6. How did Canon Corporation (read Practical Perspective 5–1) eliminate the disadvantages presented by the international product division structure?

7. A global corporation establishes a headquarters to manage its business activities in Africa and an headquarters to manage its activities in Asia. The firm is using which international organizational structure?

8. Which international organizational structure allows local subsidiaries to use discretion in developing products or services to fit local markets and at the same time allows headquarters to coordinate activities across the globe to capitalize on synergies and economies of scale?

9. Which structure enables organizations to minimize the weaknesses of the other structures?

10. Managers must be flexible to the extent they can adopt different structures to different environments. Discuss the environments that influence use of the international division, the regional structure, product division, and matrix structures.

11. Read Practical Perspective 5–5. Discuss some of the pitfalls of such reorganization.

Assignment

Obtain the most current annual report of a multinational corporation. Prepare a short report describing the corporation's structure for class presentation.

Toys `Я´ Us

C A S E   5–1

Source: Adapted from
Stuart Gannes,
"America's Fastest
Growing Companies,"
Fortune, May 23, 1988;
Holt Hackney, "How Do
You Say Toys `Я´ Us in
German?" *Financial
World,* September 5,
1989; Anthony Ramirez,
"Can Anyone Compete
with Toys `Я´ Us?"
Fortune, October 28,
1985; Robert Neff,
"Guess Who's Selling
Barbies in Japan Now?"
Business Week, December
9, 1991; *Toys `Я´ Us
1990 Annual Report;*
"Toys `Я´ Us Seeks
Bigger World Market,"
Discount Merchandiser,
July 1989; Isadore
Barmash, "Toys `Я´ Us:
1990 Outlook," *Stores,*
December 1989; Patrick
Oster, "Toys `Я´ Us:
Making Europe Its
Playpen," *Business Week,*
January 20, 1992.

Charles Lazarus founded Toys `Я´ Us on the premise that "when Mama went back to work, department stores were dead." He argued that "working women wanted a store where they could shop for their children quickly, easily, and cheaply." Toys `Я´ Us offers a warehouse full of play items. Says Lazarus, "We don't want to decide which toys you should buy. We have everything." When focusing on domestic markets, Toys `Я´ Us selects store locations where the rent is low, mainly along major highways as opposed to expensive shopping malls. The company's strategy of warehouse-size stores built away from shopping malls and slashing prices on merchandise is as effective today as it was four decades ago. Toys `Я´ Us, in essence, invented the toy supermarket. By being big, Toys `Я´ Us possesses the ability to buy merchandise at large volume discounts. Toys `Я´ Us stocks about 8,000 items and it expects to raise that level to 15,000 over time.

Toys `Я´ Us went international in 1984. The company began operating first in Canada, then it subsequently opened stores in Europe, Hong Kong, and Singapore. Japan was always tempting, but the country's Large-Store Law aimed at protecting Japan's small shopkeepers was too great a barrier to overcome . . . until December of 1991. Japan has the second largest toy market in the world. The Japanese spent $4.7 billion on toys in 1991. It was for this reason that Toys `Я´ Us launched its Japanese effort. The first Japanese store was opened on December 20, 1991, in Ami, north of Tokyo.

Toys `Я´ Us' international growth is as follows: During 1984, five stores were opened. By 1985, 13 had been opened. By 1986, 24 had been opened and by 1987, 37 had been opened. By 1988, 52 international stores were in operation, 74 by 1989, and in 1990, 97 international stores were open for business. As of January, 1992, Toys `Я´ Us was operating 497 stores in the United States, and 126 outlets overseas (including the two already opened in Japan), plus 189 Kids `Я´ Us stores. Combined, these stores generated approximately $6 billion in sales in 1991.

Everyday low pricing has been a success in Europe, since it is virtually non-existent there. Toys `Я´ Us plans to continue its aggressive pricing policy to obtain a greater market share. Toys `Я´ Us has planned to open 10 foreign stores per year from 1993 through the end of the decade. According to Lazarus, at least 100 stores might be opened in Japan alone within the next 10 years, depending on red tape and the ability to find real estate there. Toys `Я´ Us' goal for the future is to open 300+ European stores.

Q U E S T I O N S

1 Design the appropriate international organization structure for Toys `Я´ Us.
2. Why did you select that structure?
3. Will the structure be different in 10 years?

Notes

1. Joann S. Lublin, "Firms Ship Unit Headquarters Abroad," *The Wall Street Journal,* December 9, 1992, p. B1.

2. William A. Dymsza, *Multinational Business Strategy* (New York: McGraw-Hill, 1972), p. 17.

3. *Designing the International Corporate Organization* (New York: Business International Corporation, 1976), p. 17. For additional information about organizational structures refer to Michael Z. Brooke, *International Management: A Review of Strategies and Operations* (London: Hutchinson, 1986); W. H. Davidson and P. Haspeslagh, "Shaping a Global Product Organization," *Harvard Business Review* 59 (March–April 1981); C. A. Bartlett and S. Ghoshal, "Tap Your Subsidiaries For Global Reach," *Harvard Business Review,* 64 (November–December 1986); Daniel Robey, *Designing Organizations: A Macro Perspective* (Homewood, IL: Richard D. Irwin, 1982); Thomas H. Naylor, "International Strategy Matrix," *Columbia Journal of World Business* 20 (Summer 1985).

4. Adopted from *Designing the International Organization,* pp. 32–33.

5. Dymsza, *Multinational Business Strategy,* p. 23.

6. John M. Livingstone, *The International Enterprise* (New York: John Wiley, 1975): 95.

7. Adopted from *Designing the International Corporate Organization,* pp. 19–25.

8. C. A. Bartlett and S. Ghoshal, *Managing Across Borders: The Transnational Solution* (Boston: Harvard Business School Press, 1989).

9. Adopted from *Designing the International Organization,* pp. 33–36.

10. "The Discreet Charm of the Multicultural Multinational," *The Economist,* July 30, 1994, p. 58.

11. Adopted from *Designing the International Organization,* pp. 25–29.

12. Ibid., pp. 29–31.

13. Joshua Greenbaum, "View from the Top: Survival Tactics for the Global Business," *Management Review,* (October 1992): 50–51.

14. "The Discreet Charm of the Multicultural Multinational," p. 58.

15. Ibid.

16. Bartlett and Ghoshal, *Managing Across Borders.*

17. Stefan H. Robock and Kenneth Simmonds, *International Business and Multinational Enterprises* (Homewood, IL: Dow Jones-Irwin, 1983), pp. 387–388.

18. "The Discreet Charm of the Multicultural Multinational," p. 58.

19. See K. Ohmae, "The Global Logic of Strategic Alliances," *Harvard Business Review* 67 (March–April 1989): 143–154.

20. "The Discreet Charm of the Multicultural Multinational," p. 57.

21. Ibid.

22. Jeremy Main, "Making Global Alliances Work," *Fortune,* December 17, 1990, p. 121.

23. *Designing the International Corporation,* p. 36.

24. H. H. Hinterhuber and W. Popp, "Are You a Strategist or Just a Manager?" *Harvard Business Review* 70 (January–February 1992): 105–113.

25. Henry Mintzberg, *Structures in Fives: Designing Effective Organizations* (Englewood Cliffs, NJ: Prentice-Hall, 1983).

26. Jeremy Main, "The Winning Organization," *Fortune,* September 26, 1988, p. 60.

27. B. Dumaine, "The Bureaucracy Busters," *Fortune,* June 17, 1991, p. 46.

28. See John Miner, *The Management Process: Theory, Research and Practice* (New York: Macmillan, 1973), p. 270.

29. See Max Weber, *The Theory of Social and Economic Organization,* trans. A. M. Henderson and T. Parsons (New York: Oxford University Press, 1947).

30. J. Stopford and L. T. Wells, Jr., *Managing the Multinational Enterprise* (New York: Basic Books, 1972).

31. S. Ghoshal and N. Nohria, "Horses for Courses: Organizational Forms for Multinational Corporations," *Sloan Management Review* (Winter 1993): 24.

32. "The Discreet Charm of the Multicultural Multinational," p. 57.

33. Adopted from John Fayerweather, *International Business Management—A Conceptual Framework* (New York: McGraw-Hill, 1969): 185.

34. Adopted from C. A. Bartlett and S. Ghoshal, "Matrix Management: Not a Structure, a Frame of Mind," *Harvard Business Review* 68 (July–August 1990): 138–145.

IV

INTERNATIONAL HUMAN RESOURCE MANAGEMENT

The human resource management (HRM) function can contribute immensely to a firm's attainment of its goals and objectives. If properly administered, an HRM department helps the enterprise's management recruit, train and develop, and place the right people in the right places. And it helps identify the right motivational programs to keep employees working at their maximum pace. Administering the HRM function is indeed a challenging task in any organization. When the HRM function cuts across national borders, administering it becomes a monumental challenge because HRM managers face a complex set of problems that differ dramatically from those in the home country. One of the problems is selecting managers to staff the firm's foreign operations. This aspect is addressed in Chapter 6. Another problem is developing and implementing effective international programs. This aspect is addressed in Chapter 7.

Chapter Six

International Managerial Staffing

Ten years ago there were 10,000 Japanese living in Britain. Today [1991] there are at least 44,000. The tide of Japanese investment is bringing a tide of Japanese expatriates. . . . There are headaches [for the Japanese expatriates]. Top of the list for most is the language. English (or rather American) is Japan's second language. Another worry is social anarchy. Many Japanese find ethnic diversity a puzzle. The levels of violence and crime in contemporary Britain are profoundly shocking to them. Most dislike the lack of deference displayed by the poor to the rich and—even worse, in their eyes—the lack of consideration shown by the rich for the poor.[1]

Objectives of the Chapter

Regardless of whether the nature of their business is in commerce, science and technology, education, entertainment, tourism, transportation, religion, or communications, domestic enterprises that want to remain competitive, as indicated in the previous chapters, must develop strategy in response to the intense global competition they face. When a domestic corporation develops a strategy to conduct business in a foreign country, its **human resource management (HRM) function** faces a complex set of managerial problems that differ drastically from those it faces at home. One of the complex problems is selecting the most effective managers to staff the firm's international operations. The objectives of this chapter are therefore to discuss:

189

1. The international HRM function,
2. Three types of managerial personnel commonly used by international corporations to staff their foreign subsidiaries,
3. The pros and cons of each type,
4. The factors that influence the type selected.

THE INTERNATIONAL HRM FUNCTION

Basically, international human resource management (HRM) consists of an interplay among three dimensions:[2]

1. The broad function: procurement, allocation, and utilization.
2. Country categories: the home country, i.e., where the headquarters is located; the host country, i.e., where the subsidiary is located; and third countries, i.e., other countries that may be a source of labor.
3. Types of employees: home-country employees, host-country employees, and third-country employees.

The factors that differentiate international from domestic HRM are additional functions and activities, a broader perspective, more involvement in employees' personal lives, changes in emphasis as the workforce mix varies, risk exposure, and more external influences.[3]

Additional Functions and Activities

Operating in an international environment, a multinational corporation's (MNC's) HRM department has to perform numerous activities that would not be required in the domestic environment. The department must deal with international taxation, international relocation and orientation, administrative services for expatriates (employees sent from the home country to manage firms' foreign subsidiaries), host government relations, and language training.

International Taxation

Relative to international taxation, expatriates normally have both home- and host-country tax liabilities. HRM thus has to assure that there is neither a tax incentive nor a tax disincentive attached to any particular assignment.[4]

International Relocation and Orientation

International relocation and orientation entails making arrangements for predeparture training; providing immigration and travel details; providing housing, shopping, medical care, recreation, and schooling information; and finalizing compensation details such as the issuance of salary in the foreign country, determination of various overseas allowances, and taxation treatment.

Providing International Administrative Services

Providing administrative services is a time-consuming and complicated activity, in part because policies and procedures are not always clear-cut and sometimes conflict with local conditions. For example, the practice of testing employees for alcohol and drugs may be legally required in a foreign country, but illegal in the home country, or vice versa. As another example, Chinese expatriates must take an AIDS test upon return to China after being away for a certain length of time. How does a Chinese company reconcile this with the prospective expatriate who may refuse the assignment because of such conditions?

Foreign Government Relations

Relative to host government relations, it usually makes it much less difficult for HRM managers to obtain work permits and other important documents required by the expatriate if the international business enterprise maintains a good relationship with the host-country's government.

Providing Foreign Language Training

Providing verbal and nonverbal language translation services for internal and external personnel correspondence is another important activity of the international HRM. Expatriates require at least some basic knowledge of the language of the country where they will be conducting business; otherwise, how will they communicate with people there?

Broader Perspective

International HRM managers are confronted with the problem of designing and administering programs for more than one national group of employees. As such, they need to take a more global view—for example, making sure that employees are treated fairly regardless of nationality.

More Involvement in Employees' Lives

Because the international HRM department must be involved in the selection and training of expatriates, and because it must ensure that expatriates understand housing arrangements, health care, cost-of-living allowances, taxes, and so on, it becomes much more involved in their personal lives than it must with domestic employees.

Changes in HRM Emphasis as the Workforce Mix Varies

As the corporation's foreign operations mature, the HRM department may have to change its international functions. At that stage, the enterprise may be employing mostly host-country nationals. The department would no longer need to place as much emphasis on, for example, expatriate training, relocation, and tax programs. The emphasis may be on such programs as bringing host country nationals to the home office for development, and so on.

Risk Exposure

Possible terrorism in the foreign country, especially in countries where some groups hold hostile feelings toward "capitalists," or where there is a high possibility of the expatriate being kidnapped for ransom, is of great concern to international business corporations and their expatriates. The training programs administered by the HRM department must therefore include briefing the expatriate about such **risk exposure.**[5] Furthermore, preparing an employee to work abroad is very costly. This preparation investment is a high risk in the sense that many employees want to return home soon after they get to the foreign country. The international HRM department must thus make great efforts to lower the incidence of expatriates returning early from foreign assignments.

More External Influences

The type of government, the state of the country's economy, and the generally accepted practices of doing business in the host countries are factors that affect international HRM. They vary from one host country to another. The cost of labor and the extent to which labor is organized also varies from country to country.

To find the right executives to effectively manage their firms' foreign operations, managers of international HRM must spend a lot of time studying the complex situations that exist in each country. In other words, to be effective in their role, international HRM managers must do a lot of homework.

THREE APPROACHES TO STAFFING FOREIGN SUBSIDIARIES

A key problem confronting managers who make decisions regarding who should manage their enterprises' foreign operations is deciding whether to employ an expatriate, a host-country national, or a third-country citizen. Basically, an **expatriate** is a **home-country national,** usually an employee of the firm, who is assigned abroad to manage the enterprise's foreign subsidiary(s); a **host-country national** is a resident of the country where the firm's subsidiary is located, or is to be located, employed to manage the operations; and a **third-country national** is a resident of a country other the home country and the host country employed to manage the operations. A problem confronting international HRM is having to determine which approach is best suited to the needs of each particular situation. To make the right determination, HRM managers must be cognizant of the advantages and disadvantages each approach presents.

Advantages and Disadvantages of Using Expatriates

When managers of international businesses are attempting to determine if they should use an expatriate to manage a foreign subsidiary, they need to consider both the advantages and disadvantages of the approach.[6]

Advantages

Relatively Easy to Obtain People with Knowledge of the Corporation's Culture.   Using expatriates is a relatively easy way to obtain personnel with detailed knowledge of company policies, procedures, and corporate culture.[7]

Has Knowledge of the Company's Management Techniques.   Expatriates, because they have worked for the company in the home country, would be familiar with the company's management techniques and methods, as well as with the related technology and product development.

Loyalty.   The expatriate approach enables international business corporations to select people with proven loyalty to the company.

Influence at Headquarters.   It places individuals in the foreign subsidiary who are influential at the home headquarters.

Easier To Assess.   Because the expatriate has been employed with the firm for some time, it is not too difficult to assess his or her qualifications for the foreign assignment.

Foreign Image.   Using expatriates enables companies to maintain a "foreign image" in the host country, which is in some cases an important marketing strategy (many people, for example, Chinese people, like to purchase goods with foreign labels).[8]

Disadvantages

Expensive Orientation Programs Needed.   Expensive programs (which often are not successful) to orient the expatriate to the foreign county's culture and systems are required. This is not as much of a problem for large international business enterprises as it is for small- to medium-size companies that compete in the global arena. Smaller companies often do not have the financial means to establish such programs. Smaller companies can send their expatriate candidates to a private training institution, but this is also costly. Yet, without such training, small firms' expatriates are likely to make many costly blunders in conducting business abroad, thus putting them at a disadvantage. Small businesses can sometimes overcome this difficulty by entering into a partnership with a capable firm in the foreign market, however.

Unfamiliar With Foreign Environment.   Initially, even after going through the orientation program, the expatriate is **not familiar with the local culture, laws, political process, legal process, and other subtleties.** People can be taught the formal, but the informal has to be learned through field experience. This often impairs performance.

Communication Problems Abroad.   The expatriate may encounter communication problems in the foreign country, especially if he or she does not have a good command of the local verbal and nonverbal language. This also often impairs performance.

May Not Adapt to Foreign Culture.   The expatriate and/or his or her **family may not adapt to the local culture** and has to be **repatriated** (brought back to the home country) early, which is financially very expensive—not only in the sense that it was expensive to send the expatriate there (in 1990, moving an expatriate and family members from the U.S. to Europe cost about $50,000, and twice as much to Japan)[9] and expensive to prepare someone else for the assignment, but also in the sense that the expatriate may not have been very effective in the assignment.

The Best Qualified People Sometimes Do Not Want the Assignment.   It may be difficult to find highly qualified people who want to work at the foreign subsidiary.[10] This is because many employees are motivated to elevate themselves in the corporate hierarchy, and they fear that once they are in the foreign country, they may not rise as quickly through the company as if they remained in the mainstream of things at home—in the foreign subsidiary, they would be removed from the mainstream, and many people believe in the "out of sight, out of mind" syndrome. For example, Ted Patlovich, vice chairman of Loctite Corp., has indicated that "generally, people are not champing at the bit to go [on a foreign assignment]." "It is a major plus to have international experience these days, but you may get lost there," says Chuck Campbell, senior vice president of Federal Signal Corp. "You aren't as visible as the guy who is working away in front of the CEO's eyes."[11] And in a survey of personnel managers at 56 MNCs, 56 percent of the respondents believed a foreign assignment to be immaterial or detrimental to their careers.[12]

It should be noted, however, that currently it is generally believed that executives cannot elevate themselves in the organization unless they possess substantial foreign experience. For example, according to Michael Angus, chairman of Unilever PLC, "Most people who rise toward the top of our business will have worked in at least two countries, probably three."[13] It may now be less difficult to find highly qualified people for foreign assignments than in the past.

Highly qualified executives may also refuse a foreign assignment because of a dual-career family situation, which is increasing in the United States. The U.S. Department of Labor has predicted that 81 percent of all marriages will be a dual-career partnership by 1995.[14] This means that to get highly qualified executives in such a partnership, international business enterprises may have to take on the additional costly burden of having to find a job in the foreign country for the spouse or pay for some other arrangement, such as commuter marriage support. The strategies that some companies are applying to deal with this problem include intercompany networking, job-hunting/fact-finding trips, and intracompany employment.[15]

Very Expensive Incentives Required.   To get these highly qualified people to accept a foreign assignment, very expensive incentives, such as much higher salaries and benefits, are often required. (As an illustration, refer to Practical Perspective 6–1.)

Low Productivity in Early Part of Assignment.   The expatriate may not be too productive in the earlier part of the assignment because he or she needs time to adapt to the new environment.

"Badwill."   Employing foreigners could generate "badwill" among the local people, who may prefer to see citizens of their country managing the foreign subsidiary.

Expensive Repatriation Programs Needed.   Expensive programs to reorient the expatriate when he or she returns home (repatriation) are required.

Expatriate May Have an Ulterior Motive for Accepting the Assignment.   If an expatriate is resentful of his or her country's political system and/or governmental policies, his or her motivation for wanting the foreign assignment may be "escaping" from the country. In turn, at the foreign site, the expatriate's energies may be exerted toward attaining his or her objectives instead of the company's. For example, in the past, some expatriates from communist countries on assignment in democratic countries have exerted much of their energy toward finding ways to obtain political asylum in those countries.

PRACTICAL PERSPECTIVE 6-1

Expatriates Require Higher Salaries

Patrick Grossi, manager of employment and human resources information systems for CE [Combustion Engineering, Inc.], points out, "Compensation is a major concern when recruiting people for overseas work. Americans generally consider overseas employment 'above the call of duty' for periods of more than one year and expect a 40 percent increase above their existing pay schedules. This viewpoint is not shared by Europeans, who consider foreign travel and employment part of their culture and business. Consequently, it is sometimes less expensive to hire foreigners." Sometimes, however, hiring citizens of the country where the foreign operation is located is not an option. When this is the case, an alternate source of personnel is third-country nationals.

Robin Morton, director of human resources and administration at CE's Lummus Crest, Inc.

of Houston, Texas, describes how the company taps into a third country's human resources. When a contract has been consummated with a foreign customer, CE immediately investigates the supply of qualified Americans who can fulfil the requirements of the assignment. In some cases, it's impossible to find an American with suitable technical experience. "We had a project in the South China Sea," Morton recalls, "that required knowledge of rough ocean conditions for water depth considerations, and so on. We knew of an expert who had worked in the North Sea on a similar project, so we contacted him, and he agreed to help us. He was a national of the United Kingdom." A few years ago CE worked on a project in Iran. Because the political tension at that time, it was better for everyone if CE hired British or Canadian specialists in place of Americans.

Source: Chuck Oakes, "Multinational Recruitment: Stick with the Basics," *Management Review,* 77 (September 1988): 55–56.

Japanese Expatriates in the U.S. as an Illustration of the Disadvantages

An influential Japanese organization employed Matthew D. Levy, principal of WSY Consulting Group, and Soji Teramura, president of the consulting firm Teramura International, to analyze the experiences of 50 foreign-owned enterprises in the United States. The following are some of their findings:[16]

- ◆ A large majority of Japanese executives and about half of American executives find miscommunication (language barriers) to be a significant obstacle to successful operations.

- ◆ More than half of American executives, and nearly as many Japanese executives, find cultural differences in the U.S. workplace to be a problem.

- ◆ Smaller Japanese companies, which tend to be less experienced in international management, have the most difficulty managing cultural differences.

- ◆ Family adjustment and lack of preparation for life in the United States were cited as problems by about half of the Japanese executives.

- ◆ Japanese families have problems readjusting when they return to Japan.

- ◆ Some Japanese executives have problems dealing with American-style unions.

- ◆ Some Japanese executives, coming from a homogeneous society, encounter difficulties in dealing with America's culturally diverse workforce.

- ◆ Some Japanese executives have difficulty dealing with the negative feelings some American workers have toward Japanese management.

- ◆ Many Japanese executives have problems dealing with U.S. federal, state, and local government regulations.

- ◆ Some Japanese executives are not able to deal with community relations very well.

Advantages and Disadvantages of Using
Host-Country Locals

As indicated above, when managers of international enterprises are attempting to determine if they should use an expatriate to manage a foreign subsidiary, they need to consider both the advantages and disadvantages of the approach. If the disadvantages of using an expatriate outweigh the advantages, they may have to consider the option of using a host-country national. This approach, too, has advantages and disadvantages that must be considered.

Advantages

Familiar with Local Environment. Host-country nationals are already familiar with the local language, culture, and customs. They therefore do not require expensive training in language proficiency or in cultural acculturation. For example, Ted Patlovich, vice chairman of Loctite Corp., sees big advantages in having a local manager running things overseas. "Our preference is that we would rather have nationals be country managers than foreigners," Patlovich says. "The national knows his [or her] way around. He [or she] knows the lawyers, the financial people, the bankers. He knows everybody."[17]

Can Sometimes Be Productive Right Away.   Unlike the expatriate, they do not need time to **adapt** to the local environment, and can sometimes be productive from the beginning of the assignment.

Knows Local Business Subtleties.   They possess knowledge of the subtleties of the local business situation—which may be vital to the establishment of a good relationship with customers, clients, government agencies, employees, and the general public.

"Goodwill."   Having local nationals in management positions, especially at higher levels, may enhance the company's image (it develops **"goodwill"** for it), especially in strong nationalistic countries. It may also enhance host-country employees' morale. This is because they may appreciate working for a boss of the same nationality rather than a foreigner and/or they may appreciate the opportunity for growth in the organization.

Usually Less Expensive to Employ.   Employing host-country nationals is often less expensive than employing home-country or third-country nationals—especially in lower wage nations. Their salaries and other benefits packages are often lower than the expatriate's and the third-country national's. And no expensive repatriation programs are needed.

Disadvantages

Loyalty May Be to Country, Not to the Company.   It is possible that in a conflict between national policy and the company's interests, host-country managers may favor national policy over the company's interests.[18]

Often Difficult to Find Qualified People.   It is quite often difficult expecially in the less-developed countries, to find people at the local level who possess the right skills for the assignment.

More Difficult to Assess Abilities.   It is usually more difficult to assess locals' skills and abilities than to assess someone who is working for the corporation.

Does Not Understand the Corporation's Culture.   The local most likely does not possess sufficient knowledge of the firm's policies and culture, including the informal decision-making network in the home office.

Problems in Communicating with Home Office.   The local may have difficulty communicating with the home-office manager and other employees.

May Not Be Mobile.   Host country managers, once appointed, may be difficult to move; they may want to remain on the job until retirement. For example, the Japanese tend to prefer lifetime employment in the same company.

May Have Ulterior Motives.   Local managers may become bored with the job itself and concentrate on building a name and reputation in the community for themselves, thus ignoring the managerial function.

May Be Weak in Dealing with Local Government Officials.   There is the fear that a host country manager will be weak in dealing with local authorities.[19]

Expensive Training and Development Programs Needed.   To deal with the problems outlined above, expensive programs, such as assigning the local to the corporate headquarters for a lengthy period of time to orient him or her with the corporation's overall formal and informal modus operandi, may be required. This would eliminate the advantage of the local manager being productive right away. And the host-country local becomes an expatriate, thus inheriting the problems outlined above for the expatriate.

Advantages and Disadvantages of Using Third-Country Personnel

If the disadvantages of using an expatriate or a host-country national outweigh the advantages, another option managers can consider is using a third-country national to manage the foreign subsidiary. This approach, too, has advantages and disadvantages.

Advantages

Additional Source of Personnel.   Third-country nationals are a source of personnel when there is a shortage of qualified host-country and home-country nationals who are able or willing to take foreign assignments. (Refer again to Practical Perspective 6–1.)

Usually Costs Less Than the Expatriate.   The costs of maintaining third-country nationals are often less than the costs of maintaining expatriates—especially if the expatriates are from high-income nations such as the U.S. and Japan.

Greater Adaptability Than the Expatriate.   Third-country nationals from a country in the same region as the foreign assignment are likely to possess greater cultural adaptability and greater flexibility and ease of adjustment in the host country than home-country personnel. For instance, a Brazilian probably would adapt more readily in Chile than a Scandinavian. There would be even greater adaptability if the third country and the host country share a common language and relatively similar cultural background. For example, a Portuguese citizen may be able to work in Brazil more easily than could a citizen from Britain because Portuguese is the language spoken in both countries. And it would be easier for a Taiwanese to work in the People's Republic of China than it would for a French individual because Taiwan and the People's Republic of China, to a great extent, share a common culture and language (Mandarin). American companies, for instance, have over the years hired English or Scottish executives for top management positions in their subsidiaries located in countries that were former British colonies, such as Jamaica, India, and Kenya.

Advantageous When the Home Country Does Not Maintain a Good Relationship with the Host Country.   The approach is especially advantageous when the home-country government does not maintain a positive relationship with the government of the nation in which the subsidiary is located, but the third country government does. For instance, an Iranian enterprise with a subsidiary in the U.S. may be better off employing a Canadian citizen, for example, to manage the subsidiary. This is because the Iranian government's relationship with the U.S. government is not very good, and it is not as negative with Canada's government.

Disadvantages

Disadvantageous If the Employee's Country Does Not Maintain a Good Relationship with the Host Country.   There could be problems with this staffing strategy if the qualified employee available is from a country that does not really have a good relationship with the country where the assignment is to take place. For example, in certain parts of the world, animosities of national character exist between neighboring countries—for instance, India and Pakistan, Greece and Turkey, and Ireland and Northern Ireland. Transfers of third-country nationals must take such factors into account because an oversight in this area could be disastrous. For example, local workers may not like working for the third-country manager simply because he or she is from that country.

Locals May Prefer Their Own Citizens in Managerial Positions.   Another problem, which is similar to the use of the expatriate option, is associated with the desire of the host-country's government to elevate its own people to responsible managerial positions. Even if the third-country national is better qualified, the government may still prefer that a local citizen be appointed.

Appointee May Have an Ulterior Motive.   Yet another problem, also similar to the expatriate approach, is if the candidate is dissatisfied with his or her country's political system and/or governmental policies. His or her motive for wanting the assignment may be to "escape," and he or she may exert energy toward attaining this end and ignore the company's objectives.

FACTORS INFLUENCING THE CHOICE

Numerous factors influence the choice of whether to use an expatriate, a host-country national, or a third-country national. The factors include top management's staffing outlook, perceived needs, the corporation's characteristics, the characteristics of the personnel available at home, and the host country's characteristics.

Top Management's Staffing Outlook

The varying staffing views of international business corporations influence the decision. A company's view can be ethnocentric, polycentric, regiocentric, or geocentric.[20]

Ethnocentric

The **ethnocentric** view holds that key positions in the foreign subsidiary should be staffed by citizens from the parent company's home country. An enterprise develops such an outlook because its top management perceives a deficiency in the qualifications, experience, and competence of host-country nationals available to fill management positions in the foreign subsidiary. These firms thus use expatriates to manage their foreign operations. Japanese international businesses are reputed to adhere strongly to this view. For example, Japanese international business corporations have been found to employ considerably more parent-country nationals at the senior and middle management levels in their foreign operations than do American and European international business enterprises, and they do not use third-country nationals at any level of management in their foreign operations, except in Africa.[21] Procter & Gamble endured a series of painful product failures because of its (now abandoned) policy of imposing managers from headquarters on overseas subsidiaries.[22]

Polycentric

The **polycentric** view holds that key positions in the foreign subsidiary should be staffed by locals (host-country nationals). A corporation's top management holding this view will employ host-country locals to ensure that the foreign subsidiary's operation follows overall company policy.

Although Japanese international businesses have tended to apply the ethnocentric approach, some of them are starting to think polycentrically—for example, Sony now aims to give the top job in each of its subsidiaries to a manager from the host country.[23]

It should be noted that a company may behave polycentrically toward one country and at the same time behave ethnocentrically toward another. Polycentric firms send expatriates to the foreign subsidiary not only to train and develop the locals, but also to develop or enhance their managerial skills and to develop an informal communication network in the foreign market.[24] For example, Becton Dickinson promotes cross-posting of managers. They accomplish this by sending managers to different foreign subsidiaries for a period of time and have them take on general management responsibilities. This gives members of the strategy teams a broad international profile, enabling them to be more effective when making organizational decisions.[25] Histoircally, hierarchical opportunities for host-country locals in these enterprises has generally been limited to as far as top management of the local subsidiary.[26]

Regiocentric

The **regiocentric** view holds that key positions at the regional headquarters should be staffed by individuals from one of the region's countries. The firms will use expatriates to develop a regional organization and, as in the case of the polycentric approach, to enhance their skills and develop an informal communication network.[27] Hierarchical opportunity for host-country locals presented by these businesses (especially U.S. and European international business corporations) tends to be to as far as top management at the regional headquarters.[28] This opportunity evolved in part because polycentric companies came to realize that a way to keep effective local managers was to give them the opportunity for regional top-level positions that were occupied by home-country expatriates. For instance, Arthur Pappas, an American who (in 1991) heads Glaxo's regional operations in Asia, "has sent home ten Western managers since 1989, replacing them with locals or one of the growing number of Asians who work in the region but outside their home country. Among his current tasks: to train or recruit an Asian to take his place."[29]

It should be noted that international business enterprises typically do not provide locals the opportunity for growth to top-level positions in the central, home-office headquarters. The lack of this opportunity demoralizes some local and regional managers. Table 6–1 presents the managerial profile for a number of large international business corporations. As can be seen, few foreigners reach the top ranks.

Geocentric

The **geocentric** view holds that nationality should not make any difference in the assignment of key positions anywhere (local subsidiary, regional headquarters, or central headquarters); that competence should be the prime criterion for selecting managerial staff. Even though this view (referred to as the global corporation in Chapter 1), at least in theory, seems to be catching on, few international business enterprises practice it fully. For example, David dePury, co-chairman of Asea Brown Boveri, the Swedish-Swiss electrical engineering giant, informed a recent international management symposium at St. Gallen in Switzerland that few multinationals produce more than 20% of their goods and services outside their immediate or wider home market; that most boards come predominantly from one culture; and that few multinationals are ready to let their shareholder base become as global as their business.[30]

Coca-Cola Co., however, seems to fit this view. It owns and operates businesses of all sizes in more than 195 nations. Two-thirds of its 31,000 employees work outside the United States. Third-country nationals make up the majority of the international service employees, and individuals of other nationalities are in charge of more of Coca-Cola's division offices than are North Americans.[31] These corporations, too, use expatriates for development purposes. Ford Motor Co. has recently embarked on a colossal plan to turn itself into a borderless firm.[32]

Top Management's Perceived Needs

Some top managements may perceive that an expatriate would work better for them than a local, and vice versa. For example, Louis Jouanny, manager of international marketing for Grid Systems Corp., a portable computer maker in California, has stated that, "The experience we had is that you need Europeans to sell in Europe and Asians to sell in Asia. You need local people to sell locally."[33] On the other hand, Jerry Johanneson, chief operating officer for Haworth Inc., an office furniture maker from Michigan, says, "because the pricing and design of furniture systems can get complicated, and because we wanted to be certain Haworth's service would be excellent from the outset, we elected to station a U.S. national in the London office."[34]

Company's Characteristics

Companies' **characteristics that influence the choice of staffing strategy** include the following:[35]

Ownership of Foreign Subsidiaries

The type of staffing strategy an international business company adopts depends on whether the investment is for a short or a long term. If it is for a short term, the firm may utilize the expatriate approach because there is no time to develop locals; if it is for a long term, it may use a development-of-locals approach.

Company	Home Country	1989 Total Sales Billions	Sales Outside Home Country	Assets Outside Home Country	Shares Held Outisde Home Country	Management Approach
Nestle	Switzerland	$32.9*	98.0%*	95.0%*	Few	Ceo is German. Has 10 general managers, of whom five are not Swiss
Sandoz	Switzerland	8.6*	96.0	94.0	5.0%	All Swiss at top, more conservative in style than other Swiss companies
SKF	Sweden	4.1	96.0	90.0	20.0	Foreigners have cracked board and top management group
Hoffman-La Roche	Switzerland	6.7*	96.0	60.0	0.0	All-Swiss board, but next level of managers mixed
Philips	Netherlands	30.0	94.0	85.0*	46.0	Solidly Dutch company, but number of senior foreign managers is increasing
Smithkline Beecham	Britain	7.0	89.0	75.0	46.0	Joint U.S.-British management at all levels
ABB	Sweden	20.6	85.0*	NA	50.0	Moved headquarters to Switzerland; Managers are Swedish, Swiss, German
Electrolux	Sweden	13.8	83.0	80.0	20.0	Of 50 top managers outside Sweden, only five are Swedish
Volvo	Sweden	14.8	80.0	30.0	10.0	Solidly Swedish at all top management levels
ICI	Britain	22.1	78.0	50.0	16.0	40% of top 170 executives are not British; top ranks include four other nationalities
Michelin	France	9.4	78.0	NA	0.0	Secretive, centralized, with top management almost entirely French
Hoechst	W. Germany	27.3	77.0	NA	42.0	No foreigners on board, but most foreign operations are run by locals
Unilever	Britain/Neth.	35.3	75.0*	70.0*	27.0	Five nationalities on board, thoroughly stateless management
Air Liquide	France	5.0	70.0	66.0	6.0	English is official language, but it considers itself thoroughly French
Canon	Japan	9.4	69.0	32.0	14.0	Foreigners run many sales subsidiaries, but none in top ranks
Northern Telecom	Canada	6.1	67.1	70.5	16.0	Thoroughly Canadian, but has assumed U.S. identity
Sony	Japan	16.3	66.0	NA	13.6	Only major Japanese manufacturer with foreigners on board
Bayer	W. Germany	25.8	65.4	NA	48.0	No foreigners on board, but six of 25 business groups run by foreigners
BASF	W. Germany	13.3	65.0	NA	NA	Relies on local managers to run foreign operations, but none in top ranks
Gillette	U.S.	3.8	65.0	63.0	10.0*	Three foreigners among top 21 officers
Colgate	U.S.	5.0	64.0	47.0	10.0*	CEO, other top execs have had several foreign posts; many multilingual
Honda	Japan	26.4	63.0	35.7	6.9	Foreigners running offshore plants, but none at top levels at home
Daimler Benz	W. Germany	45.5	61.0	NA	25.0*	Similar to other German giants
IBM	U.S.	62.7	59.0	NA	NA	Relies on locals to manage non-U.S. operations; increasing number of foreigners in top ranks
NCR	U.S.	6.0	58.9	40.5	NA	Nationals run foreign operations, but none in top ranks

Company	Home Country	1989 Total Sales Billions	Sales Outside Home Country	Assets Outside Home Country	Shares Held Outisde Home Country	Management Approach
CPC International	U.S.	5.1	56.0	62.0	5.0*	One third of officers are foreign nationals
Coca-Cola	U.S.	9.0	54.0	45.0	0.0	Thoroughly multinational management group making big international push
Digital	U.S.	12.7	54.0	44.0	NA	Five of top 37 officers are foreign; most foreign operations run by locals
Dow Chemical	U.S.	17.6	54.0	45.0	5.0	Out of top 25 managers, 20 have experience outside U.S.
Saint-Gobain	France	11.6	54.0	50.0	13.0	Of 25 top managers, only two are not French
Xerox	U.S.	12.4	54.0	51.8	0.0	Major joint ventures with Rank, Fuji have shaped top management thinking
Caterpillar	U.S.	11.1	53.0	NA	NA	Of top five executives, four have foreign experience, including CEO-elect
Hewlett-Packard	U.S.	11.9	53.0	38.6	8.0	Five of top 25 officers not U.S. citizens; many units managed offshore
Siemens	W. Germany	36.3	51.0	NA	44.0	Some business groups managed from outside Germany by non-Germans but none on management board
Corning	U.S.	3.1*	50.0*	45.0*	NA	Company is leader in use of joint ventures to penetrate markets
Johnson & Johnson	U.S.	9.8	50.0	48.0	NA	First foreign national on board in 1989; senior managers include foreign-born
United Technologies	U.S.	19.8	49.7	26.7	NA	Because of U.S. defense business, few foreigners at top
Unisys	U.S.	10.1	49.0	31.0	10.0	Aside from Japanese joint venture, management is largely American
Merck	U.S.	6.0	47.0	NA	NA	Top management is American, but foreign nationals run overseas operations
Nissan	Japan	36.5	47.0	20.0	2.9	Foreign operations managed by locals; completely Japanese at headquarters
3M	U.S.	12.0	46.0	42.0	15.0	CEO pushing to raise foreign sales to 50% of total by 1992
DuPont	U.S.	35.5	44.0	20.0	24.0	Has two foreign directors, both Canadians, but top management is heavily American
Matsushita	Japan	41.7	42.0	NA	7.0	American named no. 2 for North America, but no foreigners in top ranks
Hertz	U.S.	6.0	40.0	41.0	0.6	CEO is Irish citizen, management thoroughly mixed
P & G	U.S.	21.4	40.0	32.0	NA	International operations chief recently named CEO

NA = Not Available   Data: Company Reports, * BW Estimates

This is a sampling of manufacturing companies with a minimum $3 billion in annual sales that derive at least 40% of those sales from countries other than their home country. It does not include state-owned companies or holding companies.

Source: W. J. Holstein et al., "The Stateless Corporation," *Business Week*, May 14, 1990, p. 103. Copyright © 1990, McGraw-Hill. All rights reserved. Used with permission.

Industry Group

Staffing strategy will vary at least between the manufacturing and service industries. Service industries such as banking, insurance, and law often require locals because they possess the knowledge of the local practices required to operate the foreign subsidiary effectively. On the other hand, manufacturing enterprises often require expatriates because they possess the technical knowledge required to develop and operate the foreign subsidiary effectively.

Technology

The level of technological sophistication and the amount of research needed to sustain it will affect the staffing strategy. If it is high, an expatriate may be required. Furthermore, if the enterprise is very secretive about, or protective of, its technology, it is likely to use expatriates because using locals may mean sharing its secret.

Market Influences

Staffing strategies will vary according to whether the market for the product is purely local or international. If the foreign subsidiary is producing for local distribution, employing managers with a local perspective may suffice. If, however, the production is for global distribution, managers with a broader perspective would be required, which expatriates or third-country nationals are more likely to possess than locals.

Stage of Foreign Subsidiary Development

Traditionally, international business corporations have staffed foreign subsidiaries with expatriates in the early stages of establishing operations in a foreign country. To some extent, this is true as well in the developed stages when it involves higher-level positions.[36] In the later **stages of subsidiary development,** at least at the lower levels, host-country nationals are employed. For example, research has revealed that in their first stage of internationalization, companies in the U.S. and Europe export their products to foreign markets. However, as the local market becomes large enough to support local manufacture of the product, home-country managers are sent to the host country to start the operations and manage them during the first few years. Subsequently, the companies replace the expatriates with host-country nationals.[37] The case of Motorola serves as an example:

> Motorola has been doing business internationally for approximately 20 years. We presently [1985] have about 160 U.S. managers serving on assignments in Europe, the Mid East, Asia, Canada, Mexico and Latin America. In virtually all our operations we use an American manager in the start-up process. We do this because it's very difficult for someone in a foreign country to acculturate

to the company's management style and objectives while starting up a facility. It's an awful lot to learn. There are exceptions to that, mainly when we have a longer-than-normal lead time to get the facility going. But a lot of our expansion has happened fairly rapidly with only 9 to 12 months to get a plant up and running.[38]

It should be noted that U.S. international businesses have the tendency to use host-country nationals at all levels of foreign subsidiary management to a much greater extent in the more advanced regions of the world than in the less advanced regions.[39] This suggests that U.S. international business corporations use the ethnocentric approach in less-developed countries and the polycentric approach in developed countries.

Organizational Structure

A company's **organizational structure** also affects its choice of staff. International business enterprises with multidomestic strategies (discussed in Chapter 3) may utilize locals more so than enterprises with global strategies, which require an expatriate's or a third-country national's global perspective. (Of course, locals can also possess a global perspective.)

Dependence on International Business

Firms with high dependence on international business may feel more secure with an expatriate managing their foreign operations. Firms with low dependence may use locals because they cost less than expatriates.

Cost-Benefit Factors

The staffing approach with the most favorable cost-benefit ratio would be chosen. There is, however, no standard formula for accurately determining the ratio. Decision makers must therefore rely on their intuition.

Style of Management

International business companies apply a staffing strategy that suits their organizational character (or corporate culture) and their **style of management.** For example, Japanese international businesses tend to staff their foreign subsidiaries' important decision-making positions with Japanese expatriates.

Characteristics of Personnel Available at Home

The choice of staffing strategy is also influenced by the **characteristics of the personnel available at home.** Are there individuals with:

- ◆ Adequate qualifications and experience?
- ◆ A proven record of previous performance?

- ◆ A commitment to international business, including aspirations for international assignments?
- ◆ The ability to adapt to cultural environments different from their own and the sensitivity to adapt to new situations?
- ◆ Family commitments that would not hinder the foreign assignment?

If the answer to most of the above questions is no, the firm may have to (1) look for them in third countries and/or in the host country, (2) implement extensive training and development programs (to be discussed in Chapter 7), or (3) do both (1) and (2).

Host-Country Characteristics

The choice of staffing strategy is also influenced by factors associated with the **host country.** The factors include the following:

Level of Economic and Technological Development

If the country's level of economic and technological development is low, it may sometimes be difficult for the company's top management to find qualified personnel locally.

Political Stability

If political stability in the country is low and nationalist sentiments are high, and there is high potential for the government to nationalize or expropriate foreign-owned companies, an enterprise's top management may feel more secure sending a expatriate. (Of course, as it is suggested in Chapter 2, many companies will not establish operations in such a high-risk country.)

Control of Foreign Investments and Immigration Policies

Nations may have a policy mandating that foreign investors place locals in managerial positions in the subsidiaries they own there. For example, as it is pointed out in Chapter 2, when Russia started to attract foreign investment in the late 1980s, it had a policy that top management in foreign-owned subsidiaries there had to be locals (Russians). Since the policy was not working, Russia has since eliminated it, allowing foreigners to assume top management positions in foreign-owned subsidiaries.[40]

Availability of Capable Managerial Personnel

If managers with the appropriate abilities and experience are not available in the host country, the corporation may have to look for them in third countries or at home, and then implement programs aimed at training and developing locals for managerial positions.

Sociocultural Setting

Will it be too difficult for an expatriate to adjust to the country's cultural, racial, language, religious, and political boundaries? If so, the firm may have to look for locals or for third-country nationals. For example, "The country you plan to expand into makes a big difference," says Steven Graubart, manager with the accounting and consulting firm Ernst & Young. "In Malaysia, Indonesia, Thailand and the Middle East, for example, hiring a local executive to run the operation might be more necessary than it would be in Canada, the United Kingdom or Hong Kong, because differences in language, social customs and government regulations are far more pronounced."[41]

Geographical Location

If the location is very isolated, it may be too difficult for the expatriate to adapt there. For example, it may be difficult to find an employee of a company in Hong Kong to accept an assignment in an isolated area of an African or a South American country. The corporation would then have to consider locals or third-country nationals.

The three sets of factors—company, home-country individuals, and host country characteristics—may interact to affect the choice of one particular staffing strategy rather than another. These factors suggest that there may be situations in which international businesses will have to adapt their selection criteria to specific situations; for example, they may sometimes have to lower their standards. For instance, a position at home may require an employee with a college degree, but in a foreign nation where college graduates are scarce and other factors dictate employing a local, the MNC may have to settle for a high school graduate.

SUMMARY

This chapter has briefly described how the international HRM function differs from the domestic HRM function. It has described three options for international business enterprises to select staff to manage their foreign operations—send someone from the home country, hire someone in host country, or hire someone from a third country—and discussed the advantages and disadvantages of each options. It also presented the factors HRM managers must consider when making a determination as to whether to use a home-country national, a host-country national, or a third-country national.

Key Terms

1. International human resource management function
2. International relocation and orientation
3. Risk exposure
4. Expatriate
5. Home-country, host-country, third-country nationals
6. Familiarity with internal aspects of the firm
7. Not familiar with local culture, laws, political process, legal process, and other subtleties
8. Family may not adapt to local environment
9. Repatriate
10. Adaptation
11. "Goodwill"
12. The ethnocentric, polycentric, regiocentric, and geocentric staffing views
13. Characteristics that influence the choice of strategy
14. Stage of subsidiary development
15. Organizational structure
16. Characteristics of personnel available at home
17. Style of management
18. Host-country characteristics

Discussion Questions and Exercises

1. Fundamentally, the international human resource management (HRM) functions consist of an interplay among three dimensions. What are the three dimensions?

2. How does the international HRM function differ from the domestic HRM function?

3. Briefly describe the three approaches to international managerial staffing.

4. Discuss some of the advantages and disadvantages of each approach.

5. You are the manager of the international HRM function for a firm that needs to assign an executive to manage a subsidiary in a foreign country. You have approached a top-notch executive who refused the assignment because he or she wishes to remain in the home office because of upward movement aspirations. How would you convince the executive to accept the assignment? What would you say to him or her?

6. What are some of the problems Japanese expatriates encounter in the U.S. environment?

7. You are the manager of the international HRM function for a firm located in the U.S. that needs to assign an executive to Iran to establish operations there. The top management of the firm is inclined to send one of its own executives. What advice would you give to the top management?

8. You are the manager of the international HRM function for a firm whose staffing view is ethnocentric. You noticed that the firm has been spending far too much money assigning expatriates to manage its foreign operations, and that the host-country nationals working for foreign subsidiaries are disgruntled because their managers are foreigners. What would you advise the firm's management to do?

9. What is the appropriate expatriate strategy for the following company characteristics?
   a. Has established foreign operations for a short period of time.
   b. Has established a banking subsidiary in foreign country.
   c. Is transferring advanced, sophisticated technology to the foreign country.
   d. Has an established foreign subsidiary in the foreign country to produce for local consumption.
   e. Is to establish a new subsidiary in the foreign country.
   f. Has developed a multidomestic strategy.
   g. Has total revenues that rely only slightly on foreign sales.

10. Discuss the host-country characteristics that influence the staffing method.

Assignment

Contact the manager of an international business corporation's international HRM function. Ask him or her to describe the company's international managerial staffing approaches. Prepare a short report for class presentation.

Japan's Uneasy U.S. Managers

CASE 6–1

Source: Excerpted from Brian O'Reilly, "Japan's Uneasy U.S. Managers," *Fortune,* April 25, 1988, pp. 245–264. Reprinted with permission from publisher. Copyright © 1988 Times, Inc., New York. All rights reserved.

Consider the Japanese salaryman. Along with tens of thousands of his countrymen, he comes to live and to work in America. His migration is born of spectacular success—the rise of his homeland as an awesome, unstoppable economic power. . . . Compared with his life in Japan, the expatriate in America seems marvelously well off. His food is cheaper, his house is bigger, and a round of golf costs a fraction of the $800-a-foursome it takes to play back home. Are things really that great? . . . . Arrayed against those physical comforts are the many problems that a stint in America can create for him, for his family, and for his career. Whether he lives in New York City, Atlanta, or Washington Court House, Ohio (pop. 12,700), he must learn to adjust to America's strange ways. More important, and more difficult, perhaps, he must preserve his Japanese character in order to fit back into Japan's homogeneous society when he returns.

This worry overshadows Japanese in the U.S. It isolates them from Americans, sometimes diminishes their performance as managers, and wreaks huge changes in their family lives. Holding themselves separate, they do not come to understand American business as well as they should. "Concern about fitting back in dictates their behavior while they are here," says professor Toshiaki Taga, director of the U.S.–Japan Management Studies Center at the Wharton School in Philadelphia. "We say they have eyes in the back of their heads. They may be negotiating with Americans, but they are really looking back to Japan." Twenty years ago, when Japan was desperately trying to assert itself in world markets, only the most promising businessmen went overseas. To be selected was a high honor. These days, when most executives can afford to travel for pleasure and even average salarymen get sent abroad to work, an overseas assignment is viewed much differently. "Now all I hear is what a disruption it is to come here," says Simon Shima, a Japanese-born executive at Coldwell Banker in Los Angeles.

Few Japanese turn down a request to relocate abroad, fearing with justification, that to do so could hurt their careers. The nearly 200,000 in the U.S. stoically accept difficulties that would send their American counterparts packing: for example, the lack of an education good enough to prepare their children for the arduous entrance examinations at Japanese universities. They suffer through countless indignities large and little. A few years ago the wife of a Japanese trade official arrived from Tokyo to her new home in Pasadena. She was alone the next evening when people in grotesque clothes and face paint began ringing her doorbell. Frightened and unable to speak English, she slammed the door, but the ringing kept up for most of the evening. The Japanese do not celebrate Halloween.

What is life like for most Japanese expatriates? The experiences of Takeru Egawa, 43, an assistant general manager at Dai Ichi Kangyo Bank in Los Angeles, and his family are fairly typical. "When I got off the plane in 1982, I couldn't understand anything the immigration agent was saying to me," Egawa says. "He yelled and yelled and then gave up." As is the case with many salarymen, Egawa's family stayed behind for three months until he got settled. By the time his wife, Yumiko, and his three young sons arrived, he had rented a house in Torrance, 20 miles from his office ("good schools, not much smog"). Finding the house was easy, he says. Landlords like the way Japanese remove their shoes, saving wear on the carpets. He was amazed at the house's size—three bedrooms on a private lot, much bigger than the small house where he lived in Tokyo. He was also amazed that Yumiko, "who had never touched a steering wheel in Japan," passed her driver's test on her first try.

Learning English has been harder than driving for Yumiko. "She is very shy," Egawa explains. She spends her days driving the children to school, cleaning, helping the children study, taking them to the park, driving one of them to a Japanese fencing academy ("It teaches good manners," says Egawa), and preparing dinner. To keep their Japanese language skills sharp, the boys are forbidden to speak English at home. Because of Yumiko's difficulty with English, her oldest son, Hirohisa, 12, helps with chores like shopping and paying the bills. In Japan, Egawa's wife would run the household and raise the children almost single-handedly while her husband pursued his career. "You don't get to see your children's faces," says Masaaki Hayashida, general manager of Komatsu America Corp., Caterpillar Tractor's main competitor. But Japanese families often become closer when they move to America. Fathers see American men playing with their children and socializing with their wives, and begin to do it themselves.

Egawa arrives home around 10 P.M. That is earlier than many salarymen, who usually go out for ritual drinking with their co-workers. . . . Egawa says he has grown to enjoy life in Los Angeles; the directness of Americans is refreshing, he says politely. But his widowed mother is living alone in Tokyo—she doesn't like Los Angeles—and Egawa feels duty-bound to return. Hirohisa is eager to get back too. He and Takehisa, 9, have stayed Japanese enough to suit their father. But Egawa worries that Katsuhisa, 5, may be picking up too much of the L.A. lifestyle. "When I yell at him," says Egawa, "he just shrugs."

A few years ago, when Japanese factories churned out goods that were cheaper and better made than American products, their foreign offices were little more than glorified order takers, barely able to keep up with demand. But the weak dollar, trade friction, and stiffer competition from Americans have all made the life of the overseas Japanese more difficult now. Their jobs have been further complicated by the problems they have managing—and mixing with—Americans who work in their offices. "The Japanese are underperforming, given the quality and innovativeness of their products," says Robert Paulson, a management consultant who heads McKinsey & Co.'s office in Los Angeles. "They are not finding it easy to operate here."

They frequently have trouble with English when they first arrive, making it hard to operate effectively with American colleagues. Although the Japanese often study English for years, they are trained mostly to read and write, not to speak. Sometimes language problems become so acute that the Japanese and American office staffs drift apart. The problems only get worse if the company conducts all important meetings in Japanese—an easy habit to fall into, since up to half the managers in a typical Japanese company's U.S. office are expatriates. By contrast, says John Q. Anderson, a McKinsey partner who specializes in international management, only about 15% of the executives who work in a U.S. company's Japanese office are American. Japanese and American managers use different methods to arrive at a consensus, often confounding both sides when they try to work together. The Japanese move slowly, soliciting everyone's opinion, while Americans prefer to thrash things out vigorously. . . .

Adopting western management methods is rarely an option for the Japanese. In fact, becoming Westernized—even by accident—is a major worry for expatriate salarymen. Americans who think going abroad gives them a little worldly polish would have a hard time comprehending what awaits the Japanese when they go home. . . . Just being absent from the clique at the home office can sidetrack a Japanese manager's career. "While he's in the U.S., all his buddies are drinking with the boss in the Ginza," says a former Mitsui executive. "You don't know if the boss is saving a place for you.". . .

Many returning Japanese feel as if they are being ostracized. Japan is such a homogeneous society that it rejects anyone out of the ordinary. Anyone suspected of picking up Western ways—becoming a tad impatient, perhaps, with the slowness of consensus-style decision-making—may be sent to a remote office until he reforms. "Even the normal Japanese man has to work hard to be part of the group," says Masayuki Kohama, a senior representative for Hitachi, in Los Angeles on his second assignment to America. "For the man who has been 13 years in the United States, it is very difficult. When all the Japanese men go out drinking together after work and you say, 'I have to go home to my wife,' they say, 'Oh, he's a guy from the United States.' " One man who had studied in the U.S. found that all the ideas he proposed to his peers in Tokyo were scorned. "Every time I spoke people would say, 'Oh, there goes the returnee again,' " he recalls. "I got so fed up I transferred to a small factory far from Tokyo. I never told anyone I had been in the United States."

Even children must hide their differences or risk teasing and bullying. . . . Expatriates worry about their children's education as much as they do their careers. Few trust American schools—often a year or two behind identical Japanese grades in subjects as critical as math—to prepare their children for admission to top Japanese universities. Almost without exception, Japanese parents send their young children to Saturday schools run by the Japanese government and local Japanese businesses. The Japanese government also subsidizes a five-day-a-week school in Queens, New York, for 450 children in grades four through nine. Keio University, one of Japan's most prestigious, recently announced its intention to establish the first Japanese high school in the U.S. The school is scheduled to open in September 1990 on the campus of Manhattanville College, north of New York City.

Some Japanese parents take a drastic approach to education: If they are assigned to the U.S., they leave their high school-age children—particularly their sons—behind. . . . Most managers separated from their children put on a brave face, as though it were routine business. But a Toyota executive with teenager in Japan admits, "It is very hard. My wife is very worried." Daughters don't get left behind quite so often. Because most parents are content to see their daughters become good housewives, they are under less pressure to be admitted to a big-name university. But they, too, pay a price for living in the U.S. "A thoroughly Westernized daughter may have trouble attracting a Japanese husband," say Jill Kleinberg, an anthropologist and management school professor at UCLA. . . .

Kazuo Sonoguchi, the Mazda plant manager, wonders about the effect of his second assignment to America on his three children, particularly his daughters. "Sometimes I feel sorry for them," he says. "I have a feeling I may have confused them." For reasons like these, Japanese expatriates and their families develop an obsession with going home, donning blinders to help preserve their identity. Few seem interested in mastering the intricacies of doing business in America or understanding the culture. They are eager to return as soon as their assignments—usually four years—are over. . . .

Once in a while a salaryman decides that he can't go home again. After six years with Mitsui & Co. Ltd. in New York, Mitsuo Kurobe quit last year. He moved to California, where he helped start several small computer and peripherals companies. . . . He is one of the few to break ranks: More than 95% go back. Men bid their Volvos goodbye, women worry about squeezing back into a tiny apartment, youngsters bone up furiously on their Japanese. Then they all pray that no one notices that they once lived in America.

QUESTIONS

1. Do Japanese international corporations tend to be ethnocentric, polycentric, regiocentric, or geocentric? What in the article led you to that conclusion?
2. Do American international corporations tend to be ethnocentric, polycentric, regiocentric, or geocentric? What in the article led you to that conclusion?
3. Describe the problems faced by Japanese expatriates in the U.S.
4. What should Japanese MNCs be doing to correct the problem?
5. Based on what you have learned in this chapter, especially about determining whether to use an expatriate or a host-country national to manage foreign subsidiaries, discuss what the Japanese MNCs are doing ineffectively.

Notes

1. "Island Hoppers," *The Economist,* September 14, 1991, p. 40.

2. P. V. Morgan, "International Human Resource Management: Fact or Fiction," *Personnel Administrator* 31, no. 9 (1986): 43–47.

3. P. J. Dowling, R. S. Schuler, and D. E. Welsh, *International Dimensions of Human Resource Management* (Belmont, CA: Wadsworth Publishing, 1994), pp. 2–10.

4. See D. L. Pinney, "Structuring an Expatriate Tax Reimbursement Program," *Personnel Administrator* 27, no. 7 (1982): 19–25.

5. See J. Kapstein "How U.S. Executives Dodge Terrorism Abroad," *Business Week,* May 12, 1986, p. 41.

6. For a current account of the problems expatriates face, see R. L. Thornton and M. K. Thornton, "Personnel Problems in 'Carry the Flag' Missions in Foreign Assignments," *Business Horizons,* January/February 1995, pp. 59–65.

7. The source of this discussion is S. B. Prasad and Y. K. Shetty, *An Introduction to Multinational Management* (Englewood Cliffs, NJ: Prentice-Hall, 1976) p. 152.

8. E. L. Miller and J. L. Cheng, "A Closer Look at the Decision to Accept an Overseas Position," *Management International Review,* 18, No. 1, (1978): 25–27.

9. Charles Siler, "Recruiting Overseas Executives," *Overseas Business,* (Winter 1990) p. 31.

10. Simcha Ronen, *Comparative and Multinational Management* (New York: John Wiley & Sons, 1986), pp. 505–554.

11. Charles Siler, "Recruiting Overseas Executives," p. 77.

12. Cecil G. Howard, "Profile of the 21st-Century Expatriate Manager," *HR Magazine*, June 1992, pp. 93–100.

13. Ibid., p. 97.

14. C. Reynolds and R. Bennett, "The Career Couple Challenge," *Personnel Journal* (March 1991): 48.

15. Ibid.

16. Matthew D. Levy and Soji Teramura, "Foreign Ownership: Japanese in U.S. Overcome Barriers," *Management Review* (December 1992): 10–15.

17. Siler, "Recruiting Overseas Executives," p. 77.

18. Prasad and Shetty, *Introduction to Multinational Management,* p. 153.

19. F. Adams, Jr., "Developing an International Workforce," *Columbia Journal of World Business* 20 (20th Anniversary Issue) (1985): 23–25.

20. H. V. Perlmutter and D.A. Heenan, "How Multinational Should Your Top Managers Be?" *Harvard Business Review* 52 (November–December 1974): 121–132. See also S. H. Robock and K. Simmonds, *International Business and Multinational Enterprises* (Homewood, IL: Irwin, 1989); and J. L. Calof and P. W. Beamish, "The Right Attitude for International Success," *Business Quarterly* (Autumn 1994): 105–110.

21. Rosalie L. Tung, "Selection and Training Procedures of U.S., European, and Japanese Multinationals," *California Management Review* 25, no. 1 (1982): 61.

22. "The Discreet Charm of the Multicultural Multinational," *The Economist,* July 30, 1994, p. 58.

23. Ibid., p. 57.

24. A. Pazy and Y. Zeira, "Training Parent-Country Professionals in Host Organizations," *The Academy of Management Review* 8, no. 2 (1983): 262–272. See also Y. Zeira and A. Pazy, "Crossing National Borders to Get Trained," *Training and Development Journal* 39 (October 1985): 53–57.

25. Denis McCauley, "How Becton Dickinson Uses Cross-Border Teams to Make 'Transnationalism' Work," *Business International,* February 26, 1990, pp. 63–68.

26. Daniel Ondrack, "International Transfer of Managers in North American and European MNEs," *Journal of International Business Studies* (Fall 1985): 1–19.

27. Ibid.

28. Ibid.

29. Ford S. Worthy, "You Can't Grow If You Can't Manage," *Fortune,* June 3, 1991, p. 88.

30. "The Discreet Charm of the Multicultural Multinational," p. 57.

31. "Corporate Coaches Support Global Network," *Personnel Journal* (January 1994): 58.

32. "The Discreet Charm of the Multicultural Multinational," p. 57.

33. Siler, "Recruiting Overseas Executives," p. 76.

34. Ibid.

35. Prasad and Shetty, *Introduction to Multinational Management,* p. 154.

36. M. Z. Brooke and H. L. Remmers, *International Management and Business Policy* (Boston: Houghton Mifflin, 1978).

37. Lawrence G. Franko, "Who Manages Multinational Enterprises," *Columbia Journal of World Business* 2, no. 8 (1973): 30–42.

38. David Pulatie, "How Do You Ensure Success of Managers Going Abroad?" *Training and Development Journal* (December 1985): 22.

39. Tung, "Selection and Training Procedures," 61.

40. R. Brady and R. Boyle, "Combustion Engineering's Dislocated Joint Venture," *Business Week,* October 22, 1990, pp. 49–50.

41. Siler, "Recruiting Overseas Executives," p. 77.

Chapter Seven

Effective International Human Resource Management

More and more organizations are realizing that it's ineffective to send people overseas without training them beforehand for what lies ahead. [The MNC should] help managers develop an accurate picture of what it is like to work overseas by employing trainers who have international exposure.[1]

Objectives of the Chapter

As indicated in Chapter 6, international business enterprises use three types of executives to staff their foreign subsidiaries: home-country nationals (expatriates), host-country nationals (locals), and third-country nationals (by definition, also expatriates). Use of host-country nationals by companies to manage their foreign subsidiaries has become more and more popular in recent years. But there is no doubt that the home country and third countries will continue to be important sources of expatriate executives used by international businesses. This is especially true as more and more multinational corporations (MNCs) transform themselves into global corporations and establish a global strategy. These expatriate executives, referred to as global managers (discussed in Chapter 1), possess the ability to readily move from country to country and perform effectively no matter where they are.

Using expatriates can be very costly, especially when the expatriate wants to return home prematurely from the foreign assignment or when the wrong person was selected for the foreign assignment—and these instances are numerous. For example, a study of U.S. MNCs revealed that incidences when expatriates had to be recalled home or dismissed from the company because of their inability to perform effectively in a foreign country were numerous. More than half (69 percent) of the firms surveyed had recall rates of between 10 and 20 percent; about 7 percent of the respondents had recall rates of between 20 and 30 percent; and 24 percent had recall rates of less than 10 percent.[2] This is consistent with another study's findings that nine of ten expatriates were significantly less successful in their assignments in Japan than they had been in their previous assignments in their home country, and four of five were considered to be failures by the home office.[3] This suggests that international business enterprises need to develop and implement effective international HRM programs. The objectives of this chapter are therefore to:

1. Discuss why many expatriates fail in their foreign assignments.
2. Propose how to reduce expatriate failures.
3. Point out how to select the right expatriate.
4. Discuss how to find and develop global expatriates.
5. Show how to administer expatriate programs.
6. Discuss expatriate compensation policy.

WHY EXPATRIATES FAIL

There are numerous reasons why many **expatriates** fail in their foreign assignments, including the foreign country's physical and social environments, and varying technical sophistication; company-country conflicting objectives and policies; overcentralization; gender; inadequate repatriation programs; and the pitfalls in the human resource planning function.

The Physical and Social Environments

When expatriates cross national boundaries, they often encounter **adaption problems** caused by both the physical and the sociocultural environments. This is especially true when these environments are at odds with the expatriate's own value system and living habits. For example, geographical distance conflicts with an individual's need to feel secure in the community, and it may result in "separation anxiety" for expatriates and their family members.[4] Such reactions may impair the expatriate's on-the-job effectiveness and lower family morale. The problem is enlarged when the expatriate is not capable of communicating with the local people in their verbal and nonverbal language.[5] These problems will affect expatriates' ability to deal with individuals and business groups outside the subsidiary, including local partners, trade unions, bankers, and important customers.[6]

Varying Technical Sophistication

Another problem confronting expatriates is that they often encounter **differences in technical sophistication** in the foreign country, which conflict with their expectations. This becomes a critical problem when an expatriate views the technical differences as insurmountable.[7] Yet another problem confronting expatriates is when they attempt to apply managerial and organizational principles that were successful in the home country in the foreign country. This will cause considerable frustration for the expatriate because differences in the local culture usually prevent effective implementation.[8]

MNC–Country Conflicting Objectives and Policies

Expatriates also run into problems caused by their having to act as a link between corporate headquarters and the foreign subsidiary, and their being responsible for implementing the objectives and policies that the home office formulates. The problem occurs especially when the **objectives and policies conflict** with the managerial situation viewed by the expatriate manager and with the managerial mandates imposed on him or her by the local government.[9] That is, the expatriate manager must often conduct the subsidiary's operations within the constraints imposed by the immediate situation and the local government.

Overcentralization

Another problem confronting expatriates derives from the home office overcentralizing decision making. If the **expatriate manager's authority is visibly constrained,** his or her chances of establishing and maintaining an effective relationship with local associates are diminished. This is especially true in host environments where individuals place a high value on authority—if the expatriate manager lacks it, he or she, in the eyes of locals, loses credibility.[10]

Gender

Still another problem is cultural resistance to expatriate women managers. **Cultural biases against women** in some host countries (especially in the Middle East, Japan, and Latin America) may deter the acceptance of women as managers. Subordinates in such host-country subsidiaries may interpret the assignment of a woman executive to mean that the central headquarters has low regard for its business with that subsidiary. They may also worry that a woman will have less influence over decisions at headquarters; that is, they may feel that she will have less autonomy in local negotiations, and will thus be less able to represent the subsidiary in local transactions.[11] It should be noted, however, that, as it will be indicated shortly, using female expatriates is becoming less and less of a problem—especially when she is viewed by locals as having the authority to make decisions.

Repatriation

There is the special problem of **repatriation** (reassigning the expatriate back home). A survey revealed that only a few of the responding companies had a formal **repatriation policy**. Thus, most did not have a program aimed at helping the returning employee readjust to the home country's environment, which is a problem for many people.[12] Another survey revealed that employees found reentry into their home country and home company more difficult than the initial move to the foreign culture. This is in part because the managerial skills which they had enhanced abroad generally were neither recognized nor utilized by the home-country organization. The returnees saw themselves as being most effective when they integrated their foreign with their home-country experiences and actively used these new skills. But their colleagues evaluated them most highly when they did not have characteristics of "foreigners" and did not use their cross-cultural learning in their domestic jobs.[13] In fact, the experience expatriates acquire in the foreign assignment often make them more marketable outside the present corporation.[14]

The problem is enlarged when the technological advances made at home may make the expatriate's functional abilities obsolete.[15] It is also enlarged when the returnee finds that he or she has **missed opportunities** in the organization. For example, an investigation of returnees showed that returning managers encountered problems in the sense that important career and professional opportunities had passed them by.[16] Many expatriates have returned home only to find that their peers had been promoted ahead of them to higher-level positions.[17] Other problems include returnees' complaints that the length of their foreign assignment adversely affected their lifestyles, their ability to plan for their future professional careers, and their children's education.

Some returnees complained about losing social and professional prestige on returning home. For example, in a country where the cost of living is relatively low, coupled with the higher salary expatriates normally draw, the executive may have had a very large house with servants, children in an expensive "best" private school, and may have been in top management at the subsidiary. Now, back home, where the cost of living is relatively high, the employee may have to settle for a smaller house, no maids, and sending the kids to a less expensive, lower-quality school. And he or she is no longer in a focal position at work—even if the executive is promoted upon return, in many cases he or she may feel professionally "demoted," as the new position usually does not allow the same type of freedom and stimulation that the foreign position did.[18] Also, the repatriate and his or her repatriate family may experience **"reverse culture shock"** on return, as the environment is no longer as familiar as it was when they left.[19] Or the assignment may have been in an European cultural center and the returnee is assigned to a remote rural town.

These repatriation problems may hinder the expatriate's performance abroad, or, as pointed out in Chapter 6, the better-qualified executives may not even accept the foreign assignment, forcing companies to assign less-qualified people.

Pitfalls in the Human Resource Planning Function

The above reasons for expatriate failures stem in part from poor human resource planning. A study revealed that there are many pitfalls in the human resource planning function in U.S. multinationals, which help cause expatriate failures.[20] The human resource planning function in many U.S. international business enterprises tends to suffer because of several major limitations.

Lesser Role Assigned to Human Resource Planning

It has been found that **human resource managers generally play a less active role in companies' overall planning processes** than do managers of other functions.[21] Evidence suggests that business failures in foreign countries are often linked to poor management of human resources.[22]

Inadequate Selection Criteria for Foreign Assignments

A study of international business enterprises' practices in selecting personnel for foreign assignments showed that international corporations with lower failure rates tend to use **criteria specifically appropriate for selecting expatriate personnel.** The study also revealed that most U.S. MNCs do not yet possess such criteria.[23] Another study showed that most U.S. international businesses use technical competence as the primary criterion for selecting expatriate personnel. This practice derives from two primary reasons: one, the difficulty in identifying and measuring attitudes appropriate for cross-cultural interaction; and two, the self-interest of the selectors. Relative to the self-interest, since technical competence usually prevents immediate failure on the job, particularly in high-pressure situations, the selectors play it safe by placing a heavy emphasis on technical qualifications.[24]

There is an abundance of research showing that while technical competence is the most important factor in the overall determination of success, relational abilities appeared to increase the probability of successful performance considerably, and lack of relational skills was found to be a principal cause for expatriate failure. It has been found that U.S. MNCs seldom emphasize the relations skills criterion in the expatriate selection decision.[25]

Failure to Consider the Family Situation Factor

Another important reason for expatriate failure is the family factor. This refers to the **inability of the expatriate's family to adapt to living and work-**

ing in the foreign country. This creates stress for the expatriate's family members, who then create stress for the expatriate, often resulting in failure.[26] The majority of the respondents in a survey of personnel administrators indicated that they recognized the importance of this factor to successful performance in a foreign assignment, yet few U.S. MNCs actually take it into consideration in the selection decision.[27] Of 80 U.S. multinationals surveyed, 52 percent of them interviewed spouses as part of the selection procedure for managerial positions, and only 40 percent interviewed spouses for technical-oriented positions.[28] The same study revealed that those U.S. multinationals that conducted interviews with the candidate and his or her spouse to determine his or her suitability for the foreign assignment experienced significantly lower incidents of expatriate failure than those that did not.

Lack of Adequate Training for Foreign Assignments

Among the 80 U.S. MNCs surveyed, only 32 percent of the respondent firms had **formalized training programs to prepare candidates for foreign assignments.** Most of the firms that did sponsor training programs used environmental briefing programs only. When used alone, environmental briefings are inadequate for preparing expatriates for assignments requiring extensive contact with the local community in the foreign country. The use of more rigorous training programs could significantly improve the expatriate's performance in an overseas environment, thus minimizing the incidence of failure.[29]

However, it should be pointed out that attempting to change the behavior of experienced managers could be an insurmountable task for a company's training system. First, prospective expatriates who do not possess a background in the behavioral sciences generally do not consider the training function to be an effective agent. Second, many prospective expatriates are inclined to believe that they are more familiar with the organizational environment and problems, both at the headquarters and at the foreign subsidiary, than the training department, and thus feel that they do not need its help. Third, a prospective expatriate whose past behavior has proven to be highly successful is difficult to convince that similar behavior may be dysfunctional in the foreign assignment. Fourth, prospective expatriates may consider such training efforts as criticism of their past behavior; they may also interpret it to mean that top management has doubts about their ability to adapt their behavior on their own volition. Fifth, their workload in the midst of preparation for their transfer may not leave sufficient time for intensive training program. Finally, top managers tend to underrate the need for such training.[30]

Duration of Assignment and Performance Evaluation[31]

Foreign assignments with a short duration are not highly conducive to effective performance because the expatriate is not allowed sufficient time to become acquainted with and **adapt to the new environment.** Many international businesses, especially American companies whose management tends to be short-range-oriented, expect immediate results from their expatriates. These MNCs evaluate expatriates who do not produce positive results right away as low on performance. This practice is not reasonable because expatriates do need time to adapt. As has been proposed, to mitigate the acculturation problem and to avoid costly mistakes, expatriates should be exempted from active management activities during the first six months after arrival in the foreign market.[32] The amount of time expatriates require for adaptation has been projected to be six months, broken down into four phases: the **initial phase, disillusionment phase, culture shock phase, and positive adjustment phase.**[33] These are depicted in Table 7–1. It should be noted that the model presented in Table 7–1 is general, and that some people are not able to pull out of the culture shock phase.

The Expatriate Adaptation Process	TABLE 7–1 ◆
The Initial Phase	When the expatriate transfers to the foreign assignment, the newness of the culture creates a great deal of excitement for him or her.
The Disillusionment Phase	After about two months, the novelty of the new culture wears out, and day-to-day inconveniences caused, for example, by different practices in the local culture and not being able to communicate effectively create disillusionment for the expatriate.
The Culture Shock Phase	After about two months of the day-to-day confusions the expatriate faces a cultural shock. By now the expatriate is ready to go back to his or her old, familiar environment.
The Positive Adjustment Phase	If the expatriate remains, at about month four of the assignment, he or she begins to adapt, and by month six he or she feels more positive about the foreign environment; he or she, however, does not attain the "high" of the first two months, but not the "low" of the next two months.

Source: Adapted from K. Oberg, "Culture Shock: Adjustment to New Cultural Environments," *Practical Anthropology* (July-August 1960): 170–182.

Underutilization of Women as Sources of Expatriates

The option of using **women expatriates is underutilized** by international businesses. A 1983 study of 686 U.S. and Canadian firms revealed that only 3 percent of expatriate managers were women.[34] (The October 21, 1994 edition of *The Wall Street Journal*, p. A1, reported this figure to now be 5 percent.) This underutilization of women for foreign assignments may derive from the presumption that male managers in foreign countries, as pointed out earlier, culturally do not accept women as business partners and equals. While such barriers do exist, male managers in many countries do make a distinction between foreign women professionals and local women—many male managers may not accept local females in managerial roles but will accept foreign females. For example, in a survey of female expatriates, many of the respondents indicated that they were viewed by locals as foreigners who happened to be women, and they also said that the added visibility of being the first female manager in the region gave them greater access to clients because of the curiosity factor.[35] (As an illustration, refer to Practical Perspective 7–1.)

This suggests that MNCs need to explore the possibilities of utilizing female expatriates more than in the past. As noted earlier, many expatriates fail because of a shortage of relational skills. These skills are abilities generally ascribed to female managers. It has been found that women managers, compared to their male counterparts, experienced significantly lower levels of boundary-spanning stress; that is, women were more adept in coping with the pressures and strains resulting from the foreign environment.[36]

The writer's own experience in developing and managing an administrative division at a Native American reservation also provides support for the contention that women are more adaptable than men in a culture much different from their own. Several years ago the writer was employed by a Native American tribe to aid in developing a division in the tribal organization. At the conclusion of the development (three years later), the division employed the writer (a male) and 15 females. The males who had been hired quickly became frustrated with the cultural differences and left, but many of the females who were hired were much more tolerant and stayed.

JAPANESE MNCs' EXPATRIATION PRACTICES

In a comparative study of the expatriate selection and training procedures of U.S. and Japanese MNCs, it was found that Japanese MNCs experienced a significantly **lower incidence of expatriate failure** than U.S. MNCs. 86 percent of the Japanese companies reported a recall rate of less than 5 percent (in the U.S., 24 percent reported a recall rate of less than 10 percent), 10 percent reported a recall rate between 6 and 10 percent, and 14 percent reported a recall rate of between 11 and 19 percent.[37] The study's results

PRACTICAL PERSPECTIVE 7–1

An American Businesswoman's Guide to Japan

"Japanese men aren't used to dealing with woman as equals in a business setting," says Diana Rowland, author of the book *Japanese Business Etiquette*, and owner of a San Diego-based cross-cultural consulting firm. "They are uncomfortable simply due to a lack of experience." That lack of experience can severely handicap an American woman executive working in Japan—but it can also be an asset. "I've been asked at meetings if I'm married and when I say no, then I've been asked why I don't want to be," Rowland says. "You just have to gracefully deal with these questions and move on."

As intrusive as they may appear, personal questions help a Japanese businessman determine how serious a woman might be about the project at hand. After all, lingering in his mind is the idea that a woman would rather be home, not on the job. Why an American woman would choose to work rather than raise a family is almost incomprehensible to the Japanese. It doesn't jibe with their cultural experience of what a woman ought to do.

In Japan, where gender roles are rigidly defined, most Japanese women choose to root their identities in motherhood and marriage. . . . Some Japanese businessmen—especially those accustomed to dealing with Americans—sidestep the "female issue" altogether, preferring to somewhat desexualize their image of American women. "There are three kinds of people in Japan: men, women, and foreigners," says Nancy Noyes, who ran Salomon Brothers' hedge desk in Tokyo for six months in 1988. "In the Japanese male's mind, I was not a woman, but a foreigner."

Many American businesswoman say the sheer uniqueness of being a woman is an advantage in Japan. "Once I asked my Japanese associates how they felt about working with me," says a 32-year-old stockbroker for a large U.S. brokerage firm. "They said it was so easy to remember me because they'd always get Bob confused with Jim, Jim confused with John and John mixed up with Bob.". . . More and more Japanese men are discovering that they actually like working with American women. "As a group, we're probably more diplomatic and less threatening than American men," Rowland says. "Japanese men don't perceive us as trying to dominate them, nor do they feel the need to be overly competitive with us."

Source: Excerpted from Deidre Sullivan, "An American Businesswoman's Guide to Japan," *Overseas Business* (Winter 1990): 50–55.

provide numerous insights into the strengths of Japanese MNCs relative to their strategies in the human resource management function.

Importance of the Human Resource Function

The human resource function is centralized, and the head of the personnel division reports directly to the CEO.[38] The human resource division wields considerable authority in the overall aspects of the corporation's operation, such as recruitment, career development, evaluation, promotion, and the compensation of all employees.

Long Duration of Foreign Assignments

The average duration of foreign assignments in Japanese corporations is 4.67 years.[39] (Foreign assignments in U.S. companies are usually for three years or less.) During the first year of his or her foreign assignment, the Japanese expatriate focuses mainly on adaptation activities. In the second year, the expatriate becomes more active in managerial activities, but this year is still considered a period of adjustment. In the third year, the expatriate begins to function at full capacity.

Support System at Corporate Headquarters

Japanese firms provide a comprehensive support network established for the purpose of setting the expatriate's mind at ease once he or she arrives at the foreign market. The support network includes a division whose sole purpose is to look after expatriates' needs, including the provision of mental and financial support; a mentor system, which implies certain obligations and responsibilities on the part of the corporation toward the expatriate; the showing of greater concern for the total person, including the company's trying to find reasons for expatriates who went to the foreign country alone to periodically visit the headquarters or some other operation in Japan, enabling them to visit their families at the same time; and a practice of having expatriates who have been around for a long time provide assistance to the new expatriate.[40]

Criteria for Selecting Expatriates

Because the prospective expatriate has usually been with the enterprise for many years, managers of Japanese international firms normally have access to the information required to assess the candidate's suitability for the foreign assignment. The strong group orientation and the after-hours socializing practices of Japanese corporations enables managers to become familiar with employees' family background. And most Japanese companies keep a detailed personnel inventory on all their career staff.[41]

Training for Foreign Assignments

The system of lifetime employment and the long-range perspective of many Japanese firms results in their investing large sums of money to train and develop employees for future foreign assignments. The results of a study indicated that 57 percent of the Japanese MNCs surveyed sponsored formal training programs for their expatriates. The programs, in general, consist of the following components: language training, general training, field training, graduate programs in a foreign country, in-house training programs, and use of external agents.[42] The study also revealed that American MNCs tend to be reluctant to invest as much as Japanese firms do in such programs because employment in them tends to be short-term—if they invest in an employee's development and he or she leaves, the company will not recapture the costs.[43]

The above suggests that Japanese firms place much greater emphasis on preparing expatriates than do American firms. This may be because Japan's large population, in a small country with relatively few natural resources, forces it to rely on international business much more so than the U.S., which is a large country with an abundance of resources. Japanese firms must therefore invest more in preparing expatriates than American firms—although the changes that have taken place throughout the globe during the past couple of decades is making American firms more and more dependent on international business. Relative to effective preparation of expatriates, Japanese firms thus have an advantage over American firms, in part because of the programs the Japanese have implemented and in part because they hold a wider global business perspective.

It should be noted, however, that Japanese expatriation practices are not devoid of problems. For example, the lengthy foreign assignments often create problems in the children's education, and if the family adopts new cultural traits in the foreign country, they may be ostracized by the community for deviant behavior when they return to Japan. Furthermore, there is an increasing reluctance among the younger generation in Japan to undertake a foreign assignment.[44] (Refer again to Case 6–1 in Chapter 6.)

EUROPEAN MNCs' EXPATRIATION PRACTICES

As in the case of Japan, European MNCs have a much lower expatriate recall rate than U.S. MNCs. It has been found that 59 percent of the European MNCs had a recall rate of less than 5 percent (76 percent of the Japanese MNCs reported a recall rate of less than 5 percent, and 24 percent of the U.S. MNCs reported a recall rate of less than 10 percent), 38 percent had a recall rate of between 6 and 10 percent, and 3 percent had a recall rate between 11 and 19 percent.[45] The executives interviewed believed that the strong global orientation of the organization is a primary reason for the low expatriate failure rate. This orientation derives in part from the **"spirit of internationalism"** among European people. This spirit is attributed to several factors.[46]

Smallness of European Markets

Domestic markets in European nations tend to be small in size. Therefore, historically, firms have had to export in order to expand their market size. On the other hand, the vastness of the U.S. has historically been able to sustain most firms' growth objectives. Thus, in the past, many U.S. firms for the most part did not encounter the need to transact business in foreign markets. European firms, in general, have therefore developed a much greater global perspective than have American firms.

Europeans Like to Travel Abroad

Europeans, in general, tend to travel to foreign countries extensively. Due to the smallness and close proximity of European nations, Europeans are naturally exposed to numerous foreign people and cultures, and they learn multiple languages—unlike Americans, who tend to learn only their home language. Europeans therefore tend to develop an international perspective to a much greater extent than do Americans, whose huge nation keeps them at home because it provides variety in climate and scenery.

A Tradition of Interaction in Foreign Lands

European traditions and economic conditions have for many centuries encouraged interaction in foreign markets, and even emigration to foreign lands. America has not, to the extent that Europe has, developed such a tradition.

A History of Colonization

In Europe, there is a legacy of "the empire"; the colonization of nations throughout the globe—for example, Portugal, Spain, England, and France once colonized much of the world. As such, European commercial enterprises have a long history of establishing operations in foreign nations, and have thus accumulated a vast wealth of experience in dealing with people in other nations. Many European expatriates are therefore assigned to foreign markets where everything is already well established.

This "spirit of internationalism" thus provides European international businesses a large pool of individuals who can easily be developed for cross-nation assignments. This spirit also makes European spouses more adaptable to foreign cultures than American spouses. In addition, as in the case of Japanese MNCs, European MNCs possess a long-range orientation and have a low rate of turnover among managerial personnel. As a result, they are also willing to invest heavily in training and development programs and they have designed comprehensive expatriate support programs.[47] Therefore, in general, it seems as if European corporations, as in the case of their Japanese counterparts, have a greater pool of adaptable employees to transfer to foreign nations than do American businesses. Nevertheless, European companies also now face expatriation problems, such as needing to assign expatriates who are from dual-career families.

IMPLICATIONS OF U.S., JAPANESE, AND EUROPEAN MNCs' EXPATRIATE PRACTICES

Based on the above analysis of the problems in human resource planning in many U.S. international business enterprises, and of the comparative strengths of their Japanese and European counterparts, the following expatriate staffing implications may be drawn:[48]

1. Top management in international firms must pay a great deal more attention to the international HRM function. It should have adequate representation in the overall corporate strategic planning function.
2. Since inadequate relational skills contribute heavily to expatriate failures, managers making the expatriate selection decision need to pay more attention to this selection criterion.
3. Top management in international businesses must sponsor rigorous training programs aimed to prepare expatriates for the foreign assignment. This means choosing the right program for the right person and for the right nation. Since the expatriate's lack of sensitivity to the foreign country's culture is a primary reason for his or her failure, the programs must include cross-cultural sensitivity development. The programs should also address the repatriation problems.
4. Top management may have to be flexible regarding the length of the foreign assignment. In some situations, a short-term assignment may be appropriate—for example, an expatriate is sent abroad to repair some aspect of the manufacturing facilities in the foreign site. In other situations, however, such as sending an expatriate to develop a new foreign market, a longer-term assignment may be appropriate.
5. International business enterprises must also develop programs to attend to the needs and aspirations of expatriates, and eliminate the information gap so that expatriates do not feel too alienated from their old atmosphere. In this respect, the following ideas have been proposed:[49]

    ◆ A mentor program should be established to keep abreast of the expatriate's career progression throughout his or her international and domestic experience.

◆ The international business enterprise should establish a unit in its HRM function for career planning, meeting regularly with expatriates and repatriates.

◆ The firm's home office should maintain contact with expatriates by sending them newspapers, company newsletters, and mail.

6. Since the family is a prime reason for expatriate failures, managers making the selection decision must assess the expatriate's spouse and children to ascertain their adaptability to the foreign country.

7. International enterprises need to use women in their foreign operations to a much greater extent then they do now.

Incorporating the above framework into the international business enterprise's overall human resource management strategies will have positive consequences. It is likely to reduce the incidences of ineffective or poor expatriate performance. MNCs can no longer rely solely on technology to gain a competitive edge in international markets; they must also rely on international human resource management planning, because the organization and technology are managed and operated by people.

REDUCING EXPATRIATE FAILURES

In essence, **expatriate failures can be reduced** by selecting the right person and implementing programs for assessing a prospective expatriate's effectiveness potential, finding and developing global executives, preparing expatriates, and providing effective compensation.

Selecting the Right Expatriate

As suggested above, expatriate failures can be reduced by **selecting the right person** for the assignment. As previously indicated, "when an expatriate manager fails in a foreign assignment, it is usually not due to technical incompetence; it is due to improper selection."[50] To select the right expatriate for the assignment, David Pulatie, [in 1985] vice president and director of employee relations–personnel international at Motorola, Inc., recommends the following steps:[51]

1. Do an extremely sophisticated job of selecting the people you send to the foreign country—not only the expatriate, but his or her family as well. This requires private, extensive interviews to evaluate each candidate's family situation, lifestyle, and financial picture. For example, if the expatriate has family problems or schooling, medical, or financial responsibilities, adjustment overseas will be difficult. The expatriate will not be able to devote his or her full attention to the assignment.

2. Find out why the candidate wants the foreign assignment, what he or she expects to get out of it, and if the expectations are realistic (see

the accompanying cartoon), what his or her attitude is about living in a foreign country, and what his or her tolerance is.

3. Select only top-notch, proven people. This will help in both the expatriation and repatriation processes (to be discussed later).
4. Familiarize the expatriate and the accompanying family members with the country they are going to (to be discussed later).
5. Set up an administrative branch with the sole function of supporting your international staff (as previously discussed).

Rosalie L. Tung, a professor of international business at Simon Fraser University in Canada, has developed a flowchart of the expatriate selection process (see Figure 7–1).[52] Her model contains several notable features.[53] First, by requiring information about whether the position could be filled by a host-country national, it brings up the issue of employee nationality. Second, the model follows a low-risk strategy in selecting expatriates. Third, the model takes a contingency approach to selecting and training expatriates in that it recognizes that varying assignments require different degrees of interaction.

Assessing Expatriates' Effectiveness Potential

It is apparent from the preceding sections that individuals being considered for foreign assignments require certain characteristics that would not be required for local assignments. As executive search consultants agree, to be effective, expatriate managers must be patient, listen well, and have respect—and perhaps even enthusiasm—for other cultures.[54] "You are looking for someone who is an open minded person who is quite flexible and tolerant of other ways of doing things," says Kai Lindholst, managing partner for Egon Zehnder International Inc., a leading executive search firm. "If the person can only eat at McDonald's every day of the week, why go abroad? If the expatriate manager has a family also making the move, they must share in the enthusiasm in order for the relocation to work. Uprooting a family can be traumatic. . . . Most overseas managers seem to know of at least one divorce resulting from an overseas assignment."[55]

Based on existing published research, Professors Mark Mendenhall and Gary Oddou developed a framework outlining the **special characteristics required by expatriates**.[56] Their framework consists of four dimensions as components of the expatriate adjustment process. The four dimensions and subfactors are outlined in Figure 7–2. If a prospective expatriate demonstrates weakness on those dimensions, he or she may not be adaptable in a foreign culture. Professors Mendenhall and Oddou also identified some techniques currently available to test the strengths and weaknesses in the dimensions and subfactors outlined in Figure 7–2.[57]

Relative to the self-oriented dimension, assessors already possess the means of evaluating technical expertise. They have access to various

◆ CARTOON ILLUSTRATION 7–1   **An Expatriate's Dream**

Source: Eileen Daspin, "Managing Expatriate Employees," *Management Review* (July 1985): 47. Copyright © 1985, Eileen Daspin. All rights reserved. Reprinted with permission.

The Expatriate Selection Process   FIGURE 7-1 ◆

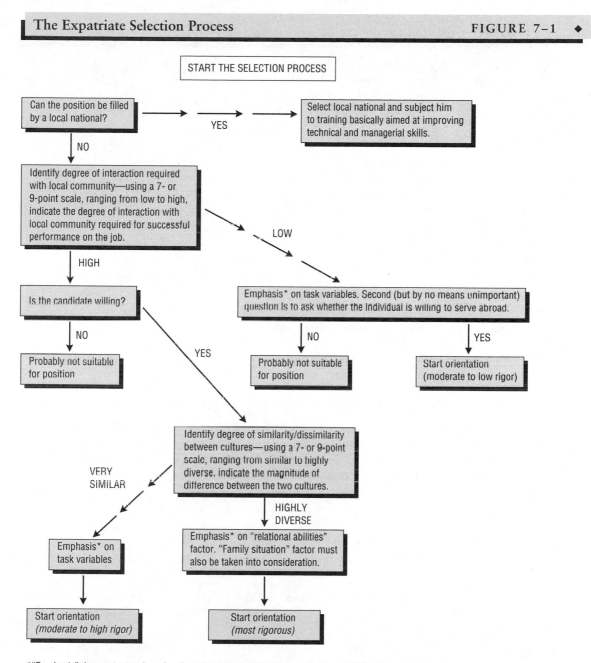

START THE SELECTION PROCESS

Can the position be filled by a local national? → **YES** → Select local national and subject him to training basically aimed at improving technical and managerial skills.

NO ↓

Identify degree of interaction required with local community—using a 7- or 9-point scale, ranging from low to high, indicate the degree of interaction with local community required for successful performance on the job.

LOW →

HIGH ↓

Is the candidate willing?

Emphasis* on task variables. Second (but by no means unimportant) question is to ask whether the individual is willing to serve abroad.

NO ↓   **YES** →

Probably not suitable for position

NO ↓   Probably not suitable for position

YES ↓   Start orientation (moderate to low rigor)

Identify degree of similarity/dissimilarity between cultures—using a 7- or 9-point scale, ranging from similar to highly diverse, indicate the magnitude of difference between the two cultures.

VERY SIMILAR ↙   **HIGHLY DIVERSE** ↓

Emphasis* on task variables

Emphasis* on "relational abilities" factor. "Family situation" factor must also be taken into consideration.

Start orientation *(moderate to high rigor)*

Start orientation *(most rigorous)*

*"Emphasis" does not mean ignoring the other factors. It only means that it should be the dominant factor.

Source: Rosalie L. Tung, "Selection and Training of Personnel for Overseas Assignments," *Columbia Journal of World Business* 16, 1 (Spring 1981): 73. Copyright © 1983, JAI Press Inc. Used with permission from JAI Press Inc. All rights reserved.

◆   FIGURE 7–2   **Dimensions of the Effective Expatriate**

The Self-Oriented Dimension

◆ Has the ability to replace pleasurable activities at home with similar, yet different activities in the foreign culture. For example, can replace baseball in the United States with soccer in Brazil.

◆ Is able to deal with the stress that the foreign culture generally produces for expatriates. He or she has "stability zones," e.g., mediation, writing in diaries, engaging in favorite pastimes, and religious worship, to which he or she can retreat when conditions in the host culture become overly stressful.

◆ Possesses the necessary technical competence.

The Others-Oriented Dimension

◆ Is able to develop long-lasting friendships with locals. The close relationship aids local mentors in guiding the expatriate through the intricacies and complexity of the new culture, e.g., the local mentor provides feedback that helps the expatriate understand local worker expectations and attitudes, and helps the expatriate in his or her efforts to train and develop local replacements.

◆ Is able to communicate with locals (he or she has a good command of the local language). This enables the expatriate to become more familiar and intimate with locals; to create and foster interpersonal relationships.

The Perceptual Dimension

◆ Has the ability to understand why locals behave the way they do and to make correct attributions about the causes of locals' behavior. This helps the expatriate predict how the locals will behave toward him or her in the future.

◆ Is nonjudgmental and nonevaluative when interpreting the behavior of locals. Seeks to update his or her perceptions and beliefs as new information arises.

The Cultural-Toughness Dimension

◆ Is able to adapt to the toughness of the specific culture (e.g., it may be more difficult for a Canadian expatriate to adapt in Nigeria than in England).

Source: Adapted from M. Mendenhall and G. Oddou, "The Dimensions of Expatriate Acculturation: A Review," *The Academy of Management Review* 10, no. 1 (1985): 39–47. Used by permission of the Academy of Management.

psychological tests and evaluation techniques, as well as to numerous instruments to measure stress levels and stress reducing programs. To assess the others-oriented dimension, assessors can solicit in-depth evaluations from a prospective expatriate's superiors, subordinates, friends and acquaintances. Regarding the perceptual dimension, there are numerous psychological tests available to measure the rigidity and flexibility of an individual's perceptual and evaluative tendencies. These tests include the Cognitive Rigidity Test, the F-test, the Guilford-Zimmerman Temperament Survey, and the Alport-Vernon Study of Values. The prospective expatriate's **cultural-toughness dimension** can be assessed on the basis of the toughness of the specific country in concert with the above needs. That is, the assessor should feel confident that the applicant's scores on the battery of evaluation scores are high enough to handle the specific country.[58]

Professor S. Ronen also identified a group of categories of attributes for expatriate success. The group includes the following: tolerance for ambiguity, behavioral flexibility, nonjudgmentalism, cultural empathy and low ethnocentrism, interpersonal skills, belief in the mission, interest in foreign experience, willingness to acquire new patterns of behavior and attitudes, adaptive and supportive spouse, stable marriage, and nonverbal communication skills.[59] A supportive spouse and a stable marriage are important because the expatriate will need someone with whom he or she can talk about his or her work frustrations—in the foreign country there may be many frustrations, and the spouse may be the only one available with whom the expatriate can talk about them. The above framework also applies to the evaluation and selection of third-country nationals, who, because they are being assigned to a foreign country, are in essence expatriates, and even to the evaluation of host-country locals who are being expatriated to the home office for development.

However, it should be pointed out that psychological testing is not without criticism. There is considerable debate among scholars and practitioners about the reliability and accuracy of tests in predicting cross-cultural adjustments.[60] Furthermore, since these tests were developed in the U.S., they may be "culture bound" and may have even less reliability and accuracy when applied to non-Americans.[61] Also, in some countries (Australia, for example) use of psychological tests is very controversial.[62]

Determining the effectiveness potential of expatriates is further inhibited by a nation's legal system. In some countries a candidate may not be asked about his or her religion, smoking habits, drug and alcohol consumption habits, and other such behaviors about which an assessor needs to know in order to make a determination as to whether or not the candidate will adapt in certain countries. For instance, an individual who needs to smoke and consume alcohol may not adapt well in some Middle East countries, such as Saudi Arabia.

Finding and Developing Global Expatriates

Many international business enterprises, especially global corporations, require a group of executives who are ready to perform effectively in foreign assignments when and where needed (in Chapter 1, this kind of expatriate was referred to as a **global manager**). Where do global corporations get such expatriate managers? Professor Cecil G. Howard identified a general recruitment and developmental process consisting of four sources: domestic operations; managers currently on a foreign assignment; external sources, including worldwide competitors; and educational institutions.[63]

Domestic Operations

A source available to international firms for recruiting and developing global expatriates is their home operations. The following are the steps an MNC can use when developing expatriate managers from its domestic operations:

1. Identify potential expatriate managers within the parent company at early stages of their careers. In other words, find out which young managers might do well in international assignments. To overcome the disadvantages of using host-country nationals (as discussed in Chapter 6) to manage local subsidiaries, before they make the appointment, many corporations first assign the local to headquarters for training and development. These individuals are thus excellent sources.

2. Prepare an individual development plan for each prospective expatriate manager. This entails conducting a training and developmental needs analysis, including discussions with the potential expatriate's supervisor and peers. (Development should include the characteristics identified in Figure 7–2.)

3. Give those selected as prospective expatriate managers training and skills development related to potential foreign assignments. The training and development should include practical on-the-job experience in a foreign site. (Practical Perspective 7–2 describes the development programs implemented by some international business enterprises.)

The domestic operations approach has at least three advantages: the MNC has a captive pool to tap; those selected are expected to be in tune with the corporate culture and its managerial philosophy; and the process of assigning those selected to foreign projects helps to eliminate those not really qualified for global managerial assignments. There are disadvantages, however. The process is quite costly and time-consuming, and there is a strong possibility that some of the trained executives will sell their newly acquired skills to another international business firm.

Managers Currently on Foreign Assignment

Another source available to corporations for recruiting and developing global expatriates is people working in their foreign subsidiaries. Using this approach involves the following steps:

PRACTICAL   PERSPECTIVE   7–2

Younger Managers Learn Global Skills

A growing number of global-minded U.S. companies are giving fast-track managers a global orientation much sooner in their careers. . . . "It's a pretty significant trend," says David Weeks, a researcher who is completing a Conference Board study of 130 large multinational companies in the U.S., Europe and Japan. The study found "a certain sense of urgency" among American companies about "trying to build an internationally experienced cadre of executives," Mr. Weeks says.

A number of European and Japanese corporate giants have already installed elaborate training and career-tracking mechanisms to develop such executives. Unless U.S. companies equip their best managers with global skills at younger ages, "they are going to come up short" in global competition, warns Michael Longua, Johnson & Johnson's director of international recruiting. . . .

American Express Co.'s Travel Related Services unit gives American business-school students summer jobs in which they work outside the U.S. for up to 10 weeks. [It] Also transfers junior managers with at least two years experience to other countries. Colgate-Palmolive Co. trains about 15 recent college graduates each year for 15 to 24 months prior to multiple overseas job stints. General Electric Co.'s aircraft-engine unit will expose selected midlevel engineers and managers to foreign language and cross-cultural training even though not all will live abroad.

Honda of America Manufacturing Inc. has sent about 42 U.S. supervisors and managers to the parent company in Tokyo for up to three years, after preparing them with six months of Japanese language lessons, cultural training and lifestyle orientation during work hours. PepsiCo Inc.'s international beverage division brings about 25 young foreign managers a year to the U.S. for one-year assignments in bottling plants. Raychem Corp. assigns relatively inexperienced Asian employees (from clerks through middle managers) to the U.S. for six months to two years.

Source: Excerpted from Joann S. Lublin, "Younger Managers Learn Global Skills," *The Wall Street Journal,* March 31, 1992, p. A1.

1. Survey eligible expatriate managers worldwide. It should be noted that the managers in the foreign subsidiaries do not necessarily have to be expatriates; they can be locals who have been developed or are being developed for local managerial assignments. Many international business enterprises, especially those with a multidomestic and global strategies, have training and development programs aimed at developing local managers. For example, Procter & Gamble asked the Chinese University of Hong Kong to develop a training program for young managers in its plant in Guangzhou, China. Japan's Matsushita's Human Development Center in Singapore trained more than 500 employees in 1990–1991.[64]
2. Identify the needs for further training and development for those who wish to fit a new and more demanding managerial role in the future.
3. Prepare independent development plans for those willing to fit the new managerial role.
4. Provide the skills and knowledge identified on the independent development plans.
5. Place expatriate managers in worldwide subsidiaries.

This approach, because the candidates are already working abroad, can be somewhat less expensive and less time-consuming than developing domestic talent, and they (other than the host-country nationals) have proven adaptability in a foreign culture. However, finding these individuals and administering and coordinating the development process can be a problem if the corporation's subsidiaries are geographically dispersed.

External Sources

Using this approach involves recruiting and developing people with foreign experience from outside sources. The steps in this recruitment and development process are as follows:

1. Recruit qualified individuals from competing and noncompeting companies, both at home and in foreign countries. Executive-search firms may be helpful in this respect.
2. After selection, identify the training and development they need to fit into the new corporate culture.
3. Prepare an individual development program.
4. Provide the required skills and knowledge.
5. Place them in strategic foreign management positions.

The advantages of this approach include the fact that the new employee brings seasoned foreign management experience and personal maturity, reducing training and development costs and time. However, the search can be very expensive—the executive search companies, also known as "headhunters," charge a very high finder's fee. And the new hiree may take a long time to fit in the new corporate culture—or he or she may not fit at all.

Educational Institutions

Another source for recruiting and developing global expatriates is colleges and universities. Many colleges and universities in the home country, especially in the United States, have recently implemented or are currently implementing programs aimed at internationalizing their students, including offering degrees in international business and programs encouraging students to undertake part of their college studies in a foreign nation. For example, Gillette International has implemented a program to groom executives to fill global management positions. Initially, Gillette worked with New York City–based AIESEC (an international student exchange program) in identifying students for recruitment into the program. Today, the personnel director and general manager for each of the company's worldwide operations are responsible for identifying the top business students in prestigious universities internationally.[65] (Appendix 7:1 presents a detailed description of Gillette's trainee program aimed at developing global managers.)

The college recruiter is, however, encouraged to become familiar with the college's international program. This is because the effective college international program should be designed to equip its students with professional skills, including cross-cultural sensitivity and linguistic skills. But this is not the case in all colleges. The programs in some colleges are designed to simply develop a narrow functional specialization and a parochial perspective to managing in a foreign culture.

EXPATRIATE PREPARATION PROGRAMS

Basically, before a selectee is sent to the foreign site, he or she needs extensive preparation. This means that international businesses require an **expatriate preparation program** and a program administrator who can effectively administer such a program. Fundamentally, the preparation program should consist of four phases: understanding the corporate international environment, pre-expatriation, expatriation, and repatriation.[66]

The Corporation's International Environment

Before he or she can properly administer an expatriation program, the **program administrator** must become totally familiar with:

1. The enterprise's foreign involvements, including operations, investments, business goals, and strategies.
2. The staffing needs of overseas operations, including qualifications, duties, the expected duration of the assignment, and the goals and objectives of the position. For example, is the expatriate needed to simply run the day-to-day operations, or to develop new operations, or to train locals for managerial positions, or to simultaneously run the

operations and develop locals? Each job may require different skills (this will be discussed more thoroughly in Chapter 11).

3. The environmental aspects of the nation where the assignment is to take place, such as geographic isolation, level of urbanization, economic development, culture, political and legal systems.

The above knowledge will enable the program administrator to: (a) better understand the organization's international commitments, (b) determine the skills, objectives, and relative hardships of foreign assignments, (c) make better selections for foreign positions, and (d) better judge the level of adjustment and readjustment necessary in each case.[67]

Pre-Expatriation

In the **pre-expatriation** phase, the selectee becomes involved in the preparation process. The objective of this phase is to make sure that:[68]

1. The individual has a complete understanding of the foreign assignment, including its purpose, goals, objectives, duties, and its relationship to his or her career objectives.
2. He or she is aware of the realities of expatriation, including the professional and personal problems foreign assignments often cause. This should include making the expatriate and family aware (but not "scared to death") of the potential psychological and emotional strains created by being separated from friends and other family members. In other words, the expatriate and family should be made aware of all the advantages and disadvantages of the foreign assignment.
3. The expatriate and his or her family are educated and oriented about their temporary foreign home before leaving. The orientation should include the elements discussed in the following paragraphs.

Cultural Briefing

This should include the country's cultural traditions, history, government, economy, living conditions (including foods, education, medical, and entertainment), climate, and clothing requirements. Books, maps, brochures, films, and slides would help in this respect.

Assignment Briefing

This briefing includes details about the length of the assignment, vacation policy, holidays, allowances, tax consequences, and repatriation policy, as well as the expatriate's tentative workplan, the basis of his or her evaluation, and his or her authority and degree of autonomy in the foreign operations.

Relocation Requirements

Shipping, packaging, storage, and home disposal and acquisition should be addressed.

Language Training

Introducing the selectee to the country's language is essential. Not only does it help in the communication process in the country, but it also helps him or her better understand the country's culture. The language training methods commonly used include instruction at a language school and do-it-yourself kits such as records, cassette recordings, and books.

Expatriation

The **expatriation** phase takes place while the expatriate is working in the foreign operations. It involves communication and information delivery. It is imperative that the home office:

1. Keep the expatriate well informed about domestic operations and plans—different time zones and the location of the assignment being out of the organizational mainstream make it easy for the home office to ignore the expatriate and make him or her feel professionally and personally isolated, thus increasing anxiety. Periodically bringing the expatriate to the home office for a meeting would help in this respect.
2. Review and discuss the expatriate's performance and career path. This should include reemphasizing the assignment's purpose and what the expatriate can expect to gain upon returning home. This is feedback and motivation.

Repatriation

After a lengthy assignment in a foreign country, the **repatriate** and the repatriate family will encounter a high level of pressure and anxiety. The longer the assignment, the greater the pressure and anxiety. Upon the expatriate's arrival home, the following must be done:[69]

1. Provide intensive organizational retraining for the repatriate. The retraining should provide information on policy and procedures changes, shifts in corporate strategy, new and promoted personnel, and a detailed description of his or her new position. (Of course, if the expatriate phase has been carried out effectively, this would not be too difficult.) Furthermore, he or she should not be pushed into a new position and be expected to produce immediately, but should be given ample time to adjust. Also, the new position should, as much

    as possible, be challenging and utilize the skills acquired in the foreign assignment.

2. Provide some form of financial counseling for the family, especially when there is a reduction of income.

3. Provide housing assistance. If the repatriate has not sold his or her house and instead rented it, help him arrange to have the house vacated and prepared for the family to move into it. If he or she has sold the house, help him or her obtain a new one, including a low-interest loan, a lump-sum bonus, or compensation for increased housing prices.

4. So that the repatriate's children can continue receiving the quality education which they received in the foreign country, assist the repatriate financially when similar schooling at home is more expensive.

5. Some repatriates and repatriate families experience personal and psychological problems readjusting. Help pay for psychological consultation.

EXPATRIATE COMPENSATION

Ineffective **expatriate compensation** can also lead to expatriate failures. Thus, international firms need to establish policy for effective management of expatriate compensation. To do so requires knowledge of the foreign country's laws, customs, environment, and employment practices, as well as with the effects of currency exchange fluctuations and inflation on compensation. And, within the context of changing political, economic, and social conditions, it also requires an understanding of why certain allowances are necessary and must be provided. For example, an assignment in an hostile or undesirable environment would require greater compensation than an assignment to a friendly, desirable environment.

    Basically, expatriate compensation policies seek to satisfy numerous objectives:[70]

- ◆ The policy should be consistent and fair in its treatment of all categories of expatriate employees.
- ◆ The policy must work to attract and retain expatriates in the areas where the corporation has the greatest need.
- ◆ The policy should facilitate the transfer of expatriates in the most cost-effective manner.
- ◆ The policy should be consistent with the overall strategy and structure of the organization.
- ◆ The compensation should serve to motivate employees.

When designing the policy, a decision must be made about whether to establish an overall policy for all employees or distinguish between home-country nationals (expatriates) and host-country and third-country nationals. Currently, it is common for international businesses to distinguish between them; they even distinguish between the types of expatriates—for example, different policies may be set on the basis of length of assignment or on the type of function to be carried out.[71] In all cases, the policy should be based on the notion that the expatriate must not suffer a loss due to his or her transfer.

Expatriate Base Salary

MNCs tend to use the expatriate's home-country base salary as the primary component for determining his or her package of compensation for undertaking the foreign assignment. They tend to use third- and home-country nationals' home salary base to determine their compensation when they are selected for the assignment. Listed below is a comparison of managers' annual pretax compensation (as of 1991) in some Asian countries. The amounts, which are estimates of total compensation for middle managers of MNCs in the region, are not adjusted for variations in cost of living.[72] (Of course, these costs are likely to be higher today.)

Country	Annual Pretax Compensation
Hong Kong	$67,939
South Korea	$62,421
Taiwan	$60,388
Singapore	$57,110
Malaysia	$37,781
Thailand	$36,057
Indonesia	$29,440

It would thus be less expensive for a Hong Kong company to hire a host-country manager for its subsidiary in Indonesia or a third-country manager from Thailand or Malaysia—of course, other factors, as discussed in Chapter 6, must be taken into consideration.

The conditions that force compensation policies to differ from those used for home-country expatriates include inflation-cost of living, housing, security, school costs, and taxation.[73] Furthermore, home-country expatriates often require a salary premium as an inducement to accept the foreign assignment or to endure the hardships of the foreign transfer. In the United States, when an international business enterprise has determined the type of hardship, it can refer to the U.S. Department of State's *Hardship Post Differentials Guidelines* to ascertain the appropriate level of premium compensation.

It should be noted that this practice of international businesses paying a higher salary to expatriate managers than to host- or third-country managers can demotivate the former two categories, especially when they have an equal level of authority and responsibility. Thus, a problem currently confronting MNCs is how to deal effectively with such inequities. Some management thinkers feel that MNCs should have a global standard policy relating to compensation; that is, regardless of the varying costs of living existing in countries, all of the corporation's managers in all countries should be compensated on the basis of a standard global salary range based on the level of authority and responsibility. This, of course, is highly arguable and extremely difficult to implement.

Taxation

For the expatriate, a foreign assignment can mean being **double-taxed**—by the home country and in the foreign country governments. (This problem, however, is mitigated in the United States by Section 911 of the Internal Revenue Service Code, which has an exclusion provision permitting a $70,000 deduction.) International firms are subject to varying tax rates throughout the globe. The rates are different from country to country, and they change within countries from time to time. For example, the maximum marginal rate in Belgium was 72 percent in 1985 and 70.8 percent in 1988; in the United States it was 50 percent in 1985 and 33 percent in 1988.[74] (Current rates may be different.) A corporation's compensation packages must consider how specific practices can be adjusted in each nation to provide, within the context of the corporation's overall policy, the most tax-effective, appropriate rewards for expatriate, host-country, and third-country managers.

Benefits

Benefits such as pension plans, medical, and social security are difficult to transfer across national borders. When considering expatriate benefits, international enterprises need to consider numerous issues, including:[75]

- ◆ Whether or not to maintain expatriates in home-country programs, particularly if the company does not receive a tax deduction for it.
- ◆ Whether companies have the option of enrolling expatriates in host-country benefit programs and-or making up the difference in coverage.
- ◆ Whether host-country legislation regarding termination affects benefit entitlements.
- ◆ Whether expatriates should receive home-country or host-country social security benefits.
- ◆ Whether benefits should be maintained on a home-country or host-country basis, who is responsible for the cost, whether other bene-

fits should be used to offset any shortfall in coverage, and whether home-country benefit programs should be exported to local nationals in foreign countries.

U.S. firms' home-country expatriates generally remain under their **home-company's benefit program.**[76] Relative to social security, there is an agreement between the U.S., Canada, and several European countries which eliminates dual social security coverage of citizens from one country working in another on a temporary basis. In some nations, however, expatriates must participate in local social security programs. In these cases, the international companies normally incur the additional costs.[77]

Allowances

International businesses generally pay expatriates certain allowances. These include cost-of-living, housing, education, and relocation allowances. **Cost-of-living allowances** pay the expatriate for differences in expenses between the home and the foreign country. Housing allowances aim to help the expatriate maintain his or her home-country living standards. Education allowances aim to give assurance to the expatriate that his or her children will receive at least the same education they would receive in the home country. Relocation allowances usually pay for the expatriate's moving, shipping, and storage expenses, temporary living expenses, and other related expenses.[78]

The preceding discussions suggest that international business enterprises tend to apply an ethnocentric compensation policy—the home-country expatriate, as previously indicated, receives compensation and benefits that are different from those received by third-country and host-country managers. However, as companies become more and more globally oriented, they will begin to rely more and more on third-country managers to manage global operations. These firms will thus begin applying a geocentric compensation policy, that is, a more globally uniform compensation and benefits package.

SUMMARY

This chapter has discussed several reasons why expatriates fail, including the foreign country's physical and social environment, varying technical sophistication, gender, inadequate repatriation programs, and the pitfalls in the HR planning function. Based on Japanese, European, and U.S. MNCs' expatriation practices, a framework for reducing expatriate failure was presented. Other ways to reduce expatriate failure were also introduced, including a framework for selecting the right person for the foreign assignment. Also presented were frameworks for finding and developing effective expatriates, for administrating expatriate programs, and for administrating expatriate compensation.

Key Terms

1. Expatriates
2. Adaptation problems
3. Differences in technical sophistication
4. Company–country conflicting objectives and policies
5. Visibly constrained authority of expatriate managers
6. Cultural bias against women
7. Repatriation
8. Repatriation programs
9. Missed opportunities
10. Skills acquired in foreign country not used at home
11. Reverse culture shock
12. Human resource managers play a less active role in companies' overall planning process
13. Inadequate selection criteria for foreign assignments
14. Inability of expatriate's family to adapt to foreign environment
15. Lack of adequate training for foreign assignments
16. Expatriates need time to adapt
17. The initial, disillusionment, culture shock, and positive adjustment phrases
18. Underutilization of women as expatriates
19. Lower incidents of expatriate failure experienced by Japanese MNCs than by U.S. MNCs
20. The "spirit of internationalism"
21. Reducing expatriate failure
22. Selecting the right expatriate
23 Assessing expatriates' effectiveness potential
24. Cultural-toughness dimension
25. Finding and developing global managers
26. Expatriation programs and program administrators
27. Pre-expatriation, expatriation, and repatriation programs
28. Expatriate compensation policy
29. Double taxation
30. Home-country's benefit package
31. Cost-of-living allowances

Discussion Questions and Exercises

1. Discuss the fundamental reasons why expatriates fail.
2. You are the manager of the international HRM function for a firm whose top management is assigning an executive from the home office to head one of the firm's foreign subsidiaries. Relative to the cultural adaptation phases, what would you advise the top management?

3. What are the international staffing implications drawn from the Japanese, European, and U.S. MNCs' expatriate practices?

4. Referring back to exercise 2, what question would you ask the top management to be sure that the right expatriate has been selected?

5. To be effective, consultants agree, expatriates require certain characteristics. What are those characteristics?

6. Discuss the significance of the self-oriented, others-oriented, perceptual, and cultural-toughness dimensions in the selection of expatriates.

7. Discuss the four sources for recruiting and developing a pool of global expatriates.

8. Discuss the pre-expatriation, expatriation, and repatriation administration programs.

9. What type of knowledge is required for the effective administration of expatriate compensation?

10. What is meant by "a global standard policy" relating to compensation?

Assignment

Contact the manager of the HRM function for an MNC. Ask him or her to describe his or her company's policy relating to expatriate development. Prepare a short report for your class.

Managing Expatriate Employees

CASE 7–1

Source: Eileen Daspin, "Managing Expatriate Employees," *Management Review* (July 1985): 47–49. Copyright © 1985, Eileen Daspin. All rights reserved. Reprinted with permission.

Pamela Paley has worked for Citicorp since 1981. She started as an assistant manager in the commercial real estate and finance division when she was 25. Today [1985], instead of handling 15 accounts like her peers in the New York office, who have no more staff than a secretary and an assistant, Paley is the director of commercial credit for Citicorp-Citibank Thailand. She has ten people reporting to her, has virtual autonomy in making decisions, designs credit card programs for Diners Club and Mercantile Bank, and is charged with developing Citibank's consumer credit card strategies for an entire country. Paley estimates that, to date, her one-year tour in Bangkok has accelerated her career by at least four years.

"The exposure has been tremendous," she says. "It's an opportunity I would never have had in New York because we are so big and departmentalized. I've had the opportunity to take the ball and run with it. Things are already set up in the States. Here, I'm doing it." Paley and her husband Kenneth relocated to Bangkok when he was asked to open the Chesebrough-Ponds' Thai marketing office in 1983. With the cost-of-living allowance provided them by their respective companies, the Paleys can afford to belong to a country club in Bangkok, and have a live-in maid and a chauffeur. It is a lifestyle they both readily admit would be beyond their means in the U.S.

The Paleys' story is not atypical, and explains better than any recruiting brochure the allure of international work. For most expatriates, a "plum" foreign assignment can bring untold opportunities to advance financially and professionally, travel, meet new people, and be exposed to different cultures. It can also confer the instant status that comes only with being an American living abroad. Says Walter Sonyi, the executive vice-president and partner of Goodrich and Sherwood, a management consulting firm, "Executives living abroad are kingpins. They are sent to countries to open or run an entire office; they develop broad management skills; they are furnished housing, maids, company cars and fancy offices." But living abroad is not always non-stop glamour and career advancement. The same expatriates who transfer overseas to visit exotic places and bring American ingenuity to the far corners of the earth are often unprepared for the cultural gulfs that, if ignored, can throttle both business deals and social relationships.

"The whole culture in Thailand is so different," says Kenneth Paley, "even their way of thinking. To get a marketing project done will take three to four times as long [as it would in the U.S.]." Something as simple as a translation can create huge problems: It took one year and three different advertising agencies to come up with a suitable Thai equivalent for Vaseline Intensive Care, the Chesebrough body lotion product. . . . Learning to deal with such subtle social and cultural differences cannot be overemphasized, says Greg Edwards, senior personnel services representative at McDonnell-Douglas in St. Louis. "You have to learn their customs." . . . To prepare expatriates for the shock of discovering that touching a Thai on the head is considered a major insult, or that Australian grocery stores close at one o'clock on Saturday and don't reopen until Monday morning, McDonnell-Douglas shows a series of films to introduce employees to ways of interacting with different cultures. The series includes films on bridging the culture gap, how to deal with culture shock, family problems, and how to make reentry into the U.S. as painless as possible.

Aside from cultural problems, expatriates face other adjustment dilemmas abroad. Some feel that what they gain in autonomy, broad management skills, and independence, they lose in technical expertise. "The big disadvantage to working overseas is that you don't know what is going on in America," says Walter Sonyi. "The perception is that American marketing know-how moves at such a rapid pace that if you are out of its mainstream, your skills are obsolete." But William Gembus, who spent five years overseas in Brussels and Germany with the accounting firm Price Waterhouse, disagrees with that point of view: "There's more to jobs than technical expertise. The individual becomes broader culturally and gains unique management experience."

In general, most people accept overseas assignments to develop broad skills and get hands-on, nuts-and-bolts experience that would be impossible to gain in a large operation. With small offices and little support staff, executives are forced to become involved in all aspect of the business. They learn how an organization runs and how to run an organization. . . . But living abroad can also put strains on personal relations. Most expatriate couples transfer overseas when the husband secures an international assignment. Since hiring for foreign executive-level positions is done in the U.S., unless the wife can find a job while they are still in America, she will likely remain unemployed for the entire length of the overseas tour. The Paleys say they were lucky that Citibank was able to create a position for Pamela in Bangkok. "We met a lot of people who can't believe we both have good jobs," says Kenneth Paley. "You see a lot of couples that come over in which the husband has a job and the wife doesn't, and it can be very tough domestically." In the absence of familiar support systems and friends, many marriages suffer and break up.

To help prepare employees to deal with potential problems of working and living abroad, some U.S. companies have developed sophisticated screening and training programs for the executives they send overseas. McDonnell-Douglas, which sends abroad employees at every level from mechanic to vice-president, began its formal screening process when it started up operations in Saudi Arabia. The program involves a process of close questioning about personal habits, political and religious beliefs, family situations, medical histories, and alcohol or drug abuse problems. "We try to talk to people to see if there are red flags of concern, either for the company or individual," says McDonnell's Greg Edwards. "We weed situations out." One aspect the McDonnell-Douglas program emphasizes that individuals and other companies often ignore is reentry. Most expatriates never even consider that coming home after a long absence could be as difficult as going abroad was in the first place. "The trouble starts when they come back to the United States," says Walter Sonyi of Goodrich & Sherwood, which handles out-placement for expatriates reentering the U.S. job market. "They were big shots abroad. Back home, they're nobodies. They go from an affluent lifestyle to one of comparative poverty. They've often lost some of the skills that made then valuable to go overseas. They are no longer on the cutting edge of their industry. . . ."

Unlike other executives, who are usually offered outplacement services because of personality differences with superiors or because of performance problems, expatriates are usually the victims of an "out of sight, out of mind" mentality. When there are no jobs waiting for them, they are offered outplacement as "compensation" in addition to the normal severance package. . . . To avoid problems such as this, McDonnell-Douglas encourages its employees to come home at least once a year, and provides round-trip airfare for their overseas employees. They also encourage individuals to establish contacts within their departments. While they are away, they can correspond with this person and keep their name "alive" in a firm. "International assignments tend to be on the periphery of the activities of most U.S. companies," says William Gembus. "There isn't a great deal of focus on the careers of international assignees. Naturally, when you're not in the mainstream, it can create problems when you come back. Lost political connections can hamper adjustment. I suppose most companies should think more about those adjustment aspects."

At the same time, these pressures take their tolls on marriages. In the year they've been part of Thailand, Pamela and Kenneth Paley have befriended two couples whose marriages split up under reentry tensions. "One couple got back home to San Francisco after having had a great lifestyle in the Far East. They faced the San Francisco housing market and couldn't fit a nice house into a small apartment." When added to hundreds of other problems they encountered in their homecoming, the couple split up. The overseas assignment, then, is an attractive way for an individual to advance rapidly and learn, but it is not an assignment without risks. They are, however, avoidable. Preparation serves all parties involved.

QUESTIONS

1. Based on what you have learned in this chapter with respect to the global expatriate, in what way is Pamela Paley's experience valuable to Citicorp?
2. How does Pamela Paley's experience contradict one of the reasons top-notch executives sometimes give for refusing a foreign assignment?
3. What are the major points the article brings out about expatriate preparation programs? How do they compare with what you have learned in this chapter?
4. Walter Sonyi said that, "The big disadvantage to working overseas is that you don't know what is going on in America." Based on what you have learned in this chapter, how would you solve this problem?

Notes

1. Neal Nadler, "How Do You Insure Success of Managers Going Abroad?" *Training and Development Journal* (December 1985): 24.

2. Rosalie L. Tung, "Selection and Training of Personnel for Overseas Assignments," *Columbia Journal of World Business* 16, no. 1 (Spring 1981): 69–78.

3. E. Harari and Y. Zeira, "Training Expatriates for Assignments in Japan," *California Management Review* 20, no. 4 (1977): 56–61.

4. D. A. Heenan, "The Corporate Expatriate: Assignment to Ambiguity," *Columbia Journal of World Business* (May–June 1970): 49–54.

5. A. J. Almaney, "Intercultural Communication and the MNC Executive," *Columbia Journal of World Business* 9, no. 4 (1974): 23–28.

6. A. Rahim, "A Model for Developing Key Expatriate Executives," *Personnel Journal* (April 1983): 312–317.

7. Heenan, "The Corporate Expatriate."

8. F. E. Cotton, "Some Interdisciplinary Problems in Transferring Technology and Management," *Management International Review* 13, no. 1 (1973): 71–77.

9. Rahim, "A Model for Developing Key Expatriate Executives."

10. Heenan, "The Corporate Expatriate."

11. D. N. Israeli, M. Banai, and Y. Zeira, "Women Executives in MNC Subsidiaries," *California Management Review* 23, no. 1 (1980): 53–63.

12. J. Alex Murray, "International Personnel Repatriation: Culture Shock in Reverse," *MSU Business Topics* 2, no. 3 (1973): 59–66.

13. Nancy J. Adler, "Re-entry: Managing Cross-Cultural Transitions" (paper presented at the annual meeting of the Academy of International Business, October 1980).

14. L. Clague and N. B. Krupp, "International Personnel: The Repatriation Problem," *The Personnel Administrator* (April 1978): 32.

15. See Rosalie L. Tung, "Career Issues in International Assignments," *The Academy of Management Executive* 2, no. 3 (1988): 241–244.

16. Cecil G. Howard, "The Expatriate Manager and the Role of the MNC," *Personnel Journal* 10, no. 10 (October 1980): 830–844.

17. Michael G. Harvey, "The Other Side of Foreign Assignments: Dealing with the Repatriation Dilemma," *Columbia Journal of World Business* 17, no. 1 (Spring 1982): 53.

18. D. W. Kendall, "Repatriation: An Ending and a Beginning," *Business Horizons* (November-December 1981): 23.

19. Harvey, "The Other Side of Foreign Assignments."

20. Rosalie L. Tung, *Strategic Management of Human Resources in the Multinational Enterprise* (New York: John Wiley & Sons, 1984).

21. P. Lorange and D. C. Murphy, "Strategy and Human Resources: Concepts and Practices," *Human Resource Management* 22, no. 1–2 (1983): 111–113.

22. R. L. Desatnick and M. L. Bennett, *Human Resource Management in the Multinational Company* (New York: Nichols, 1978).

23. Tung, "Selection and Training of Personnel."

24. Edwin L. Miller, "The Selection Decision for an International Assignment: A Study of Decision-Makers' Behavior," *Journal of International Business Studies* 3, no. 2 (1972): 49–65.

25. Tung, "Selection and Training of Personnel."

26. G. M. Harvey, "The Executive Family: An Overlooked Variable in International Assignments," *Columbia Journal of World Business* (Spring 1985): 84–91.

27. Rosalie L. Tung, "Selection and Training Procedures of U.S., European, and Japanese Multinationals," *California Management Review* 25, no. 1 (1982): 57–71.

28. Tung, "Selection and Training of Personnel."

29. Tung, "Selection and Training Procedures."

30. Harari and Zeira, "Training Expatriates."

31. For extensive coverage of this topic, refer to Charlene Marmer Solomon, "How Does Your Global Talent Measure Up? (International Personnel Performance Measures)," *Personnel Journal* 73 no. 10 (October 1994): 96–108.

32. Harari and Zeira, "Training Expatriates."

33. J. T. Gullahorn and J. E. Gullahorn, "An Extension of the U-Curve Hypothesis," *Journal of Social Sciences* 19, no. 3 (1963): 33–47.

34. Nancy J. Adler, "Cross-Cultural Management Research: The Ostrich and the Trend," *The Academy of Management Review* 8, no. 3 (1983): 226–232.

35. Ibid.

36. Tung, "Selection and Training of Personnel."

37. Tung, "Selection and Training Procedures."

38. J. C. Baker, K. Ryans, and G. Howard, *International Business Classics* (Lexington, MA: D.C. Heath and Co., 1988), pp. 283–295.

39. Ibid.

40. Ibid.

41. Ibid.

42. Tung, "Selection and Training Procedures."

43. Ibid.

44. Tung, *Strategic Management of Human Resources.*

45. Rosalie L. Tung, *The New Expatriate* (Cambridge, MA: Ballinger, 1988), pp. 161–172.

46. Ibid.

47. Ibid.

48. Adapted from Rosalie L. Tung, "Human Resource Planning in Japanese Multinationals: A Model for U.S. Firms," *Journal of International Business Studies* 15, no. 2 (Fall 1984): 139–150.

49. Tung, *The New Expatriate.*

50. Paul E. Illman, *Developing Overseas Managers and Managers Overseas* (New York: Ama Com, 1980), p. 15.

51. David Pulatie, "How Do You Ensure Success of Managers Going Abroad?" *Training and Development Journal* (December 1985): 22–23.

52. Tung, "Selection and Training of Personnel."

53. P. J. Dowling and R. S. Schuler, *International Dimensions of Human Resource Management* (Boston: PWS-KENT Publishing, 1990), p. 53.

54. Charles Siler, "Recruiting Overseas Executives," *Overseas Business* (Winter 1990): 31.

55. Ibid.

56. M. Mendenhall and G. Oddou, "The Dimensions of Expatriate Acculturation: A Review," *The Academy of Management Review* 10, no. 1 (1985): 39–47.

57. For another framework on assessing expatriate candidates refer to Charlene Marmer Solomon, "Staff Selection Impacts Global Success," *Personnel Journal* (January 1994): 88–101.

58. Mendenhall and Oddou, "The Dimensions of Expatriate Acculturation."

59. S. Ronen, "Training the International Assignee," in *Training and Career Development,* ed. I. Goldstein (San Francisco: Jossey-Bass, 1989), p. 438.

60. I. Torbioro, *Living Abroad: Personnel Adjustment and Personnel Policy in the Overseas Setting* (New York: John Wiley, 1982).

61. H. L. Willis, "Selection for Employment in Developing Countries," *Personnel Administrator* 29, no. 7 (1984): 55.

62. P. J. Dowling, "Psychological Testing in Australia: An Overview and an Assessment," in *Australia Personnel Management: A Reader,* ed. G. Palmer (Sidney: Macmillan, 1988): 123–135.

63. Cecil G. Howard, "Profile of the 21st Century Manager," *HR Magazine* (June 1992): 97–100.

64. Ford S. Worthy, "You Can't Grow If You Can't Manage," *Fortune,* June 3, 1991, p. 86.

65. Jennifer J. Laabs, "How Gillette Grooms Global Talent," *Personnel Journal* (August 3, 1993): 64–76.

66. N. Sleveking, K. Anchor, and R. C. Marston, "Selecting and Preparing Expatriate Employees," *Personnel Journal* (March 1981): 197–200. See also Solomon, "Staff Selection Impacts Global Success"; and J. L. Calof and Paul W. Beamish, "The Right Attitude For International Success," *Business Quarterly* (Autumn 1994): 105–110.

67. Harvey, "The Other Side of Foreign Assignments," p. 54.

68. Sources: R. L. Thornton and M. K. Thornton, "Personnel Problems in 'Carry the Flag' Missions in Foreign Assignments," *Business Horizons* (January–February 1995): 59–65; Harvey, "The Other Side of Foreign Assignments," p. 56; Cecil G. Howard, "How Relocation Abroad Affects Expatriates' Family Life," *Personnel Administrator* (November 1980): 71; Michael A. Conway, "Reducing Expatriate Failure Rates," *Personnel Administrator* (July 1984): 31–34; David M. Noer, *Multinational People Management* (Bureau of National Affairs, Inc., 1975).

69. Sources: Harvey, "The Other Side of Foreign Assignments," p. 58; Clague and Krupp, "International Personnel: The Repatriation Problem," p. 32.

70. Dowling and Schuler, *The International Dimensions of Human Resource Management,* p. 117.

71. Ibid.

72. Cited in Ford S. Worthy, "You Can't Grow If You Can't Manage," p. 84.

73. Dowling and Schuler, *International Dimensions of Human Resource Management*, pp. 120–121.

74. Ibid., p. 124.

75. Ibid., p. 125.

76. Ibid.

77. Ibid., p. 126.

78. Ibid., p. 129.

Appendix 7:1   *How Gillette Grooms Global Talent*

Source: Jennifer J. Laabs, "How Gillette Grooms Global Talent," *Personnel Journal* (August 3, 1993): 64-76. Copyright August 1993. Reprinted with permission from ACC Communications, *Personnel Journal*. All rights reserved.

Finding managers to run international operations can be difficult. Gillette takes a more proactive approach. In anticipation of future hiring needs, the company has implemented an international trainee program that develops managers who have a global mind-set.

As I sat down to discuss Gillette's strategy for developing global managers at its international headquarters, I couldn't help thinking that the future of global business management was sitting right across the table from me. To my right sat Christopher Makhele from South Africa. Opposite me, sat Heidi Rosser from New Zealand. Next to her was Suzana Naik from India. To my left was Kirill Matveev from Russia.

Although the city was Boston, it seemed as if the day's agenda should have centered on world relations or some other intriguing international topic. Rather, the subject of our meeting was to discuss Gillette's international-trainee program—a unique strategy that the organization uses to develop young managers to work in Gillette's operations worldwide.

In the mid-'80s, Gillette made a significant recruitment and management-development decision. In addition to parachuting high-priced executives in on a just-in-time basis to supply talent for its global operations, the company decided to develop managers internally. Nine years ago, Gillette's international human resources department implemented its international-trainee program. The program supplies the company with a steady stream of managerial talent from within its own ranks.

Since the program started, 113 trainees have passed through the program on their way to Gillette jobs worldwide. Of those 113 graduate trainees, 60 still are working for Gillette—a 53% retention rate. Trainees who have *graduated* from the program have returned to work in Gillette facilities in their home countries, later to become part of the organization's global management team. Many graduates have risen within the ranks to such positions as general manager, controller, production manager and personnel director.

Gillette's international-trainee program helps the company meet its need for internationally minded employees, allowing it to succeed in the world marketplace. For creating and implementing this outstanding business strategy, PERSONNEL JOURNAL has awarded Gillette the 1993 PERSONNEL JOURNAL Optimas Award in the *Global Outlook* category.

GILLETTE'S RAPID EXPANSION CREATES A NEED FOR MANAGERS

Gillette is a globally focused, consumer-products company that has had more than 90 years' experience in the international marketplace. The firm competes in three major consumer businesses: personal grooming products for both men and women, stationery products, and small electrical appliances. Some of the company's products include brand names as Braun™, Oral-B™, Jafra™, Liquid Paper™ and Paper Mate™. Gillette distributes its products through wholesalers, retailers and agents in more than 200 countries and territories worldwide.

The company holds 60% of the domestic razor-blade market, but has expanded steadily its blade market share overseas. In the past two years, Gillette has created, through joint ventures and acquisitions, a nearly captive market in China and India. During 1992, Gillette entered into joint ventures with razor-blade companies in Russia, Poland and China. Gillette also is rolling out its Braun and Oral-B products in Eastern Europe and Asia.

The organization continues to expand internationally by tapping into other new and existing markets. Its growth in markets abroad has continued to outpace its solid performance in the U.S. International markets now generate approximately 70% of Gillette's total sales and operating profit. This figure has grown by six percentage points in the past five years.

In his April 1993 address to stockholders, Gillette Chairman Alfred M. Zeien confirms the company's plans for further expansion: "Each of the core businesses is on the same aggressive growth track in heading to the year 2000." Currently Gillette has 57 manufacturing facilities in 28 countries. More than 75% of its employees work outside the U.S. This rapid expansion has created a need for individuals specifically trained to work in Gillette operations. Through strategic planning, the company already has a training program in place to supply the necessary employees.

THE INTERNATIONAL-TRAINEE PROGRAM BEGAN WITH INTERNS

Gillette's international-trainee program first started in 1983, when the company hired students from countries outside the U.S. to come to Boston as interns. New York City-based AIESEC (an international student-exchange program) helped Gillette identify the students. At the time, Gillette's reasons were purely philanthropic. After a few years, however, the company's HR staff realized that some of the student interns took positions with Gillette in their home countries after graduation.

At the same time, Gillette was expanding its operations in Latin America and lacked English-speaking, entry-level managers to fill positions in those countries. After a few years, Frank O'Connell, vice president of human resources for Gillette International, realized that he could turn the internship program into a traineeship program. The objective was to bring recent graduates to Boston specifically to groom them for Gillette jobs in their home countries. For a few years, O'Connell, who initiated the program, continued to identify foreign students through AIESEC. Now the personnel director and general manager for each of the company's worldwide operations are responsible for identifying the top business students in prestigious universities internationally.

What do they look for in prospective trainees? Trainees must be:

- University graduates from a business background
- Adaptable, having good social skills
- Younger than 30 years old
- Mobile and internationally career-oriented
- Single
- Fluent in English
- Enthusiastic and aggressive.

Junior trainees typically work at the Gillette subsidiaries in their home countries for six months. After that, Gillette management may choose to transfer them to one of the firm's three international headquarters for 18 months. The headquarters are in Boston, London and Singapore. The assignments usually depend on which world region their subsidiaries fall into.

Gillette now also hires senior trainees—individuals who have had more than two years' experience working for Gillette. While in training, trainees get $1,000 (net) per month, paid housing and transportation to and from work, medical insurance, tuition reimbursement, vacations and bonuses.

Gillette has four primary divisions and subsidiaries. Its divisions and subsidiaries are: the North Atlantic Group, the Stationery Products Group, the Diversified Group and the International Group. The International Group makes and markets the company's shaving, personal-care and stationery products and staffs the operations throughout the world, except for Western Europe and North America. Gillette's International Group consists of three geographic regions: 1) Latin America, Africa, Middle East; 2) Eastern European; and 3) Asian Pacific. The Asian Pacific headquarters are in Singapore. The headquarters for the Africa, Middle East, Russia and Eastern European areas are in London. The company's Latin-American and International headquarters are in Boston.

The trainee program is essentially the same in each headquarters location, although currently there are fewer trainees in London and Singapore than in Boston, where the program originated.

There currently are 28 students in the program. Four are in London, three are in Singapore and 21 are in Boston. The trainees come from Argentina, Brazil, China, Colombia, Egypt, Guatemala, India, Indonesia, Malaysia, Morocco, New Zealand, Pakistan, Peru, Poland, Russia, South Africa, Turkey and Venezuela.

The intent of the program isn't to fill short-term vacancies, according to O'Connell. He says that his objective is to hire and develop people who want careers with global proportions. "We're looking for people who look at international assignments as a challenge, not as a burden," says O'Connell.

Once they hire on at Gillette, program graduates usually work in their local Gillette facility for six months. After that, based on their performance up to that point, trainees may spend 18 months at one of the three Gillette headquarters. Upon completion of their terms, graduates return to their home countries to take entry-level-manager positions. If the graduates continue to be successful, they usually move on to assignments in other countries. Eventually, they end up back in their home countries as general managers or senior operating managers.

"Clearly, we're looking for these people to be our next generation of expatriates," O'Connell says. Many who have graduated from the training program five to six years ago now hold mid- to senior-management positions within Gillette. Beyond expatriate assignments, the company looks toward these individuals as the organization's future senior international leaders.

Expatriate experience is common throughout the organization. Of the 40 top Gillette executives, approximately 80% have had at least one foreign assignment. More than half of these executives have worked in at least three countries. From 1985 to 1992, more than 470 employees participated in more than 660 expatriate assignments. Today, the 269 employees on expatriate assignment represent 38 home countries and 47 host countries.

This kind of international experience makes better managers, according to Gillette executives. Zeien also stated in the shareholder address: "I contend that the transferability of management is the glue that holds the various parts of the company together." Gillette typically shares skills and resources among business units to optimize performance.

The trainee program's goal is to develop talented individuals to work in all the company's facilities worldwide. However, the focus of the program for the past few years has been on recruiting managers for its operations in developing countries. This coincides with the company's expansion into those areas.

"If we didn't have this program, we wouldn't be as successful in those developing countries," O'Connell explains. Gillette considers its manager trainees the second level of *bench strength* of its international management team.

Before implementing this program, Gillette didn't put as much effort into developing managers from the ground up as it does today. Although there always has been a need for managers who have had international experience, the firm's heavy expansion into many different countries has created a greater need for them during the past seven years.

"The program has been instrumental in helping us expand geographically," says Gaston (Tony) R. Levy, executive VP for Gillette's International Group. Levy says that he thinks that this program should continue indefinitely because the organization continually needs good managers.

Although Gillette had a long-time presence in such areas as Western Europe and Central America, it didn't begin breaking ground in the areas of Asia, Africa, the Middle East and Eastern Europe until the past few years. "Where are the Polish, Russian or Chinese managers going to come from?" O'Connell asks. "They certainly aren't going to come from here [in Boston]." Gillette needs managers who know how to work effectively in those countries.

Gillette has just entered into a joint venture with a company in Shanghai, China. To fill the seven managerial positions that will be available there, O'Connell says that he'll have to pull managers from other countries, such as Australia, England and France. He says that he's hoping that some of the former trainees will be able to step into the positions that these people have left behind and can hit the ground running. "We would like the companies in those countries managed by people who are familiar with Gillette," O'Connell says.

He adds, "It's a way of eliminating the need to hire expensive U.S. expatriates, but it takes time. It takes from five to 10 years before we see these people rising into the middle- to senior-management ranks of our overseas operations."

Although it costs $20,000 to $25,000 per trainee per year, expatriates can cost five to 10 times that. The total trainee-program budget in Boston alone is $1 million per year. O'Connell estimates that he could hire only three expatriates for that amount of money. Although it may take longer to develop employees in this way, he says that the cost is worth it to Gillette. "This is the core of our international recruiting. All of our efforts and resources are directed toward this program," O'Connell says.

TRAINEES PERFORM REAL JOBS WHILE ON ASSIGNMENT

The international trainees perform jobs that someone else would have to fill if they weren't there. O'Connell estimates that if the 21 trainees who currently are on assignment in Boston were gone tomorrow, the company would have to hire 10 to 12 people to replace them. As some of the lower-level assistant positions in the company's headquarters become vacant, O'Connell works with other managers to fill those spots with trainees rather than local professionals.

For example, one Boston-based financial analyst recently had received a promotion into another job within Gillette. Rather than recruiting a local professional to fill the financial-analyst position, O'Connell probably will bring in two trainees from developing markets.

Convincing managers to take trainees hasn't always been easy. "In the beginning, I used to beg the managers here to take a trainee," O'Connell says. "They often would say, 'No. I don't have time to wet-nurse some young kid. We're moving too fast.'" As time passed and managers worked with trainees, they began to see not only the immediate value of the trainees but also their long-term value to the organization as a whole. Gillette now has made working with trainees part of many manager's job descriptions. "Now they come to my office and say, 'Jose is about to return to Colombia in five months. Where's his replacement? I can't live without someone,'" O'Connell says.

Here's how the program works on a day-to-day basis. Gillette's international HR staff pairs trainees with a Gillette executive mentor in one of the organization's five major business areas. They include: marketing, finance, manufacturing, personnel, and market research and sales. The two biggest areas for trainees are the finance and marketing groups, followed by manufacturing, human resources and sales. Trainees typically work in two of these areas during their training assignments.

No matter which business areas the trainees work in while in training, they have two main objectives:

+ To learn everything they can about that particular functional area
+ To learn how to work effectively within the Gillette organization.

For example, Henry D. Mauer, financial-planning manager for the Latin-American group based in Boston, currently oversees three senior trainees from Colombia, Argentina and Venezuela. The trainees help produce monthly financial reports for the Latin-American markets and analyze capital-expenditure requests. "Those are the types of things they may not get exposed to in their home countries, especially if they're from a smaller market," Mauer says.

Once they've finished with their assignments, trainees can expect to go back to their countries and take jobs as senior analysts or supervisors. Which jobs Gillette offers them depend on how well they've done during their assignments and how big the markets are in their home countries.

By working in headquarters offices, trainees see a different side of the organization than they see in their individual countries. "They get a real perspective of the corporation and how it works," Mauer says. "People in the various markets have a tendency to look at us in headquarters and wonder what we do. While they're here, they see how we add value."

Trainees have interaction with the most-senior executives of the company. When they return to their home countries, and throughout their careers at Gillette, trainees agree that they'll be more knowledgeable about how the headquarters staff works. They also will know whom to call when they need to get information.

"People get a better understanding of what the company is by being here," says Maria M. Vallejo, a senior trainee. She says that people who work at Gillette in her home country, Colombia, often are reluctant to call headquarters because they often don't know anyone there. Having had experience working in headquarters helps the business run more smoothly.

As a junior trainee in 1986, Vallejo worked under O'Connell in the international-personnel group. Now on an expatriate assignment, Vallejo works for Mauer in finance. With an educational background in economics, Vallejo had wanted to go into finance as a junior trainee, but there had been no openings in that group. That wasn't unusual. Although HR tries to match trainees with assignments in the functional areas that interest them most, it isn't always possible. Gillette managers assume that all experience is good experience and will be useful to them as they progress.

While in her personnel assignment, Vallejo focused on compensation and later returned to Colombia as a compensation supervisor. Having been successful in compensation, she's back in Boston, learning about finance. About her experience as a trainee, Vallejo says, "By coming here, you feel more a part of what Gillette is."

Miné Ozuak, on the other hand, wanted a personnel traineeship. Ozuak, who's from Turkey, had worked there for three years as an executive secretary at Gillette. In that position, she followed personnel matters, then formally transferred to personnel in 1992. There, she became a benefits supervisor and later received a traineeship in Boston. As the personnel trainee in Boston, Ozuak administers the intentional-trainee program on a daily basis. In addition to working closely with O'Connell and learning personnel concepts, she processes visas, makes housing arrangements, provide orientation for new trainees and generally serves as a troubleshooter.

In addition to their daily jobs, trainees participate in monthly seminars on such topics as dressing for success, finance for nonfinancial managers and presentation skills. Gillette places a top priority on presentation skills, so it allows trainees to sit in on some of the important meetings that take place at the headquarters offices. Many trainees make presentations to managers while on assignment, which helps them hone their presentation skills.

"We learn a lot by observing managers in the budget- and strategic-planning meetings and presentations," says Rosser, the trainee from New Zealand. "I think that this is a positive step that the program's taking, and I hope it develops further." Matveev, the Russian trainee, agrees. Sometimes they've participated in preparing presentations with their managers. "If you actually are present for those meetings with your manager, you see the whole picture. You see how your project—your particular little brick—fits into the wall," Matveev says.

Kenneth B. White, director of marketing research for Gillette's international-business management in Boston, currently oversees one trainee: Semih Yalman from Turkey. As a trainee, Yalman helps White conduct retail audits and compile data consolidations of advertising research for all Gillette brands. In addition, he's helping put together an international market-research data bank, which will hold information for all the company's individual markets.

Because market research is complex and specialized, White usually spends the first four months bringing each new trainee up to speed with terminology and operational procedures. "After that, we spend a fair amount of time together, but he or she has to be able to work independently. It's an open-door kind of thing," White says. As a prerequisite, trainees must be computer-literate.

"Good English-language and writing skills also are important to me," White explains. He remembers one particular trainee who had a heavy Portuguese accent and was difficult to understand. The trainee also had poor writing skills. It was a daunting combination of skill problems because the trainee needed to make many interdepartmental calls from the headquarters office during his tenure and needed to dash off faxes, reports and memos. Managers evaluate trainees for all of these skills.

"Trainees aren't clerks, and they aren't analysts. They do a little bit of both jobs in an energetic way," says White. "These are very real jobs, and the trainees are measured carefully while they're here. If they don't make it in the trainee program, then they aren't recommended when they leave. They can't come here for 18 months and goof off." Trainees receive two performance reviews at nine-month intervals while they're on assignment.

To most trainees, goofing off would be a waste of valuable time. "This is the opportunity of a lifetime," says Jorge Andrino, a trainee from Guatemala who's working in the marketing group in Boston. Andrino had gone to school in the U.S. before hiring on with Gillette in his home country. So had Jan Rafal Saykiewicz, a trainee from Poland.

Most of the trainees, however, have had limited experience with different customs and with people from cultures other than their own. "For many of them, this is their first time away from their home countries," O'Connell says. "They come here, and live and work with people from more than 15 different countries. It's like a United Nations."

Levy says that the benefits of the experience directly affect the trainees' professional lives. "They live for a year and a half with people from different cultures and naturally become more open-minded managers when they go back to their own countries or to any other country," he says.

Because of their cultural differences, trainees sometimes have problems learning to live with one another at the company-provided apartment complex. Junior trainees share an apartment with two other trainees of the same gender. Senior trainees get their own apartments. Sometimes the problems have to do with religious practices or interpersonal differences. These problems, however, have been rare, according to O'Connell. He has learned that it's better to have at least three or four trainees in training at the same time. Because they're all in the same boat, they tend to help each other out with any difficulties that arise.

Despite their cultural differences, most trainees develop a true sense of camaraderie with their fellow trainees. "It's pretty ingenious. We work together, we eat together, we live together and we socialize together. When you first come here, it's the differences between us that you notice. In the end, the similarities are more obvious than the differences," Rosser says.

The trainees say that they also develop a deep appreciation for Gillette and how the company operates. They like the hands-on experience that the program gives them. "I needed a lot of practical experience because I had never worked before I graduated from school," says Naik, the trainee from India. "It's really a good experience."

Makhele says that he has learned more in the six months that he's been in the program than he had in the nearly two years that he spent in Gillette's operations in South Africa. "Right now, I feel that with what I've learned here, I could go back to South Africa and be an exceptional employee. It's been intensive."

INTERNATIONAL TRAINING BREEDS SUCCESS

Gillette executives agree that the program is a success. For every 10 trainees who go through program, Gillette generally extends permanent job offers to nine of them. Of those nine, eight will usually accept. Of the eight who accept, six stay with the firm longer than a year after returning to their home countries. Sometimes trainees are lured away by job offers from other companies back home. It isn't unheard-of for trainees to receive job offers of double or triple their salaries, according to O'Connell. "We believe that if we can keep them for one year after they return home, then we'll have them for their entire careers."

To encourage them to stay with Gillette, O'Connell meets with trainees and tells them to expect job offers, especially in their first year. "I ask them to commit to working for us for one year," he says. Within that time, the graduate trainees have moved back home, have had a performance review, a salary upgrade and sometimes a job move.

Whenever O'Connell (or another company executive) travels to Gillette subsidiaries in other countries, he makes a point of visiting with ex-trainees. This helps foster a management *clique* concept, so that graduates continue to know that they're part of the organization's international-management team.

In the company's 1992 annual report, Zeien wrote that the company's world-class products and people are fundamental to continuing to build a successful worldwide enterprise in a challenging business environment.

Whether the international-trainee program helps contribute to that success or not remains a question yet to be answered. One thing seems certain. Although it may not be possible to look at any one face within the Gillette organization and see the future of global business, it may be possible to look at the newest faces on the firm's management team and see a brighter future for Gillette.

BUILDING A GLOBAL MANAGEMENT TEAM

Rome wasn't built in a day. Neither was Gillette's international management team. According to Gillette Chairman and CEO Alfred M. Zeien, it takes at least 25 years to build an international management corps that possesses the skills, experience and abilities to take a global organization from one level of success to the next.

Gillette, through its senior management team, has learned that developing managers through international assignments helps the business grow. The firm's International Trainee Program (see main story) is one of the company's key strategies for building its worldwide management corps. Its other key international staffing strategy is hiring and developing foreign nationals to staff its operations globally. Many of these managers have become part of Gillette's growing expatriate corps.

Interestingly, fewer than 15% of the company's expatriates are natives of the U.S. At least 85% of Gillette's expatriates come from one of the other 27 countries in which it has operations.

For the most part, Gillette hires foreign nationals to staff management positions in countries other than the U.S. Often, however, the organization first identifies these individuals while they're studying at U.S. universities for their MBAs. The new hires typically work at Gillette's Boston headquarters for a year, then return to their home countries, much like trainees in the International Trainee Program.

After working in their home countries for about four years, Gillette typically moves managers on to other countries and other assignments. As Gillette managers build their international experience, they also teach and develop other potential managers within the organization.

Often these managers with international experience are prime candidates for positions that open up when the company enters into new markets or into joint ventures. Such was the case with its new joint venture last fall with a company in China. Because Gillette first began planning the joint venture in China more than four years ago, it began identifying individual managers then who would be right for assignments in that new business.

As Gillette expatriate Bob McCusker puts it, "Gillette has a lot of resources that we can apply to our new ventures." McCusker, currently on assignment in Pakistan, says that he finds it gratifying when individuals who work in a new Gillette venture in one area go on to help develop new ventures in other areas.

Gillette's policy of giving its managers international experience attracts individuals seeking international careers. Gillette managers constantly are on the lookout for individuals who show interest and promise in moving through the Gillette organization worldwide. "One of my responsibilities is to look for people who are promotable internationally," says Jorgen Wedel, president of Braun USA and a native of Denmark. "We need people who have a more global understanding of the business, and we need managers who can manage that business. I think it's one of the key responsibilities of management today."

Dieu Eng Seng agrees. Seng is the area vice president of Oral-B, Asia Pacific. A native of Singapore, Seng's past service with Gillette has included assignments in Australia, Singapore, China, Hong Kong, Malaysia and the U.S. "One of my key objectives is to identify, recruit and develop competent managers. I'm confident that from these good people will generate a flow of business growth and profits into the future."

International management teams clearly aren't built in a day. They aren't even built in a year. In Gillette's case, careful planning and constant attention to international development, however, can yield employees that support and grow a business successfully from one decade to the next.

Part Five

CROSS-CULTURAL COMMUNICATION AND NEGOTIATIONS

Communication is the process of transmitting information, ideas, and attitudes (a message) from one person (the sender) to another (the receiver). In practice, this is an extremely difficult process to apply effectively because receivers often do not interpret messages as intended by the sender; messages are often not understood or are misunderstood. This occurs when senders encode messages using words, symbols, and concepts/ideas that are unfamiliar to the receiver or receivers. Unfamiliarity results especially when senders' and receivers' frames of reference and means of communication have been developed in different cultures. Cultures typically develop unique ways of communicating; they develop formal languages, idioms, slang, jargon, nonverbal (body language) means of communication, as well as norms and values, which are unique to their own culture.

And they develop unique ways of conducting and negotiating business. This uniqueness makes communicating, and conducting and negotiating business across nations/cultures, challenging tasks for international managers. International managers who possess strong skills in this area are likely to be far more successful in international management than those who possess weak skills. Chapter 8 discusses cross-cultural communication, and Chapter 9 cross-cultural business practices and negotiations.

Chapter Eight

Cross-Cultural Communication

Stiff and ill at ease at first [at a training program], the Japanese said little, and some of what they said was hard to understand. The Americans talked too much and wondered when the Japanese would make a contribution. . . . [Professor Hirotaka Takeuchi from Hitotsubashi University, Japan] explained to the others why the Japanese spoke so little. . . . Unlike Americans, who like to jump in and grab control of a meeting, said Takeuchi, the Japanese prefer to wait and listen; the higher their rank, the more they listen. This group of Japanese were the elite, he explained, and therefore listened a lot. He added that the Japanese have a not-so-subtle saying: "He who speaks first at a meeting is a dumb ass."[1]

Objectives of the Chapter

Effective communication across nations/cultures can only take place when the sender encodes the message using language, idioms, norms and values, and so on, which are familiar to the receiver or when the receiver (or receivers) is familiar with the language, idioms, and so on, used by the sender. Attaining familiarity of language, slang, norms and values, and so on, across nations/cultures is by no means an easy task because words and concepts are often not easily translatable (and sometimes not translatable at all) from one culture to another. For example, the concept of "self-fulfillment" is well understood in the American culture, but such a concept is not translatable to many cultures throughout the world, who understand better the concept of "group-fulfillment." Furthermore, words often have different meanings when translated into another language. For instance, America's General Motors Corporation advertised on many of the automobiles it produced that the body was made by Fisher ("Body by Fisher"). The Flemish interpreted it to mean "Corpse by Fisher." The above suggests that communication is bound to create many problems for people conducting international/cross-cultural business. And international managers cannot generally be effective if they do not possess strong **cross-cultural communication** skills. Therefore, the objective of this chapter is to:

1. Discuss the communication process (ideation, encoding, transmission, and decoding) in an international/cross-cultural context.
2. Discuss the cultural and language barriers and the ways of dealing with them, including use of translators.
3. Discuss the ways to develop the ability to communicate effectively across cultures.

THE CROSS-CULTURAL COMMUNICATION PROCESS

Figure 8–1 presents the communication process. Basically, communication is the process of conveying a message (a concept or idea) from one party to another or others. The message can be transmitted orally (spoken words), visually (written words), or nonverbally (body/facial expressions). Concepts have different meanings and different levels of importance in different cultures throughout the globe, and many societies have adopted a **unique language** or multiple unique languages (for example, China has more than 50 distinct spoken languages, such as Beijingnese, Cantonese, Shanghainese). Since meanings and languages vary so much from one culture to another, people conducting business across cultures and languages will often encounter communication difficulties that they would not encounter in their own culture and language. Therefore, to communicate effectively across cultures and languages, international business people must develop the ability to adapt to the differences. Lacking this ability, they will often find themselves in embarrassing situations.[2]

Relative to differing verbal languages, **English appears to be emerging as the language of choice in conducting business** across countries. Nevertheless, cross-cultural, cross-nation communication problems still remain. This is because different cultures have developed **different social values.** Thus, a concept perceived in a certain way in one culture is perceived differently in another. Also, different cultures have developed different nonverbal languages. Therefore, differing gestures and facial expressions still present cross-cultural communication problems. Furthermore, "it is blind provisionalism to believe that English will continue to be used everywhere for all occasions."[3]

The Communication Process	FIGURE 8–1 ◆

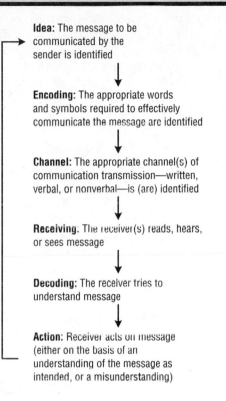

Idea: The message to be communicated by the sender is identified

Encoding: The appropriate words and symbols required to effectively communicate the message are identified

Channel: The appropriate channel(s) of communication transmission—written, verbal, or nonverbal—is (are) identified

Receiving. The receiver(s) reads, hears, or sees message

Decoding: The receiver tries to understand message

Action: Receiver acts on message (either on the basis of an understanding of the message as intended, or a misunderstanding)

This means that quite often international business is conducted between parties who speak a different language (either verbal or nonverbal, or both). When senders of messages and the receivers speak a different language, communication barriers arise. To help eliminate the verbal and nonverbal barriers, the parties involved in the communication process must often employ a **language translator.** The ensuing sections describe the ideation, encoding, transmission, and decoding stages of the communication process in an international/cross-cultural context; discuss effective translation skills; propose a framework for communicating across countries using the English language; and propose ways to develop cross-cultural communication skills.

The Ideation Stage

At the ideation stage, senders (communicators) must identify clearly and specifically what it is that they want the receivers (the listeners) to do as a result of the communication—that is, they must determine what their objective is.[4] Is it to get the receiver(s): To buy a product or service? To perform a certain task? To sign a contract? To find a solution to a problem? To approve a solution to a problem? To provide certain information? To approve a certain recommendation?

When individuals are communicating in cultures different from their own (and realistically, differences do not occur only across nations; they can often be found within nations, as well as within nations' regions, cities/towns, and in cities such as New York, within blocks and even apartments in the same building), they should ask themselves two basic questions: In light of the culture, is the objective realistic? In light of the culture, is the time frame realistic?

Realistic Objective

A society's culture determines to what extent an **objective is realistic.** For example, an objective requiring that the receiver carry out the sender's directives may not be realistic in small power distance cultures such as Sweden, Norway, and Israel, where individuals culturally expect to participate in decision making. It may, however, be realistic in large power distance cultures such as France, where individuals culturally expect to be directed. (See Practical Perspective 8–1.) Objectives to sell beef in India and

PRACTICAL   PERSPECTIVE   8–1

An Illustration of Cross-Cultural Communication Ineffectiveness

Behavior	Attribution
American: "How long will it take you to finish this report?"	American: I have asked him to participate.
	Greek: His behavior makes no sense. He is the boss. Why doesn't he tell me?
Greek: "I don't know. How long should it take?"	American: He refuses to take responsibility.
	Greek: I asked him for an order.
American: "You are in the best position to analyze time requirements."	American: I press him to take responsibility for his actions.
	Greek: What nonsense! I'd better give him an answer.
Greek: "10 days."	American: He lacks the ability to estimate time; this time estimate is totally inadequate.
American: "Take fifteen days. Is it agreed? You will do it in 15 days?"	American: I offer a contract.
	Greek: These are my orders: 15 days.

In fact, the report needed 30 days of regular work. So the Greek worked day and night, but, at the end of the 15th day, he still needed to do one more day's work.

Behavior	Attribution
American: "Where is the report?"	**American:** I am making sure he fulfills his contract.
	Greek: He is asking for the report. Both attribute that it is not ready.
Greek: "It will be ready tomorrow."	
American: "But we had agreed it would be ready today."	**American:** I must teach him to fulfill a contract.
	Greek: The stupid, incompetent boss! Not only does he give me the *wrong orders*, but he doesn't even appreciate that I did a 30-day job in 16 days.
The Greek hands in his resignation.	The American is surprised.
	Greek: I won't work for such a man.

Source: H.C. Triandis, *Interpersonal Behavior* (Monteray, CA: Brooks/Cole Publishing Company, 1977), p. 248. Copyright © 1977 Brooks/Cole Publishing Company, a division of International Thomson Publishing Inc., Pacific Grove, CA 93950. Reprinted with permission of the publisher.

pork in Israel would not be realistic. An objective to sell toothpaste that makes teeth sparkling white may not be realistic in many parts of Southeast Asia where betel nut chewing is an elite pastime and stained teeth are a symbol of high esteem. An objective to mass-sell Western-style, sitting-height toilet bowls in China, where ground-level bowls are widely used (to use, one squats over them), would not be realistic at this stage of China's economic transformation. An objective to obtain a signature on a lengthy (many pages) contract may be realistic in America, where it is an accepted practice, but not in Japan, where verbal contracts ("a gentleman's agreement"/"a handshake") or written contracts consisting only of a few pages are the accepted practice.

An objective to obtain a firm employee commitment to a project in Islamic cultures—which exist anywhere from North Africa to the Middle East to Indonesia—may not be as realistic as it is in Western cultures such as America. This is because Islamic cultures tend to be guided by a fatalistic view that events are controlled by external forces ("God wills it") and they therefore have no power to make things happen, whereas the latter cultures tend to be guided by a master-of-destiny view that events are controlled by people themselves. An objective to discuss business during a lunch or dinner meeting in many parts of Asia, Europe, and South America, where such meetings are used mainly for the development of social relations, may not be a realistic objective, but it may be realistic in North America, where such meetings are typically held for the purpose of discussing business.

Realistic Time Frame

Culture also determines what is a **realistic time frame.** Different cultures hold different concepts of time. In some cultures, for example, Germany and Switzerland, timetables are exact and precise, and people tend to meet deadlines. In some cultures, including some Latin American and African cultures, individuals possess a relatively more relaxed attitude toward time; unlike in America, time is not a commodity and the completion of tasks moves relatively slow. Deadlines given to employees in these cultures often will not be met and often will demotivate them. The objective to build a bridge in, for instance, a 24-month span of time is therefore more realistic in the former cultures than in the latter.

The Encoding Stage

After the message to be communicated has been ascertained, the next step is to determine and organize the words, expressions, and nonverbal signals needed to communicate the message effectively. Language and cultural differences existing among nations—and often within nations, for example, Canada has two official languages, Switzerland has four, and China, as previously indicated, has more than 50 different dialects—create difficulties in identifying the words, expressions, and nonverbal signals required to communicate effectively across nations and cultures. Therefore, the encoding process for cross-cultural communication must take into consideration many language and cultural differences existing throughout the globe. Some of the differences are discussed below.

Language

Unique idioms, slang, similes, metaphors, and jargon are components of languages which people use without being aware that they are doing so, and many are not easily translatable from one language to another. For example, the promotional term "come alive with Pepsi" in the U.S. means to become invigorated or energetic, whereas when translated into German, it communicates the thought of "coming alive from the grave with Pepsi." Even though the Latin word *nova* actually means new, the Nova label on Chevrolet's Nova automobile was interpreted by many Spanish-speaking individuals to mean "doesn't go" (*no va*). Who would buy a car that does not go? America's Colgate-Palmolive Company introduced its Cue brand of toothpaste in French-speaking countries. The word *cue* in French translates into a pornographic word that offends many French-speaking people. How does a non-English-speaking person using a language translation dictionary readily translate the English term "as easy as duck soup" or "a ballpark figure" or "a monkey on my back" or "a pain in the neck" into his or her language? How does an English-to-Russian translator interpret such terms as "consumer market" or "market-driven economy" to a Russian?

Even within a language many **words have different meanings** to different people. For example, Parker, the well-known maker of ballpoint pens, had to change its advertising in Latin America after learning that *bola*, the Spanish translation of ball, does not mean ball in all Spanish-speaking countries; in some it actually means "revolution" or "lie." In America, "tabling" something means postponing it; in England it means discussing it now. In Canada, a "pothole" is where one goes swimming; in New York City it is where one smashes an automobile's wheels and shock absorbers. Imagine the embarrassment of an American named Randy, who when visiting in England approached a lady at a social gathering and introduced himself: "Hi, I'm Randy." In England, to be "randy" means to be sexually aroused. And when United Airlines entered the Pacific market, one of United's inflight magazine covers showed Australian actor Paul Hogan wandering through the Outback. The caption read, "Paul Hogan Camps It Up." Hogan's lawyer called United Airlines to let them know that "camps it up" is Australian slang for "flaunts his homosexuality."[5]

Letter Characters and Alphabets

Letter characters and alphabets also differ among some cultures. Chinese and English letter characters and alphabets, for example, are very different. The Japanese language is a mixture of two syllabaries, *kana* and *kanji*. *Kana* is the phonetic sounds of the 113 possible syllables and *kanji* are Chinese characters that stand for sound plus meanings. To read a Japanese newspaper, the reader must know 2000 *kanji* characters, and the reader who knows 4000 characters is considered well educated. The Japanese language consists of about 40,000 picture characters. To overcome the problem created by having so many characters, many newspapers are published using *kana* interpretations, which are easier to understand.[6] (This may help explain why the Japanese culturally prefer oral over written communication and short as opposed to long written communication.) Such differences also make language interpretations difficult.

For example, when America's Coca-Cola Company initially introduced its beverage in China, only its Coca-Cola label appeared on the can. Since "Coca-Cola" is not translatable into the Chinese language, to write the label in Chinese, local vendors used Chinese letter characters to phonetically spell the sound of "Coca-Cola." The characters the vendors selected actually meant "bite the wax tadpole." To deal with this problem, Coca-Cola's translators eventually selected a group of characters that are interpreted by the Chinese to mean "may the mouth rejoice" and now place those characters on the cans along with the English characters.[7]

Effective translation of languages is therefore vital in cross-national business negotiations, in promotion and labeling, as well as in writing of contracts and reports, in written and/or oral communications between domestic and foreign employees, and in the general management of foreign subsidiaries.

Expressions and Nonverbal Communication

Certainly, expressions and nonverbal communication play an important role in cross-cultural encoding. For example, U.S. movie-making firms export movies and television programs made for American audiences. Usually, these must be modified by dubbing in the local language. Accurate language translation is therefore essential. But what is also important is the nonverbal communication contained in the films. For example, the ways of depicting affection in American-made movies and television programs are viewed by some cultures as being offensive. Gestures are widely used as a means of communication in films and television programs, and the same sign has different meanings across different cultures. Some gestures may offend many foreign viewers and must therefore be edited out or somehow isolated before the film is distributed in the foreign culture. For example, Americans form a circle with their index finger and thumb to communicate that something is "OK." Imagine the embarrassment of a former U.S. president who visited Brazil, stepped out of the airplane, and made that gesture to a waiting crowd of Brazilians. The same sign in Brazil means that one is interested in having sex. The same OK sign means zero in France and is a symbol for money in Japan. In many cultures, including America and China, pointing one's thumb up is a gesture meaning "good" or "great," but in Australia it is a crude gesture.

The Role of Formality and Informality in Communication

Cultures vary in their **requirements for formality and informality,** and these variations also affect cross-cultural communication encoding. Some cultures, especially America and Australia, value informality in communication, but most cultures throughout the world value formality.[8] Individuals in cultures that value informality place low importance on the use of rank, status, and position in communication, and often use first names when communicating with each other, even in business settings. On the other hand, individuals in cultures that value formality place high importance on the use of last names, titles, and other indications of rank and status in communication.

For example, in Italy many people are addressed as *Dottore* or *Dottoressa,* whether or not they hold the Ph.D. degree, and an individual can hold such a title by simply holding a college degree. In many Latin American cultures, the title is more important than the name. Therefore, the title *Inginero* (Engineer), for instance, is used before the person's last name (Inginero Vargas, for example). The French demonstrate status, rank, and privilege by the type and kind of language used in correspondence. They often use flowery, effusive, complex syntax when communicating with higher ranking individuals. The French do not use the term "Dear" to begin a letter; the letter would simply start with the person's name, for instance, "P. Rousseau." In France individuals can work together in the same place for many years and still greet each other with a formal handshake and by the formal name—for example, "Bonjour, M. Rousseau." In Germany, a doctor is addressed as "Herr Doctor," not "Doctor Schilling," and one does not use first names until invited to do so.

In many cultures rank and status is shown by seating arrangements, by the way individuals enter a room, and by who speaks first. In Japan, for instance, the oldest male is normally the most senior, and he must not be the first to enter a room; he is preceded by his assistants, and followed by other assistants, and he sits in the middle. Correspondence to people of higher status must be written individually, and mass mailings are often disliked because they emphasize efficiency over the honoring of individuals' rank and position. People in cultures that value informality, such as Americans, often become frustrated when forced to pay deference to someone simply because of his or her status (family ties, schooling, age, etc.), and not because of the person's accomplishments.

How Much Information Is Needed?

Individuals in some cultures, such as Japan, France and Germany, can be categorized as, in general, conservative or risk-avoidant. These individuals make decisions slowly, avoid risks, and dislike ambiguity (conditions of uncertainty and ambiguity make them feel uncomfortable). They therefore have a strong need for much detail and information. On the other hand, people in some cultures, such as Singapore, America, and Australia, feel relatively more comfortable with risk and ambiguity, make decisions more quickly, and require less detail and information.[9]

Language Translation

The above suggests that cross-cultural, cross-national communicators, to communicate effectively, must make certain that the language used, including the words, symbols, slang, formal and informal behaviors, as well as nonverbal behaviors, is the one that will be understood by the receiver(s). In conducting global business, business people often do not possess command of the language necessary to communicate effectively with foreign associates. These senders therefore have to find a way to convert the language they understand into the language understood by the foreign associates (the receivers).

Translating one language into another is a huge problem confronting cross-cultural, cross-national communicators. To overcome translation problems of communications, international business people often use the **dual-translation** approach. This involves using a translator in the home country interpreting the message into the foreign language, and before the message is communicated, another translator in the foreign country interpreting the message back into the home country's language. For example, a communicator transmitting a message from the United States to an Angolan in Angola, (where Portuguese is spoken) first has a translator of English to Portuguese in the United States interpret the message from English to Portuguese. The translated message is then sent to a translator of Portuguese to English in Angola to be interpreted back to English. The sender will transmit the message after he or she has been assured that the translated message will be understood by the receiver(s) as intended.

The Translator's Role

Basically, a translator acts as an interpreter for two or more people who wish to communicate with each other but speak different languages. The interpretation may involve written messages, verbal (oral) messages, nonverbal messages, or a combination of the three types. The translator's job is very complex, as he or she must effectively decode the sender's message and encode it into the receiver's language, and then decode the receiver's (now the sender's) reply and encode it into the sender's (now the receiver's) language. (See Figure 8–2.)

Oral Translators.   There are two types of oral translators: those who are engaged in simultaneous interpretations and those involved in sequential interpretations.[10]

Simultaneous oral interpreters are usually used by speakers in formal presentation situations, such as conferences, where the audience (the receivers) and the speaker (the sender) communicate using a different language. In this situation, the translator interprets the sender's formal presentation and passes it on to the audience. (This type is used in United Nations' meetings.) Usually, the speaker communicates a small group of words, pauses to allow the interpreter to translate them and pass them on to the audience, and so on. For example, the writer recently spent three weeks lecturing in English at a university in Shanghai, China. The lecture topic was current Western management theory and research. The audience consisted of the university's management professors, some high-level executives from Chinese business enterprises, and several of the university's management graduate students. Most of the participants did not understand English or

Cross-Language Interpretation

FIGURE 8–2 ◆

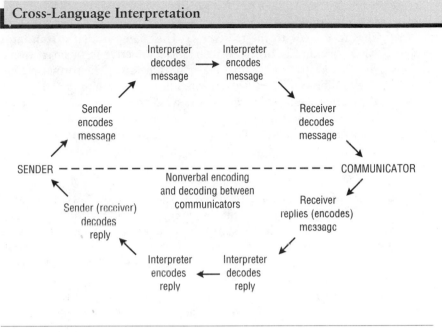

Source: Adapted from Lyle Sussman and Denise M. Johnson, "The Interpreted Executive: Theory, Models, and Implications," *Journal of Business Communication* 30, no. 4 (1993): 421.

their understanding was weak. The presentations therefore required use of a translator. Two Mandarin-speaking graduate students at the university who also spoke English fairly fluently were assigned to the writer to act as translators. Both students were management majors who had studied Western management theory. They acted as translators in shifts—the lectures were daily from 9 AM to 4:30 PM with an hour and a half for lunch, and it is virtually impossible for one person to be effective in a translator's role for such a long period of time. The writer made formal presentations with many pauses to allow the translator to interpret the message and pass it on to the audience.

Sequential oral interpreters are typically used by clients involved in cross-language business negotiations and social functions. Unlike the simultaneous interpreter, the sequential interpreter normally requires negotiation and diplomatic skills, the ability to transmit personality and style as well as knowledge of the language and culture.

The Effective Translator

It is obvious that the lack of an effective translator will lead to problems. Several factors help define the **effective translator.**[11]

Characteristics of the Message Itself.   The translator is aware of the underlying substantive content of the message—both implicit and explicit—the sender wishes to convey to the receiver(s). This suggests that a translator with a business background is likely to be more effective in business transactions than a translator with a liberal arts background. The former is likely to be more familiar with business jargon, idioms, etc., than the latter. For instance, the former is more likely to know what the business term "a ballpark figure" means than the latter. On the other hand, the translator with the liberal arts background may be more effective at social gatherings where a broad range of topics are typically discussed than the translator with the business background.

Characteristics of the Language Involved.   The translator is familiar with the sociolinguistic properties of the languages, including formality (discussed above), the role of gender, status, verb tense and standard syntax in the language. For example, the effective translator knows that it is not inappropriate to use first names in small power distance societies, but it is in large power distance societies, where use of titles is customary. For instance, as previously indicated, in America bosses and subordinates often communicate with each other on a first-name basis, but not so in France, where titles are used.

Interpreter's Relationship with the Client.   The translator has personal involvement and familiarity with the client and the topic to be communicated. For example, when the writer was lecturing in China using two translators, both were familiar with the topic. A problem that arose, however, was that the writer did not meet with the interpreters prior to beginning the lectures to orient them specifically to what was going to be covered. Interpreters not familiar with the specific contents of the message ahead of time can cause interruptions in the flow of the communication and even translation errors.

Context.   The time, place, and purpose of the meeting have an effect on a translator's effectiveness. Negotiations for high stakes taking place in an hostile environment and that must be accomplished in a short period of time will create much stress for the translator (for the communicator as well), which in turn will reduce his or her (as well as the communicator's) effectiveness. Negotiations should therefore be arranged in such a way that they cause minimum stress for the translator (and the communicator).

Interpreter's Skills.   The effective translator has command of the languages being interpreted, active listening skills, is sensitive to explicit as well as implicit meanings, and the ability to bridge cultural gaps. These skills must be optimum. Many language specialists believe that to master a language, especially idiomatic meanings, slang, and so on, it is necessary to live in the foreign country for a few years. As a matter of fact, many expatriate professional translators periodically return to their native country for a period of time so that they can **update their translation skills.** They believe that after being away from their native country for a while they lose translation ability in the sense that idioms, slang, jargon, and cultural behaviors change rapidly.

For instance, in America, the meaning of the word "gay" not too long ago was generally taken to mean happy; today many people use the word to describe a homosexual male. The word "bad" has historically meant just that; today, in describing an individual's behavior, in some situations, such as in sports, the word is actually used to describe "good." For example, a basketball player is "bad" if he or she possesses "good" playing skills. His or her being so good makes it "bad" for the opposing team—therefore, he or she "is bad." And within the past few decades, the slang word used to describe unconventional individuals in America changed from "bohemian" to "beatnik" to "hippie."

As an illustration, at a recent social gathering in New York, the writer met an expatriate from Portugal whose profession is translating English to Portuguese and Portuguese to English for businesses. She writes business contracts, is involved in oral translations, and so on. She said that, to maintain her translating skills, she goes back to Portugal every year and a half or so, and lives there for about six months, spending that time updating her Portuguese language skills. She believes that if a professional translator is away from the foreign language for much longer than a year and a half, his or her effective translation skills will diminish.

Characteristics of the Parties.   The translator is familiar with the personal styles, idiosyncracies, and communication strengths, including encoding and decoding abilities, of the parties for whom he or she is interpreting.

Cultural Norms and Values.   The effective translator is familiar with the cultural norms and values of both cultures. For example, some cultures are high context and some are low context. When conducting business, people in **high-context cultures,** including the Chinese, Korean, Japanese, Vietnamese, Arab, Greek, and Spanish cultures, (1) establish social trust first, (2) value personal relations and goodwill, (3) make agreements on the basis of general trust, and (4) like to conduct slow and ritualistic negotiations.[12] People in these cultures prefer that messages not be structured directly, that they do not get right to the point and state conclusions or bottom lines first. Instead, they prefer that a message be indirect, building up to the point and stating conclusions or bottom lines last.[13] On the other hand, individuals in **low-context cultures,** including the Italian, English, North American, Scandinavian, Swiss, and German cultures, (1) get down to business first, (2) value expertise and performance, (3) like agreement by specific, legalistic contract, and (5) like to conduct negotiations as efficient as possible.[14] Individuals in these cultures prefer that messages be structured directly; that they get immediately to the point and state conclusions or bottom lines first.[15]

The translator will have the ability to guide the communication flow accordingly, and when the parties for whom he or she is acting as intermediary are opposites (one is high context and the other low context), the translator will possess the ability to educate his or her clients accordingly and to apply the most viable communication customs. For instance, if a Japanese business person is competing with other companies to obtain a contract from a German company, the German customs are likely to be the most applicable. If, however, a German business person is competing with other companies to obtain a contract from a Japanese company, the Japanese customs are likely to be the most applicable.

Identify the Right Audience

To encode their messages effectively, senders must ascertain the correct receivers and the message must appeal to them.[16] In many cultures, those persons to be involved in the decision or action phase are not readily obvious. Tailoring a message just to the obvious receivers and appealing just to them can often create communication problems. A culture's views on authority, rank, and group definition often forces a sender to include additional or different **primary audience** members—those who will be receiving the message directly. It also often forces a sender to include a **secondary audience**—those who will hear about the message, need to participate in decision making, or are affected by the message.

The sender must also determine who the key decision makers in the audience are. These could include superiors and subordinates, influential officials, opinion leaders, power brokers, contacts, tribe or sect members, or family members. How are the power brokers identified? In Western cultures, an individual's power is demonstrated by how much "proactivity" he or she brings to a situation. In Asia, the powerful do not reveal their inner feelings and thoughts, and they display their authority by the silence and stillness they maintain in response to situations. In Latin America, those in power are often also poets and musicians, and they are trusted because they are able to reveal their inner feelings and thoughts in an eloquent manner. The message must be tailored to these audiences and appeal to their motivations.

Appeal to Receivers' Motivations

Motivations are affected by the economic and political conditions confronting the audience. Obviously, an American sending a message to a group of locals in Rwanda about his or her mansion in California or his or her recent vacation in Hong Kong probably will not be heard; they probably would hear a message about how to solve their hunger and other problems. That message also probably would not be heard by a group of individuals who are politically repressed; a message explaining how to attain more freedom would probably be heard by these people.

Individuals' motivations are also influenced by culture. For example, people in high masculinity cultures, such as America, Austria, and Switzerland, may be motivated by material wealth and accumulation, while people in low masculinity cultures, such as Denmark and Norway may value a clean environment and altruism more than material wealth. Thus, a message promising material wealth may be heard more by listeners from a high masculine culture than listeners from a low masculine culture. People in weak uncertainty avoidance cultures, such as Israel, America, and Denmark, may be motivated by task enhancement, career advancement, achievement, and challenge, while people in strong uncertainty avoidance cultures, such as France, Portugal, and Greece, may be motivated by job security and a safe work environment. Therefore, listeners from weak uncertainty avoidance cultures may be more interested in a message promising challenging tasks than listeners from strong uncertainty avoidance cultures. People in low-individualism cultures, such as Japan, may be more motivated by group relationships than by career advancement, while people in high-individualism cultures, such as Australia and America, may be motivated more by challenging work than by group relationships. A message promising individual rewards would probably be more appealing to listeners from high-individualism cultures than listeners from low-individualism cultures.

Furthermore, some individuals, culturally, have a negative attitude toward work activities and a positive attitude toward leisure, community, religious, and family activities. The message must therefore appeal to these attitudes, otherwise, it may be difficult to get such people to listen.

English as the Language of Communication in Global Business

As indicated above, English appears to be emerging as the universal language for conducting international business. To deal with this evolution, many countries' governments now require that English be taught in their education systems, and in countries whose governments do not mandate the study of English, many students study English for competitive advantages in the job market. As a result, **English is often the second or third language** for many business people throughout the globe. This, however, does not mean that these people are proficient in the use of the English language. Many of these individuals have learned English by reading and listening, and therefore possess a weak ability to communicate in English. Many understand only **dictionary (literal) translation** meanings. Therefore, quite often a correspondence in English from foreign business associates is the consequence of considerable time and effort on their part. Thus, given a choice, most receivers with English as a second or third language would probably prefer to communicate in their native language, and appreciate your acknowledgement of their first-language skills.

This suggests that senders from English-speaking countries should, when possible, attempt to communicate using the foreign receivers' language. They should learn the foreign language or at least have the communication translated. At the very least, senders should communicate some phrases using the foreign language. This shows respect for their culture, acknowledges that there are differences, and informs them that they are not viewed as a branch of the English-speaking nation.[17]

Although it is important that senders from English-speaking countries make some use of other languages, they should also be sensitive to the struggle that receivers whose English is their second or third language encounter with the English language, and should attempt to maximize their use of English (practice makes perfect). Figure 8–3 provides some ground rules for communicating in English with receivers whose knowledge of English is secondary to their native language.

Identifying the Right Transmission Channel Stage

Typically, a message may be transmitted in writing, orally, and nonverbally (body/facial expressions). Ongoing advancements in the communications technologies present new means of transmitting messages. Written messages can now be transmitted via mail, computer, fax, and electronic mail. Oral messages can be transmitted via meetings, telephone, and video teleconferencing. Nonverbal messages can be sent via meetings and video teleconferencing. Some of these communication channels are not available in many countries, especially in many of the less-developed countries.

Written or Spoken Message?

Regardless of the channels available, the sender must decide whether to transmit the message in writing or orally. Cultural norms affect the decision. Some cultures prefer written messages and others prefer spoken messages. Individuals in high-context cultures, which value trust, tend to prefer spoken communication and agreements; confirming an idea in writing may be taken as an indication that you think their word is no good. On the other hand, people in low-context cultures, which value efficiency, tend to prefer written communication and agreements.[18] Also, as indicated earlier, many people who understand English as a second or third language learned it by reading and listening, and they have not developed a strong command of the language. These receivers may therefore feel more comfortable with written communication than with oral communication, because written communication gives them more time to understand the message. Certainly, the literacy level of the audience also affects the decision. If there is a high illiteracy rate, oral messages would be more effective than written messages.

A Framework for Dealing with Language Differences   FIGURE 8–3 ◆

◆ Keep your communications simple, short, and to the point. Do not use complicated English words. Monosyllables are fine, if they say what you mean.

◆ Try to eliminate all words that have more than one meaning (i.e., does "right" mean "correct," "the opposite of left," or to "re-do"?).

◆ Don't make nouns into verbs.

◆ Don't use industry-specific jargon, acronyms, or abbreviations. Avoid all "professional-ese." There simply are no equal translations.

◆ Use action words and verbs to describe exactly what you mean (i.e., don't say "take the bus"; instead, say "ride the bus"), and avoid word pictures unless they are exactly what you mean (don't say, "walk me through this again," or "run that by me again").

◆ Always start out and stay formal unless and until your correspondent informs you to do otherwise; use titles, last names, and so forth.

◆ Avoid humor: It doesn't translate well. What is hysterically funny in one culture can be meaningless in another.

◆ Eliminate all slang, idioms, and sport-dominated terms from your English. Business English is loaded with them, and terms like "give me a ballpark figure," "hit a home run," "pinch hit for me in the morning," "that idea is from left field," "he really threw me a curve ball," "I'll touch base with you tomorrow" all have absolutely *no meaning* in cultures where they don't play baseball.

◆ On the telephone and in person, speak slowly, simply, and deliberately. Show respect and empathy. Never shout to be understood.

◆ On long-distance communications the rule should be only one communication per item or question. A comprehensive fax of 15 major points and sub-points requiring a response, in English, to a group-oriented culture will either engender no response at all (they will be overwhelmed at the task), or can cause a delay of anywhere between several months to a decade or two.

◆ Be realistic: They don't speak English, they have to translate the document, they have to consider it as a group, and then find someone available who speaks English to retranslate their final answer back to you.

Source: Dean Foster, "Business Across Borders: International Etiquette for the Effective Global Secretary," *The Secretary,* October 1992, p. 24. Copyright © 1992 Stratton Publishing and Marketing Inc. All rights reserved. Used with permission.

Format of Messages

There is no universal written message format. For example, standard paper sizes differ among many countries. The standard letter-size paper in the United States is 8.5″ × 11″; in Europe, the page is longer, but in many countries it is narrower and shorter. This can create filing, printing, duplicating, and other problems. The physical format of the message must be adapted to different cultures. Similarly, presentation formats, including presentation length, timing, number of visual aids, flamboyance, and the nature of interaction with the audience, also vary among cultures.[19]

Body Language

Body language, including eye contact, physical distance and touching, hand movements, pointing, and facial expressions, which vary across cultures,[20] also affects the transmission of a message.

Eye Contact. Eye contact between superiors and subordinates is avoided in many Southeast Asian cultures because it is a sign of disrespect. On the other hand, in Western cultures avoiding eye contact is a sign of disrespect. Therefore, an American and a Malaysian subordinate may very well view each other as being disrespectful when the American attempts to make eye contact and the Malaysian avoids it.

Physical Distance and Touching. In Asia, once a relationship is established between individuals, **physical distance** is placed between them, and **touching** or display of emotions are substantially reduced. On the other hand, in Latin America, once a relationship is established between individuals, physical distance between them is reduced, and touching and display of emotions are increased.

Hand Movements. Some cultures make greater use of **hand movements** when communicating than others. For example, Italians tend to use their hands extensively, while Americans make limited use of hand movements—they believe that use of too much hand movement while communicating orally distracts the receiver(s), thus impairing communication.

Pointing. **Pointing** with the index finger is rude in some cultures, including those of Sudan, Venezuela, and Sri Lanka. Pointing your index finger toward yourself is insulting in Germany, the Netherlands, and Switzerland.

Facial Expressions. Russians do not use **facial expressions** very much and Scandinavians do not use many gestures. This does not mean that they are not enthusiastic.[21]

Transmission of Messages Through Mediators

Messages (written, spoken, and nonverbal) are typically sent directly to the receiver(s). In some situations in some cultures, it is not wise to send messages directly to the receiver(s); it is wise to use a **mediator**—the encoder sends the message to a mediator (a third party), who in turn conveys it to the receiver(s). For example, sincere Americans are often factually blunt and frank, even if it upsets the other person.[22] The Japanese, however, culturally do not practice nor accept overt criticism and bluntness well. In Japan, to be sincere means having concern for the emotional, not the factual. In fact, not to be offensive (a concern for the emotional), a Japanese receiver may not even say "no" to a request from a sender with which he or she does not want to comply; instead, he or she would respond "maybe" (which really means "no" in Japan). Therefore, when a message being transmitted to a Japanese receiver must contain critical and blunt facts, it is better to submit it through a mediator. The bluntness is mitigated because the message was only indirectly passed from the sender to the receiver.

In Japan, when use of a mediator or message is too impractical, the Japanese use **informal get-togethers** to discuss formal matters. At the informal meeting's setting (often after work hours in bars, nightclubs, and restaurants), serious matters can be obscured as entertainment. Discussions in such settings can be semi-serious and hint of disagreements (the message can be blunt, but not too blunt), which would be unwelcome in formal settings.

Communication Principles

There is no doubt that the ability to communicate across cultures and languages is one of the most important skills required in global managers and business people. Professors Ronald E. Dulek, John S. Fielden, and John S. Hill, all with the University of Alabama, devised a three-set series of cross-cultural communication "do's" and "don'ts."[23] These are outlined in Figure 8–4. The three sets of principles are: **Conversational principles,** those that senders must remember in all aspects of cross-cultural communication; **presentation principles,** those applicable when making oral presentations to a foreign audience; and **written principles,** those which must be remembered when transmitting written messages across cultures.[24]

The Receiving-Decoding Stage

In cross-cultural communication, decoding by the receiver of signals is subject to social values and cultural variables not necessarily present in the sender. Therefore, the most effective way to understand cross-cultural communication is to focus on the decoding process and the role of perception in communication. Communication itself is best understood from the perspective of the receiver, not the sender, nor the channel or the encoded message itself.[25] This means that transmission of a message is by itself not communication; a conscious perception of signals at the receiver's end is necessary for communication to have occurred.

This suggests that an effective sender of a message understands the receiver's perceptions, which in essence means that he or she is both an encoder and a decoder. For effective communication to take place when the sender does not understand the receiver's perceptions, the receiver must understand the sender's perceptions; he or she is both an encoder and a decoder. Either the sender or the receiver (or both) must have knowledge of the other's **environmental, cultural, sociocultural, and psychocultural con-**

◆   **FIGURE 8-4   Do's and Don'ts of Cross-Cultural Communication**

Conversational Principles

1. *High-context* cultures need to know as much as possible about the sender, such as what makes him or her "tick," and the company he or she represents. Conversations about the sender's family, company, and current events are used to "warm up" relationships. And these people like to know about senders even before they meet them.
2. Foreigners who learn English often learn only formal English. These people therefore have difficulty in comprehending jargon, slang, etc. Thus, the sender should speak slowly, clearly, and simply, and he or she should avoid use of jargon, slang, cliches, and idioms.
3. It is good manners and diplomacy to learn and speak a few phrases using your host's language.
4. Pay close attention to the body language and tone of voice. Communicating disinterest or impatience will embarrass or insult many people. Loud oral communication is socially unacceptable in many parts of Asia and the Middle East, but it is acceptable in many parts of Europe and Central America.

Presentation Principles

1. Americans tend to like spontaneous, unrehearsed presentations. In most other nations, however, such presentations convey the impression that the speaker has not bothered to prepare sufficiently, thus demonstrating disrespect for the audience. Disrespect is further shown when a speaker writes on the blackboard or on transparencies during the presentation. Customized presentations are therefore appreciated in most cultures.
2. Be sensitive to the fact that different audiences in different cultures behave differently during presentations. In Japan, for example, during presentations, business people generally sit quietly and nod their heads to indicate that they understand— not that they agree. When they frenzily talk amongst themselves, it is an indication that the speaker has said something offensive. Also, be sensitive that in many cultures the audience's not looking at you while you speak does not mean that they are disinterested—in America, the audience's not looking at the speaker is a sign of disinterest.
3. Design your presentation's length, completeness, and interruptability to the culture and language capabilities. For example, Americans, Swiss, and Germans like fast-paced, efficient presentations. Most cultures, however, prefer slower, more deliberate presentations. Slower speaking paces are definitely mandatory when a

texts. Thus, when the amount of such knowledge is small on both sides, communication ineffectiveness results.

For example, in American culture it is quite acceptable to pass food at a dinner table using one's left hand, but in some Middle East cultures it is quite unacceptable. If an American transacting business in the

translator is needed or when the audience does not have good command of the language which the speaker is using. Also, never show any sign of impatience when a member of the audience who does not have command of your language is struggling or is clumsy in encoding a question. In *high-context* cultures, presentations should be short, separate segments, with questions and answers in between. In *low-context* cultures, America, for instance, questions are usually reserved for the end of the presentation.
4. Match age and rank of presenter to the audience's cultural expectations. For example, in *high-context* cultures age and seniority is a major indicator of status and wisdom. Thus, a young speaker in these cultures may not be appreciated. For instance, a young American executive sent by an American firm to negotiate a business deal may be taken to mean that the firm is not too concerned about the business deal.

Writing Principles

1. In *low-context* cultures, where efficiency is highly valued, written communication should be organized in such a way that the central point is immediately and directly stated. In *high-context* cultures, where efficiency is valued less, the communication should be less focused on getting the job done and more personally revealing. For example, people in *high-context* cultures will not read a detailed contract; they feel that no one will be so ill-bred as to camouflage anything in fine print.
2. The style should be adapted to cultural preferences. For example, individuals in *high-context* cultures place great emphasis on respect and politeness, and writing etiquette requires that subordinates are asked to "consider" performing a task or "if at all possible" complete a task. Arab and Latin American cultures tend to be poetic in their writing styles, and communications are filled with exaggerations, colorful adjectives, and metaphors. People in many cultures think that Americans tend to demonstrate egocentricism by overusing "I" and "my."
3. If the message is important, whenever possible, enclose a translation in the receiver's native language. Translations are both helpful to the receiver and diplomatic.

Source: Adapted from Ronald E. Dulek, John S. Fielden, and John S. Hill, "International Communication: An Executive Primer," *Business Horizons,* January–February 1991, 21–24. Copyright © 1991 JAI Press Inc. Used with permission from JAI Press Inc. All rights reserved.

Middle East is aware of this custom, when out to dinner or lunch with local clients, he or she will pass food only with his or her right hand. Doing so will permit communication between the American and the locals to proceed smoothly (a communication barrier is not established). If, however, the American is not aware of the custom and passes food with his or her left hand, it will offend the locals and the communication flow is impaired (a communication barrier is established). If, however, the local is aware that Americans instinctively pass food with either hand, depending on which is more convenient (efficient), and the local is "understanding," the communication flow may proceed smoothly (no communication barrier is built).

In reality, it may be difficult to find "understanding" locals, as most will expect you to come to their territory prepared. For instance, if you are an American conducting business in China out to dinner with local business clients, it may be difficult to find one whose respect you will not lose if you ask for a fork (which is customary in America), as opposed to eating with chopsticks (which is customary in China). Also, it may be amusing if at first you are clumsy using chopsticks (as well as clumsy in using Chinese phrases, such as saying "good morning" in Chinese, which you are expected to use); in a long-term relationship, however, the clumsiness will cease to be amusing, and it may actually become a handicap. Of course, if the above transactions were taking place in America, the Chinese clients would have to be understanding, and they might have to use a fork as well. But even in this situation, ultimately, it might depend on who needs whom the most. It might be wise for the American to show courtesy by occasionally taking the Chinese visitors to a local Chinese restaurant where they can use chopsticks. Of course, it may be wise for the Chinese hosts to occasionally take visiting Western clients to a local Western restaurant where they can use forks. This would symbolize a show of mutual understanding and respect for both cultures. And it certainly would be intellectually self-enhancing if one learned to do it either way.

The Nature of Received Signals

Receivers take **signals** transmitted by senders, decode them, and try to understand them. The receiver-decoded signal is a "sign" constructed of two parts: the signifier and the signified.[26] A **sign** is a signal that is recognized, structured into a category and assigned meaning. The **signifier** is the sound or shape of the signal, which is sensorially perceived without meaning attached to it yet; the **signified** is the meaning attached to the signifier. "The linkage of new, unattributed signifiers to already-existing signifieds is a large part of the process of decoding communication messages."[27] Cross-cultural communication is ineffective "when signs are not recognized because they differ from the signs in the culture-driven repository."[28] (See Figure 8–5.)

Attaching Meaning to Signals   FIGURE 8–5   ◆

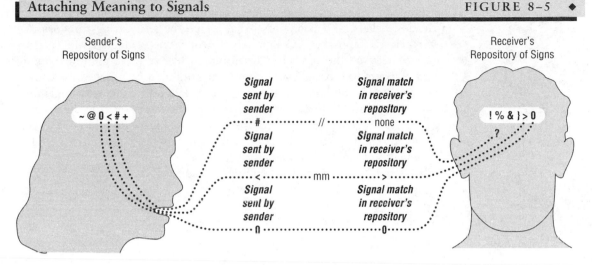

Sender's Repository of Signs

~ @ 0 < # +

Signal sent by sender
············· // ············· none ·······

Signal match in receiver's repository

Signal sent by sender
< ············ mm ············· >

Signal match in receiver's repository

Signal sent by sender
0 ·············· 0 ········

Signal match in receiver's repository

Receiver's Repository of Signs

! % & } > 0

?

The # signal sent does not match a corresponding sign in the receiver's repository (?). Thus, no communication has taken place (//). The sign # may signify **large** in the sender's repository, but *large* is signified by & in the receiver's repository. Therefore, for effective communication to take place, either the sender must add & to his or her repository or the receiver must add # to his or her repository.

The < signal sent is matched by the receiver with the seemingly corresponding sign > in his or her repository. Both believe that the signs are the same and communication has taken place. But ineffective communication (*mm*) has actually taken place because while the signs appear the same, they actually point in different directions. The signs < and > may signify *He's old*. But to the sender *He's old*, in a certain context, it may mean *He's not qualified for the job*, but to the receiver, in the same context, may mean that *He has wisdom and experience and is qualified for the job*. Therefore, for effective communication to take place, either the sender or the receiver must understand the contextual differences, and encode or decode the meaning accordingly.

The O signal sent matches the signal in the receiver's repository precisely. Effective communication has taken place.

Receivers of **cross-cultural messages continually adjust** and adapt incoming signifiers to the existing repository of signs, and adapt and adjust the repository of signifieds to create new signs. Thus, a competent cross-cultural receiver constantly challenges his or her repository of existing signs and expands it in order to participate in the matching of signs with the sender.[29] (Certainly, learning to eat using both a fork and chopsticks enhances cross-cultural competence.)

Therefore, to communicate effectively across cultures, the transmission of signs to a receiver must take into account the cultural factors—values, attitudes, beliefs, and behaviors—that shape the structuring categories of the receiver's repository. Cognitively learned knowledge of the cultures involved may be the basis for developing effective cross-cultural competence. Barriers to cross-cultural communication can be reduced by knowledge and understanding of varying cultural factors, along with a genuine desire to communicate effectively across cultures. All of this means that "intercultural communication competence is the encoding and decoding of attributed signifieds to signifiers in matches that correspond to signs held in the other communicator's repository."[30]

It should be noted that to communicate effectively across cultures also requires good listening skills—one must be able to listen to spoken as well as to nonverbal (such as facial expressions) messages. Thus, an impatient American who constantly looks at his or her watch is not likely to communicate effectively across cultures.

DEVELOPING CROSS-CULTURAL COMMUNICATION COMPETENCE

Professor Linda Beamer of California State University—Los Angeles has developed a model for the purpose of describing the process of **developing cross-cultural communication competence**.[31] The model proposes five levels of learning: acknowledgement of diversity, organizing information according to stereotypes, posing questions to challenge the stereotypes, analyzing communication episodes, and generating "other culture" messages. The intent of the learning process, according to Professor Beamer, "is to develop the ability to decode effectively signs that come from members of other cultures, within a business context, and to encode messages using signs that carry the encoder's intended meaning to members of other cultures."[32] The five levels do not cease to exist once attained; they are continually revisited in the process of learning. This means that newer differences in a culture are constantly being discovered. The ensuing sections describe Professor Beamer's model.

Acknowledging Diversity

At this level of learning, the learner becomes aware of cultural differences. He or she addresses the initial issue of perception—the recognition that formerly unknown and unrecognized signs are being sent. Individuals in homogeneous, high-context cultures, who possess limited experience of cultural diversity, need to start by acknowledging the diversity of signifiers for signifieds already understood. At this level, definitions of basic concepts for discussing diversity are important, such as "bias," "ethnocentricity," "stereotype," "value," and "culture." Especially when discussing signifiers, language is the most apparent cultural difference—but it does not always generate **cultural fluency.**

Organizing Information According to Stereotypes

At this level, **stereotypes** that distinguish a particular culture and its members are identified. Stereotypes are normally simple or brief. For example, "Americans are efficiency oriented"; "Latin Americans place the well-being of family members and friends ahead of organizational efficiency"; "the French are rude to non-French speaking visitors." Stereotypes provide some familiarity with a culture, and they may be helpful and even accurate to some extent, but they are myopic insights that reveal only *part* of the entire culture. Therefore, knowledge of a culture's stereotypes does not mean understanding of a culture, and it may actually be an obstacle to the development of cross-cultural communication competence. Stereotypes fail to challenge the signs within their own repository of meanings—they fail to ask if some other signified can be associated with the signifier. One must progress beyond this level of cross-cultural communication.

Posing Questions to Challenge the Stereotypes

At this level, **stereotypes are challenged.** The learner asks questions about, for instance, how members of a business enterprise describe that organization, their relationships to one another and to their material environment, and their position in relation to the universe. Asking questions is apt to disclose attitudes that are crucial for understanding business activities, such as individuals' attitudes toward time, status and role, obligations in relationships, responsibility and the decision-making processes, the role of law, and the role of technology. Basically, questions challenge stereotypes, and can be patterned to probe what members of a culture "value, how they behave in certain circumstances because of their values, what their attitudes are toward institutions in their society and toward events beyond their control."[33] Primary and/or secondary research will help provide answers to the questions.

Professor Beamer developed a framework outlining several questions that must be answered. The questions relate to the cultural differences in behavior and attitude that affect business communication. The framework develops five areas of value orientations: thinking and knowing, doing and achieving, the self, social organization, and the universe.[34]

Thinking and Knowing

This value orientation relates to how people in a culture obtain, organize, and communicate information about the culture. A group of questions about the culture must be answered:

1. *Ways to know.* In some cultures, an individual only knows something when it is conceptualized and abstracted; in others, what a person knows is contingent on first-hand experience.
2. *Activity that results in knowledge.* In some cultures, knowing is attained by probing, questioning, and atomizing; in others it is attained by mastering a received body of knowledge to the point where it may be reproduced.
3. *Extent of knowledge.* In some cultures, everything is knowable; in others, the indescribable nature of some things precludes their being known totally.
4. *Patterns of thinking in the culture.* Some cultures use mainly cause-and-effect patterns; they value planning, and their conceptualizations, language, and institutions divulge linear thinking patterns. Other cultures stress "context in patterns of thinking: the interconnections and relationships between things are important and a lattice or net pattern emerges."[35]

Doing and Achieving

This orientation relates to activity and achievement. Some cultures identify goals, work to achieve them, and are results-oriented; other cultures emphasize the present, commemorate simply being, and are relationship-oriented. Furthermore, some cultures apply a sequential approach to the completion of tasks (for example, they can serve only one customer at a time), while others apply a simultaneous approach (they can serve several customers at a time). Some cultures have more tolerance for uncertainty and ambiguity than others. And some cultures view luck as a significant influencer of outcomes; other cultures assign little or no importance to luck.

The Self

The self value refers to the relative importance of individualism versus interdependence. In cultures where individual efforts are rewarded, personal competitiveness is high; in interdependent cultures where people are not interested in individual achievement and groups are rewarded, competitiveness may be detestable. In some cultures age is more important than training and experience, but not in other cultures. When hiring people, in some cultures there is greater preference for one sex over the other.

The Organization of Society

Cultures' value orientations related to social structure contrast. The contrasts include: (a) a tendency toward temporary versus permanent group membership; (b) preference for private ownership of material goods versus community ownership; (c) a tendency to distrust form versus a preference for form; (d) a more egalitarian versus a more hierarchical structure; and

(e) a general practice of approaching authority directly versus using a mediated link to authority. These orientations affect the format, organization, and tone of business communication documents, as well as interpersonal communication.

The Universe

Cultural contrasts in this respect include humans dominating nature versus nature dominating humans; time being linear versus time being cyclical; human activity at the center of the universe versus divine beings at the center of all activities; change as good versus change as bad; and death as the end of life versus death as merely a part of life.[36]

Analyzing Communication Episodes

The understanding obtained by challenging cultural stereotypes can be utilized to analyze events in actual situations. Situations may reveal effective communication, ineffective communication, or both. As the situation is analyzed, new meanings for communication behavior can be ascribed. At this point of developing cross-cultural communication abilities, "learning focuses on depth of understanding, and application of the abstractions in level three [posing questions to challenge the stereotypes] during the plotting of a culture's value orientations."[37] The pool of questions about a culture's values is cultivated and enlarged with the addition of new insights from particular communication cases. This increases competence in both encoding and decoding cross-cultural messages.

Generating "Other-Culture" Messages

At this level, the communicator becomes cross-culturally competent "when messages may be encoded and directed as if from within the new culture and when messages from the new culture may be decoded and responded to successfully."[38] He or she has developed the ability to "become the other." At this level of cross-cultural competence, communicators continually evaluate **"other-culture" messages** against the **repository of signs** they have stored in their mental databases. They possess the ability to modify the database or match incoming signs and messages to those already known. They are "able to manipulate information received as well as information stored and to make linkages between levels of understanding."[39]

SUMMARY

This chapter has presented the communication process in an international/cross-cultural context. How cross-cultural communicators (senders) construct ideas to be communicated is influenced by the receivers' culture. The same concepts will be perceived differently across cultures. Thus, what works in one culture will not necessarily work in another, and adaptations must be made. The words, gestures, symbols, idioms, jargon, and slang a sender uses to communicate an idea are also affected by the particular receivers' culture. Different societies use different languages and social behaviors to communicate. Therefore, for effective communication to take place, the appropriate adaptations must be made.

The means—written, oral, or nonverbal—of transmitting the message is also affected by the receivers' culture. Culturally, some people prefer oral communication and others prefer written communication. Some cultures prefer flamboyant, flashy presentations, other cultures are offended by such presentations. The cross-cultural communicator must use the means most fitted to the receivers' culture. In essence, the sender of the message must know and use the words, concepts, and behaviors that the receivers will understand. Which means that, to be effective, a cross-cultural communicator must learn to be both a sender and a receiver.

Key Terms

1. Cross-cultural communication
2. Unique written, oral, and non-verbal languages
3. Unique social customs and behaviors
4. English as the language of communication in global business
5. Language translator
6. Realistic objectives
7. Realistic time frame
8. Same word, different meanings
9. Requirements for formality and informality
10. Dual-translation
11. Simultaneous and sequential oral translators
12. Effective translator
13. Updating translator skills
14. High-context and low-context cultures
15. The audience's motivations
16. Primary and secondary audiences
17. Dictionary translation
18. English as a second or third language
19. Body language
20. Eye contact, physical distance, and touching
21. Hand movements, pointing, and facial expressions
22. Mediators
23. Informal get-togethers
24. Conversational, presentation, and written principles
25. Environmental, cultural, sociocultural, psychocultural contexts
26. Signal, sign, signifier, and signified
27. Cross-cultural message adjustment
28. Developing cross-cultural communication competence
29. Cultural fluency
30. Stereotyping

31. Challenging cultural stereo-   33. Repository of signs
    types
32. "Other-culture" messages

Discussion Questions and Exercises

1. What are the major causes of cross-cultural communication ineffectiveness?

2. Discuss some of the factors that affect the development of an idea to be communicated across cultures.

3. Discuss some of the major factors that must be considered when encoding a message to be sent across cultures.

4. An American executive's firm has just completed negotiating a business deal with a company in Japan. You have been employed to help him or her write the contract. What would you advise your client to do?

5. Discuss some of the ways expressions and nonverbal communication affect the cross-cultural encoding process.

6. How do "formality" and "informality" affect the cross-cultural encoding process?

7. An American executive who is preparing to communicate with a French audience enlists your services to help him or her write the substance of the message. With respect to the amount of information a culture requires, what would you advise your client to do?

8. Discuss the dual translation process.

9. Discuss the two types of translators.

10. Discuss the factors that describe an effective translator.

11. You are an executive from a low-context culture preparing a message to be delivered orally to an audience from a high-context culture. How would you structure the message?

12. Discuss the role audience motivation plays in encoding messages.

13. English appears to be emerging as the language of global business. You are from England and you are going to speak to an audience whose English is a second or third language. Discuss the "do's" and "don'ts" of delivering the message.

14. Discuss the ways culture affects the selection of the right transmission channel.

15. How are mediators useful in cross-cultural transmission of messages?

16. What are the fundamentals of the three communication principles?

17. "The most effective way to understand cross-cultural communication is to focus on the decoding process and the role of perception in communication." Explain this statement.

18. Differentiate between "a sign," "the signifier," and "the signified."

19. Discuss how cross-cultural communication competence is developed.

Assignment

Select a short story written in English and write a dictionary translation of the story into a foreign language that you do not understand. Then have someone who speaks both English and the foreign language fluently interpret it back to English. How does the back translation compare with your translation? Share the experience with your classmates.

The Efficient Cross-Cultural Communicator

CASE 8–1

Source: Excerpted from Dean Foster, "Business Across Borders: International Etiquette for the Global Secretary," *The Secretary,* October 1992, p. 20. Copyright © 1992 Stratton Publishing and Marketing Inc. All rights reserved. Used with permission.

I was speaking recently with an American manager quite down in the dumps and befuddled over the fact that cooperation from the Mexicans, with whom his office did a great deal of work, was becoming increasingly difficult. He just could not figure out why. I asked him to outline all major changes he could think of that occurred around the time that cooperation began to change and he admitted that he had replaced his assistant around the same time. "Was this assistant responsible for communications between your office and the Mexicans?" I inquired, and got a positive response. "Is your new assistant similarly responsible?" Yes, he said.

By the look of things, the new assistant was certainly doing her job. There was no doubt about the efficiency of the letters, e-mails, faxes, and the like that went out like clockwork to the Mexico office. In fact, the new assistant had streamlined the communications system within the office significantly. Now there was a specific form to be used for different types of letters, more precise, straight to the point, and usable for mailing lists. Different criteria were now used for sending out different types of correspondence, time periods had been established that would automatically signal certain types of correspondence to be released to certain individuals, and so forth. Then I looked at the previous assistant's correspondence. It certainly was more cumbersome: Each letter was individually written, following no predetermined form, and was quite customized, depending upon to whom it was written and the circumstances. In fact, each correspondence usually acknowledged the individual to whom it was being written in quite personal ways. All correspondence seemed to be about 30 percent greetings, with much inquiry into the health and happiness of the reader's business and family. The significant issues—the reason for the letter in the first place—usually were embedded somewhere in the middle of all this, and constituted only about half of the total letter. A final 20 percent was spent at the end, once again, on all sorts of non-business-related issues, from hoping to see you next month in

Guadalajara, to the recounting of a memorable meal that was shared the last time they were together.

Comparing these two very different styles of correspondence, my American manager friend agreed that he regretted replacing his former assistant, but that the company simply couldn't grow spending so much time and resources on old-fashioned, inefficient patterns and systems of communication. I asked him if Mexico constituted an important market for him. He answered that more than 80 percent of his business was with Mexico.

QUESTIONS

1. Discuss how the concept of low-context and high-context cultures led to this problem.
2. Assume that you are a consultant hired by this manager to solve the problem. What would you advise the manager to do?

The Elusive System

CASE 8–2

Source: Roderick MacLeod, *China, Inc.: How to Do Business with the Chinese* (Toronto: Bantam Books, 1988), pp. 33–35. Copyright © 1988 by Roderick MacLeod. Used by permission of Bantam Books, a division of Bantam Doubleday Dell Publishing Group, Inc.

GBAH, the General Bureau of Animal Husbandry, is a division of the huge Chinese Ministry of Agriculture. It received its first grant from the UNDP—the United Nations Development Program—shortly after China joined the UN. It was a grant to study the feasibility of irrigation in the Mongolian grasslands, but one condition of the grant required the GBAH to demonstrate that it had adequate systems for safeguarding and accounting for the funds. So the GBAH reluctantly allocated some of the precious funds to employ a Western consulting firm to show them the systems they should have. That's what I was in China for, in part—to snag opportunities like that for my firm—so I was delighted. Since we looked upon it as an entry to the "China market," which we believed to be potentially huge and profitable, we scoured our worldwide resources for a UNDP expert and for Chinese-speaking staff.

Even though the fee would adequately compensate only for one, we sent a team of four people, a UNDP and cattle-farming expert, two Chinese-speaking consultants, and me, for the purpose of doing a bang-up job that we could use as a future reference.

We arrived as scheduled and went to the Beijing Hotel as directed. We weren't expected. It took a couple of hours to get somebody from the GBAH, accompanied by a person from the ministry's Foreign Affairs Department, down to the hotel to work on the problem, and it took another twelve hours to get the four of us into rooms in the Yanjing Hotel, a couple of miles away and several steps down on Beijing's prestige scale. Sitting for fourteen hours in the barroom of the Beijing Hotel, anxious and helpless, unwashed and unloved, is not the best way to start coping with combined jet lag and culture shock.

The next day the GBAH officials came to the hotel, and the day was spent going over the contract, discussing arrangements, and having a con-gratulatory banquet. The day after that, twenty Mongolian accountants arrived to be trained in the UNDP accounting requirements. They looked like country people, and farm people: weather beaten faces, callused hands, worn Mao jackets, and the bemused expressions country people have all over the world on their first visit to the city. Each was the accountant for his "Banner" (Mongolian communes are called Banners, evoking images of troops of wild horsemen, although they are really political and economic units of up to several hundred thousand people) and thus was a responsible and experienced official.

We got to work, proud of the charts and tables we had laboriously drawn by hand and labeled in Chinese, and of the overhead projector we had brought along for displaying them. The two Chinese-speaking consultants had been told what to say by the expert, they had spent a week or more at the difficult task of translating it from English to Chinese, and they were ready to give all-day lectures in Chinese. The expert and I sat in ready to answer questions or help out as we could. The Mongolians listened quietly, diligently taking notes, for two days.

The third day the GBAH officials were back and a long discussion with the two Chinese-speaking consultants delayed the opening of the session. It appeared that what the Chinese were being told wasn't what they had con-tracted to find out. The Mongolians sat idly in the meeting room for another several hours while we tried to find out what the GBAH wanted, and tried to convince them that they knew all there was to know and should be satisfied. The GBAH wasn't satisfied.

We stayed up all night, literally. The expert and I redid the lectures and charts, and the other two did their best to put them into Chinese. Ordinarily, it takes at least three times as long to put a lecture into Chinese as it does for the expert to write it in English. They didn't have that much time; they did it between eleven at night and seven in the morning.

The next day was a tiring one, and at the end of it the expert, who didn't like Chinese food, went off to call on his country's ambassador. (He hap-pened to be Irish, but that's incidental; it seemed to me that all citizens of small countries treated their embassies in Beijing as homes-away-from-home.) The rest of us worked away at the charts and transparencies and lectures, and fell into bed exhausted.

Next day the GBAH officials were back. It still wasn't right. Since it was Saturday (the Chinese work a six-day week) we gave the Mongolians a long weekend and spent Saturday and Sunday trying to get it right. Except for the expert: He worked Saturday and then went to the embassy for Saturday night and Sunday.

Monday morning there was a conference to see if we were getting it. The expert said there were only so many ways you could slice up one piece of cake, and he thought they'd tried them all. The GBAH still wasn't satisfied. The Mongolian accountants had typically impassive faces, but not so much so that their irritation and frustration weren't showing through.

It went on and on like that. The GBAH had spent their money and wanted what they had paid for. The Mongolians wanted to be sure that they could measure up in the frightening new world of international agencies. We had our professional pride in our work, and also visions of future assignments driving us, and we were determined to get it right. Except for the expert, who spent more and more time at the embassy.

Finally, everybody was exhausted and the allotted time was up. The GBAH officials put a good face on it, saying the Chinese equivalent of "it had been a learning experience." Everybody went home, hurt and sad.

QUESTIONS

1. Based on what you learned in this chapter, what do you believe went wrong in this case? In answering the question, you should relate to the communication process.
2. How could the problem have been avoided?

Notes

1. Excerpted from Jeremy Main, "How 21 Men Got Global in 35 Days," *Fortune*, November 6, 1989, p. 71.

2. See, for example, David Ricks, *Big Business Blunders: Mistakes in Multinational Marketing* (Homewood, IL: Dow Jones-Irwin, 1983).

3. R. E. Dulek, J. S. Fielden, and J. S. Hill, "International Communication: An Executive Primer," *Business Horizons* 34, no. 1 (1991): 20.

4. This discussion draws from Mary Munter, "Cross-Cultural Communication for Managers," *Business Horizons* (May–June 1993): 69.

5. J. R. Zeeman, "Service—The Cutting Edge of Global Competition: What United Airlines is Learning in the Pacific." Remarks before the Academy of International Business Annual Meeting, Chicago, IL, November 14, 1987.

6. L. S. Dillon, "Japanese Rules for Communication," *Personnel Administrator* 19 (January 1984): 92.

7. "Going International, Part 1, Bridging the Culture Gap," video by Copeland Griggs Productions, San Francisco, California.

8. This discussion draws from Dean Foster, "Business Across Borders: International Etiquette for the Effective Global Secretary," *The Secretary*, October 1992, pp. 20–24.

9. Ibid., p. 24.

10. This discussion draws from Lyle Sussman and Denise M. Johnson, "The Interpreted Executive: Theory, Models, and Implications," *The Journal of Business Communication* 30, no. 4 (1993): 415–434.

11. This discussion draws from Sussman and Johnson, ibid., pp. 419–420.

12. Edward T. Hall, "How Cultures Collide," *Psychology Today* (July 1976): 67–74.

13. Munter, "Cross-Cultural Communication for Managers," p. 74.

14. Hall, "How Cultures Collide," pp. 67–74.

15. Ibid., p. 74.

16. This discussion draws on Munter, "Cross-Cultural Communication for Managers," p. 73.

17. This discussion draws from Foster, "Business Across Borders," p. 24.

18. Munter, "Cross-Cultural Communication for Managers," p. 74.

19. Ibid., p. 75.

20. Ibid.

21. Ibid., p. 76.

22. This discussion draws from Jon P. Alston, "*Wa, Guanxi,* and *Inhwa:* Managerial Principles in Japan, China, and Korea," *Business Horizons* 32, no. 2 (March–April 1989): 27–28.

23. Dulek, Fielden, and Hill, "International Communication," pp 21–24.

24. Ibid., p. 21.

25. This discussion draws from Linda Beamer, "Learning Intercultural Communication Competence," *The Journal of Business Communication* 29, no. 3 (1992): 285–303.

26. L. A. Saussure, *Course in General Linguistics,* trans. R. Harris, cited in Beamer, ibid., p. 247.

27. Beamer, "Learning Intercultural Communication Competence," p. 387.

28. Ibid.

29. Ibid., p. 289.

30. Ibid.

31. Ibid., pp. 291–301.

32. Ibid., p. 291.

33. Ibid., p. 294.

34. Ibid, pp. 296–300.

35. Ibid., p. 296.

36. Ibid., p. 300.

37. Ibid.

38. Ibid., p. 301.

39. Ibid.

Chapter Nine

Cross-Cultural Business Practices and Negotiations

Around a conference table in a large U.S. office tower, three Americans sat with their new boss, Mr. Akiro Kusumoto, the newly appointed head of a Japanese firm's American subsidiary, and two of his Japanese lieutenants. The meeting was called to discuss ideas for reducing operating costs. Mr. Kusumoto began by outlining his company's aspirations for its long-term U.S. presence. He then turned to the current budgetary matter. One Japanese manager politely offered one suggestion, and an American then proposed another. After gingerly discussing the alternatives for quite some time, the then exasperated American blurted out: "Look, that idea is just not going to have much impact. Look at the numbers! We should cut this program, and I think we should do it as soon as possible!" In the face of such bluntness, uncommon and unacceptable in Japan, Mr. Kusumoto fell silent. He leaned back, drew air between his teeth, and felt a longing to "return East". . . . In overseas settings American business people are being compared increasingly to Japanese people. . . . Local business people deal with both Americans and Japanese, sometimes choosing between the two. In such settings, relative differences between American and Japanese are most apparent. Since America's future in international business depends in part on the quality of these overseas relationships, it is time to hold up a mirror to American ways, warts and all.[1]

Objectives of the Chapter

In this era of globalization of business activities, managers from one country will often be conducting business with and/or sitting at negotiating tables with managers from other nations and cultures. Conducting business and negotiating in one's own culture are complex tasks; they are, however, far more complex when they are conducted across cultures. Each side tends to have perceivable differences in ways of conducting business, language, dress, preferences, and legal and ethical considerations. Understanding and minding the cultural variables of the country where business transactions are taking place is one of the most important aspects of being successful in any international business endeavor. A lack of understanding and/or disregarding the variables will most likely lead to failure. Practical Perspective 9–1 presents an illustration of how an internationalizing firm's not heeding to local culture (Disney's managers insisted on doing things the way they did them at home) leads to problems. The objectives of this chapter are therefore to discuss:

1. The ways business practices vary across cultures.
2. The ways negotiating tactics vary across cultures.
3. The ways negotiating styles vary across cultures.
4. The negotiating styles in numerous countries.

CROSS-CULTURAL BUSINESS PRACTICES

As corporations become increasingly international and competition for global markets increases, business managers who are not attentive to cultural differences will not be able to function in foreign markets effectively—they will make their companies less competitive. Thus, effective international managers have learned how varying cultural practices across societies affects business and management practices and how to adapt to the differences. Learning something about the culture of a country before transacting business there shows respect, and those who understand the culture are more likely to develop successful, long-term business relationships than those who do not.[2] The ensuing section discusses business practices in a cross-cultural context.

The Impact of Culture on Business Practices

Approaches to conducting business vary from culture to culture, making the practice of business at the international level much more complex than in the home market. Some factors that affect **cross-cultural business** include time, thought patterns, personal space, material possessions, family roles and relationships, competitiveness and individuality, and social behavior,[3]

PRACTICAL PERSPECTIVE 9–1

Blundering Mouse

Europe got its first taste of the management style of Walt Disney Co. when Joe Shapiro started kicking in a door at the luxury Hotel Bristol here [Paris]. It was 1986, and Disney was negotiating with the French government on plans to build a big resort and theme park on the outskirts of Paris. To the exasperation of the Disney team headed by Mr. Shapiro, then the company's general counsel, the talks were taking far longer than expected. Jean-Rene Bernard, the chief French negotiator, says he was astonished when Mr. Shapiro, his patience ebbing, ran to the door of the room and began kicking it repeatedly, shouting, "Get something cheap to break!" Mr. Shapiro doesn't remember the incident, though he adds with a laugh, "there were a lot of histrionics at the time." But Disney's kick-down-the-door attitude in the planning, building and financing of Euro Disney account for many of the huge problems that plague the resort, which currently loses $1 million a day because of sky-high over-head and interest payments on loans. . . .

The irony is that even though some early French critics called the park an American cultural abomination, public acceptance hasn't been the problem. European visitors seem to love the place. . . . Euro Disney's troubles, instead, derive from a different type of culture clash. Europe may have embraced Mickey Mouse, but it hasn't taken to the brash, frequently insensitive and often overbearing style of Mickey's American corporate parent. . . . Disney's contentious attitude exacerbated the difficulties it encountered by alienating people it needed to work with, say many people familiar with the situation. Its answer to doubts or suggestions invariably was: Do as we say, because we know best. "They were always sure it would work because they were Disney," says Beatrice Descoffre, a French construction industry official who dealt with the U.S. company. "Disney," adds a colleague, "came here like the Marines going to Kuwait."

Source: Peter Gumbel and Richard Turner, "Fans Like Euro Disney But Its Parent's Goofs Weigh the Park Down," *The Wall Street Journal*, March 10, 1994, pp. A1, A12.

as well as whether a culture is high-context or low-context (discussed in Chapter 8).[4]

Time

"Time Equals Money" versus Relationships.   Some cultures, America, for example, perceive time as a commodity and an asset, and a very high importance is placed on it—**"time equals money."** The conservation of time is therefore an efficient process in these cultures. Punctuality is expected behavior; tardiness is unacceptable behavior. People in other cultures, however, do not place as much of a premium on time and punctuality; to them, time does not equal money, and tardiness is quite acceptable; and in some cultures punctuality is viewed as unreasonable behavior. Individuals in these cultures place a much greater premium on relationships and a more relaxed lifestyle than they do on time and punctuality.

Thus, business people in these cultures generally would be offended by individuals applying time-oriented behavior in business transactions; they prefer that an amicable relationship be established before business is conducted. For example, Charles Ford, commercial attaché in Guatemala, has said that:

> The inexperienced American visitor in Guatemala often tries to force a business relationship. The abrupt "always watching the clock" style is often ineffective in Guatemala. A more informed business person would engage in small talk about Guatemala, show an interest in the families of his or her associates, join them for lunch or dinner, and generally allow time for a personal relationship to develop. This holds true for Latin America in general.[5]

Schedules.   Schedules are important to individuals in some cultures, but relatively unimportant to people in other cultures. In other words, individuals in some cultures possess a "it must be done by tomorrow" mentality, but people in other cultures possess a "when it gets done is when it is done" mentality. Furthermore, in some cultures what task gets done first depends on task importance factors, but in some cultures it depends on other factors, such as relationship. For instance,

> In the Arab East, time does not generally include schedules as Americans know and use them. The time required to get something accomplished depends on the relationship. More important people get fast service from less important people, and conversely. Close relatives take absolute priority, nonrelatives are kept waiting.[6]

Therefore, telling someone in the Middle East that something must be done now or by the end of the day or by tomorrow may often prove to be a mistake. The recipient of the direction may stop work because he or she is placed under pressure and/or because he or she may view the person issuing the directive as being rude or "too pushy."

Time and Decision Making.   Some cultures take a long time to make important decisions; other cultures make important decisions quickly.

Consequently, low-level managers in cultures that take a long time to make important decisions often try to heighten their work status by taking a long time to make routine decisions. And foreign managers who try to make important decisions quickly in these cultures are likely to downgrade their importance in local people's eyes. For example,

> In Ethiopia, the time required for a decision is directly proportional to its importance. This is so much the case that low-level bureaucrats there have a way of trying to elevate the prestige of their work by taking a long time to make up their minds. (Americans in that part of the world are innocently prone to downgrade their work in the local people's eyes by trying to speed things up.)[7]

Thought Patterns

Some cultures' thought patterns are circular. **Circular cultures** believe that since individuals can see what has happened in the past, their past is ahead of them, and since they cannot see into the future, their future is behind them. Many people in these cultures view change as being bad, thus they do not see business opportunities that lie ahead. In contrast, some cultures' thought patterns are linear. **Linear cultures,** America, for example, view the past as being behind them and the future in front of them. Individuals in these cultures tend to view change as being good and attempt to take advantage of the business opportunities they foresee in the future. Circular-oriented people are likely to view a future-oriented person's behavior as forward and aggressive. Thus, people in linear cultures are far more open to new ideas and the setting of objectives than are people in circular cultures.

Personal Space

Cultures generally develop informal rules on the distance individuals remain from one another in face-to-face interactions. People in some cultures, America, for example, prefer a wide distance from those with whom they are involved in face-to-face communication, and they usually feel uncomfortable when the distance is narrow. In contrast, people in some cultures, Arabs, for instance, prefer a very short distance between themselves and those with whom are communicating, and they feel offended or rejected by those individuals who maintain a wide distance or keep backing away.

For example, Americans tend to feel comfortable in the following zones of space: zero to 18 inches for comforting or greeting; 18 inches to four feet for conversing with friends; four to 12 feet for conversing with strangers; and more than 12 feet for public space (standing in lobbies or reception areas). Venezuelans generally prefer much closer space and might view it as rude if someone backs away. On the other hand, the British tend to prefer more distant space and might view it as rude if one moves too close.[8]

Material Possessions

How individuals value material wealth varies from culture to culture. For example, individuals in high masculinity cultures tend to value **material possessions** more than do people in low masculinity cultures, who tend to place greater value such things as a clean environment and a sense of equity/fairness. Individuals in some cultures, America, for example, equate success with material wealth—expensive clothes, automobiles, and houses, large offices, expensive furnishings, and so forth. Individuals in many cultures, however, place relatively little importance on material possessions and view the flaunting of wealth as disrespectful. For example,

> Middle East businessmen look for something else—family, connections, friendship. They do not use the furnishings of their office as part of their status system; nor do they expect to impress a client by these means or to fool a banker into lending more money than he should. They like good things, too, but feel that they, as persons, should be known and not judged solely by what the public sees.[9]

The American notion that "money talks" is therefore far from true in many cultures. Furthermore, some cultures use material possessions differently from America. For example, the Japanese take pride in relatively "inexpensive but tasteful arrangements that are used to produce the proper emotional setting."[10] Europeans are embarrassed when guests compliment them on their personal possessions; they are not likely to value an object because of its monetary worth—they appreciate an object for its age, beauty, and form; for example, objects that have been in the family for a long time.[11] Therefore, in most cultures, when one comments about the value of someone's material possessions, the comment should reflect the aesthetic value, as opposed to the monetary value, of the possession.

Family and Friendship Roles

In many cultures, family roles are highly traditional and personal. Members of the family have predictable, designated roles and a responsibility for maintaining the status quo. In these cultures, family responsibilities have greater influence on members' behavior than do work situations and business interactions; family-related matters are more important than work-related matters. On the other hand, in some cultures, especially America, work matters often take precedence over family matters. Relative to friendship, Americans tend to make friends quickly and become disassociated from them just as fast. In many countries, however, in general, friendships are formed more slowly, but once made they are deeper, last longer, and involve real obligations—friends, as well as family, tend to provide some sort of social insurance. For example,

It is important to stress that in the Middle East and Latin America your "friends" will not let you down. The fact that they personally are feeling the pinch is never an excuse for failing their friends. They are supposed to look out for your interests.[12]

Competitiveness and Individuality

Competitiveness and individuality are values considered natural by Americans. For example, statements often made by the late Vince Lombardi, a famous, highly successful American football coach, characterizes many Americans' view on competition: "Winning isn't everything, it is the only thing." Many cultures, including European cultures, however, reject this behavior; they instead emphasize team and consensus values; they value modesty, team spirit, and patience. Individuals in these cultures are therefore likely to be offended by those who apply **haste and aggressive behavior** in the pursuit of business transactions; they prefer business relationships that have a more relaxed atmosphere.

Social Behaviors

Numerous social habits, such as eating, types of foods eaten, gift giving, and greetings vary from culture to culture.

Eating.   Behaviors such as noisy eating and belching are quite acceptable in some cultures and totally unacceptable in others. Eating noisily and belching means that the meal is being enjoyed, and not doing so may actually be offensive to the hosts because one is telling them that the meal is not enjoyable. In some cultures, spitting residuals on the table, such as chicken bones and shrimp shells, while eating—either at home or at a restaurant—is appropriate behavior. Removing the residuals with your fingers and placing them on the table is actually crude behavior to people in these cultures. (The French, who think Americans are repulsive because they switch forks from one hand to the other while eating, might find these types of behaviors to be quite gross.)

Foods.   Types of foods vary from culture to culture, and what foreigners in a culture are expected to eat when dining with local hosts can be a traumatic cultural shock to many. For example, in China ceremonial lunches and dinners often consist of about 15 courses, and sometimes more. Chinese hosts typically expect guests to try at least a bit of each course—not doing so would be offensive. China, with a land-base smaller than Canada's, has a population of about 1.2 billion people (about 25% of the world's population). How, one might wonder, is such a population kept fed? One way is by being efficient; by not wasting foods and maximizing use of the foods "Mother Nature" provides. Thus, people in China generally eat a greater variety of foods than do people in most Western cultures. Therefore, a foreign guest should not be too surprised when he or she finds foods such as fish heads, chicken heads, chicken feet, and "night duck" soup (bat soup) included in the 15 or so courses.

Furthermore, an American in France might not enjoy snails, a popular local dish, and might not enjoy blood pudding sausages, which are popular in Portugal; nor might he or she enjoy "fragrant meat" (dog meat) eaten in Taiwan or horse meat once eaten in some parts of Italy. Some global travelers who have participated in such lunches or dinners may advise you that in such situations it is best to just eat and not ask what it is. This writer's own experience, however, has been that it is polite and diplomatic to ask what it is, but asking must be in a polite, curious, inquisitive way (the hosts appreciate that you have taken an interest in their culture); never, however, ask in a "What is that?" tone of voice, which may make it sound as if you find it strange that they would eat such a thing.

Gift Giving. In some cultures, gifts are expected, and failure to present them is considered an insult, whereas in other cultures, offering a gift is considered offensive. For example, gifts are rarely exchanged in Germany and are usually inappropriate—although small gifts may be appropriate. In some cultures, the present is given during the initial visit, while in others it is given afterwards. In some cultures, the gift is given in private, whereas in other cultures it can be given in public. For instance, in Japan, where gift-giving is an important part of doing business (it helps symbolize the depth and strength of a business relationship), the exchanging of gifts usually takes place at the first meeting. The gift given to a Japanese associate should consist of multiple contents that can be shared with the group.

The type of gift given also varies from one culture to another. For example, white flowers are typically not given in Asia, where the color white is symbolic of death. In China, giving a clock shakes the superstitious. The phrase "to give a clock" sounds like a Chinese expression that means "to care for a dying patient."[13] In Belgium, gift-giving is not a normal custom—flowers may be given as a gift when invited to someone's home, but do not bring chrysanthemums, as they are used mainly for funerals.

Greetings. Knowledge of a culture's greeting behavior is important because first impressions are important to the development of relationships. Many cultures use a handshake as a major form of greeting, some use a hug, some a combination of a handshake and a hug, but some cultures do not greet by touching. For example, Australians and Americans use a strong handshake, but the French use a light, gentle, single shake. Many Latin European cultures greet with an *abrazo*—a combination of handshake, hug, and shoulder pats. The Japanese greeting involves a bow, and the Laotian greeting involves bringing palms together in prayer-like form and bowing.[14]

High-Context versus Low-Context Cultures

Some cultures are high-context and some are low-context. The degree affects the business tempo in the society. As discussed in Chapter 8, in the transaction of business, people in **high-context cultures**, including the Chinese, Korean, Japanese, Vietnamese, Arab, Greek, and Spanish cultures, establish social trust first, value personal relations and goodwill, make agreements on the basis of general trust, and like to conduct slow and ritualistic negotiations.[15] On the other hand, individuals in **low-context cultures**, including the Italian, English, North American, Scandinavian, Swiss, and German cultures, get down to business first, value expertise and performance, like agreement by specific, legalistic contract, and like to conduct negotiations as efficiently as possible.[16] The following is the advice an American Embassy attache gave to an executive from America (a low-context culture) seeking to do business in a high-context, South American Spanish-speaking country:[17]

1. "You don't do business here the way you do in the States; it is necessary to spend much more time. You have to get to know your man and vice versa."
2. "You must meet with him several times before you talk business. . . ."
3. "Take your price list and put it in your pocket. . . . Down here price is only one of the many things taken into account before closing the deal. In the United States, your past experience will prompt you to act according to a certain set of principles, but many of these principles will not work here. Every time you feel the urge to act. . . suppress the urge. . . ."
4. "Down here people like to do business with men who are somebody. In order to be somebody, it is well to have written a book, to have lectured at a university, or to have developed your intellect in some way. The man you are going to see is a poet. He has published several volumes of poetry. Like many Latin Americans, he praises poetry highly. You will find that he will spend a good deal of business time quoting his poetry to you, and he will take great pleasure in this."
5. "You will also note that the people here are very proud of their past and of their Spanish blood, but they are also exceedingly proud of their liberation from Spain and their independence. The fact that they are a democracy, that they are free, and also that they are no longer a colony is very, very important to them. They are warm and friendly and enthusiastic if they like you. If they don't, they are cold and withdrawn."
6. "And another thing, time down here means something different. It works in a different way. You know how it is back in the States when a certain type blurts out whatever is on his mind without waiting to see if the situation is right. He is considered an impatient bore and

somewhat egocentric. Well, down here, you have to wait much, much longer, and I really mean much, much longer, before you can begin to talk about the reason for your visit."

7. "There is another point I want to caution you about. At home, the man who sells takes the initiative. Here, they tell you when they are ready to do business. But, most of all, don't discuss price until you are asked and don't rush things."

Business Customs in China, Japan, and South Korea

People transacting business across cultures must be sensitive to the above dynamics, as well as to varying business customs. Culture affects business behavior and customs. This section describes how *guanxi* affects business culture and customs in China, how *wa* affects business culture and customs in Japan, and how *inhwa* affects business culture and customs in South Korea. Some other interesting business customs from around the world that differ from country to country are presented in Table 9–1. Note that the descriptions in Table 9–1 are generalizations. Not all residents of a country necessarily adhere to those customs—especially the immigrants in a country. For example, many people in Australia are from another country, such as China and Italy. These people may adhere to the customs of their country of birth.

Guanxi

The Chinese are excessively polite, but are tough bargainers; they like to entertain and expect reciprocal dinner parties; and they avoid all unnecessary physical contact. In China, contracts are binding only if the conditions present at time the contract is signed are also present when the contract is executed.[18]

A major dynamic of Chinese society is *guanxi*, which refers to the special relationships two people have with each other.[19] The two individuals who share this relationship assume that each is fully committed to the other; that they have agreed to exchange favors, even when official commands mandate that they act neutrally. The *guanxi* relationship, even though it is preferred, does not have to be between friends. In the relationship, an individual who refuses to return a favor loses face and becomes known as untrustworthy. Foreigners wishing to do business in China who have not established a *guanxi* relationship may very well have to deal with uninterested officials. When the relationship is between two people of unequal rank, the relationship favors the weaker person. The weaker person can claim inadequacy and ask for special favors that he or she does not have to reciprocate equally. The unequal exchange gives respect and honor to the stronger party who voluntarily gives more than he or she receives. Thus, to do business in China effectively, good personal connections must

Business Customs Around the World	TABLE 9-1 ◆

Australia	Business is almost always conducted over drinks, and it is considered rude to buy out of turn. Australians like to be addressed by their titles.
Austria	Austrians prefer to be addressed by their titles and consider it rude if a business associate tries to pick up the tab for a lunch or dinner they have initiated. They enjoy discussing art, music, as well as skiing.
Belgium	Belgians like to get down to business immediately and are very conservative and efficient in their approach to business meetings. One must address French-speaking Belgians as "monsieur" or "madame," while Dutch-speaking Belgians must be addressed as "Mr." or "Mrs."
Egypt	Egypt is dominated by the Moslem faith, and their business customs reflect such. Business is slow-paced and the red-tape is limitless. Egyptians take offense at refusals and at the use of direct negatives.
France	Conducting business in France in August is difficult, because most people are taking their vacation. The French use titles until use of first names is proposed; in negotiations, they like to debate issues; they like to show their intellect and to challenge your intellect. To successfully sell the French requires convincing them of the merits of the product/service through intellectual debate, not through flashy, high-powered presentations. They employ sophisticated table manners.
Germany	One should expect much handshaking, but in order of the person's importance in the enterprise. Germans insist on using titles, seldom use first names, use surname preceded by title, dislike small talk, and are very punctual. Germans are competitive negotiatiors who get straight to the point and leave little room for debate. German executives tend to have an engineering and science background, and one must therefore appeal to their technical tastes—glitzy presentations are thus likely to fail. They do not strongly emphasize the development of personal relationships with business associates—they value their privacy and keep business and private matters separate.
Greece	The Greeks are famous for their extensive bargaining and for never discussing business without a cup of coffee. Building a personal rapport with Greeks is important. Business entertaining normally takes place in the evening at a local tavern, and

◆   **TABLE 9–1   Business Customs Around the World,** *continued*

	spouses are often included. It is important that a business relationship based on trust be built. Government plays an important role in business, which means that one must work through bureaucracy. Business is highly personalized—family connections, political connections, and business connections. How one connects is often more important than the quality of the product/service. In Greece, negotiations are not finished even after the contract has been awarded—a contact is viewed as an evolving document of agreement.
Guatemala	A luncheon set for a specific time means that some guests may arrive 10 minutes early, while others may be 45 minutes late.
India	Business is conducted at an extremely leisurely pace, therefore Indians are very patient, unlike their American counterparts. When invited to dinner, one should accept and pass the food with the right hand only and expect to be asked many personal questions—which Indians see as a sign of politeness. Indians avoid discussing political issues with their business contacts.
Ireland, Republic of	Do not confuse it with Northern Ireland or the United Kingdom—it is politically and culturally distinct from both.
Italy	Italians use a handshake for greetings and goodbyes. Unlike in the U.S., men do not stand when a woman enters or leaves a room, and they do not kiss a woman's hand—this is reserved for royalty. Appearance and style are very important to Italian business people. The appeal and polish of a presentation reflect the quality of the product/service or the firm itself. Italian business people are confident, shrewd, and competent negotiators, and they tend to rely mainly on their instincts, and not as much on the advice of specialists.
Malaysia	Most Malaysians are Muslims, thus do not eat pork, nor drink alcohol, and do not party on Friday night, the eve of the Muslim sabbath. They are very status and role conscious, and therefore do not readily mingle at social gatherings, particularly so if men and women are together at the same gathering.
Netherlands	The Dutch as competitive negotiators who get straight to the point and there normally is little conflict or debate.
Nigeria	Business is slow-paced and never conducted over the telephone.
Pakistan	The Islamic faith is a dominant factor in Pakistani life, therefore in business as well. It is a male-dominated country where women are highly confined to the domestic sphere; hence

Pakistani men are uncomfortable or may even refuse to transact business with a woman. They refuse alcohol, cigarettes, and pork. One should never try to take a picture of a Pakistani without his or her permission.

Portugal

One must take the time to establish a rapport with Portuguese business associates.

Saudi Arabia

Business is informal, slow paced, and male-dominated. The Saudies are insulted if forced to deal with a representative rather than with the main person. When invited to a Saudie home, never bring flowers or gifts to the lady of the house, never eat or drink with the left hand, and never praise their house furnishings unless you would like to receive them as a gift the following day.

South Africa

Business people like to discuss politics with their peers, and they are generally ultra-conservative.

Spain

The Spanish work long days and break appointments often. The business lunch is an important part of conducting business in Spain, and great ceremony is applied in lunch meetings. Lunches stretch from 2:30 PM to 5:00 PM, then work until 8:30 PM or 9:00 PM. These lunches are used to develop the relationship required before business can be conducted.

Thailand

Thailand's traditional greeting is the *wai*, which is made by the placement of both hands together in a prayer-like position at the chin and bowing slightly. The gesture means "thank you" and "I am sorry" as well as "hello." The higher the hands, the more respect is symbolized. The fingertips, however, should never be raised above the eye level. Failure to return a *wai* is equivalent to refusing to shake hands in the West. In Thailand it is considered offensive to place one's arm over the back of the chair in which another person is sitting, and men and women should not show affection in public. First names are used, and last names are reserved for very formal occasions or in writing.

United Kingdom

In the U.K., never sit with the ankle resting on the knee; one should instead cross his or her legs with one knee on top of the other. Avoid backslapping and putting an arm around a new acquaintance. Use titles until use of first names is suggested. Gift-giving is not a normal custom in the U.K. The British are very civil and reserved, they do not admire overt ambition and aggressiveness, and are offended by hard-sell tactics. They

◆   **TABLE 9–1   Business Customs Around the World,** *continued*

do not brag about their finances or positions. And they are good negotiators, but do not have a high regard for bargaining in general.

United States   Americans often feel that the European practice of meticulous-ly cultivating personal relationships with business associates slows the expedient conduct of business; they agree that time is money, and the Europeans waste time. Business comes first, and friendship or pleasure comes later, if at all.

Source: Excerpted from David Altany, "It Takes Cultural Savvy," *Industry Week,* October 2, 1989; M. Katherine Glover, "Do's and Taboos: Cultural Aspects of International Business," *Business America,* August 13, 1990, p. 3; and Dean Foster, "Business Across Borders: International Etiquette for the Effective Secretary," *The Secretary,* October 1992, p. 23.

be established first. Note that the decision-making process in China is slow even when bureaucracy is circumvented by *guanxi*. This is because decisions in China are made hierarchically, and superiors in each *guanxi* link must agree.[20]

Wa

The Japanese entertain exhaustively, but in a very businesslike manner. To them, business is family, and therefore they are usually selfless—unlike the cutthroat business styles of many Americans. The Japanese, like the Chinese, avoid physical contact as much as possible, and they require even more space than Americans. No matter how poorly negotiations may be going, the Japanese see direct negative statements as rude and offensive. They consider it rude to be late for a business meeting, but it is quite acceptable to be late for a social occasion. The Japanese bow is a well-known form of greeting; it symbolizes respect and humility. When receiving a business card, observe it carefully, acknowledge it with a nod that you have taken in the information, and make a relevant comment or ask a polite question about it. In other words, treat the card as you would treat its owner—with respect. When presenting the card, use both hands and position the card so that the recipient can read it. The information should be printed in Japanese on the reverse side of the card.

The Japanese concept of *wa* necessitates that members of a group, be it a work team, a company, or a nation, cooperate with and trust each other. Thus, the Japanese usually prefer, or even demand, that business dealings occur among friends, and do not like to deal with strangers. Therefore, proper introductions are crucial when business relationships are launched. Before business transactions can begin, the Japanese must first place the foreigner within some group context (a *wa* relationship must be established).[21] Furthermore, in Japan telling the truth, or, as it is called in America, "laying one's cards on the table," does not work well because it may upset someone and threaten the group's *wa*. The Japanese thus prefer ensuring harmony and goodwill over the truth, as well as long-term over short-term relations.[22]

Inhwa

South Korean business behavior is heavily influenced by **inhwa**, which stresses harmony; linking of people who are unequal in rank, prestige, and power; loyalty to hierarchical rankings; and superiors being concerned for the well-being of subordinates.[23] Corporations are viewed as a "family" or a "clan." As a consequence, Korean business people prefer to establish personal ties with strangers before they transact business deals with them. Unlike the Japanese, but like the Chinese, the binding of Koreans' relationships is between individuals, and thus there is no strong loyalty to the organization—they will readily change companies when it is beneficial to them. *Inhwa* relationships are long-term and require a long time and much patience to cultivate. Once relationships have been established, they must be continually maintained and strengthened. Business contracts are interpreted through the personal relationships of those who agree; therefore, an agreement is only as good as the personal relations that made it possible—thus, lawyers should not take over from the originators.

Furthermore, in Korea contracts are not simply documents indicating mutual obligations and rights; they are declarations of intentions supported by the integrity of the signers. As a result, renegotiation of contracts is expected behavior in Korea. Koreans do not consider a contract binding if conditions change. Since the emotional aspects are more valuable than the contents of a contract, foreigners must cultivate a strong relationship with their Korean associates prior to signing a contract. And the original signers should be prepared to continually maintain that relationship and interest in the project after the contract has been signed, because a change of those in power could lead to problems.

It should be noted that government officials direct much of Korea's economy, thus, most major ventures require the support of one or more governmental offices. Foreign business people must establish relationships in government circles as well. Senior Korean officials deal only with other senior officials, not junior officials. Therefore, if the Korean company is using its president as the negotiator, the foreign corporation should use its president as well. Also, Koreans do not like bad news, and when it must be delivered, it should be done toward the end of the work day and unexpectedly.[24]

Cross-Cultural Generalizations: A Caveat

The international business person should be aware that while the culture influences the mode of doing business in a country, the introduction of new technology changes culture. Historically, cultural borrowing between countries has been common. Strategists should thus be cautious about older information on a nation's culture, since it may be outdated. They should also be aware that generalized information about nations serves mainly as a stereotype, and stereotypes are useful mainly as starting points for analysis. Ultimately, specific situations must analyzed and considered to make the final decision. For example, it may be true that Americans tend to regard time as money, but not all of them do.

Cross-Cultural Adaptation: A Caveat

Those who offer advice on international negotiations advocate adaptation—an attempt to obtain approval from members of a foreign culture by trying to become behaviorally more similar to them (**"When in Rome, do as the Romans do"**). This advice is based on research findings that when individuals were perceived as more similar in areas of beliefs, attitudes, dialect style, and socioeconomic class, they were viewed more favorably. These advocates do not specify a degree of adaptation, however. Other research findings suggest that the positive relationship between similarity and attraction may only be true at moderate levels of similarity, and that substantial levels of adaptation actually result in negative relationships.[25] In other words, if one does not attempt to adapt to local culture, a negative relationship will occur, as it will if one attempts to adapt too much. It is therefore moderate adaptation that leads to a positive relationship. A possible explanation for this is that substantial adaptation efforts may be perceived as presumptuous, while moderate adaptation efforts may reflect respect and sensitivity to the local culture without appearing presumptuous.[26]

For example, a male Japanese executive conducting business in Texas may actually be offensive if at a business meeting with his traditionally dressed Texan associates dresses in traditional Texas clothes (big hat, big boots, and so forth). In the same context, an American conducting business in Malaysia may offend some Malaysians if he or she dresses in traditional Malaysian clothes. Simply acknowledging and respecting that traditional dress style differs in many countries would suffice. Not violating local rituals, such as hurrying the conducting of business in a culture where business activities typically are not hurried, will result in a better relationship. Furthermore, a male Texan conducting business in India may actually command respect if he dresses in traditional Texas clothes—it would be interesting to the locals.

CROSS-CULTURAL NEGOTIATIONS

Negotiating across cultures is far more complex than negotiating within a culture because foreign negotiators have to deal with differing negotiating styles and cultural variables simultaneously. In other words, the negotiating styles that work at home generally do not work in other cultures. Thus, **cross-cultural business negotiators** have one of the most complicated business roles to play in organizations. They are often thrust into a foreign society consisting of what appears to be "hostile" strangers. They are put in the position of negotiating profitable business relationships with these people or suffering the negative consequences of failure. And quite often they find themselves at a loss as to why their best efforts and intentions have failed them.

How Not to Fail in International Negotiations

Negotiators in a foreign country often fail because the local counterparts have taken more time to learn how to overcome the obstacles normally asso ciated with international/cross-cultural negotiations. Failure may occur because of time and/or cost constraints. For example, a negotiator may be given a short period of time to attempt to obtain better contract terms in country A, where negotiations typically take a long time, than the terms to which country B agreed. A negotiator may simply feel that "what works in the home country is good enough for the rest of the world," which is far from the truth—in fact, strategies that fail to take into account cultural factors are usually naive or misconceived. Typically, the obstacles to overcome include:

- **Learning the local language,** or at least being able to select and use an effective language translator.
- **Learning the local culture,** including learning how the culture handles conflict, its business practices (as previously discussed), and its business ethics, or at least being able to select and use an effective cultural translator.
- Becoming well prepared for the negotiations, that is, along with the above, the negotiator must have a thorough knowledge of the subject matter being negotiated.

Thus, effective cross-cultural negotiators understand the cultural differences existing between all parties involved; and they understand clearly that not understanding the differences serves only to destroy potential business success.[27]

How Much Must One Know About the Foreign Culture?

Realistically, it is nearly impossible to learn "everything" about another culture (although it may be possible if one lives in the culture for several years).

This is because each culture has developed, over time, multifaceted structures that are much too complex for any foreigner to understand totally. Therefore, foreign negotiators need not require total awareness of the foreign culture; they do not need to know as much about the foreign culture as the locals, whose frames of reference were shaped by that culture. However, they will need to know enough about the culture and about the locals' negotiating styles so as not to feel uncomfortable during (and after) negotiations.[28] Besides knowing enough not to fail, they also need to know enough to win. For example, in negotiations between Japanese and American business people, Japanese negotiators have sometimes used their knowledge that Americans have a low tolerance for silence to their advantage.

In other words, for negotiation to take place, the foreigner must at least recognize those ideas and behaviors that the locals intentionally put forward as part of the negotiation process—and the locals must do the same for the foreigners. Both sides must be capable of interpreting these behaviors sufficiently to distinguish common from conflicting positions, to spot movement from positions, and to respond in ways that sustain communication.[29] Practical Perspective 9–2 describes negotiating with the Chinese. Tables 9–2 and 9–3 present the recommended behavior for negotiating with the Japanese, and Table 9–4 for negotiating with the French. Appendix 9–1 presents the negotiating styles of various European nations, and Appendix 9–2 presents the negotiating style in Asia. (Both appendices are presented at the end of the chapter.) It cannot, however, be overemphasized that these are stereotypes or generalizations, which can only serve as starting points in understanding a culture. Not all individuals in a culture adhere to these practices. Thus, ultimately, cross-cultural negotiators must determine their counterparts' personal motivations and agendas and adapt the negotiation style to them.

The purpose of the ensuing sections is therefore to develop a cross-cultural negotiations process. The process includes both strategy and tactics. Basically, **strategy** refers to a long-term plan, and **tactics** refers to the actual means used to implement the strategy.[30]

STRATEGIC PLANNING FOR INTERNATIONAL NEGOTIATIONS

Strategic planning for international negotiations involves several stages: preparation for face-to-face negotiations, determining settlement range, selecting the form of negotiations, determining where the negotiations should take place, deciding whether to use an individual or a group of individuals in the negotiations, and learning about the country's views on agreements/contracts.

PRACTICAL PERSPECTIVE 9–2

Negotiating With the Chinese

Foreign business people often complain about the length of the negotiation process in China. Efficiency needs to be improved and the process speeded up, but foreigners also have to keep in mind that the pace of life in China is slower than in, for example, the U.S. After all, Americans have a reputation for the quickest pace of life in the world. They move in a hurry and are results oriented. To ensure a smooth negotiation process, it is important that foreign negotiators know about their counterparts. They should know, for example, whether their Chinese partners have the legal capacity or authority to negotiate or conclude a deal, whether they fully understand all aspects of the transaction, and so on.

Foreigners also need to realize that they cannot deal with a government entity in China in the same way they might deal with a home-country government entity or company. In addition, the Chinese have their own way of doing business. For foreign companies, the key is to differentiate between big, fundamental issues and minor, insignificant ones. For example, in a negotiation

between an American and a Chinese party, the Chinese insisted that the contract be based on the Chinese format, while the Americans thought that their format was more sophisticated. A seesaw battle ensued. The solution was to use the Chinese format as a basis for the contract, but to make changes whenever necessary. The American side finally took to China a draft based on the Chinese format but marked with additions and changes.

On looking back, the question of which format to use seems a minor issue. But the underlying point is that negotiations will not work if one party tries to overpower the other. For many Chinese companies, doing business with the West is a new experience. Lacking experience—and confidence—they want to hold on to something familiar. Once they gain experience, they will relax more. One more point: foreign companies can help shorten the negotiation process by doing their homework before making the journey to China. They should consult their legal counsel before they bring up issues for discussion with the Chinese.

Source: Jia Zhao, "Doing Business with China," *East Asian Executive Reports*, January 1991, p. 10.

◆   **TABLE 9-2   Recommended Behavior for Negotiating with the Japanese**

Employ

◆ Use "introducer" for initial contacts (e.g., general trading company).
◆ Employ an agent the counterpart knows and respects.
◆ Ensure that the agent/advisor speaks fluent Japanese.

Induce

◆ Be open to social interaction and communicate directly.
◆ Make an extreme initial proposal, expecting to make concessions later.
◆ Work efficiently to get the job done.

Adapt

◆ Follow some Japanese protocol (reserved behavior, name cards, gifts).
◆ Provide a lot of information (by American standards) up front to influence the counterpart's decision making early.
◆ Slow down your usual timetable.
◆ Make informed interpretations (e.g., the meaning of "it is difficult").
◆ Present positions later in the process more firmly and more consistently.

Embrace

◆ Proceed according to information-gathering, *nemawashi* (not exchange) model.
◆ "Know your stuff" cold.
◆ Assemble a team (group) for formal negotiations.
◆ Speak in Japanese.
◆ Develop personal relationships, respond to obligations within them.

Improvise

◆ Do homework on the individual counterpart(s) and circumstances.
◆ Be attentive and nimble (improvising entails different behaviors for different Japanese).
◆ Invite the counterpart to participate in mutually enjoyed activities or interests (e.g., golf).

These are examples, not a complete listing, of attitudes and behaviors implied by a negotiator's use of each strategy.

Source: Stephen E. Weiss, "Negotiating With 'Romans'—Part 1," *Sloan Management Review* (Winter 1994): 58. Copyright © 1994, Sloan Management Review Association, Massachusetts Institute of Technology, Sloan School of Management. Used with permission. All rights reserved.

How to Behave During Negotiating Sessions in Japan	TABLE 9–3 ◆

◆ Don't get too involved with details of the contract too early in the session. The Japanese may feel that the details can be worked out as the relationship continues to grow.

◆ Try not use an aggressive approach to selling your idea. Japanese feel that your idea or product should speak for itself. A low-key approach is better.

◆ Don't interrupt when someone is speaking. This considered rude by most Japanese.

◆ Try to be formal. Do not ask if it would be O.K. to call them by their first names or if everyone can take off their suit coats to relax. This type of atmosphere or approach tends to give the Japnese a feeling of a lack of sincerity.

◆ Always bring as much information as possible about your plans and your firm. Published articles are of great advantage.

◆ Better not approach the Japanese alone. Send a group (two or three) to conduct negotiations. This is a sign of earnestness to the Japanese. Make certain you send the appropriate individuals who can make the decisions.

◆ Do not demand an immediate decision on points covered in the meetings. As most decisions are made in groups, the Japanese team needs time to compare notes and discuss matters.

◆ Do not be offended if the Japanese tend to inquire about your religious or political beliefs. These are common questions used in Japan because they are interested in knowing as much about you and your company as possible. It is a confidence builder.

◆ If you get stuck on a point, don't continue to beat away on it. Move on to other points and come back when the other team has had time to think about it.

◆ Keep reviewing those points that were agreed upon during the meeting, trying to move forward in a constructive manner.

◆ Maintain good communication with your interpreter. The interpreter may be able to inform on the progress of the contact or perhaps possible conflicts that may be avoided.

◆ Speak slowly and with patience. Do not rattle off numbers to indicate your knowledge of the project. Numbers can be studied in detail by the Japanese at a later date.

◆ Be prepared for misunderstandings and clarify the points with sincerity and willingness to assist.

◆ Don't cover difficult points first on the agenda. Work toward a common ground, but be flexible enough to realize that ground may totally change before the contract is signed.

Source: Robert T. Moran, *Getting Your Yen's Worth: How to Negotiate with Japan, Inc.* (Houston, TX: Gulf Publishing, 1985), pp. 123–124. Copyright © by Gulf Publishing Company. Used with permission. All rights reserved.

◆ TABLE 9–4   **Recommended Behavior for Negotiating with the French**

Employ

- ◆ Employ an agent well-connected in business and government circles.
- ◆ Ensure the agent/advisor speaks fluent French.

Induce

- ◆ Be open to social interaction and communicate directly.
- ◆ Make an extreme initial proposal, expecting to make concessions later.
- ◆ Work efficiently to get the job done.

Adapt

- ◆ Follow the French protocol (greetings and leave-takings, formal speech).
- ◆ Demonstrate an awareness of French culture and business environment.
- ◆ Be consistent between actual and stated goals and between attitudes and behavior.
- ◆ Defend views vigorously.

Embrace

- ◆ Approach negotiation as a debate involving reasoned argument.
- ◆ Know the subject of negotiation *and* broad environmental issues (economic, political, social).
- ◆ Make intellectually elegant, persuasive yet creative presentation (logically sound, verbally precise).
- ◆ Speak in French.
- ◆ Show interest in the counterpart as an individual but remain aware of the strictures of social and organizational hierarchies.

Improvise

- ◆ Do homework on the individual counterpart(s) and circumstances.
- ◆ Be attentive and nimble (improvising entails different behaviors for different French).
- ◆ Invite the counterpart to participate in mutually enjoyed activities or interests (e.g., dining out, tennis).

These are examples, not a complete listing, of attitudes and behaviors implied by a negotiator's use of each strategy.

Source: Stephen E. Weiss, "Negotiating With 'Romans'—Part 1," *Sloan Management Review* (Winter 1994): p. 58. Copyright © 1994 Sloan Management Review Association, Massachusetts Institute of Technology, Sloan School of Management. Used with permission. All rights reserved.

Preparation for Face-to-Face Negotiations

Generally, at the preparation stage, the issues to be identified are common interests, desired outcomes, possible conflicts (and tactics for handling them), participants' abilities and limitations, business markets, financial status, participants' reputation, and similar products/services.[31] Typically, the negotiating strategy that is effective in the home market will have to be modified for negotiating with foreign businesses; as indicated above, cultural factors, business customs, and ethical standards of the foreign country must be considered.[32] For instance, in negotiating with the Chinese, Americans want to agree on specific terms first while the Chinese want to determine general principles (the "spirit of the contract") and then discuss specifics. In other words, Americans tend to be concerned with short-term goals, such as profits, while the Chinese are more concerned with long-term interests, such as the procurement of American technology and business techniques.[33]

Determining a Settlement Range

At this phase, a negotiation or **settlement range** (all possible settlements a negotiator would be willing to make) must be established. The "least acceptable result" (LAR) and a "maximum supportable position" (MSP) must be identified. In this respect, the Japanese have a saying, *"Banana no tataki uri,"* which means "ask outrageous prices and lower them when fared with buyer objections."[34] Establishing a range provides negotiators the ability to make concessions, and therefore more flexibility in the negotiations. Some cultures, Russians, for example, view concessions as a sign of weakness, not gestures of goodwill or flexibility. To be able to establish a reasonable negotiating range, an accurate analysis on the nature of all relevant markets must be conducted.[35] If there are other options, that is, if either the seller or the buyer has other forms of leverage or enticement, he or she may not need to make as many concessions, or may not need to make any concessions at all.

Form of Negotiations

International negotiations can take place via telephone, telex, or fax; face-to-face video conferencing; face-to-face in-person negotiations, and use of third parties.[36] Using a telephone, telex, or fax is relatively inexpensive, but because it lacks personal presence, it is usually not a viable approach in important negotiations.

Global video teleconferencing can be an effective negotiating form. There is face-to-face communication, yet, unlike face-to-face in-person negotiations, negotiators do not have to travel to strange physical environments and the costs of airfare and lodging are saved. However, the development of global video conferencing technologies is still at an early stage. It is not yet widely used by negotiators, but as technological advancements are made, its use is more likely. Note that video conferencing will not be a viable form for all face-to-face negotiations. In many cultures, carrying out certain rituals and ceremonies are an important part of negotiations, and in many negotiating situations in-person presence is needed. Thus, in important negotiations, the **face-to-face in-person** form is the most widely used, and it is likely to continue to be. Using a **third party** in face-to-face in-person negotiations sometimes works best, especially when one or both of the parties involved are not knowledgeable about cross-cultural negotiations, and when there is much political and/or social hostility between the two countries involved in the negotiations.

Where Should Negotiations Take Place?

Negotiations can take place in the home country, in the counterpart's home country, or at a neutral site. Most negotiators would prefer that negotiations take place on their home turf. Familiar surroundings and easy access to information provide more leverage; fatigue and stress associated with travel to the foreign country are not experienced; and, of course, lower travel costs are incurred.[37] On the other hand, negotiating in the foreign country does have its advantages, such as sometimes receiving certain concessions because you have endured the burdens of traveling. And quite often it is a good idea to base decisions on site observations—for example, it is a good idea to see the plant where your product is going to be manufactured. A neutral site that is equally advantageous to both parties is often ideal. For example, an American executive from Park Avenue in New York City may not adapt well in a village in the Amazons, Brazil, and an executive from this village may not adapt well in New York City. Thus a negotiating site that falls between the two extremes may be the most viable.

Individual or Team Negotiations?

An organization can assign one individual or a group of individuals to conduct the negotiations. The obvious advantages of using **one person** are that it cheaper and a decision can be made quickly. An obvious disadvantage is that one person may not have sufficient ability to deal with the other side, which typically consists of a group of experts and negotiating specialists—an advantage of the group approach. Furthermore, in some cultures, Japan, for instance, not using a group may be interpreted to mean that you are not very serious about the negotiation or the business deal. Also, the individual negotiator often finds himself or herself pressed to make a decision when it is not the right time to do so. In a group, the members can always take a break to confer, therefore "buying time" to assess the situation and develop new strategies and tactics (the Japanese typically use this method because their decisions usually require group consensus). Thus, in negotiating situations where cost and speed of a decision are more important than the other factors, use one negotiator; otherwise use a group of experts and negotiating specialists.

To help speed up decision making a bit and still have access to expert input, a **team of negotiators** can be used, but one member is given full negotiating authority (Americans generally use this approach). Of course, the other side may know this. And in the negotiations game, for tactical reasons, both parties try to learn who the decision maker is. In this respect, American decision makers usually reveal themselves quickly because they tend to be very active in the negotiations. On the other hand, Japanese decision makers are usually not very active in the negotiations—they simply remain silent and listen. It should also be noted that the Japanese tend to include several young executives in the negotiations team simply for exposure and on-site development purposes.[38]

What Are the Country's Views on Agreements/Contracts?

Countries existing on a high commercial level have generally developed a working base on which agreements can rest. The base may be on one or a combination of three types:[39]

1. Rules that are spelled out technically as laws or regulations.
2. Moral practices mutually agreed and taught to the young as a set of principles.
3. Informal customs to which everyone conforms without being able to state the exact rules.

Some cultures favor one, and some another. Americans, for example, rely heavily on written contracts, and they tend to consider the negotiations ended when the contract is signed. Many societies, however, do not place much importance on written contracts; they rely more on the development of a social relationship. And in many cultures, Greece, for instance, a signed contract is simply a starting point for negotiations, which end only when the project is completed—the clauses in the contract are subject to renegotiation. Thus, the international negotiator must understand the nature of the other country's **views and practices relating to agreements and contracts.**

TACTICAL PLANNING FOR INTERNATIONAL NEGOTIATIONS

Tactical planning for international negotiations involve determining how to obtain leverage, use delay, and deal with emotions.

Leverage

In negotiations, it is generally accepted that the more options you have the more **leverage** you have and the more concessions your opponents may be willing to make. For example, if you are negotiating with the Argentinean government to establish a manufacturing subsidiary in Argentina, and the Argentinean negotiators know that their site is the only viable one you have, they will not make any concessions, and are likely to ask for some concessions. But if the Argentinean negotiators believe that you can just as easily set up the subsidiary in Peru or Brazil, and they need the technology—as most Third World nations do—they are likely to be willing to make concessions.

Third World countries appear to have leverage over multinational corporations. This is because they have control over access to their own territory, including markets, the local labor supplies, investment opportunities, sources of raw materials, and other resources that multinational corporations need or desire. China, for instance, is developing rather fast economically these days. Its 1.2 billion prospective customers, along with its relatively inexpensive cost of labor, make China an attractive place for many foreign companies to establish operations. This, it seems, would give Chinese negotiators considerable leverage, and concessions would often have to be made by foreign negotiators. This may be true in some cases, but in many instances, multinational corporations have negotiating advantages because they possess the capital, technology, managerial skills, access to global markets, and other resources that governments in the Third World need for economic development.[40]

Delay

Applying **delay tactics** is another form of leverage. If you walk away from the negotiations and your opponents become overly anxious, they may be willing to make some concessions. On the other hand, if you become anxious before your opponent does, you may have to make some concessions. Furthermore, the pause in the negotiations enables you to rest and recuperate, assess progress, obtain other information, and reformulate strategy.[41] In this context, patience is generally recognized as being a key personal attribute in negotiators. Americans tend to be low on patience, while the Japanese tend to be high. As an illustration, refer to Practical Perspective 9–3.

Emotions

Even though behavior in negotiations is mainly intuitive, it should never be judgmental. To be able to listen to other negotiators, one should exclude his or her subjective opinions, preconceptions, and emotional filters. By becoming aware of your **emotions,** you can learn to change your reactions and avoid being manipulated by others or by the emotions themselves—you prevent emotion from controlling a negotiation. On the other hand, if you negotiate solely on the basis of logic, you will miss emotional signals sent out by the other negotiator. Thus, the key to negotiations is to be perceptive of feelings (yours and theirs) without being reactive.[42] As an illustration, refer again to Practical Perspective 9–3.

PRACTICAL PERSPECTIVE 9–3

Don't Just Sit There—Do Something!

A close friend and executive in a large Japanese company spoke very frankly to me one day. He said, "You Americans are fond of the expression 'Don't just sit there—do something.' Once in a while, you should reverse that advice. We Japanese would prefer to say 'Don't just do something—sit there.' Contemplation may be more productive than action."

It is true that U.S. businessmen have always been action-oriented. Only when rushing to an endless series of appointments and conferences do they really feel productive. For many, to be in perpetual motion seems to be their ultimate goal. It was Santayana who once observed that Americans are possessed by an obscure compulsion that will not let them rest, that drives them on faster and faster — not unlike a fanatic who redoubles his effort when he has lost sight of his goal. The greatest compliment that can be paid a U.S. executive is to call him dynamic. . . .

Furthermore, foreign visitors are startled by Americans' typically low tolerance of silence. Most Asians, in contrast, can endure long periods during which nobody says anything. They feel that these opportunities for organizing and evaluating one's thoughts may be the most productive in any conference or negotiation.

Their relative inability to tolerate long periods of silence has gotten many American negotiators into serious trouble when the other side feels no comparable frustration and tension. As one foreign consultant cautions, "This is a bad trait indeed when the negotiation game is being played in a boardroom in Rio or in a Ginza nightclub, and when the other side is playing by Brazilian or Japanese rules."

The international vice president of a large U.S. corporation confessed to his own experience with the consequences of failing to understand foreign negotiating patterns. He said, "In one of my company's deals overseas, our buyer was sitting across the table from the Japanese manufacturer's representative for the purpose of bidding on an item in which we were interested. Following the usual niceties, our man offered $150,000 per batch. On hearing the bid, the Japanese sat back and relaxed in his chair to meditate. Our buyer, interpreting this silence to be disapproval, instantly pushed his offer higher. It was only after the session was over that he realized he had paid too much."

It is true that Americans are considered an outspoken lot. Masaaki Imai contrasts this with the behavior of his own countrymen in saying, "Sitting mute is clearly a minus at the Western conference, while silence is still silver, if not golden, in the Japanese mind-set. Many Japanese sit silent throughout the conference. Nobody thinks the worse of them for that. They are like oxygen; their views may not be visible, but they are making a positive contribution nonetheless."

Unless and until American business leaders can learn to live more comfortably with silence, and to value thinking and listening as highly as mere physical activity, foreign executives will enjoy an easy advantage. It has been suggested that top U.S. executives keep a tiny replica of the giant Buddha of Kamakura, Japan, on their desks at all times. Its typical posture of quiet and peaceful meditation should serve as a constant reminder that great leaders are remembered for their thoughts as well as their deeds.

ETHICAL CONSTRAINTS

Business ethics and corporate social responsibility, which are discussed in Chapter 13, place constraints on negotiators. For example, a negotiator's **ethical concerns** for honesty and fair dealings regardless of the power status of negotiating parties will affect the outcome. As it will be pointed out in Chapter 13, there is no global standard or view of what is ethical or unethical behavior in business transactions—what is viewed as unethical behavior in one culture may be viewed as ethical in another culture, and vice versa. For instance, if a negotiator on one side "pays off" an influential decision maker on the other side to obtain a favorable decision, it would be an unethical (and illegal in the U.S.) business practice in some cultures, but it would be quite acceptable in other cultures.

SUMMARY

This chapter has discussed how differing cultural views on time, material possessions, family roles, relationships, and so forth, affect the ways one transacts business across societies. For example, in America, "time is money," but in many parts of the world, people value relationships more than time. Thus, the "hurry up" business approach used by Americans would not be effective in, for instance, Spain, where establishing a relationship is more important than "time equals money." The practices in a number of countries were briefly discussed. Also discussed was how negotiating styles vary from culture to culture. If a cross-cultural negotiator does not become familiar with, and adapts to, the style of the society where he or she is negotiating for business contracts, the consequence is likely to be failure. Issues related to strategic and tactical planning for international negotiations were addressed. The negotiation styles of numerous nations were examined.

Key Terms

1. Cross-cultural business practices
2. "Time is money"
3. Circular- and linear-oriented cultures
4. Material possessions
5. Haste and aggressive behavior
6. High-context and low-context cultures
7. *Guanxi, wa,* and *inhwa* relationships
8. "When in Rome, do as the Romans do"
9. Cross-cultural negotiations
10. Learning the local language and culture
11. Strategic and tactical planning for international negotiations
12. Settlement range
13. Face-to-face in-person negotiations
14. Use of a third party in negotiations
15. Individual versus team negotiations
16. Countries' views on agreements/contracts
17. Leverage
18. Delay tactics
19. Emotions
20. Ethical considerations

Discussion Questions and Exercises

1. Discuss how a culture's views on "time is money," relationships, and material possessions affect cross-cultural business transactions.

2. Discuss the affect of a culture's thought patterns—linear or circular—on cross-cultural business activities.

3. "Winning isn't everything, it's the only thing." Discuss this statement in a cross-cultural context.

4. Discuss some of the ways social customs differ across cultures.

5. Describe the business tempo for the following cultures: Greece, Spain, Italy, England, and Germany.

6. Discuss the major business dynamics of China, Japan, and South Korea.

7. How does one avoid failing in cross-cultural negotiations?

8. You are the vice president of marketing for Y Co., You need to send an executive to Brazil to negotiate a contract. Your firm's personnel files indicate that one of your marketing executives has a college degree with a major in Brazilian culture. Would you feel comfortable sending this executive to Brazil to negotiate the contract? Why?

9. You are the negotiator for a firm that wishes to negotiate a contract in a foreign country. What must you do before you depart?

10. What are the forms of international negotiations?

11. You are a cross-cultural consultant specializing in negotiating in Japan and China. Two clients come to you for guidance—one on Japan and the other on China. In broad terms, what would you tell your clients to do?

12. As a classroom exercise, your professor will appoint two groups of at least five students each. One group will act the part of a team of negotiators sent to China by a U.S. company that makes automobiles to negotiate a contract with Chinese government officials and business people. The company has decided to establish a subsidiary in the People's Government of Yue Cheng District Shaoxing (about 200 miles southwest of Shanghai) to manufacture automobile parts to be sold back to the parent company in the U.S. The group has decision-making authority. *If available, these actors should be students who are U.S. citizens.*

   The second group is to represent the Chinese side. This group is represented by the district head and vice-head, who are concerned with the long-range economic development of their district, and by three top-level local factory executives who are seeking to import the manufacturing technology, which they need to update their current unproductive operations. This group also has decision-making authority. *If available, these actors should be students who are from an Asian nation or some nation other than the U.S.*

   The demands are as follows:

   ◆ The Chinese side wants Chinese managers in charge of the subsidiary; the American side feels that the Chinese do not yet have managers capable of managing this type of advanced technology and wants Americans in charge.

   ◆ The Chinese side does not want the parent company to repatriate any profits for ten years (they want profits to be reinvested in China); the Americans, who have short-range pressures to increase employee salaries and issue dividends to stockholders, want to be able to repatriate profits after two years.

   ◆ The Chinese want the American side to pay for all the expenses of building a new plant or refurbishing an old one; the Americans feel that since they are contributing technology, which is very important to China's economic development, the Chinese side should pay for the entire investment.

In 45 minutes or less, the two groups should negotiate an agreement in class. The groups should draw on this chapter, including Appendix 9–2 and Practical Perspective 9–2, as well as on previous chapters, especially those on international human resource management. After the agreement is negotiated, hold a class discussion relating to the negotiating difficulties and possible compromises.

Assignment

Select a country that was not extensively discussed in the chapter. Research the literature on the country, and prepare a short report on how to transact business there— the do's and don'ts. Present your findings (in three to five minutes) to your class.

The Impatient American Sales Manager

CASE 9–1

Source: Harvard Business Review, Edward T. Hall, "The Silent Language in Overseas Business," *Harvard Business Review,* 3, no. 3 (May–June 1960): 93–96.

A Latin American republic had decided to modernize one of its communication networks to the tune of several million dollars. Because of its reputation for quality and price, the inside track was quickly taken by American company "Y". The company, having been sounded out informally, considered the size of the order and decided to bypass its regular Latin American representative and send instead its sales manager. The following describes what took place. The sales manager arrived and checked in at the leading hotel. He immediately had some difficulty pinning down just who it was he had to see about his business. After several days without results, he called at the American Embassy where he found that the commercial attaché had the up-to-minute information he needed. The commercial attaché listened to his story. Realizing that the sales manager had already made a number of mistakes, but figuring the Latins were used to American blundering, the attaché reasoned that all was not lost. He informed the sales manager the Minister of Communications was the key man and that whoever got the nod from him would get the contract. He also briefed the sales manager on methods of conducting business in Latin America and offered some pointers about dealing with the minister.

The next day the commercial attaché introduced the sales manager to the Minister of Communications. First, there was a long wait in the outer office while people kept coming in and out. The sales manager looked at his watch, fidgeted, and finally asked whether the minister was really expecting him. The reply he received was scarcely reassuring, "Oh yes, he is expecting you but several things have come up that require his attention. Besides, one gets used to waiting down here." The sales manager irritably replied, "But doesn't he know I flew all the way down here from the United States to see him, and

I have spent over a week already of my valuable time trying to find him?" "Yes, I know," was the answer, "but things just move much more slowly here."

At the end of about 30 minutes, the minister emerged from the office, greeted the commercial attaché with a *doble abrazo*, throwing his arms around him and patting him on the back as though they were long-lost brothers. Now, turning and smiling, the minister extended his hand to the sales manager, who, by this time, was feeling rather miffed because he had been kept in the outer office so long. After what seemed to be an all too short chat, the minister rose, suggesting a well-known café where they might meet for dinner the next evening. The sales manager expected, of course, that, considering the nature of their business and the size of the order, he might be taken to the minister's home, not realizing that the Latin home is reserved for family and very close friends.

Until now, nothing at all had been said about the reason for the sales manager's visit, a fact which bothered him somewhat. The whole setup seemed wrong; neither did he like the idea of wasting another day in town. He told the home office before he left that he would be gone for a week or ten days at most, and made a mental note that he would clean this order up in three days and enjoy a few days of Acapulco or Mexico City. Now the week had already gone and he would be lucky if he made it home in ten days. Voicing his misgivings to the commercial attaché, he wanted to know if the minister really meant business, and, if he did, why could they not get together and talk about it?

The commercial attaché by now was beginning to show the strain of constantly having to reassure the sales manager. Nevertheless, he tried again: "What you don't realize is that part of the time we were waiting, the minister was rearranging a very tight schedule so that he could spend tomorrow night with you. You see, down here they don't delegate responsibility the way we do in the States. They exercise much tighter control than we do. As a consequence, this man spends up to 15 hours a day at this desk. It may not look like it to you, but I assure you he really means business. He wants to give your company the order; if you play your cards right, you will get it."

The next evening provided more of the same. Much conversation about food and music, about many people the sales manager had never heard of. They went to a night club, where the sales manager brightened up and began to think that perhaps he and the minister might have something in common after all. It bothered him, however, that the principal reason for his visit was not even alluded to tangentially. But every time he started to talk about electronics, the commercial attaché would nudge him and proceed to change the subject.

The next meeting was for morning coffee at a café. By now the sales manager was having difficulty hiding his impatience. To make matters worse, the minister had a mannerism he did not like. When they talked, he was likely to put his hand on him; he would take hold of his arm and get so close that he almost "spat" in his face. As a consequence, the sales manager was kept busy trying to dodge and back up.

Following coffee, there was a walk in a nearby park. The minister expounded on the shrubs, the birds, and the beauties of nature, and at one spot he stopped to point at a statue and said: "There is a statue of the world's greatest hero, the liberator of mankind!" At this point the worst happened, for the sales manager asked who the statue was of and, being given the name of a famous Latin American patriot, said, "I never heard of him," and walked on . . . . The sales manager did not get the order.

QUESTIONS

1. It appears as if the sales manager did not follow the commercial attaché's instructions. What do you believe were the attaché's instructions?
2. The sales manager was sent to a foreign country to negotiate a business contract. Discuss what should have be done before he or she was sent to the foreign country.

A Failed Cross-Cultural Negotiation Attempt

CASE 9–2

Source: Alex Blackwell, "Negotiating in Europe," *Hemispheres*, United Airlines (July 1994): 43.

An Italian director of a construction company went to Germany to negotiate for a project. He began the discussion with a presentation of his company that vaunted its long history and its achievements. The German managers first looked startled, then bored, then they excused themselves and walked out the door, without even listening to the Italian manager's offer.

QUESTIONS

1. Discuss what you believe went wrong.

The Long Printed Contract

CASE 9–3

Source: Arthur M. Whitehill, "American Executives Through Foreign Eyes," *Business Horizons* (May–June 1989): 46.

There is a popular story making the rounds of Japanese business circles. So legalistic was the representative of an American candy company that he ruined his chances to establish a potentially profitable joint venture with a Japanese corporation. The product was a top-quality, prestige chocolate with a fine reputation already established in the United States. The goal was to establish a plush retail outlet on Tokyo's glittering Ginza. Many days were spent by the U.S. company's legal department in drawing up a lengthy, complete contract *before* their representative packed his bags for a trip to Tokyo.

He was proud of the leather-bound, printed contract with almost 50 pages of fine print. No detail had been omitted. All that was lacking were the two signatures needed to launch the new enterprise.

With no knowledge of the Japanese language or culture, the U.S. representative faced a half dozen Oriental negotiators. He had a copy of the contract for each member of the Japanese team. But he was crushed when not one of them even opened the impressive legal document before them. Instead, a pleasant and inconclusive discussion of general business conditions in the two countries took up the whole afternoon. No decision on the proposed joint venture was made then—nor was the possibility ever discussed again.

QUESTIONS

1. Discuss what you believe went wrong.

Notes

1. Richard G. Linowes, "The Japanese Manager's Traumatic Entry into the United States: Understanding the American-Japanese Cultural Divide," *Academy of Management Executive* 7, no. 4 (1993) 21–22.

2. M. Katherine Glover, "Do's and Taboos: Cultural Aspects of International Business," *Business America*, August 13, 1990, p. 3.

3. Adapted from R. Knotts, "Cross-Cultural Management: Transformations and Adaptations," *Business Horizons* (January-February 1989) 29–33.

4. This idea draws from Edward T. Hall, "How Cultures Collide," *Psychology Today*, July 1976, pp. 67–74.

5. "Do's and Taboos" p. 3.

6. Edward T. Hall, "The Silent Language in Overseas Business," *Harvard Business Review* (May–June 1960): 87.

7. Ibid.

8. Mary Munter, "Cross-Cultural Communication for Managers," *Business Horizons* (May-June 1993): 77.

9. Hall, "The Silent Language," p. 90.

10. Ibid.

11. John Hill and Ronald Dulek, "A Miss Manners Guide to Doing Business in Europe," *Business Horizons* (July-August 1993): 50.

12. Hall, "The Silent Language," p. 90.

13. Frederick H. Katayama, "How to Act Once You Get There," (Pacific Rim, 1989) *Fortune*, p. 88.

14. Munter, "Cross-Cultural Communication for Managers," p. 77.

15. Hall, *Beyond Culture* (Garden City, NY: Doubleday, 1976).

16. Ibid.

17. Hall, "The Silent Language," p. 96.

18. Cindy P. Lindsay and Bobby L. Dempsey, "Ten Painfully Learned Lessons About Working in China: The Insights of Two American Behavioral Scientists," *Journal of Applied Behavioral Science* 19, no. 3 (1983): 265–276.

19. This discussion draws from Jon P. Alston, "*Wa, Guanxi,* and *Inhwa*: Managerial Principles in Japan, China, and Korea," *Business Horizons* 32, no. 2 (March–April 1989): 28–29.

20. Ibid., p. 29.

21. Ibid., p. 27.

22. Ibid.

23. Ibid., pp. 29–30.

24. Ibid.

25. Cited in June N. P. Francis, "When in Rome? The Effect of Cultural Adaptation on Intercultural Business Negotiations," *Journal of International Business Studies* (Third Quarter, 1991): 403–428.

26. Ibid.

27. Dean Allan Foster, *Bargaining Across Borders* (New York: McGraw-Hill, 1992), p. 5.

28. Ibid.

29. Stephen E. Weiss, "Negotiating With 'Romans'—Part 1," *Sloan Management Review* (Winter 1994): 52.

30. Hokey Min and William Galle, "International Negotiation Strategies of U.S. Purchasing Professionals," *International Journal of Purchasing and Materials Management* (Summer 1993): 43.

31. Trenholme J. Griffin and W. Russell Daggatt, *The Global Negotiator* (New York: Harper Business Publishers, 1990, p. 74.

32. Min and Galle, "International Negotiation Strategies," p. 42.

33. Robert O. Joy, "Cultural and Procedural Differences That Influence Business Strategies and Operations in the People's Republic of China," *SAM Advanced Management Journal* (Summer 1989): 31.

34. Griffin and Daggatt, *The Global Negotiator*, p. 77.

35. Min and Galle, "International Negotiation Strategies," p. 43.

36. Ibid., pp. 43–44.

37. Ibid.

38. Ibid., p. 44.

39. Hall, "The Silent Language," p. 93.

40. Shah M. Tarzi, "Third World Governments and Multinational Corporations: Dynamics of Host's Bargaining Power" (n.d., n.p.), p. 237.

41. Griffin and Daggatt, *The Global Negotiator*, p. 120.

42. Ibid., p. 106.

Negotiating in Europe   Appendix 9–1

The following are generalizations, based on expert opinion, about the negotiating style found in Europe's major markets:

GERMANY

In the preliminary stages of negotiations, German managers are often tough, cold, and impassive. They grill their prospective partners on all the technical aspects of their businesses, and it's bad luck for them if they don't have all the answers. "A mistake at this stage means that you're lost," comments cross-cultural negotiating consultant Prabhu Guptara, chairman of ADVANCE: Management Training Ltd. in London. Once they are satisfied about technical matters, they begin to feel they can trust them. The difficulty at this point is to make German managers change their position. "At times they can stick to one point and refuse to budge," says [Ann] Bengtsson [a management consultant based in Stockholm]. Still, consultants agree that German managers are, in

Source: Alex Blackwell, "Negotiating in Europe," *Hemispheres*, United Airlines (July 1994): 43–48. Reprinted with permission from *Hemispheres*, the inflight magazine of United Airlines, Pace Communications Inc., Greensboro, N.C. and the author.

general, quite practical at this stage. Finalizing a negotiation is not difficult with German mangers. However, it is important to know if the person you are dealing with has the authority to close the deal. Germans believe in "consensus management," comments [Vincent] Guy [a consultant specializing in international business communication with Canning International Management Development in London]. Patience may be required to get the final word.

ITALY

Human relationships are most important here. Italian managers need to feel that they can get along as well with their foreign partners as they would with managers from Italian companies. Initial negotiations with Italians can include a lot of idle talk and some chess playing. These preliminaries will last until they feel secure and comfortable. When they do, the negotiation process actually starts. But here the foreign businessperson may be baffled by circumlocutions: Italian managers may take ages to get to the point, Guptara points out. But be sure not to interrupt. As far as Italians are concerned, they are simply giving you the benefit of a complete understanding of their position. Concluding a negotiation with Italian managers can go quite quickly. But a surprise may be in store for the foreign manager because of the fluid nature of Italian corporate hierarchy. Titles mean relatively little in Italian companies, and very often the person who would normally have decision-making authority turns out to need approval. "Watch for someone sitting on the sidelines who's said nothing so far," warns Bengtsson. That person may leap into the fray at the end, make some changes, and then conclude the negotiation.

FRANCE

The French have their own way of doing most things, and negotiation is no exception. As a result, the French do not quite fit into the North-South dichotomy. The art of diplomatic negotiations was invented in France in the 14th century, and the French embrace that long tradition. Yet because French education stresses mathematics and logic, doing business is a highly intellectual process for French managers. "They see the negotiating process as a means to solve a logical problem," points out Robert Moran, professor of cross-cultural communication and international studies at the American Graduate School of International Management in Glendale, Arizona.

French managers will have carefully prepared for the negotiations, but they will generally begin with some light, logical sparring. "The French love discussion and often handle negotiating as though it were a debate," Moran adds. In general, French managers don't like to work on one point at a time. "They like to outline the entire structure of a potential agreement abstractly," explains Guptara. "Then they look at the details briefly, moving quickly from one to another." Throughout the preliminary and middle stages of negotiating, the French manager will judge the partners carefully on their intellectual skills, their ability to reply quickly and with authority. As one French businessman puts it, "sometimes I am more impressed by a brilliant sally than by a well-reasoned argument." But generally one has to be able to do both. Because the details come last in French negotiations, the finalizing stage can be very tricky. "French managers tend to slip in little extras when finalizing, like executive bonuses," comments Bengtsson. It's important to insist on what one wants at this stage, and be prepared to refuse, even if days have been spent getting to this point.

SCANDINAVIA

While it is always difficult to generalize about four separate nations like Norway, Sweden, Finland, and Denmark, consultants agree that the business culture is quite similar in these countries. Scandinavian managers tend to be frank, open, and relatively sincere. They like to get right down to work, and expect their partners to do the same. This makes the preliminary stages relatively brief, but the foreign manager should not confuse Scandinavian frankness with the easy establishment of a relationship of trust. "If the foreign manager becomes too friendly too quickly, the Scandinavian partner will construe this as weakness," comments Bengtsson. In fact, time must be taken to develop a real relationship. In the middle stages of negotiations, foreigners may be surprised to find a Scandinavian manager become inflexible, sticking to a technical point. "These are often not negotiable in Scandinavia," Guptara says. "It is best to research technical questions carefully beforehand to be prepared for the Scandinavian's reaction." After this stage, finalizing is usually relatively quick and simple.

SPAIN

Preliminaries to negotiations in Spain may take several days. The foreign businessperson may be asked to spend a day touring the city, having long meals, with business barely being mentioned. Here the establishment of a good, friendly relationship with a partner precedes all else. "It is very important not to appear impatient, not to seem in a hurry to get it over with," says Thorne. The foreigner should show interest in Spain and its culture, without being unctuous. When finally the Spanish managers get down to business, the negotiation process can be elaborate and theatrical. "Sometimes a Spanish manager will just storm out of the room, right in the middle of negotiations," Bengtsson says.

One has to be prepared for long and complex discussions in the middle stages. It is important at this time to earn the respect of the Spanish manager, with intelligence and straightforward replies. Finalizing can be difficult in Spain because of the strict hierarchy in Spanish companies. Approval may take a long time.

BRITAIN

British manager managers tend to be curious negotiators. They tend to be open in preliminary stages of negotiations, and they like to get down to work fairly quickly. They are very practical and well prepared. Yet in the middle stages of negotiations, British managers may become "a bit vague," Bengtsson points out. Sometimes they can become cagey about details, refusing to provide information. Here the foreign manager must be patient. Finalizing can be complex in Britain because it may take time and more negotiating to get approval from the right people. Patience and tact are required in order to reach a conclusion.

THE NETHERLANDS

Dutch managers are generally among the most cosmopolitan of Europe's business people, consultants agree. With a long history of trade, the Dutch are experienced at adapting to foreign cultures. They are likely to be familiar with customs in a foreigner's country and to change their negotiating style accordingly. It is possible to offend your Dutch partners, though. Beating around the bush and too much dallying will eventually make the Dutch manager annoyed and ultimately distrustful. They appreciate efficiency above all.

EASTERN EUROPE

The countries of Eastern Europe are rapidly learning modern negotiation techniques, but it is too early to analyze cultural differences, Moran points out. These countries need to attract business from all the industrialized nations, and that makes the negotiating process somewhat special. The same general rules apply in Eastern Europe as they do in all international negotiations. Be polite, earn the trust and respect of the partner, and you will succeed. All the consultants agree that this approach applies everywhere in the world.

Appendix 9–2   *Asian Bargaining Tactics*

Excerpted from Christopher Engholm, "Asian Bargaining Tactics: Counter Strategies for Survival," *East Asian Executive Reports*, July 1992, pp. 9, 22–25, and August 1992, pp. 10–13. Copyright © 1992, International Executive Reports, Ltd. and Christopher Engholm. Reprinted with permission. All rights reserved.

Westerners can enhance their negotiating power in Asia by recognizing a set of *strategic archetypes* used by Asian negotiators. Most Asian negotiators imitate military tactics developed in China thousands of years ago and passed down through mentor-apprentice relationships. Eight strategic archetypes are commonly encountered in Asia.

STRATEGY 1. PLAYING THE ORPHAN

Use humility to make them haughty. Sun Tzu

Throughout Asia, one encounters business situations in which the Asian company claims to be weaker and more vulnerable than it really is. The Asian side claims it is a small or backward company in order to elicit sympathy in the form of concessions. This seems odd to North American executives who typically try to convince a negotiating partner that their company is large and powerful. Sun Tzu taught: "Even though you are competent, appear to be incompetent." Sun Tzu's commentator, Mei Yaochen, elaborated: "Give the appearance of inferiority and weakness, to make [your enemy] proud."

Asians may open a negotiation by dwelling on their company's vulnerabilities, small size, and other feigned weaknesses, to swell Westerners' confidence and induce them to ask for less in return for the concessions that the Westerners are prepared to request. Some Westerners might think the orphan strategy is an expression of Asian humility. Instead, it often conceals a hidden agenda. For example, a claim of weakness is soon followed by a request that the foreign side ease its credit terms to lighten the financial burden on the Asian side. Or, the Asians demand conciliatory "favors" outside the contract.

STRATEGY 2. TEAM-DRIVEN INTELLIGENCE GATHERING

Comparisons give rise to victories. Sun Tzu

By the comparisons of measurements, you know where victory and defeat lie," Cao advises in *The Art of War*. What Asian counterparts can find out about a Western company will be used against the company during negotiations—how large or small the company is, what sort of technological know-how it possesses, and the tone of its financial muscle. A concerted effort may be underway to transfer to the Asian side as much of the company's know-how as possible, free of charge.

Westerners who have negotiated in Asia report that Asians value detail in formulating their business decisions; they consider information gathering to be the heart of a negotiation. However, what they call a "know-how exchange" often becomes "information rape," with the Asian side planning to reverse-engineer a Western product from the outset of collaboration with the firm. The effort will be a concerted team objective. If Western negotiators are not on guard against it, their firm is likely to find itself the victim of information rape.

The Asians' objective of sharing in a company's know-how without paying for it may be partially cultural in origin. In Asia, no notion of proprietary know-how took root; new technology was shared by all. Knowledge was kept public, and to imitate or adopt someone else's methodology was considered virtuous, and a great compliment to the person who created it. Borrowing another person's know-how was considered to be neither thievery nor unethical. The Japanese have long conducted a policy of "selective borrowing" from foreigners. Industrial Japan borrowed extensively from the West and adapted Western production and quality control techniques to its own needs.

All of this is *not* to suggest that Asia hasn't developed technologies on its own; its well-known inventions through the centuries had dramatic effects on all of civilization. Today, technological innovations travel back and forth across the Pacific with amazing frequency. The flow of innovation, however, is moving faster toward the East than toward the West. Japanese companies, for example, purchased over half of American high-technology firms that were sold during a 30-month period from 1989 to 1991, according to a study by the Economic Strategy Institute, a Washington think tank. Increasingly, North American corporations have found it necessary to forge "strategic alliances" with Asian companies (mostly Japanese) in order to acquire know-how from Asia, rather than vice versa. Facilitating the flow of technical information and human know-how has proven easier said than done.

STRATEGY 3. THE HAUGHTY BUYER

The customer is God.

Sellers of products and services in the West defer to their buyers to some degree but sellers and buyers ultimately deal with one another as social equals. Not so in Asia: buyers and sellers differ fundamentally in social status.

In North America, buyers and sellers maintain a somewhat adversarial relationship; in order to get a lower price, buyers ask vendors to bid against each other, and sellers seek out those buyers who will pay a premium price. When monetary advantage can be found elsewhere, buyers have few qualms about terminating their relationship with a seller. Business is business.

In much of Asia, however, buyers and sellers forge longer-term bonds of trust and partnership. Sellers tend to respond to every wish and whim of their buyers. In Japan, and increasingly in Korea, as well as other parts of Asia, the customer is not only king, but God. Here's the hitch, though. Asian buyers look after their suppliers in ways their North American counterparts do not.

Asian sellers tend to *overserve* their buyers because they can trust them to stay loyal if times get tough. A buyer might pay an above-market price, find a seller new customers, and—you guessed it—help to [protect] the seller's business from foreign competitors. In Japan, the relationship between buyer and seller is based on *amae* (a paternalistic, dependent relationship). Paternalistic buyer-seller bonds are hard to break, especially for a newcomer in the market.

Westerners' typical unwillingness to accept the lower-status position of suppliers in Asia and to enter into paternalistic relationships with buyers is a primary reason, though not the sole one, that American executives often hear their potential Asian customers say, "We'll contact you when we are prepared to buy," which means, "Thanks anyway." Asian buyers are not exactly "haughty" as part of a strategy; they are demanding, and possibly condescending, because of conditioning.

To sell, Westerners may have to enter *amae*-like relationships and accept the lower status. They have to satisfy what they may consider unreasonable demands—fast delivery, costly product modifications, and strictly enforced quality specifications, for example. Some companies have perished trying to meet the rigorous requirements of being sellers in Asia. Still, there are ways to lasso buyers without losing the corporate shirt.

STRATEGY 4. OUTLASTING THE ENEMY

It is easy to take over from those who have not thought ahead. Li Quan in The Art of War

Asian negotiations can, as the Chinese saying goes, be like "grinding a rod down to a needle." When the Taoist concept of *wu wei* (nonassertion) is applied to business negotiation, the strategy is to seek long-term success through minimal short-term effort: state a position and wait, hoping that opponents will yield on concessions in order to close the deal. Time is NOT money for Asian negotiators; it's a weapon.

Asian negotiators often open a negotiation, extend an invitation to visit their country, supply some technical information, and dedicate time and resources to forging an agreement. Unfortunately, the final contract remains elusive. Some Japanese investors, according to a number of American real estate developers I know, will sit down with them and sign on for a mutually beneficial deal, but problems set in at the last minute, when they balk and push for concessions. Then they initiate delay tactics, all the while pushing for more and more concessions in the grey areas of the contract. The foreign side often gives in because a costly delay may jeopardize firm financial commitments.

When Asian negotiators use delay tactics that push foreigners to the brink of anger, they may be seeking more than concessions. They may be testing the Westerners' commitment to a deal or their accountability. They may want to clarify the unequal status between buyer and seller. By delaying, they send a message that their interest may be waning; the Westerners may weaken in their resolve to hold out for a stated price.

I've seen this strategy used on youthful foreigners (myself included) as a way of testing their will and trying to intimidate them—to put them in their youthful place. Another possible reason for delay is that an Asian wants to kill a deal without losing face and hopes that the Westerner will take a hint and walk away as a friend, not a frustrated foe.

STRATEGY 5. HIDDEN IDENTITIES

The inscrutable win, the obvious lose. Du Mu in The Art of War

In the city of Hefei, in China's Anhui Province, I came across two Canadian representatives of a water purification equipment company. They were to have an important meeting with local import officials the following morning in the conference room at our hotel.

I met them the next day as they emerged confidently from their meeting. I also recognized a past acquaintance, the leading official from the Ministry of Foreign Economic Relations and Trade. After he left the hotel, I complimented the Canadians on obtaining a meeting with such a prominent official and suggested that this official's presence indicated significant interest in the water purification system on the part of the Chinese.

"Who, him?" one of the Canadians blurted. "He said he was just our interpreter for the meeting!"

This high official had concealed his true identity in order to eavesdrop on the Canadians in the guise of an interpreter. They had been burned by the hidden identity strategy.

Although a meeting in Asia usually begins with an exchange of business cards and handshakes, the true identities of the real decision makers on the Asian negotiating team may remain unknown—sometimes indefinitely. Ascertaining precisely who the key players are and how much influence they wield is difficult because some persons may vanish and later reappear at a banquet or sightseeing excursion.

The hidden identity strategy may also involve sudden changes among the Asian side's negotiating personnel. The number of Asian negotiators may swell over time, while the foreign side generally depends on the same team throughout. Being forced to defend a proposal before a new team can be maddening or can lead to making extra concessions or giving up some that have already been won. More innocently, the Asian negotiator whom the company hosted in the West for a factory visit and a side trip to Disneyland may have suddenly moved to another division of the Asian company. All the concessions won with him are now gone, and the process must start all over again with a new negotiator. In China, this problem has been exacerbated by the massive reorganization that has taken place since the Tiananmen Square massacre.

It would be unfair to Asians, however, not to mention that the same problem occurs in North America for different reasons. With the constant merging of North American companies and the high turnover of their executives, whether through departure, relocation, or promotion, the appearance of new negotiators can be difficult and disconcerting for Asians who desire to forge long-term, ongoing relationships with Western companies.

STRATEGY 6. THE TRUST GAME

Honey in mouth but dagger in heart. Chinese saying

A well-known American cable television company recently signed a deal with a comparable cable network in Taiwan. The agreement was based on a royalty to be paid by the Taiwanese company to the U.S. company for each television show aired. To guarantee its 10 percent share, the American company requested that the contract enable it to periodically view the Taiwanese company's accounting books.

The president of the Taiwanese company took the request as a grave insult. He was livid and nixed the entire deal, which had taken months to put together. "The American company is implying that we are liars," he railed. "If the Americans can't trust us, then we won't trust them!"

The irony is that *most* Taiwanese companies (this one included) keep two, or even three, sets of books, and a demand to have the accounting records made public in a deal of this size would be reasonable anywhere else in the world.

As part of what I call the trust game, the Asian doesn't want to trust the Westerner, but reacts negatively to any suggestion that the mistrust is mutual. Asians may even purposefully personalize negotiations in order to give Westerners a feeling that trust has been generated, and thus lure them into a deal; Westerners may find they are being called "old friend" at the second meeting. The Asian side's personalization of the negotiation may be a good thing for the long-term relationship between the two companies. However, it may be merely a tactic to obtain proprietary information about the firm—its size and past endeavors, the price and marketability of its products, its experience in Asia, and so on. Trust has to work both ways.

The trust game in Asia can be especially brutal on "middlemen" and firms that share their technology. "When the hares have been killed, the hounds are cooked," as the Chinese say. That is, the middlemen are discarded once they have fulfilled their purpose. I recommend that middlemen sign a bomb-proof contract with the manufacturer they represent, guaranteeing them total exclusivity to rep the product in Asia. They should conclude the contract before they disseminate information or quote prices of equipment among potential Asian customers.

Often Asian customers will contract the manufacturer directly and attempt to cut the middlemen out. The motive may not be to avoid paying an added commission, but simply to forge a relationship directly with the manufacturer and get closer to its technology.

In another trust game, the Asian side signs a "symbolic agreement." The Asians win over the Western firm by signing a well-drafted contract but then fail to *implement* what they have agreed to do. Some Asians may sign a "symbolic contract" knowing full well that governing bodies with oversight of the venture will not accept the conditions of the deal. Requests for major revisions in the contract arrive soon after.

A recent case in Korea involved the purchase of agricultural goods from the United States. The goods were refused by Korean Customs. The Korean customer had guaranteed that the government would enact a regulation allowing the import of the goods long before the contract was signed. Unfortunately, the Korean government was unwilling to enact the law. The deal died, along with a shipment of perishable product.

STRATEGY 7. SACRIFICE SOMETHING SMALL FOR SOMETHING BIG

Cast a brick to attract a piece of jade. Chinese saying

In this strategy, Asian counterparts attempt to trick Westerners into trading something significant for something insignificant. An Indonesian or Chinese joint venture partner might assure a Western company of access to a large untapped market or offer unlimited numbers of inexpensive workers in exchange for cash, technology, and worker training.

Many gullible Westerners have fallen victim to this strategy, believing the numbers that appear in feasibility studies presented by the Asians. The market may be both smaller than the numbers claim *and* quite inaccessible despite promises of access. The building space and land offered may appear to be a real break but would cost a bundle to upgrade.

Some Asian managers desire to link up with a foreign firm to gain the benefits that accrue to an Asian factory that forges a joint venture with a foreign company. In China, for example, these benefits can include the right to hire and fire workers, the unilateral right to buy imports without government approval, and the right to pay more to workers than regular Chinese enterprises can, thus allowing the manager to attract more workers with higher skills.

Some foreign companies have been asked by Chinese enterprises to form a joint venture but to station only one foreign manager in China—an easy way for the Chinese enterprise to enjoy the benefits of being a "foreign-invested enterprise." They sign a contract to manufacture and sell a foreign product, but the interests of the foreign partner become secondary to their own the moment the contract is signed.

A weak Asian company can obtain a new lease on life by merging with an unsuspecting, richer foreign partner. Even a near-bankrupt Asian company gains leverage over its Asian competitors by becoming a partner of a large foreign company. "If you forge alliances with strong partners, your enemies won't dare plot against you," Cheng Shi comments in *The Art of War*. For the foreign company, having an Asian partner with this objective usually leads to disaster.

STRATEGY 8. THE SHOTGUN APPROACH

Foreign business negotiators most often experience the "shotgun approach offer" when dealing with individual overseas Chinese entrepreneurs (briefcase companies); their locale is just about all of Asia except Japan and Korea. The Westerners begin by presenting a product for sale to the Asian side, and within minutes they find themselves talking about transferring technology, transferring a management model, and setting up a manufacturing joint venture in Asia. They have been lured off course by the "shotgun strategy."

We don't need to dwell long on this tactic; most of us have dealt with it in some form on our home turf. Chinese Malay business people might negotiate like the proverbial used car salesmen of the West; they want a deal, any deal, *now*. Owners of Asian "trading companies" tend to work along and to negotiate as individual (one-person) companies.

They start by saying, "I can get you anything in Asia that you want. Bamboo furniture, tropical fish, orchids, anything. My brother has an orchid farm near Kuala Lumpur, you know." "Okay, okay," you say, "let's concentrate on orchids. Can you get 8,000 stems by February?"

"Well, I don't know, 8,000 is a lot of orchids. Let me call my brother. Maybe we start slow with about 200 per week."

Your expected sigh only triggers another onslaught.

"We should grow orchids here! Set up a greenhouse. Start small. Big profit. You make a mint. Why didn't you guys think of it? It'll be like having the right to print money!"

You sigh again and balk at the whole idea of collaborating at all.

These dealmakers try to make Westerners feel guilty about not trusting them. In fact, the obstacle in the negotiation is that they can't perform what they originally claimed they could do. Wise Westerners stay polite and collected, and they keep communication lines open. Getting irate is the only sin that Westerners can commit in dealing with these "pushy" overseas Chinese: it robs Westerners of face and gets their name around as a company to avoid.

VI

P a r t   S i x

CROSS-CULTURAL COORDINATION

Some managers make decisions participatively; they involve those subordinates who will be affected by the decision in the decision-making process. Others make decisions authoritatively; instead of involving subordinates who will be affected by the decision, they make the decision by themselves. One theory posits that a manager's approach is influenced by national culture. Another theory is that the approach is influenced by specific situations in all cultures. This is discussed in Chapter 10. American-based theories posit that participative leadership behavior produces better results than authoritative behavior. However, in many cultures, authoritative behavior produces better results. Culture also has an effect on employee motivation. In some cultures, employees are motivated by the opportunity to obtain challenging work, but in other cultures, they are motivated by the opportunity to socialize. Cross-cultural leadership and motivation are discussed in Chapter 11.

Chapter Ten

Cross-Cultural Decision Making

Bosses in France tend to be Napoleonic. Graduates as a rule of one of the elite Grands Ecoles, they are expected to be brilliant technical planners, equally adept at industry, finance and government. They can be vulnerable to surprise when the troops below fail to respond to orders from on high. Stiff hierarchies in big firms discourage informal relations and reinforce a sense of "them" and "us." Managers in Italy tend to be more flexible. Firms' rules and regulations (where they exist) are often ignored. Informal networks of friends and family contacts matter instead. Decision making tends to be more secretive than elsewhere, and what goes on in a meeting is often less important than what happens before and after.[1]

Objectives of the Chapter

In essence, every aspect of management (planning, organizing, staffing, coordinating, and controlling), in one form or another, involves decision making. Decision making is thus the manager's most difficult task, and when managers cross national borders and cultures, the task becomes even greater. This is because people in different cultures view problems differently and apply unique decision-making processes. (As illustrations, read Practical Perspectives 10–1, 10–2, and 10–3.) **A decision or a decision making process that works in one culture is often ineffective in another culture.** Furthermore, different situations also require different decision-making styles. The objectives of this chapter are therefore to discuss:

1. The decision-making process in a cross-cultural context.
2. The differing cultural factors that affect managers' decision-making style, authoritative/consultative or participative.
3. The varying environmental factors/situations that affect the decision-making style.

THE DECISION-MAKING PROCESS: A CROSS-CULTURAL PERSPECTIVE

Basically, when making decisions, managers in organizations apply either a programmed or a nonprogrammed decision-making process. Both processes are affected by the culture of the society in which the decision is being made.

PRACTICAL PERSPECTIVE 10–1

Choosing a Local Manager in Russia

In choosing a general manager [in Russia], Western companies are often misled by the false conventional wisdom that insists there never was such a thing as effective Soviet management. Considering the enormous handicaps imposed on them by perennial shortages and centralized command and control, the general managers of many Soviet enterprises accomplished wonders. These managers still have no training in Western management theory and practice, of course, but their own Russian management style, deeply rooted in the resilient culture of the Russian *mir*, or collective, has its own considerable strengths. For example, Russian executives are often strong personal leaders who practice hands-on, walk-around, face-to-face management. They develop direct bonds of loyalty with employees at all levels. They also practice a unique form of decision making that combines consultation and command by alternating periods of open, widespread discussion of options with moments of strong, top-down authority in making final decisions.

Source: P. Lawrence and C. Vlachoutsicos, "Joint Ventures in Russia: Put Locals in Charge," *Harvard Business Review* (January–February 1993): 45.

PRACTICAL PERSPECTIVE 10–2

Decision Making in Japan

"Adjustment to Japan has been much easier than I thought," Ted Owens told his wife about a year after their move from the United States. Ted had been sent by an automobile company in Detroit to see if he could establish production facilities for transmission systems that would be built in Japan and imported to the United States. Having been told that negotiations take a long time in Japan, he was not disappointed that it had taken a year for a major meeting to be set up with the key Japanese counterparts. But the Japanese had studied the proposal and were ready to discuss it this morning, and Ted was excited as he left for work. At the meeting people discussed matters that were already in the written proposal that had been circulated beforehand. Suddenly it occurred to Ted that there was an aspect of quality control inspection that he had left out of the proposal. He knew that the Japanese should know of this concern since it was important to the long-range success of the project. Ted asked the senior person at the meeting if he could speak, apologized for not having already introduced the quality control concern he was about to raise, and then went into his addi-tion to the proposal. His presenta-tion was met with silence, and the meeting was later adjourned with-out a decision having been made on the whole manufacture-impor-tation program. Since Ted thought that a decision would be made that day, he was puzzled. What was the reason for Ted's difficulty? The big cultural mistake on Ted's part was in his method of introducing the new issue about quality control. In Japan (and, in general, Southeast Asia) people do not like surprises at meetings. Most information sharing and introduction of new ideas takes place in one-on-one meetings between the person such as Ted and his Japanese counter-parts who would be involved in the decision. After all corrections, modifications, and additions are made in these interactions, the addition to the proposal can be put on the agenda of a later meeting at which all the people involved in the project would be present. But at that point, everyone in the meeting has had extensive opportunities to study the addition to the proposal. No one will be embarrassed by an aspect of the proposal that might affect them but about which they are unprepared to comment.

Source: Excerpted from R. W. Brislin et al., *Intercultural Interactions: A Practical Guide*, vol. 9 (Newbury Park, CA: Sage Publications, 1986), pp. 164–165, 182. Copyright © 1985, Sage Publications, Inc. Used with permission. All rights reserved.

PRACTICAL PERSPECTIVE 10-3

The Quiet Indonesian

Machmud had recently been promoted to a position of authority and was asked to represent his company and Indonesia's needs at the head office in Butte, Montana. Relationships with fellow workers seemed cordial but rather formal from his perspective. He was invited to attend many policy and planning sessions with other company officials where he often sat, rather quietly, as others generated ideas and engaged in conversation. The time finally came when the direction the company was to take in Indonesia was to be discussed. A meeting was called to which Machmud was invited to attend. As the meeting was drawing to a close after almost two hours of discussion, Machmud, almost apologetically, offered a suggestion—his first contribution to any meeting. Almost immediately, John Stewart, a local vice president, said, "Why did you wait so long to contribute? We needed your comments all along." Machmud felt that John Stewart's reply was harsh. In Indonesia, the group often comes before any action of the individual. Machmud was acting as one would in a meeting in his home country. Rather than standing out as an idea-person seeking attention, suggestions are often quickly presented toward the close of a meeting, with hope that little attention will be paid to the originator of the idea.

Source: Excerpted from R. W. Brislin et al., *Intercultural Interactions: A Practical Guide*, vol. 9 (Newbury Park, CA: Sage Publications, 1986), pp. 169, 185. Copyright © 1986, Sage Publications, Inc. Reprinted with permission. All rights reserved.

The Programmed Decision-Making Process

The **programmed decision-making process**, which is by far the most commonly used in organizations, entails making decisions based on precedent, custom, policies and procedures, and training and development. An advantage of this approach is that the basis for a decision can be pretested for efficiency, which reduces risk and stress for decision makers ("I followed the procedures manual," "I did it the way it is supposed to be done," or "I did it the way it is always done"). A disadvantage of this approach is that when the organization's environment changes, the programmed bases for decision making often become obsolete and ineffective, which can lead to decision-making ineffectiveness. Of course, some of the advantages and disadvantages are culturally determined. For example, people in some cultures do not like too much challenge; they prefer a structured environment that provides certainty, and become frustrated in ambiguous, challenging situations. People in other cultures prefer challenge and become bored in an environment that provides too much structure. (This will be discussed in more detail later in this chapter.)

The Nonprogrammed Decision-Making Process

The **nonprogrammed decision-making process** entails analyzing current data and information, obtained through a systematic investigation of the current environment, for the purpose of identifying and solving a problem. Two approaches to this process are rational decision making and "satisficing."

The Rational Decision-Making Process

In Western culture, the steps in the rational decision-making process are as follows: (1) through investigation, define the problem, (2) identify a set of minimum criteria on which to base the decision, (3) identify multiple viable choices, (4) quantitatively, evaluate each viable choice on the basis of each criterion, and select the optimum choice, the one with the highest quantitative value, and (5) implement the choice. In Western culture, the "ideal" decision model thus presumes an optimum choice among viable alternatives.

The Satisficing Decision-Making Process

The satisficing approach assumes that there is an incompleteness of information; that is, decision makers do not possess the information necessary to optimize.[2] Therefore, they *satisfice*; they select the first choice that meets some minimum criteria, that is, the first choice that is "good enough." They do not identify multiple viable choices. An advantage of satisficing over the rational approach is that it is quicker and thus less expensive. A disadvantage is that you may be foregoing a better solution.

The Impact of Culture on Nonprogrammed
Decision Making

The validity of the nonprogrammed decision-making process as a prescription for decision-making behavior is affected by culture. Culture has been defined as "... the interactive aggregate of common characteristics that influence a group's response to its environment."[3] Since the characteristics vary from group to group, people in different cultures are likely to have different preferences for a certain state of affairs, for specific social processes, and for "general rules for selective attention, interpretation of environmental cues, and responses."[4] As such, people in different cultures view and react to problems differently. What is rational in one culture may be irrational in another, and vice versa. In a broad context, we do not know whose views are right.[5] Presented below are some examples of how contrasting views affect the decision making process.

Problem Recognition

The master of destiny and fatalistic cultural concepts described in Chapter 1 affect problem definitions. Managers in **master of destiny cultures** tend to perceive most situations as problems to be solved, and seek improvement through change. On the other hand, managers in **fatalistic** societies tend to accept situations as they are and do not seek improvement or change; they believe that fate or God's will intervene in decision making. The American society is an example of the master of destiny culture, and Indonesia an example of a fatalistic society.[6] American decision makers would thus act faster on a problem than would Indonesian decision makers.

Criteria

Some cultures possess a "collective" orientation (discussed in Chapter 1 and to be discussed later on in this chapter as "low individualism") and some an "individualistic" orientation (also discussed in Chapter 1 and to be discussed later on in this chapter as "high individualism"). The collectivist orientation implies that individuals in the culture possess a group orientation; they emphasize group objectives in arriving at decisions, the rights of both current and future generations, and group harmony and discipline. In contrast, the individualistic orientation implies emphasizing the functional definition of relationships, utilitarianism in problem solving, a shorter time perspective, and the freedom to choose and compete.[7] Decision makers in the two cultures are thus likely to use different criteria to make a decision. For example, collectivist decision makers may use maintaining group harmony as the major criterion on which to base the decision; in contrast, individualistic decision makers may use cost-benefit as the major criterion (evident in the U.S., an individualistic society).

Information Gathering

As pointed out in Chapter 1, decision makers in some cultures rely on "hard facts" and data as bases for a decision. The nonprogrammed approach to decision making would therefore be applied in these cultures. In many cultures, however, decision makers do not place a high premium on factual information and data; instead, they rely more on their instincts as a basis for decision making. Since decision makers in these cultures rely on their intuition, they would not be highly receptive to the application of the nonprogrammed decision-making process.

Choice and Implementation

Because group consensus is generally required, decisions in collectivist societies normally take a long time to make. The process of obtaining consensus is often more important than the choice itself. In contrast, choice and implementation decisions in individualistic societies are normally made quickly. This because decision makers tend to be autocratic and make decisions by themselves (the ensuing sections will discuss this more thoroughly). Furthermore, decision makers in individualistic cultures are likely to select the most economically efficient choice. On the other hand, decision makers in collectivist societies are likely to select a choice that does not offend members of the group.

In some cultures, decision makers are very methodical and carefully evaluate numerous alternative choices before making a selection; in other cultures, decision makers use an incremental approach—they discuss alternatives in a preplanned sequence, making decisions as they go along. Furthermore, as will also be discussed in the ensuing sections, individuals in some cultures take greater risks than individuals in other cultures. For instance, in deciding on a foreign market entry strategy, decision makers in the lower-risk-taking cultures may select the safer exporting approach; decision makers in the higher-risk-taking cultures may select a riskier approach, such as producing abroad.

DECISION-MAKING BEHAVIOR: AUTHORITATIVE OR PARTICIPATIVE?

Decision makers use two basic types of decision making behavior: authoritative and participative. Decision makers using **authoritative behavior** decide alone what is to be done and/or how it is to be done and tell subordinates; however, they may consult their subordinates about decisions before they finalize them. Using **participative behavior**, decision makers ask their subordinates what should be done and/or how it should be done, and together they reach an agreement and/or a consensus. Both approaches have advantages and disadvantages.

An advantage of the authoritative approach is that decisions can be made quickly. A disadvantage, however, is that not involving the subordinates in the decision-making process can lead to their demoralization, which often leads to decision sabotage and slow implementation. An advantage of the participative approach is that it can lead to greater subordinate satisfaction and performance, especially when participation makes work more challenging for them, and the multiple input obtained from the subordinates can result in higher quality decisions than those made authoritatively by one person. A disadvantage is that the decision process can take too long, although this disadvantage can be offset by the decision not being sabotaged and therefore quicker implementation.

Rensis Likert has hypothesized that authoritative decision making leads to "mediocre" organizational performance, consultative to "good" organizational performance, and participative to "high levels of productivity."[8] It should be noted, however, that the concept of authoritative or participative decision-making behavior is explained from a Western cultural perspective. Some cultures may not even possess such a perspective. In other words, many concepts are not readily transferrable across cultures. For example, many people in Western cultures perceive the authoritarian decision maker in a negative way: "Who made him/her king/queen?" But in some cultures, the same decision-making behavior is perceived favorably: "By dictating to me, he/she is communicating God's will to me, so I feel good."

Furthermore, many Westerners perceive participative decision-making behavior positively. In many cultures, however, it is **perceived negatively**: "He/she is asking me what I think . . . doesn't he/she know how to do his/her job? It's not my responsibility to make decisions." In these cultures, the participative decision maker loses credibility in subordinates' eyes, and may even frustrate and demoralize them. For example, in their study of Mexican workers in a Mexican plant and of American workers in a U.S. plant, cross-cultural management researchers T. Morris and C. M. Pavett concluded that U.S. management systems do not have to be applied in the Mexican plant to extract the same level of production as in the U.S. plant. They found that the management systems used in the two plants

> reflect some of the salient cultural differences between the U.S. and Mexico. Americans have been characterized as less accepting of authority, autocratic decision making and unequal power distributions [to be discussed in the ensuing sections] than are people of Mexico. . . . Mexican workers are characterized as expecting an authority figure to make decisions and assume responsibility.[9]

It should be noted that in applying participative decision making, some managers apply the management by objectives (MBO) approach, while others apply the *ringi* approach. The use of these approaches is also dictated by culture. The major features of a typical **MBO** program are as follows:[10]

1. Manager and subordinate meet and together set objectives for subordinate.
2. Manager and subordinate attempt to establish realistic, challenging, clear, and comprehensive objectives related to organizational and personal needs.
3. Criteria for measuring and evaluating the objectives are agreed upon by both the manager and the subordinate.
4. The manager and the subordinate establish review dates when objectives will be reexamined.

5. The manager plays less the role of a judge and jury and more of a coaching, counseling, and supportive role.
6. The overall process depends on results accomplished and counseling subordinates and not on activities, errors, and organizational requirements.
7. After establishing goals and objectives and identifying the activities necessary to accomplish them, subordinates are allowed to pursue their goals and objectives essentially in their own manner. However, as indicated above, there are periodic reviews by the manager. The subordinate also reviews his or her own progress.

Many decision makers, especially in Japanese organizations, use a group-oriented process known as *ringi* to establish objectives. The **ringi** participative approach is as follows:[11]

1. All subordinates who are to be involved in the execution of the decision must have the opportunity to voice their views.
2. The manager meets with the group responsible for carrying out the decision.
3. During the meetings, all issues are considered and all members of the group contribute to the discussion of options, facts, and philosophy underlying the decision. Therefore, when a decision is reached, everyone involved knows what he or she must do. And because everyone has agreed to the decision, its execution can proceed quickly.

The MBO process is likely to work best in "individualistic" cultures such as the U.S., where individuals tend to prefer to work on their own, and the *ringi* process is likely to work best in group-oriented, "collectivist" cultures such as Japan, where people tend to like to work in groups.

Subordinates' views on how they should be utilized in the decision-making process vary from culture to culture, as do managers' views. For example, French executives tend to assume that the authority to make decisions is a given right of office and a privilege of rank, and therefore make decisions authoritatively. On the other hand, executives in the Netherlands, Scandinavia, and the United Kingdom expect their decisions to "be challenged, discussed or, more probably, made on a consultative, group basis in the first place."[12]

Which approach works best? It is, as suggested above, contingent on many factors. The aim of the ensuing sections is to explain the concept of **contingency decision-making behavior**. Different situations and cultures require dissimilar behavior, and decision makers therefore have to be flexible in their decision-making style when confronted with varying situations and when crossing national boundaries and cultures. Failure to apply the right decision-making behavior will result in ineffective decisions, which in turn will make the enterprise less competitive in the global economy.

DECISION-MAKING BEHAVIOR: TWO CONTINGENCY FRAMEWORKS

Decision makers who are not bound to just one approach or style are often confronted with the problem of determining which decision-making behavior (DMB)—authoritative/consultative or participative—is applicable in a situation. Using several existing theories, concepts, and research findings, the ensuing sections develop two contingency DMB frameworks that can assist cross-cultural managers in determining the appropriate DMB for specific situations and cultures. The first framework, labeled **the country-related cultural factors framework**, identifies certain national cultural dimensions and their impact on DMB. Basically, this framework is "**culture-specific**"; it assumes that different societies possess distinct and relatively stable cultures that serve as determinants of the DMB.[13] The second contingency framework, labeled **the universal factors model**, identifies various situations and their impact on DMB. This model is "**culture-free**"; it assumes that certain situational factors have an impact on DMB in all cultures.[14]

The Country-Related Cultural Factors Framework

A key study used in developing *the country-related cultural factors framework* was conducted by Professor Geert Hofstede. Professor Hofstede developed a typology consisting of four national cultural dimensions by which a society can be classified: power distance, uncertainty avoidance, individualism, and masculinity.[15] (These were discussed in Chapter 1.) As pointed out in Chapter 1, Professor Hofstede and his colleague, Michael Bond, subsequently identified a fifth dimension, labeled the *Confucian dynamism* dimension.[16] The ensuing section describe these five cultural dimensions and discuss whether DMB tends to lean toward authoritative/consultative or participative (see Figure 10–1). Figure 10–2 lists the 50 countries included in Professor Hofstede's study and their cultural classification, as well as the Confucian measure for 18 of the 50 countries.

DMB *as a Factor of the Country's Power Distance*

As indicated in Chapter 1, Professor Hofstede found that some of the countries included in his study are classified by a moderate-to-large **power distance** cultural dimension. Individuals dominated by this dimension, according to him, tend to accept centralized power and depend heavily on superiors for structure and direction. Professor Hofstede also noted that different laws and rules for superiors and subordinates are accepted. Therefore, authoritative DMB probably would be preferred by subordinates dominated by this cultural dimension. On the other hand, Professor Hofstede found that some nations are classified by a *moderate-to-small power distance cultural dimension*. Individuals dominated by this dimen-

The Country-Related Cultural Factors Model	FIGURE 10–1 ◆

Factors	DMB>
Large power distance	A
Small power distance	P
Low individualism	A
High individualism:	
Employees show low concern for organization's well-being	A
Employees show high concern for organization's well-being	P
Strong uncertainty avoidance	A
Weak uncertainty avoidance	P
Confucianism	A
High masculinity	A
Low masculinty	P

DMB> – Decision-making behavior leaning toward
A = Authoritative; P = Participative

sion do not tolerate highly centralized power and expect to be consulted in decision making. Furthermore, Professor Hofstede remarked that status differences (large power distance) in these countries are suspect. Thus, subordinates in these cultures probably would favor participative, or at least consultative, DMB. For example, subordinates in the United States, a moderate power distance society, tend to favor consultative DMB.

Cross-cultural researcher O. J. Stevens conducted a research project including MBA students from Germany, Great Britain (both small power distance societies), and France (a large power distance society). This study provides some support for the above propositions about a country's power distance measure influencing DMB. He asked the students to write their diagnosis of and solution to a case problem. The majority of the French referred the problem to the next higher authority—they sought direction. The British handled the problem. The Germans attributed it to a lack of formal policy and proposed establishing one.[17] Studies by researchers S. Kakar and by L. Williams, W. Whyte, and C. Green also lend support for these conclusions.[18] Professor Kakar reported that the paternal type of superior-subordinate relationships, especially in the form of assertive behavior, dominates the authority relations in organizations in India, a large power distance society. He attributed this pattern to sociocultural factors, as well as to the hierarchical development of modern work organizations in India. Professor Williams and his colleagues concluded that in societies where there are small power differences, such as Sweden, Austria, and Israel, subordinates and managers are highly interdependent in the completion of

◆ **FIGURE 10-2**   **Cultural Profile of Fifty Countries**

Country	PD	IN	MA	UA	CF
Argentina	LG*	LO	ST	ST	—
Australia	SM	HI	ST	WK*	LO
Austria	SM	HI	ST	ST	—
Belgium	LG	HI	ST*	ST	—
Brazil	LG	LO	ST*	ST	HI
Canada	SM	HI	ST*	WK	LO
Chile	LG	LO	WK	ST	—
Colombia	LG	LO	ST	ST	—
Costa Rica	SM	LO	WK	ST	—
Denmark	SM	HI	WK	WK	—
Ecuador	LG	LO	ST	ST	—
Finland	SM	HI	WK	ST*	—
France	LG	HI	WK*	ST	—
Germany (F.R.)	SM	HI	ST	ST	LO
Great Britain	SM	HI	ST	WK	LO
Greece	LG	LO	ST	ST	—
Guatemala	LG	LO	WK*	ST	—
Hong Kong	LG	LO	ST	WK	HI
Indonesia	LG	LO	WK*	WK	—
India	LG	LO	ST	WK	HI
Iran	LG	LO	WK*	ST*	—
Ireland	SM	HI	ST	WK	—
Israel	SM	HI	ST*	ST	—
Italy	LG*	HI	WK*	ST	—
Jamaica	LG*	LO	ST	WK	—
Japan	LG	LO	ST	ST	HI
Korea (S.)	LG	LO	WK*	ST	HI
Malaysia	LG	LO	ST*	WK	—
Mexico	LG	LO	ST	ST	—
Netherlands	SM*	HI	WK	WK*	HI*
Norway	SM	HI	WK	WK	—
New Zealand	SM	HI	ST	WK	LO

tasks, and status differences are downplayed. In cultures where there are large power differences, such as the Philippines, Mexico, and Venezuela, a more autocratic management style is not only more common, but also expected by subordinates.

DMB *as a Factor of the Country's Individualism Measure*

Professor Hofstede found that many societies are classified by a moderate-to-low **individualism** (collectivist) cultural dimension. Low individualism societies are tightly integrated, and individuals belong to "in-groups" from

Country	PD	IN	MA	UA	CF
Pakistan	LG	LO	ST*	ST	LO
Panama	LG	LO	WK*	ST	—
Peru	LG	LO	WK*	ST	—
Philippines	LG	LO	WK	WK	LO
Portugal	LG	LO	WK*	ST	—
So. Africa	LG*	HI	ST	WK	—
Salvador	LG	LO	WK*	ST	—
Singapore	LG	LO	WK*	WK	HI
Spain	LG	HI	WK*	ST	—
Sweden	SM	HI	WK	WK	LO
Switzerland	SM	HI	ST	ST*	—
Taiwan	LG	LO	WK*	ST	HI
Thailand	LG	LO	WK	ST*	HI
Turkey	LG	LO	WK*	ST	—
Uruguay	LG	LO	WK*	ST	
United States	SM*	HI	ST	WK	LO
Venezuela	LG	LO	ST	ST	—
Yugoslavia	LG	LO	WK	ST	—

PD = Power Distance; IN = Individualism; MA = Masculinity;

UA = Uncertainty Avoidance; CF = Confucianism

LG = Large; SM = Small; HI = High; LO = Low;

ST = Strong; WK = Weak

* But near the line that divides the two extremes.

Note: The PD, IN, MA, and UA dimensions are adopted from Geert Hofstede, "The Cultural Relativity of the Quality of Life Concept," *Academy of Management Review* 9(3) (1984): 391–393. The CF dimension is adopted from G. Hofstede and M. H. Bond, "The Confucius Connection: From Cultural Roots To Economic Growth," *Organizational Dynamics* (Spring 1988): 12–13. This study categorized only 18 countries.

which they cannot detach themselves. People think in "we," as opposed to "me," terms and obtain satisfaction from a job well done by the group. Since most of the societies that measured low individualism also measured large power distance (as shown in Figure 1-5, Chapter 1), the DMB applied by decision makers in organizations in these countries probably leans toward the authoritative.

On the other hand, Professor Hofstede concluded that some nations are classified by a *moderate-to-high individualism cultural dimension.* Individuals in these societies look primarily after their own interests. Since employees in these cultures often consider their own objectives to be more important than the organization's, decision makers are likely to apply DMB leaning toward the authoritative, as evidenced by the authoritative/consultative DMB usually applied by decision makers in U.S. organizations, a country with a high individualism measure. And, as Practical Perspective 10–4 indicates, the management of Japanese MNCs tend to behave authoritative with American executives working for their subsidiaries in the U.S. In these societies the subordinates themselves probably would prefer that participative or at least consultative DMB be applied. This contention is based on Professor Hofstede's conclusion that, for these individuals, a high quality of life means individual success and achievement, which is perhaps best attained in organizations whose decision makers apply participative DMB. Therefore, in societies with a high individualism measure, decision makers in organizations whose employees are strongly concerned with the enterprise's well-being probably apply DMB leaning toward the participative.

The above contentions are partially supported by Jackofsky and Slocum. They aregue that in low individualism cultures, employees attach more importance to structure than to freedom in their jobs and are more emotionally and morally involved with their organizations than employees in cultures that stress high individualism.[19]

DMB as a Factor of the Country's Uncertainty Avoidance Measure

Many societies, Professor Hofstede found, are classified by a *moderate-to-strong* **uncertainty avoidance** *cultural dimension*. Individuals in these cultures feel uneasy in situations of uncertainty and ambiguity and prefer structure and direction. Therefore authoritative DMB, because the uncertainty involved in decision-making is assumed by someone else, probably would be preferable to these subordinates. Professor Hofstede has proposed that improving the quality of life for employees in these societies implies offering more security and perhaps more task structure on the job. On the other hand, Hofstede found that numerous countries are classified by a *moderate-to-weak uncertainty avoidance cultural dimension*. People in these cultures tend to be relatively tolerant of uncertainty and ambiguity and require considerable autonomy and low structure. Since it allows for some degree of autonomy, participative DMB probably would be preferred by subordinates dominated by this dimension.

This conclusion is supported by cross-cultural researchers R. N. Kannungo and R. Wright, who discovered that many managers in Britain, a weak uncertainty avoidance culture, placed much greater importance on individual achievement and autonomy than managers in France, a strong uncertainty avoidance society. The French valued competent supervision, sound company policies, fringe benefits, security, and comfortable working conditions.[20] This suggests that British subordinates prefer participative DMB and the French authoritative DMB.

PRACTICAL PERSPECTIVE 10–4

The Authoritative Japanese Management

There are now an estimated 25,000 American managers working for Japanese companies in the United States, and by and large they seem to be unhappy and demoralized a lot. The Japanese need American executives' expertise to sell their products in the United States and are willing to pay top salaries to get them. But in company after company, the Americans complain about a system of subtle and debilitating discrimination in which they are treated as necessary but inferior outsiders—without the authority to get things done and lacking upward mobility. . . . This is hardly surprising, given the chasm that separates the American and Japanese corporate cultures. The qualities admired in American managers—ambition, risk taking, independence—are handicaps in Japanese companies, where group cooperation and a strict decision-making hierarchy prevail. Japanese managers generally choose a company for life, and they move up the corporate ladder very slowly, and according to seniority rather than ability. . . .

Japanese companies have been described as Machiavellian bureaucracies where absolute loyalty is demanded. . . . As a result, the Japanese have a hard time dealing with the mobility of American executives, whose tendency to move from company to company to take advantage of better opportunities makes their loyalty automatically suspect and breeds distrust. . . . A study on the organization of Japanese subsidiaries in the United States by the Boston Consulting Group shows that while the formal corporate chain of command includes American executives at the second and third level, the actual decision-making system cuts out the Americans altogether. "You have a situation in which business is conducted at night on the telephone in Japanese between Japanese," says Kazuo Nomura, who is consul for the Boston Consulting Group and helped put the study together. "They come back in the morning and tell the Americans what has been decided, and sometimes they even make it seem like the Americans made the decision."

Source: Excerpted from Leah Nathans, "A Matter of Control," *Business Month* (September 1988): 46, 50.

DMB *as a Factor of Confucianism*

As it was pointed out earlier and in Chapter 1, research by Professors Hofstede and Bond revealed a fifth cultural dimension by which societies can be classified, labeled the *Confucian dynamism* dimension. This dimension applies mainly to East Asian cultures based on **Confucian** philosophy (the People's Republic of China, South Korea, Japan, Hong Kong, and Singapore)[21] As indicated in Chapter 1, Confucianism is not a religion, but a system of practical ethics; it is based on a set of pragmatic rules for daily life derived from experience. The key tenet of Confucian teachings is that unequal relationships between people create stability in society.

In essence, individuals in Confucian-based organizations are forced to adhere to rigid, informal group norms and values, which include the subservient relationships aspects of Confucianism described in Chapter 1. Since individuals are so strictly bound to group norms, decision makers in organizations based on the Confucian cultural dimension, in reality, apply authoritative DMB. Support for this contention is provided by cross-cultural studies conducted by K. H. Chung and by W. S. Nam, who found that South Korean managers demonstrate the Confucian virtues of loyalty and obedience to authorities; by G. W. England and R. Lee and by J. Harbron, whose studies revealed that South Korean managers tend not to adopt systems of shared management and power equalization within organizations. It is also supported by research conducted by L. W. Pye and by R. H. Solomon, who described Chinese subordinates as passive and as preferring that others make decisions for them.[22]

As discussed earlier, Japanese managers use a participative approach labeled *ringi*. Many Japanese managers, however, prior to the group's meeting, "discuss" the issue or decision one-on-one with individual members (refer again to Practical Perspective 10–2). In essence, the *ringi* method appears to be subtle authoritative decision making—not only does the manager enforce rigid group norms and values, but so do the group's members. The real objective of participative decision making is to generate and allow the introduction of varying views and alternative choices. The group-oriented cultures, however, tend not to allow the introduction of views that differ from the group's norms and values—which, in a Westerner's view, translates into repressive, authoritative behavior. In fact, a trend currently catching on in Japan is Japanese executives' seeking employment in foreign companies where they can be more autonomous.[23]

DMB *as a Factor of the Country's Masculinity Measure*

Many countries, Professor Hofstede found, are classified by a *moderate-to-strong masculine cultural dimension*. Societies classified by this dimension stress material success and assertiveness and assign different roles to males and females. Males are expected to carry out the assertive, ambitious, and competitive roles in the society; females are expected to care for the nonmaterial quality of life, for children, and for the weak—to perform the society's caring roles. In such societies a male might be the manager of finance, and a female might be his secretary; a role reversal would be an exception to the rule. In strong masculine countries where such behavior is perceived as inequitable, mandating authoritative DMB emphasizing reduction of such social inequities would probably be applied in many organizations. One finds evidence of this in recent programs in the U.S., a society with a moderate to strong masculine dimension, which enacted programs such as the Equal Pay Act of 1963, Title VII of the Civil Rights Act of 1964, and affirmative action and equal employment opportunity; in Japan, with its very strong masculine culture, which enacted the Employment Opportunity Law of 1986; and in Great Britain, another high masculinity culture, which enacted strong equal opportunity laws in 1976. Furthermore, the assertive behavior of male managers is likely to lead them to making decisions authoritatively.

Professor Hofstede also concluded that numerous nations are classified by a *moderate-to-weak masculine cultural dimension*. Societies classified by this dimension stress interpersonal relationships, a concern for others, and the overall quality of life, and define relatively overlapping social roles for males and females. In these cultures, neither male nor female need be ambitious or competitive; both may aspire to a life that does not assign great value to material success and that respects others—both may perform the society's caring roles. Male secretaries, female truck drivers, and male nurses would be far more acceptable in such societies than they would in societies classified by a strong masculine cultural dimension. According to Professor Hofstede, improved quality of work life for individuals in these societies means offering opportunities for developing social relationships on the job, which is perhaps best accomplished through participative/consultative DMB. Sweden, a weak masculine society, which generally exhibits participative DMB, is a good example. Findings by cross-cultural researchers B. M. Bass and L. Eldridge provide support for Professor Hofstede's contention. They discovered that successful managers in Denmark (a low masculine society) emphasized societal concerns in decision making, whereas successful American, British, and German (all high masculine societies) managers strongly valued a profit motive.[24]

Other Support for the Country-Related Cultural Framework

Numerous theorists accept the country-related cultural factors model.[25] They conclude that managerial attitudes, values, and beliefs are functions of a society's culture, and many studies support these theorists' contention. **Cross-cultural** researchers A. Sorge and M. Warner, for example, found substantial differences between West German and British factories with respect to shape of organizations, functional differentiation and integration mechanistics, basic features of industrial systems, and the process of education; they attributed these differences to distinct national technical cultures.[26] Researchers M. Maurice, A. Sorge, and M. Warner analyzed matched factories in France, West Germany, and Great Britain and proposed that organizational processes of differentiation and integration interact with the processes of educating, training, recruiting, and promoting manpower; that these processes develop within an institutional logic that is distinct to a society; and that nationally different shapes of organization result.[27]

Cross-cultural researcher D. Gallie studied the work attitudes of employees in four oil refineries owned by a multinational corporation. The refineries, two situated in Great Britain and two in France, were matched for technology and size. Professor Gallie found considerable contrast in the attitudes of workers and their relations with management; he attributed the differences to national culture.[28] Professor A. Laurent researched employees in a multinational enterprise in different nations and found that the employees retained their culturally specific work behaviors despite the existence of common management policies and procedures.[29]

Researcher P. Blunt studied an organization employing about 160 people in Brunei to determine whether or not the employees' values compared with Brunei's national values of large power distance, strong uncertainty avoidance, and low individualism. Brunei was not included in Hofstede's study, but Professor Blunt equated Brunei with similar countries in the region which Hofstede had categorized as such. Blunt found that commonalities did exist between the firm's employees and Brunei's national values. For example, employees showed a considerable unwillingness to make a decision without referring it to the most senior manager in the organization—an indication that the employees were exhibiting large power distance and strong uncertainty avoidance.[30]

Researchers E. F. Jackofsky and J. W. Slocum, Jr. examined published sources to ascertain whether or not the behaviors of two French CEOs, three West German CEOs, two Swedish CEOs, one Taiwanese CEO, and three Japanese CEOs compared with their respective country's culture as identified in Hofstede's study. Although they detected a few deviations, for the most part they found commonalities in the CEOs' behavior and their country's value system.[31] The above cited cross-cultural studies thus provide strong support for the "cultural-specific" theory.

Questions About the Country Factors Framework

Despite support for the country-related cultural factors framework, many unanswered questions remain. For example, how does the framework apply to **multicultural centers,** such as the U.S. and Canada? For instance, British Americans can be individualistic and Japanese-Americans collectivistic; German-Americans can have strong uncertainty avoidance and Swedish-Americans weak uncertainty avoidance. From a global perspective, can we even conceptually define the meaning of the labels used, such as uncertainty avoidance? Are not the more educated members of societies generally better equipped to deal with conditions of high uncertainty than the less educated members? If so, does this framework apply only to the less-educated members of the society? In the same sense, does the framework apply more to the lower-level members of an organization than to the upper-level members?

Furthermore, how does this framework apply to the Economic Man, Theoretical Man, Political Man, Religious Man, Aesthetic Man, and Social Man personal values of decision makers existing in societies?[32] For instance, the Theoretical Man, who relies on tangible evidence in seeking the truth, would probably have low tolerance for power from above and high tolerance for uncertainty. The Religious Man, who relies on the intangible and mysticism (faith), would probably have higher tolerance for power from above and lower tolerance for uncertainty. The Economic Man is practical and concerned with what is immediately useful, the Social Man is driven by benevolence, the Political Man is driven by challenge, and the Aesthetic Man is driven by savoring the moment's beauty—would not these individuals also have different tolerances for different decision-making styles and would not they themselves apply different decision-making behaviors? For instance, would not the more liberal values of the Aesthetic Man generate more participative decision-making behavior than would the more power-oriented values of the Political Man? These questions thus lead us to the universal factors framework.

The Universal Factors Model

Many theorists argue that, irrespective of a society's culture, individuals are forced to adopt attitudes and behaviors that comply with the imperatives of industrialization.[33] (As an illustration, read Practical Perspective 10–5.) These theorists believe that other transnational factors affect DMB in all countries. For example, management theorists V. Vroom and P. Yetton contend that participation is not an ideological or cultural phenomenon, but an "instrumental" phenomenon. They propose that U.S. managers use participation to enhance both quality and acceptance.[34] Therefore, many cross-cultural theorists adhere to a universal factors framework, which posits that DMB is influenced not as much by broad cultural factors as by varying situational factors, such as **subordinates' work environment, motivation, maturity level, and managerial level and functions.** These situations and the DMB behavior associated with each are discussed below. (See Figure 10–3.) It should be noted that numerous management textbooks, especially those addressing leadership, list many other situations that affect DMB. These few were selected to illustrate the framework.

PRACTICAL PERSPECTIVE 10–5

Participative Management Comes to the Far East

Taiwan and South Korea, the two heavyweights among the newly industrialized economies, face not so much a quantitative shortage as a qualitative one: The skills its managers have are simply no longer appropriate for the changing competition they face. As wages have risen, the region's traditionally low-tech companies have had to move into higher-value-added products dependent upon expertise—overseas marketing sophistication, for instance—that their old-line managers often do not have. As authoritarian governments in both countries loosened up, workers began to challenge their bosses for the first time, creating a whole new set of managerial problems. Says Lee Hak-chong, a dean at Yosei University in Seoul: "Democratization has produced a tough and loud labor force." The search for more of the right kind of managers is challenging some of the region's most basic values. . . .

A new wave of thinking is bringing forward a fresh generation of managers, men like Ng Pock Too and Nelson An-ping Chang. After getting an MBA degree from New York University, Nelson Chang went back to Taiwan. He heads an innovative computer services firm and a large cement manufacturing company that his father founded in 1954. . . . Chang, 38, could easily fill the part of the omnipotent dictatorial boss, the role favored by his father's generation. He has instead renounced that style because he thinks it stifles productive ideas. Says he, proudly: "I am a participative manager." The participation can get rough. To make certain that his senior executives take issue with him, Chang sometimes deliberately sets overambitious goals that they must argue against—or suffer penalties if the objectives are not met.

Belatedly, the region's universities are trying to respond. . . . Business schools are broadening curriculums in response to criticism that they have been turning out narrow specialists. At the National University of Singapore, business majors will now [1991] be required to take courses in such areas as psychology and Japanese culture. Chow Kit Boey, director of the school's Centre for Business Research and Development, says professors are now challenging students to become more "participative" and "free-thinking."

The Universal Factors Model	FIGURE 10–3 ◆

Factors	DMB>
Subordinates' Work Environment:	
Crisis conditions	A
Ambiguous conditions	A
Competent individuals	Pe
Individuals' Motivation:	
Need for affiliation individuals	Ac
Need for achievement individuals	Pe
Need for power individuals	Pe
Individuals' Maturity Level:	
Low maturity individuals	A
Low-moderate-maturity individuals	Ac
Moderate-high-maturity individuals	P
High-maturity individuals	Pe
Managerial Level and Functions:	
Upper-level managers	Pe
Lower-level managers	A
Structured functions	A
Unstructured functions	P

DMB> = Decision making behavior leaning toward

A = Authoritative; Ac = Authoritative/Consultative;

P = Participative; Pe = Participative/Extensive

The Subordinates' Work Environment

Regardless of national culture, in crisis situations and in conditions where a group of individuals are under extreme pressure to perform a difficult task or survive in a hostile atmosphere, they generally prefer that the decision maker behave in a directive manner.[35] A decision maker who authoritatively makes and communicates decisions to correct the undesirable conditions is likely to be welcomed. Individuals confronted with ambiguous or unclear assignments also generally prefer a manager who provides much structure, clearly defining roles and expectations.[36] On the other hand, in situations where individuals feel competent, an effective decision maker is likely to be one who asks them to participate extensively in the decision-making process. This is because competent people, those with a higher degree of perceived ability relative to the task demands, usually have low tolerance for authoritative behavior.[37]

Individuals' Motivation

In many societies, some individuals are motivated by the need for affiliation, some by the need for achievement, and some by the need for power.[38] Individuals whose primary motivator is the need for affiliation are interested in warm, friendly relationships, social interaction, communication and collaboration. Such people generally dislike to make unpopular decisions, even when it is necessary for organizational effectiveness. These individuals may not like the responsibilities that come with participative decision-making behavior, and they may prefer authoritative DMB with consultation. People motivated by the need for achievement are interested in attaining specific objectives, will work hard to achieve them, and tend to be more interested in personal success. It is likely that these individuals will want to be very involved in making decisions. People motivated by the need for power are interested in controlling and influencing situations; they like to get things done through people, and they like to teach and inspire other individuals. Since such people want to have an impact on the organization, they are probably would prefer to participate extensively in the decision-making process—although they themselves may prefer to apply authoritative DMB with their subordinates.

Individuals' Maturity Level

According to theorists Paul Hersey and Kenneth Blanchard, individuals function at four maturity levels: low maturity, low-to-moderate maturity, moderate-to-high maturity, and high maturity.[39] Individuals at a low maturity level have an negative attitude; they are unwilling and unable to assume responsibility. With such people, the effective manager applies directive (authoritative) DMB. Some individuals attain a low-to-moderate maturity level. These people are willing to assume responsibility, are confident, have a positive attitude, but lack the skills to make decisions. A combination of directive (authoritative) and supportive (consultative) DMB would work best with them. The manager, engaging in both kinds of DMB and through two-way communication, tries to improve the subordinates' decision-making abilities.

Some individuals develop to a moderate-to-high maturity level. Through coaching, training and development, they have acquired the ability to make decisions, but are unwilling to do so because of a lack of confidence. Participative DMB, which provides strong emotional support and encouragement and helps build confidence, would work well with these individuals. People with a high maturity level are able, willing, and possess the confidence to make decisions. Because they are at a maturity level where they need little direction and little emotional support, these individuals are likely to prefer a participative approach that allows them a great deal of responsibility in the final decision. Hersey and Blanchard's theory thus suggests that DMB is not a factor of national culture, but a factor of individuals' differing maturity level in their culture.

Decision-Making Level and Functions

Regardless of national culture, lower-level decision makers generally provide more direction than do upper-level decision makers; upper-level decision makers normally delegate more than those at a lower-level.[40] This means that upper-level decision makers apply participative DMB more so than lower-level decision makers, and lower-level decision makers apply authoritative DMB more so than upper-level decision makers. Decision makers for functions such as production, especially when the tasks are structured, tend to be directive and apply authoritative behavior. Decision makers for functions such as sales, where much of the employees' work is self-initiated, usually apply participative DMB.[41]

Other Support for This Model

Cross-cultural researchers P. C. Bottger, I. G. Hallein, and P. W. Yetton explored the effects of task structure and leader power on participative leadership across Australian, African, Papua-New Guinea and Pacific Island managers. They reported that "differences in leadership style between developed and developing nation managers would appear to arise from instrumental considerations, rather than cultural or ideological ones."[42] Researcher D. B. Stephens studied textile workers in three plants in Peru and in three plants in the United States. He concluded that

> the cultural differences assumed to affect management processes in different countries may not transfer completely to the management context or may be attenuated by a somewhat universal management experience. . . . Based on this research there is little reason to conclude that leader styles are much different in Peru than in the U.S.[43]

Some Problems with This Framework

The above discussion has presented some ideas that may aid decision makers in determining the appropriate DMB for certain situations in all national cultures. One problem in applying the above framework is reconciling the conflicting demands of a situation. For example, when a crisis confronts a group of achievers, which behavior would be most appropriate? Another problem is how to identify individuals' motivation at all levels—not all upper-level managers are willing to delegate authority to the lower-levels, nor do all lower-level managers want to behave autocratically. Furthermore, some organizational behavioralists have questioned the utility of complicated situational theories as a means of improving managerial effectiveness.[44] They believe that these theories can only be applied when the manager has time to analyze the situation and select the style that works best. But managers, according to those behavioralists, are so busy making decisions and responding to crises in a hectic and fragmented fashion that they do not have adequate time to evaluate the situation. The complexity of managing in the international environment is likely to increase, which means that managers will have even less time to analyze and apply a situational approach in the international environment than they do in the domestic one.

WHICH FRAMEWORK IS CORRECT?

Since the two frameworks are well supported by existing literature, can they both be correct? An analysis of the study by Professors Jackofsky and Slocum, cited earlier, can be used to lend support to both models. They found that in some instances the behavior of one of the French CEOs was influenced more by his own personal characteristics than by his country's cultural characteristics. This CEO acted boldly in acquiring two competing firms—behavior that stands in marked contrast to France's culture of strong uncertainty avoidance (conservative behavior). He also decentralized management in the acquisitions—conduct that also is opposed to France's large power distance culture. Professors Jackofsky and Slocum, surmised that this CEO's behavior of not conforming to national culture eventually led to his demise—which supports the country-related cultural factors framework. However, this CEO's behavior also violated the universal factors framework. This contention is based on the idea that often acquisitions are made when the firm being acquired is encountering difficulties (crisis), and that ambiguous conditions often arise in newly acquired firms. In such situations, the universal framework proposes application of directive DMB,[45] yet the CEO decentralized decision making. This CEO's unorthodox behavior, which led to his failure within the company, thus also can be interpreted to support the universal framework.

The other CEO, also eventually released from his position, generally conformed to France's national culture. He made conservative decisions (high uncertainty avoidance behavior), even when his firm was confronted with crisis conditions. However, his behavior also contradicts the universal framework, which proposes that individuals confronted with a crisis generally prefer an authoritative manager who makes decisions that communicate potential for correcting the situation. This CEO did make a somewhat bold decision in trying to cut 9,000 jobs to save money. But this action seems to go against both models. It violates the universal framework in the sense that the solution does not develop hope for subordinates confronted with crisis conditions, and it violates the country-related framework in the sense that the French display strong uncertainty avoidance and search for security; eliminating 9,000 jobs certainly does not make one feel secure.

The cases of these French CEOs, therefore, lend validity to both frameworks—as does Professor Herbert Simon's famous, older work. He discusses the "zone of acceptance" concept, which is the extent a subordinate accepts another's decisions as governing his or her behavior. Individuals with a wide zone accept more; individuals with a narrow zone accept less. Professor Simon proposes that the zone is socially determined and varies with the social situation, which in some ways equates with the country-related framework. On the other hand, he notes that "there are wide differences, too, among different types of employees in their expectation of authority relations in their positions. Professional men and skilled workmen are apt to have relatively narrow zones of acceptance."[16] This provides support for the universal framework.

Even though we know that both frameworks can be used to help predict DMB in organizations, we do not know yet which one is the best predictor. That is, we do not know when the determinants in one framework have a greater impact on DMB than the determinants in the other. Are there any situations (for example, crisis) that make the determinants in one framework more dominant than the determinants in the other? For example, would the two French CEOs discussed above have been more effective if their behavior emphasized the universal model's determinants when they seemed the most relevant and the country-related determinants when they seemed the most appropriate? How is such a determination made? It seems that, to make such a determination, managers require a great deal of managerial savvy, including global, cross-cultural savvy.

IMPLICATIONS OF THE TWO FRAMEWORKS FOR CROSS-CULTURAL DECISION MAKING

The two frameworks developed in this chapter are still being refined; but they do have some implications for cross-cultural decision making. The country-related cultural factors framework can serve as a general starting point for analysis. For example, it may be accurate to state that culturally the British tend to be highly individualistic and the Portuguese tend to be less individualistic. But it would be risky to make a blanket decision based on this belief, as not all British rank high on individualism, nor do all Portuguese rank low on individualism. Thus, ultimately, each specific situation must be studied. For instance, when the Japanese Honda Motor Company penetrated the European market, it discovered that it is not sufficient to have abstract knowledge about a foreign country—a deeper understanding must be developed. Honda learned the importance of adopting a locally oriented approach and building up a new way of doing work in the host country. As its success indicates, Honda learned how to blend its corporate culture with the cultural background of the host nation.[47]

The two frameworks also imply that cross-cultural decision makers need to determine to what extent individuals in different situations and cultures tolerate or expect different DMB. They also imply that effective cross-cultural decision makers are flexible in their approach to making decisions in different situations and across cultures; they understand that the behavior that works in one situation or culture will not necessarily work in another. Historically, managers doing business across foreign borders, in part because they did not adopt managerial styles appropriate to specific situations and cultures, have made many costly blunders.[48] For example, David Pulatie, vice president and director of employee relations—personnel international at Motorola, Inc., stated that there has been a tendency on the part of American managers to simply go into nation X, Y, or Z and try to introduce the American mentality and decision making without considering the reactions of the host country's citizens.[49] In view of the huge costs managerial blunders can generate in the global economy, it is imperative that international decision makers learn and apply the appropriate managerial behavior to the situation and culture.

Before a corporation sends someone abroad, it must identify the effective management style for that place and, as indicated in Chapters 6 and 7, select and train the right person for the assignment. For example, Reynolds International's training director, Thomas Kruse, explained that in order to determine the right management style for a country, they rely on managers who have worked there before, and they talk to Peace Corps volunteers who have worked in the country. They also obtain information from the American Management Association in New York, which offers country profiles and arranges seminars in which natives of a specific nation provide information on management styles that work in their country.[50] In the long run, the investment of time and effort put into assessing the situation, culture, and appropriate managerial behavior will be recaptured by avoiding costly blunders.

SUMMARY

This chapter has discussed the programmed and the nonprogrammed decision-making processes in a cross-cultural context, including a discussion on how a society's culture affects the rational decision-making process. The MBO and *ringi* participative decision-making approaches were also described in a cultural context. Two frameworks, each presenting several factors that influence decision-making behavior (DMB)—authoritative or participative—were discussed. The country-related cultural factors framework proposes that certain cultural dimensions affect DMB. The universal factors framework posits that certain specific situational factors affect DMB in all cultures. Questions about how to apply both frameworks were posed. The implications of both frameworks were put forth—mainly that cross-cultural decision makers, to apply the appropriate DMB, must understand each situation and culture thoroughly.

Key Terms

1. An effective decision-making process in one culture may be ineffective in another
2. Programmed and nonprogrammed decision making
3. "Master of destiny" and "fatalistic" cultures
4. Authoritative and participative decision making
5. Participative DMB is perceived negatively in many cultures
6. Contingency decision making
7. The country-related cultural factors framework
8. The universal factors framework
9. The "culture-specific" and "culture-free" theories
10. MBO and *ringi*
11. Power distance
12. Uncertainty avoidance
13. Masculinity
14. Individualism
15. Confucianism
16. Cross-cultural research
17. Multicultural centers
18. Subordinates' work environment
19. Individuals' motivation
20. Individuals' maturity level
21. Decision-making level and function

Discussion Questions and Exercises

1. Discuss the ways culture affects programmed and nonprogrammed decision making.
2. Discuss the fundamentals of the country-related cultural factors and the universal factors frameworks.
3. What type of DMB, authoritative or participative, would you apply in the following cultures:
   a. Large power distance
   b. Low individualism
   c. Strong uncertainty avoidance
   d. Low masculinity
   e. High Confucianism
4. What type of DMB, authoritative or participative, would you apply in the following situations:
   a. Crisis conditions
   b. Subordinates are motivated by the need for affiliation
   c. Subordinates function at a high level of maturity
   d. Subordinates carry out the sales function
5. Discuss the problems with the country-related cultural factors and the universal factors frameworks.

6. Fundamentally, what do the two frameworks tell the global manager?

7. Analyze Figure 10–3, and based on the country-related cultural factors framework, determine the appropriate DMB—authoritative or participative—for each of the 50 countries.

Assignment

Interview an executive involved in international business. Ask the executive to describe his or her experiences in making decisions across cultures. Did he or she apply the country-related factors framework or the universal factors framework? Prepare a short report for class discussion.

CASE 10–1

Source: Ken Hodgson, "Adapting Ethical Decisions to a Global Marketplace," *Management Review* (May 1992): 55.

Cultural Traditions

If you are involved in business with Third World countries, you need to understand three widespread traditions that affect business transactions: the inner circle, future favors and gift exchange.

INNER CIRCLE

Communal societies divide people into two groups: those with whom they have relationships, and those with whom they have none—the goal being group prosperity and protection. There are the "in" people and the "out" people. The "ins" are family; the "outs" are strangers. In East and West Africa, inner circles can be true relatives, comrades or persons of similar age or region. In China, they may be those who share the same dialect; in India, members of the same caste. These are not unlike the "old boy networks" in the United States. The effect in many of these countries is to restrict social and business dealings to those with whom the business person has safe, trusting relationships.

FUTURE FAVORS

The system of future favors operates within the inner circles. In Japan it is known as "inner duty," in Kenya, "inner relationship," and in the Philippines, "inner debt." In these traditions, the person is obligated to another to repay the favor sometime in the future. Some form of favor or service will repay the earlier debt; this repayment then places the grantor of the original favor under future obligation. Lifelong shifting obligations create relationships of trust and are the basis for doing business.

GIFT EXCHANGE

In many non-Western circles, the gift exchange tradition has evolved into a business tool: Gifts begin a process of future favors. They are an immediate

sign of gratitude or hospitality, but upon acceptance, they generate an obligation that the recipient must someday repay.

QUESTIONS

1. Discuss some of the ways the above cultural traditions affect the rational
   decision-making process described in this chapter.

From Napa Valley, California to Paris, France

C A S E   10–2

Source: This case was
created by the author.

John Terwilick, an executive for Shonteur, Inc., a wine wholesaler based in
Massachusetts, was appointed to head Shonteur France, Inc., a subsidiary in
Paris, France. The subsidiary had been established to procure wines in
Europe for distribution in the U.S. market. The subsidiary employs 179 peo-
ple. The employees are mostly locals (French), but numerous employees are
from Germany, Spain, and Portugal—which are sources of European wines.
The company selected Terwilick for the assignment because of his successful
experience managing another wine sourcing subsidiary in Napa Valley,
California.

Over the years Terwilick has attended many management development
seminars, where he was taught that participative management, involving
employees in the decision-making process, would produce wonders. It did
work well for him at the Napa Valley subsidiary, and it helped establish his
reputation at the Massachusetts headquarters as an effective manager. These
days, however, to climb to the top of a corporation's headquarters, managers
require extensive cross-cultural experience—that is, experience managing
diverse cultures. In view of this current managerial trend, Terwilick, with the
goal of a high-level appointment at corporate headquarters, happily accepted
the appointment in France.

Terwilick was determined to be at least as successful in France as he had
been in Napa Valley. Upon assuming his managerial post as the head of the
French subsidiary, Terwilick began applying basically the same managerial
style he had applied in Napa Valley. For example, he began delegating some
of his decision-making duties to the French supervisors, and in making major
decisions, he often solicited their input—he involved them in the decision-
making process. Terwilick had been taught in management development programs and learned through experience at Napa Valley that this would
improve employee morale, and thus productivity. To his surprise, however, he
noted that the French supervisors nonverbally expressed anxiety, dissatisfaction, and low morale. Terwilick thought to himself: "What is wrong here?
What is the problem?"

QUESTIONS

1. What did the company do wrong in sending Terwilick overseas?
2. Can you help Terwilick solve the problem with which he is confronted?

Notes

1. "The Business of Europe," *The Economist,* December 7, 1991, p. 64.

2. See Herbert A. Simon, *Administrative Behavior* (New York: The Free Press, 1976).

3. Geert Hofstede, *Culture's Consequences: International Differences in Work-Related Values* (Beverly Hills, CA: Sage Publications, 1980), p. 19.

4. D. K. Tse et al., "Does Culture Matter? A Cross-Cultural Study of Executives' Choice, Decisiveness, and Risk Adjustment in International Marketing," *Journal of Marketing* 52 (October 1988): 82.

5. See R. Theobald, "Management of Complex Systems: A Growing Societal Challenge," in F. Feather, ed., *Through the 1980s: Thinking Globally, Acting Locally* (Washington, D.C.: World Future Society, 1980), pp. 42–51.

6. Nancy J. Adler, *International Dimensions of Organizational Behavior,* 2d ed. (Boston: PWS-KENT Publishing, 1991), p. 162.

7. Tse et al., "Does Culture Matter?" p. 82.

8. Rensis Likert, *The Human Organization: Its Management and Values* (New York: McGraw-Hill, 1967).

9. T. Morris and C. M. Pavett, "Managing Style and Productivity," *Journal of International Business Studies* (First Quarter): 1992, 177.

10. Anthony P. Raia, "A Second Look at Management Goals and Controls," *California Management Review* (Summer 1966): 49–58; and Peter F. Drucker, *The Practice of Management* (New York: Harper & Row, 1954).

11. J. Johnston, "*Ringi:* Decision Making Japanese Style," *Management Review* 70 (May 1981): 15–21.

12. R. Neale and R. Mindel, "Rigging Up Multicultural Teamworking," *Personnel Management,* January 1992, p. 37.

13. See J. Child and A. Kieser, "Organizations and Managerial Roles in British and West German Companies: An Examination of the Culture-Free Thesis," in C. Lammers and D. Hickson, eds., *Organizations Alike and Unlike* (London: Routledge and Kegan Paul, Ltd., 1979), pp. 251–271.

14. See Child and Kieser, "Organizations and Managerial Roles in British and West German Companies," W. Heydebrand, *Comparative Organization: The Results of Empirical Research* (Englewood Cliffs, NJ: Prentice-Hall, 1973); D. J. Hickson, C. J. Hinings, and J. P. Schwitter, "The Culture-Free Context of Organization Structure: A Tri-National Comparison," *Sociology* 8 (1974): 59–80; M. Haire, E. E. Ghiselli, and L. W. Porter, *Managerial Thinking: An International Study* (New York: John Wiley, 1966).

15. Hofstede, *Culture's Consequences* Geert Hofstede, "The Cultural Relativity of the Quality of Life Concept," *Academy of Management Review* 9(3) (1984): 389–398.

16. G. Hofstede and M. Bond, "The Confucius Connection: From Cultural Roots to Economic Growth," *Organizational Dynamics* (Spring 1988): 5–21.

17. Cited in Geert Hofstede, "Motivation, Leadership, and Organization: Do American Theories Apply Abroad?" *Organizational Dynamics* (Summer 1980): 42–62.

18. S. Kakar, "Authority Patterns and Subordinate Behavior in Indian Organizations," *Administrative Science Quarterly* 16 (1971): 93–101; L. Williams, W. Whyte, and C. Green, "Do Cultural Differences Affect Workers' Attitudes?" *Industrial Relations* 5 (1966): 105–117.

19. E. F. Jackofsky and J. W. Slocum, Jr., "CEO Roles Across Cultures," in D. C. Hambrick, ed., *The Executive Effect: Concepts and Methods for Studying Top Managers* (Greenwich, CT: JAI Press, 1988).

20. R. N. Kannungo and R. Wright, "A Cross-Cultural Comparative Study of Managerial Job Attitudes," *Journal of International Business Studies* 14(2) (1983): 115–129.

21. Hofstede and Bond, "The Confucius Connection."

22. K. H. Chung, "A Comparative Study of Managerial Characteristic of Domestic, International, and Governmental Institutions in Korea," paper presented at the Midwest Conference of Asian Affairs, Minneapolis, Minn., 1978; W. S. Nam, "The Traditional Pattern of Korean Industrial Management," ILCORK working paper no. 14, Social Science Research Institute, University of Hawaii, 1971; G. W. England and R. Lee, "Organizational Goals and Expected Behavior Among American, Japanese, and Korean Managers: A Comparative Study," *Academy of Management Journal* 14 (1971): 425–438; J. Harbron, "Korea's Executives Are Not Quite the New Japanese," *The Business Quarterly* 44 (1979): 16–19; L. W. Pye, *The Spirit of Chinese Politics* (Cambridge, MA: MIT Press, 1968); R. H. Solomon, *Mao's Revolution and Chinese Political Culture* (Berkeley, CA: University of California Press, 1971).

23. "Changing Jobs Catching On in Japan," *Focus Japan*, March 1993, p. 6.

24. B. M. Bass and L. Eldridge, "Accelerated Managers' Objectives in Twelve Countries," *Industrial Relations* 12 (1979): 158–171.

25. See M. Crozier, *The Bureaucratic Phenomenon* (London: Tavistock Publications, 1964); S. M. Davis, *Comparative Management: Cultural and Organizational Perspectives* (Englewood Cliffs, NJ: Prentice-Hall, 1971); R. Nath, "A Methodological Review of Cross-Cultural Research," *International Social Science Journal* 20(1) (1968): 35–62; W. Glasier, "Cross-National Comparisons of the Factory," *Journal of Comparative Administration* (May 1971): 67–83; Hofstede, "Culture's Consequences;" Haire, Ghiselli, and Porter, *Managerial Thinking.*

26. A. Sorge and M. Warner, "Culture, Management and Manufacturing Organizations: A Study of British and German Firms," *Management International Review* 21 (1981): 35–48.

27. M. Maurice, A. Sorge, and M. Warner, "Societal Differences in Organizing Manufacturing Units: A Comparison of France, West Germany, and Great Britain," *Organization Studies* 1 (1980): 59–86.

28. D. Gallie, *In Search of the Working Class* (London: Cambridge University Press, 1978).

29. A. Laurent, "The Cultural Diversity of Management Conceptions," *International Studies of Management and Organization* (Spring 1983): 75–96.

30. P. Blunt, "Cultural Consequences of Organization Change in a Southeast Asian State: Brunei," *The Academy of Management Executive* 2(3) (1988): 235–240.

31. Jackofsky and Slocum, "CEO Roles Across Cultures."

32. See W. D. Guth and R. Tagiuri, "Personal Values and Corporate Strategy," *Harvard Business Review* (September–October 1965): 126.

33. See R. E. Caves, "Industrial Organization, Corporate Strategy and Structure," *Journal of Economic Literature* 18 (1980): 317–334; Hickson, Hinings, and Schwitter, "The Culture-Free Context of Organization Structure"; W. Heydebrand, "Comparative Organization: The Results of Empirical Research" (Englewood Cliffs: Prentice-Hall, 1973).

34. V. Vroom and P. Yetton, *Leadership and Decision-Making* (Pittsburgh: University of Pittsburgh Press, 1973); F. Heller and B. Wilpert, *Competence and Power in Managerial Decision-Making* (New York: John Wiley & Sons, 1981).

35. See A. W. Halpin, "The Leadership Behavior and Combat Performance of Airplane Commanders," *Journal of Abnormal and Social Psychology* 49 (1954): 19–22; E. P. Torrence, "The Behavior of Small Groups Under Stress Conditions of Survival," *American Sociological Review* 19 (1954): 751–755; M. Mulder and A. Stemering, "Threat, Attraction to Group, and Need for Strong Leadership," *Human Relations* no. 16 (1963): 317–334.

36. E. Burack, *Organizational Analysis: Theory and Applications* (Hinsdale, IL: Dryden Press, 1975), pp. 315–318.

37. See A. S. Ashour and G. England, "Subordinates' Assigned Level of Discretion as a Function of Leader's Personality and Situational Variables," *Journal of Applied Psychology* 56 (1972): 120–123; A. C. Filley, R. House, and S. Kerr, *Managerial Process and Organizational*

Behavior, 2d ed. (Glenview, IL: Scott, Foresman and Co., 1976), p. 215; F. Heller, *Managerial Decision Making: A Study of Leadership Style and Power Sharing Among Senior Managers* (London: Tavistock Publications, 1971).

38. See D. C. McClelland, "Business Drive and National Achievement," *Harvard Business Review* 40 (July–August 1962): 35–42; D. C. McClelland, *The Inner Experience* (New York: Irvington, 1975).

39. P. Hersey and K. Blanchard, *Management of Organizational Behavior,* 4th ed. (Englewood Cliffs, NJ: Prentice-Hall, 1982).

40. See F. Heller and G. A. Yukl, "Participation, Managerial Decision Making, and Situational Variables," *Organization Behavior and Human Performance* 4 (1969): 227–241; W. W. Tornow and R. R. Pinto, "The Development of a Managerial Job Taxonomy: A System for Describing, Classifying, and Evaluating Executive Positions," *Journal of Applied Psychology,* 61 (1976): 410–418; R. A. Webber, *Time and Management* (New York: Van Nostrand-Reinhold, 1972).

41. See J. K. Hemphill, "Job Descriptions for Executives," *Harvard Business Review* 37 (September–October 1959): 55–67; R. Stewart, *Contrast in Management* (Maidenhead, Berkshire, England: McGraw-Hill U.K., 1976); B. M. Bass, "A System Survey Research Feedback for Management and Organizational Behavior," *Journal of Applied Behavioral Science* 12 (1976): 151–171; Heller and G. A. Yukl, "Participation, Managerial Decision Making, and Situational Variables" Webber, *Time and Management.*

42. P. C. Bottger, I. G. Hallein, and P. W. Yetton, "A Cross-National Study of Leadership: Participation as a Function of Problem Structure and Leader Power," *Journal of Management Studies* 22, no. 4, (July 1985): 365.

43. D. B. Stephens, "Cultural Variation in Leadership Style: A Methodological Experiment in Comparing Managers in the U.S. and Peruvian Textile Industries," *Management International Review* 21, no. 3 (1981): 54.

44. See M. W. McCall, Jr., "Leaders and Leadership: Of Substance and Shadow," in J. Hackman, E. E. Lawler, Jr., and L. W. Porter, eds., *Perspectives on Behavior in Organizations* (New York: McGraw-Hill, 1979).

45. E. P. Torrence, "Behavior of Small Groups."

46. H. A. Simon, *Administrative Behavior.*

47. H. Sigiura, "How Honda Localizes its Global Strategy," *Sloan Management Review* 31, no. 1 (Fall 1990): 77–82.

48. See D. Ricks, *Big Business Blunders: Mistakes in Multinational Marketing* (Homewood, IL: Dow Jones-Irwin, 1983).

49. D. Pulatie, a section of "How Do You Ensure Success of Managers Going Abroad?" *Training and Development Journal* (December 1985): 22–23.

50. T. Kruse, a section of "How Do You Ensure Success of Managers Going Abroad?" *Training and Development Journal* (December 1985): 23.

Chapter Eleven

Cross-Cultural Leadership and Motivation

"Companies tend to take good advice on contractual and legal problems but don't tend to take account of the cultural problems," [Stephen] Burke [Dusseldorf-based director of recruitment consultants Michael Page International] said. Not clearly understanding the way people work and the attitudes they have towards work can cause real difficulties, as [Michael] Howlin [a barrister with Dickson Minto in Edinburgh] explained: "For example, in a highly unionized country such as Italy, even when a company is acting fairly, the workforce may be suspicious because there is a tradition of conflict." However, "there are no real differences in work aspirations between nationalities, more differences in the way such aspirations are expressed," explained Rosemary Neale, managing consultant with Warwick Weston. . . . "For instance, British and American workers felt that to do well they had to work longer hours and stay late to show commitment, whereas Scandinavians felt that working beyond your allotted hours just demonstrated that you were not doing your job right." "There are also differences in management style. A French executive, for example, will tend to make the assumption that the authority to make decisions comes as a right of office, whereas Dutch, British or Scandinavian managers expect a more consultative, team approach to decision-making."[1]

Objectives of the Chapter

Basically, *leadership* is the act of one person guiding another or others toward the attainment of an objective, and *motivation* is the act of the leader providing the incentives necessary to induce the follower or followers to attain the objective. Leadership and motivation are therefore interrelated and interdependent. However, the leadership style and the types of inducements to which individuals respond vary from one culture to another. Thus, the managerial behavior that works well in one culture will not necessarily work well in another. For example, culturally, the French and the Swedish tend not to respond to the same leadership style. Americans and Japanese tend to be driven by somewhat different motivations.

Therefore, managers of multinational corporations are likely to be ineffective if they attempt to rashly transfer the leadership style and inducements that work in their home country to the management of subsidiaries in other countries. This means that, along with having to adapt their business, negotiation, and communication approaches to different cultures, cross-cultural managers must adapt their leadership style and motivation inducements to different cultures as well. The objectives of this chapter are therefore to:

1. Discuss how culture affects leadership style.
2. Point out that American-based leadership theories do not have global application.
3. Describe the traits, abilities, and behavior leaders require in varying international strategic situations.
4. Discuss how culture affects motivation.
5. Point out that American-based motivation theories do not have global application.
6. Discuss how work goals vary across cultures.

CROSS-CULTURAL LEADERSHIP

There are some universal leadership similarities. For example, managers throughout the globe tend to want to be more proactive and to get work done by applying less authority, and those with greater rates of career advancement view themselves as possessing greater effective intelligence.[2] However, in most cases, national boundaries make a substantial difference in managers' goals, inclination for taking risks, pragmatism, interpersonal skills, and leadership style.[3] This is because, overall, the environments that affect leader-subordinate relations vary across countries and cultures.[4] What is valued in one society in terms of leadership behavior may not be valued as much in another society. For example, the ambitious behavior of American managers is valued less by the British than it is by the Americans.[5]

PRACTICAL PERSPECTIVE 11–1

Leaders Require Cultural Sensitivity

Global corporations are those that consider all nations as sources of managerial, leadership, and technical resources. Glaxo, a pharmaceutical corporation headquartered in London, has intentionally spread its operations throughout the globe in pursuit of cultural diversity and human resource talent. It has research centers in the United States, Italy, Japan, and France.

Cross-country partnership means that open-minded leaders must coordinate activities in Glaxo plants. An authoritarian style or a best way technique is not suited to Glaxo's approach to cultural diversity. Glaxo's work force, managers, and orientation are built on the premise that cultural values must be respected and can be utilized to the advantage of the enterprise.

Source: Adapted from Paul Girolami, "Why Glaxo Seeks Cultural Diversity," *World Link*, September–October 1990, pp. 108–109.

Therefore, to be effective, **cross-cultural managers** are often required to assume different **leadership styles,** depending on the culture with which they are interacting. (For illustration purposes read the case of Glaxo in Practcal Perspective 11–1.) It should be noted, however, that, as pointed out in Chapter 10, cross-cultural managers may sometimes find themselves confronted with situations in which other factors are more important determinants of the appropriate leadership style than cultural factors. For example, a manager confronted with the need to make a decision very quickly may not have the time to involve employees who culturally want to be involved in the decision-making process.

American-Based Management Theories

Popular **American-based leadership theories** include Douglas McGregor's *Theory X versus Theory Y manager* and Rensis Likert's *System 4 management.*[6] Fundamentally, these theories advance the notion that participative leadership behavior is more effective than authoritarian leadership behavior. As it was pointed out in Chapter 10, this may be true more in small power distance cultures, such as the United States and Denmark, than in large power distance cultures, such as France, Mexico, Spain, and Turkey, where employees tend to expect authoritative leadership.

Relationship-Oriented and Task-Oriented Leadership

In leader-subordinate relationships, some leaders are by nature *relationship-oriented* and some *task-oriented*. *Relationship-oriented leaders* place much more emphasis on maintaining a good relationship with their subordinates than they do on the performance of tasks. *Task-oriented leaders* place more importance on the performance of tasks than they do on maintaining a good relationship with their subordinates.[7] Robert R. Blake and Jane S. Mouton surveyed 2,500 managers from the United States, South Africa, Canada, Australia, the Middle East, and South America, who were participating in Managerial Grid seminars. Most agreed that the ideal leadership style was an integration of the relationship and task orientations, but when these managers described their actual behavior on the job, the practice was more task-oriented than relationship-oriented.[8]

However, culture has an impact in this respect as well. For instance, Indian leaders have been found to emphasize the task orientation.[9] Also, using the Least Preferred Coworker (LPC) questionnaire, it was found that high-performing managers in the Philippines had a low score (task-oriented) while their counterparts in Hong Kong had a high score (relationship-oriented).[10] In a study of American, Indian, and Japanese managers, the Japanese managers felt that they received more social support from their superiors than did the American and Indian managers, and for Americans and Indians, relatives were more important providers of social support.[11] The Chinese, as Practical Perspective 11–2 indicates, also prefer relationship-oriented leadership.

Initiating Structure and Consideration

Leadership behavior similar to the task and relationship orientations is *initiating structure*, which refers to the leader's efforts in organizing and getting things done, and *consideration*, which relates to the extent of trust, friendship, respect, and warmth that a leader extends to subordinates.[12] It was once believed in the United States that leaders applying consideration behavior were more effective than those applying structure. However, this leadership behavior, too, is affected by culture. For example, it has been found that consideration behavior applied by leaders in a mixed cultural setting in New Zealand did not contribute to managers' effectiveness.[13] A twelve-nation study revealed that leaders tend to view the need for more consideration at the lower levels than at the upper levels of management—except for the French and Latin Americans, who regarded being considerate as relatively unimportant at all levels of management. Germans and Austrians viewed consideration as important at all levels. Consideration was highlighted by fast-rising but not by slow-rising managers in Italy, Spain, Portugal, and the United States, and it was deemphasized by managers with accelerated careers in Belgium, Scandinavia, France, Latin America, and India.[14]

PRACTICAL PERSPECTIVE   11–2

Managers in the People's Republic of China

Ignoring me [James A. Wall, Jr., University of Missouri] as well as her customers, the young sales-clerk slowly leafed through her paperback. This I had heard was the best-run clothing store in Nanjing, and I was waiting to talk with its manager. "He's not here," said the translator. "He's on a buying trip, so we'll have to come back later." As we left, I asked the salesclerk, "Would you be reading that book if your manager were here?" "Of course," she snapped. "He's not a cold machine. He's progressive and lets me enjoy my work. He has a reformed management style." I had just been given my first lesson in contemporary Chinese management.

This article provides some initial information about Chinese management. It is based upon interviews with 50 workers in the Jiangsu province—one of China's richest—who described their bosses' management and with approximately 120 managers from a wide variety of Chinese organizations in that province. The managers discussed not only their management styles, but also their experiences, frustrations, and joys while leading in today's China. Complementing these interviews are my observations of Chinese managers. On occasion, I sat, with a translator by my side, and observed Chinese as they led. An additional supplement came from discussions with businessmen who are operating joint venture and trading firms in the P.R.C.

"Reform" and inflation are currently the principal players on the Chinese agenda, and they intertwine in a complex fashion: When Deng Xiaoping took over as China's leader in 1978, he sought to stimulate production by increasing returns to workers, factories, and farmers. . . . There is wage reform, price reform, market reform, and management reform. To steer the economy from socialist planning into the free—prosperous—market, the government is pushing responsibility for productivity down to the peasants, managers of the factories, and street committees. Leaders are encouraged to think for themselves and to reward productive workers.

Immediately in 1978, Deng abolished the communes and replaced them with a "responsibility" system. Under this scheme, the state officially owns the land but rents it for a lengthy, indefinite period to the peasants. In payment, each peasant family agrees or "contracts" to deliver a specific amount of rice, wheat, pork, onions, etc., to the state at an artificially low price. Any surplus or "bonus" is theirs, to use or sell. . . . As agricultural "responsibility" was succeeding, Deng began to reform the factory system. For selected industries, the state created a two-tier market system in which it supplied only a portion of the raw materials to the factories at a fixed (low) price. Any additional materials must be located and purchased by the factories in the free (high-priced) market. Likewise, the state purchases only a "contracted" amount of the output from these factories. The excess can be sold in the free (higher-priced) market. . . .

Within each firm, managers are expected to "reform" their managerial practices. Officially, "rewarding each according to his need" (i.e., fixed wage rates) is a slogan of the past. Now the approach is "to reward each according to his productivity." To implement this approach, managers pay each worker an "elementary" wage . . . and supplement it with a "bonus." . . . Officially, this bonus is to be linked with worker productivity. . . . While the managers are responsible for increasing productivity, they find the power to do so is shared with the Communist Party. Within most institutions, a Party hierarchy parallels the management structure. In 1988, the Party instructed its units to hand over most of their power to the managers; yet, the majority have not done so. The party in

combination with various aspects of Deng's reform package prevent most worker transfers among firms, assign workers to their jobs, prevent managers from firing workers, and force managers to employ all workers assigned to them. . . .

Facing such a workforce, managers find managerial problems are complicated by two additional socialistic outcroppings. First is the Marxist idea that managers do not create wealth. (Translation: Management and managers have no value.) Rather, wealth is created by the workers, and any scheme that does not return all income to the workers is exploitative. Therefore, if the managers take any pay for their efforts, which of course they do, they in a sense are exploitative, not to be respected. The problem generated by this maxim pales when compared to those arising from the concept, "dictatorship of the proletariate." Here the idea is that the workers own the factories of production, that is, the firm. Therefore, the managers work for the workers, instead of vice versa; consequently, the managers should serve and care for the workers.

"Dictatorship of the proletariat" dovetails quite easily with ancient Chinese values. In the feudal system, the rulers, landowners and businessmen treated their subordinates as a large family. The superiors expected obedience, loyalty and labor from the subordinates. In return, the superiors provided food, care, and protection. Chinese society still views firms from this feudal perspective. The firm is expected to provide for the families of the workers, and managers are expected to attend to the workers' personal problems. Reared under these traditional values and 40 years of socialism, Chinese managers willingly accept their paternal roles. . . .

Chinese managers, it seems, are squeezed into power positions and at the same time instructed by their government to utilize scientific management in which pay is tied to productivity. The problem, however, is that the discretionary pay (bonus) of about $5 a month is not large enough to serve as an incentive. As they recognize that they have no effective pay system, the Chinese managers, like their counterparts in the U.S., build and rely on other forms of power. And they do so quite pragmatically.

A seemingly preferred method for building power is to loosen the rules; in street jargon, managers "cut workers some slack." Specifically, managers allow cooperative workers to be tardy, take days off, sleep on the job, play cards, or earn extra income using plant tools. . . . In return for their laxness, managers expect to glean workers "on" (obligation), so that they will perform when production is necessary, and give moderate attention to quality. In Western terminology, we say the Chinese managers develop idiosyncrasy credits with each worker and then call these in as they need loyalty, hard work, and high performance. Managers labor diligently to establish and maintain a strong, warm relationship (i.e., referent power) with each worker. Since the leader traditionally is viewed as a patriarchal figure, this relationship is highly valued by the subordinates. . . . The importance of the leader-subordinate relationship cannot be overly emphasized. It enables leaders to gain worker conformity and it proves to be an important source of worker satisfaction. . . .

Reform, even though it breaks sharply from tradition, is heartily embraced by managers. Every manager emphasizes that he or she practices a "reformed" leadership style. In practice, though, most pick and choose from the reform package. . . . Many managers, workers complain, lead as they wish and then label their approaches "reformed" management. My interviews with managers in the Nanjing and Shanghai areas strongly validated this assertion. Many were autocratic, expecting subordinates to work hard without complaining. Some held that workers should work for and appreciate their "elementary" pay because it provided them with rice (i.e., life). And others admitted eschewing risk—"No achievement but no failure"—and following the rules. In all these cases, the managers re-ferred to their styles as "reformed."

Bonuses, while used and praised by most managers, are administered effectively by a small percentage. One set of managers pretends to reward productive employees with differential bonuses. Actually they spread the bonuses around arbitrarily and parrot the reform propaganda. Some only preach bonuses because they do not care to devote the time and resources to monitoring individual production levels. And others eschew bonuses because they do not want the reform system to work.

Source: Excerpted from James A. Wall, Jr., "Managers in the People's Republic of China," *Academy of Management Executive* 4, no. 2 (1990): 19–32. Used with permission from the Academy of Management. All rights reserved.

Japanese PM Theory of Leadership

American managers' authoritative leadership approach is poorly suited for Japan's group-controlled style. Building on the American task and relationship leadership ideas, during the past few decades, the Japanese have developed their own theory, labeled **the PM theory of leadership.** *P* stands for performance and *M* for maintenance. Fundamentally, in Japanese PM leadership, the P refers to leadership oriented toward forming and reaching group goals, and M refers to leadership oriented toward preserving group social stability.[15] Therefore, as in the case of the American task and relationship leadership style, *PM* is concerned with both output and people.

However, a fundamental difference between Japan's PM leadership theory and America's task and relationship leadership theory is that the Japanese emphasize groups and Americans emphasize individuals. Another fundamental difference is that in practice Americans tend to emphasize the task more than the relationship aspects of leadership, while the Japanese emphasize P and M equally. (Table 11–1 shows a comparison between some American and Japanese management styles.)

Cross-Cultural Leadership Traits, Abilities, and Behavior

Figure 1–8 in Chapter 1 and Figure 7–2 in Chapter 7 present the characteristics of effective cross-cultural, cross-national managers. Along with those characteristics, cross-cultural leaders also require certain other traits, abilities, and behaviors, as well as the ability to apply different traits, abilities, and behaviors to different leadership situations.

A Comparison of American and Japanese Management	TABLE 11–1 ◆

The American Manager	The Japanese Manager
Is a decision maker	Is a social facilitator
Heads a group	Is a member of a group
Is directive	Is paternalistic
Often has conflicting values	Has harmonious values
His/her individualism sometimes obstructs cooperation	Facilitates cooperation
Is confrontational	Avoids confrontation
Top-down communication	Top-down, bottom-up communication
His/her authority and responsibility are limited and specified	His/her authority and responsibility limits are not specified
Is held responsible for performance	Groups are held responsible for performance
Is held responsible for subordinates' poor decisions	Accepts symbolic responsibility when things go wrong
Top managers initiate problem statements and propose solutions	Top managers initiate problem statements, and those affected are involved in identifying solutions
Makes final decision	Codifies final decision
Needs to show immediate results because he/she is reviewed on a short-term basis	The longer term review period enables him/her to concentrate on long-term plans

Source: Adapted from Sang M. Lee and George Schwendiman, *Japanese Management: Cultural and Environmental Considerations* (New York: Praeger Publishers, 1982); Sang M. Lee and George Schwendiman, *Management by Japanese System* (New York: Praeger Publishers, 1982).

Innovator, Implementor, and Pacifier Leadership

Different situations require a manager with particular leadership characteristics. Three types of leaders, **the innovator, the implementor, and the pacifier,** require different characteristics (the characteristics are described in Table 11–2). Each type works best in specific situations. Figure 11–1 depicts three problem phases (situations) organizations normally encounter and the appropriate type of leader.[16]

As Figure 11–1 indicates, an organization needing an infusion of new ideas (often an organization undergoing crisis) requires a leader with the characteristics of the innovator. This is because under crisis conditions, sub-ordinates generally prefer a forceful leader who can solve the problem—leadership behavior is characteristic of the innovator. The innovator identi-fies new ideas and visions and "sells" them to the institution. Some aspects of the leadership behavior of Jack Welch, General Electric's CEO, is a good illustration of an innovator leader. He recognized the problems created by global competition and redirected GE into broadcasting, investment bank-ing, high-tech manufacturing, and other high-risk ventures. Lee Iacocca's behavior at Chrysler is another example of innovator leadership. Hired by Chrysler when it was confronted with extreme financial crisis, he came up with the radical idea of getting the U.S. Congress and the United Auto Workers to aid him in saving the company. He got the U.S. government to

---

◆ **TABLE 11-2**   **The Traits, Abilities, and Behavior of Three Types of Leaders**

The Innovator	Likes to compete and win
	Keeps on trying to succeed
	Assumes responsibility for success and failures
	Takes moderate as opposed to high risk (is bold)
	Likes to commit unit to a major course of action
	Is actively searching for new ideas to improve unit
	Seeks organizational growth
	Is motivated by the need to achieve, to be creative
	Centralizes decision making (is in control)
	Has desire to stand out from the rest of the group (dares to behave differently)
	Believes the environment can be controlled and manipulated (can "sell" his or her ideas)
	Is long-range oriented (foresees positive results in the distant future)
The Implementor	Desires to exercise power, to control and influence situations
	Is actively assertive
	Is able to get things done through others
	Has the ability to assume responsibility for decision making
	Is systematic in analysis and in problem solving
	Is able to integrate decisions and analysis

Is both long-range and short-range oriented (tends to distant needs as well as today's)

The Pacifier

Has a positive attitude toward authority figures

Has willingness to carry out administrative functions (willingness to do the "paper work")

Is interested in friendly relationships

Likes to communicate and collaborate with employees (is socially oriented)

Likes to improve the social atmosphere in the unit

Makes decisions which keep everyone moderately happy

Makes decisions based on feedback from what others have decided

Allows employees to make many of the unit's decisions (delegates decision making)

Accepts that decisions in the unit are not in harmony (individuals make conflicting decisions)

Seeks to satisfy influential individuals

Believes the environment cannot be controlled and manipulated (cannot "sell" ideas)

Makes short-range decisions (deals only with day-to-day problems)

Source: Carl A. Rodrigues, "Identifying the Right Leader for the Right Situation," *Personnel* (September 1988): 46.

---

guarantee bank loans, he put the president of the union on Chrysler's board, and he received major concessions from the union.

The new ideas introduced by the innovator often create an ambiguous atmosphere in the organization. When individuals cannot tolerate ambiguous or unclear assignments, they generally prefer to have a leader who provides systematic structure to create a stable working environment within the organization. Thus, after the new vision has been initiated, the institution needs a leader who can systematically put into operation the desired changes; someone whose personality is similar to the implementor's. Some aspects of the behavior of Alfred Sloan, Jr., serves as an example of implementor leadership. He generated structure in General Motors after William C. Durant conceived the company. Sloan was a talented operations executive

◆ **FIGURE 11–1   Contingency Leadership Cycle**

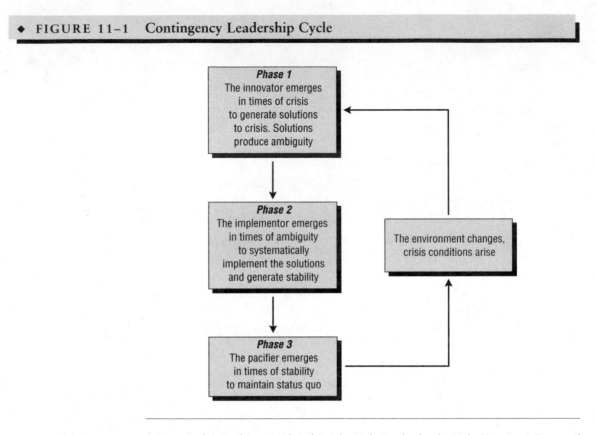

Source: Carl A. Rodrigues, "Identifying the Right Leader for the Right Situation," *Personnel* (September 1988): 44.

who also possessed competency in financial and organizational matters. He studied the situation at GM and prepared the "Organizational Study," a program proposing a new organizational and business philosophy for GM.[17]

When the organization has attained a certain stability and daily operations are running smoothly, members usually feel more competent and feel that they can perform the task at hand. The higher the degree of perceived ability related to task demands, the less willing subordinates will be to accept strong direction and oversight. In this situation, an organization needs a pacifier-oriented leader. In some respects, the leadership of Reginald H. Jones, Jack Welch's predecessor at General Electric, illustrates pacifier behavior. Prior to the advent of Welch into the top position, Jones emphasized the role of corporate statesman.[18] It should be noted that, as Figure 11–1 shows, when a crisis arises again, the leadership cycle is repeated.

Managerial Strategy and Application of the Three Leader Types			TABLE 11-3 ◆

| | Type of Leader Needed | | |
Managerial Strategy	**Innovator**	**Implementor**	**Pacifier**
Expatriate to create a new subsidiary abroad	X		
Expatriate to operationalize the new subsidiary		X	
Expatriate to train locals for managerial positions		X	
Expatriate to transfer autonomy to local managers			X
Home-office manager to monitor subsidiary activities			X
Expatriate/local manager to solve crisis in subsidiary	X		
Expatriate/local manager to operationalize solution		X	
Local manager to carry out activities under conditions of stability			X

Managerial Strategy and Application of the Three Leader Types

Table 11–3 depicts foreign subsidiary managerial strategy and application of the three types of leaders. As Table 11–3 shows, when a company needs to send an expatriate abroad to start a new subsidiary, an individual with the innovator's creative characteristics probably would work best. But once the innovator has conceived the idea for establishing the subsidiary, an individual with the implementor's capabilities to systematically operationalize the innovator's ideas and to train locals for managerial positions would probably work best (many innovators do not possess the implementor's characteristics). Once the implementor has fully developed the subsidiary and local managers, a pacifier-oriented leader is needed to transfer managerial duties to the locals. Subsequently, a manager with the characteristics of the pacifier is needed at the firm's headquarters to monitor the foreign subsidiary's activities. This type of manager is needed because he or she will not interfere as much in local activities as would the innovator and the implementor, who are hands-on managers.

Some individuals possess the characteristics of both the innovator and the implementor. Thus, instead of sending two individuals, one who has been properly developed to act both ways would be the most cost efficient. And some individuals actually possess the traits, abilities, and behavior of all three types—as three-dimensional leaders, they know when it is time to create, when it is time to rally others to get the creation operationalized, and when to stay out of the way. Three-dimensional leaders would therefore be the ideal. They, however, are hard to find—but can be developed.

It should also be noted that national culture also has an impact on the appropriate leadership style. For example, small power distance individuals, because they want more control over their affairs, would be open to the relatively "hands-off" managerial approach of the pacifier leader type. On the other hand, large power distance individuals are likely to appreciate the strong "hands-on" managerial approach of the implementor leader type. And in comparison with weak uncertainty avoidance people, strong uncertainty avoidance people, since they have relatively low tolerance for ambiguity, probably would prefer the structure the implementor provides, and probably would be closed to the innovator's creative thinking.[19]

CROSS-CULTURAL MOTIVATION

In discussing the topic of *motivation,* some individuals may argue that there are no major differences in what motivates people across countries; that people everywhere, in general, are the same and respond to the same stimuli. This may be true in some respects, but not in all. Certainly, just about all individuals are driven by such basic needs as food, water, air, and shelter. However, people are also driven by psychological needs, such as self-esteem and social status needs. Psychological drives tend to be *culture-specific*; the stimuli to which an individual responds differs across cultures. For example, people in individualistic-oriented cultures, such as America, may work toward **self-actualization** as an **end,** while people in collectivistic-oriented cultures, such as China, may work toward self-actualization as a **means** to an **end—to serve society/the group better.**

Many of the popular motivation theories were developed by Western scholars using Western subjects and concepts. The ensuing sections discuss some of these theories in a cross-cultural context.

A Comparison of Western and Southeast Asian Motivation Theories

More than three decades ago, Douglas McGregor proposed that managers adhere to one of two opposing theories about people: *Theory X* and *Theory Y.*[20]

Theory X

Basically, Theory X posits that the average human being has an inherent dislike of work and will avoid it if he (or she) can. Because of this human characteristic of dislike of work, people must be coerced, controlled, directed, or threatened with punishment to get them to put forth adequate effort toward the achievement of organizational objectives. The average human being prefers to be directed, wishes to avoid responsibility, has relatively little ambition, and wants security above all.

Theory Y

Theory Y puts forth that the expenditure of physical and mental effort in work is as natural as play or rest. External control and the threat of punishment are not the only means of bringing about effort toward organizational objectives. People will exercise self-direction and self-control in the service of objectives to which they are committed. Commitment to objectives is a function of the rewards associated with their achievement. The average human being learns, under proper conditions, not only to accept but to seek responsibility. The capacity to exercise a relatively high degree of imagination, ingenuity, and creativity in the solution of organizational problems is widely, not narrowly, distributed in the population; under the conditions of modern industrial life, however, the intellectual potential of average human beings is only partially utilized.

Several years ago Geert Hofstede, the European researcher, analyzed these two theories in the context of Southeast Asian culture. He believed that McGregor's assumptions, which are common to both theories, stem from America, an individualistic and masculine society. Hofstede outlined the assumptions on which McGregor's theories rest as follows:[21]

- ◆ Work is good for people. It is God's will that people should work.
- ◆ People's potentialities should be maximally utilized. It is God's will that you and I should maximally use our potentialities.
- ◆ There are "organizational objectives" which exist separately from people.
- ◆ People in organizations behave as unattached individuals.

Theory T and Theory T+

Professor Hofstede proposed that America's assumptions do not apply in the collectivist (low individualism), large power distance Southeast Asian cultures. He replaced them with Southeast Asian assumptions.[22]

Southeast Asian assumptions:

- ◆ Work is a necessity but not a goal itself.
- ◆ People should find their rightful place, in peace and harmony with their environment.
- ◆ Absolute objectives exist only with God. In the world, persons in authority positions represent God, so their objectives should be followed.
- ◆ People behave as members of a family and/or group. Those who do not are rejected by society.

◆   **TABLE 11–4   Southeast Asian Management**

Theory T: There is an order of inequality in this world in which everyone has his or her rightful place. High and low are protected by this order, which is willed by God.

Children have to learn to fulfil their duties at the place where they belong by birth. They can improve their place by studying with a good teacher, working with a good patron, and/or marrying a good partner.

Tradition is a source of wisdom. Therefore, the average human being has an inherent dislike of change and will rightly avoid it if he or she can.

Theory T+:   In spite of the wisdom in traditions, the experience of change in life is natural, as natural as work, play or rest.

Commitment to change is a function of the quality of the leaders who lead the change, the rewards associated with the change, and the negative consequences of not changing.

The capacity to lead people to a new situation is widely, not narrowly distributed among leaders in the population.

The learning capacities of the average family are more than sufficient for modernization.

Source: Geert Hofstede, "The Application of McGregor's Theories in Southeast Asia," *Journal of Management Development* 6, no. 3 (1987): 16. Copyright © 1987 MCB University Press. Used with permission. All rights reserved.

Professor Hofstede proposed that since these assumptions are culturally determined, McGregor's Theory X and Theory Y distinction becomes irrelevant in Southeast Asia. He developed a **Southeast Asian distinction** (although he qualifies his distinction in that he is a European and may thus have made cultural mistakes). Theory X and Theory Y are mutually exclusive opposites. Unlike the American distinction, the Southeast Asia distinction that Professor Hofstede proposed, which he labeled **Theory T and Theory T+** (*T* standing for traditional), is a complementary one—Theory T and Theory T+ fitting harmoniously together. According to Professor Hofstede, Southeast Asian management could be as outlined in Table 11–4.[23] Theory X posits that people dislike work and will avoid it if they can, and Theory T contends that people dislike change and will avoid it if they can. This suggests that both Theory X and Theory T propose that all people would attempt to avoid challenging work. A difference, however, is that Theory T espouses development of people, while Theory X advocates control. Theory T+ indicates that in spite of the wisdom of tradition, the experience of change in life is natural, and, similar to Theory X, it is the function of the leader to coerce those who resist change.

People in cultures throughout the world thus behave in dissimilar ways because of the differences in how they view their environment. Their thinking is partly conditioned by national cultural factors, which are passed on from one generation to the next. It would therefore be a critical mistake for an international manager to attempt **to apply a set of motivational techniques on a worldwide basis**—to reiterate, what works in one culture does not necessarily work in another. Of course, people's thinking does not remain static from generation to generation. Cultural factors do change gradually over time as new technologies are introduced into the society. For example, the new economic systems introduced into the former communist nations are changing the ways managers lead and what motivates employees. (For illustration purposes, refer again to Practical Perspective 11–2 and review the case of China presented in Practical Perspective 11–3.)

Chinese Social Motivation versus Western Individual Motivation

The *Hierarchy of Needs* theory developed by Abraham H. Maslow proposes that certain individual needs serve as motivators.[24] Maslow contended that people are first motivated by activities that aim to satisfy their *basic needs*. Once these needs are reasonably satisfied, they seek to satisfy the next level, their *safety needs*. Subsequently, they satisfy the next higher level, their *social needs*. Once the social needs are reasonably satisfied, the individuals satisfy their *esteem needs*. And once these are reasonably satisfied, they satisfy their *self-actualization needs*, which, according to Maslow, is the highest level of the needs hierarchy.

Maslow's theory has not been empirically verified, however. In fact, it has been widely criticized. Such terms as "belonging" and "esteem" are vague. The meaning of "satisfaction" is unclear. For example, after a big meal an individual would be full, and he or she, according to the theory, would not be motivated by food. However, this is not true in all cases—some individuals may still remain motivated by food because they have a memory and the ability to anticipate the future when hunger could occur again. Also, there is no evidence that gratification of one need activates the next higher need, and there is little support for the proposition that the level of satisfaction of a need diminishes its importance as a motivator.[25] In an international context, the hierarchy has been criticized as being based on Maslow's personal choice—American individualistic, middle-class values that put self-actualization and autonomy on top.[26] Furthermore, a study by cross-cultural management researchers Haire, Ghiselli, and Porter concluded that workers in different cultures tend to have a different hierarchy of needs. For example, managers in the United States and Italy ranked security as being relatively less important than other needs (basic needs were

PRACTICAL PERSPECTIVE   11–3

Money Works Wonders in China

Attracting workers [in China] can be a lot easier than holding on to them. Money is king in contemporary China. Workers will jump to other companies for a $5 raise. Stories abound of women from the inner provinces arriving to work long, backbreaking days for a few years and then returning home flush with cash to start businesses or to start up a local gentry. To provide some stability to their workforces, companies are moving to individual contracts. "We want total commitment from our workers," says Mr. Yen of Xian-Janssen [Pharmaceutical Ltd., a China-U.S. joint venture]. "They have to sign a pledge. Signing something is very significant here. So once they sign, they are committed."

"Have them sign it before training takes place, so you can protect your investment," advises Ralph McIntyre, area director for Asia of Mine Safety Appliances Co. in Pittsburgh. Incentives also help restrain potential wanderers and boost performance. "Simple performance-related incentives works best," says Mr. [Andrew] Mok [vice president] of Philips [Inc., the Hong Kong subsidiary of a Dutch multinational]. "If a unit exceeds its target, the members get extra money. Some of our partners refuse to use incentives, and you can see a marked difference in output." The disinclination to take individual action or responsibility is another trait that can be tackled via incentives. "Anyone who takes a risk is immediately rewarded," says Xian-Janssen's Jerry Norkskog. "I don't care how wrong the risk is."

Of course, even money takes time to move attitudinal mountains. Rich Brecher of the U.S.-China Business Council cites an American company that recently took over a state-run enterprise. The plant now has one expatriate officer on the floor with hundreds of Chinese workers. The transformation from communism to capitalism is proving slow. "That guy can't do everything," observes Mr. Brecher. "The workers have to understand that all decisions don't have be made by the president. But that takes years to teach." All the time and effort will be worth it, however, if China continues shedding communism as an economic philosophy. Companies with well-trained management teams and workforces in place stand to enjoy a great advantage over those who are delaying [entering China] until they can see exactly how Premier Deng Xiaoping's long march to capitalism pans out.

Source: Excerpted from John R. Engen, "Getting Your Chinese Workforce Up to Speed," *International Business*, August 1994, p. 44.

omitted from the study); in India, Spain, and Germany, security ranked as relatively more important.[27] Maslow's individual-based theory thus does not have universal application. The ensuing section demonstrates how the theory has a different application in the Chinese culture.

I-Ching: Beyond Self-Actualization

Professors David V. Gibson and Francis Woomin Wu of the University of Texas at Austin and Fordham University, respectively, have used the *I-Ching* to form what they label the ***social interaction paradigm of human cooperative behavior.*** The *I-Ching* ("The Book of Change") was written by ancient Chinese philosophers and social leaders between 3000 and 1000 B.C. and was interpreted by Confucius (551–479 B.C.). (*I-Ching* has also been translated to mean "The Bible of Practicality.") The social interaction paradigm, which is used to explain the inherent cooperative culture behind the economic success of the Pacific Rim economies, extends the hierarchy of needs beyond the self-actualization need.[28] Professors Gibson and Wu state:

> Maslow's theory of human needs is not comprehensive enough to address the complexity of business and social communication required by increased human interaction and the emerging global economy. It does not provide a paradigm for social interaction in relation to real-world problems of the coming decades. Although Maslow's theory describes "love" as an important motivation, it refers mostly to "self-centered" social needs, or love receiving. "Society-based" social needs for undertaking cooperative tasks for the survival and prosperity of collectives from the level of groups to nations are not mentioned. Although these collectives are important in coordinating individual effort toward mutual benefit, the formation of social entities, such as organizations or communities, cannot be fully explained in terms of individual self-actualization or love and belongingness needs.... Instead, individual effort which is directed toward developing larger cooperative entities may result in the satisfaction of others' needs rather than just the needs of oneself. Collectives may actually restrain the individual from actualizing his/her own talent and power in order to facilitate intra- and inter-organizational cooperation. When individuals act in ways which they perceive as rational in terms of pursuing their own goals, they may actually be disadvantaging themselves and others at the collective level.... Striving for high social needs without regard for immediate personal gain is symbiotic with the *I-Ching* philosophy which emphasizes that as social beings, people must deal with social responsibilities throughout their lives. The greatest social welfare is achieved though the joint efforts of individuals creating better social and physical environments in which others can actualize their capacities. Greater value is placed on the ability to lead individuals and groups to cooperative output than on the actualization of one's own individual talent.[29]

To help illustrate the above quotation, assume that an American corporation's headquarters executive who monitors the activities of the firm's subsidiary in Japan notices that a young Japanese employee has strong capabilities and is highly productive. To reward the employee, the executive decides to promote him/her to a managerial position in charge of the group. This would be a mistake because it would demoralize both the capable employee and the group; it would disturb the group's *wa* (discussed in Chapter 9). The disruption of the group's harmony would result from the violation of the accepted Japanese practice of promoting elders, and from the violation of the Japanese practice of rendering rewards to groups, not to an individual member of the group—even if his/her performance is out-standing. And individual members of the group do not want to be singled out for exceptional performance. In Japan, individuals adhere to the notion that "The nail that sticks out will be hammered down" (the similar Chinese saying is "The bigger trees catch the wind"). This means that a group member who receives individual recognition will be ostracized and emotionally punished by the group.

The Chinese symbol of the dragon, which depicts the Eastern thought that the ultimate aim of the individual is to contribute to the larger collective, derives from the *I-Ching*.[30] The **dragon** symbolizes both individual freedom (it can fly) and the creation of shared social benefits (its flying through the clouds causes rain, which benefits all). Thus, as symbolized by the dragon, "individual self-actualization is not an end in itself, but merely a preparation for the more noble goal of contributing to the betterment of society."[31] Therefore, the social interaction paradigm of human cooperative behavior suggests that personal freedom is a necessary step toward social cooperation.

Professors Gibson and Wu's addition of the stages of the social interaction paradigm of human cooperative behavior to Maslow's theory of human needs is depicted in Figure 11–2. The following discussion describes the additional stages.[32]

Stage 6: Social Awareness

The stage of **social awareness,** understanding human/social needs outside one's own individual-based ends, furnishes a base for interorganization cooperative behavior, and for molding effective strategies to merge human endeavors to solve difficult problems. Confucian philosophy posits that the most effective leaders often possess humble origins where they were exposed to basic human needs. Such origins equip leaders with the ability to recognize the needs of others.

Stage 7: Social Contribution

Social contribution refers to the mixture of striving to fulfil other people's needs while simultaneously pursuing one's own personal growth and social power. At this stage, an individual searches for opportunities that benefit the **collective.** He or she looks for "win-win" situations.

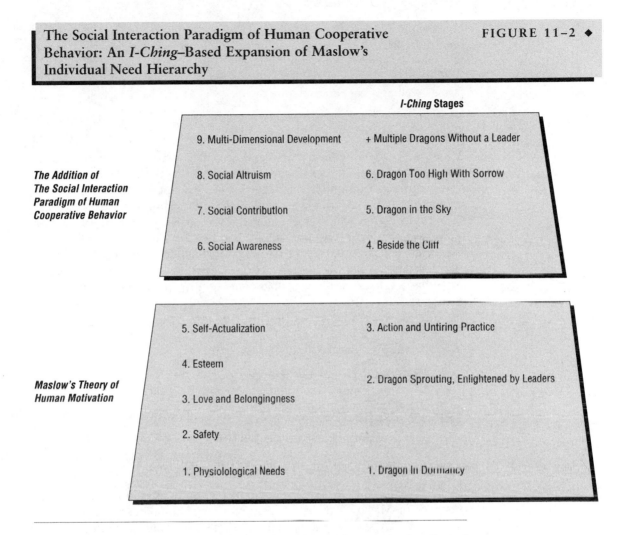

The Social Interaction Paradigm of Human Cooperative Behavior: An *I-Ching*–Based Expansion of Maslow's Individual Need Hierarchy

FIGURE 11–2 ◆

I-Ching **Stages**

The Addition of The Social Interaction Paradigm of Human Cooperative Behavior

9. Multi-Dimensional Development   + Multiple Dragons Without a Leader

8. Social Altruism   6. Dragon Too High With Sorrow

7. Social Contribution   5. Dragon in the Sky

6. Social Awareness   4. Beside the Cliff

Maslow's Theory of Human Motivation

5. Self-Actualization   3. Action and Untiring Practice

4. Esteem

     2. Dragon Sprouting, Enlightened by Leaders

3. Love and Belongingness

2. Safety

1. Physiolological Needs   1. Dragon In Dormancy

Source: David V. Gibson and Francis Woomin Wu, "The Social Interaction Paradigm of Human Cooperative Behavior: Societal Motivation Beyond Maslow's Need Hierarchy," *Proceedings of the Fourth International Conference on Comparative Management,* National Sun Yat-sen University, Taiwan, 1991. Reprinted with permission from Professor David V. Gibson. All rights reserved.

Stage 8: Social Altruism

At this stage, an individual's major concern is the functioning of society. He or she acts to generate vital long-term benefits for others without wanting or needing to acquire reward(s) for himself or herself. **Social altruism** must be voluntary, and the individual must expect little overt appreciation because the beneficiaries are usually not aware of, or do not appreciate, the long-term benefits of his or her efforts. Social altruism requires the support of a wide range of people with influence. This support is generated in Stage 7, where the individual builds networks of organization and community ties, as well as a cooperative spirit.

Stage 9: Multidimensional Development

A key facet of **multidimensional development** is **"stepping aside,"** that is, leaving an important position and distributing political and economic power across public and private sectors. One downplays one's social power by helping others develop their leadership abilities and networks, so that many individuals, besides the dominant few, will have strong intra- and interorganizational connections and social power. This philosophy magnifies the effectiveness of cooperative action through intensified participation, and it stimulates the sharing of rewards. Consequently, a society's benefits are enhanced because more people contribute to the common good, and greater stability is attained because power and rewards are diffused and individuals network across multiple leaders and groups.

As shown in Figure 11–2, *I-Ching* articulates the stages of leadership development by using the dragon as a metaphor:

1. *Dormant*: Dragon in dormancy.
2. *Growth*: Dragon sprouting, enlightened by leaders.
3. *Actualization*: Action and untiring practice.
4. *Take-off*: Beside the cliff.
5. *Service-delivering*: Dragon in the sky.
6. *Leading*: **Dragon too high with sorrow,** with a compensation strategy of multiple dragons capable of governing themselves.

The *I-Ching's* dormant stage compares with the physiological and safety stages of Maslow's theory; the growth stage compares with Maslow's love and esteem stages; and the actualization stage compares with Maslow's self-actualization stage. As indicated in Figure 11–2, the *I-Ching's* stages 4, 5, and 6 are not captured by Maslow's theory.[33]

Professors Gibson and Wu also develop their theory from the perspective of Buddhism. They divide Buddhism into two sects: *Hinayana,* which stresses the importance of self-restraint, and *Mahayana,* which stresses selfless devotion to society. Basically, Hinayana compares with self-actualization in Maslow's theory in the sense that it underscores the energy it takes to contain one's mind and to exercise one's full physical and mental strength. Hinayana compares with the *I-Ching's* later stages in the sense that it requires great initiative and compassion for others.[34]

The leadership motivation of the *I-Ching* contrasts with Western leadership motivation. Western leaders tend to be motivated by the need for power, while Asian leaders tend to be motivated more by a need resembling the Western need for affiliation.[35] The Asian leaders' "sorrow" (stage 6) derives from their having to make decisions that affect others—Western leaders generally do not experience such "sorrow." In other words, leaders motivated by the philosophy of the *I-Ching* lack the arrogance typically demonstrated by Western leaders.

Cross-Cultural Behavior Modification

All organizations throughout the globe seek to attain organizational effectiveness. Effectiveness, however, may be defined differently across cultures. For example, in American organizations, effectiveness is often measured by profits, but in some cultures profits are less important than other measures, such as quality of life (for instance, a clean, safe environment). One thing that is common throughout the globe, however, is that the attainment of organizational effectiveness requires employees to practice behavior desired by the organization. For instance, the export division of an international company requires certain staff to be present at certain times to process certain documents in a certain way. If the staff decide not to be present at those times or decide to process the documents in their own way, organizational ineffectiveness may result. The company therefore needs to be assured that the staff will be present when needed and that they will process the documents in the specified way. This means that the organization must have programs in place to **modify the behavior** of employees—to develop employee behavior that conforms to the organization's needs.

All organizations attain the desired member behavior through reward and punishment techniques. But the importance level attached to the rewards and punishments varies across cultures. For example, giving money as a reward for desired behavior or not giving money because of undesired behavior may be a highly effective behavior modifier in some cultures but not as effective in other cultures. In some cultures, the prospect of being rewarded with a big individual office may encourage an employee to work hard and to conform to the behavior desired by the organization. But in other cultures it may not—for instance, American managers may work hard for such a reward, but Japanese managers are quite satisfied with a small individual office or simply sharing an office with other employees. In the same context, employees in some cultures are motivated by the prospect of being rewarded with challenging work and more job responsibility, while employees in other cultures may be motivated more by job security—for example, British workers may be motivated more by challenging work, and French workers may be motivated more by job security.

Total Quality Management and Empowerment

Relative to the awarding of challenging work as a reward, today's popular **Total Quality Management** (TQM) concept advances the notion of

empowering employees (usually in groups) as a means of improving organizational effectiveness.[36] Fundamentally, TQM calls for giving employees more challenging work. It is believed that employees must be given the responsibility for deciding the most effective and efficient way to service the organization's customers (both internal and external customers). However, individuals in some cultures are more receptive (or less receptive) to TQM/empowerment programs than individuals in other cultures.[37] For example, people in collectivistic (low individualism) societies are likely to work much better in groups than people in high individualism societies, who tend be competitive and prefer to work on their own. (A TQM framework is described in Chapter 14.)

Furthermore, TQM and empowerment theories assume that individuals will take the initiative in getting things done. However, individuals in strong uncertainty avoidance cultures are likely to take less initiative than individuals in weak uncertainty avoidance cultures, and vice versa. This is because taking initiative normally means taking risk, and people in weak uncertainty avoidance cultures tend to take greater risk than people in strong uncertainty avoidance cultures.[38] For instance, "industrial democracy" in Sweden, a weak uncertainty avoidance culture, was initiated in the form of local experiments and was subsequently given a legislative framework. But in Germany, a strong uncertainty avoidance culture, industrial democracy was initiated by a legislative framework first and then localized in organizations.[39] Also, individuals in some cultures tend to perceive managers' efforts to apply TQM/empowerment programs as efforts to manipulate them. (Practical Perspective 11–4 describes Motorola's efforts to implement TQM/empowerment programs in its Malaysian and Florida plants.)

PRACTICAL PERSPECTIVE 11–4

Importing Enthusiasm

Inside Motorola Inc.'s glistening walkie-talkie plant in Penang [Malaysia], the atmosphere resembles a high school sports department. Group shots of exuberant Malaysian production workers, charts with performance statistics, and morale-boosting slogans line the walls. A trophy case is filled with awards hauled back from quality competitions across the U.S. and Asia by teams with names such as "Orient Express" and "Road Runners." The messages are hammered home: We are a family. This is your company. This is a grand global experiment in plant management by one of the best-run American companies. The methods used to promote worker excellence at the Penang plant are a big part of Motorola's blueprint for developing a well-trained, motivated, and highly productive workforce, especially in emerging markets such as China and Vietnam.

This is potentially frightening news for American and even Japanese workers, who think they still have a lock on more demanding jobs. But in Motorola's case, the company is trying to allay that fear by improving the productivity and motivation of workers in its U.S. plants as well. And Motorola is using lessons learned in Penang to boost the morale and involvement of workers back home. . . . The [Penang] plant's quality control program . . . relies in part on the thousands of recommendations it receives from workers. Last year, employees submitted 41,000 suggestions for improving operations, which resulted in $2 million in savings. "Here," says Managing Director Ko Soek King, "everyone marches in the same direction."

The Motorola approach means a great deal in a developing country such as Malaysia, where workers are used to being treated by management as disposable robots. To the typical American worker, though, it may sound more like the usual corporate motivational pap. But the "I Recommend" program, so successful in Malaysia, is also part of Motorola's approach to boost quality in the U.S. That's especially so at the company's 2,300-worker factory in Plantation, Fla., which makes products simi-

lar to those in Penang. The goal, pursued by Motorola worldwide, is to get employees at all levels to forget narrow job titles and work together in teams to identify and act on problems that hinder quality and productivity. The Plantation plant now displays lists of star employees, and managers hand out everything from "golden attitude" pins to cash bonuses for good ideas. New applicants are screened on the basis of their attitude toward "teamwork."

But getting them to match the Malaysians' enthusiasm hasn't been easy. "The whole plant in Penang had this craving for learning," says Jerry Mysliwiec, director of manufacturing in Plantation, who spent three years in Penang in the late 1980s. "People in the U.S. are less trusting and believing." And at first, many of the recommendations that came in weren't very helpful. Recalls Craig Kenyon, another manager in Plantation: "They were things like 'Move the garbage can from point A to point B.' " After a slow start, "empowerment" is starting to take hold in Florida, too. . . . The U.S. and Malaysian workers share one reason to stay on their toes: fear of losing their jobs. Not long ago, a quality team was assembled in Florida to examine a component production line whose workers' morale was at rock bottom. Hourly output was one-third of the counterpart line in Penang. The Plantation team boosted output by nearly 150% by, among other things, reducing 18 work stations to 6. Now, a product change and a highly automated line are giving the team a new goal: to find new jobs for the workers no longer needed.

Malaysians also must stay alert. Just as the Penang plant had its origins as a source of cheap labor, the workers' fear is that Motorola someday could shift work to an even cheaper locale. So managers are trying to increase the plant's share of R&D and looking for ways to boost efficiency even further. Says Managing Director Ko: "I con-

stantly tell them that we will lose out to other places if we aren't cost-competitive." Ko knows firsthand about the coming competition. Her next post is Tianjin, China, where she will be in charge of a new factory. "In China, we are starting with people with a higher level of technical training," she says. "I give them five years before they catch up with us." If that's an accurate prediction, workers in both the U.S. and Malaysia will have even more reason to keep hustling. For both production workers and engineers, staying competitive is the only real job guarantee in the global economy.

Source: Excerpted from Peter Engardio and Gail DeGeorge, "Importing Enthusiasm," *Business Week, 21st Century Capitalism,* special edition, 1994, pp. 122–123. Copyright 1994, McGraw-Hill, New York. Used with permission.

WORK GOALS AND VALUES VARY ACROSS CULTURES

In the industrialized world, the role of work in an individual's life is extremely important. What sort of work goals do people seek? About three decades ago, Frederick Herzberg, an American researcher, identified numerous work goals, including salary, work conditions, security, supervision, achievement, and recognition, and the importance level individuals attach to them.[40] Professor Herzberg's findings posit that factors such as an increase in pay, improvement in working conditions, more security, and improved supervision do not motivate employees to increase production, but they will demotivate employees and cause them to produce less when perceived as inadequate. What motivates employees, according to Professor Herzberg's findings, is the presence of factors such as opportunity for personal growth, challenging work, and recognition—but the lack of these factors does not cause demotivation. It should be noted that his research subjects were professionally homogeneous (accountants and engineers)

Americans. Does the importance level employees attach to various **work goals vary across countries?**

Do Work Goals Vary Across Cultures?

To obtain an answer, Itzhak Harpaz, a researcher at the University of Haifa, Israel, surveyed employees from seven countries. The countries and the number of respondents from each country were as follows: Belgium (*n* = 450), Great Britain (*n* = 773), Germany (*n* = 1,278), Israel (*n* = 973), Japan (*n* = 3,226), Netherlands (*n* = 996), and the U.S. (*n* = 1,000). The employees were asked to rank eleven work goals.[41]

The results are shown in Table 11–5. As Table 11–5 shows, employees in Belgium, Great Britain, Israel, and the U.S. ranked "interesting work" as the most important facet of their work lives, and employees in Japan, the Netherlands, and Germany ranked it second or third respectively. The Japanese employees ranked "match between person and job" as the most important facet of their work lives, employees in the Netherlands ranked "autonomy" as the most important, and German employees ranked "pay" as number one. "Pay" was ranked number two in Belgium, Great Britain, and the U.S., number three in Israel, and number five in Japan and the Netherlands. Thus, as Table 11–5 depicts, while the "interesting work" value is fairly consistent across the seven nations, many of the other values are not. For example, "autonomy" was ranked number one in the Netherlands, four in Belgium and Israel, eight in the U.S., and ten in Britain.

An interesting point in this study is that Japan was the only country Geert Hofstede classified as a collectivist (low individualism) society. People in these cultures value group harmony to a greater extent than do people in high individualism societies. This would help explain why "match between person and job" was ranked the number one work value by the Japanese employees—being in the right job helps maintain harmony. Israel and the Netherlands were the only countries classified by Hofstede as feminine societies—the others were classified as masculine societies. According to Hofstede, people in feminine cultures strongly value the maintenance of good interpersonal relations, and people in masculine cultures tend to need to perform and to assert themselves.[42] Israel and the Netherlands were the only two of the seven societies included in this study to rank the "good interpersonal relations" work value higher than the "pay" work value.

The results of the above study indicate that the importance people place on work goals tends to vary from culture to culture. It should be noted that the study included only advanced industrialized countries. Therefore, those work goals that match across cultures may be generalizable only to advanced countries. Thus, the same study conducted in industrially less-advanced countries is likely to produce different results—if people are not well fed or are relatively illiterate, they may not rank "interesting work" or "challenging work" very high, and may rank money very highly. For

◆ TABLE 11–5 Mean Ranks and Intracountry Ranking of Work Goals

Work Goals	Belgium	Britain	Germany	Israel	Japan	Nether-lands	USA
Opportunity to learn	5.80[a] 7[b]	5.55 8	4.97 9	5.83 5	6.26 7	5.38 9	6.16 5
Interpersonal relations	6.34 5	6.33 4	6.43 4	6.67 2	6.39 6	7.19 3	6.08 7
Opportunity for promotion	4.49 10	4.27 11	4.48 10	5.29 8	3.33 11	3.31 11	5.08 10
Convenient work hours	4.71 9	6.11 5	5.71 6	5.53 7	5.46 8	5.59 8	5.25 9
Variety	5.96 6	5.62 7	5.71 6	4.89 11	5.05 9	6.86 4	6.10 6
Interesting work	8.25 1	8.02 1	7.26 3	6.75 1	7.38 2	7.59 2	7.41 1
Job security	6.80 3	7.12 3	7.57 2	5.22 10	6.71 4	5.68 7	6.30 3
Match between person & job	5.77 8	5.63 6	6.09 5	5.61 6	7.83 1	6.17 6	6.19 4
Pay	7.13 2	7.80 2	7.73 1	6.60 3	6.56 5	6.27 5	6.82 2
Working conditions	4.19 11	4.87 9	4.39 11	5.28 9	4.18 10	5.03 10	4.84 11
Autonomy	6.56 4	4.69 10	5.66 8	6.00 4	6.89 3	7.61 1	5.79 8

[a]Mean ranks are shown in the upper left corner of each cell.
[b]The rank of each work goal within a given country is shown in the lower right corner of each cell. Rank 1 is the *most* important work goal for a country, and rank 11 is the *least* important.

example, cross-cultural researchers Philip Hughes and Brian Sheehan interviewed Eastman Kodak employees in Australia and Thailand work sites to determine what they valued most about their work. Australian employees valued interesting and challenging work, and Thai employees valued work primarily for the friends with whom they worked.[43] (Practical Perspective

| Rankings of Work Values in the U.S.A., Russia, and Taiwan | | | | | | TABLE 11-6 ◆ |

	U.S.A. 1990–1991		Russia 1991		Taiwan 1990–1991	
	M	F	M	E	M	E
Full appreciation of work done	2	1	8	7	1	4
Feeling "in" on things	8	7	9	2	3	8
Sympathetic help on personal problems	9	10	1	8	8	6
Job security	1	3	5	6	6	1
Good wages	4	5	7	10	4	2
Work that keeps you interested	3	2	10	3	2	5
Promotion and growth in organization	5	4	6	1	7	3
Personal loyalty to workers	6	8	2	4	9	9
Good working conditions	7	6	3	9	5	7
Tactful disciplining	10	9	4	5	10	10

M = The rankings of the work goals manager believed their employees valued
E = The rankings by the employees

Source: Adapted from Colin P. Silverthorne, "Work Motivation in the United States, Russia, and the Republic of China (Taiwan): A Comparison," *Journal of Applied Social Psychology* 22 no. 20 (1992): 1634. Copyright © V. H. Winston & Son, Inc., 1992. Used with permission. All rights reserved.

11–3, presented earlier, illustrates how money is very important to Chinese workers.)

The Full Appreciation of Work Done

The work values included in the above study are not all inclusive—there are other work values. For example, Professor Colin P. Silverthorne of the University of San Francisco conducted a study to compare employee work motivation in the U.S., Russia, and Taiwan. Professor Silverthorne's study contained some work values that were not contained in Professor Harpaz's study, for instance, "Full appreciation of work done." The results of Professor Silverthorne's study are included in Table 11–6.

Professor Silverthorne asked managers in the three countries to rank the ten work values based on how they believed their employees would rank them.[44] Their rankings are indicated by *M* in Table 11–6. The professor then asked the managers' employees to rank the same ten values. Their rankings are indicated by E in Table 11–6. Note that American employees ranked "Full appreciation of work done" as number one and "interesting work" (ranked number one in the Harpaz study) as number two. Note also that "Full appreciation of work done" was ranked number seven by the Russian employees and number four by the Taiwanese, and "interesting work" was ranked number five by the Taiwanese. As illustrated in Table 11–6, American managers' and employees' rankings are far more closely matched than are the Russians' and the Taiwanese's matchings. One explanation as to why U.S. managers' and employees' rankings are more closely matched may be that U.S. management theories and managerial development programs, which have been administered in Russia and Taiwan to a lesser extent, have in the past several decades sensitized American managers to the fact that organizational effectiveness depends on their being aware of motivating factors. This suggests that when international corporations hire locals to manage their foreign subsidiaries, their HR managers must make sure that the locals are put through the appropriate development programs.

Work Values: A Study of a Chinese Factory

Addressing the problem of cross-cultural human resource management, Professors John C. Beck and Martha Nibley Beck conducted a study of a factory in China whose top management was experimenting with cross-cultural management.[45] The factory, located in southern China in the town of Zhongshan, was operated by a Hong Kong subsidiary of a Japanese corporation. One part of the plant was managed by local Chinese managers, another part by Hong Kong managers, and a third part by Japanese expatriates. The factory was originally built by the Communist government to produce cardboard boxes. In the late 1970s, it was purchased by the Hong Kong Japanese subsidiary to manufacture small electronic consumer goods for foreign markets, such as the U.S., Japan, and Europe. Due to rising costs at home, the Japanese firm began to utilize this factory more and more in the mid-1980s.

In order to produce "Japanese-quality" products, the Hong Kong subsidiary's top management decided to mix the managerial style at the factory. Top management attempted to implement a mix of the Japanese, Hong Kong, American, and mainland Chinese styles. The factory was divided into three different sections. The first section, which consisted of the first and second floors of the plant's largest building, was managed by a supervisor from mainland China. The second section, which consisted of the third and fourth floors, was overseen by Hong Kong managers. And the third section, which consisted of the fifth floor, was overseen by two Japanese supervisors.

Before conducting their own study, Professors Beck and Beck interviewed the Hong Kong's subsidiary's top management. They were informed that the section run by the mainland Chinese supervisors was sloppy and lazily managed. The section operated by the Hong Kong managers was highly productive, but somewhat ramshackle and disorganized. And the section operated by the Japanese supervisors, "just like the Japanese," was clean, efficient, and highly coordinated. The professors thus concluded that Hong Kong top management believed that the managers with superior skills which had proven effective in one culture could be applied effectively in another cultural setting. Professors Beck and Beck subsequently studied the situation at the factory. Their findings and conclusions are described below.

Differences Between the Three Sections

Chinese Managers.   The first section was managed by a mainland Chinese supervisor left over from the factory's cardboard box–producing days. This section contained the facilities for producing the plastic casings the firm uses in its radios and stereo headsets. The production technology was simple and required little labor from the eight workers in the section. The mainland Chinese manager was thus assigned to a section with very low production technology. The section, according to the professors, appeared to live up to its reputation of being similar to Chinese-managed factories, which are usually unkempt and lackadaisically operated. The workers appeared to take little interest in their jobs.

Hong Kong Managers.   The second section, operated by the Hong Kong managers, consisted of 180 floor workers. The majority of these employees spent their working hours arranged along two assembly lines, assembling small radios and portable cassette players. The Hong Kong managers were therefore assigned to a more advanced production technology. The professors observed that the emphasis in this section appeared to be on speed of production, and little attention was being paid to tidiness—there was debris of all types. There were shelves where workers were supposed to leave their shoes after replacing them with rubber slippers—which was mandatory. But most of the employees did not take off their shoes and did not put on the rubber slippers. The Hong Kong managers told the professors that it was **"mandatory," but not "required"** (organizations often have policies mandating certain behaviors that are not enforced by management, and employees practice a different behavior). The professors also observed that managers publically "scolded" employees when they made mistakes.

Japanese Managers.   The third section, managed by the Japanese expatriates, contained 103 line workers. They were responsible for producing polyvaricon capacitors, tiny coil-like components utilized in small audio electronic devices. The Japanese managers were thus assigned to a very advanced production technology. According to Professors Beck and Beck, this section demonstrated a glaring contrast to the first and second sections.

The room was very clean and orderly. All employees were mandated, as well as required, to take off their shoes and put on their rubber slippers. There were no exceptions, and all the shoes were tidily arranged in the proper area. Unlike the Hong Kong managers, the Japanese managers did not apply rushed behavior nor public scolding.

Which Sections Were Most Successful?

Professors Beck and Beck sought to determine which sections were the most effective. The professors omitted the first section from the analysis because it contained so few employees. Thus, only sections two and three (Hong Kong and Japanese managers) were analyzed. They centered their analysis around determining worker satisfaction, and disaggregating levels of dissatisfaction determined by the nature of the task and factors specifically related to managerial tactics on the part of the supervisors. Their investigation used in-depth interviews and broad-scale questionnaires.

The Second Section (Hong Kong Managers).   According to the professors, the workers in the second section were "old" employees who had been well trained in all aspects relating to the line. The section was doing very well, quality standards were being met, and most days the workers produced more than their quotas.

The Third Section (Japanese Managers).   The third section had a high employee turnover, which is very costly to the company. Thus, employees in the second section were more satisfied (or less dissatisfied) than the employees in the third section.

Differences Attributed to Management Styles

Professors Beck and Beck attribute the differences to the leadership styles applied by the Hong Kong and Japanese managers. The employees in the second section were more satisfied with their leaders than were the employees in the third section. The styles used by top managers in the second and third sections differed. The leadership approach used by the managers in the second section adhered to local culture; the approach applied by the managers in the third section did not. For example, the Chinese and Japanese societies share the traditional value of removing one's shoes before entering a home and walking on the floor. However, in China the value is loosely followed, while in Japan it is rigidly followed. Thus, the professors found, the Japanese managers' rigid insistence that the employees in the third section follow this practice irritated them and led to resentment (dissatisfaction). As noted earlier, the Hong Kong managers in the second section did not enforce this value, so thre was no employee resentment (no dissatisfaction).

Professors Beck and Beck also concluded that whether managers practiced **open criticism** also affected employees' satisfaction level. The Japanese managers practiced quiet, nonaccusatory behavior, while the Hong Kong managers practiced open criticism. Culturally, the practice of public scolding (*ma ren*) is quite acceptable in China, while in Japan such practice is highly unacceptable. The Chinese view such practice as open communication, and view the practice of quiet, subtle criticism as "sneakiness" or lack of open communication. The Japanese managers' subtle approach thus contributed to employee dissatisfaction.

Somewhat related to the above practice, the management of a large department store in Xian, China, selects its forty worse sales clerks each year and has them write self-criticisms and analyze their shortcomings. The managers then hang a plaque over their work place with a picture.[46] This observation, as well as Professors Beck and Beck's observation, took place in the 1980s. This writer visited two model Chinese factories in Shanghai in June 1994. At each factory there were large glass cases with large color pictures of individual employees (such as mechanical engineers who work alone) and of groups of employees being recognized as outstanding employees and groups of the month. This may mean that employees' work values in China are changing or that Chinese values differ from region to region.

FLEXIBILITY IN CROSS-CULTURAL LEADERSHIP AND MOTIVATION

As suggested above, there are no leadership and motivation theories with clearly global application. The following section discusses how leadership styles and motivation approaches differ in Germany, France, the Netherlands, and Chinese societies.[47] (How the leadership style differs between the U.S. and Japan was discussed earlier.)

Leadership and Motivation Approaches

Germany

In Germany, highly skilled and responsible workers do not necessarily require a manager to "motivate" them, American-style. These workers expect their superiors, who generally possess an engineering background, to assign their tasks and to be the expert in solving technical problems. German workers thus require little supervision. This means that German organizations would require relatively fewer supervisors than would organizations in many other cultures. For example, a comparison of similar organizations in Germany, Britain, and France showed that Germans have the highest rate of personnel in productive roles and the lowest in both leadership and staff roles.

France

Unlike Americans the French do not think in terms of managers versus non-managers. Rather, they think in terms of cadres versus noncadres. One becomes a member of a cadre by attending the right schools, and remains a member for the rest of his or her life. Furthermore, regardless of task, cadres possess the privileges of a higher social class, and it is very rare for noncadres to cross the ranks.

The Netherlands

Leadership in the Netherlands is different from what it is in the United States. Leadership in America presupposes assertiveness, as opposed to consensus and modesty in the Netherlands. However, in the Netherlands there are time-consuming ritual consultations to conserve the appearance of consensus and modesty.

Chinese Societies

Chinese business people living/operating in other than mainland China countries, such as Taiwan, Singapore, and Hong Kong, tend to prefer economic activities in which large gains can be attained with few human resources. They employ few professional managers. They do employ their sons and sometimes daughters who have graduated from prestigious business schools, but they continue running the family business the Chinese way. (As an illustration of an exception, refer to Practical Perspective 11–5.) They keep their enterprises small because of their perception that nonfamily employees will not be loyal and if they are competent they will start their own business. This type of view is found in the history of Chinese society, where there have been no formal laws, only formal networks of influential people steered by general principles of Confucian virtue. The authorities were often unreliable, thus no one could be trusted except one's family.[48]

The above suggests that international managers are confronted with an enormous challenge. They are faced with the complex task of having to determine the leadership style and the motivation preferred by different people in different cultures, and adapt to them appropriately. This suggests that effective international managers must be highly versatile; they must know how to manage in multicultural settings. (The development of these global managers was discussed in Chapter 7.)

SUMMARY

This chapter has proposed that the appropriate leadership style and the motivational incentives a cross-cultural manager applies are for the most part determined by the culture in which he or she is managing. But in some

PRACTICAL   PERSPECTIVE   11–5

First Pacific's Pearls

For all their money-making abilities, the ethnic Chinese business clans have a major weakness. They jealously keep decision-making within the family. Only by marriage into the patriarch's clan can a nonfamily employee acquire real power within the group. . . . This reluctance to share power or wealth limits the ability of many Chinese-owned businesses to grow and assures that many will suffer under inept heirs. Indonesian multibillionaire Liem Sinoe Liong is a glaring exception to the rule. The Indonesian surname of the Liem family's Chinese name is Salim. Based in Jakarta, Liem/Salim's main business, Salim Group, has holdings in everything from cement to noodles.

In the late 1970s Liem/Salim encouraged his son, Anthony Salim, to recruit nonfamily talent. Anthony Salim approached Manuel Pangilinan, a young investment banker then working for American Express Bank in Hong Kong. Pangilinan was a Filipino who was educated in Jesuit schools before receiving an M.B.A. from Wharton in 1968. Would Pangilinan set up a Hong Kong-based investment arm for the Liem family? He would. In 1981, at age 35, Pangilinan acquired for the Liem/Salims a tiny Hong Kong finance company for $1.5 million. From this seed has sprouted Hong Kong–based First Pacific Co. Ltd., an emerging trans-Asia conglomerate that probably earned over $120 million after taxes in 1994, on sales of about $3.5 billion. . . .

"The Salims are unique," says Pangilinan. "They are one of the few Chinese groups that's recognized the distinction between ownership and management." And profitably so. Their 35% holding in First Pacific is currently worth $400 million, and Manny Pangilinan is considered a member-in-very-good-standing of the extended Liem/Salim family.

Source: Excerpted from Andrew Tanzer, "First Pacific's Pearls," *Forbes*, February 13, 1995, pp. 48, 50.

---

situations, as discussed in Chapter 10, other factors may supersede the cultural factors in importance as the determinants of the appropriate style and incentives. The chapter also suggested that United States–based theories do not have cross-cultural application. And it concluded that culture also influences the degree of importance people place on work values.

Key Terms

1. Cross-cultural leadership
2. American-based leadership and motivation theories
3. The PM theory of leadership
4. Innovator, implementor, and pacifier leadership
5. Self-actualization
6. To serve society better
7. Application of one approach on a worldwide basis
8. Theory T and Theory T+
9. Southeast Asian management
10. Social interaction paradigm of human cooperative behavior
11. *I-Ching*
12. The dragon
13. Social awareness, social contribution, and social altruism
14. Multidimensional development ("stepping aside")
15. "Dragon too high with sorrow"
16. *Hinayana* and *Mahayana*
17. Collective
18. Cross-cultural behavior modification
19. Total quality management and empowerment
20. Work goals vary across cultures
21. "Mandatory" but not "required"
22. Open criticism

Discussion Questions and Exercises

1. What is the notion of Theory X and Theory Y and System 4 management with respect to leadership style? Do you agree? Why?

2. What is the impact of culture on empowerment?

3. You are a cross-cultural training specialist. Your client is a global corporation that has employed you to train one of its home country employees who is being prepared to manage the corporation's foreign subsidiary in the Philippines. At home, the employee has been an effective manager by applying a "relationship-oriented" leadership style. What would you tell the employee?

4. You are the HR manager assigned to recruit three top-level managers for three of the company's foreign subsidiaries. One of the subsidiaries is in the strategic planning stages and has not yet been started. The second subsidiary has recently been started amid much chaos. The third subsidiary has been established and is now operating under conditions of stability. For each subsidiary, describe the leadership characteristics each manager requires to be effective. Discuss why you chose those characteristics.

5. How do Theories X and Y differ from Theories T and T+?

6. The assumptions on which Theories X and Y are based do not apply in Southeast Asia. Why not?

7. Maslow's hierarchy of needs theory does not have global application. Discuss this statement.

8. How does Maslow's hierarchy of needs theory differ from the social interaction paradigm of human cooperative behavior?

9. How are work goals affected by culture?

10. You are a cross-cultural training specialist. Your client is a global corporation that has employed you to train one of its home country employees who is being prepared to manage the corporation's foreign subsidiary in mainland China. With respect to motivation and work values, what would you tell the employee?

Assignment

Contact a manager who has had experience managing an enterprise in a foreign country. Ask him or her to share his or her experience relative to leadership and motivation in the particular country. What were the differences he/she perceived? Prepare a brief report for presentation in class.

Putting on the Ritz

When Horst H. Schulze stood before the core staff of the Ritz-Carlton, Hong Kong, last August, he gave his usual talk about team ownership and the need to correct "challenges" (a euphemism for problems) as soon as they occurred. After speaking animatedly for 50 minutes, the German-born Schulze asked a young man trained as a bellhop, "In what hotel did you work previously?" The young man smiled broadly and answered in perfect English, "My pleasure, Mr. Schulze." Reflects Schulze, 53, "In that culture, they want to say yes and are eager to please, but they didn't get what I was saying at all."

Shaking his head at the memory he adds, "I knew at that moment I had seriously underestimated what it would take to operate in the Far East. I was used to a quick start: Going in with a cross-trained team 10 days before opening and putting the finishing touches on the local staff and then leaving. I will never do that again." As president and COO of the Atlanta-based Ritz-Carlton Hotel Co., one of the world's most renowned hotel-management companies, Schulze has high standards, yet he doesn't expect any more from his employees than he does from himself. Before the grand opening of a new luxury hotel or resort, Schulze flies in to conduct orientations personally. He dons blue jeans to work alongside his employees, ensuring that every detail is letter perfect.

That drive for excellence helped the Ritz-Carlton became the first and only company to capture the U.S. Commerce Department's Malcolm Baldrige National Quality Award in 1992. . . . Schulze attributes much of the victory to the Ritz-Carlton's infusing its 14,000-employee organization with a team

CASE 11–1

Source: Excerpted from Echo Montgomery Garrett, "Putting on the Ritz," *World Trade,* April 1994, pp. 52–56. Copyright © 1994, World Trade magazine. Used with permission. All rights reserved.

spirit and a sense of individual empowerment. For example, any employee is authorized to spend as much as $2,000 to satisfy a disgruntled guest. Although that award-winning management style brought the rapidly expanding company international kudos, Schulze only recently learned that doesn't necessarily translate into ready acceptance. "Our first efforts in the international market were opening two hotels in Australia," he says. "Because we spoke the same language, in my mind it wasn't going to be any different than managing a hotel in California. In hindsight, however, the Australians viewed teams and total quality management with a great deal of skepticism. They have been won over to the Ritz-Carlton way now, but it took about a year before they no longer thought of it as " 'a bunch of American hype.' "

After his epiphany in Hong Kong, Schulze—a slim elegant man who is decidedly passionate about the hotel business—is still firmly committed to hiring locals to run the hotel. "They have an understanding of the local culture that outsiders cannot possibly attain quickly enough," he says. However, to ensure that Ritz-Carlton corporate culture isn't lost in the equation, the core staff of locals will now be hired a full year before the hotel is scheduled to open. "There is such a thing as a different culture," says Schulze, who began in the hotel business as a 17-year-old busboy in Germany and came to the U.S. in 1965 to work with Hilton. . . . "We knew that, yet we didn't fully appreciate the importance of it until Hong Kong. Now, we are being careful to teach the Ritz-Carlton culture while allowing the locals to combine it with their own so as to better relate it to their compatriots in their style."

Throughout most of the 1980s, Schulze had his hands more than full with expansion in the U.S. Then, when the luxury hotel market took a major hit with the collapse of the real estate market, he began to look to export Ritz-Carlton's credo: "We are ladies and gentlemen serving ladies and gentlemen." Besides the foreign properties in Hong Kong and Australia, the 11-year-old, privately held company . . . currently operates a resort in Cancun, Mexico and is scheduled to open the Hotel Arts Barcelona this month. The latter is the company's first property in Europe. (It doesn't own the rights to the Ritz-Carlton name in France, England, Spain or Canada.) And the Spaniards employed in Barcelona received a year-long training within the organization.

At the moment, Schulze is primarily focusing on expanding Ritz-Carlton's franchise in the Pacific Rim. "That's where most of our opportunity is, because that's where the business traveler is going," he says. "We go to the strategic locations because we want to build loyalty with our existing customers. The Pacific Rim and Asia are the most dynamic regions in the global economy and represent the cornerstone for our second decade of development." The Ritz-Carlton broke ground in Osaka, Japan in December and has agreements to provide technical service and support for properties in Tokyo, Jakarta, Nagoya, Singapore, Bangok, Kuala Lumpur, Seoul, Auckland and Bali. The company established a development office in Hong Kong and is negotiating to develop properties in Shanghai, Cheju Island, Guangzhou, Taipei, Melbourne, Pusan, Manila, a second site in Tokyo, Beijing, Shenzhen, Gold Coast and Adelaide, Australia.

The Ritz-Carlton's reputation . . . is one of its most precious assets. . . . "Our guests expect a certain level of service and having demands met on time is one of the keys," says Schulze. "However, in Hong Kong that same rapidity is viewed as rude and intrusive. It was hard to convince them that Europeans and Americans who sat in a restaurant for two or three hours for lunch would not be coming back." Overcoming such skepticism and suspicion is paramount to the company's overseas success. In this case, Schulze discovered that the Chinese have a great respect for written information. By showing Hong Kong employees the extensive surveys the company had done regarding guests' requirements, he was able to convince the staff that speed is paramount.

Among the most difficult hurdles he faced in Hong Kong was convincing the staff that management valued their input. Schulze always opens orientation by declaring imperiously, "My name is Horst Schulze. I am president of this company, and I am very important." After a dramatic pause, he adds, "And so are you. You are equally important." In the U.S., that statement was met with approval and nods. In Hong Kong it was met with disbelief. "When I started setting silverware on the tables in the restaurant the day before orientation started, the Chinese supervisors said, 'Why are you doing that? The workers come tomorrow.' " Recalls Schulze, "They couldn't fathom the idea of leading by example—a management technique we take for granted in the U.S. Understanding the idea of mutual respect was difficult, too. They were used to being the boss, period."

Companies that use management styles readily accepted in the U.S. must gird themselves for such battles. Schulze noticed that although the Hong Kong Chinese were clearly unconvinced that team management would work initially, they were loath to admit their disbelief. In Mexico, he knew immediately that the employees were dubious. "When I was working through the mission statement with the dishwashers, a practice I complete with each department, I asked if they had any questions," says Schulze. "The Mexicans were very open about their lack of faith in individual empowerment. They questioned everything, but they were also quicker to rally to our ways once they understood that we were sincere." In hindsight, Schulze believes it has taken the Australians almost three years to get with the Ritz-Carlton program. "That was completely our fault. Because English was the language there, I took it for granted that they understood us."

QUESTIONS

1. What type of leader—an innovator, an implementor, a pacifier, or a combination of two or three—do you believe Mr. Schulze is? Which facts in the article led to your conclusion?
2. Do you believe Mr. Schulze is an effective cross-cultural leader? Why?
3. Why did the Australians view teams and TQM with skepticism?

The New Chief Auditors

C A S E   11–2

Source: Fredric William
Swierczek, "Culture and
Training: How Do They
Play Away from Home?"
*Training & Development
Journal* 42, no. 11
(November 1988): 76.
Copyright © November
1986, American Society
for Training and
Development. Reprinted
with permission. All
rights reserved.

Mr. Chartchai is a the new chief auditor of a large agro-business [in Thailand]. He is 29 and has an MBA from Thammasat University. He is recognized as a hard worker who accomplishes his tasks quickly and competently. He amazed his manager by studying for the MBA and finishing so quickly. This is one of the reasons he was selected to be the chief auditor. There are 10 other auditors in the department. Mr. Chartchai has been working in the department for seven years and has several close friends. He has thought of being the top manager in the department for a long time, and has taken charge of the department very fast. Now that he is in charge, he wants things done his way. He takes a very strong interest in the smallest details of what the auditors do. He also keeps after the other staff. He feels that this is "his" department and that he is responsible for everything that goes right and everything that goes wrong.

Sometimes he has to complain to his friends. They keep doing things their own way, not his. He feels bad when he does it, but he has decided that running the auditing department the way it is suppose to be run is more important than friendship. From his business studies, he learned that management is not a popularity contest. Still, he would like to keep his friends and to enjoy the work and their activities after work. He misses the sense of closeness, but being a manager, he feels, is worth the sacrifice.

QUESTIONS

1. Thailand is medium on power distance, low on individualism, and high on Confucianism. Is the chief auditor's leadership behavior the appropriate one for the culture? Why?
2. Does Mr. Chartchai's behavior contrast or support the *I-Ching* philosophy? How?
3. Do you believe Mr. Chartchai will be an effective manager? Why?

The Rewarded Chinese Olympic Stars

C A S E   11–3

Source: Excerpted from
"China: New Rich," *The
Economist,* October 10,
1992, p. 36.

For China's Olympic stars, the gold medals around their necks in Barcelona were just a forecast of what was to come. As symbolism of China's invincibility in the swimming pool and on the ping-pong table, the athletes returned home to be showered with gold and cash to an estimated value of $182,000 each, tax-free.

In a country where the average annual income [in 1992] is under $400, it was perhaps inevitable that the awards provoked feelings of envy and claims from other professionals. Rocket scientists pointed out that the launch of a Long March rocket carrying an Australian communications satellite was also considered a patriotic victory. As a result, 20 rocket scientists have each been awarded 5,000 yuan (about $900).

QUESTIONS

1. Discuss the case within the context of the hierarchy of needs framework described in this chapter. How does the rocket scientists' behavior relate to the *I-Ching* philosophy?
2. Discuss the scientists' work values.

Volvo's Enriched Job Strategy

Volvo executives decided that one way to improve job conditions is through a job enrichment program. Volvo experimented with this idea by converting its Uddevalla, Sweden, plant to a job-enriched facility. Automobiles are built in small workshops by teams of approximately 12 autonomous workers. Each team member is trained to be capable of doing every job the team is responsible for in building the automobile. There are very few supervisors in the plant. Thus, members of the team learn from and receive feedback from the other members—not from supervisors. Volvo declared the experiment at Uddevalla a success and implemented it at its three other plants in Sweden. Volvo found the program motivational, efficient, and profitable.

QUESTIONS

1. Using a cultural perspective, why do you think the program worked so well at Volvo?
2. Do you believe the program would work as well with American employees at a U.S. car builder? Why?

CASE 11–4

Source: Adapted from William E. Nothdurft, "How to Produce Work-Ready Workers," *Across the Board,* September 1990, pp. 47–52.

F. Suzanne Jenniches at Westinghouse

F. Susanne Jenniches, who previously was a high school biology teacher, joined Westinghouse in 1975 as an associate test engineer. As of 1992, she was general manager of Westinghouse's Civil Systems Division. On motivation, Ms. Jenniches stated, "I believe the best thing you can do for people in terms of recognizing and rewarding them is to give them a higher level of responsibility and authority. That doesn't necessarily mean a promotion to

CASE 11–5

Source: Adapted from "F. Suzanne Jenniches," *Industry Week,* March 2, 1992, pp. 32–36.

top management, because many people don't want that kind of responsibility—many of them want more technical responsibility, more recognition of their technical expertise, or to be a team leader."

QUESTIONS

1. Based on what you have learned in this chapter, does Ms. Jenniches's belief about motivation have universal application? Why?

Notes

1. "Foreign Bodies," *CA Magazine*, November 1993, p. 21.

2. B. M. Bass et al., *Assessment of Managers: An International Comparison* (New York: Free Press, 1979).

3. Ibid.

4. V. Terpstra, *The Cultural Environment of International Business* (Cincinnati, OH: Southwestern, 1978).

5. P. T. Terry, "The English in Management," *Management Today* 1, no. 11 (1979): 90–97.

6. Douglas McGregor, *The Human Side of the Enterprise* (New York: McGraw-Hill, 1960); Rensis Likert, *The Human Organization: Its Management and Value* (New York: McGraw-Hill, 1961).

7. Robert R. Blake and Jane S. Mouton, *The Managerial Grid* (Houston, TX: Gulf Publishing, 1964).

8. Cited in Bernard M. Bass, *Bass & Stogdill's Handbook of Leadership: Theory, Research, & Managerial Applications,* 3d ed. (New York: The Free Press, 1990), p. 796.

9. Ibid.

10. M. Bennett, "Testing Management Theories Culturally," *Journal of Applied Psychology* 62 (1977): 578–581.

11. J. M. Ivancevich, D. M. Schweiger, and J. W. Ragan, "Employee Stress, Health, and Attitudes: A Comparison of American, Indian, and Japanese Managers," paper presented at the annual meeting of the Academy of Management, Chicago, 1986.

12. See V. V. Baba and M. E. Ace, "Serendipity in Leadership: Initiating Structure and Consideration in the Classroom," *Human Relations* 42 (June 1989): 509–525.

13. L. R. Anderson, "Management of the Mixed-Cultural Work Group," *Organizational Behavior and Human Performance* 31 (1983): 303–330.

14. Bass et al., *Assessment of Managers.*

15. Mark F. Peterson, "PM Theory in Japan and China: What's in It for the United States," *Organizational Dynamics* (Spring 1988): 22.

16. This discussion draws from C. A. Rodrigues, "Identifying the Right Leader for the Right Situation," *Personnel* (September 1988): 43–46; C. A. Rodrigues, "The Situation and National Culture as Contingencies for Leadership Behavior: Two conceptual models," in S. B. Prasad, ed., *Advances in International Comparative Management*, vol. 5 (Greenwich, CT: JAI Press, 1990); and C.A. Rodrigues, "Developing Three-Dimensional Leaders," *Journal of Management Development* 12, no. 3 (1993): 4–11.

17. J. P. Wright, *On a Clear Day You Can See General Motors* (Grosse Pointe, MI: Wright Enterprises, 1979).

18. R. Mitchell, "Jack Welch: How Good a Manager?" *Business Week*, December 14, 1987, pp. 92–95.

19. For a more complete discussion of this topic, see C. A. Rodrigues, "Application of High-Quality Leadership as an International Competitive Advantage," in A. J. Ali, ed., *How to Manage for International Competitiveness* (Binghampton, NY: The Haworth Press, 1992).

20. Cited in Geert Hofstede, "The Applicability of McGregor's Theories in Southeast Asia," *Journal of Management Development* 6, no. 3 (1987): 16.

21. Ibid., pp. 16–18.

22. Ibid., p. 17.

23. Ibid., pp. 17–18.

24. Abraham H. Maslow, "Theory of Human Motivation," *Psychological Review* 50 (July 1943): 370–396.

25. J. C. Williams, *Human Behavior in Organizations* (Cincinnati, OH: South-Western Publishing, 1982), pp. 80–81.

26. Geert Hofstede, "The Cultural Relativity of the Quality of Life Concept," *Academy of Management Review* 9, no. 3 (1984): 396.

27. M. Haire, E. E. Ghiselli, and L. W. Porter, *Managerial Thinking: An International Study* (New York: John Wiley & Sons, 1966).

28. David V. Gibson and Francis Woomin Wu, "The Social Interaction Paradigm of Human Cooperative Behavior: Societal Motivation Beyond Maslow's Need Hierarchy," *Proceedings of the Fourth International Conference on Comparative Management* (1991), Taiwan, National Sun Yat-sen University. Used with permission from professor David V. Gibson. All rights reserved.

29. Ibid., p. 99.

30. Ibid.

31. Ibid.

32. Ibid., pp. 100–101.

33. Ibid., p. 101.

34. Ibid.

35. For a discussion on the three learned motivation needs, the need for achievement, the need for power, and the need for affiliation, refer to David C. McClelland, *The Achieving Society* (Princeton, NJ: Van Nostrand Reinhold, 1961).

36. See Carl A. Rodrigues, "A Framework for Defining Total Quality Management," *Competitiveness Review* 5, no. 2 (1995); and Richard S. Johnson, *TQM: Leadership for Quality Transformation* (Milwaukee, WI: ASQC Quality Press, 1993).

37. See Carl A. Rodrigues, "Employee Participation and Empowerment Programs: Problems of Definition and Implementation," *Empowerment in Organizations: An International Journal* 2, no. 1 (1994): 29–40

38. See Bass et al., *Assessment of Managers;* Geert Hofstede, *Culture's Consequence: International Differences in Work-Related Values* (Beverly Hills, CA: Sage Publications, 1980).

39. Geert Hofstede, "Motivation, Leadership, and Organization: Do American Theories Apply Abroad? *Organizational Dynamics* (Summer 1990): 57.

40. Frederick Herzberg, "One More Time: How Do You Motivate Employees?" *Harvard Business Review* 46 (January–February 1968): 53–62

41. Itzhak Harpaz, "The Importance of Work Goals: An International Perspective," *Journal of International Business Studies* 21, no. 1 (First Quarter 1990): 81.

42. Hofstede, *Culture's Consequence.*

43. Philip Hughes and Brian Sheehan, "Business Across Cultures: The Comparison of Some Business Practices in Thailand and Australia," *Asian Review,* Institute of Asian Studies, Chulalongkorn University (1993): 263.

44. Colin P. Silverthorne, "Work Motivation in the United States, Russia, and the Republic of China (Taiwan): A Comparison," *Journal of Applied Social Psychology* 22, no. 20 (1992): 1631–1639.

45. This discussion draws from John C. Beck and Martha Nibley Beck, "The Cultural Buffer: Managing Human Resources in a Chinese Factory," *Research in Personnel and Human Resources Management,* Suppl. 2 (Greenwich, CT: JAI Press, 1990), pp. 89–107.

46. Adi Ignatius, "Now if Ms. Wong Insults a Customer, She Gets an Award," *The Wall Street Journal,* January 24, 1989, p. 1.

47. This discussion draws from Geert Hofstede, "Cultural Constraints in Management Theories," *The Academy of Management Executive* 7, no. 1 (1993): 81–94.

48. See also Andrew Tanzer, "First Pacific's Pearl's," *Forbes,* February 13, 1995, pp. 48, 50.

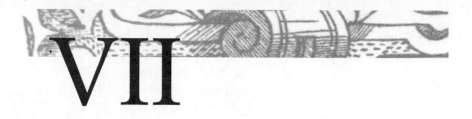

VII

P a r t   S e v e n

INTERNATIONAL CONTROL

The intention of the control process is to enable managers to compare actual activities with planned activities. Planning (discussed in Chapter 3) and controlling are thus closely linked. When the organization establishes tactical objectives (discussed in Chapter 3), management must establish feedback mechanisms to verify that those objectives are being attained. The question, however, is how much control? The aim of this part is to address the question of how much control in a global context. When corporations establish subsidiaries in foreign countries, their headquarters' managers must decide how to best maintain control over foreign activities; how to be assured that activities in foreign markets are being carried out as planned. Headquarters' managers are therefore confronted with the task of deciding whether to give the subsidiaries autonomy (loose, decentralized control) or make decisions at home (rigid, centralized control), or, since either extreme is ineffective, how to attain a balance between the two. Chapter 12 discusses this aspect of control.

C h a p t e r   1 2

Headquarters–Foreign Subsidiary Control Relationships

12

Chapter Twelve

Headquarters–Foreign Subsidiary Control Relationships

American Telephone & Telegraph Co., grappling with slow growth in the U.S., is setting up foreign units with their own chief executive officers to pursue the potentially huge new markets in Asia, Europe and Latin America. The new CEOs, one has already been appointed to head the Asian operations, will have power to set up individual country operations, set up pricing for AT&T products and services, and even hunt for mergers and joint ventures to help AT&T's global expansion.[1]

Objectives of the Chapter

When businesses establish operating **subsidiaries** in foreign countries, their headquarters' managers must establish an effective **headquarters–foreign subsidiary control relationship.** Traditional management thinking is that a relationship may be one of **centralization,** in which headquarters' managers do not give much autonomy to the subsidiaries' managers, and they make most of the important decisions about local operations. Or it may be one of **decentralization,** in which the subsidiaries' managers are given a great deal of autonomy and they make most of the important decisions relating to local operations. Both centralized and decentralized controls have pros and cons. Contemporary management thinking promulgates the control relationship in terms of three headquarters–foreign subsidiary governance mechanisms: "centralization" (a top-down hierarchical relationship), "formalization" (a bureaucratic, prescribed procedures relationship), and "nor-

427

mative integration" (a relationship that relies neither on centralization nor formalization, but on shared overall behavior). The appropriate control relationship is contingent on cultural and situational factors.

Regardless of the thinking they adopt, headquarters managers of effective international business enterprises must establish the headquarters–foreign subsidiary control relationship that best attains the overall goals and objectives of the corporation. The objectives of this chapter are therefore to:

1. Discuss centralized and decentralized headquarters–foreign subsidiary relationships.
2. Describe the factors that affect the decision of whether to establish a centralized or a decentralized relationship.
3. Describe centralization, formalization, and normative integration relationships.
4. Discuss the cultural and situational factors that influence use of the three relationships.
5. Discuss how a balanced relationship is accomplished.

GLOBAL CONTROLS: CENTRALIZATION AND DECENTRALIZATION

To maintain proper control systems, an appropriate organizational structure (discussed in Chapter 5) is essential. Along with identifying the appropriate structure, headquarters management must decide whether the headquarters–foreign subsidiaries relationship should be centralized or decentralized. In a centralized system, most of the important decisions relative to local matters are made by the headquarters management. In a decentralized system, managers at the subsidiary are given the autonomy to make most of the important decisions relative to local matters.

Both approaches have advantages and disadvantages. For example, it is difficult for the headquarters managers located in Paris, France to know what type of benefits best meet the expectations of workers in a subsidiary located in Rio de Janeiro, Brazil. Local managers would know best. Joanne Webster, human resource director for Gupta Corporation, a 260-employee software company based in Menlo Park, California, stated that she has seen multiple kinds of organizational structures and now views her own ideal: "At my last company, Europe was operated like a separate company that mirrored the United States. When we were acquired, it all went into corporate in the United States, which had the responsibility for overseeing everything, even the salary surveys." Webster now finds herself leaning toward establishing human resource departments in geographic areas, with managers handling employee relations and training, but reporting to her office. Webster does not believe that "we in the United States can develop the expertise in all the employment regulations. We would want to hire someone closer to the action. They would have that expertise and base their compensation and benefits on what works in Europe."[2]

Also, foreign markets now change rapidly, and since local managers are closer to the market, they are able to keep abreast of local changes more than headquarters managers. The case of AT&T illustrates this point.

> AT&T employs about 54,000 workers in foreign markets, of which about half are in AT&T's traditional lines of equipment and communication services and the rest in its NCR computer unit. But local management is spotty, and equipment and long-distance businesses report up through separate units based in Basking Ridge, N.J. Virtually all major decisions are made in the U.S., requiring foreign proposals to snake their way up through myriad departments before getting approval. "That's much too far from our customers" to achieve on-site, rapid decision-making, said Victor Pelson, chief of AT&T Global Operations. "The market is changing very rapidly."[3]

Decentralizing such decisions would therefore be advantageous. On the other hand, when decision making is decentralized, judgments made by local managers may sometimes have negative consequences for other subsidiaries and/or may not be the best decision when the overall firm's objectives are considered. For instance, a decision made by managers at the Rio de Janeiro subsidiary to pay generous benefits to their workers may demoralize workers in other subsidiaries if they perceive their benefits to be comparatively unfair. Centralized decision making would thus enable headquarters' managers to consider the consequences of a decision on all of the firm's subsidiaries. Centralization, in this respect, would be advantageous.

As another example, managers of a subsidiary with decision-making power may decide to expand their subsidiary's market. In their efforts, they may unknowingly (or knowingly) be competing with another of the firm's subsidiaries. For example, in the 1980s, top management at such firms as Ford, IBM, Digital Equipment, and Texas Instruments saw their increasingly important international operations become slow-moving clones of corporate headquarters. Little communication or coordination occurred among regions. Even worse, country organizations sometimes spent more energy competing with each other than they did fighting with the competition.[4] In its fiscal year ending March 1994, Japan's Matsushita realized nearly 50 percent of its $64.3 billion in sales in overseas markets, and its foreign factories supplied two-thirds of the goods sold abroad. Matsushita lets its plants set their own rules, fine-tuning manufacturing. Many of Matsushita's overseas plants are beginning to compete with the company's factories back in Japan.[5]

Centralized control would help avert such a situation, and it would be advantageous in this respect. On the other hand, centralized controls requiring local managers to obtain permission to apply their creativity may actually inhibit local initiatives that would benefit the overall organization. The case of Japanese corporations' practices illustrates how centralization can be disadvantageous.

Unwillingness to give foreigners much clout could put Japanese companies at a disadvantage. Even at Uniden, where 277 out of 10,000 employees work in Japan, Japanese executives run all the foreign subsidiaries, and most key decisions are made at headquarters. Overcentralized management compounds the problem. Taku Ogata, an advisor on China for Nomura Research Institute Ltd. and author of a Japanese bestseller, *The Secret of Success in China,* thinks the unwillingness of Japanese companies to give authority to foreign executives is causing them to fall behind their Western competitors in China. Westerners hire Chinese managers, turn them loose, and reward them lavishly if they do well. By contrast, Japanese companies hesitate to hire Chinese at high levels, and Chinese prefer to work for Western companies, because pay is better.[6]

Headquarters managers are therefore often confronted with the problem of deciding whether to maintain central control over decisions relating to the firm's foreign subsidiaries or allow local managers to use their own discretion in decision making. Of course, when an organization adopts an approach, it does not adhere to it rigidly; it changes approaches when needed. For example, when an enterprise operating on a decentralized basis is confronted with the need to transform itself due to environmental changes, headquarters management will centralize decision making. But after the transformation has been accomplished, central management may again decentralize decision making to the local subsidiaries to enable them to establish strong **local presence**. The case of Berkel illustrates this point.

> Maatschappij Van Berkel's Patent N.V., a Dutch-based MNC supplier of weighing and food processing equipment, took action to meet competitive cost pressures by transforming itself into a sales and service firm. To manage the complicated process of rationalizing its manufacturing and engineering activities and phasing in an outsourced product line, Berkel temporarily adopted a highly centralized decision-making structure. But once the transformation was accomplished, the headquarters loosened control over its national operating companies and resumed the more autonomous decision-making style that in the past had helped to build a strong local presence.[7]

The case of Berkel presents a factor that influences whether headquarters managers centralize or decentralize decision making. Some of the traditional factors used by top management to determine whether to centralize or decentralize are outlined in Table 12–1.[8] The ensuing sections present contemporary thinking relative to headquarter–foreign control relationships.

HEADQUARTERS–FOREIGN SUBSIDIARY GOVERNANCE MECHANISMS

A contemporary idea on headquarter-subsidiary governance (control) relationships (HSRs) has been discussed by business professors Sumantra Ghoshal and Nitin Nohria, from INSEAD, France and Harvard Business

	Traditional Determinants of Centralization and Decentralization TABLE 12–1 ◆
Industry	Firms in an industry which requires product consistency across many foreign markets (such as firms with a global strategy) tend to centralize control. On the other hand, firms in an industry which must produce to suit the needs of specific foreign markets (such as firms with a multidomestic strategy) tend to decentralize decision making. This is because the former needs much more central coordination than the latter.
Type of Subsidiary	Foreign manufacturing subsidiaries are likely to be more controlled by headquarters' managers than foreign marketing subsidiaries. This is because manufacturing technologies tend to be consistently applicable across foreign markets, and can therefore be centrally coordinated. On the other hand, marketing technologies generally require a great deal of cross-cultural adaptation, which is generally best accomplished by local managers.
Function	International functions such as finance and accounting are likely to be more centrally controlled than functions such as hiring local workers. This is because top management generally likes to control "the purse" (money), and local managers would have a better grasp on the local labor market than central headquarters' managers.
Range of Subsidiary's Product and Market	Those foreign subsidiaries which provide a wide range of products for diverse markets tend to be less centrally controlled than those which provide uniform products for uniform markets. This is because the latter is not too complicated for headquarters' managers to control, while the former would be too complex for central managers to control, and local managers are best able to make adaptations required by the diverse markets.
Number and Size of Subsidiaries in a Market	Companies with a few large subsidiaries in a foreign area tend to decentralize more so than firms with many small units. This is because many small units in a market would require more central coordination among the units than would a few large units, which can more easily coordinate matters among themselves.
Ownership Structure	Partially owned foreign subsidiaries, for example, joint ventures, are more likely to be less centrally controlled than wholly owned foreign subsidiaries. This is because the expertise, such as knowledge of local culture, markets, and legal systems, often lies in the foreign partner, while in the wholly owned subsidiary the expertise often lies in the home office.
Date of Acquisition	Newly acquired foreign subsidiaries which continue manufacturing their old product lines under their same managers tend

◆   **TABLE 12-1   Traditional Determinants of Centralization and Decentralization (*continued*)**

	to be less centrally controlled. This is because the old managers possess the expertise. However, when the subsidiary subsequently grows and begins to expand into other products and markets, central control increases. This is because central expertise and coordination is now needed.
Headquarters' Interest and Expertise	The greater the headquarters management's personal interest in the subsidiary and the greater expertise in the subsidiary's business area, the greater central control over the foreign subsidiary it maintains, and vice versa.
Distance	Distant foreign subsidiaries tend to be less centrally controlled—although, as indicated earlier, advances in global communications technologies made in recent years have shortened the distance.
Environment	Subsidiaries located in countries with environments which are unfamiliar to headquarters management tend to be given greater autonomy than those which are located in familiar environments. Also, if the foreign subsidiary is located in a dynamic, changing local environment, the tendency is for headquarters' management to decentralize. This is because local management is more familiar with the local environment and is more in touch with the rapid changes which take place locally than headquarters' management, and is therefore better able to cope.
Corporate Goals	If the goal of headquarters managers is to maintain maximum power, then more central control is applied. If it is to maximize local market share, however, control tends to be decentralized. This is because local managers are generally more familiar with the local market conditions, and are therefore better equipped to carry the growth objective.
Ownership	If the enterprise is owned and managed by a few individuals, these managers may maintain a closer watch over their foreign interests than would professional managers of an enterprise which is owned by a large number of stockholders. (Of course, the other factors must also be considered.)
Headquarters' Confidence in Subsidiary's Management	When the confidence in the foreign subsidiary's managerial abilities increases, decision making tends to become more shared and less dictated by headquarters' management. And vice versa, when it decreases, the tendency is to apply central controls.
Success of the Subsidiary	If the foreign subsidiary is perceived as being highly successful, headquarters' control tends to lessen. But when things are not

	going well locally, headquarters management becomes more involved and centralist.
Intersubsidiary Transactions	A firm with a substantial volume of intersubsidiary transactions tends to be centralized. This is because when organizational effectiveness depends on several subunits, central coordination is usually required.
Importance of Foreign Market	Headquarters management may want to monitor an important foreign market very closely. Therefore, control over a foreign subsidiary in that market would be more centralized than it would be for subsidiaries located in markets which are of less importance.
Foreign Laws	The government of the nation in which a foreign subsidiary is located may require that the subsidiary be managed by locals. Central control would thus be less.
Individuals	If managers of the foreign subsidiary require autonomy, the tendency is to apply less central control. Attempts to control these individuals from the headquarters would result in ineffectiveness. On the other hand, some individuals, culturally, prefer that decisions be centrally made.

School, respectively. They described the relationships in terms of three basic headquarters-subsidiary **governance mechanisms:** centralization, formalization, and normative integration.[9] According to them, centralization concerns the role of formal authority and hierarchical mechanisms in the company's decision-making processes; **formalization** represents decision making through bureaucratic mechanisms such as formal systems, established rules, and prescribed procedures; and **normative integration** relies neither on direct headquarters involvement nor on impersonal rules but on the socialization of managers into a set of shared goals, values, and beliefs that then shape their perspectives and behavior.[10] (Organizations that adopt the matrix organizational structure, discussed in Chapter 5, also tend to adopt the normative integration approach.) The ensuing sections present two schemes that identify factors to help determine the right headquarters–foreign subsidiary control relationship. The first scheme posits that national cultural dimensions affect the relationship. The second proposes that certain situational factors influence the relationship in all countries.

The Country-Cultural Scheme

As discussed in Chapter 1, cross-cultural researcher Geert Hofstede[11] proposed a paradigm to study the impact of national culture on individual behavior. He developed a typology consisting of four national **cultural dimensions** by which a society can be classified: power distance, individualism, uncertainty avoidance, and masculinity. He later added a fifth dimension—Confucianism. The ensuing section indicates whether the headquarters-subsidiary relationship (HSR) with subsidiaries located in these cultures leans toward low or high centralization (C), low or high formalization (F), or low or high normative integration (NI). (See Figure 12–1.)

Power Distance

Moderate to Large Power Distance.   Individuals in societies dominated by this dimension tend to accept centralized power and depend heavily on superiors for direction. Therefore, an HSR leaning toward high C probably would be preferred by subsidiary managers who are dominated by this cultural dimension.

Moderate to Small Power Distance.   Individuals in societies dominated by this cultural dimension do not tolerate highly centralized power and expect to be consulted, at least, in decision making. Further, Hofstede remarked

---

◆ **FIGURE 12–1   The National-Cultural Framework**

Cultural Determinants	Headquarters–Foreign Subsidiary Control Relationship
Large power distance	HC
Small power distance	LC, HF, or HNI
High individualism	HC or HF
Low individualism	LF, HNI
Strong uncertainty avoidance	HF or HC
Weak uncertainty avoidance	LC or HNI
Confucianism	LF, HC, HNI
High masculinity	HF
Low masculinity	LC, HNI

C = centralization; F = formalization; NI = normative integration; H = high; L = low

Source: Carl A. Rodrigues, "Headquarters-Foreign Subsidiary Control Relationships: Three Conceptual Frameworks," *Empowerment In Organizations: An International Journal,* 3, no. 3 (1995). In print.

that status differences in these countries are suspect. Thus, subsidiary managers who are dominated by this cultural dimension probably would favor an HSR leaning toward low C, high NI, or high F.

A research project including MBA students from Germany, Great Britain (both small power distance societies), and France (a large power distance society)[12] provides some support for the conclusions about a country's power distance measure influencing HSR. The students were asked to write their own diagnosis of and solution to a case problem. The majority of the French referred the problem to the next higher authority—they sought direction (high C). The British handled the problem (low C or high NI-like behavior), and the Germans attributed it to a lack of formal policy and proposed establishing one (high F).

Individualism

Moderate to High Individualism.   Individuals in societies dominated by this dimension think in "me" terms and look primarily after their own interests. Since these individuals often consider their own objectives to be more important than the organization's, the HSR that evolves in subsidiaries managed by people influenced by this cultural dimension probably leans toward high C or high F.

Moderate to Low Individualism.   Low individualism societies are tightly integrated and individuals belong to "in-groups" from which they cannot detach themselves. People think in "we" as opposed to "me" terms and obtain satisfaction from a job well done by the group. Individuals in these societies are controlled mainly by the group's norms and values. These people would therefore require less formal structure than individuals who think in "me" terms. An HSR leaning toward high NI would thus fit these societies.

Findings by some researchers lend support to the above contentions. These researchers concluded that control systems in the U.S. (a high individualism culture) are designed under the assumption that workers and management seek "primary control" over their work environments.[13] Primary control is manifested when employees with individualistic tendencies attempt to shape the existing social and behavioral factors surrounding them, including co-workers, specific events, or their environments, with the intention of increasing their rewards.[14] Thus many employees exhibit behaviors and establish goals that may diverge from those desired by the organization. For these reasons, control systems consisting of rules, standards, and norms of behavior are established to guide, motivate, and evaluate employees' behavioral performance (high F).[15] On the other hand, organizations in Japan (a low individualism culture) rely more on "secondary controls," controls that rely mostly on informal peer pressure (high NI).[16] And Japanese corporations with subsidiaries in the U.S. tend to give American managers working for them little or no authority.[17]

Uncertainty Avoidance

Moderate to Strong Uncertainty Avoidance.   Individuals in these cultures feel uneasy in situations of uncertainty and ambiguity and prefer structure and direction. Therefore, because it tends to reduce uncertainty for individuals, managers of subsidiaries who are influenced by this cultural dimension probably would prefer an HSR leaning toward high F or high C. Professor Hofstede has proposed that improving quality of life for employees in these societies implies offering more security and perhaps more task structure on the job (high F).

Moderate to Weak Uncertainty Avoidance.   Hofstede found that in countries dominated by a moderate to weak uncertainty avoidance cultural dimension, individuals tend to be relatively tolerant of uncertainty and ambiguity; they do not require as much high C or high F as do people in strong uncertainty avoidance cultures. Thus, an HSR leaning toward low C or high NI, since it provides more challenge than does high C and high F, probably would be preferred by managers of subsidiaries who are dominated by this cultural dimension.

For example, it has been found that managers in Britain, a weak uncertainty avoidance culture, tend to value achievement and autonomy (low C or high NI-like behavior) and managers in France, a strong uncertainty avoidance society, value competent supervision, sound company policies, fringe benefits, security, and comfortable working conditions (high C and high F).[18] It has also been found that French managers do not believe matrix organizations (discussed in Chapter 5), which tend to apply high NI-like behavior, are feasible; they view them as violating the principle of unit of command.[19]

Confucianism

As it was pointed out in Chapter 1, individuals in East Asian cultures (the People's Republic of China, South Korea, Japan, Hong Kong, and Singapore) are also influenced by the Confucian cultural dimension. In essence, individuals in Confucian-based organizations are forced to adhere to rigid, informal group norms and values (high NI-like relationship). Since individuals are so strictly bound to group norms, organizations based on the Confucian cultural dimension probably apply less formalization (low F) than do organizations in the West. This contention is partially supported by research findings that organizations in China, where the Confucian influence is still strong, tend to be far less formalized than Western organizations.[20] There is evidence that Confucian-based organizations apply high C. For example, it was found that South Korean managers demonstrate the Confucian virtues of loyalty and obedience to authorities, and that they tend not to adopt systems of shared management and power equalization within organizations.[21] Chinese subordinates have been found to be passive, preferring that others make decisions for them (high C).[22]

Masculinity

Moderate to High Masculinity. Societies dominated by this dimension stress material success and assertiveness and assign different roles to males and females. Males are expected to carry out the assertive, ambitious, and competitive roles in the society; females are expected to care for the non-material quality of life, for children, and for the weak—to perform the society's caring roles. In strong masculine countries where people perceive such behavior as being inequitable, HSR leaning toward high F emphasizing reduction of such social inequities would probably be preferred. One finds evidence of this in recent programs in the U.S., a society with a moderate to high masculine cultural dimension—the Equal Pay Act of 1963, Title VII of the Civil Rights Act of 1964, affirmative action and equal employment opportunity programs; and in Japan with its very high masculine culture—the Employment Opportunity Law of 1986.

Moderate to Low Masculinity. Hofstede also concluded that those nations dominated by a low masculine cultural dimension stress interpersonal relationships, a concern for others, and the overall quality of life, and define relatively overlapping social roles for males and females. In these cultures, neither male nor female need be ambitious or competitive; both may aspire to a life that does not assign great values to material success and respects others. According to Professor Hofstede,[23] improved quality of work life for individuals in these societies means offering opportunities for developing relationships on the job, which is perhaps best accomplished through low C or high NI-like HSR. For example, people in Sweden, a low masculine society, generally prefer organic (low C, NI-like) organizational structures, and they like to be involved in the decision-making process.

The Situational Scheme

The above presented a cultural scheme as a means of determining HSRs. However, as pointed out in Chapter 10, the scheme serves mainly as a generalization—as a starting point for analysis—and many organizational theorists[24] have argued that, irrespective of a society's culture, individuals are forced to adapt attitudes and behaviors that comply with the imperatives of industrialization. This means that HSRs are affected more by situational factors than cultural factors. Thus we arrive at the **situational scheme**. See Figure 12–2.

The Subsidiary's Local Context

Professors Ghoshal and Nohria believe that headquarters-subsidiary relationships are not identical for all subsidiaries throughout the company; that each headquarters-subsidiary relationship can be governed by a different combination of the three mechanisms (C,F,NI); and that companies adopt

◆ FIGURE 12–2   **The Situational Framework**

Situational Determinants	Headquarters–Foreign Subsidiary Control Relationship
The Subsidiary's Local Context	
Low complexity; low level of resources	HC, LF, LNI
Low complexity; high level of resources	LC, HF, HNI
High complexity; low level of resources	MC, LF, HNI
High complexity; high level of resources	LC, MF, HNI
The Organization's Size	
Large-scale organization	HF
Large-scale organization with global strategy	LC, HC, HNI
Large-scale organization with multidomestic strategy	LC, HF
Small-scale organization	HNI or HC
Organizational Function	
R&D-like functions	HNI, LC, LF
Production-like functions:	
With multidomestic strategy	HF
With global strategy	HNI, MC
Cash management-like functions	HC, HF
Organization under Crisis Conditions:	
In an environment of scarcity	HC or HF
In an environment of abundance	LC, HNI
Management's Preference:	
Likes to maintain strong control	HC
Likes to maintain stability	HF
Likes to maintain adaptability, flexibility	HNI

C = centralization:	F = formalization:	NI = normative integration:
H = high;	L = low;	M = moderate

Source: Carl A. Rodrigues, "Headquarters-Foreign Subsidiary Control Relationships: Three Conceptual Frameworks."

different governance modes to fit each **subsidiary's local context.** The local context, according to them, can vary in a number of ways, but two of the most important ways are **environmental complexity** (the level of technological dynamism and competitive intensity) and the **amount of local resources** available to the subsidiary.[25] Some subsidiaries may be managing advanced technologies (computers, for example) in a very competitive market (high environmental complexity), while others may be managing older technologies (steel production, for example) in a stable market (low environmental complexity). Some subsidiaries may have an abundance of resources, while others have scarce resources. Professors Ghoshal and Nohria developed a scheme that matches headquarter-foreign subsidiary control relationships (HSRs) to subsidiary contexts. The scheme is as follows:[26]

1. Low environment complexity and low levels of local resources dictate a high level of centralization and low levels of formalization and normative integration.
2. Low environment complexity and high levels of resources dictate a low level of centralization and high levels of formalization and normative integration.
3. High environment complexity and low resource levels indicate a moderate level of centralization, a low level of formalization, and a high level of normative integration.
4. High environment complexity and high resource levels indicate a low level of centralization, a moderate level of formalization, and a high level of normative integration.

Size of the Organization

The **size of the organization** has been found to be a factor in determining HSRs. Large-scale organizations have tended to apply structural relationships leaning toward high F and small-scale organizations tend to apply a high NI-like or a high C structural relationship.[27] However this factor is influenced by the organization's strategy. Some international businesses establish a global strategy. The global corporation uses all of its resources against its competition in a very integrated fashion. All of its foreign subsidiaries and divisions are highly interdependent in both operations and strategy. As an expert said:

> In a global business, management competes worldwide against a small number of other multinationals in the world market. Strategy is centralized, and various aspects of operations are decentralized or centralized as economics and effectiveness dictate. The company seeks to respond to particular local market needs, while avoiding a compromise of efficiency of the overall global system.[28]

Companies that apply the global strategy include IBM in computers, Caterpillar in large construction equipment, Timex, Seiko, and Citizen in watches, and General Electric, Siemens, and Mitsubishi in heavy electrical equipment. Many corporations that adopt the global strategy approach also adopt the matrix organizational structure. In the matrix structure there is extensive cooperation between all the operating subsidiaries. Therefore, the global corporation relies on an HRS with a combination of low C, high C, and high NI.

Many international firms establish a multidomestic strategy. The multidomestic firm has a different strategy for each of its foreign markets. In this type of strategy, "a company's management tries to operate effectively across a series of worldwide positions with diverse product requirements, growth rates, competitive environments and political risks. The company prefers that local managers do what is necessary to succeed in R&D, production, marketing, and distribution, but holds them responsible for results."[29] In essence, this type of corporation competes with local competitors on a market-by-market basis. A multitude of American corporations use this strategy, for example, Procter & Gamble in household products, Honeywell in controls, Alcoa in aluminum, and General Foods in consumer goods. Large organizations that adopt a multidomestic strategy tend to apply low C; but for accountability reasons, they also tend to rely on bureaucratic (high F) HSRs.

Type of Organizational Function

It has been found that the internal aspects of the organization are also determinants of structural relationships.[30] Some subunits apply high organic, NI-like relationships while other subunits in the same organization apply high C or F relationships. Thus, functions such as R&D subsidiaries, because their functional effectiveness often depends on an integration of numerous individuals' ideas, probably function more effectively with a relationship leaning toward low F, low C, and high NI. Subunits such as production, a function that usually requires high structure to ensure production efficiency, probably work best with a relationship leaning toward high F—this, however, may be more so for corporations with a multidomestic strategy than companies with a global strategy. To ensure overall production efficiency, global corporations often integrate production across all subsidiaries by use of the matrix organization structure, thus applying a high NI with some degree of central coordination (moderate C). Functions such as cash management are usually centralized (high C) and formalized (high F). For example, Broken Hill Proprietary Co. Ltd., a U.S.-based producer/distributer of minerals, petroleum, and steel, has centralized cash management in the corporation, but has decentralized and localized the management of resource gathering, marketing, and distribution.[31]

Organizations under Crisis Conditions

Numerous studies have revealed that organizations confronted with **crisis conditions**—environmental hostility, turbulence, and financial adversity—tend to increase the formalization and standardization of procedures, to place greater emphasis on previously established rules, and to centralize and involve fewer people in the decision-making process.[32] In other words, headquarters managers of organizations confronted with crisis conditions usually apply an HSR leaning toward high F or high C. It has been found, however, that this occurs more frequently when the organization exists in an environment of scarcity than when it exists in an environment of munificence (abundance).[33] Organizations confronted with crisis conditions in an environment of abundance tend to decentralize (low C, high NI-like behavior).

Management's Preference

Culturally, management may like to maintain strong control over activities (high C); strong organizational stability, and thus a bureaucratic system (high F); or a flexible, adaptable organization, and therefore an interactive approach (high NI). The U.S.-based giant corporation, Johnson & Johnson, is an illustration of a company whose management has over the years developed a corporate culture that promotes decentralization, but encourages managers to act in a global concerted fashion when necessary.

> Johnson & Johnson is performing an act that defies gravity. It runs no fewer than 33 major lines of business, with an astounding 168 operating companies in 53 countries. And runs them well. Johnson & Johnson may have mastered the art of decentralized management better than any other company in the world. Long before the rest of Corporate America made "empowerment" a management buzzword, J&J was practicing it. As early as the 1930s, longtime chairman Robert Wood Johnson pushed the idea of decentralization. Believing that smaller, self governing units were more manageable, quicker to react to their markets, and more accountable, the son of a J&J co-founder encouraged such early mainstays as Ethicon Inc., a sutures maker, and Personal Products Co., the feminine-hygiene business, to operate independently.[34]

International Managers Must Consider Both Schemes

As it was pointed out in Chapter 10, both the cultural and the situational schemes are well supported by research. Therefore, when making a decision about the right headquarters–foreign subsidiary control relationship, international managers will have to consider both the situational and the cultural schemes. When international managers make a mistake and select the wrong HSR, it usually costs their company a great deal of money to correct the wrong, and there will be other costs as well, such as low employee morale. Either extreme—too much centralization and too little decentralization, or too little centralization and too much decentralization—eventually leads to managerial problems. Hence, international managers must seek to attain a **balance between centralized and decentralized headquarters–foreign subsidiary control.**

A FRAMEWORK FOR ATTAINING
A BALANCED HSR

As is indicated in Practical Perspective 12–1, "no company can operate effectively in the global arena by centralizing key decisions and then farming them out for implementation." As Kenichi Ohmae, head of McKinsey's office in Tokyo, proposes,

> The conditions in each market are too varied, the nuances of competition too complex, and the changes in climate too subtle and too rapid for long-distance management. No matter how good they are, no matter how well supported analytically, the decision makers at the center are just too far removed from the intricacies of individual markets and the needs of local customers.[35]

But decentralizing key decisions creates its own problems, and no company can operate effectively for a long period of time through a totally centralized or a totally decentralized control relationship. In other words, as classical U.S. management principles indicate, there must be a balance between centralization and decentralization (this means that Johnson & Johnson, previously described, may not be as decentralized as the media make it out to be). This means that a major problem confronting headquarters' managers is how to attain an HSR with balanced centralization and decentralization; how to obtain assurance that decisions made by subsidiary managers are in tune with the enterprise's overall objectives, and that decisions made by headquarters management are not sabotaged by subsidiary management. The ensuing section describes a framework for attaining a balanced HSR.

Due Process as a Means of Attaining Balanced HSRs

Historically, when headquarters managers made decisions (such as establishing strategic plans) that had to be executed by subsidiary managers, many managers relied on implementation control mechanisms such as incentive compensation, monitoring systems, and rewards and punishments. W. Chen Kim, associate professor of strategy and international management, and Renee A. Mauborgne, research associate of management and international business, both at INSEAD, France, conducted extensive research to ascertain what it takes for multinationals to successfully execute global strategies. The subsidiary top managers they interviewed indicated that these implementation control mechanisms alone are not sufficient nor effective; that they were not particularly motivating and were easy to dodge and cheat.[36]

The subsidiary managers indicated that effective implementation requires that due process be exercised in the global decision-making process. The due process is depicted in Figure 12–3. Basically, due process means: (1) that the head office is familiar with subsidiaries' local situations; (2) that two-way

PRACTICAL PERSPECTIVE 12–1

Planting for a Global Harvest

No company can effectively operate on a global scale by centralizing all key decisions and then farming them out for implementation.... The conditions in each market are too varied, the nuances of competition too complex, and the changes in climate too subtle and too rapid for long-distance management. No matter how good they are, no matter how well supported analytically, the decision makers at the center are just too far removed from the intricacies of individual markets and the needs of local customers.

The strength of a global corporation derives, in no small measure, from its ability as a full-fledged insider to understand local customers' needs.... Effective cultivation of global markets requires more than the removal of absentee landlords. Decomposing inevitably creates its own problems. The more successful a company is at bringing both operational and strategic responsibility down to the regional or local level, the more likely it is that local or regional concerns, attitudes, affinities, and allegiances will shape the decisions of its far-flung managerial cadre.... Maintaining a vital corporate identity in a global environment is no trivial exercise. Formal systems and organizational structures can help, but only to the extent that they nurture and support intangible ties.

Training programs, career-path planning, job rotation, company-wide accounting, evaluation systems that are fair across national borders, and electronic data-processing systems take on heightened importance as globalization proceeds. Most important, however, is a system of values that all employees in all countries and regions unquestioningly accept.... It [the global corporation] serves its customers in all key markets with equal dedication. It does not shade things with one group to benefit another. It does not enter markets for the sole purpose of exploiting their profit potential. Its value system is universal, not dominated by home country dogma, and it applies everywhere....

The more dispersed your people and the closer the attention they must pay to local customers and markets, the more they need to escape the center's rigidities while retaining its shaping values. Colonial administrators—and early global managers—in the old, pyramidal organizations had only crude means to help their people strike an appropriate balance. For the most part, they used brute force: distance and poor communication softened rigidity, and the threat of penalty reinforced shared values. Today brute force is neither necessary nor effective. A new form of organization, organic and amoebalike, makes that balance far easier to achieve. . . .

[Companies in an advanced stage of global operations development] must denationalize their operations and create a system of values shared by company managers around the globe to replace the glue a nation-based orientation once provided. The best organizations operate in this fashion and, as a result, devote much of their "corporate" attention to defining personnel systems and the like that are country neutral. In a genuinely global corporation, everyone is hired locally. No matter where individuals in an amoebalike structure are, they can communicate fully and confidently with colleagues elsewhere. Building this level of trust takes time because building shared values takes time. You can try to speed things up by asserting policies and mandating values, but it does not work. . . .

Building a global organization based on values, not on a pyramid of authority, is, first and foremost, a time-consuming exercise in culture: nurturing trust on a person-to-person level and learning what will and will not grow in some particular patch of garden. The culture of an organization is like the soil; a business is like a tree growing in the soil; and profits are like the fruits of the tree. An effective corporation will have the same kind of soil, with the same Ph, in all the regions of the world where it operates. And in that soil will grow similar kinds of trees. If you put the wrong seeds in this or that patch of ground, if you try to grow someone else's kind of tree, if you play fast and loose with the mergers and acquisitions game and just want to steal the fruits without planting or fertilizing anything—that is, if you do not take the time to grow healthy trees in the spots suitable for them—you will never be able to reap a proper long-term harvest.

Few, if any, companies have been able to force radically different kinds of trees to root strongly and grow well in precisely the same soil. If you want to harvest a variety of fruits, then you have to plant each tree in its appropriate setting. You need a healthy environment, with the right leadership style, accounting and planning systems, evaluation and reward systems, and so on. For global companies, this means looking at organizational issues in a new way. No longer is the key question how to combine disparate business units into divisions or sectors based solely on assumed similarities among customers or markets. The far more important questions is how to combine disparate businesses into coherent culture units that provide a common soil in which the businesses can flourish.

Source: Reprinted by permission of *Harvard Business Review*. An excerpt from Kenichi Ohmae, "Planting for a Global Harvest," *Harvard Business Review* (July–August 1989): 136–145. Copyright © 1989 by the President and Fellows of Harvard College. All rights reserved.

communication exists in the global strategy-making process; (3) that the head office is relatively consistent in making decisions across subsidiary units; (4) that subsidiary units can legitimately challenge the head office's strategic views and decisions; and (5) that subsidiary units receive an explanation for final decisions.[37] This model basically means that organizations can attain a balance between centralization and decentralization if they apply extensive **vertical and horizontal communication** throughout the overall system. Application of the **matrix organization structure** (discussed in Chapter 5) can help attain this type of communication. More is needed, however. Practical Perspectives 12–1, 12–2, and 12–3 suggest that the development of corporate global core values, which cut across all foreign subsidiaries, would help provide a balance.

Global Corporate Culture and Core Values as a Means of Attaining Balance

Some cross-cultural researchers have broken down the meaning of corporate culture into symbols, heroes, and rituals, which they defined as organizational **practice,** and into **values,** such as good/evil, beautiful/ugly, normal/abnormal, rational/irrational. These researchers contend that corporate cultures "reflect nationality, demographics of employees and managers, industry and market; they are related to organization structure and

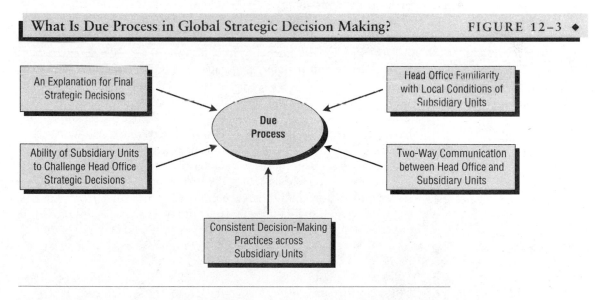

What Is Due Process in Global Strategic Decision Making?   FIGURE 12-3 ◆

An Explanation for Final Strategic Decisions

Head Office Familiarity with Local Conditions of Subsidiary Units

Due Process

Ability of Subsidiary Units to Challenge Head Office Strategic Decisions

Two-Way Communication between Head Office and Subsidiary Units

Consistent Decision-Making Practices across Subsidiary Units

Source: W. Chan Kim and Renee A. Mauborgne, "Making Global Strategies Work," *Sloan Management Review* (Spring 1993): 12. Copyright © 1993, Sloan Management Review Association. Used with permission. All rights reserved.

PRACTICAL PERSPECTIVE 12–2

Transplanting Corporate Cultures Globally

Asea Brown Boveri, Inc. (ABB), the electrical-engineering giant, is the quintessential global company. It has a clearly defined mission statement and a culture that supports the mission. . . . "We think about ABB as a company without any regard to national boundaries," says Richard P. Randazzo, who, as ABB's vice president of HR, works out of the company's Stamford, Connecticut base and oversees the company's HR operations in the U.S. "We just operate on a global basis. A lot of other companies see boundaries and barriers, but from a business standpoint, this company is intent on transcending those boundaries." Indeed, more than 50% of its sales are in Europe, 20% are in North America, 20% in Asia, and the rest are in South America and Africa. The official language is English; the official currency is the dollar. . . .

It's a highly decentralized business (the U.S. alone has 50 companies, each with its own president). Divisions treat each other as vendors and customers, invoicing one another and maintaining accounts payable and receivable from other divisions. Characterized by *Forbes* as a company that has no discernible national identity, ABB's corporate culture is one of its strong defining fea-

tures. The company embodies the phrase *think globally, act locally.* According to Randazzo, ABB's culture is focused tightly on making money. Its personality profile is a hands-on, action-oriented, travel-to-the-opportunity kind of business. Each division acts locally in response to customers and employees. But managers are required to think globally about sourcing. For example, if the dollar is strong relative to the Swedish krona, then the company sources more from Sweden because goods and services are cheaper there. When that changes, sourcing also changes.

Corporate culture mixes with the culture of the country in which ABB operates. "There's no attempt by the corporation to tell us in the U.S. how we should behave relative to our customers or to our employees," says Randazzo. (Other HR executives oversee ABB's HR operations in its different business segments and the different countries in which the company operates.) The senior management team is composed largely of Europeans, so at times they give Randazzo quizzical looks when he says that they can't ask a person's age or marital status when recruiting. "They don't understand some of the affirmative-action targets we have, but they don't attempt to influence any of that. The motivation is that we know more about the U.S. marketplace than the Germans, the Swedes or the Swiss will ever know, and therefore, we're better able to deal with it."

But cultures aren't static. They influence each other. For one, HR management plays a much more significant role in the U.S. than it does in Europe. According to Randazzo, this is the arena in which Americans have had significant influence on ABB's Europeans, addressing such issues as employee involvement, empowerment and total quality. In fact, the U.S. HR staff developed materials for conducting management training, some of

which were translated into German.

Likewise, the Europeans have influenced the Americans. They've brought a sense of business urgency to the company. They helped with downsizing, lowering the break-even point and getting the organization focused. Understanding local attitudes helps corporate cultures take root. Not all corporate cultures transplant well overseas. Companies that try to graft the Stars and Stripes forever in a foreign location will likely encounter resistance. Those that are sensitive to local attitudes and customs are bound to be more successful.

Source: Excerpted from Charlene M. Solomon, "Transplanting Corporate Cultures Globally," *Personnel Journal* (October 1993): 80–81. Reprinted with the permission of *Personnel Journal*, ACC Communications, Inc., Cosa Mesa, California. All rights reserved.

PRACTICAL PERSPECTIVE   12–3

Global Vision and Core Values

In April 1992, Chairman Riley P. Bechtel issued the company's [Bechtel Corp.] new strategic plan called *Toward 2001*. In it, he articulated his global vision and core values, making a commitment to analyze and change the corporate culture within a

global context. To be most effective, it was essential to learn about employees' beliefs and attitudes. Gaufin's HR staff issued a 102-question survey to 22,000 employees. Questions asked employees about communication, training-and-advancement opportunities, the work environment and the importance of international and domestic field experience to professional development. The staff followed up with more than 200 focus groups at the firm's domestic and international locations.

In response to the results, each large office developed specific action plans to address employee concerns, which included communication between management and employees and the availability of training programs for people at field locations. Corporatewide priorities address the areas of reward and recognition, training and development and employee participation, among others.

For example, the company is developing a communication plan to disseminate information more effectively throughout all locations, including field operations. It's reinstating a companywide newsletter that will go to all employees worldwide to help improve communication between the company and its employees. Performance appraisals are being revised to reflect the kind of culture that Bechtel wants to become. Rather than have a report-card-like performance-review form, it will be a tool to increase communication between supervisors and employees, and also help each employee reach his or her objectives. The review pro-

motes better communication because it requires employees to take the initiative to communicate with their managers. It addresses on-the-job and outside training needs.

"The survey is a way of listening to employees. It gives us ways to implement the corporate culture more effectively," says Gaufin. The 1992 survey is the baseline. Periodic surveys will provide means of measuring progress. There are a lot of challenges when it comes to implementing some of the changes, says Gaufin. For example, different cultures perceive performance reviews in different ways. "We have to be sure that we're not going against accepted practices in other parts of the world," she says. Furthermore, part of the new strategic plan focuses on empowered teams. Gaufin says that will be a challenge, too.

The 1992 survey wasn't translated into other languages, but Gaufin says they'll consider translating the next ones into Spanish and other major languages. There are just too many instances when English doesn't communicate adequately.

The survey and the desire to translate it into other languages attest to a change in corporate culture at Bechtel. "We're trying to be more open and communicative—internally as well as externally," says Morgan. "We need to understand the environment in which we operate." . . . Of course, state-of-the-art telecommunications facilitate the cultural exchange. Many employees have considerable international phone contact with each other. Video conferencing and in-person meetings with foreign colleagues build social relationships. The company also televises major company meetings to Europe.

These are key ways to convey corporate culture. In Bechtel's case, this is particularly important. As the speedy mobilization to help fight the Kuwait fires attests, employees sometimes are called on to move to another location on a few days' notice. A highly decentralized, flexible structure makes this rapid response possible. Work often is done with project teams. They form to accomplish specific tasks. U.S. expatriates, other expatriates and local nationals do the job and then demobilize. This type of work arrangement, the speed at which the company can respond, and the company's flexibility also make it imperative that employees fully comprehend the company's mission.

"Obviously, you have to communicate the company's purpose and its objectives," says Morgan. "The culture provides guidance for the employee on how the company wants to achieve those objectives." . . . In addition, the HR staff (which includes 45 people in Bechtel's corporate offices in San Francisco and 340 people in regional and area offices, and many field locations) uses pre-employment interviews to communicate some of the company's culture, particularly when hiring managers. The issue of *fit* not only involves technical skills and qualifications, but also in knowing that the employee will be comfortable with Bechtel's way of doing things. For example, all new employees sign a Standard of Conduct agreement.

Training and development are other areas in which Bechtel communicates its goals and values. Morgan, who is Australian and has lived in a variety of offshore settings, says that international training is heightened when you teach mixed groups of U.S. expatriates and local nationals. The training goes both ways. U.S. expatriates communicate the company's ideals and personality to local nationals, and the nationals transmit the host culture to the Americans.

control systems; but all of these leave room for unique and idiosyncratic elements"[38] Among national cultures, comparing "otherwise similar people," these researchers found "considerable differences in values." Among corporate cultures, the opposite was the case; they found "considerable differences in practices for people who held about the same values."[39]

Therefore, according to these researchers, the value aspects of corporate culture are attributed to nationality, but the practice aspects (symbols, heroes, and rituals) are attributed to the corporation, and the corporation **changes practices in response to environmental demands.** Since the environment changes at different times for different organizations, the practice aspects will differ from corporation to corporation, even when the values remain relatively similar. This means that individuals in the same national culture may possess broad behavioral similarities, but different practices, depending on the corporation they work for.

The development of **global corporate core values,** that is, values that cut across all subsidiaries located throughout the globe, would help provide a **balance.** For example, Asea Brown Boveri, Inc. (ABB), the electrical engineering giant, is the quintessential global company. It has a clearly defined mission statement and a culture that supports the mission. "We think about ABB as a company without any regard to national boundaries," says Richard P. Randazzo, who, as ABB's vice president of HR, works out of the company's Stamford, Connecticut base and oversees the company's HR operations in the U.S. "We just operate on a global basis. A lot of other companies see boundaries and barriers, but from a business standpoint, this company is intent on transcending those boundaries."[40]

In April 1992, Chairman Riley P. Bechtel issued Bechtel Corp.'s new strategic plan called "Toward 2001." In it, he articulated his global vision and core values, making a commitment to analyze and change the corporate culture within a global context: "The culture provides guidance for the employee on how the company wants to achieve those objectives."[41] "It's vitally important that the [transnational] company have a strong company culture," says Calvin Reynolds, senior fellow at the Wharton School of the University of Pennsylvania and senior counselor for New York City-based Organization Resources Counselors. "If you don't have a strong set of cultural principles from which to function, when people get overseas, they're so lacking clarity that no one knows where they're going."[42]

Nurturing Balance

The above suggests that a global corporation can develop a value system with global application, in which individual subsidiaries adapt practices to the local situation. As Practical Perspective 12–1 indicates, such organizational culture must be **nurtured.** David Whitwan, CEO of Whirlpool Corporation, also supports this contention. He stated that:

When we acquired Philips [a floundering European appliance business in 1989] . . . Wall Street analysts expected us to ship 500 people over to Europe, plug them into the plants and distribution systems, and give them six months or a year to turn the business around. They expected us to impose the "superior American way" of operating on the European organization. . . . If you try to gain control of an organization by simply subjugating it to your preconceptions, you can expect to pay for your short-term profits with long-term resistance and resentment. That's why we chose another course. During the first year, I think we had two people from the United States working in Europe, and neither was a senior manager. By the end of the second year, we had maybe a half a dozen U.S. managers there—again, none at the senior level. We listened and observed. We worked hard to communicate the company's vision, objectives, and philosophy to the European workforce. Building a shared understanding takes time, and we had to learn how to do that in a multilingual, multinational environment. Today we have 15,000 employees in Europe with only 10 from U.S. operations. They all report to European bosses, with the exception of Hank Bowman, executive vice president of Whirlpool Europe.[43]

Gurcharan Das, formerly chairman and managing director of Procter & Gamble India, said the same thing:

Globalization does not mean imposing homogeneous solutions in a pluralistic world. It means having a global vision and strategy, but it also means cultivating

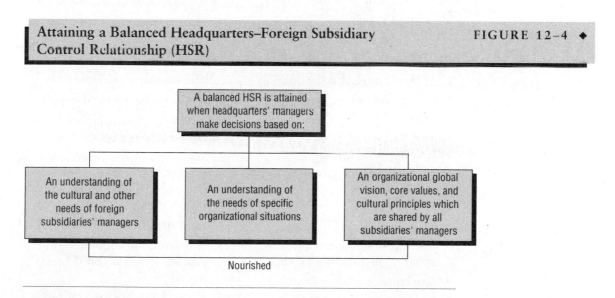

Attaining a Balanced Headquarters–Foreign Subsidiary Control Relationship (HSR)   FIGURE 12–4 ◆

Source: Carl A. Rodrigues, "Headquarters-Foreign Subsidiary Control Relationships: Three Conceptual Frameworks."

roots and individual identities. It means nourishing local insights, but it also means reemploying communicable ideas in new geographies around the world.[44]

Practical Perspective 12–3 describes Bechtel Corporation's approach to changing corporate culture within a global context. Figure 12–4 depicts the framework for attaining a balance between centralization and decentralization and therefore a balanced headquarters–foreign subsidiary control relationship.

SUMMARY

This chapter has addressed the topic of headquarters–foreign subsidiaries control relationships. It has presented the traditional concepts of centralized and decentralized headquarters–foreign subsidiaries control relationships, as well as several factors that help headquarters managers determine the appropriate relationship. It has also addressed the contemporary concepts of centralization, formalization, and normative integration headquarters–foreign subsidiary control relationships, and presented cross-cultural and situational factors that help headquarters managers determine the appropriate relationship. It has proposed that effective global corporations need to establish a balanced headquarters–foreign subsidiary relationship, and that balance can be attained through the implementation of a global corporate culture and core values.

Key Terms

1. Centralization; decentralization
2. Formalization; normative integration
3. Subsidiary
4. Headquarters–foreign subsidiary control relationships (HSRs)
5. Local presence
6. Headquarters management's confidence in the foreign subsidiaries' management abilities
7. Governance mechanisms
8. The country-cultural scheme
9. Cultural dimensions affect relationships
10. The situational scheme
11. The subsidiary's local context
12. Environmental complexity and amount of local resources
13. Size of the organization; type of organizational function; crisis conditions; and management's preference
14. Informal integration
15. A balanced headquarters-foreign subsidiaries control relationship
16. Vertical and horizontal communication
17. Matrix structure

18. Global corporate culture and core values as a balance

19. Nurturing balance

20. Practices and values

21. Corporate value system has global application

22. Adapting practices to local situation

Discussion Questions and Exercises

1. Describe the centralized and decentralized headquarters–foreign subsidiaries control relationships, and some of the pros and cons of both.

2. Foreign manufacturing and foreign marketing subsidiaries are likely to generate what types of headquarters-subsidiary relationships?

3. The function of recruiting and selecting personnel in foreign subsidiaries is likely to generate what kind of headquarters–foreign subsidiary control relationship?

4. Why are foreign subsidiaries that provide a wide range of products less centrally controlled than those that provide a narrow range of products?

5. Describe the centralization, formalization, and normative integration headquarters–foreign subsidiaries control relationships.

6. What type of headquarters-subsidiary relationship—centralization, formalization, or normative integration—fits low individualism cultures? Why?

7. Managers of foreign subsidiaries who are dominated by a small power distance cultural dimension are likely to favor a normative integration or a formalization headquarters-subsidiary relationship. Do you agree or disagree? Why?

8. You are from the headquarters of a U.S.-based company. You are assigned to create subsidiaries in France, Germany, Britain, and China. What type of headquarters-subsidiary relationships—centralization, formalization, or normative integration—would you establish in those countries? Why?

9. Describe the degrees of centralization, formalization, and normative integration in a headquarters-subsidiary relationship when the foreign subsidiary is confronted with a high environment of complexity and low levels of local resources.

10. You are the headquarters executive responsible for the financial aspects of the overall corporation. What type of headquarters–foreign subsidiary control relationship—centralization, formalization, or normative integration—are you likely to establish? Why?

11. How do global corporate cultures and core values help provide a balanced headquarters–foreign subsidiaries control relationship?

12. Top management of a global corporation that manufactures and distributes product Y has decided to divest its manufacturing operations

and concentrate on its distribution operations. How is the transformation best approached? (Refer to Practical Perspective 12–3.) Which headquarters–foreign subsidiary control relationship is likely to emerge?

Assignment

Contact a senior international executive of a corporation. Ask him or her to describe his or her company's foreign subsidiary control relationship. Write a short report for presentation in class.

CASE 12–1

Source: Reprinted by permission of Harvard Business Review. An excerpt from C. A. Barlett and S. Ghoshal, "What Is a Global Manager?" *Harvard Business Review* (September–October 1992): 125–128.

Electrolux

Global business or product-division managers have one overriding responsibility: to further the company's global-scale efficiency and competitiveness. This task requires not only the perspective to recognize opportunities and risks across national and functional boundaries but also the skill to coordinate activities and link capabilities across those barriers. The global business manager's overall goal is to capture the full benefit of integrated worldwide operations.

To be effective, the three roles at the core of a business manager's job are to serve as the strategist for his or her organization, the architect of its worldwide asset and resource configuration, and the coordinator of transactions across national borders. Leif Johansson, now president of Electrolux, the Swedish-based company, played all three roles successfully in his earlier position as head of the household appliance division.

In 1983, when 32-year-old Johansson assumed responsibility for the division, he took over a business that had been built up through more than 100 acquisitions over the previous eight years. By the late 1980s, Electrolux's portfolio included more than 20 brands sold in some 40 countries, with acquisitions continuing throughout the decade. Zanussi, for example, the big Italian manufacturer acquired by Electrolux in 1984, had built a strong market presence based on its reputation for innovation in household and commercial appliances. In addition, Arthur Martin in France and Zoppas in Norway had strong local brand position but limited innovative capability. As a result of these acquisitions, Electrolux had accumulated a patchwork quilt of companies, each with a different product portfolio, market position, and competitive situation. Johansson soon recognized the need for an overall strategy to coordinate and integrate his dispersed operations.

Talks with national marketing managers quickly convinced him that dropping local brands and standardizing around a few high-volume regional and global products would be unwise. He agreed with the local managers that their national brands were vital to maintaining consumer loyalty, distribution leverage, and competitive flexibility in markets that they saw fragmenting into more and more segments. But Johansson also understood the views of his division staff members, who pointed to the many similarities in product characteristics and consumer needs in the various markets. The division staff was certain Electrolux could use this advantage to cut across markets and increase competitiveness.

Johansson led a strategy review with a task force of product-division staff and national marketing managers. While the task force confirmed the marketing managers' notion of growing segmentation, its broader perspective enabled Johansson to see a convergence of segments across national markets. Their closer analysis also refined management's understanding of local market needs, concluding that consumers perceived "localness" mainly in terms of how it was designed or what features it offered. From this analysis, Johansson fashioned a product-market strategy that identified two full-line regional brands to be promoted and supported in all European markets. He positioned the Electrolux brand to respond to the cross-market segment for high prestige (customers characterized as "conservatives"), while the Zanussi brand would fill the segment where innovative products were key (for "trendsetters").

The local brands were clustered in the other two market segments pinpointed in the analysis: "yuppies" ("young and aggressive" urban professionals) and "environmentalists" ("warm and friendly" people interested in basic-value products). The new strategy provided Electrolux with localized brands that responded to the needs of these consumer groups. At the same time, the company captured the efficiencies possible by standardizing the basic chassis and components of these local-brand products, turning them out in high volume in specialized regional plants. So, by tracking product and market trends across borders, Leif Johansson captured valuable global-scale efficiencies while reaping the benefits of a flexible response to national market fragmentation. What's more, though he took on the leadership role as a strategist, Johansson never assumed he alone had the understanding or the ability to form a global appliance strategy; he relied heavily on both corporate and local managers. Indeed, Johansson continued to solicit guidance on strategy through a council of country managers called the 1992 Group and through a set of product councils made up of functional managers. . . .

Newly developed business strategies obviously need coordination. In practice, the specialization of assets and resources swells the flow of products and components among national units, requiring a firm hand to synchronize and control that flow. For organizations whose operations have become more dispersed and specialized at the same time that their strategies have become more connected and integrated, coordination across borders is a tough challenge. Business managers must fashion a repertoire of approaches and tools, from simple centralized control to management of exceptions identified through formal policies to indirect management via informal communication channels. Leif Johansson coordinated product flow—across his

35 national sales units and 29 regional sourcing facilities—by establishing broad sourcing policies and transfer-pricing ranges that set limits but left negotiations to internal suppliers and customers. For instance, each sales unit could negotiate a transfer price with its internal source for a certain product in a set range that was usually valid for a year. If the negotiations moved outside that range, the companies had to check with headquarters. As a coordinator, Johansson led the deliberations that defined the logic and philosophy of the parameters; but he stepped back and let individual unit managers run their own organizations, except when a matter went beyond policy limits.

In contrast, coordination of business strategy in Johansson's division was managed through teams that cut across the formal hierarchy. Instead of centralizing, he relied on managers to share the responsibility for monitoring implementation and resolving problems through teams. To protect the image and positioning of his regional brands—Electrolux and Zanussi—he set up a brand-coordination group for each. Group members came from the sales companies in key countries, and the chairperson was a corporate marketing executive. Both groups were responsible for building a coherent, pan-European strategy for the brand they represented. To rationalize the various product strategies across Europe, Johansson created product-line boards to oversee these strategies and to exploit any synergies. Each product line had its own board made up of the corporate product-line manager, who was chair, and his or her product managers. The Quattro 500 refrigerator-freezer, which was designed in Italy, built in Finland, and marketed in Sweden, was one example of how these boards could successfully integrate product strategy.

In addition, the 1992 Group periodically reviewed the division's overall results, kept an eye on its manufacturing and marketing infrastructure and supervised major development programs and investment projects. Capturing the symbolic value of 1992 in its name, the group was chaired by Johansson himself and included business managers from Italy, the United Kingdom, Spain, the United States, France, Switzerland, and Sweden. . . .

The building blocks for most worldwide companies are their national subsidiaries. If the global business manager's main objective is to achieve global-scale efficiency and competitiveness, the national subsidiary manager's is to be sensitive and responsive to the local market. Country managers play the pivotal role not only in meeting local customer needs but also in satisfying the host government's requirements and defending their company's market positions against local and external competitors.

The need for local flexibility often puts the country manager in conflict with the global business manager. But in a successful transnational like Electrolux, negotiation can resolve these differences. In this era of intense competition around the world, companies cannot afford to permit a subsidiary manager to defend parochial interests as "king of the country." Nor should headquarters allow national subsidiaries to become the battleground for corporate holy wars fought in the name of globalization.

QUESTIONS

1. What type of headquarters-subsidiary relationship did Johansson establish?
2. Did he nurture corporate culture across the firm's subsidiaries? If so, how?

Notes

1. John J. Keller, "AT&T to Give Foreign Units More Autonomy," *The Wall Street Journal,* December 13, 1993, p. A3.

2. Cited by Stephanie Overman, "Going Global," *HRM Magazine,* September 1993, pp. 49–50.

3. Keller, "AT&T to Give Foreign Units More Autonomy," p. A4.

4. P. Dwyer et al., "Tearing up Today's Organization Chart," *Business Week/21st Century Capitalism,* p. 81 (1994 Special Issue).

5. Brendan R. Schlender, "Matsushita Shows How to Go Global," *Fortune,* July 11, 1994, p. 162.

6. Dwyer et al., "Tearing up Today's Organization Chart," p. 90.

7. John Dupuy, "Learning to Manage World-Class Strategy," *Management Review* (October 1991): 40.

8. The factors contained in Table 12–1 are adapted from Richard D. Robinson, *Internationalization of Business: An Introduction* (New York: The Dryden Press, 1984), pp. 268–269.

9. Sumantra Ghoshal and Nitin Nohria, "Horses for Courses: Organizational Forms for Multinational Corporations," *Sloan Management Review* (Winter 1993): 28.

10. Ibid.

11. Geert Hofstede, *Culture's Consequences: International Differences in Work-Related Values* (Beverly Hills, CA: Sage, 1980).

12. Cited by Geert Hofstede, "Motivation, Leadership, and Organization: Do American Theories Apply Abroad?" *Organizational Dynamics* (Summer 1980): 60.

13. J. R. Weisz, F. M. Rothbaum, and T. C. Blackburn, "Standing out and Standing in— The Psychology of Control in America and Japan," *American Psychologist* 39 (1984): 955–969.

14. R. N. Bellah et al., eds., *Individualism and Commitment in American Life* (New York: Harper & Row, 1987).

15. W. G. Ouchi, "The Relationship Between Organizational Structure and Control," *Administrative Science Quarterly* 22 (1987): 95–113.

16. Weisz et al., "Standing out and Standing in."

17. Leah Nathans, "A Matter of Control," *Business Month,* September 1988, pp. 46–52.

18. R. N. Kannungo and R. W. Wright, "A Cross-Cultural Comparative Study of Managerial Job Attitudes," *Journal of International Business Studies* 14(2) (1983): 115–129.

19. Cited by Hofstede, "Motivation, Leadership, and Organization," p. 60.

20. S. G. Redding and D. S. Pugh, "The Formal and the Informal: Japanese and Chinese Organizational Studies," in S. R. Clegg, D.C. Dunphy, and S. G. Redding (eds.), *The Enterprise and Management in East Asia* (Hong Kong: Center for Asian Studies, 1986).

21. K. H. Chung, "A Comparative Study of Managerial Characteristics of Domestic, International, and Governmental Institutions in Korea." Paper presented at the Midwest Conference of Asian Affairs, Minneapolis, Minn., 1978; W. S. Nam, *The Traditional Pattern of Korean Industrial Management* (ILCORK working paper No. 14, Social Science Research Institute, University of Hawaii, 1971); G. W. England and R. Lee, "Organizational Goals and Expected Behavior Among American, Japanese, and Korean Managers: A Comparative Study," *Academy of Management Journal* 4 (1971): 425–438; J. Harbron, "Korea's Executives Are Not Quite the New Japanese," *The Business Quarterly* 44 (1979): 16–19.

22. R. H. Solomon, *Mao's Revolution and Chinese Political Culture* (Berkeley, CA: University of California Press, 1971).

23. Geert Hofstede, "The Cultural Relativity of the Quality of Life Concept," *Academy of Management Review* 9(3) (1984): 389–398.

24. R. E. Caves, "Industrial Organization, Corporate Strategy and Structure," *Journal of Economic Literature* 18 (1980): 64; M. Haire, E. Ghiselli, and L. W. Porter, *Managerial Thinking: An International Study* (New York: John Wiley, 1966); D. J. Hickson et al., "The Culture Free Context of Organization Sructure: A Tri-National Comparison," *Sociology* 8 (1974): 59–80.

25. Ghoshal and Nohria, "Horses and Courses: Organizational Forms Multinational Corporations."

26. Ibid.

27. H. Aldrich, *Organizations and Environments* (Englewood Cilffs, NJ: Prentice-Hall, 1979); L. Greiner, "Evolution and Revolution as Organizations Grow," *Harvard Business Review* (July–August 1972): 41.

28. Thomas Hout, Michael E. Porter, and Eileen Rudden, "How Global Companies Win Out," *Harvard Business Review* (September–October 1982): 103.

29. Ibid.

30. P. R. Lawrence and J. W. Lorsch, *Organization and Environment: Managing Differentiation and Integration* (Cambridge, MA: Division of Research, Graduate School of Business Administration, Harvard University, 1967).

31. "Decentralizing for Comptitive Advantage," *Across the Board* 31 (January 1994): 26.

32. R. E. Miles, C. C. Snow, and J. Pfeffer, "Organization Environment: Concepts and Issues," *Industrial Relations* 13 (1974): 244–264; K. Weick, *The Social Psychology of Organization* (Reading, MA: Addison-Wesley, 1969); R. F. Zammuto, "Growth, Stability, and Decline in American College and University Enrollments," *Educational Administration Quarterly* 19(1) (1983): 83–89.

33. M. Yasai-Ardekani, "Effects of Environmental Scarcity and Munificence on the Relationship of Context to Organizational Structure," *Academy of Management Journal* 32(1) (1989): 131–156.

34. Excerpted from Brian O'Reilly, "J&J Is on a Roll," *Fortune*, December 26, 1994, pp. 178–192; and Joseph Weber, "A Big Company That Works," *Business Week*, May 4, 1992, p. 125.

35. Kenichi Ohmae, "Planning for a Global Harvest," *Harvard Business Review* (July–August 1989): 136.

36. W. C. Kim and R. A. Mauborgne, "Making Global Strategies Work," *Sloan Management Review* (Spring 1993): 11.

37. Ibid.

38. G. Hofstede et al., "Measuring Organizational Cultures: A Qualitative and Quantitative Study Across Twenty Cases," *Administrative Science Quarterly* 35 (1990): 286–316, 311.

39. Ibid., p. 312.

40. Charlene M. Solomon, "Transplanting Corporate Cultures Globally," *Personnel Journal* (October 1993): 80–81.

41. Ibid.

42. Ibid.

43. Regina Fazio Maruca, "The Right Way to Go Global: An Interview with Whirpool CEO David Whitwan," *Harvard Business Review* (March–April 1994): 139.

44. Gurcharan Das, "Local Memoirs of a Global Manager," *Harvard Business Review* (March–April 1993): 38.

VIII

Part Eight

INTERNATIONAL
ETHICS

In international business, a great deal of attention has been paid in recent years to business ethics and corporate social responsibility. International companies are increasingly being held accountable for the contributions they make to society, as well as to the extent their employees adhere to an appropriate code of ethical conduct. Thus, in the future, international business managers will be expected to address crucial social issues in a preventive manner and to maintain a high standard of ethical behavior. Such attention, however, has been mainly in the United States. Even though other advanced nations have made some progress in this area, there still exists a considerable gap between the United States and the rest of the industrialized world. Chapter 13 addresses the topic of cross-national business ethics and social responsibility.

Chapter 13
Cross-National Ethics and Social Responsibility

459

Chapter Thirteen

Cross-National Ethics and Social Responsibility

In the Third World, many nations—and their bribe-takers—have never known life without bribery. Countries such as Indonesia, Malaysia, China, India, Nigeria and Thailand are known for having government officials that are easily bribable. "In the U.S., the social lubricant is alcohol," says [A Rushdi] Siddiqui [an international trade lawyer]. "In many Third World nations, it's gifts." Sometimes these gifts can be as much as 10% of the cost of the project.[1]

Objectives of the Chapter

When managers of corporations begin to formulate strategy to conduct business across nations, they must possess a thorough understanding of their firms' views on business ethics and social responsibility, as well as the views of each nation in which the firm wishes to transact business. Views on what is ethical or unethical in business transactions vary from company to company, as well as from country to country. For example, the practice of bribery in business transactions is acceptable in many countries, and in many situations it is expected and needed to supplement a low-wage structure, while in some countries it is unacceptable and illegal. And in the United States, managers must understand that under the U.S. Foreign Corrupt Practices Act (FCPA) of 1977 it is illegal to practice the act of bribery not only in the U.S., but in other countries as well, even if it is an acceptable business practice there.

Views on what actions denote corporate social responsibility also vary from company to company, as well as from country to country. For example, some executives feel that they must not be judgmental and should adhere to countries' varying views. Following this view, an executive of a U.S. multi-national corporation (MNC) would hire female managers at home because it is the right thing to do, but would not do so for the firm's operations in Saudi Arabia. This is because in Saudi Arabia it is not an acceptable practice to hire female managers for most jobs.[2] Others feel that there should be a universal guideline; MNCs should apply one view on social responsibility in all nations. Therefore, adhering to this view, the executive of the U.S. MNC would hire female managers in Saudi Arabia—which conflicts with Saudi Arabia's views. Dealing with conflicting ethical norms between home and host country, as well as defining and applying social responsibility in cross-national settings, is thus a huge problem confronting the managers of MNCs. Therefore, the objectives of this chapter are to:

1. Describe what ethics are, including legality and social acceptability.
2. Examine the considerations and complications in complying with foreign ethical practices.
3. Examine some of the events leading to the passage of the FCPA.
4. Examine the impact of the FCPA on MNCs.
5. Discuss social responsibility in a cross-national context.

CROSS-NATIONAL ETHICS

Some business people believe that what is **ethical or unethical** is governed by the legality of the situation and by the social aspects of the situation (what members of the society generally accept as being **"right" or "wrong"**). For example, if it is illegal to practice the act of bribery in a country, and a firm's manager bribes someone there to obtain a favor, it would be unethical, and the violator could be prosecuted under the law. And if **bribery** is not illegal in a country, but it is known to be generally **socially unacceptable**, it would be unethical to practice it; the violator would be punished not by formal law, but by informal means, such as by negative publicity and/or by customers boycotting the firm's product or service.

Regarding the social aspects of the situation, many cultures establish informal ethical principles or moral standards that define "right" and "wrong" conduct. However, what is right or wrong is difficult to define conclusively and agree upon in any culture—for example, in the U.S., some Americans believe legal abortion is right, others think it is wrong. And what is right or wrong is far more difficult to define conclusively and agree upon among the different cultural environments throughout the globe. This is because different societies are confronted with different opportunities and constraints, and to cope, each society develops a unique culture and standard of ethics. As result, what is right and wrong may differ dramatically from one culture to another. This means that managers of MNCs will often find themselves with conflicting ethical responsibilities; that is, one's own nation's standard of ethics often collides with those of other nations. For example, the practice of bribery in business transactions is acceptable in Thailand, but not in the United States. An American executive transacting business in Thailand would thus be confronted with conflicting ethical responsibilities.

In part because of these conflicting ethical responsibilities, the actions of many U.S. MNCs have been subjected to considerable criticism, which in turn has led to a wide range of negative consequences, such as bad publicity, consumer boycotts, lawsuits, and government intervention, such as the passage of the Foreign Corrupt Practices Act (to be discussed later in this chapter).

BRIBERY AND PAYOFFS ABROAD

An investigation in the early 1970s by the U.S. Securities and Exchange Commission (SEC) into illegal corporate contributions to President Nixon's campaign fund discovered that many corporations had made substantial illegal contributions during the 1972 presidential election campaign. Subsequent investigations in 1976 and 1977 by the SEC revealed that instances of undisclosed, questionable, or illegal corporate payments, both domestic and foreign, were widespread—major MNCs regularly made **"payoffs"** abroad to foreign government officials and politicians in the course of conducting business.[3] The SEC investigation generated other investigations by the Senate Foreign Relations Committee, the Internal Revenue Service (IRS), and the departments of Defense and State (Department of Defense corporations had been a major source of payoffs abroad). These investigations, too, revealed that many U.S. MNCs regularly made questionable or illegal payments to foreign government officials and politicians in order to secure business.

The difficulties and pressures MNCs face in conducting business with foreign government officials and politicians were presented in testimony before a U.S. Senate Foreign Relations Subcommittee by then chairman of Gulf Oil Corporation, Bob R. Dorsey. Mr. Dorsey described his dealings with then finance chairman of South Korea's Democratic Republican Party, S. K. Kim: "He (S. K. Kim) happens to be as tough a man as I've ever met. I have never been subjected to that kind of abuse."[4] When Mr. Kim first approached Mr. Dorsey, his demand was $1 million. Later, Mr. Kim demanded $10 million from Mr. Dorsey in the form of a campaign contribution to his political party. Mr. Dorsey said, "He (Kim) left little to the imagination as to what would happen to Gulf's $300 million investment, most of it in refining and petrochemicals, if the company would choose to turn its back on the request."[5] Mr. Dorsey haggled the $10 million extortion demand by Mr. Kim down to $3 million, making it a total of $4 million to save $300 million in assets in South Korea.[6]

Another case that helps illustrate the difficulties and pressures MNCs face in transacting officials and politicians involved Exxon in Italy. Italy is noted for a government and political system in which approvals, permits, and licenses are issued extremely slowly, and perhaps disapproved, when payments (called *bustarella*) are not made to the proper officials. Exxon had large refineries in Italy producing oil products for sale in Italy and in the entire European Union. Between 1963 and 1972, Exxon admitted making payments of over $29 million to Italian political parties. In the wake of the ongoing SEC investigation into such foreign payments, Exxon suspended any further payments to Italian political parties. Subsequently, rate increases requested by Exxon during the period when OPEC was drastically raising the price of crude oil were ignored. As a result, the once profitable Exxon subsidiaries in Italy generated large losses.[7]

The investigations caused many board members of MNCs to become concerned about their exposure and liability to lawsuits brought by stockholders. U.S. Internal Revenue Service officials were concerned about the apparent laxity of independent auditing firms in pointing out such questionable and many times sizeable payments. And the SEC felt that "when a company receives substantial benefits as a result of a payoff or, if its continued operations are subject to extortion, investors are entitled to know."[8] Assertions were made at the time that "the SEC had embarked on a typical American exercise in ethnocentrism—imposing its own moral judgements on foreign governments and U.S. international corporations."[9]

Forms of Bribery

Basically, a bribe can be defined as *a payment in any form (cash or gift) for the purpose of influencing action by a government official in order to obtain or retain business.* Bribes can be classified as "whitemail bribes" or as "lubrication bribes."

Whitemail Bribes

Whitemail bribery refers to payments made to induce an official in a position of power to give favorable treatment where such treatment is either illegal or not warranted on an efficiency, economic benefit scale. Fundamentally, a key point in this type of bribery is that the payment be intended to induce the official "to do or omit doing something in violation of his lawful duty, or to exercise his [or her] discretion in favor of the payor's request for a contract, concession, or privilege on some basis other than merit."[10] These payments, when exposed, can lead to scandals, fines and so on. Payments of this nature have historically been "buried" in the books of MNCs, or concealed in some other ways. (Practical Perspective 13–1 presents some illustrations of whitemail bribes.)

PRACTICAL PERSPECTIVE 13–1

Wandering into Ethical No-Man's Land

When American business people ventured abroad, a common view is that they're wandering into an ethical no-man's land, where each encounter holds forth a fresh demand for a "gratuity," or baksheesh. William C. Norris, who founded and for many years headed Control Data Corporation, says, "No question about it. We were constantly in the position of saying how much we were willing to pay" to have a routine service performed overseas. Norris recalls frequently facing situations such as: "The computer is on the dock, it's raining, and you have to pay $100 to get it picked up. . . ."

In South America, firms often face a "closed bidding system" when dealing with that region's large, nationalized companies, says John Swanson, a senior consultant of communications and business conduct at Dow Corning Corporation. He says that his company has been locked out of the South American market at times because it refused to pay the bribes necessary to get that business.

In Japan, bids for government construction jobs are routinely rigged, according to one former U.S. government official who asked to remain anonymous—a result of Japanese firms purchasing "influence" from politicians. Donald E. Peterson, former chairman and chief executive officer of the Ford Motor Company, cites ethical challenges in much of the developing world. "Give me a military dictator with absolute power, and it doesn't matter if he's South American or African or Asian—you've got problems."

Source: Excerpted from Andrew W. Singer, "Ethics: Are Standards Lower Overseas?" *Across The Board*, September 1991, p. 31. Copyright © 1991, Conference Board, Inc., New York. Reprinted with permission. All rights reserved.

Lubrication Bribes

This type of bribe is typically described as payment to facilitate, expedite, or speed up routine government approvals or other actions to which the firm would legally be entitled. Such payments are generally made to minor officials, for example, to custom agents or licensing clerks. Another trait of **lubrication bribes** is that the amounts are generally smaller than whitemail bribes, although there have been cases where large lubrication-type payments were made. The number and acceptability of the practice of lubrication bribes is much greater than that of whitemail bribes. Officials in many Third World countries are especially noted for requiring "grease" in order to make their political and administrative wheels turn. Somewhat similar to waiters or waitresses in America who receive a low salary and rely on customers' tips to supplement their income, in many countries, numerous officials receive a low salary and rely on "grease" payments to supplement their income.

Extortion

A distinction can be made between bribery an extortion. Bribery is offered by an individual or a corporation seeking an unlawful advantage, while **extortion** is force exerted in the other direction—an official seeking payment from an individual or corporation for an action to which the individual or corporation may lawfully be entitled. Gulf Oil's dilemma in South Korea is an example of extortion.

To Bribe or Not to Bribe?

When a manager crosses a nation's borders to conduct or negotiate business, he or she will sometimes be confronted with the need to decide whether or not to practice the act of bribery. Figure 13–1 presents some questions whose answers can help international executives make such a decision. Figure 13–2 presents a perspective on how to conduct business legally in foreign countries.

The U.S. Foreign Corrupt Practices Act of 1977

The revelations by the SEC and Senate Foreign Relations subcommittee investigations of U.S. MNCs' "whitemail bribery" practices abroad, and the concern for the negative image such practices generated for the U.S., helped plant the seed that eventually produced U.S. Senate Bill 305, the **Foreign Corrupt Practices Act (FCPA).** (See Practical Perspective 13–2.) The FCPA was passed and signed into law in 1977. Its purpose was twofold:

1. To establish a worldwide code of conduct for any kind of payment by United States businesses to foreign government officials, political parties, and political candidates.
2. To require appropriate accounting controls for full disclosure of firms' transactions.

The law applies even if such payments are common practice (viewed as an ethical practice) in the country where they are made. Some of the basic provisions of the FCPA are as follows:

| Questions to Determine Whether or Not to Bribe | FIGURE 13–1 ◆ |

Legal Questions

1. What are the legal consequences in the parent country?
2. How comprehensive is the law of the host country? What is the enforceability of its law?
3. Will the corporation be liable to its competitors for financial damages (such as unfair practice, restraint of trade)?
4. Will the company be held liable by stockholders in the host or parent country?

Moral Questions

1. What is the company's policy regarding overseas payoffs? Will it cause any deviation from standard practice?
2. If the questionable payment is disclosed, will it damage the public image of the company in the parent country?
3. Will the payoff activity affect employee morale of the company at home or overseas?
4. What is the custom in the host country?
5. Does the public opinion of the host country carry the same weight as it does in the parent country?

Economic Questions

1. How does the expected gain compare with the company's total earnings?
2. What is the cost of payoff as a percentage of total revenue? Is it a one-time payment or a periodic contribution?
3. Is the company diversified in many countries?
4. Will the payoff trigger other host countries to make the same demand?
5. Will the payoff action cause retaliation from competitors?

Personal Questions

1. Will top management find out about the payoff? If so, am I subject to censure?
2. Am I likely to be held personally liable for such action?
3. Does the company carry insurance to pay my legal fees if I am found guilty of violating a law?
4. Will disclosure of payoff harm my reputation and make it difficult to obtain or retain a management position in the future?
5. How would my family and friends react to disclosure of such activity?

◆ FIGURE 13–2   **Conducting International Business Legally**

◆ Rigorously learn about the culture, the business practices and the laws of your host country—not just the customs and niceties. Talk with others who have done business there and with local lawyers. Contact the area group that represents American and indigenous interests, often a local chamber of commerce with a joint agreement with the U.S. Chamber of Commerce. Seek out the commercial attaché in the U.S. embassy.

◆ Hire a local journalist to do a comprehensive local media search. Do not rely solely on the U.S. business press. You need to know how much attention is being paid to corruption and if criminal charges have ever been brought—in short, how seriously bribery and corruption are regarded in your host country.

◆ Perform a due diligence investigation of everyone who will work for the company as an agent, representative, distributor, licensee and joint venture partner. Examine the reputation, especially honesty. Enter into a specific contract delineating the person's responsibilities as they pertain to company policies and the Foreign Corrupt Practices Act. The person must sign a detailed statement promising not to engage in bribery. This prudent step could lessen both your company's liability and your personal liability.

◆ For all managers: Clearly enunciate your corporate policies regarding bribery and U.S. law to your employees with direct and indirect sales responsibilities overseas. Restate them often—annually, at least. Each time, employees should complete and sign a detailed worksheet and a declaration that they have read and understood the policies; they know these papers go into their dossiers.

Source: Barbara Ettorre, "Why Overseas Bribery Won't Last," *Management Review* (June 1994): 24.

◆ It is a criminal offense for a firm to make payments to a foreign government official, political party, party official, or candidate for political office in order to secure or retain business in another nation.

◆ Sales commissions to independent agents are illegal if the business has knowledge that any part of the commission is being passed to foreign officials.

◆ Government employees whose duties are essentially ministerial or clerical are excluded, so expediting payments to persons such as customs agents and bureaucrats are permitted. (Thus, the FCPA does not apply to small "lubrication" bribes.)

◆ In addition to the antibribery provisions that apply to all businesses, all publicly held corporations that are subject to the SEC are required to establish internal accounting controls to assure that all payments abroad are authorized and properly recorded.[11]

The penalty levied on the business enterprise for not complying with the FCPA was set at $1 million for each count. The penalty levied on individual members of the corporation found guilty of making the illegal payment is a fine of up to a $10,000 and/or five years imprisonment, with the added provision that the firm may not pay or reimburse the employee for the fines levied on them. Thus, the FCPA calls for both civil and criminal penalties.

Enforcement of the FCPA was assigned to two federal agencies: the SEC and the Department of Justice. The SEC's responsibility included enforcement of the record keeping and accounting control provisions of the FCPA, and civil authority to enforce the prohibitions against foreign bribery by U.S. publicly held corporations. The Department of Justice was given the responsibility to enforce the criminal penalties for corporate bribery of foreign officials, and the authority to bring civil actions against domestic concerns whose securities are not registered with the SEC.

Over the years, numerous companies have been fined. For example, in the late 1980s, Young & Rubicam Inc., the New York-based advertising agency, and three of its executives were indicted on a conspiracy charge under the FCPA. The U.S. government contended that the firm had "reason to know" that one of its Jamaican agents was paying off that country's Minister of Tourism to obtain advertising business. In order to avert a lengthy trial, the corporation paid a $500,000 penalty, says R. John Cooper, vice president and general counsel of Young & Rubicam. And several years ago, Control Data Corporation was prosecuted by the U.S. government under the FCPA for making payments in Iran. In 1978, Control Data Corporation pleaded guilty to three criminal charges that it made improper payments to unnamed foreign officials. It was fined $1,381,000 by the U.S. Customs Services.[12]

Complaints from MNCs Over the FCPA

The major areas of concern communicated by U.S. multinational corporations over the FCPA were as follows:

- ◆ The FCPA placed them at a competitive disadvantage because companies from other countries, as well as from the host country, were not bound by the FCPA laws, and could continue making whitemail payments to secure business, thus putting them at a competitive advantage. (See Practical Perspective 13–3.)
- ◆ The accounting burden of internal controls, along with the vagueness of this section of the law, make the MNCs' duty and liability difficult to assess.
- ◆ MNCs complain that the FCPA forces them to become political tools of the U.S. government because they have to exert its will in the world through their economic power.

PRACTICAL PERSPECTIVE   13–2

The Murky Land of the FCPA

The Foreign Corrupt Practices Act (FCPA) became law in 1977, in the wake of foreign bribery scandals involving U.S. companies that shook the governments of Belgium, the Netherlands, Honduras, Italy, and Japan. One of the most notorious incidents involved an estimated $25 million in concealed payments made overseas by Lockheed Corporation in connection with sales of its Tristar L-1011 aircraft in Japan. This culminated in the resignation and subsequent criminal conviction of Japanese Prime Minister Kankuie Tanaka.

The FCPA, which makes it a crime for U.S. corporations to bribe officials of foreign governments to obtain or increase business, is controversial, in part, because it seeks to forge a distinction between "bribes" (which it deems illegal) and "gratuities" (which the FCPA permits). The difference is murky, according to the FCPA's critics.

"The law marked the difference between gratuities paid to low-level officials and payments made to authorities," writes Duane Windsor in his book, *The Foreign Corrupt Practices Act: Anatomy of a Statute.* "In many countries a payment to a customs official is a matter of course and a matter of economic necessity. A customs official may backlog an order or hinder a shipment by elaborately checking each imported item. The detrimental effect to the shipment is obvious. In response, lawmakers sought to delineate gratuities and bribes very clearly. But in reality the delineation of gratuities was so vague that some people felt it had a chilling effect [on business]."

Source: Excerpted from Andrew W. Singer, "Ethics: Are Standards Lower Overseas?" *Across The Board,* September 1991, p. 33. Copyright © 1991, Conference Board, Inc., New York. Reprinted with permission. All rights reserved.

Furthermore, a report issued in 1978 by the Export Disincentives Task Force, created by the White House to find ways of improving the negative balance of trade between the U.S. and other nations, pointed to the FCPA as being potentially harmful. This statement, which was made one year after passage of the FCPA, was based on interviews with executives of U.S. MNCs who claimed that their firms lost export business because of compliance with the FCPA.

PRACTICAL PERSPECTIVE   13-3

Can We Litigate Morality?

Passed in the late '70s in the wake of the Watergate [the investigation that lead to President Richard M. Nixon's resignation] and the overseas bribery scandals, the Foreign Corrupt Practices Act (FCPA) made it a felony for U.S. companies to obtain business by paying off foreign government officials. From its inception, the FCPA has been controversial. "Managers in other countries often chuckle at the United States hoping to export its morality in the form of the Foreign Corrupt Practices Act," says Gene Laczniak, management professor at Marquette University in Milwaukee.

"It's anachronistic in today's world," says William Norris, the former Control Data [Corporation] chief. "It's like the antitrust laws in many ways. The world has passed it by." [The antitrust laws] worked fine as long as the U.S. economy was an isolated system, say critics. But now antitrust laws may be inhibiting large U.S. firms from competing in the international arena. In any case, says Norris, most U.S. companies don't want to become involved in activities such as bribing foreign officials.

R. John Cooper, executive vice president and general counsel of Young & Rubicam Inc., makes a similar argument. The FCPA was enacted at a time when the competitive position of U.S. companies in the world was stronger—than it is today, Cooper points out. In 1970, the United States was the source of 60 percent of the world's direct foreign investment. By 1984, according to the United Nations, that figure dropped to 12 percent. Japanese, European, and East Asian firms have picked up much of the slack, launching economic forays even into America's own backyard. The United States risks becoming economically hamstrung by statutes such as the Foreign Corrupt Practices Act, suggests Cooper. "We have to reexamine some of these high-toned notions." According to Cooper, with increasingly heated international competition, the act is out of date. It puts too much of a burden on U.S. corporations to know everything about their foreign agents—a burden not shouldered by foreign competitors.

Yet another problem with the FCPA was that it was not too clear with respect to the use of foreign subsidiaries to transact business. For example, Boeing Corporation sold its planes abroad through a distributorship, Overseas International Distributors Company, which was registered as a Netherlands company, but doing business out of Geneva. Overseas International Distributors bought planes from Boeing after obtaining orders for the aircraft from officials in the Middle East. Finally, many MNCs saw the FCPA as landmark legislation could beget more legislation, thus hindering the ability of the U.S. MNCs to deal effectively in the global marketplace. Overall, many U.S. MNCs saw the FCPA as another stumbling block to an already complex situation of competing in the global arena.

1988 Amendments to the FCPA

In early 1981 and again in early 1983, the U.S Senate attempted to repair some of the uncertainties associated with the FCPA. The Senate's proposed amendments were rejected by the House of Representatives. The amendment finally passed as a section of the Omnibus Trade and Competitiveness Act of 1988. The amendment clarifies various provisions of the FCPA, consolidates most of the enforcement responsibilities for bribery violations into the U.S. Department of Justice, and increases the civil and criminal penalties for violating the FCPA. Relative to the accounting aspects of the FCPA, the amendment limits future criminal liability to intentional actions to circumvent the internal accounting control system or falsify the corporation's books. With respect to payments made through third parties, the amendment eliminates the "reason to know" standard and modified the "knowing" standard. Under the act, "knowing" is defined to entail the substantial certainty or conscious disregard of a high probability that the third-party payment will become a bribe.[13]

Relative to enforcement of the FCPA, the amendment increased the civil and criminal penalties for violations. Criminal penalties were increased from $1 million to $2 million for corporations, and from $10,000 to $100,000 for individuals. The maximum imprisonment remained five years. A civil penalty of $10,000 for individuals was established and may not be paid by the corporation. All jurisdictions for enforcing the antibribery provisions of the FCPA were consolidated within the Department of Justice. The SEC remained responsible for civil enforcement of the records and internal accounting control provisions of the FCPA.[14]

An Alternative Payoff Approach

Many international executives do not view the FCPA as hindering their competitiveness in the global marketplace. (See Practical Perspective 13–4.) These executives enhance their competitiveness by improving their enterprises' technical expertise, their customer service, and their responsibility to

PRACTICAL PERSPECTIVE 13–4

Keeping the Cutting Edge Sharp

Because the Foreign Corrupt Practices Act has been such an entrenched influence, many U.S. companies have ceased to regard it as a stumbling block. "I've never had a manager say, 'We can't do business because we're limited by the Foreign Corrupt Practices Act,' " says Raymond V. Gilmartin, chairman, president and CEO of Becton Dickinson and Company and board chairman of the Ethics Resource Center. "We are not at a competitive disadvantage at all."

It would seem so. A manufacturer of medical devices and diagnostic systems and supplies, the New Jersey-based company generates 44 percent of its $2.6 billion in revenues from overseas. In 1985, that figure was 25 percent. Gilmartin says foreign sales are growing twice as fast as domestic. But Gilmartin is the first to say that any company doing business beyond America's borders has to keep sharply focused on doing the lawful thing.

Before, echoing the thoughts of many U.S. companies, Becton Dickinson felt it was "an ethical company with ethical employees," Gilmartin says. "We said we wanted to do the right thing, but it became clear that we must use training and reinforcement." Accordingly, Becton Dickinson is using interactive workshops for the first time—small group exercises and case studies that train employees to recognize ethical dilemmas and to work them through. The company is also revising its written code of conduct, making it more "understandable, readable and practical," says Gilmartin. "I've also made it clear in speeches that in no way do we want you, the employee, to compromise your personal integrity. But we are going beyond that. We are serious. We are giving recognizable managerial support."

When doing business abroad, Gilmartin says, an aggressive approach works best. A company should "make it clear right upfront" to any prospective foreign client that it doesn't give payoffs. "If our principles seem to preclude us from certain business, we'll forego this opportunity—but we won't give up," he states. "We will try other avenues."

Source: Excerpted from Barbara Ettoree, "Why Overseas Bribery Won't Last," *Management Review* (June 1994): 22. Copyright © 1994, American Management Association, New York. Reprinted with permission. All rights reserved.

PRACTICAL PERSPECTIVE   13–5

Tolerance of Bribery by Countries Overseas Is Waning

There are signs that the tolerance of bribery by countries overseas is waning, even as experts caution that the practice is still widespread. "There have been some reforms, but bribery is at a level that is still unacceptable," says Michael Slattery Jr., an investigator at Kroll Associates, an international investigation firm. Nevertheless, U.S. professionals who deal with foreign nationals report that emerging business and government classes around the world are gradually adopting a new attitude. These educated people—many of them seeking democratization in their home countries—are coming to regard bribery as ultimately ruinous to their economies.

Robert McNamara, former head of the World Bank, has stated that democratization of countries, growing intolerance of their citizenry toward illicit payments and increased media scrutiny have produced a climate more conducive to address bribery seriously than at any time in the past 40 years. The Clinton Administration has put bribery on the international agenda by urging industrial nations to adopt strict antibribery laws comparable to those of the United States. It has put the issue before the Organization for Economic Cooperation and Development

(OECD), whose 26 member nations comprise 16 percent of the world's population and two-thirds of its goods and services. There have also been high-level private initiatives against bribery with widespread international support.

The trouble is, some American business executives and expatriate consultants have not gotten the message. They are mired in old thinking, even as they regard foreign competition as having an automatic edge or as they ignore admonitions that bribery is no longer necessary or desirable to conduct business. Consider China. There are two ways for foreign companies to do business there—legally, by dealing directly with the appropriate ministry and avoid agents, or illegally, by hiring an agent, usually a relative of the minister. The former takes longer; the latter moves more quickly when payments help smooth the red tape. Notably, Chinese nationals say there is a more important result: Once a company has gotten business via illegal payments, it is difficult to shed the image of corruption. Expectations have been created, and it is almost impossible for a company to get out from under a corrupt reputation.

"As we look to do business in China, we're investigating our advisors," says Raymond V. Gilmartin, chairman, president and CEO of Becton Dickinson and Company. Gilmartin says the company is seeking outside consultants and China hands who have reputations for honesty and who counsel foreign companies that they don't have to bribe to get business. . . . Experts say that, because of insensitivity to gradually changing attitudes, it is just a matter of time before a major U.S. company will be embarrassed by another big bribery scandal. . . . North Americans at home and abroad "seem to be largely of the opinion that the world operates as it always has—that the Asia Pacific region is a corrupt environment," says Gary Edwards, president of the Ethics Resource Center, a nonprofit Washington consultancy with extensive contacts overseas. Edwards says that Americans feel the way to do business there is "through agents and intermediaries willing and able to pay the necessary bribery" to secure business.

"This contrasts with some Asian nationals who are telling us that in many of their markets, that's not necessary," Edwards continues. "The practice is increasingly viewed as unacceptable and destructive to their economies." He says that with advent of such global media as Cable News Network, citizens abroad see how business is done ethically in other countries and realize that bribery usually is an established practice in underdeveloped nations. Lynn Paine, an associate professor specializing in management ethics at the Harvard Business School, notes that foreign nationals participating in her management seminars and roundtables are "so much more vocal these days" about their efforts to clean up corruption at home. "In the mid-'80s, I rarely heard anyone saying that developing countries would resent [bribery]," Paine continues. "Now, they are asking for respect. A lot of participants say you don't really have to bribe. . . ." She goes on to say, "Many countries are learning from their own experience. You cannot build trust if you have corruption, and you cannot build economic enterprise unless you have trust."

the customer through quality. Furthermore, there are indications that the practice of bribery is not as widespread as it once was; it seems to be waning (see Practical Perspective 13–5). And when these executives must make some sort of payment to obtain a favor, they do not pay "private individuals"; instead, they make payments to institutions, such as contributions to build schools, hospitals, medical clinics, or agricultural projects.[15] Payments of this nature obtain favors and goodwill for the MNC; they also improve the local situation, such as by increasing local employment. This payment approach, thus, does not improve only one person's bank account; instead, the payment is shared with the community.

CROSS-NATIONAL SOCIAL RESPONSIBILITY

Social responsibility has been defined as "the notion that corporations have an obligation to constituent groups in society other than stockholders and beyond that prescribed by law or union contract."[16] Corporate social responsibility therefore means that a firm's actions must take into account not only the well-being of the stockholders, but also the well-being of the community, the employees, and the customers. Figure 13–3 presents the **ten commandments of corporate social responsibility.** With respect to MNCs' cross-national social responsibility, many international business executives condone the concept of cultural relativism, while others condone the concept of universalism.

Cultural Relativism

Cultural relativism holds that "no culture's ethics are any better than any other's."[17] Under this standard there are no international "rights" or

---

◆ FIGURE 13–3   The Ten Commandments of Social Responsibility

    I. Thou Shall Take Corrective Action Before It Is Required.
    II. Thou Shall Work with Affected Constituents to Resolve Mutual Problems.
    III. Thou Shall Work to Establish Industrywide Standards and Self-Regulation.
    IV. Thou Shall Publicly Admit Your Mistakes.
    V. Thou Shall Get Involved in Appropriate Social Programs.
    VI. Thou Shall Help Correct Environmental Problems.
    VII. Thou Shall Monitor the Changing Social Environment.
    VIII. Thou Shall Establish and Enforce a Corporate Code of Conduct.
    IX. Thou Shall Take Needed Public Stands on Social Issues.
    X. Thou Shall Strive to Make Profits on an Ongoing Basis.

Source: Larry D. Alexander and William F. Matthews, "The Ten Commandments of Corporate Social Responsibility," *Business and Society Review*, 50 (Summer 1984): 62–66.

"wrongs." Thus, if Thailand tolerates the bribery of public officials, then Thai tolerance is no worse than American or German intolerance. If Switzerland is liberal with respect to insider trading, then Swiss liberalism is no worse than American restrictiveness.[18] These executives would therefore not support the FCPA.

But the concept of cultural relativism can backfire. For example, suppose a U.S. corporation invents a product and patents it. Patent piracy is wrong (and illegal) in the U.S., but it is not wrong in some nations (and if it is illegal, culturally, it is not enforced). What if a company in one of these countries pirated the patent? Would the executives in the company from which the patent was pirated simply write the loss off as, "Oh well, that's culture?" As illustration, some enterprises in China readily pirate U.S. firms' copyrighted computer software, movies, and music and put phony American labels on consumer products (see Practical Perspective 13–6). If the American pirated firms' executives adhered to the cultural relativism concept, they would not complain about the Chinese firms' pirating practices because they are not viewed as being unethical in China. However, U.S. trade representatives are currently (1995) applying strong pressure on Chinese government officials to implement and enforce policies that preclude Chinese enterprises from undertaking such activities.[19] Suppose also that a U.S. MNC is manufacturing in Bangladesh using cheap child labor. Use of child labor in such a way is not tolerable in America, but it is tolerable in Bangladesh. What happens to the MNC when the U.S. press gets hold of the information and promulgates it among the U.S. public? Will it result in a boycott? It therefore seems that the concept of cultural relativism is often not very practical.

Universalism

On the other hand, the concept of **universalism**, a rigid global yardstick by which to measure all moral issues (for example, the FCPA), is often not very practical either. This is because its application would show disrespect for valid cultural differences and different economic needs. For example, people in the U.S. do not tolerate manufacturing facilities that disperse health-damaging smog. Under the concept of universalism it would be unethical to transfer such manufacturing facilities to another country. But in countries where people are starving, economic development may be more important than health, and such manufacturing facilities would thus be welcome. A manager guided by the cultural relativism view would export such manufacturing facilities to the starving country. But, as mentioned above, it is likely to backfire.

For example, U.S.-based Union Carbide established gas production facilities in Bhopal, India. In its U.S. plants, Union Carbide was required by the government to install expensive accident-prevention systems. The government of India did not require such systems. In the 1980s, an accident at the

PRACTICAL   PERSPECTIVE   13–6

The Risks Are Rising in China

China's flagrant piracy of American pop music, movies, and computer software is more than the biggest rip-off in global commerce. It's also the latest evidence of the growing and increasingly visible risks confronting Western and Asian companies doing business in the People's Republic. None of these risks— galloping inflation (21% last year), erratic policy shifts, rampant corruption, a penchant for treating contracts like disposable Kleenex tissues, or the immediate prospect of even greater turmoil following the demise of 90-year-old supreme leader Deng Xiaoping—are new. Nor do they undercut the long-term logic driving businesses to stake a claim in what could within 15 years become the world's largest market. In the past two years, U.S. corporations have poured nearly $4.3 billion into China. What could well slow the flow of that investment are the prominence of companies running into trouble, the size of their potential losses, and growing awareness of just how deeply rooted China's problems are.

McDonald's, for instance, is being evicted from its prime site in Beijing despite a 20-year lease that has 17 years left to run. Lehman Brothers is suing two state corporations for failing to pay nearly $100 million of losses in foreign-exchange trading. And a group of Japanese, German, and Italian banks has been reduced to begging Beijing to make good on some $600 million of defaulted loans they made to state enterprises.

Nowhere are the stakes bigger—or less amenable to a quick lasting solution—than the current U.S.-China dispute over heisted copyrights. More than a trade war, think of this fight as a clash of civilizations. The new American economy, with its edge in handling information technology, confronts an ambitious Asian giant with a voracious appetite for capital, know-how, and export markets—and a primitive legal system that lacks almost any concept of the Western notion of intellectual property. Says Kenneth DeWoskin, a University of Michigan business school professor and China specialist: "Most Chinese do not understand the notion of intangible assets like brands or copyrighted material. We're in for a long siege on these issues."

Beijing would have a hard time fixing the situation if it wanted to: It has devolved economic power upon the provinces, which control the pirate factories and the courts. Further complicating matters, senior politicians, military men, and their families are often involved in the pirating industries. Says Howard Lincoln, chairman of Nintendo of America: "We have evidence that government officials have ownership stakes in companies doing the counterfeiting." One of the most egregious violators of Nintendo's copyright is state-owned Tianjin New Star Electronic Co., whose president heads a department in the Ministry of Electronics and Machinery. New Star has even sought to raise equity capital in the U.S. to expand its illegal operations.

Showbiz products such as Madonna recordings and Mickey Mouse films grab the spotlight, but intellectual property of corporations with manufacturing plants in China is equally at risk. To get into the PRC, companies must disclose to authorities details of their products and processes. Says DeWoskin: "Chinese research and design institutes look for the best technology in the country and spread it around. They also examine plans and specifications of new ventures, so there's bound to be some leakage."

Indeed, after DuPont introduced into China its Londax herbicide, which curbs weeds in rice fields, it decided in 1992 to open a $25 million plant in Shanghai to make the product. By then state-owned Chinese competitors had jumped into the market with cheaper knockoffs of DuPont's weed killer. Shortly after Pilkington opened a plant in China to make architectural glass, a state glass factory sent an order for production equipment to Germany—complete with detailed and obviously filched plans emblazoned with Pilkington's name. Johnson & Johnson, which got into China early to make prescription drugs, constantly has to ferret out counterfeit versions of its products. Smart investors are careful not to bring their latest technology into China.

Protecting a brand name in the China market often resembles a mission impossible. A bogus Chinese breakfast cereal product called Kongalu Cornstrips has a trademark and packaging identical to that of Kellogg's cornflakes. A small Chinese computer manufacturer, Mr. Sun, has appropriated the trademark of Sun Microsystems for its machines. And mineral water drinkers in China can enjoy Pabst Blue Ribon Water. As for videos, movies, compact disks, and computer software, virtually the entire Chinese market is a pirate's den because Beijing denies market access to most of the legal products. Nor is there much shame about the grand larceny, which costs U.S. companies more than $1 billion a year. According to a report issued by the U.S. Trade Representative's office, "Anyone can walk into a store in

Beijing and buy a pirated copy of Microsoft's popular widows software package. The store simply copies it onto a few blank floppy disks while you wait."

In plain sight of policemen, Chinese music fans can pick up on the streets of major cities the latest CDs by such artists as Whitney Houston, Billy Joel, and Kenny G—for the equivalent of $1.70. Though PRC authorities have staged a few raids on retailers, they have done nothing to stop 29 high-tech factories in southern and central China that can turn out a total of 75 million CDs annually for a market that absorbs only about five million disks. Much of their output is exported, robbing U.S. companies of sales in other markets. These flagrant violations of intellectual property is what prompted Mickey Kantor, the chief U.S. trade negotiator, to slap stiff tariffs worth some $1 billion on Chinese products. In the trade equivalent to a surgical airstrike, however, the U.S. targeted such items as cellular phones, fishing rods, and bicycles, which would hurt the PRC without causing pain for American companies

and consumers. The Chinese retaliated with rhetoric about defending their "national dignity" and retaliatory tariffs that also would have little real effect. Example: China threatens to impose punitive import duties on U.S. cigarettes, most of which are smuggled into the PRC anyway.

The crisis atmosphere has at least sent everyone back to the bargaining table. . . . Can a solution emerge? Optimists point to Taiwan. Only a dozen years ago that island nation harbored a vigorous underground export industry that skillfully copied leading global brands. A visitor could buy good-looking knockoffs of Rolex watches in the back streets of Taipei. The counterfeiting abated once Taiwanese companies developed their own intellectual property and thus a deeper appreciation of its value. Given time and a few more knocks in the game of global trade, the Chinese too should eventually come to see piracy as more expensive than it's worth. Until then, expect it to remain one more reason to cast a cautious eye on China's red-hot but risky market.

Bhopal plant killed over 3,000 people and injured thousands of others.[20] The press coverage of the Union Carbide incident was very negative. Many Americans felt that Union Carbide, knowing the dangers of not taking preventive measures, had a moral obligation to have taken them in India, even if India did not require them and could not afford them. These Americans thus adhere to the concept of universalism. On the other hand, many Americans adopted the concept of cultural relativism—they felt that Union Carbide did not have the right to interfere with Indian government matters.

Thus, developing, implementing, and controlling cross-cultural business ethics and social responsibility programs is an enormous challenge confronting the managers of MNCs. The problem is enlarged by the press sometimes persuading MNCs to impose their social responsibility on their manufacturing subcontractors. For example, Starbucks Coffee has agreed to adopt a "code of conduct" that must be adhered to by its coffee suppliers and may help workers in Guatemala and other Third World nations. Starbucks' management made the decision after stores in British Columbia, Canada and the U.S. were targeted in a February, 1995 leafletting blitz. The protesters were concerned about "harsh working conditions, paltry pay and human rights violations on Guatemalan coffee plantations."[21] (As an illustration, read Practical Perspective 13–7.) The press therefore often asks MNCs to reject the concept of cultural relativism and apply the concept of universalism.

PRACTICAL   PERSPECTIVE   13–7

The Supply Police

Home Depot desperately wants to avoid a new strain of public-relations disaster. The Christmas-week NBC show asserting that Wal-Mart's "Buy American" program misleads consumers also leveled a more sinister charge: that children as young as 9 churn out clothes for the nation's largest retailer in Bangladeshi sweatshops. Other big-name U.S importers aren't waiting to see whether the public buys Wal-Mart's denials. Instead they're making sure their own suppliers are free of environmental, human rights or other potential embarrassments. The supplier police had better hurry. Jeff Fiedler, the AFL-CIO official who helped NBC mug Wal-Mart, says that he's drawing beads on a dozen new targets, including apparel and dress-shoe companies.

Suddenly, "going global" invites a hazard nobody mentioned back in B-school. Activists pushing a variety of causes have discovered that exposing corporate exploitation will accomplish what tamer strategies, such as leafleting annual meetings, have not. Scrutiny by labor unions, activists and socially conscious investors is forcing importers to monitor not just their foreign subsidiaries but their far-flung network of independent suppliers—and their suppliers' as well. Says Donna Katzin of the Interfaith Center on Corporate

Responsibility, "Just because companies don't make a product themselves doesn't relieve them of all obligations. . . ."

Is it fair to hold Third World suppliers to U.S. standards of conduct? Even many of those who say it is admit to ambivalence about imposing their values on countries and companies halfway around the world. "It's easy to take cynical views of American corporations," says Northwestern University business ethicist David Messick. "But what gives us the right to decide at what age people in Bangladesh should work?" . . . To which image-conscious executives might answer: why take risks? As the Wal-Mart case demonstrates, even perceived transgressions can lead to big embarrassment. . . .

Several companies have made pre-emptive strikes to avoid similar pratfalls. Last March, Sears said it wouldn't import forced-labor products from China. Phillips-Van Heusen explicitly threatens to terminate orders to apparel suppliers that violate its broad ethical, environmental and human rights code. And Dow Chemical asks suppliers to conform not just to local pollution and safety laws, but to the often tougher U.S. standards. At least one major U.S. company acted merely to stamp out falsehoods: persistent rumors that McDonald's suppliers grazed their cattle on cleared rainforest land finally led it to ban the practice in writing. Executives may well take the increased scrutiny as a sign of an antibusiness conspiracy.

But three distinct types of tactics are now evident. Socially conscious investors and mainstream religious groups promote the positive message that companies should extend their own high standards to all their business partners. Environmentalists and other activists tend toward the more direct pressure that comes from naming names. Union officials are taking a more investigative approach to locate human rights and other violations, including schemes in which foreign manufacturers, especially in China, circumvent U.S. textile quotas by misidentifying the country in which their goods were made. Unions have approached a number of companies about these issues; most pledges to enforce appropriate rules and have avoided negative publicity.

Exasperated importers say they can't possibly patrol the world. For openers, there is no central repository of information about exporters. "How can you know what's happening in Bangladesh when everyone between here and there has reason to lie?" says John Schultz, president of Ethical Investments, which helps bleeding-heart investors pick stocks. Some charges of misbehavior reach the United States through regional groups like Hong Kong's Committee for Asian Women, which exposes beatings and other factory abuses. But in a global market of component parts, generic goods and layers of middlemen, it's hard to keep score. "I can't control the factory that supplies my supplier," says Russell Berrie, whose New Jersey company is a big buyer of trinkets from China. . . .

How can importers behave honorably—or at least watch their backs? The model of aggressive enforcement is Levi Strauss & Co., which last March laid down tough standards of conduct to its 600 suppliers worldwide. After inspecting each one, the company ditched about 30 suppliers and exacted reforms from an additional 120. Levi Strauss also pulled out of Myanmar, citing that government's pervasive human rights violations. And in Bangladesh, where factories routinely employ youngsters under the legal age of 14, the company struck a bargain to protect 40 children who would have been fired under its new rules. That could have impoverished entire families. Instead Levi Strauss will help to educate the kids while local suppliers pay them regular wages until they turn 14.

Separating right from wrong overseas doesn't guarantee a company high praise at home. Just ask Nike, which ran afoul of cultural relativism late in 1992. *Harper's* magazine printed a U.S. labor activist's dissection of a pay stub for an Indonesian woman; she netted the equivalent of $37.46 a month for making sneakers. Later, an article in the *Far Eastern Economic Review* reported that Indonesians who make Nikes earn far more than most workers lucky enough to get jobs in the impoverished country. "American focus on wages paid, not what standard of living those wages relate to," says Nike's Dusty Kidd. But such argument misses the point. When it comes to social responsibility, it's not enough for a company to be right. It also has to convince its increasingly touchy customers.

TOWARD THE GLOBALIZATION OF BUSINESS ETHICS

The American approach to business ethics is unique. In comparison with other capitalistic societies, it is more individualistic, legalistic, and universalistic.[22] In other words, issues of business ethics are far more visible in the United States than they are in other capitalistic societies. This may be because there are far more laws regulating business in the U.S. than there are in other capitalistic countries. Therefore, the American public reads and hears far more about business misconduct than do people in other countries. Hence, the "ethics gap" between the United States and the rest of the developed world is considerably large.[23]

Some strides toward closing the ethics gap have been made in Europe and, on a much smaller scale, in Japan. In 1987, a group of 75 European business executives and academics established the European Business Ethics Network (EBEN), and the first European business journal, *Ethica Degli Affari,* was published in Italy. Since the mid-1980s, ethics research centers have been established in Britain, Belgium, Spain, Germany, and Switzerland. In 1989 and 1991, the Institute of Moralogy sponsored international ethics conferences in Kashiwa City, Chiba Ken, Japan.[24] Notwithstanding, as pointed out above, a considerably large ethics gap between the U.S. and other advanced nations still exists.

The Impact of Culture on the Business Ethics Visibility Gap

America is one of the most individualistic cultures in the world. As it was indicated in earlier chapters, people's decisions in individualistic cultures tend to be guided by self-interests, as opposed to group interests. On the other hand, managers in group-oriented cultures tend to reflect less their personal moral guidance and more their shared understanding of the nature and scope of the corporation's responsibilities—and the enterprise's moral expectations are shaped by the norms of the community, not the personal values and reflections of the individual.[25] This helps explain why there are far more laws regulating business in the U.S. than there are in other advanced nations, and it helps explain why there is such a large business ethics gap between the U.S. and other nations.

This suggests that globalization of business ethics (application of the concept of universalism) is far away and that the concept of cultural relativism still prevails. Thus, as the integration of the global economy increases, effective international managers develop a "better appreciation of the differences in the legal and cultural context of business ethics between the United States and other capitalist nations, and between Western and Asian economies as well."[26]

SUMMARY

This chapter discussed cross-national ethics and social responsibility. It proposed that certain business practices, such as bribery, are viewed as unethical in some cultures, but ethical in others. The practice of bribery and "payoffs" by numerous U.S. MNCs led to the passage of the Foreign Corrupt Practices Act of 1977. Managers of many MNCs complained that the act, because it precluded them from bribing or "paying off" officials in foreign countries to obtain "favors," even if it was an acceptable practice in the country, put them at a competitive disadvantage with foreign competitors who were not bound by the act. The chapter also discussed cross-national corporate social responsibility. It proposed that some international executives condone the concept of "cultural relativism," which holds that no culture's ethics are any better than any other's; that there are no international "rights" or "wrongs." It was suggested that the practice of cultural relativism often backfires. Some international executives condone the concept of "universalism," which holds that there should be a global yardstick by which to measure all moral issues. This approach often leads to a show of disrespect for valid cultural differences. The media often influence MNCs to reject cultural relativism and apply the concept of universalism. There is a large business ethics gap between the U.S. and other advanced nations; Americans are exposed to far more business misconduct issues than are people in other advanced countries.

Key Terms

1. Ethical or unethical; "right" or "wrong"
2. Bribery
3. Socially acceptable or unacceptable
4. "Payoffs"
5. *Bustarella*
6. Whitemail bribes; lubrication bribes
7. Conflicting ethical responsibilities
8. Extortion
9. The Foreign Corrupt Practices Act
10. Cross-cultural social responsibility
11. Cultural relativism; universalism
12. The ten commandments of corporate social responsibility
13. Business ethics gap
14. Business ethics visibility gap

Discussion Questions and Exercises

1. How do some business people make a determination on what is ethical or unethical?
2. Why is it a problem to define what is ethical or unethical across cultures?
3. What is meant by "conflicting responsibilities"?
4. Differentiate between "whitemail" and "lubrication" bribes, and extortion.
5. Why do so many international business people pay lubrication bribes?
6. What was the major purpose of the Foreign Corrupt Practices Act?

7. What were some of the major complaints from U.S. international executives over the Foreign Corrupt Practices Act?

8. The top management of a U.S. MNC has decided to build a manufacturing facility in a city in country X. A city bureaucrat in country X has approached the executive responsible for implementing top management's decision. The bureaucrat informed the executive that a permit to build in the city is extremely difficult to obtain and it is a very lengthy process; that he has "a friend" on the city council who, for U.S. $200,000, would be able to get the council to issue the permit immediately. It is important to the top management that the permit be issued, and that, for competitive reasons, it be issued as fast as possible. Time is thus very important to the MNC. You are the executive. What would you do?

9. With respect to cross-national social responsibility, what are the potential negative consequences of the practice of cultural relativism and universalism?

10. From a social responsibility perspective, what are the potential negative consequences associated with home-country corporations using manufacturing subcontractors abroad?

11. Why is there a relatively large business ethics gap between the U.S. and other advanced nations?

Assignment

Contact an international executive in a MNC and ask him or her to describe his or her company's policy pertaining to cross-national ethics and social responsibility. Prepare a short report to be shared with the class.

Bribery and Extortion in International Business

CASE 13–1

Source: Louis T. Wells, Jr., Harvard Business School, Harvard University. Used with permission.

The following caselets have been disguised, but reflect actual events with which I [Louis T. Wells, Jr.] am familiar or which have been reported in the press.

1. You are in charge of trying to secure a contract for the sale of U.S. telecommunications equipment worth about $40 million to the communications and transport ministry of a Latin American country with a military government. European firms are also eager for the contract. Quality differences in the products of the various suppliers are not important. A local accountant, who has helped you with government negotiating in the past, suggests to you that the company might receive the contract if it were to be willing to deposit $2 million in the Swiss bank account of the general in charge of the ministry.

2. You are responsible for negotiating with an African government the terms under which your company would build and operate a battery plant in the country. You have U.S. counsel and know a local law firm with two Harvard-trained principals. However, other Americans who have successful investments in the country suggest that you hire the local Speaker of the House, who is a lawyer, to help represent you in the negotiations. You are aware that the House must eventually approve the agreement you negotiate.

3. Your U.S. company has a major petroleum investment in a non-Arab oil country. All foreign investors have been notified that their contracts (covering taxes, royalties, and so on) will be reviewed in the light of events in other countries. A lawyer, who is the brother of the vice president, offers his services to your firm in the upcoming renegotiations. The proposed fees are about 25% higher than those that might be asked by a U.S. law firm.

4. You have just been put in charge of a U.S. subsidiary in a developing country and have discovered that the previous manager has been paying $40 to immigration officials each time the residence permit of U.S. employees is to be extended There is no official basis for the charge and it has been paid each time in cash. You are told other foreign companies and even private U.S. foundations pay similar fees.

5. You are a vice president for international operations of a U.S. company. One of your new managers of a rapidly expanding subsidiary in a developing country reports the following experience: A tax collector visited the firm with a bill for the firm's annual income tax. Although the bill seemed a bit high, based on the accounts earlier submitted to the government, the manager told the collector that he would authorize a check to the Treasury. The collector pointed out that the total due could be discussed and he was sure that some less costly arrangement could be worked out. The manager replied that he prefered to accept the Treasury's calculation and had a check made out. Two weeks later, the manager receives a registered letter from the collector saying that an error had been made and that the company owed about 35% more. A bill was enclosed, but the letter mentioned that the tax collector would be happy to discuss the matter further.

6. You are the U.S. manager of a local subsidiary in a developing country. As you are leaving the country for a brief visit to headquarters, the clerk at the counter for the local airline you are using points out that you have overweight luggage. (This was not a surprise to you, since you are carrying home Christmas presents for your and your wife's families, but you know some international airlines have dropped the weight limit or would simply over-look the small amount of excess weight.) You ask the charge and hear that it is $75. When you look hesitant, the clerk suggests that $5 might actually take care of the matter.

7. You are on a consulting trip to a Latin American country and discover a very fine suit in a smart downtown shop. You ask about the price and discover that it is 9000 pesos. The clerk explains that that would be $75, if you will pay in dollars You realize that it is $300 at the official rate of exchange that you encountered at the airport and at banks.

8. The American manager of one of your Latin American subsidiaries has been kidnapped by a leftist political group. You are informed that he will be released unharmed if you will have your company run an ad in the local newspaper presenting the group's criticism of the government in power, if you will provide $100,000 of food for distribution to the poor, and pay $1 million in ransom to the group. You discover that the ransom payment would be illegal in the country.

QUESTIONS

1. What would you do in each of the above cases?
2. Why?

America's New Merchants of Death

CASE 13–2

Source: William Ecenbarger, "America's New Merchants of Death," *Reader's Digest* (Canadian version), April 1993, pp. 85–92. Reprinted with permission from the April 1993 *Reader's Digest.* Copyright © 1993 by the Reader's Digest Assn., Inc.

In Germany three women in black miniskirts set up a display table beside a Cadillac in the centre of Dresden. In exchange for an empty pack of local cigarettes, they offer passersby a pack of Lucky Strikes and a leaflet that reads: "You just got hold of a nice piece of America. Lucky Strike is the original . . . a real classic." Says German physician Bernhard Humberger, who monitors youth smoking: "Adolescents time and again receive cigarettes at such promotions."

◆ A Jeep decorated with the yellow Camel logo pulls up in front of a high school in Buenos Aires. The driver, a blond woman wearing khaki safari gear, begins handing out free cigarettes to 15-and 16-year-olds on their lunch recess.

◆ In Malaysia a man responds to a television commercial for "Salem High Country Holidays." When he tries to book a trip, he is refused by the office manager, who later admits that the $2.5 million-a-year operation exists only to advertise Salem on TV. This promotes Salem cigarettes without technically breaking the law.

◆ At a video arcade in Taipei, free American cigarettes are strewn atop each game. "As long as they're here, I may as well try one," says a pony-tailed high-school girl in a Chicago Bears T-shirt. Before the United States entered the Taiwanese cigarette market, such giveaways were uncommon at spots frequented by adolescents.

A *Reader's Digest* investigation covering 20 countries on four continents has revealed that millions of children are being lured into nicotine addiction by American cigarette makers. In several nations U.S. tobacco companies have been fighting legislation that curtails cigarette use by minors and are cleverly violating the spirit of curbs on advertising. Their activities clearly show a cynical disregard for public health. But the most shocking finding is that children are being seduced into smoking in the name of America itself. In some countries tobacco companies never would have gained a foothold without the help of a powerful ally: the U.S. government.

Although sales in the United States have dropped for eight years straight, and by the year 2000, only one in seven Americans will likely smoke, sales elsewhere have more than tripled since 1985. Smoking rates in the Third World are climbing more than two percent a year. Most alarming is the rise in youth smoking. In the Philippines 22.7 percent of people under 18 now smoke. In some Latin American cities, the teenage rate is an astonishing 50 percent. In Hong Kong, children as young as seven are smoking. Why are the young so important? Because millions of adult smokers either kick their habit or die each year, the cigarette industry depends on attracting new customers. Most smokers begin between ages 12 and 16; if a young person hasn't begun by 18, he or she is unlikely ever to smoke.

"Tobacco is a growth industry, and we are gaining in volume and share in markets around the world," Philip Morris assured stockholders in its 1991 annual report. "Growth prospects internationally have never been better," gushed Dale Sisel, chief executive officer of R.J. Reynolds (RJR) Tobacco International, at last summer's international tobacco conference in Raleigh, N.C. "We all produce and sell a legal product that more than one billion consumers around the world use every single day."

Unmentioned at the conference was the fact that smoking is one of the leading causes of premature death, linked to cancers of the mouth, lung, esophagus, kidney, pancreas, bladder and cervix, as well as to heart disease. Or that according to the World Health Organization, tobacco will prematurely kill 200 million who are now children and eventually wipe out 10 percent of the world's population. This grim prospect is due in no small part to the spectacular U.S. invasion of overseas markets. More than 50,000 medical studies have demonstrated these hazards. Yet the tobacco gurus assembled at Raleigh referred to the "debate" and "controversy" over smoking.

"People need to know precisely how American companies and their government are promoting smoking among the world's children," says Dr. Carlos Ferreyra Nunez, president of the Argentine Association of Public Health. "If they knew the full story, I believe they would stop this outrage."

Here is that story.

PERVASIVE INFLUENCE

Developing countries are unusually vulnerable to cigarette advertising. Until recently some of them sold tobacco only through government monopolies, with little or no attempt at persuasion. And because most of these countries don't have effective antismoking campaigns, many of their people are surprisingly innocent of the link between tobacco and disease. In Manila we even found cigarettes sold at a snack bar operated by the local Boy Scouts. Many governments, moreover, are reluctant to wage antismoking wars because they're addicted to tobacco taxes. Argentina gets 22.5 percent of its tax revenue from tobacco; Malawi, 16.7 percent.

Into this climate of naivete and neglect, U.S. tobacco companies have unleashed not only the marketing wizardry that most Americans take for granted but other tactics they wouldn't dare use in the U.S. market.

In Malaysia, *Gila-Gila,* a comic book popular with elementary-school students, carried a Lucky Strike ad. Teenagers going to rock concerts or discos in Budapest are regularly met by attractive women in cowboy outfits who hand them Marlboros. Those who accept a light on the spot also receive Marlboro sunglasses.

Tobacco advertising is more pervasive in many other parts of the world than in the United States. African merchants can get their shops painted to look like a pack of Marlboros. The Camel logo adorns taxis and store awnings in Warsaw. Christmas trees in Malaysian discos are trimmed free by Kent— with balls and stars bearing the Kent logo. In Mexico one in five TV commercials is for cigarettes. On an average day, 60 spots for American brands appear on Japanese TV, many of them during programs watched by teens.

Although their marketing budgets are secret, tobacco companies have bolstered their spending for international advertising, adding substantially to the $4 billion allocated yearly for the United States. "It's crucial for them," says Richard Pollary, professor of marketing at the University of British Columbia. "Familiarity in advertising breeds trust." Tobacco spokesmen insist that cigarette advertising draws only people who already smoke. But an ad executive who worked until recently on the Philip Morris account, speaking on condition of anonymity, disagrees. "You don't have to be a brain surgeon to figure out what's going on. It's ludicrous for them to deny that a cartoon character like Joe Camel is attractive to kids."

Dr. John L. Clowe, president of the American Medical Association, says: "It is clear that advertising fosters tobacco use among children. And despite tobacco-industry denials, ads like Joe Camel are especially appealing to adolescents, equating smoking with sexual prowess, athleticism, even success." Numerous independent studies support this view. They show that cigarette advertising creates an environment in which young people are more likely to smoke. That may explain why the U.S. Centers for Disease Control found that smokers between ages 12 and 18 prefer Marlboro, Newport and Camel—three of the most advertised brands.

"BRAND STRETCHING"

Like the United States and Canada, some of the progressive developing countries have banned cigarette commercials on TV and radio. This doesn't stop the tobacco companies, however. To keep their logos before the public, they resort to "brand-stretching"—advertising nontobacco products and services named after their brands. Most of these items have special appeal to young people: Marlboro jeans and jackets, for example. In Malaysia a music store called Salem Power Station wraps customers' tapes and CDs in plastic bags bearing the Salem logo, and television carries a rock-video show called "Salem Powerhits." A Budapest radio station broadcasts a rock program called the "Marlboro Hit Parade," and in China, Philip Morris sponsors the "Marlboro American Music Hour."

Rock concerts are especially effective. One of the live performances under tobacco sponsorship (Sales in Seoul) was by Paula Abdul, who is popular among teens. Stars who have appeared in televised concerts underwritten by the industry include Madonna (Sales in Hong Kong) and Dire Straits (Kents in Malaysia). Sports sponsorship is even more insidious, for it implies that smoking and fitness go together. Tobacco logos are blazoned on events of every description, from cycling in Morocco to badminton in Indonesia. There's the Salem Open Tennis Tournament in Hong Kong and the Kent International Sailing Regatta, to name just a couple. American tobacco companies spent $100 million sponsoring sports in 1992—double the 1985 total.

Tobacco companies regularly skirt laws against TV commercials. In Shanghai, Philip Morris airs spots for "The World of Marlboro" at the end of American sitcom reruns. Except that cigarettes aren't mentioned, the ad is identical to a Marlboro commercial: The Marlboro man and his horse splash across a stream, the man dismounts and gazes towards mountains that look like the Rockies. One of the most misleading forms of brand-stretching is the "travel" ad. In Thailand, where all cigarette advertising is forbidden, an ad appeared in the Bangkok *Post* for "Kent Leisure Holidays." It showed the company's logo and offered "A Pleasure Trip." A Thai doctor phoned to book the trip, but was turned down. He was told the cruise ship was in the Caribbean and wouldn't be in Bangkok for at least two years.

Unfortunately many of the children who succumb to brand-stretching find habits that begin as cobwebs end as steel cables. At a McDonald's in Malaysia, Sunil Ramanathan, 16, finishes off a Big Mac, lights a Marlboro and inhales deeply. He says he's smoked since he was ten. "I know smoking is bad for me, but I can't stop. I try to quit, but after one day I start again."

EASY ACCESS

Just off Taipei's bustling Keelung Road, high-school students begin filing into the Whisky A Go-Go disco about 9 p.m., and soon the room is a sea of denim. On each table are free packs of Salems. Before long, overhead fans are fighting a losing battle with the smoke. "American tobacco companies spend more than a quarter of a billion dollars every year giving away cigarettes, many of which are smoked by children and teenagers," says Joe Tye, editor of the newsletter *Tobacco Free Youth Reporter*. "If they can get a youngster to smoke a few packs, chances are he'll be a customer for life."

The companies say adult establishments such as discos cannot legally admit minors. The industry insists it instructs distributors of free samples to screen out the underaged. "It doesn't work," says Cecilia Sepulveda, a tobacco expert with Chile's Ministry of Public Health. "We estimate that 40 percent of 13-year-olds in Santiago smoke." Of seven under-18 students assembled at the Beltram High School in Buenos Aires, five say they have been offered free Camels. None was asked his age. One, Ruben Paz, 16, said he got his from a "blond, American-looking girl" handing out cigarettes from "the Camel Jeep" at the school door.

Young black-marketers hawk single cigarettes to their peers. Ten-year-olds in the tin-roofed kampongs of the Malaysian jungle can buy a Salem for eight cents. Students at the St. Ignatius School in Santiago buy cigarettes for ten cents at carritos, handcarts that also sell candy and soft drinks near the school. Although increasingly controlled in the United States, vending machines are used widely abroad. They were rare in East Germany, but since reunification U.S. and British companies have installed tens of thousands. In parts of Japan, machines sit on almost every corner.

SELL AMERICA

"Many African children have two hopes," says Paul Wangai, a physician in Nairobi, Kenya. "One is to go to heaven, the other to America. U.S. tobacco companies capitalize on this by associating smoking with affluence. It's not uncommon to hear children say they start because of the glamorous lifestyle associated with smoking." Cigarette advertising outside the United States focuses heavily on U.S. life-styles; indeed, the ads are seen as a way of learning about America itself. A letter from secretarial students in China appeared in the Petaluma, Calif., *Argus-Courier:* "Every day we listen to the 'Marlboro American Music Hour.' We enjoy Elvis Presley and Michael Jackson. We smoke American cigarettes and wear American clothes. We are eager to gain more information about American life."

To hear the children of the rest of the world tell it, everyone in America smokes. The truth is, the United States has one of the *lowest* smoking rates— 25.5 percent of the population. Yet because of U.S. advertising, American cigarettes are considered a gauge of style and panache. In Bangkok, Thai youths sew Marlboro logos on their jackets and jeans to boost their status. At the city's Wat Nai Rong High School, 17-year-old Wasana Warathongchai says smoking makes her feel "sophisticated and cosmopolitan, like America." She lumps Marlboros with "jeans and denim jackets, Pizza Hut, everything we like about America."

FRIENDS IN HIGH PLACES

The theme of last summer's Raleigh conference was "The Tobacco Industry to the Year 2000," and on hand were two experts from the U.S. Department of Agriculture to help the industry sell tobacco overseas. . . . Wait a minute.

Didn't the American government decide in 1964 that cigarettes are a major cause of death and disease, and doesn't the U.S. government discourage its own citizens from smoking? Then how can it encourage people of other nations to smoke? For many years Japan, Korea, Taiwan and Thailand imposed stern trade restrictions on imported cigarettes. But in the early 1980s, American tobacco companies joined forces with the Office of the U.S. Trade Representative (USTR) to crack these Asian markets.

The weapon Washington wielded was Section 301 of the Trade Act of 1974. It empowers the USTR to retaliate—with punitive tariffs—against any nation thought to have imposed unfair barriers on American products. In September 1985 the USTR began an investigation of Japanese trading practices. Senator Jesse Helms, from the tobacco-growing state of North Carolina, then stepped in on behalf of the tobacco industry. Helms dispatched a letter to Prime Minister Yasuhiro Nakasone, intimating he could not support a substantial U.S. defence presence in the Pacific or help stem the tide of anti-Japanese trade sentiment in Congress unless Japan opened its cigarette market.

"I urge that you establish a timetable for allowing U.S. cigarettes a specific share of your market," Helms wrote. "I suggest a total of 20 percent within 18 months." Three months later the Japanese government agreed to open its markets more. During this same period, tobacco companies enlisted two former aides to President Ronald Reagan—Michael Deaver and Richard Allen—as lobbyists. Deaver received $250,000 for pressing Philip Morris's case in South Korea and in a meeting with President Chun Doo Hwan. That country yielded to a Section 301 action in May 1988. By 1990 tobacco-industry clout had opened markets in Taiwan and Thailand.

The results have been devastating. Before the Americans arrived, smoking rates were declining slightly in Japan, but since 1987, cigarette consumption by minors has increased 16 percent. Among Taiwanese high school students, the smoking rate climbed from 19.5 percent in 1985 to 32.2 percent in 1987. Between 1988 and 1991, the number of Thai smokers ages 15 to 19 increased 24 percent, with similar increases for Korean high school boys. "We were making headway in discouraging smoking, but all has been washed away by the flood of American advertising," says David D. Yen, chairman of an antismoking group in Taiwan. "We want your friendship, but not your tobacco."

The U.S. cigarette business is booming. Exports are soaring, factories being built. And at the end of the rainbow lies China, with 300 million smokers—30 percent of the world market. "This vastly larger marketplace means a whole new world of opportunities," RJR's Dale Sisel told the Raleigh conference. Expansion abroad, he continued, would "pave the way for a bigger and brighter future." That kind of talk makes Argentina's Dr. Ferreyra Nunez quake with anger. "American tobacco companies know their product causes death. Yet they promote smoking among children. What must these people think? Don't they have children of their own?"

QUESTIONS

1. Are the cigarette companies behaving ethically?
2. Would you consider the free samples of cigarettes these companies give to teenagers in foreign countries a form of bribery? Please explain your answer.
3. Based on what you have learned in this chapter regarding cross-national social responsibility, are these MNCs behaving in a socially responsible fashion?
4. Do you believe this problem can be solved? What are your thoughts?

Notes

1. John Kimelman, "The Lonely Boy Scout," *FW,* (Fall 1994), p. 50.
2. Thomas Donaldson, "Global Business Must Mind Its Morals," *The New York Times,* February 13, 1994, p. F11.
3. O. Ronald Gray, "The Foreign Corrupt Practices Act: Revisited and Amended, *Business and Society,* Spring 1990, p. 11.
4. P. Nehemkis, "Business Payoffs Abroad: Rhetoric or Reality?" *California Management Review*, (Winter 1975): 13.
5. Ibid.
6. Ibid.
7. Ibid.
8. Ibid., p. 6.
9. Ibid.
10. W. A. Label and J. Kaikati, "Foreign Antibribery Law: Friend or Foe?" *Columbia Journal of World Business*, (Spring 1980): 46.
11. Gray, "The Foreign Corrupt Practices Act," p. 14.
12. Andrew W. Singer, "Ethics: Are Standards Lower Overseas?" *Across the Board,* September 1991, p .33.
13. Ibid., pp. 15–16.
14. Ibid., p. 16.
15. Kent Hodgson, "Adapting Ethical Decisions to a Marketplace," *Management Review* (May 1992): 56–57.
16. Donna J. Wood, "Corporate Social Performance Revisited," *Academy of Management Review* 16 (October 1991): 691–718.
17. Donaldson, "Global Business Must Mind Its Morals."
18. Ibid.
19. David E. Rosenbaum, "China Trade Rift with U.S. Deepens," *The New York Times,* January 29, 1995, p. 1.
20. R. C. Trotter, S. G. Day, and A. E. Love, "Bhopal, India and Union Carbide: The Second Tragedy," *Journal of Business Ethics* 8 (1989): 439–454.
21. Sarah Cox, "Starbucks Pours One for Coffee Workers," *Monday Magazine* (Victoria, B.C., March 16–22) 1995: 6
22. David Vogel, "The Globalization of Business Ethics: Why America Remains Distinctive," *California Management Review* 35, no.1 (Fall 1992): 30.
23. Ibid., pp. 35–37.
24. Ibid., p. 35.
25. Ibid., pp. 46–47.
26. Ibid., p. 49.

IX

P a r t   N i n e

INTERNATIONAL MANAGEMENT: A FUTURE PERSPECTIVE

It seems certain that the word "globalization" will continue to be used extensively, that companies will conduct their business activities in a highly interconnected world, and that in this "shrinking world" managers will need to reengineer organizations that can respond quickly to developments in foreign markets. Total quality management (TQM) is a managerial technique that many organizations are attempting to implement as a way of coping with these global changes. TQM, this chapter proposes, can be achieved only when the organization develops the ability to cater to customers' needs; monitor the internal and external environments on an ongoing basis to obtain and disseminate information needed by empowered group decision makers; establish and maintain an atmosphere where there is strong vertical and horizontal communication, collaboration, and cooperation

C h a p t e r   1 4
Total Quality Management and Implementation Challenges

among individuals in internal units, as well as among individuals in external units; develop and maintain a bond and a "sense of ownership" among employees; and develop and maintain ongoing training programs. Implementing such a program is a challenge to managers of any organization in any country, and it is even more challenging when they attempt to implement it across nations.

Chapter Fourteen

Total Quality Management and Implementation Challenges

New markets, rapid advances in communications, and new sources of brainpower and skilled labor are forcing businesses into their most fundamental reorganization since the multidivision corporation became standard in the 1950s. "We're talking about a new order, a sea of change, that will go on for the rest of my career," says [Richard J.] Callahan [CEO of U.S. West International]. "It's almost like Halley's Comet arriving unannounced." Senior managers are struggling to adapt themselves and their organizations to the 21st century business world that's rapidly taking shape. Boundaries will be even less important than they are today. The rate of technological progress will accelerate, with breakthroughs in biotechnology or digital electronics coming from such unexpected places as Israel, Malaysia, or China. At the same time, the huge demands of the new middle classes and their governments will revive such supposedly mature businesses as household appliances and power-plant construction. All this means that business opportunities will explode—but so will competition as technology and management know-how spread beyond brandname companies to new players in Asia and Latin America. Thriving in this fast-paced environment requires a new kind of company and a new kind of CEO. Just as much of the world is embracing a liberalized

497

economic model, so businesses of all stripes seem to be converging on a common management model to run their far-flung operations. Although that model is still a work in progress, the outlines of what is likely to be the early 21st century's world standard are beginning to take shape. This model will rely on Western-style accounting and financial controls, yet stress Japanese-style teamwork. It will value ethnic diversity, though less from high-mindedness than pragmatism. It will be centrally directed by multicultural, or at least cosmopolitan, executives who will set overall tone and strategy but give entrepreneurial local managers a long leash.[1]

Objectives of the Chapter

Within the past few decades, as suggested in previous chapters, many countries throughout the globe have made substantial progress toward achieving their industrialization objectives. As a result, intensive global competition has evolved, and it is expected to continue to intensify. Total quality management (TQM) is a tool or a management technique that numerous organizations have implemented, or are attempting to implement, to cope with these environmental changes. For example, recent evidence indicates that "80 percent of American Fortune 500 companies have undertaken major initiatives in quality. An equal percentage have formulated corporate strategies during the last seven years. The percentages are probably similar throughout the industrialized world."[2] The concept of quality has been discussed by numerous writers.[3] The term TQM has many meanings. In general, however, it refers to an organization having a long-term commitment to ongoing improvement of quality throughout its whole system, with all employees at all levels in all subunits and subsidiaries actively participating.[4] It also means an organization producing goods and/or services that meet or exceed consumers' expectations at the lowest possible cost,[5] as well as doing things right the first time.[6] According to quality management writer J. M. Juran, quality consists of two basic dimensions: "product performance that results in customer satisfaction" and "freedom from product deficiencies, which avoids customer dissatisfaction."[7]

The American Society of Quality Control supports the term "management of quality" to mean the activities that are generally associated with quality improvement in the organization.[8] Built into the TQM concept is the notion that all employees in the organization provide a service, not only to the external customer, but also to their colleagues. Therefore, the customer is anyone for whom a service is rendered—both inside and outside organizational boundaries.[9] The Baldrige Award also helps describe TQM. Building on the quality concept, the Baldrige Award was established in 1987 to provide a systematic national framework for assessing quality levels in U.S. companies. In Britain, the concept of quality is described by

British Standard 5750 and in the European Union by ISO 9000, and by such labels as quality improvement program (QIP), total customer delight (TCD), and total customer satisfaction (TCS). In Japan it is described by such labels as total quality control (TQC) and quality circles (QC).

Thus there are many definitions of TQM, but there does not seem to exist a general framework that defines the abilities (or characteristics) an organization must possess in order for TQM programs to be effective.[10] Many organizations fail in their attempts to implement TQM programs, and many of the successfully implemented TQM programs eventually failed because the companies were not able to maintain them. This suggests that "simply being aware of the new management paradigms or being willing to act on them will not produce competitive advantage. International competition demands not only a knowledge of what is required to be a global player, but also superior ability to implement that knowledge."[11] The objectives of this chapter are therefore to:

1. Describe a general TQM framework.
2. Describe the challenges/barriers managers face in implementing and in maintaining such a framework.

TOTAL QUALITY MANAGEMENT: A FRAMEWORK

As suggested above, **total quality management (TQM)** means an organization being more efficient and effective than its competitors. The ensuing sections propose that this can be achieved only if the organization attains and maintains the abilities described below (see Figure 14–1). It should be noted that, as it will be demonstrated, these abilities are all interdependent, and neglecting any one is thus likely to lead to ineffective TQM programs.

Responsive to Customer Needs

The effective TQM organization is culturally highly responsive to the needs of markets; it does not produce first, then find markets for its goods. Its managers ask: "What does the world really need that our company can and should provide?"[12] For example, Honda Motor Company, a Japanese firm that since 1948 has grown into a huge international corporation, places utmost importance on localization. According to its retired chairman Hideo Sugiura, localization means "developing, manufacturing, and marketing products best suited to the actual and potential needs of the customers and to the social and economic conditions of the marketplace."[13] Professors R. Blackburn and B. Rosen interviewed executives at organizations that have won the Baldrige Award in order to codify these organizations' human resource policies and practices. In discussing the Baldrige Award–winning

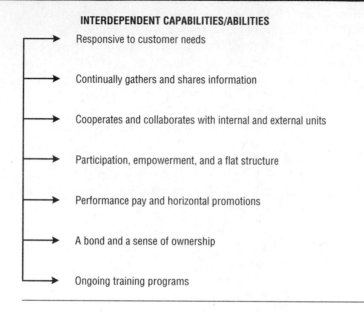

◆ FIGURE 14–1   **Characteristics of the TQM Organization**

companies, Blackburn and Rosen cite **customer satisfaction** as a characteristic of the TQM culture.[14] And, as cited earlier, the responsibility for customer satisfaction in a TQM organization must lie with all employees at all levels. It should be noted that the meaning of quality varies among countries, and even among people in countries. Many people are more concerned with **value** (the usefulness, desirability, or worth of a thing[15]) than with **quality.** As Jack Welch, General Electric's CEO, has observed,

> Everywhere you go, people are saying, "Don't tell me about your technology, tell me your price." To get a lower price, customers are willing to sacrifice the extras they used to demand. The fact is, many governments are broke, and people are hurting, so there is an enormous drive to get value, value, value.[16]

Continually Gathers Information

The above characteristic suggests that effective TQM organizations require the ability to gather vast amounts of information from many parts of the world. They must be able to obtain information about what customers or prospective customers want, where and when. To react effectively, they require information about their capabilities, as well as the ability to get the information to where it is needed. This means that effective TQM organizations have developed **cybernetic**[17] and **scanning**[18] systems to obtain and disseminate the needed information.

Cybernetic System

The concept of cybernetics includes such processes as information transmission, processing, and storage.[19] Basically, cybernetic behavior requires that a focal unit monitor internal occurrences on an ongoing basis, but not as much for the purpose of control as for the purpose of coordinating effective and efficient problem-solving/decision-making activities. For example, computer monitoring has often been used by managers to control and punish employees. At Hughes Aircraft, however, computer monitoring is used to gather information about production and quality strategy that provides needed information to a diverse team of workers.[20]

Scanning System

Scanning behavior involves monitoring the external environment. The term "environment" has been defined as the relevant physical and social factors outside the boundary of an organization which are considered during organizational decision making.[21] Environmental scanning should be a continuous process.[22] Analysis of the social, economic, technological, political and regulatory aspects of the global environment is ongoing. The analysis involves the examination of current and potential changes and the ways those changes affect the organization.[23] When a monitoring focal unit finds that the environment is dictating change, organizational transformation activities are initiated. Organizations that are unable to effectively scan and react to their environment are likely to decline when faced with more capable competition. It has been found that top-level managers in high-performance companies scan their environment more often and broadly in response to strategic uncertainty than do their counterparts in low-performance firms.[24] The performance of many of today's organizations thus relies on how effectively they respond to their external environment.[25]

For example, to help monitor the internal occurrences and the external technological environment and to nourish the domestic and international transfer of technology, Japan formed the Japan Industrial Technology Association at the macro level. This organization helps facilitate the dissemination and exchange of technical information between the Agency of Industrial Science and Technology research laboratories and foreign countries. It attempts to keep abreast of technological developments at home and abroad, and it facilitates the transfer of technical information and technology between the source and the potential user.[26] In Japanese companies managers are trained to make competitive intelligence everyone's business.[27] In the U.S., General Electric has been a pioneer in the application of the scanning system. In fact, in the past it has sold information obtained from the global marketplace through its scanning system to other enterprises.

Many organizations have not applied this type of organization in the past because the costs would have been huge. Today, however, the advent of enormous communications technologies that generate information at relatively low cost should enable more organizations to implement this type of system. Obviously, customer satisfaction cannot be attained unless, first, the organization knows what the customer wants, and second, it is able to get this information to the employees at all levels who are responsible for customer satisfaction. TQM thus requires such an information-gathering system.

Cooperates and Collaborates with Internal and External Units

Internal Cooperation and Collaboration

Systems-approach management, popularized in the 1960s,[28] posits that all subunits in an organization are interrelated and that positive decisions made in one unit often have a negative impact on other units, thus leading to an unhealthy internal atmosphere. It was proposed that managers could improve organizational efficiency if they considered the effect their decisions might have on other units and averted the foreseen negative consequences. This requires managers to get feedback from all of those whom the decision might affect. This type of decision-making approach therefore requires downward, upward, and horizontal communication within the organization, as well as a focal point to coordinate the communication. In this respect, American scholar Rensis Likert developed the "linking-pin" concept of a strong vertical and horizontal organizational communication link.[29]

The effective TQM organization has thus developed a culture in which there is much cooperation, communication, and collaboration among individuals within the organization, and quite often with individuals in other organizations. In such an environment, managers and employees do not work at cross-purposes. For example, in efforts to obtain acceptance of and mobilize support for their new visions, some U.S. corporations have applied a variation of the linking process. Bank of America established a program, labeled the Management Forum, to link all levels in order to obtain support for its new vision. The program's objective was to provide tools to the top 100 executives by which they would link others to generate support.[30] Southwestern Bell linked 55,000 employees and spouses in 57 locations via satellite.[31] Professors Blackburn and Rosen found that the Baldrige Award–winning organizations practice this type of information-sharing behavior.[32]

External Cooperation and Collaboration

As noted above, the effective TQM organization often cooperates, collaborates, and communicates with individuals in other organizations, and it often forms **strategic alliances** with competitors.[33] For example, Phillips and DuPont collaborate to develop and manufacture compact discs.[34] AT&T has links with many of the world's biggest telephone and electronics companies; IBM has created an alliance council of key executives who meet monthly to keep track of more than 40 partnerships throughout the globe; and Boeing has taken on three Japanese allies—the heavy industry divisions of Fuji, Mitsubishi, and Kawasaki—to make a new plane.[35] And, as indicated in Chapter 4, Toyota and General Motors, General Electric and Salelni (an Italian construction firm), and MW Kellogg Co. of Houston and China Petrochemical International Corporation (SINOPEC) have formed such collaborative ventures.[36] Organizations enter such an arrangement to share costs and risks, to gain additional technical and market knowledge to complement each other, to serve an international market, to strengthen themselves against other competitors, and to develop industry standards together.[37]

Basically, organizations attain greater efficiency by being aware of the available resources in their internal units (subsidiaries, divisions, departments, and so on), as well as in external units (other companies, governments, and so on), and forming mutually beneficial alliances that make wise use of those resources. For example, a subunit in the organization suddenly requires additional production capacity. Instead of investing resources to acquire it, the focal monitoring unit knows of available production capacity in another internal or external unit and arranges a mutually beneficial alliance between the two units to use the idle capacity.

The organization also attains greater efficiency by focusing on its strengths; it does what it can do best and contracts for other needed functions. For instance, a firm's strength may be engineering and design. Instead of doing manufacturing, it would be efficient for the firm to farm it out to a company whose strength is manufacturing. For example, as pointed out in Chapter 3, Apple vice president Al Eisenstat said, "If I can loop off one area of activity and say, 'Gee, I can join with such and such company,' then I can focus my resources on what I do best."[38] Firms such as Apple, Nike, and IBM's PCs have established themselves as design, engineering, and marketing companies, farming out much of their manufacturing to those who are able to do it cheaper and better. Maatschappij Van Berkel's Patent N.V., a Dutch-based multinational supplier of weighing and food processing equipment, met competitive cost pressures by outsourcing its manufacturing and engineering activities and transforming itself into a sales and service company.[39] As Jack Welch of GE put it, "tomorrow's organization will be boundaryless. It will work with outsiders as closely as if they were insiders."[40] Organizations that do not possess the ability to work with outsiders will not be as competitive and as capable of serving the customer as those that do. This TQM characteristic is thus dependent on the organization's ability to continually gather information about internal and external occurrences, as well as on the ability to share information openly.

Participation, Empowerment, and a Flat Structure

Professors Blackburn and Rosen found that Baldrige Award winners apply participative management, empower groups, and have a flat organizational structure.[41] (As an illustration, read Practical Perspective 14–1.)

PRACTICAL PERSPECTIVE   14–1

Ford's Ambitious Global and Product Plans for the '90s

Ford has ambitious plans to expand global activities in all three of its product areas—vehicles, components, and financial services—while maintaining a lean staff and production base. To get there, Ford's people must develop broader capabilities and learn to work together in teams. Flexibility is the key word.

Looking to the future, Ford's specific goals for the remainder of the 20th century include establishing production bases in China and other Asia/Pacific markets, growing worldwide component sales by 50%, increasing engineering productivity by 50%, maintaining a 70/30 split between automotive and financial profits, maintaining strong technical and design capabilities, and increasing cash reserves to prepare for the next downturn, which may come in 1997. Between now and 1998, Ford will spend more than $30 billion to bring new cars and trucks to market, including capital investments for plant upgrades. This equals outlays during the last five years, but it'll get more bang for its bucks because there'll be more new products—and heavier costs to meet clean-air and safety demands. For plans to introduce 14 new cars and trucks—including the new Mustang, Contour/Mystique "world" cars and Windstar minivan—just over the next 24 months alone. Moreover, Ford says this will be accomplished with fewer people, not more. Overall, Ford employs 140,000 in the U.S., including 96,000 hourly workers. It expects to hire 12,000 to 13,000 new workers in the next three years to replace those who retire or otherwise leave, but still keep employment at today's level.

Ford's vision of the future involves the merging of customer satisfaction, employee satisfaction and profitability. If these objectives are met, market share will take care of itself, says Edward E. Hagenlocker, executive vice president–Ford North American Automotive Operations (NAAO). "Part of the strategy we're working on within NAAO that will be implemented over the next year focuses heavily on empowering people," Mr. Hagenlocker says. To facilitate this environment, Ford is shifting from strong functional organizations such as marketing, accounting, engineering and manufacturing, to empowered teams with authority to function as independent units.

Source: Excerpted from Stephen E. Plumb, "Trotman Team Eyes Ford's Future," *Ward's Auto World* (November 1993): 25–26.

Participation

Participative management is a "cover-all" term meaning such activities as setting goals, solving problems, direct involvement in decision making, and including employees in consultation committees, representation on policy bodies, and selection of new co-workers.[42] It has been argued that participative management is an ethical imperative.[43]

The effective TQM organization uses a **participative** approach in decision making, either in the initial stages of the decision or at least in the implementation stages. It does so because participation offers a number of benefits.[44] One is that people will accept a decision more readily when they were involved in making it. Another is that diverse input often leads to a high-quality decision. Yet another is that it helps develop an environment of trust, which helps develop an achievement orientation among employees. For example, observation of a General Motors plant revealed that both the workers and their union were very enthusiastic about the new emphasis on quality—participating in determining high-quality standards provides workers with a feeling of self-worth and dignity.[45] It is also beneficial in the sense that it is the lower level employees who are close to the customer, and they thus know better what the customer wants—as has been proposed, in the old days, the "tool maker" and the "tool user" were one and the same. The "tool maker" could thus easily judge what would best serve the "tool user."[46] According to Professors Babbar and Rai, managers can facilitate institutional involvement by regularly discussing environmental issues and information gathered through scanning.[47]

Group Empowerment

Effective organizations consist of smaller, more adaptable, interdependent, parallel problem-solving and information-sharing, relatively self-sufficient subunits.[48] For example, in recent years many U.S. enterprises have began applying a managerial form labeled "team self-management."[49] Other labels include "self-managed work teams" and "quality circles."[50] Today about one in five U.S. employers use self-management teams, and by the end of the 1990s, experts predict, 40 to 50 percent of all U.S. workers could be managing themselves through such mechanisms.[51]

The basic idea of team self-management is that members of the team possess a high degree of decisional autonomy and control of activities (**empowerment**), which were previously a prerogative of management.[52] Professors Blackburn and Rosen[53] cite Pauline Brody, chairwoman of Xerox's Quality Forum, who stated that human resources practices in TQM organizations must be congruent with corporate culture, including a shift from working as individuals to working as teams. Performance measurement and evaluation are based on team goals. In Japan, this team orientation is referred to as total quality control (TQC) or *Jidka*.[54]

Ad Hoc Group Empowerment

Many of the organization's decisions are made in what has been labeled an "*ad hoc* center," which is defined by task-relevant, specialized knowledge; centers of control, authority, and communication are problem-specific and dependent on where the expertise to solve a problem rests.[55] Another label used is "problem-solving groups."[56] The Baldrige Award–winning companies studied by Blackburn and Rosen practice this behavior. Charles Sabel, a sociologist at Massachusetts Institute of Technology, describes this type of organization as a geometric form that has no identifiable top or bottom (the Mobius strip organization), "a body that constantly turns on itself, in an endless cycle of creation and destruction."[57] As contended by Kenan Sahin, president of Kenan Systems Corp., a Cambridge, Massachusetts software consulting firm, in this type of organization managers will have to change gears readily, following those who know most about the subject.[58] Therefore, a skilled scientist, marketer, or engineer who is a manager on one project may have to be a follower on the next. Raymond Miles, a professor of management at the University of California at Berkeley, describes this idea as a network where managers function like switchboard operators, coordinating the activities of employees, suppliers, customers, and joint-venture partners.[59]

When a problem arises, an *ad hoc* **group** consisting of members who possess the relevant knowledge is formed by a coordinator to serve temporarily as decision makers. The group, which may consist of shop-floor workers, managers, technical experts, suppliers, and customers, come together to do a job and then disband, with everyone going back to their regular jobs or to the next assignment. For example, large construction firms such as Bechtel, Fluor, and Brown & Roothand pick groups of employees and outside contractors with the right skills for each new dam, refinery, or airport. Becton Dickinson, according to its CEO Gilmartin, organize their own cross-functional **teams** including not only their own people but also vendors, suppliers, and people from other divisions.[60]

The above means that the organization requires a system to keep track of people and their skills. For example, Cypress Semiconductor, a San Jose, California, maker of specialty computer chips, has developed a computer system that keeps track of its 1,500 employees as they criss-cross between different functions, teams, and projects. Apple is developing a computer network called Spider, a system that combines a network of personal computers with a video-conferencing system and a database of employee records. A manager assembling a team can call up profiles of employees who are stationed anywhere in the world. A color photo of the person can be seen on the screen, where he/she works, who reports to him/her, to whom he/she reports, and his/her skills. If the manager wants to interview a candidate in, for instance, Frankfurt, the manager can call the person over the Spider network and talk with him/her in living color on the computer screen.[61]

Basically, participative management and empowerment generates an organizational culture that challenges workers. Professors Babbar and Rai proposed that the organization "must challenge employees and engage them intellectually so as to optimize the use and development of human resource."[62] Clearly, one of the stronger components of TQM is a commitment to the development of human resources. Babbar and Rai indicated that "Managers can make this possible by providing the necessary infrastructure required to bring out the best in their employees and building in mechanisms for them to use in order to draw from the environment. This in turn should facilitate continuous improvement in basic processes and raise the productivity of individuals."[63] This aspect of TQM is thus dependent on the organization's ability to gather and openly share information, as well as to apply participative management and empowerment in a genuine way.

Relatively Flat Organizational Structure

The effective TQM organizational structure is relatively **flat.** That is, there are fewer managerial layers than in traditional hierarchical organizations. This is because, as Tom Peters has been quoted saying, "A twelve-layer company can't compete with a three-layer company."[64] In part this is because paying many managers at many levels and the slowness of hierarchal decision making in tall structures would make organizations existing in a dynamic environment less efficient and hence less competitive. Also, an organization can only create an atmosphere of maximum creativity if it reduces hierarchical elements to the minimum and creates a corporate culture in which its vision, company philosophy, and strategies can be implemented by employees who think independently and take the initiative.[65] Furthermore, as management scholar Henry Mintzberg proposed in his explanation of *adhocracy*, many levels of administration restrict the organization's ability to adapt.[66]

A flatter structure is made possible by the enormous advancements in communications technologies, which, as the well-known management expert Peter F. Drucker noted, enables managers to communicate with a far wider span of individuals than was possible in the past.[67] Spans of control thus give way to spans of communication. For example, at Cypress Semiconductor, CEO T. J. Rodgers has a computer system that enables him to keep abreast of every employee and team in his rapidly moving, decentralized, constantly changing organization. Each of his 1,500 employees maintains a list of 10 to 15 goals such as "Meet with marketing for product launch" or "Make sure to check with customer X." Noted next to each goal is when it was agreed upon, when it is due to be completed, and whether it is completed yet or not. Mr. Rodgers stated that he can review the goals of all the employees in about four hours, which he does each week. He searches only for those falling behind, and then contacts them not to scold but to ask if there is anything he can do to help them accomplish the goal.[68]

It should be noted that the *path-goal theory* suggests that wide spans are possible if the employees are well trained and experienced.[69] This aspect of TQM therefore depends on the developmental aspects of the participation and empowerment components, as well as on training and development programs (to be discussed later). The participative-empowerment aspects of TQM therefore depend on a flat structure.[70] One of the characteristics of the TQM culture identified by Blackburn and Rosen is "a wide span of control."[71]

While effective TQM organizations are relatively flat, they still maintain the three basic management levels: institutional, administrative, and operational.[72] The institutional level still monitors the organization's internal ongoing and the external environment and establishes objectives and policies to align the two; the administrative level still interpolates structure or improvises, that is, it implements the policies and objectives in its respective subunit; and the operational level still uses the structure provided to keep the organization operating effectively. However, the fixed actors at these levels, as previously indicated, use participative management and empowerment, and decisions at these levels are often made by problem-specific, *ad hoc* groups and by relatively autonomous groups.

Performance Pay and Horizontal Promotions

In effective TQM organizations, the reward system is viewed by employees as being equitable. Basically, employees' perceptions of equity affect their decisions to join, remain, and produce for a firm. Equity includes an external and individual process.[73] External equity refers to employees' perception of how they are rewarded in proportion to the external market, and individual equity relates to employees' perception of how they are rewarded in proportion to their individual performance.[74] If rewards are perceived to be inequitable, employees are likely to leave; if they stay, they are likely to be low producers.

Performance Pay

Individual equity suggests that "better workers should receive higher wages on the same job than poorer workers."[75] This wage differentiation supposedly helps motivate workers to produce closer to their maximum potential.[76] This suggests that the effective TQM organizational culture require some form of a pay-based-on-performance system.

Performance pay became a major area of strategic management change in the 1980s.[77] In a survey of over 1600 U.S. organizations, 75 percent indicated having some form of incentive scheme, with more plans having been introduced in the past five years than in the previous twenty years.[78] Performance pay is distinct from "merit pay" in that it is systematic and open; employees have at least some awareness of the criteria being applied to measure performance and the consequent rewards. Using the merit-pay approach, increases are often based on arbitrary management decision.[79]

R. Semler, CEO for the Brazilian firm Semco S/A, reported that at his company, employees at the lower level can actually, through incentives, earn more money than middle-level employees.[80] According to Blackburn and Rosen (previously cited), Baldrige Award winners offer a variety of formal and informal financial and nonfinancial rewards for individuals and teams. However, it has been found that intrinsic job motivation declined when extrinsic rewards, such as pay, were involved,[81] and workplace participation and job enrichment were far more closely associated with employee motivation than pay.[82] This means that this TQM factor is dependent on the participation, group involvement, and empowerment factors. As Frederick Herzberg found, money does not motivate workers, but it does demotivate them when it is viewed as being inequitable or inadequate; what motivates them is challenging work, and so on.[83]

Horizontal Promotions

As people move from one team to another, they and the firm consider their careers and pay in new ways. Instead of slowly climbing up the organizational ladder (the TQM organizational structure is flat), workers and managers make more lateral moves, acquiring expertise in different functions such as marketing or manufacturing. Becton Dickinson, for example, is trying out lateral promotions for those who do well in teams, rotating, for example, a financial person into a marketing or manufacturing job. In 1990, in one division the company rotated ten managers out of 50. They received a raise and change of title, just as they would with a regular promotion, but they were not necessarily put in charge of any more workers.[84] As previously indicated, at Semco, quite often associates make higher salaries than the coordinators and partners, and they are able to increase their status and compensation without entering the management line. This aspect of TQM depends on the flat component because a tall organization's promotion opportunities will disrupt the system and will inhibit application of empowerment.

A Bond and a Sense of Ownership

The effective TQM organization requires high **employee commitment.** In high-commitment organizations, the relationship between labor and the organization is expanded "well beyond the traditional arrangement [high compliance]. The employee becomes committed to the organization and its goals, and is matched by an additional commitment by the employer to the employee's welfare."[85] Similarly, it has been proposed that "provision must be made to ensure that each member (called an associate) is bonded to the organization as a whole and to the position held. Moreover, the position must be bonded to the organization."[86]

However, the bonds must not be unbreakable. If an employee is committed to a course of action, and he or she subsequently finds that course is no longer suitable, the employee is encouraged to develop a new suitable course and submit it through the approval process. For example, one U.S.-based firm depends on mechanical organizational behavior for attaining efficiency. The mechanics are agreed upon through a participative process. If, however, an employee later becomes bored or disenchanted with the mechanical job, he or she is encouraged by management to develop a new and more interesting way of accomplishing the task and to submit a proposal through the agreed upon process. Once the change is agreed upon, the new way becomes part of the routine. The firm's executive with whom the writer spoke claimed that this behavior may be temporarily inefficient (while the employee is redefining his/her job), but in the long run it is highly efficient. This suggests that the TQM organization is paradoxical—it resembles the organic form in the sense that it is flexible and adaptable and at the same time it resembles the bureaucratic form in the sense that it must adhere to many processes—not rigid rules and procedures, however.

To enhance commitment, effective TQM organizations develop a "**sense of ownership**" in their employees. The sense of ownership makes employees less afraid of losing their jobs. This in turn makes them object less to learning about new technology and proposing process improvements.[87] For example, to help develop such a sense, Semco S/A (previously discussed) issues profit sharing in each division twice a year divided equally among employees, and every month, each employee gets a balance sheet, a profit-and-loss analysis, and a cash-flow statement for his/her division. Furthermore, the company provides additional job security for employees who have been with the company for more than three years or who are over 50 years old. Wal-Mart gives everybody a piece of the action. Through profit sharing, incentive bonuses, and stock purchase plans, all the people who handle the goods and the customers have a direct stake in doing well.[88] In Japan, layoffs are less common for those employed under Japanese-style tenured employment. Thus, because they generally are not afraid of losing their jobs, employees are not usually opposed to learning about new technology and suggesting process improvements.[89] Organizational improvement and change to serve the customer better is an imperative of TQM.

Ongoing Training Programs

Fundamentally, TQM culture requires a change "from a focus on results to a focus on continuous improvement of the processes that deliver the results."[90] TQM thus requires developing more flexible cultures and structures, new organizational practices, and **socializing employees** to them. It has been proposed that continuous improvement in basic processes and raising the productivity of employees can be facilitated by challenging them and engaging them intellectually. Managers can make this possible "by providing the necessary infrastructure required to bring out the best in their employees and building in mechanisms for them to use in order to draw from the environment."[91]

Training programs are a primary mechanism through which organizations socialize employees to new organizational values; they also signal an organization's desire for greater employee involvement and its reciprocal commitment to increasing employee welfare. TQM requires the empowerment of workers and the reduction of managers' relative power.[92] It has been suggested that such a power shift and cultural change can cause increased aggression for all parties and severe problems with authority relationships.[93] The training programs must address this problem. For example, in a discussion of the implementation of a Japanese-style just-in-time (JIT) system in American organizations, it was proposed that "The greater the number of high-quality training programs related to power shifting between management and workers, the faster its [JIT] rate of adoption and the better the firm's performance."[94] As Blackburn and Rosen reported, "the Baldrige companies focus their training efforts on quality. Their quality training programs are comprehensive, well funded, and fully supported by top management."[95] Of course, since the environment is constantly changing and TQM organizations respond to changes, training programs to change the organization's culture must be ongoing.

CHALLENGES IN IMPLEMENTING AND MAINTAINING TQM PROGRAMS

Basically, effective implementation and maintenance of a TQM program requires a new organizational culture.[96] Organizational culture is not easily changed, however. **Organizational culture** has been defined as the "pattern of basic assumptions that a given group has invented, discovered, or developed in learning to cope with its problems of external adaptation and internal integration, and that have worked well enough to be considered valid, and therefore to be taught to new members as the correct way to perceive, think and feel in relation to those problems."[97] Organizational culture is thus defined by the organization's members' frames of reference, which are articulated and codified by organizational statements of purposes, policies, myths, stories, and rituals.[98] The meaning of organizational culture has been broken down into **practice,** such as symbols, heroes, and rituals, and into **values,** such as good/evil, beautiful/ugly, normal/abnormal, rational/irrational. The value aspects of organizational culture are determined by national culture, and the practice aspects are determined by the organization as a means of adapting to environmental demands for change.[99] The notion of culture thus presents numerous challenges to the implementation and maintenance of TQM programs across cultures.

How Are the Practice and Value
Aspects of Culture Changed?

To implement TQM programs, do organizations need to change both the practice and value aspects of organizational culture? How are the practice aspects changed? For example, it has been noticed that a firm's traditions "frequently have their origins in the ideology of an entrepreneurial founder who set out both a strategic perspective on the task of the organization and a philosophy on the form of the labor process to accomplish it."[100] Thus, when implementing change, past design choices are likely to influence the type of job design and coordination and control strategies chosen.[101] Professors Bartlett and Ghoshal have shown how an organization's administrative heritage and ingrained management norms constrain its ability to reconfigure itself.[102] Similarly, Professor R. E. Quinn's competing values model provides one means of examining how **different value orientations** underlying organizational culture affect design choices. Some organizations possess flexibility-oriented values, which emphasize decentralization and differentiation, and some possess control-oriented values, which emphasize centralization and integration.[103] The former is likely to encounter much less difficulty in implementing TQM programs than the latter. How do the latter organizations deal with the implementation difficulties?

Professors Quinn and Kimberly have indicated that no organization is likely to reflect only one value; instead, organizations reflect a combination of values, although one could be more dominant than the others.[104] This suggests that an organization may apply strong controls in a certain function, for example, finance, and at the same time apply looser controls in another, for instance, marketing or R&D. How do organizations attempting to implement such programs address the need for different approaches for different functions?

How are the value aspects changed? For example, the education system in the U.S. fosters individual efforts and in Germany and Japan it fosters group harmony and cooperation. Therefore, to implement TQM, which requires group cooperation, do the U.S. and similar cultures need to transform their education system? In light of the fact that Americans and people in similar cultures tend to adhere strongly to the individualistic approach, how is the transformation accomplished?

Organizations that have implemented TQM programs rely heavily on **informal group controls.** It has been suggested that in American-like cultures people join group activities voluntarily "on the basis of enlarged benefits that will accrue to them for participation, balanced against the loss of individual freedom that is surrendered to the group."[105] How do organizations address employees who do not want to participate in group activities because they do not want to lose their individual freedom? The Japanese are forced, in many instances, to become members of groups others feel are appropriate for them.[106] Can people in American-like cultures be mandated to join groups? Even if they could be, it may not be effective—as has been proposed, employee involvement "with **voluntary membership** status works best for the firm [boldface added]."[107] And research shows that the effectiveness of self-managed work teams is not uniformly positive.[108] How do managers of organizations attempting to implement and maintain effective TQM programs confront these challenges?

How Are Participation and Team Programs Implemented in Resistant Cultures?

As it was pointed out in Chapter 1, societies consist of multicultural dimensions: large or small power distance, strong or weak uncertainty avoidance, group-oriented or individualistic, and so on. Individuals dominated by a **large power distance** and/or **a strong uncertainty avoidance** cultural dimension (for example, the French) do not necessarily want the responsibilities that come with the participation and empowerment aspects of TQM programs. And people dominated by an **individualistic cultural dimension** (for example, Americans) do not fit well into the team aspects of TQM programs.

Japan, for example, is a **group-oriented culture**. Implementation and maintenance of such programs would thus be possible there. However, Japan is also a large power distance culture (employees prefer direction), which suggests that it would not be possible there. But the popular press reports that such programs have been effectively implemented in Japan. How? Or is it that Japanese organizations do not really apply these programs in the way they are understood in the West? For instance, it has been observed that there is strong social pressure in Japan to make "voluntary" suggestions for improvement in the work place.[109] Some companies such as Nissan have a quota of suggestions for each employee that must be met each month.[110] Further, Japanese managers use peer pressure to force employees to master their jobs in order not to call attention to themselves too often.[111] These kind of pressures cause stress for the workers—Japanese or American.

Also, many people like to be consulted on decisions, but do not necessarily want to participate in making them. Furthermore, it has been proposed that for participation to work, there has to be enough time, issues must be relevant to workers' interests, employees must have the ability to participate, and the organizational culture must support employee involvement.[112] In this dynamic environment there is not always enough time, and when quick decisions are needed, it is often best that one person make them. Also, a multitude of studies have looked at the participation-performance relationship. When the results of numerous studies are examined closely, it seems as if participation has only a moderate impact on variables such as motivation, productivity, and job satisfaction.[113] How do organizations address these **barriers** to the implementation and maintenance of TQM programs?

What If Customers Do Not Want to Pay for TQM?

Major cultural changes and structural change efforts are very expensive and time-consuming due to the need to build **trust,** develop skills, and overcome resistance. For example, shifting from a mechanistic to an organic form is time consuming and costly because of the requirement that lower level employees, supervisory personnel, and middle managers be retrained in the knowledge, skills, and abilities needed to carry out their new roles. These changes disrupt existing power and status networks, making resistance likely as well as costly and time consuming to overcome.[114] Also, organizations incur substantial ongoing training costs after their initial investment because of the need to continually update employee knowledge and skills.[115]

In other words, quality is expensive, and ultimately the consumer must bear these expenses. What if customers do not want to pay for these costs? Or what if consumers can get the product for less from companies that do not incur as many costs in implementing such programs? What if customers no longer want to pay for TQM? For example, Baldrige Award winner Wallace Company's customers eventually rebelled at paying higher prices to fund the costs of the firm's quality program. The enterprise lost money, laid off employees, and was forced to operate in Chapter 11.[116] If the latter occurs, what happens to the "bond" aspects of TQM? How will these problems be dealt with?

Can Organizations Really Guarantee Quality?

Labels such as "A TQM Organization" or "A Baldrige Award Winner" or "An ISO 9000 Company" symbolize the organization's commitment to quality both at the employee level and the organizational level. The label therefore becomes organizational worth; it becomes a "rubber stamp."[117] Is such a guarantee possible? Some of the firms included in Peters's and Waterman's famous list of "excellent" corporations soon after turned out not to be so excellent, and TQM organizations tend to fail very quickly.[118] Wallace Wilson, CEO of Wilson Industries, has been cited as saying: "I think some companies use it [TQM] and promote it strictly for marketing advantages. They hype it and talk about it, but it really isn't valid. If you talk to their people, they really do not believe in it and they really are not doing that much."[119] Following her investigation of two firms in England that failed in their attempts to implement quality programs, researcher Carole Brooke questioned whether quality techniques can be taken seriously: "Could it be that heavy emphasis on quality symbols and ritual processes can mask what is 'really' going on and that experience may contradict the quality objectives, resulting in organizational shambles?"[120] How can organizations address this problem?

Can TQM Be Implemented in New, Small Firms?

Another question has to do with entrepreneurship. According to Professor Henry Mintzberg, the entrepreneur, who is functional in smaller, newer enterprises and does not work well in a structured organization, centralizes decision-making and has little interest in employee involvement.[121] Does this mean that TQM programs cannot be implemented in new, small organizations?

What If Those in Power Refuse to Relinquish Power?

Still another question has to do with individuals' need for power and empowerment. Many people are motivated by the need for power.[122] What if such individuals do not want to surrender their power? How do organizations deal with these individuals? Can they be taught the practice of empowerment? Furthermore, if these individuals refuse to relinquish power, how will organizations establish a flatter structure?

In Strategic Alliances, How Can Trust Be Built?

As indicated in the TQM framework, to be effective in the global marketplace, organizations must often enter into strategic alliances. However, strategic alliances are typically laden with tensions, most of them run into trouble at some point, and tensions tend to arise between each parent company.[123] The success rate of alliances is not documented, but Jordan D. Lewis, a consultant based in Washington, D.C., believes it is not high. "The biggest reasons for failure," he said, "are corporate cultures and misplaced control. Cultural differences can also be magnified by a strategic alliance."[124] How do managers address this problem?

How Is an International Telecommunications Network Established?

For firms seeking to compete in the global marketplace, managing information technology and systems presents monumental challenges.[125] One challenge is that global information technology managers must understand the overall global strategy of the parent company, as well as the strategy of each of the business units. Another challenge involves establishing an **international telecommunications network.** This is a complex and frustrating undertaking. Telecommunications service offerings, pricing schedules, and policies differ from country to country. Furthermore, telecom services must be arranged separately with each regional PTT office (national public utility organizations, similar to AT&T in North America). Each PTT has different rules and regulations, and often different languages.[126] These are just a few of the challenges involved in establishing a global cybernetic and scanning system required for effective TQM. How will managers meet these challenges? As has been proposed, "few companies have really mastered the skills of gathering and exploiting information from around the world."[127]

IS TQM REALLY ATTAINABLE?

These questions suggest that while we may know that TQM programs are imperative for organizational effectiveness, there is still much to be learned about what such programs really are and what they are really for. Are they a **quick-fix** business solution? Are they a methodology? It has been inferred that TQM is neither; that it is an attitude, a set of values; that there is very little discussion in the literature of what is required in order for TQM to work.[128] This chapter has attempted to show what is needed. Notwithstanding all the barriers, the concept of total quality management is still valuable. It provides, at least, a framework for thinking in terms of organizational and managerial improvement.

SUMMARY

This chapter has suggested that as global competition continues to intensify, organizations must look for ways to serve customers better than the competitors. One way is by developing better managerial capabilities. One managerial tool that can aid organizations in this respect is total quality management (TQM). A TQM framework was described. Many questions need to be answered, however, before such a framework can be effectively implemented and maintained.

Key Terms

1. Quality; value
2. Total quality management (TQM)
3. Customer satisfaction
4. Cybernetic; scanning
5. Internal cooperation and collaboration
6. External cooperation and collaboration
7. Alliances
8. Participation; empowerment
9. Flat structure
10. Teams; ad hoc groups
11. *Jidka*
12. Performance-based pay
13. Horizontal promotions
14. Commitment
15. A sense of ownership
16. Socializing employees to new organizational values
17. Barriers
18. Organizational culture
19. Practice; values

20. Different value orientations
21. Informal group controls
22. Voluntary membership
23. Individualistic cultures
24. Group-oriented cultures
25. Labels
26. Trust
27. International communications network
28. Quick fix

Discussion Questions and Exercises

1. Describe the general meaning of total quality management (TQM).
2. Describe the difference between *quality* and *value*.
3. You are an international management consultant hired by a domestic firm in Sweden. The firm's top-level management is aware of the opportunities and threats that are emerging throughout the global marketplace. In light of these changes, management has decided that the firm must internationalize its operations. As has been emphasized in this and other chapters, to remain competitive in this changing world, many businesses will have to develop superior international management skills. As the consultant, prepare for the firm's management:
   a. An outline of the capabilities/abilities the firm will need to develop to be effective in international management.
   b. An outline of the difficulties/barriers the management will face in implementing those capabilities/abilities and in maintaining them.

Assignment

Contact an executive of an international organization who has extensive international management experience. Ask him or her to describe the future international management challenges he or she foresees. Prepare a short report to share with the class.

Managing Without Managers

Semco S/A is one of Brazil's fastest growing companies. According to its CEO, Ricardo Semler, its management programs are based on three fundamental values: democracy, profit sharing, and information. These values function in a complex circle, each dependent on the other two. Relative to democracy, or employee participation, Semco believes that workers who control their working conditions are going to be more satisfied than those who do not. Semco found four big obstacles to effective participative management: size, hierarchy, lack of motivation, and ignorance.

Semco's participative programs did not work when the units were large because there were "too many managers in too many layers holding too many

C A S E   14–1

Source: Draws from R. Semler, "Managing Without Managers," *Harvard Business Review* (September–October 1989), p. 78.

meetings." To overcome the size barrier, Semco reduced each production unit to a limit of about 150 people. The short-range effect of this breakup was higher costs due to duplication of efforts and loss of economies of scale. The long-range effect, however, was sales doubling in one year; inventories falling from 136 days to 46; the unveiling of eight new products which had been stalled in R&D for two years; and increased productivity, which allowed Semco to reduce its workforce by 32 percent through attrition and retirement incentives. The smaller size put Semco's employees in touch with one another so they could coordinate their work. The smaller size also enabled Semco to eliminate the hierarchical pyramid, which tends to emphasize power, promote insecurity, distort communications, hobble interaction, and make it extremely difficult for people who plan and the people who execute to move in the same direction. Furthermore, Semco abolished dress codes, norms, manuals, rules, and regulations, replacing them with the rule of common sense and putting its employees in the position of using their own judgment.

The status and money hierarchical managers enjoy, Semco concluded, are the biggest obstacle to participative management. Semco, therefore, designed an organizational circle with three management levels—one corporate level and two operating levels at the manufacturing units. The central circle contains five people, labeled counselors (not CEO, EVP), who integrate the company's movements. The second circle contains the heads of eight divisions. These heads are called partners (not VP, and so on). The third circle consists of all the other employees, called associates. The associates do the research, design, sales, and manufacturing work. They have no one reporting to them on an ongoing basis. Some of them, however, are permanent and temporary team and task leaders called coordinators. There are therefore four titles in three management layers: counselors, partners, coordinators, and associates.

QUESTIONS

1. Is Semco in tune with management in the future as described in the chapter?
2. Discuss how Semco's management styles compares with the TQM framework.
3. The chapter presented numerous barriers to the implementation of TQM programs. Describe the ways Semco dealt with some of the barriers.

Notes

1. B. Dwyer, P. Engardio, Z. Schiller, and S. Reed, "Tearing Up Today's Organizational Chart," *Business Week*, 21st Century Capitalism (1994 Special Issue), p. 81.

2. T. Q. Spitzer and B. Tregoe, "Thinking and Managing Beyond the Boundaries," *Business Horizons* (January–February 1993), p. 36.

3. See F. F. Reichheld, and W. E. Sasser, Jr., "Zero Defections: Quality Comes to Services," *Harvard Business Review* (September–October, 1990), pp. 105–111; G. Taguchi and D. Clausing, "Robust Quality," *Harvard Business Review* (January–February 1990), pp. 65–75.

4. R. Collard and G. Sivyer, "Total Quality," *Personnel Management* (May 1990), Factsheet 29.

5. W. E. Deming, *Out of the Crisis* (Cambridge, MA: Massachusetts Institute of Technology, Center for Advanced Engineering Study, 1986); and A. V. Feigenbaum, *Total Quality Control* (New York: McGraw-Hill, 1983).

6. H. J. Harrington, *The Improvement Process: How America's Leading Companies Improve Quality* (New York: McGraw-Hill, 1987).

7. J. M. Juran, *Planning for Quality* (New York: The Free Press, 1988), p. 332.

8. S. Cavalery and K. Obloj, *Management Systems: A Global Perspective* (Belmont, CA: Wadsworth Publishing, 1993), p. 176.

9. Collard and Sivyer, "Total Quality."

10. This framework builds on Carl A. Rodrigues, "A Framework for Defining Total Quality Management," *Competitiveness Review,* Vol. 5, No. 2 (1995).

11. Spitzer and Tregoe, "Thinking and Managing Beyond the Boundaries," p. 36.

12. W. G. Bennis, "Managing the Dream: Leadership in the 21st Century," *Training: The Magazine of Human Resources Development,* Vol. 27 (May 1990): 48.

13. H. Sugiura, "How Honda Localizes Its Global Strategy," *Sloan Management Review,* Vol. 32, No. 1 (1990), p. 78.

14. R. Blackburn, and B. Rosen, "Total Quality and Human Resources Management: Lessons Learned from Baldrige Award-Winning Companies," *The Academy of Management Executive,* Vol. 7, No. 3 (1993), pp. 49–66.

15. J. J. Kaufman, "Total Quality Management," *Ekistics,* Vol. 56, No. 337 (July–August 1989), pp. 182–187.

16. "Jack Welch's Lessons for Success," *Fortune* (January 26, 1993), p. 86.

17. For more information on this concept, see A. T. Schick, "Toward the Cybernetic State," *Public Administration in Time of Turbulence,* D. Waldo, ed. (New York: Chandler Publications, 1971).

18. For more information on this concept see R. Vernon, "The Product Cycle Hypothesis in a New International Environment," *Strategic Management of Multinational Corporations: The Essentials,* H. B. Wortzel and L. H. Wortzel, eds. (New York: John Wiley and Sons, 1985).

19. J. Klir, *Cybernetic Modelling* (Princeton, NJ: D. Van Nostrand, 1965).

20. T. L. Griffith, "Teaching Big Brother to Be a Team Player: Computer Monitering and Quality," *The Academy of Management Executive,* Vol. 7, No. 1 (1993), pp. 73–80.

21. R. B. Duncan, "Characteristics of Organizational Environments and Perceived Environmental Uncertainty," *Administrative Science Quarterly,* Vol. 17, No. 3 (1972), pp. 313–327.

22. S. Babbar and A. Rai, "Competitive Intelligence for International Business," *Long Range Planning,* Vol. 26, No. 3 (1993), pp. 103–113.

23. P. M. Fahey and V. K. Narayanan, *Macroenvironmental Analysis for Strategic Management* (St. Paul, MN: West Publishing, 1986).

24. D. L. Daft, J. Sormunen, and D. Parks, "Chief Executives Scanning Environmental Characteristics, and Company Performance: An Empirical Study," *Strategic Management Journal,* Vol. 9, No. 2 (1988), pp. 123–139.

25. P. M. Ginter, and W. J. Duncan, "Macroenvironmental Analysis for Strategic Management," *Long Range Planning,* Vol. 23, No. 6 (1990), pp. 91–100.

26. S. Gee, *Technology Transfer, Innovation, and International Competitiveness* (New York: John Wiley and Sons, 1981).

27. Babbar and Rai, "Competitive Intelligence for International Business," p. 110.

28. See C. W. Churchman, *The Systems Approach* (New York: Dell Publishing, 1968).

29. R. Likert, *New Patterns of Management* (New York: McGraw-Hill, 1961).

30. R. N. Beck, "Visions, Values, and Strategies: Changing Attitude and Culture," *The Academy of Management Executive,* Vol. 1, No. 1 (1987).

31. Z. E. Barnes, "Change in the Bell System," *The Academy of Management Executive,* Vol. 1, No. 1 (1987).

32. Blackburn and Rosen, "Total Quality and Human Resources Management: Lessons Learned from Baldrige Award-Wining Companies."

33. See K. Ohmae, "The Global Logic of Strategic Alliances," *Harvard Business Review* (March–April 1989).

34. G. Hamel, L. Y. Doz, and C. K. Prahalad, "Collaborate with Your Competitor—and Win," *Harvard Business Review* (January-February 1989).

35. J. Main, "Making Global Alliances Work," *Fortune* (December 17, 1990), p. 121.

36. R. Ajami, "Designing Multinational Networks," *Making Organizations Competitive*, R. H. Kilmann and I. Kilmann, eds. (San Francisco: Jossey-Bass, 1991).

37. J. G. Wissema, and L. Euser, "Successful Innovation Through Inter-Company Networks," *Long Range Planning*, Vol. 24 (December 1991), pp. 33–39.

38. B. Dumaine, "The Bureaucracy Busters," *Fortune,* (June 17, 1991), p. 46.

39. J. Dupuy, "Learning to Manage World-Class Strategy," *Management Review* (October 1991), p. 40.

40. Dumaine, "The Bureaucracy Busters," p. 46.

41. Blackburn and Rosen, "Total Quality and Human Resources Management: Lessons Learned from Baldrige Award-Winning Companies."

42. J. L. Cotton, D. A. Vollrath, K. L. Froggatt, M. L. Lengnick-Hall, and K. R. Jennings, "Employee Participation: Diverse Forms and Different Outcomes," *The Academy of Management Review,* Vol. 13, No. 1 (1988), pp. 8–22.

43. M. Shashkin, "Participative Management Is an Ethical Imperative," *Organizational Dynamics* (Spring 1984), pp. 5–22.

44. See S. P. Robbins, *Organizational Behavior* (Englewood Cliffs, NJ: Prentice-Hall, 1993).

45. R. E. Cole, "Quality Improvement in the Auto Industry: Close But No Cigar," *California Management Review,* Vol. 33, No. 5 (1990), pp. 71–85.

46. J. M. Juran, and F. M. Gryna, Jr., *Quality Planning and Analysis* (New York: McGraw-Hill, 1970).

47. Babbar and Rai, "Competitive Intelligence for International Business," p. 109.

48. J. W. Dean, Jr., and G. I. Susman, "Strategic Responses to Global Competition: Advanced Technology, Organizational Design and Human Resources Practices," *Strategy, Organization Design, and Human Resource Management,* C.C. Snow, ed. (Greenwich, CT: JAI Press, 1989).

49. C. C. Manz and H. P. Sims, Jr., "Leading Workers to Lead Themselves: The External Leadership of Self-Managing Work Teams," *Administrative Science Quarterly,* Vol. 32 (1987), pp. 106–128.

50. R. F. Magjuka, "Survey: Self-Managed Teams Achieve Continuous Improvement Best," *National Productivity Review* (Winter 1991/1992), pp. 51–57.

51. J. S. Lublin, "Trying to Increase Worker Productivity, More Employers Alter Management Style," *The Wall Street Journal* (February 13, 1992), p. B1.

52. P. K. Mills, "Self-Management: Its Control and Relationship to Other Organizational Properties," *The Academy of Management Review,* Vol. 8 (1983), pp. 445–453.

53. Blackburn and Rosen, "Total Quality and Human Resources Management: Lessons Learned from Baldrige Award-Winning Companies," p. 50.

54. R. Chase and N. Aquilino, *Production and Operations Management* (Homewood, IL: Irwin, 1989).

55. K. E. Weick, "Theorizing About Organizational Communication," *Handbook of Organizational Communication,* L. L. Putnam, K. H. Roberts, and L. W. Porter, eds. (Newbery Park, CA: Sage Publications, 1987).

56. Magjuka, "Survey: Self-Managed Teams Achieve Continuous Improvement Best."

57. Dumaine, "The Bureaucracy Busters," p. 42.

58. Ibid., p. 50.

59. Ibid., p. 42.

60. Ibid.

61. Ibid., p. 41.

62. Babbar and Rai, "Competitive Intelligence for International Business," p. 109.

63. Ibid.

64. J. Braham, "Money Talks," *Industry Week* (April 17, 1989), p. 23.

65. H. H. Hinterhuber, and W. Popp, "Are You a Strategist or Just a Manager?" *Harvard Business Review* (January–February 1992), pp. 105–113.

66. H. Mintzberg, *Structures in Fives: Designing Effective Organizations* (Englewood Cliffs, NJ: Prentice-Hall, 1983).

67. J. Main, "The Winning Organization," *Fortune,* September 26, 1988, p. 60.

68. Dumaine, "The Bureaucracy Busters," p. 46.

69. R. T. Keller, "Test of the Path-Goal Theory of Leadership with Need for Clarity as a Moderator in Research and Development Organizations," *Journal of Applied Psychology* (April 1989), pp. 208–212.

70. K. Shelton, "People Power," *Executive Excellent* (December 1991), pp. 7–8.

71. Blackburn and Rosen, "Total Quality and Human Resources Management: Lessons Learned from Baldrige Award-Winning Companies," p. 51.

72. See D. Katz and R. L. Kahn, *The Social Psychology of Organizations* (New York: John Wiley and Sons, 1966).

73. M. J. Wallace and C. H. Fay, *Compensation Theory and Practice* (Boston: PWS-Kent, 1988).

74. Ibid.

75. Ibid., p. 18.

76. W. F. Cascio, "Do Good or Poor Performers Leave? A Meta-Analysis of the Relationship Between Performance and Turnover," *The Academy of Management Journal,* Vol. 30, No. 4 (1987), pp. 744–762.

77. See S. Kessler, and F. Bayliss, *Contemporary British Industrial Relations* (Basingstroke: Macmillan, 1992).

78. J. McAdams, "Performance-Based Pay Reward Systems: Towards a Common Fate Environment," *Personnel Journal* (June 1988), pp. 103–113.

79. Kessler and Bayliss, *Contemporary British Industrial Relations.*

80. R. Semler, "Managing Without Managers," *Harvard Business Review* (September–October 1989).

81. E. L. Deci, "The Effects of Contingent and Non-Contingent Rewards and Controls on Intricate Motivation," *Organizational Behavior and Human Performance,* Vol. 8 (1972), pp. 217–219.

82. N. P. Lovrich, "Merit Pay and Motivation in the Public Workforce: Beyond Technical Concerns to More Basic Considerations," *Review of Public Personnel Administration,* Vol. 7, No. 2 (1987), pp. 54–71.

83. F. Herzberg, F. Mausner, and B. B. Snyderman, *The Motivation to Work* (New York: John Wiley and Sons, 1959).

84. Dumaine, "The Bureaucracy Busters," p. 42.

85. R. E. Walton, *Up and Running: Integrating Information Technology and the Organization* (Boston: Harvard Business Press, 1989), p. 81.

86. K. D. MacKenzie, "Holonomic Processes for Ensuring Competitiveness," *Making Organizations Competitive,* R. H. Kilmann and I. Kilmann, eds. (San Francisco: Jossey-Bass Publishers, 1991), p. 244.

87. C. Johnson, "Japanese Style Management in America," *California Management Review,* Vol. 31, No. 4 (1988), pp. 34–45.

88. "Wal-Mart," *Business World,* ABC-TV, April 21, 1991.

89. Johnson, "Japanese Style Management in America."

90. Blackburn and Rosen, "Total Quality and Human Resources Management: Lessons Learned from the Baldrige Award-Winning Companies," p. 50.

91. Babbar and Rai, "Competitive Intelligence for International Business," p. 109.

92. Walton, *Up and Running: Integrating Information Technology and the Organization.*

93. L. Hirschhorn, and T. N. Gilmore, "The Psychodynamics of Cultural Change: Learning from the Factory," *Human Resources Management,* Vol. 28 (1989), pp. 211–233.

94. S. M. Young, "A Framework for Successful Adoption and Performance of Japanese Manufacturing Practices in the United States," *The Academy of Management Review,* Vol. 17, No. 4 (1992), pp. 692.

95. Blackburn and Rosen, "Total Quality and Human Resources Management: Lessons Learned from Baldrige Award-Winning Companies," p. 55.

96. Much of this discussion is excerpted from Carl A. Rodrigues, "Employee Participation and Empowerment Programs: Problems of Definition and Implementation," *Empowerment in Organizations: An International Journal,* Vol. 2, No. 2 (1994), pp. 29–40.

97. E. Schein, "Coming to a New Awareness of Organizational Culture," *Sloan Management Review* (Winter 1994), p. 3.

98. P. Shrivastava and S. Schneider, "Organizational Frames of Reference," *Human Relations,* Vol. 37 (November 10, 1984), pp. 795–805.

99. G. Hofstede, B. Neuijen, D. D. Ohavy, and G. Sanders, "Measuring Organizational Culture: A Qualitative and Quantitative Study Across Twenty Cases," *Administrative Science Quarterly,* Vol. 35 (1990), pp. 311–312.

100. J. Child, "Managerial Strategies, New Technology and the Labor Process," *New Technology as Organizational Innovation,* J. M. Pennings, and A. Buitendam, eds. (Cambridge, MA: Balinger, 1987), p. 171.

101. M. R. Kelley, "Programmable Automation and the Skill Question: A Reinterpretation of Cross-National Evidence," *Human Systems Management,* Vol. 6 (1986), pp. 141–147.

102. C. A. Bartlett and S. Ghoshal, *Managing Across Borders: The Transnational Solution* (Boston: Harvard Business School Press, 1989).

103. R. E. Quinn and J Rohrbaugh, "A Spatial Model of Effectiveness Criteria: Towards a Competing Values Approach to Organizational Analysis," *Management Science,* Vol. 29 (1983), pp. 363–367.

104. R. E. Quinn and J. R. Kimberly, Jr., "Paradox, Planning and Perseverence: Guidelines for Managerial Practice," *Managing Organizational Transitions,* J. R. Kimberly and R. E. Quinn, eds. (Homewood, IL: Dow Jones-Irwin, 1984), pp. 295–313.

105. S. P. Sethi, N. Namiki, and C. L. Swanson, *The False Promise of the Japanese Miracle: Illusions and Realities of the Japanese Management System* (London: Pitman, 1984), p. 243.

106. Ibid.

107. R. F. Magjuka, "Should Membership in Employee Involvement Programs Be Voluntary?" *National Productivity Review* (Spring 1992), p. 208.

108. See, for example, J. L. Cordery, W. S. Mueller, and L. M. Smith, "Attitudinal and Behavioral Effects of Autonomous Group Working: A Longitudinal Field Study," *The Academy of Management Journal,* Vol. 34, No. 2 (1991), pp. 464–476.

109. J. Junkerman, "We Are Driven," *Mother Jones* (1982), pp. 21–40.

110. "The Darker Side of Japanese Management," *Frontline,* PBS-TV New Documentory (1984).

111. K. Susaki, "Japanese Manufacturing Techniques: Their Importance to U.S. Manufacturers," *Journal of Business Strategy,* Vol. 5 (1985), pp. 10–19.

112. R. Tannenbaum, I. R. Weschler, and F. Massarik. *Leadership and Organization: A Behavioral Science Approach* (New York: McGraw-Hill, 1961).

113. For example, J. W. Graham and A. Verna, "Predictors and Moderators of Employee Responses to Employee Participation Programs," *Human Relations* (June 1991), pp. 551–568; and K. L. Miller and P. R. Monge, "Participation, Satisfaction and Productivity: A Meta-Analytic Review," *The Academy of Management Journal,* Vol. 29, No. 4 (1986), pp. 727–753.

114. Child, "Managerial Strategies, New Technology and the Labor Process."

115. P. L. Nemetz and L. W. Fry, "Flexible Manufacturing Organizations: Implications for Strategy Formulation and Organization Design," *The Academy of Management Review,*

115. P. L. Nemetz and L. W. Fry, "Flexible Manufacturing Organizations: Implications for Strategy Formulation and Organization Design," *The Academy of Management Review,* Vol. 13 (1988), pp. 627–638.

116. Blackburn and Rosen, "Total Quality and Human Resource Management: Lessons Learned from Baldrige Award-Winning Companies," p. 61.

117. C. Brooke, "Symbols and Shambles: Quality and Organizational Change," *Proceedings of Organizations and Symbols of Transformation,* Standing Committee on Organizational Symbolism, Barcelona, Spain (June 27–30, 1993).

118. E. E. Lawler III, S. Mohrman, and G. E. Ledford, Jr., "The Fortune 1000 and Total Quality," *National Productivity Review* (Autumn 1992), pp. 501–515.

119. R. C. Hill, "When the Going Gets Rough: A Baldrige Award Winner on the Line," *The Academy of Management Executive,* Vol. 7, No. 3 (1993), pp. 78–79.

120. Brooke, "Symbols and Shambles: Quality and Organizational Change," p. 4.

121. H. Mintzberg, "Strategy Making in Three Modes," *California Management Review,* Vol. 16, No. 1 (1973), pp. 44–53.

122. D. C. McClelland, *The Inner Experience* (New York: Irvington, 1975).

123. J. Bleeke and D. Ernst, "The Way to Win in Cross-Border Alliances," *Harvard Business Review* (November–December 1991), p. 135.

124. Martha H. Peak, "Developing an International Style of Management," *Management Review* (February 1991), p. 33.

125. S. L. Huff, "Managing Global Information Technology," *Business Quarterly* (Autumn 1991), p. 71.

126. Ibid., p. 73.

127. Dwyer et al., "Tearing Up Today's Organization Chart," pp. 83–84.

128. A. Wilkinson, "TQM and Employee Development," *Human Resource Management Journal,* Vol. 2, No. 4 (1992), pp. 1–20.

X

P a r t   T e n

INTEGRATIVE CASES

This part contains seven cases: "Euro Disneyland," "Sony in America," "Thai Chempest," "The Case of the Floundering Expatriate," "Levi's Says Goodby to China," "Nissan U.K.: A Worker's Paradox?" and "McDonald's Conquers the World."

In each chapter, this textbook has presented practical perspectives, exercises, and cases which, along with the instructor's lectures, will help students understand the chapter's contents. The seven cases in this part will help students develop an integrated understanding of the textbook's contents. These cases should be read and analyzed after students have read all the chapters and practical perspectives, and completed all the exercises and previous cases.

To help students develop an integrated view, the instructor will provide a set of questions for each case to guide them in the analysis. The instructor may also assign individual and group exercises, which aid in the integrative development process. The integration will be enhanced if the analyses are discussed in class.

Euro Disneyland *Integrative* Case One

By the late 1980s, Europe was seen as the upcoming economic superpower of the twenty-first century. Trade restrictions were being methodically removed, and plans were being made to convert to one European currency unit. The "new Europe" was purported to be the next major area of growth and wealth accumulation.

The Disney company wanted to be part of Europe's future. In order to take full advantage of these changes the management knew they had to get in early. In 1987, the decision was made to go ahead with a major development plan. With revenues springing to life from the American parks and Tokyo Disneyland an unqualified success, Disney under Michael D. Eisner began to plan for its next major expansion—Euro Disneyland.

BACKGROUND

Euro Disneyland was not a new idea. It was simply the most recent manifestation of the Walt Disney Company's theme park strategy—the latest phase in Disney park evolution. Its predecessors can be directly traced back to Anaheim, California (1955), Orlando, Florida (1970), and Tokyo Disneyland in Japan (1982).

By the beginning of the 1950s, the Walt Disney Company was well established as a film studio. It had developed this success by utilizing a new film technology, animation, and developing an endearing cast of animated "stars"—Mickey Mouse, Goofy, Donald Duck, Snow White. Starting with short film subjects in the 1920s, or cartoons, the Disney organization was developing full-length animated films by the late 1930s. The broad acceptance of the Disney films by the American public, the strict adherence to high-quality production standards, the development of new film techniques, and the continuing creation of popular animated characters were key factors in establishing the success of the studio. Interestingly, the Disney animated cast would have a profound effect on the development of the theme parks.

The "Great Man"

The Disney studio was an entrepreneurial enterprise with its foundation in the arts. Founded by Walt Disney, it had his mark on every endeavor. There are few other such clear examples in American industry of the "Great Man" model. As a company, it developed as a patriarchal institution with Walt and his brother Roy controlling everything. With Walt Disney from the beginning, Roy Disney concentrated on the financial aspects of the burgeoning empire and allowed Walt, the creative sibling, to concentrate on the animation and marketing aspects. This partnership was extremely successful. The two Disneys built one of the most impressive design/marketing machines in the history of American business. Disney logos, shirts, animations, books

Source: This case was prepared by Dr. Tunglung Chang, assistant professor of marketing and international business at New Jersey Institute of Technology, with the assistance of his former graduate student, Mr. Edward Healy. The information came from various periodicals, books, and the company's financial reports. The case was developed for class discussion rather than to illustrate effective or ineffective management practices. Printed with permission. All rights reserved by Dr. Tung.

the history of American business. Disney logos, shirts, animations, books and films pervade our culture and are recognized throughout the world.

Walt Disney realized early on that his park would have a distinct advantage over every other amusement park in the world. He knew he could develop a strong relationship with the characters his studio had developed. No other park had universally recognized hosts like Mickey Mouse, Goofy, or Donald Duck, and its own one-hour TV show on Sunday nights with which to promote it. No other park could command the loyalty of thousands of children on the opening day. His cast of celluloid characters and their well-documented adventures became the park's most important marketing tool.

Management Orientation and Philosophy

Perhaps the most unique aspect of the Disney studio was its close adherence to the philosophy of its founder Walt Disney. Unlike the other Hollywood studios at the time, Disney made sure that the studio maintained a strict moral environment. He was adamant that the studio and the products generated by the entire Disney corporation be closely associated with family values and a wholesome American image.

The Disney corporate attitude that evolved was a direct reflection of the personal beliefs of the founder. This legacy continued long after Walt Disney's death. During staff meetings, "executives clinched arguments by quoting Walt like Scripture or Marx." Taking a chapter from Chairman Mao of China, the Disney company eventually produced and distributed a little book with Walt's sayings.

A second important aspect of management philosophy developed by Walt Disney and maintained long after his death was the refusal to pay the enormous amounts demanded and received by movie talent at the time. Walt Disney believed that the studio should concentrate on wholesome family-oriented pictures that were produced within a relatively limited budget. It was this wholesomeness and tight financial control that became the hallmark of the Disney Company.

The success of Disneyland was immediate. Despite strenuous objections from Roy, who believed the company should remain focused on films, Disneyland generated record crowds from opening day. So successful was the park that all construction loans were retired within nine months.

Walt Disney never advertised his park in the media. The only communication used was through the television programs being generated for the ABC network. Despite this self-imposed (and frugal) limitation, the public media offered wide coverage because of the park's uniqueness and its devotion to cleanliness and family values. Within a short period, it became an American icon for family entertainment.

The success of the park was directly attributable to the brilliant vision of Walt Disney. From the start, it was his devotion to the development of

| Growth Rate in Los Angeles and California, 1950–1960 | | | TABLE 1 ◆ |

	1950	1960	Percent Change in Population
Los Angeles	1,970,358	2,479,015	25.8%
California	10,586,223	15,717,204	48.5%

Source: Information Almanac, 1992.

the idea of a theme park and the scrupulous way in which it was constructed and maintained that ensured its success.

Southern California—1950s

Another factor in its success was the the location in which the Disney studios and subsequently Disneyland were built. The choice of Anaheim in Orange County as a site for the first Disney theme park had as much to do with the location of Disney Studios in Burbank, California, as it did with the rapid growth of the Los Angeles area in the 1950s and 1960s.

Even so, the choice and timing couldn't have been better. Not only was Southern California rapidly developing as an area of high technology and modern industry (electronics, aircraft, and military), but it had become a modern-day mecca for tourists seeking a vacation in the land of Hollywood and the home of the big-screen movie. It had become an important vacation destination. The construction of Disneyland was able to exploit these trends and reinforce the image of a California vacation playland.

The "baby boom" was also of importance. Starting in 1946, America enjoyed a rapid increase in the number of children. By 1955, the first wave of this burgeoning group would be nine years old—the perfect age for Disney products (films, TV shows, products) and attending the new park. As this wave increased in number, Disneyland grew and prospered. The Disney planners were aware of this change and they took full advantage of it.

STRATEGIC DECISIONS IN EACH DEVELOPMENT STAGE

From Cartoons to the Theme Parks

The evolution of the Walt Disney Company can be clearly divided into various growth phases with each phase delineated by strategic decisions. The first phase was Walt Disney's commitment to films and animations. Although he had intended originally to be a movie producer when he moved from Kansas City to Hollywood, he soon realized the advantages of concentrating his efforts in what he knew. The second phase began when the studio, now well financed, chose to enter the full-length movie market.

Although the studio still made cartoons, it poured resources into the development of the full-length movies. The successes that followed (*Snow White*, 1937; *Pinocchio, Fantasia*, 1940; *Bambi*, 1942) illustrate the wisdom of this decision.

The third major strategic decision had the most direct impact on Euro Disneyland. In 1953, Walt Disney made the decision to build a theme park. It was his desire to combine the Disney Corporation's orientation toward family values and a wholesome environment with an amusement park that led to development of the first Disney theme park—Disneyland in California. The success of Disneyland (California) was directly responsible for the decision to build a second park in Florida, Walt Disney World. The idea of an East Coast park had been with Walt Disney from the beginning and he felt certain that it would have to be located somewhere in Florida.

The Magic Formula—EPCOT and MGM/Disney and Hotels

The fourth strategic decision was to develop an entire area, a cluster of Disney attractions, focused on one geographic area. The Florida location became the first test site. The Disney Company eventually developed three major theme parks surrounded by Disney theme hotels. The various theme parks would offer attractions to a much wider audience, and the hotels would offer Disney hospitality to a captive audience. This combination was to prove very successful.

The first ancillary park was EPCOT, the dream of the founder, Walt Disney. He had envisioned a city of the future where Americans could go to get a glimpse of the shape of things to come. EPCOT was to be a living social experiment that would embrace the latest technologies. Although he passionately believed that EPCOT would be even more significant than the Walt Disney theme park, he died before construction could begin.

In developing the Orlando region as a tourist center, Disney management was aware of how successful Universal Studios in California had been in attracting vacationing tourists. In Florida, Disney had both the land and the desire to create a theme park based on the movies. The result was a joint venture with MGM to develop a theme park similar to the one offered by Universal Studios in California.

Marketing Planning and Promotion

Both Disneyland and the Orlando Disney World/EPCOT/MGM complex had struck a nerve in American culture. Like EPCOT and MGM/Disney, they offered an escape to a contrived, safe, simpler time when the streets were clean and the inhabitants (Disney refers to them as "cast members"— a reference to their cinematic background) well trained and polite. This combination was both profitable for the Disney Company and attractive to Americans, as well as a growing number of foreigners.

Walt Disney also believed that the park would never be "finished." As new advances in science or new artistic developments were achieved, they would be incorporated into the park. In an interview with the Hollywood *Citizen-News*, he explained, "the park means a lot to me. It's something that will never be finished, something I can keep developing, keep 'plussing," and adding to. It's alive. It will be a live, breathing thing that will need changes."

The marketing of Disney theme parks centered on the uniqueness of each park, the tie-in with Disney characters, and the constant change of attractions. Walt Disney had developed an attraction that was to become an American institution—a familiar place of wholesome fantasies. It would be a safe, clean, friendly environment where scenes were ever-changing and families could enjoy a day together. This was exactly how the parks were marketed—a place from the past to escape to and feel safe and secure.

The American Fit

The Disney theme parks were designed for Americans—from Davy Crockett's Frontierland right down to the Mississippi Riverboat Ride. Walt Disney wanted his parks to be closely aligned with America's past . . . and future. In order to achieve an American "feel," he chose a scene out of American folklore—a reproduction of a Midwestern town at the turn of the century (circa 1890–1910). Victorian buildings (undersized for additional warmth and sense of community), horse-drawn trams, and spotless walks populated by friendly guides became the standard. Disney's Main Street was the recreation of the ideal typical American town drawn from the movie maker's imagination.

The entire park was surrounded by a reduced-scale railroad based on a turn-of-the-century American model. The system would offer a powerful historical image and tie the park together with transportation services to various points along the park's perimeter. It would also serve as a barrier to the outside world.

Breaking off from the square were four American theme areas— Fantasyland, Adventureland, Frontierland, and Tomorrowland. Most of the attractions would be related to either the animated characters the studio had created and developed or geographic images of the fantasies the films had created. This intertwining of theme park attractions with Disney characters gave Disneyland a tremendous advantage over other park operators. America had grown up with the studio's cast of characters. This association allowed the park to be more than just a collection of amusement rides. It was an "American experience" where the visitor could actually enter into one of Disney's fantasies.

The importance of the movie-making experience was also important in the planning of the attractions. Drawing on his expertise in making movies, Walt Disney felt the park should be structured like a film with a strong sense of continuity. He wanted the visitor to move through the park much like a camera moves from scene to scene—another trait that sets it apart from the ordinary amusement park. Americans are comfortable with movies and accepted the park's structure as natural.

Driven by Walt Disney's creativity and marketing savvy, and drawing heavily on the Disney Studios theatrical and animation design skills, Disneyland, Walt Disney World, EPCOT, and the Disney/MGM studios quickly developed a powerful identity of their own, unique to anything that had ever been developed. So phenomenal was the acceptance of the parks by the American public, they became a powerful symbol of both modern American entertainment and American culture.

GLOBAL EXPANSION

The success of the Disney theme parks in the United States encouraged management to consider expanding abroad. This was not a new idea. When Walt Disney was planning the Orlando complex, he commented to one of his aides that he could see a time when these (Disney World) parks were scattered throughout the world.

The first foreign commitment came during the leadership of "Card" Walker. Walker had joined the Disney Studios as a messenger boy in 1938 and literally worked his way to the top. Following the deaths of Walt Disney and Roy Disney, E. Cardon Walker became the chief executive officer (1976–1983). He was a "flinty, strait-laced Idaho-born Mormon" who made studio decisions based on what he thought Walt would want. Quick to ridicule underlings in public and impervious to any point of view but his own, he is credited with losing touch with modern taste, resulting in the the poor performance of the studio's offerings.

One of his successes, however, was entering into an agreement with the Oriental Land Company to build a Disney theme park in Japan. In keeping with the tight-fisted financial philosophy of the Disney Company, the agreement was structured as a franchise.

Competitive Advantage

The World Franchise—Disney Products

The greatest advantage enjoyed by the Disney Company is the worldwide public awareness of the products of the company. Children and their parents throughout the world know the images of Mickey Mouse and Goofy. The company has always maintained the highest quality in any of their offerings. As a result, the images and products of the Walt Disney Company are synonymous with quality and high-value entertainment.

The most important part of this worldwide Disney franchise is the cast of characters created by Walt Disney and carefully developed over the succeeding decades. Each character is an easily identified symbol that can be quickly associated with any Disney project. This instant identification capability gives Disney a deep-rooted competitive advantage.

This quality entertainment is not limited to the theme parks. Disney's movies, such as the recent *Aladdin*, have enjoyed strong support in the theater and then strong sales as after-market videotapes. The Disney company is now extending the market for *Aladdin* products and the preceding *Beauty and the Beast* product line by developing Sega and Nintendo games.

Television has projected Walt Disney's animation throughout the world. The development of world communications has had a dramatic effect on developing the Disney mystique. "The company gospel is that entertainment delivery systems can become obsolete, but what is always in demand is the entertainment that travels throughout them." This philosophy has served them well in their expansion.

Deep Pockets—Cold Cash

The other important competitive advantage enjoyed by the Disney management is a healthy balance sheet. The Disney Company is not highly leveraged. Michael Eisner, the current CEO, "is fanatical about not overpaying. Armed with lots of cash and a balance sheet that would support billions in added debt, Disney has looked carefully at CBS Inc., Mattel Inc., a host of record companies and many other businesses before backing off." The company has the capability of borrowing billions of dollars and this access to capital gives the company market clout.

Consumer Needs and Wants

The success of the California park in 1955 and the Florida park in 1970 clearly indicates that the Disney Company very effectively filled an American need. Both parks provide a pleasant escape from the realities of modern life. They take visitors back to another time when everything was clean and everybody pleasant, where simply by moving from one area to another, the visitor can enjoy singing mechanical bears or a spaceship ride to the planets. Fantasy is not only encouraged, but cultivated.

EPCOT gives the visitor a chance to see the state of the art in science and a sense of things yet to come. It challenges as much as it entertains and educates. It is in every way a Disney experience. MGM/Disney brings the visitor face to face with the movie and television industries. It satisfies the fascination Americans have for two of the most creative industries. There is a question, however, as to whether American tastes can be extended throughout the world. The Disney management made the decision that "Yes it can." Time will tell.

Competition

Walt Disney never felt that the traditional amusement park was competition for his planned Disneyland. He drew a sharp distinction between the usual

"Great White Way" and his idea of a theme park. He was also adamant about not including the traditional Ferris Wheel in his park, despite all of the advice he received from park operators that you needed one to attract people. Although the traditional amusement park does not offer much competition to a theme park, that is not to say there are no other theme parks. Besides the traditional amusement parks that dot the country, Disneyland and Walt Disney World are facing a growing list of competitors. Disneyland had Knotts Berry Farm, a well-established theme park, as a competitor for years. Both parks project a wholesome, family image. It is the development of Universal Studios theme parks, however, that have intensified the pressure on the Disney offerings.

Located in the Los Angeles area, Universal Studios offered the tourist an inside peek at the movies. As the technical sophistication of the movies increased, the exhibits developed by Universal became more like the Disney exhibits. The increasing success of the California park encouraged Universal to expand into new markets.

Tokyo Disneyland

In 1982, the Disney Company entered into an agreement with the Oriental Land Corporation (a joint venture between Mitsui Real Estate Development Co. and Keisei Railway Co.). Oriental Land felt that there was a need for a world-class theme park in Japan. Japan, which had worked so hard during the 1950s, 1960s, and 1970s, had reached economic superpower status. What was missing was recreational opportunity. Oriental Land wanted to fill it.

Franchise Agreement

The agreement with the Disney Company was simple. Disney would design the park and supply expertise in return for a royalty of 10% of the gate and 5% of concessions. Disney would also make sure that the Tokyo park was a close duplicate of the two American parks. Oriental Land wanted the genuine article—Disney Americana.

Oriental Land Company would carry the entire risk of constructing the park. Disney, on the other hand, would limit its risk to the cost of design and providing park expertise. Given the cost of the park (180 billion yen, approximately $1.5 billion), Disney had struck a shrewd bargain. The company felt it could determine whether or not a Disney theme park could be exported while at the same time assuming very little risk.

Disney's Concerns

It was obvious that the Disney management was concerned about constructing a theme park, using Disney characters and Disney trademarks, in an Asian country and in a cold environment. They were uncertain as to how well the Disney images, so popular with American audiences for generations, would be accepted by a foreign culture.

With regard to the cultural challenge, Disney was able to prepare the Japanese market with a flood of cartoons, TV shows, movies, and cartoon characters. By the time the park was complete, Disney images were well known and growing in popularity in all segments of the Japanese population. The image of Mickey Mouse had become so popular that even Emperor Hirohito wore one on his wristwatch.

The location of the park was another matter. Walt Disney had expressed strong doubt as to ever building a theme park in a northern climate. He saw no way to keep the park open for fewer than twelve months a year and still generate a cash flow sufficient to meet park expenses. The California and Florida parks were able to remain open for twelve months of the year because they were in a warm climate. Would the Tokyo park be able to overcome this limitation?

Physical Adjustments

Although similar to the two American parks in most important features, Tokyo Disneyland does make heavy use of bilingual signs. In addition, the park includes a number of Japanese food entrees on the menu (along with hamburgers, French fries, and hot dogs, of course).

Because of climatic differences, Tokyo being much father north than either Anaheim or Orlando, the park designers enclosed waiting areas to protect visitors from the elements. In addition, a number of the rides have covers over them to protect riders. These changes permitted the park to effectively operate twelve months out of the year.

Cultural Adjustments

In addition to the architectural changes to Tokyo Disneyland, there were also cultural and ethnic changes. "Melvin, Buff and Max, the antlered commentators at the Country Bear Jamboree, speak in the grave basso profundos of Kurosawa samurais" rather than the country twang found in the American parks. Alice in Wonderland was given Asian features. Frontierland was changed into Westernland (the Japanese don't like frontiers). Finally, the center of the entire park, Main Street, was renamed the World Bazaar. These differences are relatively minor, however. The spirit and essence of the park are strictly Disney.

Financial Performance

After a slow start, the theme park was enthusiastically accepted by the Japanese. In 1987 over one million school children, who normally would have been taken to the shrines of Japan, were brought to the park. Although financial numbers are not available, Oriental Land is pleased with its investment.

◆   TABLE 2   Temperature and Precipitation

| | Average Temperature (F degrees) | | | | Annual Precipitation |
| | January | | July | | |
	Max.	Min.	Max.	Min.	(inches)
France	42	32	76	55	22.3
Japan	47	29	83	70	61.6

Source: The World Almanac & Book of Facts, 1992.

Impact on Company's Strategy

The success of Tokyo Disneyland had one important effect on the Disney company's plans for expansion. Just as the success of Disneyworld had convinced Walt Disney to build a second park in Florida, the success of Tokyo Disneyland convinced Disney management to build a second park—a European park. Since there were certain similarities between the climates and the regions, management felt that if the Disney theme park idea worked in Japan, then surely it would work in Europe.

Euro Disneyland—The Second Venture

Michael D. Eisner was the driving force behind Euro Disneyland. Early in his career at Disney, Eisner had made a great success by increasing the admission fare at the American Disney parks by 100% to generate much needed capital. He reasoned correctly that an increase in the cost of admission would not discourage tourists from visiting the parks. He understood that Disney was one of the world's most powerful consumer franchises and was unique in the world of amusement parks, and that people would pay to see it. This increase in park admission charges alone achieved a $450 million gain to pretax profits with no drop in attendance.

His second move was centered on the Walt Disney World complex in Florida. Sensing that the Orlando park area was not being properly exploited, he increased the number of hotel rooms on Disney property by 6,700 (4,400 owned directly by Disney). These strategies were successful. Disney reported earnings increased from $22 million in 1984 to $824 million in 1990.

In 1987, the decision was made to go ahead with a major development plan. The company envisioned a Disneyland-type theme park surrounded by theme hotels. This was the same formula used in Orlando. Once the hotel and park were firmly established, Disney would begin the second phase. This included the second and third theme parks, and the office complex and housing project.

Euro Disneyland Goals

The goals for the new Euro Disneyland were fairly straightforward. Management wanted to:

1. Meet the goal of 11 million visitors at the end of one operational year.
2. Generate a profit from the theme park and the hotels by the end of the third operational quarter and continue to expand profits in each succeeding quarter.
3. Develop the financial foundation with the theme park and its supporting hotels so as to continue with the second phase (an American-like office park complex and another theme park—MGM/Disney) and the third phase (a housing project and a second theme park).
4. Have all of the elements of the project reinforce each other, thereby making the sum of the parts greater than the individual parts themselves and subsequently increasing tourist activity.

Key Concern 1—Site Location

The first strategic decision facing management was where to build it. If the Euro Disney theme park was to open in April of 1992, the choice of site had to be made. In 1987, during the early planning stages, the selection came down to a beet farm 20 miles east of Paris and two sites in southern Spain. David Lawday wrote in *U.S. News & World Report*, "at first, Disney was unsure whether to land in Spain or in France. Barcelona offered a sunnier climate—and cheerier populace—but Disney was ultimately swayed by France's superior infrastructure and quicker access to the 12 nation European Community's 320 million consumers. Paris not only boasts two international airports but a high-speed rail system that covers the country." Lawday adds, "in the future, this train will rush passengers from Britain via the Channel Tunnel and from the population heart of Germany."

The French government agreed to extend the suburban Paris subway directly to the park. Since Paris was a major vacation destination, it was felt that many tourists would be tempted to visit the park. Taken together—the location, the infrastructure, and the generous incentives offered by the French government—the Disney management was swayed. There was still a vexing problem, however: the weather.

Key Concern 2—Climate

Unlike the location of the two American parks, the Paris region was considered a temperate climate with cold winters. For the most part, many of Disney's concerns were neutralized by the success of the Tokyo park, but there remained some anxiety as to whether the park would generate sufficient crowds during the winter months.

Since the Japanese park faced the same problem, Disney designers made similar adjustments in the Euro park design (extensive sheltered areas and numerous fireplaces). Management was now fairly certain the French would support the park in November, December, and January. The French government condemned the land used for sugar beet growing, and the project began.

Euro Disney Personnel

Robert Fitzpatrick, an American and a "tall bespectacled man of cosmopolitan bearing and enormous charm," was selected as the president of Euro Disney. His appointment was considered a masterstroke of personnel placement. Known as the former president of the California Institute of the Arts, director of the Olympic Arts Festival, and professor of French at the University of Maine, his charm and fluency in French (and his French wife) were seen as a means of demonstrating Disney's commitment to French culture.

The park, Euro Disneyland, has come close to meeting its goal of 11 million visitors for the first year of operation. The park has not, however, been able to meet hotel occupancy and expenditures per visitor projections. These are far below expectations and are placing a strain on the theme park's finances. This poor showing also drew Disney's California-based senior management directly into the crisis in late 1993.

Exacerbating the financial shortfall is a heavy debt burden (approximately $3.7 billion) incurred by the Disney Company to build the Euro park. Denominated in French francs, it has become a victim of the French government's strategy of keeping interest rates high so as to protect the value of the franc.

The Disney management is now desperately trying to determine the cause for the park's weak performance and develop a strategy to reverse it. The determination of a solution, however, will be neither simple nor easy because the nature of the problem is neither clear nor apparent. What is clear is that Disney management is facing an unexpected crisis situation—what should they do about Euro Disney?

Sony in America *Integrative* Case Two

Akio Morita and a friend founded Tokyo Telecommunications Company (name translated) in Tokyo in 1945 and incorporated it in 1946. It manufactured communications equipment for Japanese telephone and telegraph companies and for the national railroad. From the beginning it stressed quality production and heavy investment in R&D. It started research on consumer goods in 1947 and brought out its first product, a tape recorder, in 1950. It brought out a transistor radio in 1955 and a pocket-sized version in 1957; the latter became its first export product and was quite successful in the U.S. and Europe. It introduced the world's first fully transistorized television set in 1959.

Source: William A. Stoever, Keating-Crawford Professor of International Business at Seton Hall University. This case was prepared as a basis for class discussion rather than to illustrate effective or ineffective management practices. Printed with permission. All rights reserved by Professor Stoever

INTERNATIONAL EXPANSION

The company's early successes in exporting, combined with the Japanese government's drive to increase exports, stimulated its efforts to internationalize. It changed its name to Sony in 1958 because it wanted a shorter name that would be easier for foreign customers to remember. It began establishing overseas subsidiaries and joint ventures in 1960 and expanded rapidly. Among the most important were:

- Established Sony Corporation of America (originally a marketing company) in 1960 (U.S.A.)
- Incorporated Sony Overseas S.A. in 1960 (Switzerland)
- Established Sony Tektronix Corp. in Japan as joint venture with Tektronix Inc. to produce oscilloscopes in 1965 (U.S.A.)
- Set up Sony (U.K.) Ltd. in 1968 (U.K.)
- Established CBS/Sony Group Inc., a 50-50 joint venture with Columbia Broadcasting System (CBS) in 1970 to manufacture and market musical equipment in Japan (U.S.A.)
- Set up Sony G.m.b.H. (1970) (which became Sony Deutschland G.m.b.H. in 1980) (West Germany)
- Established Sony Trading Company in 1972 to identify products manufactured in the U.S.A. and Europe and market them in Japan
- Established its first manufacturing facility outside Asia in San Diego, California, in 1972 to assemble television sets (U.S.A.)
- Set up Sony France S.A. in 1973 (France)
- Established Sony Eveready, Inc. in Japan in 1975 as a joint venture with Union Carbide Corp. to import and sell Union Carbide's high-performance dry cells (U.S.A.)
- Acquired Wega Radio and Wega Hi-Fi, a highly reputed manufacturing group in 1975 (West Germany)
- Established Sony Prudential Life Insurance Co., Ltd. in 1979 as joint venture (51% owned by Prudential Life Insurance Co. of America) to sell life insurance in Japan

- Established Sony/Wilson, Inc. in 1979 as joint venture with Pepsico, Inc. (U.S.A.) to import and sell Wilson sporting goods in Japan
- Acquired hard disk technology and operations from Apple Computer Inc. (U.S.A.) in 1984 to produce hard disks in Japan and market them in the U.S.A.
- Sony Corp. of America acquired Digital Audio Disc Corp. from CBS/Sony Group Inc. in 1985 (U.S.A.)
- Entered joint venture agreement in 1985 with Vitelic Corp. (U.S.A.) to obtain Vitelic's proprietary CMOS memory technology in exchange for agreement to manufacture Vitelic products for sale by Vitelic
- Acquired CBS Records Inc. and CBS Inc.'s share of CBS/Sony Group Inc. for approximately U.S. $2 billion in 1988 (U.S.A.)
- Acquired (bought out) Materials Research Corporation in 1989 (U.S.A.)
- Purchased all the outstanding common stock of Columbia Pictures Entertainment, Inc. and of the Guber-Peters Entertainment Company (a Columbia affiliate that produced movies and TV fare) for approximately $3.6 billion and assumption of $1.5 billion of Columbia's debt (1989) (U.S.A.)
- Sony Music Entertainment Inc. (SMEI, formerly CBS Records) established Columbia House Company as 50-50 joint venture with a subsidiary of Time-Warner Inc. (U.S.A.) to market music and home-video products in the U.S. and Canada (1991)

Over the years Sony also set up 100% subsidiaries or joint ventures in Australia, Austria, Belgium, Brazil, Canada, Denmark, Hong Kong, Italy, Korea, Malaysia, Netherlands, Panama, Saudi Arabia, Singapore, Spain, Taiwan and Thailand.

These companies show an evolution in Sony's strategy over the years. Its first overseas subsidiaries were marketing organizations to sell products manufactured in Japan. Its early joint ventures were for the purpose of obtaining technology for its home plants.

It set up its *sogo shosha* (Sony Trading Company) partly to diversify and partly because its overseas representatives found some good-quality foreign products it could sell back home. It could channel these products to its growing chain of retail outlets (which eventually reached 8,000) and eliminate middlemen's commissions. This move also helped it deflect growing criticism of Japan's closed market.

Its first overseas manufacturing facilities were necessitated because upward revaluations of the yen, a reaction against the flood of Japanese goods, and the possibility of protectionism threatened to make exports from home uncompetitive. Later overseas manufacturing was to get closer to its markets and to find the lowest-cost production locations.

Many later acquisitions and joint ventures were for product diversification. Some later acquisitions of foreign companies were to gain additional returns on technology it had developed. Materials Research Corp., for example, had been floundering until it obtained an infusion of capital, technology, R&D, and market credibility from Sony's buyout.

In 1991 Sony had a total of 16 manufacturing plants: nine in Japan, four in Europe, and three in the U.S.A. Its sales breakdown was 29% in the U.S., 28% in Europe, 26% in Japan, and 17% in the rest of the world.

MARKETING PHILOSOPHY

Sony has always been product-driven and indeed has no market research facility. It allows its R&D and product people to follow their heads and develop the products they want to develop; it believes these are the products that will sell. One such product developed without any prior market research was the Sony Walkman, a small radio with earphones that could be carried in a person's pocket or belt and played in public places while doing other activities; it was a notable success. Morita once said, "We don't market products that have already been developed; rather, we develop markets for the products we make." The company is willing to sell off (or write off) investments in products that "don't work."

Sony has several times demonstrated its willingness to cut prices and profit margins in order to build market share. For example, in fall 1990 it cut prices on automobile compact disk players, which had been a major profit generator. An executive of an American competitor surmised that this was preparatory to pruning its line to make room for new products. Another said it should also help solidify Sony's brand name and image.

LONG-TERM PERSPECTIVE

Sony has been willing to take a long-term view of its investments in both R&D and production facilities. Sometimes its thoroughness and deliberate pace have worked to its disadvantage, however. For example, it started developing its betamax system for videocassette recorders (VCRs) in 1960 but didn't bring it to market until 1976. Then it hoped to reserve the market for itself and so failed to license the tape technology to other manufacturers. Soon thereafter its archrival Matsushita Electric Co. brought out VCRs using the VHS system, which it licensed widely and which eventually became the industry standard. Although many observers considered Sony's system superior, it never captured more than about a sixth of the market and ceased production in 1986. The company ended up having to write off a large portion of its R&D investment in the product.

THE QUESTION OF CHEAP LABOR

An ongoing question at Sony was whether to open production facilities in less-developed countries (LDCs) in order to take advantage of cheap labor.

Mexico was one of the countries that had approached the company to offer subsidized plant sites, tariff exemptions for components for products to be re-exported, and subsidies for training of labor. Such an offer would be especially attractive for products that had reached life cycle maturity, such as Sony's core of consumer electronics. But the company's top management was concerned about difficulties in rapidly imparting its product and technology innovations, maintaining its quality edge, and preserving its top-market image. It was especially concerned that products manufactured or assembled in Third World countries might damage the reputation of the ones originating in Japan and other industrialized countries. Thus when it announced plans in 1990 to expand existing capacity and open new plants in Singapore, Malaysia, and Thailand, these were mainly to serve internal markets in Southeast Asia. Sony also wasn't convinced that LDC assembly plants would insulate it from the harmful effects of currency fluctuations, especially at times when the yen was strengthening. As a generalization, its Japanese managers were more reluctant than its foreign managers to entertain the possibility of LDC production.

MANAGEMENT PROBLEMS

Sony's overseas top management was all Japanese until 1972, when the company concluded it would have to internationalize its outlook and management practices. One of its first foreign top executives was an American, Harvey Schein, who became president of Sony Corp. of America. However, this and other non-Japanese appointments created some problems. The foreign executives had been accustomed to taking charge and making rapid, more or less unilateral decisions, and they chafed when they had to clear their major moves with Tokyo headquarters, especially since decisions there were made by the slow, collegial *ringi* process. There were also communications problems between headquarters and the foreign subsidiaries, due partly to difficulties of getting timely translations and partly to failures to understand what executives of the other nationality really *meant* by what they said. At any rate, Harvey Schein resigned in 1977. Akio Morita selected another American to replace him, a man considered to be more amenable to cooperating with Japanese executives.

A 1990 survey identified factors causing dissatisfaction among senior American executives in Sony and other Japanese and other foreign-based companies:

- ◆ Lower compensation than their counterparts in American-based companies
- ◆ Less upward mobility—the "bamboo curtain" keeping them out of the top ranks
- ◆ Less true decision-making power than their high public profiles would seem to signify, i.e., a concern not to become mere tokens or figureheads

- ◆ The reluctance of Japanese top managers to allow their American middle managers to design and carry out statistically sound market assessments before commiting large sums to development and production of new products
- ◆ The feeling that there was always a Japanese in the shadows double-checking every move by the Americans
- ◆ Cultural barriers that are seemingly insurmountable regardless how much effort the American executive makes to learn the language and customs of his corporate overlords

In the late 1980s Sony began trying to create a hybrid Japanese-American structure based largely on personal rapport. It believed the new style could correct deficiencies typical of American managers such as a lack of communication with workers and poor management of pay scales. It also declared that its policy was to be "global localization," under which local companies were to obtain a global perspective on their operations while operating largely on their own and preserving their internal cultures. Materials Research Corp., for example, retained most of its American top management after it was bought out. However, almost all the American executives of Columbia Pictures left their positions shortly after Sony purchased it in 1989. One who remained was the chairman of the television division, Gary Lieberthal, who signed a highly lucrative long-term contract and was appointed a Columbia director in 1990. However, he unexpectedly announced his retirement at the end of 1991 at age 46. Sony officials said the retirement was voluntary.

In 1991 all 18 of the parent company's senior, representative, and managing directors were still Japanese nationals. (These are different classes of directors under Japanese law.) Sixteen of its 19 directors were Japanese, two were American, and one was Swiss. Its highest-ranking American executive was Michael P. Schulhof, vice chairman of Sony-USA and a director of Sony Corp.

STOCKHOLDERS

Sony's stock is traded on the Tokyo Stock Exchange and also on the New York Stock Exchange (in the form of American depository receipts, or ADRs) and other foreign exchanges, and 37% of its shares were owned by foreigners. Its dividend payouts have been low by American standards, but American shareholders were willing to hold the stock as long as its growth prospects remained bright. However, American stockholders are quicker to react to the prospect of falling earnings than Japanese, and one disadvantage of having its ADRs traded on the NYSE is that it could come under heavier selling pressure in the face of a threat. In fact its stock fell from a high of 65¾ in 1989 to a low of 31⅜ in 1991.

THE MOVE INTO THE ENTERTAINMENT INDUSTRY

Sony began diversifying into entertainment-related companies in the latter part of the 1980s for several reasons. Competition heated up in the consumer electronics business, making it harder for the company to maintain sales and profit growth in its core businesses. Morita noted the example of Kodak, which has made much more money on its film than its cameras. Even after the market for VCRs and tape and disk players reached saturation, consumers would keep buying tapes and disks. Profit margins on those items could run up to 50%. The company believed it could find synergy by producing the tapes and compact disks to be played on its electronic hardware. It also believed it could create synergy between the Japanese and American entertainment industries by acquiring production companies in both countries, especially since American producers were acknowledged to be the world's leaders in entertainment. Finally, it viewed its move into Hollywood as an important test of American receptivity to an expanded Japanese role in U.S. culture.

At the same time Michael Schulhof was engineering the acquisitions of CBS and Columbia Pictures acquisitions, rival Matsushita was similarly motivated to acquire MCA Corp., owner of Universal Studios, for $6.1 billion in 1990. Some observers criticized both Sony's and Matsushita's acquisitions, saying the Japanese parent companies grossly overpaid for them. They also said the companies were spreading themselves too thin and going beyond their areas of special competence. Sony's core of developing and manufacturing leading-edge electronics and other up-market products was a very different business from recruiting and managing artists and selling music recordings.

At least Sony recognized that its American entertainment business would have to be managed in the American way. Hence Peter Guber, the driving force behind Guber-Peters, was made CEO of a new entity, Sony Pictures. His management style was much more tumultuous and free-spending than that of the buttoned-down engineers and accountants who ran the parent company and most of its subsidiaries. He spent over $1 billion on movie and TV production in his first two years, gambling that such movies as *Hook, Bugsy Siegel,* and *Prince of Tides* would take in hundreds of millions, enough to cover the multimillion-dollar compensation to stars like Dustin Hoffman, Madonna, Jack Nicholson, and Warren Beatty and still have something left over for the company to cover its costs and show a profit. He also started plans for a "Sonyland" theme park similar to Disneyland.

THE SITUATION IN LATE 1991

As shown above, Sony's major commitments from 1988 through 1991 were almost all in the U.S., where it had invested almost $6 billion to acquire full ownership of CBS Records and Columbia Pictures and to set up its joint venture with Time-Warner. It took on more than $2 billion debt to finance these acquisitions.

Unfortunately much of the world entered a substantial recession just as these transactions were being completed. Demand for audiovisual equipment in Japan was sluggish, and the parent company's export competitiveness was damaged by the continuing high value of the yen, causing its revenues to decline at home. Consumer spending in the U.S. and Europe also fell off sharply, especially for discretionary items. The hoped-for synergy between Sony's Japanese and American entertainment businesses was very slow to materialize. Vigorous discounting by competitors in the U.S. and Europe drove down prices and profits. Sony was especially vulnerable to such declines because of its heavy debt service payments, and its net income fell 5% in the quarter ending in June 1991. The company's financial officers imposed measures designed to cut costs by 10%, and they told Guber to shelve the plans for the Sonyland theme park.

Integrative Case Three   Thai Chempest

Source: William A. Stoever, Keating-Crawford Professor of International Business at Seton Hall University. This case was prepared as a basis for class discussion rather than to illustrate effective or ineffective management practices. Faculty members in nonprofit institutions may reproduce this case for distribution to their own students without charge or permission. All other rights reserved jointly to the author and the Society for Case Research. Copyright © 1994 by the *Business Case Journal* and William A. Stoever. Printed with permission. All rights reserved.

In January 1991 Shep Susmar, President of Agricultural Chemicals International Corporation (ACIC), had to decide whether his company should set up manufacturing with a local partner in Thailand. He had received a letter in November 1990 from Kau Ah-Wong, President of Kau Teck-Meng & Co., in Bangkok, saying that rising tariffs might make it impossible for the Kau company to continue importing one of ACIC's profitable pesticides. Mr. Kau* suggested that the two companies might begin a joint venture to do some of the processing in Thailand, a move that might be mutually profitable while also aiding the development of agriculture in his country. Mr. Susmar had to decide whether to enter into a joint venture, what problems might arise if they did enter it, and how to plan for and deal with such problems.

HISTORY OF ACIC

Agricultural Chemicals Corporation was founded in Rutherford, New Jersey, in 1960 by Tyrone Susmar, Shep Susmar's father. It specialized in developing and producing pesticides to meet the needs of individual purchasers. It kept in close contact with current and potential customers in order to learn about and supply their specialized needs. There was a steady demand since various insect species mutated rapidly and developed immunity to existing pesticides. Basically a niche marketer, the company had to keep seeking new products that the large, resource-rich chemical manufacturers did not yet produce commercially. In the late 1970s Tyrone decided that the company could support a modest R&D program that went beyond the mere combining of previously known components. Agricultural Chemicals set up a small applications-oriented research laboratory to study new infestations that kept cropping up. The laboratory had a small, top-quality staff that was highly productive. It usually developed products to order for large customers, but sometimes it produced new compounds that were marketed under the company name. Some of these were innovative enough to qualify for patents. In order to protect the technology the company established a small plant to manufacture some of these proprietary products.

Shep had started working full-time for the company in 1970 after completing a B.S. in chemical engineering. He earned an MBA part-time during the next 5 years while working in a variety of functions and took over as president in 1985.

---

* As with many Chinese, the family name was ordinarily given first, and the two given or "first" names came last.

OVERSEAS GROWTH

By the mid-1970s Tyrone realized that the company had to go international if it wanted to maintain a steady rate of growth. To signify his commitment, Tyrone changed the company name to Agricultural Chemicals International Corporation (ACIC). The markets abroad, particularly in less-developed countries (LDCs), were smaller, less mechanized, and less accustomed to the use of chemical aids than those in North America, and the giant chemical companies didn't find it worthwhile to devote a lot of effort to them. This meant that once ACIC established a market in a particular country, it could hope for several years of sales without strong international competition.

In 1978 Tyrone hired a young man named Bill Greene and gave him the title of "international manager." Greene had earned a B.S. in Chemical Engineering in 1970 and an MBA in 1976. He had had 8 years' experience in domestic and foreign sales for a large chemical manufacturer. His responsibilities in his new job were rather vaguely defined, but he seemed to have a good feeling for how to make his way.

Greene appointed area managers for Europe, the Middle East, and Asia. The Asia area manager was Mike Mingas. They were all based in New Jersey but had to spend a lot of time traveling in order to stay close to their areas. ACIC began seeking distributors in southern Europe, the Middle East, and Asia. The initial contacts were made rather haphazardly, sometimes from approaches by local companies seeking a foreign supplier and sometimes on the recommendations of intermediaries. Some of the distributors had worked out, but a few had proven to be politically unastute, incompetent, lazy, or plain dishonest. Some arrangements failed to live up to expectations because of government restrictions, lack of foreign exchange, disappointing sales, or loss of interest by the local partner. In at least one case ACIC believed the local distributor had deliberately hidden revenues and had failed to deliver ACIC's share of its profits.

Greene and the area managers had to rely on the parent company for technical assistance and staff functions. The responsibilities were not formalized; they just grew up over the years. In general, the international people had been able to get what support they needed, except on the occasions when the staff and technical people's workloads were too heavy. Some of the parent company's personnel were becoming increasingly interested in the international aspect of the business; others paid little attention to the overseas operations.

In 1980 an Italian chemical company approached ACIC seeking a license to use its processes to manufacture finished products from basic raw materials purchased in Italy. The products were sold to distributors in Italy and other EU countries. ACIC received a healthy royalty, 2 percent of gross sales of the licensed products, but in exchange it gave up the right to export to the EU from its U.S. plants. ACIC received a royalty of almost $1 million in 1990.

In 1981, following a trip by Greene and Mingas to Australia, ACIC set up a processing plant, a wholly owned subsidiary, in that country. The plant contracted with local chemical companies for purchases of particular components, which it blended into finished products and packed for shipment. Its operations followed the processes specified by the parent company. The venture lost money for the first 4 years, finally turned a profit in 1987, and paid back the original investment in 1989. It contributed almost $1 million to the parent's profit before tax in 1990, and the prospects for further growth were promising.

By the mid-1980s the Susmars and Greene recognized that ACIC would have to begin producing in more overseas markets rather than simply exporting to them. Some distributor relationships were running into trouble because of import-substitution policies and shortages of hard currencies in many LDCs. Also, ACIC foresaw heightened competition from companies in Korea, Turkey, India, and other industrializing low-wage Third World countries. However, ACIC wanted to evaluate any given country carefully before deciding whether to make an equity investment (100 percent or joint venture), to license its technology, to serve the market by exports (where allowed), or to give up the market. They hoped to start on a small scale, with a minimum commitment of capital and management time.

A condensed version of ACIC's income statements for the past 4 years is presented in Exhibit 1.

DEALINGS WITH KAU & COMPANY

In 1985 Kau Ah-Wong visited the United States. Among his goals was to find something to combat a wood-boring beetle which infested both hardwood and palm trees in Thailand and other countries of Southeast Asia and which had apparently developed resistance to the available insecticides. Mr. Kau heard about ACIC through professional contacts and called on the Susmars. Figuring there was nothing to lose, ACIC appointed Kau & Company as its distributor in Thailand and agreed to supply trial quantities of a newly developed pesticide called 3,5-D. (ACIC was waiting for a decision on its application for a U.S. patent on this compound.) The trials soon demonstrated that the new insecticide was effective in controlling the beetle. Kau didn't set up any formal marketing program, but his company began receiving commercial orders from the more progressive producers who had heard about the success of the trials. Volume was small at first, but enough to whet ACIC's interest.

Subsequently Mingas made several trips to Bangkok to help promote the relationship. By 1989 ACIC was exporting about $1 million a year of the insecticide to Thailand, which Kau was reselling for about 50 million Thai baht. (See Exhibit 2 for baht-dollar exchange rates.) Even so, Mingas believed they had barely scratched the surface of the Thai market, and Kau had not yet promoted 3,5-D elsewhere in Southeast Asia.

MR. KAU'S LETTER

Kau Ah-Wong's letter of November 1990 came as something of a shock because it seemed to indicate that ACIC's exports to Thailand were threatened. The letter noted that the government was vigorously seeking to diversify Thailand's economy by developing manufacturing industries. It intended to restrict imports of selected products in order to promote manufacturing, and it especially favored products that promoted the country's agriculture. It intended to impose tariffs of 25 to 50 percent on imports of agricultural pesticides like 3,5-D, although it would allow importation of components or ingredients at low or no duties for a while, provided that Thailand's portion of the value added was increased as quickly as possible. The Ministry of Industry wanted to restrict imports of 3,5-D immediately, but the Ministry of Agriculture and Cooperatives prevailed upon them to allow imports at a reduced level for at least one more year.

In view of this new development, Mr. Kau proposed that ACIC and Kau Teck-Meng & Company set up a joint venture to use ACIC's technology and know-how to start production of 3,5-D and other pesticides in Thailand. He even suggested a name: Thai Chemical Pesticides Corporation. He offered to supply the buildings, local sales and administrative staff, and most of the working capital, and proposed that ACIC's contribution be imported equipment, technological knowledge, the necessary engineering and staff advice and support, and some of the working capital. Kau & Company wanted somewhere between 51 and 75 percent ownership since it was contributing the bulk of the capital, physical assets, and personnel. The new company would use ACIC's processes, which would be protected to the fullest extent possible under Thai law.

GREEN'S TRIP TO BANGKOK

Shep Susmar decided not to travel to Bangkok himself, both because of domestic business pressures and because he felt that Kau's business did not justify the investment of his time. Susmar telephoned Kau that ACIC's international manager would go in his place. When Greene arrived in early December, Kau expressed some displeasure at not seeing a counterpart of equally high rank from the American company, but he was quite gracious. He showered Greene with hospitality, including visits to some of Bangkok's notorious night spots. He also took him to call on officials at the Board of Investment, the Thai Development Bank, and in the Ministries of Industry,

Agriculture and Cooperatives, and Commerce. The Board of Investment officials assured Greene that it should be no problem to get approval of a Kau-ACIC joint venture, provided of course that Thailand's rules, regulations, and procedures were followed. Officials at the Development Bank seemed to be amenable to granting a long-term loan at a concessional interest rate,* again provided that the venture satisfied the bank's criteria. Greene had heard, however, that other ministries sometimes imposed roadblocks and that the approval process could be very corruption-prone, time-consuming, and frustrating.

After a week in Bangkok, Greene returned and reported on his findings. The Kaus were a wealthy family of Chinese origin who had been in Thailand for four or five generations. They had political connections built up partly by substantial contributions to General Prem Tinsulanonda's political party (see Appendix). Nonetheless, the Chinese were a somewhat distrusted minority in Thailand, and the government might discriminate against them or a company they were associated with. Kau Ah-Wong had made several trips abroad and was fairly fluent in English. Greene liked Kau personally and thought he was probably pretty reliable.

Kau Teck-Meng & Co. had been founded by Kau Ah-Wong's grandfather and his brothers. It was a trading company that imported and exported a variety of products. Among its imports were M.A.N. trucks, Massey-Ferguson tractors, some industrial chemicals from Monsanto Corporation that it wholesaled to local plastics manufacturers, and some Japanese industrial control devices. It sold the bulk of its turnover in Thailand but exported rice and air-conditioning equipment to other nations of the Association of Southeast Asian Nations (ASEAN)** and Laos, Cambodia, and Burma. It also exported palm products and hand-carved teak furniture to the United States and to the EC. Greene could not be certain, but he had the impression that sales of ACIC's insecticide constituted 4 or 5 percent of its gross revenues.

Greene speculated that sales of the insecticide could increase markedly over the next 5 years if supplies were available; he guesstimated that sales might reach 250 million baht by 1995. He worked up a pro forma income statement, mostly based on figures from the U.S. and Italian

---

* The interest rate on loans from Thai commercial banks was about 8.5 percent to 9.0 percent at the time. The Development Bank was offering loans to qualified borrowers at 3 to 4 percentage points lower.

** The ASEAN countries consisted of Brunei, Indonesia, Malaysia, Philippines, Singapore, and Thailand. ASEAN was originally intended to be a customs union, but its members sometimes found it easier to cooperate on political matters than on economic.

plants and following American accounting principles (Exhibit 3). At present, the Thai government was requiring only that the final production stages be completed in Thailand; these were reasonably simple processes, and the necessary equipment was not too complicated or costly. Greene was aware that the government might demand that more production be moved to Thailand in the not too distant future. Nonetheless, the prospects looked good enough to suggest that ACIC consider a joint venture with as large an equity share as possible. He estimated that ACIC's initial capital expenditure need not exceed $800,000, of which about $400,000 would be for imported equipment and the rest for setup costs, expatriate expenses, etc.

Exhibit 2 and the Appendix contain information Greene collected on Thailand's economy and rules and policies on foreign investment.

ACIC'S RESPONSE

Shep Susmar held a meeting of his top domestic and international executives in mid-December 1990 to discuss the Kau proposal (which they'd already begun referring to as "Thai Chempest." He opened with these comments:

> Our friend Mr. Kau seems eager to set up an alliance with us. It looks like a possibility to me, but there are some definite problem areas. Among them:
>
> ◆ Would it be more cost-effective or less risky to continue exporting as long as the government allows it, unless they raise the tariffs higher than Mr. Kau seems to anticipate?
> ◆ Should we license our processes to Kau's organization?
> ◆ If we go the joint venture route, what possible problems might there be with the Thai business climate and government?
> ◆ What terms might Kau want, and how should we respond?
> ◆ What kind of incentives, guarantees, and other terms could we get from the government?
>
> Kau might want to be managing director or president if we went into a joint venture. We'd have to decide whether that's a good idea, or how to handle it if we decide against him. We'd also have to figure out the financing and ownership structure. We want to be careful to avoid another situation where we get ripped off, like those so-and-so's in Asiatica did to us.
>
> If we do go ahead there, we'd need a plant manager, a chief financial officer, a chief technical officer, and maybe a sales manager to start in Bangkok. An immediate question is whether these should be Americans or Thais.
>
> I need you to draft some plans for what to do about Kau's proposal. Be as specific as you can; don't use phrases like "This problem will have to be planned for." We need concrete suggestions, nuts-and-bolts details.

APPENDIX: POLITICAL AND ECONOMIC DATA ON THAILAND*

Political Structure

Thailand is a constitutional monarchy with a bicameral National Assembly. The Thai Senate includes members who are appointed and who represent constituencies ranging from labor to the military. The lower house consists of roughly 350 members who are elected for 4-year terms. The Prime Minister is appointed by the King based on the recommendations of the National Assembly. The current King, Bhumibol Adulyadej, does not possess a great deal of legislative power but does exercise strong moral leadership.

1932–1980

The modern era is generally considered to have begun in 1932 with a coup d'etat that eliminated most true powers of the King. The absolute monarchy was replaced by a constitutional government, with the support of the King. The military has continued to exert strong influence over the government from the 1932 initial coup up to the present. The name of the country was changed from Siam to Thailand in 1939. The government's effectiveness was diminished during the country's reluctant involvement in World War II as an ally of Japan and during the wars in Vietnam, Laos, and Cambodia in the 1960s and 1970s. Between 1932 and 1980 there were 26 coups and countercoups and the adoption of 13 constitutions. There were a number of military governments mixed with several attempts at democracy.

1980–1990

General Prem Tinsulanonda took power in a coup in 1980 and held it into 1988 through a series of coalition governments. He never stood for election but was able to put down coup attempts in 1981 and 1985. His governments were noted for stability (itself something of an achievement in Thailand) rather than progressive policies. His government strove to improve the environment for foreign investment.

Prem's government resigned in 1988 rather than face a no-confidence vote called by Chatichai Choonhavan's Chat Thai party. Chatichai was elected President in the subsequent elections. He formed a coalition consisting largely of the same core as Prem's coalition. There were predictions that his government would not last long, due partly to intimations that his cabinet ministers were mainly interested in feathering their own nests—corruption has long been rife in Thai governments. However, Chatichai out-

---

* The sources for the appendix material were: Business International Corporation, *Investing, Licensing and Trading Conditions Abroad,* July 1990, pp. 3–5; International Trade Administration, U.S. Department of Commerce, "Thailand," *Guide to Doing Business in the ASEAN Region,* February 1990, pp. 48–56; and current news reports.

lasted the initial expectations. He adopted a pro-business stance that bene-
fitted his cabinet as well as foreign investors.

Currency

The Thai baht was tied to the U.S. dollar during the 1950s, but it became
progressively overvalued and was eventually floated. In 1963 it was again
fixed against the U.S. dollar. Up until 1978 there were a series of devaluations in the baht's gold backing in order to maintain a relatively stable correspondence to the U.S. dollar, which was gradually losing its value against
gold. In 1978 the baht was detached from the dollar and its value pegged
to a basket of currencies. Since then it has been somewhat more stable than
the dollar (see Exhibit 2).

Foreign Investment

The government officially supports foreign investment. Multinational corporations should expect substantial delays in obtaining approvals of their
investment applications, although these should be no greater than for Thai
businesses. Thai governments have long been known for being weighted
with bureaucracy and for their slowness in making decisions. As of 1984
U.S. investment in Thailand was estimated at $4 billion, about 30 percent
of all foreign investment in the country. By 1989, however, the United States
accounted for only 8 percent of incoming investment, while Japan accounted for more than half.

The Thai Investment Law, which was passed in 1977, includes assurances against nationalization.

Foreign Equity Ownership

Industries approved for foreign investment are regulated by the Alien
Business Law of 1972, which created three separate levels of foreign ownership depending on the industry. The first level requires majority Thai
shareholders for a public corporation. The second level requires majority
Thai ownership for new investments but allows grandfathering of businesses that existed prior to the passing of the law. The third level allows
majority foreign ownership as long as an alien business license is approved.
Despite these provisions, as a practical matter 49 percent foreign ownership
has been permitted even in the most restricted industries, although recent
changes may reduce allowable foreign ownership levels.

Among the restrictions relating to specific industries are the requirements for:

- ◆ 60 percent Thai equity in businesses involved in large-scale agriculture, livestock raising, and the production of fertilizers
- ◆ 100 percent Thai equity in businesses involved in agricultural product processing and rice milling

Land Ownership

Land ownership is restricted to Thai nationals except when special allowances are granted.

Local Content Requirements

There are strict requirements for local content in the automobile and motorcycle industries, but the proportion of local content in most other industries is generally controlled by high duties on nonlocal materials.

Remittability of Funds

Firms have little difficulty in repatriating funds as long as they can establish the foreign origination of those funds. Profits may be repatriated as long as proof of tax payment is presented.

Corporate Taxes

The nominal corporate tax rate is 30 percent for companies listed on the Securities Exchange and 35 percent otherwise. Tax evasion is common among Thai companies, however, either through hiding of profits or through bribes to the tax authorities. In practice the amount of many companies' tax payments is determined by negotiations with the government.

Incentives

The Investment Promotion Act of 1977 allows certain incentives to be offered for foreign investment. Industries eligible for incentives include: agricultural products and commodities; minerals; chemicals and chemical products; general manufacturing; and others.

Because of the recent influx of foreign investment, the government is granting fewer incentives than before. It is trying to target incentives to ventures that make a strong contribution to national development. Among the criteria to be considered:

1. Location in up-country provinces
2. Efficient use of natural resources
3. Use of domestic labor and raw materials
4. Share divestiture to Thai nationals and employee share ownership
5. Advanced technology transfer
6. Mobilization of offshore funds

Incentives include but are not limited to:

◆ Guarantees against nationalization
◆ Competitive protection

- ◆ Expatriate permission
- ◆ Land ownership permission
- ◆ Tax holidays and tax loss carry-forwards

The regulations establish a special category of Target Businesses, which includes those that develop natural resources or use agricultural raw materials for export manufacturing. An investment designated as a Target Business may be eligible for additional incentives such as:

- ◆ Exemption from machinery import tax
- ◆ 50 percent reduction of import duty on raw materials used in goods for local consumption
- ◆ 5-year exemption from import duties on raw materials used in export goods
- ◆ 5-year, 90 percent exemption from business tax
- ◆ 50 percent reduction in corporate income tax for 5 years after the tax holiday or from the first income-earning year
- ◆ 10-year, 200 percent tax deduction for expenses for transport, electricity, and water
- ◆ Special depreciation rights for original installation

The regulations divide the country into three zones:

1. Bangkok and the five adjacent provinces
2. Ten provinces located near Bangkok, in the central region and on the eastern shore
3. The up-country provinces

The tax holidays, tariff exemptions, and other incentives are more generous for investments located in Zone 2 than for those in Zone 1, and the incentives for Zone 3 are substantially more generous than for Zone 2.

Labor

Thailand has a large supply of unskilled labor, but there is a shortage of skilled labor, particularly in newly introduced industries.

Patent Protection

Patents are governed by the Patent Act of 1979, which was adopted following strong pressure from the United States and other governments who objected to the flagrant copying in Thailand of products and processes that had been developed and patented in other countries. Patents may be registered by Thai nationals and nationals of countries that have provided reciprocal patent rights to Thai nationals. Patents are granted for 15 years from filing date with the possibility of cancellation after 6 years if no production is undertaken. Protection of trademarks and intellectual property has improved under this legislation, although strict enforcement still poses a problem.

Patents may be granted or recognized in Thailand only if the invention is new, involves an innovative step, and is capable of industrial application. Patents are not allowed in a variety of areas including agricultural equipment, pharmaceuticals, food, beverages, biological species, and computer programs.

One current issue is the protection of computer software and pharmaceuticals as mandated under the Uruguay round of the General Agreement on Tariffs and Trade in 1983. The United States is pushing for a quick resolution and is attempting to influence Thailand's decision through various international channels.

In late 1990 the U.S. government identified Thailand as a Priority Foreign Country that inadequately protects U.S. intellectual property under Section 301 of the Omnibus Trade and Competitiveness Act of 1988. As a result, the United States started investigating whether to institute or raise tariffs against selected imports from Thailand.

◆   EXHIBIT 1   **Agricultural Chemicals International Corporation Condensed 4-Year Statement of Earnings (Dollar Figures in Millions)**

	1990	1989	1988	1987
Sales and other revenue				
Net sales	62.2	60.5	58.7	59.8
Royalties	1.3	1.0	1.1	0.6
Total	63.5	61.5	59.8	60.4
Costs and other charges				
Cost of sales	32.0	31.1	29.7	30.0
Depreciation and amortization	8.2	8.0	7.7	7.8
Direct labor	7.8	7.8	7.5	7.7
Selling and administrative expenses	6.0	6.0	5.8	5.6
Interest expenses	3.1	2.9	3.0	2.7
Other income charges	1.0	0.9	0.9	1.1
Taxes	2.1	1.9	1.8	2.0
Total	60.2	58.6	56.4	56.9
Earnings for the year	3.3	2.9	3.4	3.5

◆ EXHIBIT 2 Financial Statistics on Thailand

	1978	1979	1980	1981	1982	1983	1984	1985	1986	1987	1988
Millions of Baht											
Total exports	83,065	108,179	133,197	153,001	159,728	146,472	175,237	193,366	233,383	299,851	403,570
Imports	108,899	146,161	188,686	216,746	196,616	236,609	245,155	251,169	241,358	334,209	513,114
Billions of Baht											
Foreign debt	48.25	56.77	74.59	92.27	123.30	132.19	155.78	158.48	172.42	175.50	128.05
Millions $											
Official reserves	2,557	3,129	3,026	2,727	2,652	2,556	2,689	3,003	3,776	5,212	7,112
Baht per U.S. $											
Official exchange	20.39	20.43	20.63	23.00	23.00	23.00	27.15	26.65	26.13	25.07	25.24
Index 1985—100											
Consumer price index	59.80	65.70	78.70	88.60	93.30	96.80	97.60	100.00	101.80	104.40	108.40

Source: International Monetary Fund, International Financial Statistics.

◆   **EXHIBIT 3**   **Thai Chempest Pro Forma Income Statement (In Millions of Baht)**

Year of operations	1st	2d	3d	4th	5th
Sales revenue	50	100	150	200	250
Cost of goods sold	35	70	105	140	175
Administrative costs	30	30	30	30	30
Depreciation and amortization*	4	4	4	4	4
PBIT	−19	−4	11	26	41
Interest*	2	2	2	2	2
PBT	−21	−6	9	24	39

*Depreciation (straight-line) @ 10% on $400,000 imported equipment and 10 million baht buildings, etc., + amortization of 40 million baht loan from government Development Bank at 5% interest, repayable in 20th year.

The Case of the Floundering Expatriate   Integrative Case Four

At exactly 1:40 on a warm, sunny Friday afternoon in July 1995, Frank Waterhouse, CEO of Argos Diesel, Europe, leaves his office on the top floor of the Argos Tower, overlooking the Zürichsee. In the grip of a tension headache, he rides the glass elevator down the outside of the mirrored building.

To quiet his nerves, he studies his watch. In less than half an hour, Waterhouse must look on as Bert Donaldson faces the company's European managers—executives of the parts suppliers that Argos has acquired over the past two years. Donaldson is supposed to give the keynote address at this event, part of the second Argos Management Meeting organized by his training and education department. But late yesterday afternoon, he phoned Waterhouse to say he didn't think the address would be very good. Donaldson said he hadn't gotten enough feedback from the various division heads to put together the presentation he had planned. His summary of the company's progress wouldn't be what he had hoped.

It's his meeting! Waterhouse thinks, as the elevator moves silently down to the second floor. How could he not be prepared? Is this really the man who everyone at corporate headquarters in Detroit thinks is so fantastic?

Waterhouse remembers his introduction to Donaldson just over a year ago. Argos International's CEO and chairman, Bill Loun, had phoned Waterhouse himself to say he was sending the "pick of the litter." He said that Donaldson had a great international background—that he had been a professor of American studies in Cairo for five years. Then he had returned to the States and joined Argos. Donaldson had helped create the cross-divisional, cross-functional teams that had achieved considerable cost reductions and quality improvements.

Loun had said that Donaldson was just what Argos Europe needed to create a seamless European team—to facilitate communication among the different European parts suppliers that Waterhouse had worked so hard to acquire. Waterhouse had proved his own strategic skills, his own ability to close deals, by successfully building a network of companies in Europe under the Argos umbrella. All the pieces were in place. But for the newly expanded company to meet its financial goals, the units had to work together. The managers had to become an integrated team. Donaldson could help them. Together they would keep the company's share of the diesel engine and turbine market on the rise.

Waterhouse deserved to get the best help, the CEO had said. Bert Donaldson was the best. And later, when the numbers proved the plan successful, Waterhouse could return to the States a hero. (Waterhouse heard Loun's voice clearly in his head: "I've got my eye on you, Frank. You know you're in line.")

Waterhouse had been enthusiastic. Donaldson could help him reach the top. He had met the man several times in Detroit. Donaldson seemed to have a quick mind, and he was very charismatic.

Source: Gordon Adler, "The Case of the Floundering Expatriate," *Harvard Business Review,* July-August 1995, 24-30. Copyright 1995 by the President and Fellows of Harvard College. All rights reserved. Reprinted by permission.

But that wasn't the Donaldson who had arrived in Zürich in August 1994 with his wife and two daughters. This man didn't seem to be a team builder—not in this venue. Here his charisma seemed abrasive.

The elevator comes to a stop. Waterhouse steps into the interior of the building and heads toward the seminar room at the end of the hall.

Waterhouse keeps thinking of his own career. He has spent most of his time since Donaldson's appointment securing three major government contracts in Moscow, Ankara, and Warsaw. He has kept the ball rolling, kept his career on track. It isn't his fault that Donaldson can't handle this assignment. It isn't his fault that the Germans and the French still can't agree on a unified sales plan.

His thoughts turn back to Donaldson. It can't be all Bert's fault, either. Donaldson is a smart man, a good man. His successes in the States were genuine. And Donaldson is worried about this assignment; it isn't as though he's just being stubborn. He sounded worried on the phone. He cares. He knows his job is falling apart and he doesn't know what to do. What can he return to at Argos in the States if he doesn't excel here in Europe?

Let Donaldson run with the ball—that's what they said in Detroit. It isn't working.

Waterhouse reaches the doorway of the seminar room. Ursula Lindt, his executive assistant, spots him from the other side. Lindt is from a wealthy local family. Most of the local hires go to her to discuss their problems. Waterhouse recalls a few of her comments about Donaldson: Staff morale on the fifth floor is lower than ever; there seems to be a general malaise. Herr Direktor Donaldson must be having problems at home. Why else would he work until midnight?

Waterhouse takes a seat in the front row and tries to distract himself by studying the meeting schedule. "Managing Change and Creating Vision: Improving Argos with Teamwork" is the title. Donaldson's "vision" for Argos Europe. Waterhouse sighs. Lindt nears him and, catching his eye, begins to complain.

"A few of the managers have been making noises about poor organization," she says. "And Sauras, the Spanish director, called to complain that the meeting schedule was too tight." Her litany of problems continues: "Maurizio, the director in Rome, came up to me this morning and began to lobby for Donaldson's replacement. He feels that we need someone with a better understanding of the European environment." Seeing Waterhouse frown, Lindt backs off. "But he's always stirring up trouble," she says. "Otherwise, the conference appears to be a success." She sits down next to Waterhouse and studies her daily planner.

The room slowly fills with whispers and dark hand-tailored suits. Groups break up and re-form. "Grüss Gott, Heinz, wie geht's?" "Jacques, ça va bien?" "Bill, good to see you . . . Great." Waterhouse makes a perfunctory inspection of the crowd. Why isn't Donaldson in here schmoozing? He hears a German accent: "Two-ten. Ja ja. Amerikanische Pünktlichkeit." Punctuality. Unlike Donaldson, he knows enough German to get by.

A signal is given. The chitchat fades with the lights. Waterhouse turns his gaze to the front as Donaldson strides up to the podium.

Donaldson speaks. "As President Eisenhower once said, 'I have two kinds of problems, the urgent and the important. The urgent are not important, and the important are never urgent.' " He laughs, but the rest of the room is silent save for the sound of paper shuffling.

Donaldson pauses to straighten his notes and then delivers a flat ten-minute summary of the European companies' organizational structure. He reviews the basics of the team-building plan he has developed—something with which all the listeners are already familiar. He thanks his secretary for her efforts.

Then he turns the meeting over to Waterhouse, who apologizes for not having been able to give the managers any notice that this session would be shorter than planned. He assures them that the rest of the schedule is intact and asks them to take this time as a break before their 4 P.M. logistics meeting, which will be run by the French division head.

The managers exchange glances, and Waterhouse detects one or two undisguised smiles. Walking out of the seminar room, he hears someone say, "At least the meeting didn't run overtime." Waterhouse fumes. He has put in four years of hard work here in Europe. This is the first year of his second three-year contract. He is being groomed for a top management position back in the States. The last thing he needs is a distraction like this.

He remembers how Detroit reacted when, a little over a month ago, he raised the issue of Donaldson's failure to adjust. He had written a careful letter to Bill Loun suggesting that Donaldson's assignment might be over his head, that the timing wasn't right. The CEO had phoned him right away. "That's rubbish, Frank," his voice had boomed over the line. "You've been asking for someone to help make this plan work, and we've sent you the best we've got. You can't send him back. It's your call—you have the bottom-line responsibility. But I'm hoping he'll be part of your inner circle, Frank. I'd give him more time. Make it work. I'm counting on you."

More time is no longer an option, Waterhouse thinks. But if he fires Donaldson now or sends him back to Detroit, he loses whatever progress has been made toward a unified structure. Donaldson has begun to implement a team-building program; if he leaves, the effort will collapse. And how could he fire Donaldson, anyway? The guy isn't working out here, but firing him would destroy his career. Bert doesn't deserve that.

What's more, the European team program has been touted as a major initiative, and Waterhouse has allowed himself to be thought of as one of its drivers. Turning back would reflect badly on him as well.

On the other hand, the way things are going, if Donaldson stays, he may himself cause the plan to fail. One step forward, two steps back. "I don't have the time to walk Donaldson through remedial cultural adjustment," Waterhouse mumbles under his breath.

Donaldson approaches him in the hall. "I sent a multiple-choice survey to every manager. One of them sent back a rambling six-page essay," he says. "I sent them in April. I got back only 7 of 40 from the Germans. Every time I called, it was 'under review.' One of them told me his people wanted to discuss it—in German. The Portuguese would have responded if I'd brought it personally."

Waterhouse tells Donaldson he wants to meet with him later. "Five o'clock. In my office." He turns away abruptly.

Ursula Lindt follows him toward the elevator. "Herr Direktor, did you hear what Herr Donaldson called Frau Schweri?"

Bettina Schweri, who organizes Donaldson's programs, is essentially his manager. She speaks five languages fluently and writes three with style. Lindt and Schweri have known each other since childhood and eat lunch together every day.

"A secretary," Lindt says, exasperated. "Frau Schweri a secretary? Simply not to believe."

Back in his office, Waterhouse gets himself a glass of water and two aspirin. In his mind, he's sitting across from Donaldson ten months earlier.

"Once I reach a goal," Donaldson says, "I set another one and get to work. I like to have things going at once—especially since I have only two years. I'm going for quick results, Frank. I've even got the first project lined up. We'll bring in a couple of trainers from the Consulting Consortium to run that team-skills workshop we talked about."

Waterhouse comes back to the present. That first workshop hadn't gone too badly—at least he hadn't heard of any problems. But he, Waterhouse, had not attended. He picks up the phone and places a call to Paul Janssen, vice president of human resources for Argos Europe. Paul is a good friend, a trusted colleague. The two men often cross paths at the health club.

A few seconds later, Janssen's voice booms over the line. "Frank? Why didn't you just walk down the hall to see me? I haven't seen you at the club in weeks."

Waterhouse doesn't want to chat. "Donaldson's first training weekend, in February," he says. "How'd it go? Really."

"Really. Well, overall, not too bad. A few glitches, but nothing too out of the ordinary for a first run. Bert had some problems with his assistant. Apparently, Frau Schweri had scheduled the two trainers to arrive in Zürich two days early to prepare everything, recover from jet lag, and have dinner at the Baur au Lac. They came the night before. You can imagine how that upset her. Bert knew about the change but didn't inform Frau Schweri."

Waterhouse has the distinct impression that Janssen has been waiting for a chance to talk about this. "Go on," Waterhouse says.

"Well, there were a few problems with the workshops."

"Problems?"

"Well, yes. One of the managers from Norway—Dr. Godal, I believe—asked many questions during Bert's presentation, and he became rather irascible."

"Bert?" Waterhouse asked.

"Yes. And one of the two trainers wore a Mickey Mouse sweater—"

"Mickey Mouse?" Waterhouse laughs without meaning to.

"A sweater with a depiction of Mickey Mouse on the front."

"What on earth does that have to do with Bert?"

"Well, Bert offered them a two-year contract after Frau Schweri advised him not to. He apparently told her he was satisfied with the trainers and, so far as he was concerned, questions about their personal habits and clothing weren't worth his time."

"Yes, and—"

"Well, there were complaints—"

"They all went to Frau Schweri?" He is beginning to see.

"One of the managers said the trainers provided too much information; he felt as though they were condescending to him. A bombardment of information, he called it. Other managers complained that Bert didn't provide enough background information. The French managers seemed to think the meeting was worthwhile. But Bert must think that because his style works with one group, the others will fall into place automatically. And everyone was unhappy with the schedule. The trainers always ran overtime, so everybody was displeased because there weren't any coffee breaks for people from various offices to network. Oh, and the last thing? All the name cards had first names and last names—no titles."

"No titles," Waterhouse says, and lets out a sigh. "Paul, I wish you'd told me all this earlier."

"I didn't think you needed to hear it, Frank. You've been busy with the new contracts." They agree to meet at the club later in the week, and they hang up. Waterhouse stares down at Donaldson's file.

His résumé looks perfect. He has a glowing review from the American University in Cairo. There, Donaldson earned the highest ratings for his effectiveness, his ease among students from 40 countries, and his sense of humor. At Argos in the United States, he implemented the cross-divisional team approach in record time. Donaldson is nothing short of a miracle worker.

Waterhouse leans back in his swivel-tilter and lets the scuttlebutt on Donaldson run through his mind. Word is that he's an *Arbeitstier*. "Work animal" is the direct, unflattering translation. He never joins the staff for a leisurely lunch in the canteen, preferring a sandwich in his office. Word is he can speak some Arabic from his lecturing days in Cairo but still can't manage a decent "good morning" in Swiss German. Word is he walks around all day—he says it's management by walking around—asking for suggestions, ideas, plans, or solutions because he can't think of any himself.

Waterhouse remembers an early conversation with Donaldson in which he seemed frustrated. Should he have paid more attention?

"I met with Jakob Hassler, vice president of human resources at Schwyz Turbines," Donaldson had said, pacing the office. "I wanted some ideas for the training program. Schwyz is the first company we acquired here; I wanted to show Hassler that I don't bite. When I opened the door, he just stood there. I offered him a chair beside the coffee table, told him to call me Bert. He nodded, so I asked him about his family and the best place to buy ski boots, and he answered but he acted so aloof. I took a chair across from him, listened to ten minutes of one-word answers, and then I finally asked him how things were going in general, to which he said, 'Everything is normal.' Can you beat that, Frank? I told him I was interested in his ideas, so he pushed his chair back and said, 'Please let me know what you expect.' I reminded him that we're all on the same team, have only two years for major change, gave him a week to get back to me with a few ideas, and you know what he said? He said, 'Ja ja.' "

At the time, Donaldson's frustration seemed to stem from the normal adjustment problems that expatriates face. But he never did adjust. Why doesn't he just give Hassler what he needs to know and get out? Waterhouse knows this; why hasn't Donaldson figured it out?

His phone rings—the inside line. It's Ursula Lindt. "Frau Direktor Donaldson just called. She said Herr Direktor Donaldson was expected home at 4. I told her you had scheduled a meeting with him for 5." She waits. Waterhouse senses that there is more to her message. "What else did she say, Frau Lindt?"

"I inquired after her health, and she said she's near the end of her rope. Bored without her work. She said they thought Zürich would be a breeze after Cairo. Then she went into a tirade. She said that they're having serious problems with their eldest daughter. She'll be in grade 12 at the international school this fall. She's applying to college. Frau Donaldson said her daughter's recommendations from her British teachers are so understated that they'd keep her out of the top schools, and she keeps getting C's because they're using the British grading scale. She reminded me that this is a girl with a combined SAT score of over 1350."

Lindt is done. Waterhouse thanks her for the information, then hangs up. Julie Ann is usually calm, collected. She has made some friends here. Something must have pushed her over the edge. And their daughter is engaging, bright. Why is this all coming to a head now?

Waterhouse recalls his most recent meeting with Donaldson, a couple of days before Donaldson's vacation in May.

"I've tried everything, Frank. I've delegated, I've let them lead, I've given them pep talks." Waterhouse remembers Donaldson sinking deep into his chair, his voice flat. "No matter what I do—if I change an agenda, if I ask them to have a sandwich with me at my desk—someone's always pissed off. We're talking about streamlining an entire European company and they're constantly looking at their watches. We run ten minutes overtime in a meeting and they're shuffling papers. I tell you, Frank, they're just going to have to join the rest of us in the postindustrial age, learn to do things the Argos way. I worked wonders in Detroit . . . . "

The clock in Waterhouse's office reads 4:45. What can he do about Donaldson? Let him blunder along for another year? And take another 12 months of . . . he closes the door on that thought. Send him back and forget? Morale on the fifth floor will improve, the Europeans will be appeased, but with Donaldson will go the training program, such as it is. Corporate will just think that Waterhouse has forgotten how to play the American way. They'll think that he mistreated their star. Can he teach Donaldson cultural awareness? With the Ankara, Moscow, and Warsaw projects chewing up all his time? You can't teach cultural savvy. No way.

He hears Donaldson enter the outer office. A hanger clinks on the coat tree. How can he work this out?

Integrative Case Five   *Levi's Says Goodbye to China*

Source: This case was prepared by William Beaver, Professor of Social Science, Robert Morris College, Coraopolis, PA. Printed with permission. All rights reserved by Professor Beaver.

What to do about human rights in China has been on a lot of people's minds lately. Continued reports of political and religious oppression, along with the revelation that China uses prison labor to produce commercial goods that are then sold in the West, is to say the least disconcerting. President Clinton, although admitting that serious human rights abuses continue, decided to renew most favored nation (MFN) trading status with China despite earlier promises to take decisive action in the human rights situation didn't show "overall significant progress." The president's decision was obviously tied to the fact that American multinationals are playing an increasingly important role in the Chinese economy and would suffer if trade sanctions were imposed.

For its part, American business has also been somewhat ambiguous about China, particularly following the events at Tiananmen Square in 1989. A few firms left, but most stayed, arguing that an American presence would eventually improve the situation. More recently only one major American company, Levi Strauss, has gone against the grain. The company has decided to end much of its business dealings in China, due to what the company called "pervasive human rights abuses." This, at a time, when American multinationals are dramatically increasing their presence in China. At last count, 2000 U.S. firms had invested roughly $6.6 billion, and corporate giants like AT&T, Motorola, and Ford are planning major investments.

MAKING THE DECISION

Levi's involvement in China was not large. It made purchases from thirty Chinese subcontractors who produced trousers and shirts, which amounted to approximately $50 million per year. In May 1993, Levi's announced that it would phase out these operations over a period of several years, although the company will continue to purchase fabric in China. However, Levi's did leave the door open if the situation changes. As one Levi's executive stated, "Our hope is that conditions will change and improve so that we can revisit our decision, at sometime in the future" (Carlton, 1993). Nevertheless, and just as important, the decision also means that Levi's has indefinitely postponed plans for more substantial direct investment.

Levi's decision to leave China was based in accord with its shared values, which provides the foundation for all the company's decision making. Since the mid-1980s under the leadership of CEO Robert Haas, Levi Strauss has redefined its business strategy. After engineering a successful LBO in 1985, Haas decided to focus on a more value-centered management that would emphasize social responsibility and employee rights. As Haas stated, "values drive the business" (Howard, 1990). These values are spelled out in the company's "aspirations statement," which serves as a guide for both management and workers.

The aspirations statement points to the need for fair treatment and respect for all employees, along with a safe and productive work environment, while always attempting to close the gap between principles and practice. "People in accord with the bottom line" (Laabs, 1992) is the way one Levi's executive put it. It should also be pointed out that the value focus has not hurt the bottom line. Levi's continues to be a highly profitable company. Nineteen ninety-three marked the seventh consecutive year of record sales, while net income rose by 36 percent over the previous year.

These values do not just apply to the U.S. but to all Levi's employees around the globe, and today Levi's is truly a global company. It now operates in over 60 countries. Half of all the company's shirts and jeans are made abroad. While one might suspect that cultural differences could interfere with the global adoption of Levi's core values, such does not appear to be the case. Although Levi's attempts to adjust to a particular culture, the company maintains that there is widespread agreement about values. This fact appears to support a growing agreement among researchers that a global value consensus is emerging, much of which focuses on individual rights.

Levi's decision to leave China was not made hastily. A company task force worked for three years on developing guidelines for doing business abroad. Not surprisingly, the standards developed reflect Levi's shared values. The standards, which became known as the "Global Sourcing Guidelines," have two parts. The first is known as the "Business Partner Terms of Engagement" and addresses specific workplace issues that Levi's international business partners can control, things like safe working conditions, length of the work week, fair wages, respect for the environment, and prohibitions against child labor. To add teeth to the guidelines company inspectors make periodic surprise visits to job sites around the globe. If violations are discovered Levi's will either require that changes be made or sever its relationship with a particular subcontractor. In this regard the company found no major violations of its workplace guidelines after making ten random inspections of its Chinese subcontractors.

Although Levi's may have found working conditions acceptable, recent reports from China regarding the apparel industry paint a different picture. For instance, in Shenzhen, female sewing factory workers put in 12-hour days plus overtime, while receiving only 2 days off per month. Pay is often below the legal minimum of 12 cents an hour. Workers usually have no health care and no compensation for injury, although recently passed legislation requires it. All this prompted the Chinese News Service to complain, "Some foreign businessmen do not care about Chinese laws. They beat and swear at our workers, treat them badly and embezzle their wages" (*Pittsburgh Tribune-Review,* April 3, 1994). Apparently the Chinese government is most upset with the behavior of businessmen from Hong Kong and Taiwan who are reportedly the worst culprits.

Safety conditions in such factories appear to be no better. There is little ventilation, since windows are often sealed and barred to prevent robberies.

Few of these factories even have fire extinguishers, and even if a factory is cited for safety violations, bribes are commonly paid to government officials to avoid fines and shutdowns. Besides bribes, officials are also reluctant to enforce existing worker protection laws for fear of scaring off foreign investment.

Lack of safety concerns produced tragedy in 1993. In November at the Zhili Handicraft Factory in Shenzhen, 84 women were killed in a fire. Many were trampled to death as workers scrambled to reach the one unlocked door—all the windows were barred. Earlier in the year a fire at another Shenzhen sewing factory killed 61 workers. Events such as these have spawned conflict. The Chinese government admits to 10,000 labor disputes in 1993 alone. However, any attempt by workers to organize independent unions are illegal, and when they are discovered, arrests usually follow, indicating that the Chinese government is still intolerant of any organized opposition.

The fact that Levi's did not find these kinds of sweatshop conditions present with its subcontractors indicates that fair workplace standards are certainly possible, if American multinationals demand and ensure that the standards are being followed. Notwithstanding, Levi's has taken action against other business partners when their standards were not being met. For example, the company withdrew from the island of Saipan because of worker abuse on the part of a subcontractor. Levi's also threatened to withdraw from two factories located in Bangladesh over the use of child labor, but changed its mind when the practice was adjusted. The situation in Bangladesh illustrates that Levi's is not inflexible when cultural differences are involved. In Bangladesh it is legal to employ children under the age of 14. Moreover, families are often dependent on these incomes for survival. Yet according to Levi's guidelines, children under 14 should not be employed. Levi's did not want the youths discharged, which would have hurt their families, but it didn't want them working either. To make the situation palatable, Levi's worked out a compromise with the local contractors in which the children would be paid while attending school, but offered full-time jobs once they turned 14. In all, the company has severed its relationship with 30 business partners and demanded changes from 120 others in various countries.

The second part of the "Global Sourcing Guidelines" deals with "country selection" and concerns larger issues that are beyond the control of Levi's business partners. Levi's maintains that it is the only company that has adopted standards for country selection. These guidelines focus on such things as political or social instability that could threaten Levi's interests, a country's impact on brand image, safety dangers to company employees, and human rights abuses. Violations of any or all of these guidelines can mean the cutting off of all business relationships in a particular country.

For 19 days Levi's China policy group scrutinized the situation and finally concluded that subcontracting in China had to be phased out.

Human rights violations were widespread and thus inconsistent with company values. As a matter of fact, a recent report by two human rights groups (Human Rights Watch–Asia and Human Rights in China) indicates that human rights abuses in China may be worse than previously thought, despite assurances from President Clinton and others that the situation is improving. Specifically, the report claims that approximately 500 more people were imprisoned as a result of Tiananmen Square than previously reported, and that 200 are still being detained in extremely harsh conditions, where torture and solitary confinement are commonplace. Moreover the report states that, "Known cases of political and religious imprisonment in China represent only the tip of the iceberg" (*Pittsburgh Tribune-Review,* May 19, 1994). Other reports indicate that in the first four months of 1994 at least 88 arrests and trials of political or religious dissidents have taken place.

China is not the first country from which Levi's has withdrawn. The company has severed all subcontractor relationships in Burma because of human rights abuses. The company also suspended its business dealings in Peru because it felt that its employees were in danger due to terrorist activity by the Shining Path guerillas. However when the danger in Peru subsided, Levi's lifted the suspension.

One inconsistency is apparent in Levi's China decision. Although Levi's is phasing out its dealings with subcontractors who produce garments, the company, as mentioned, will continue to purchase fabric in China. Why Levi's would continue to do so when it has stated that China has failed to meet its "country selection" standards is puzzling. For its part, Levi's says that it is reviewing the situation.

PROFIT OR PRINCIPLES

Critics of Levi's have charged that the decision to leave China was nothing more than a publicity stunt, ultimately aimed at luring more customers. That is, consumers will be attracted to Levi's for its stand against human rights abuses while reinforcing the company's "antiestablishment image." As one critic charged, "this was a pure business decision related to bottom line profitability" (Miller, 1993).

Levi's admitted that the decision could improve its image. Top management believes that the brand is symbolic of American culture, hence brand identity must be protected. Moreover it appears that strengthening the customer base was also a concern. As one Levi's vice president put it, "Increasingly consumers are sensitive to goods being made under conditions not consistent with U.S. values and fairness" (Dumaine, 1992).

Critics have also noted that since the company had no direct investment in China, little is being sacrificed, since the company will be able to find low-cost subcontractors in other Asian countries. In the short term such may be the case, but in the long term Levi's may be sacrificing a great deal.

China is the world's fastest growing economy; some have even predicted that in twenty years China will be the world's largest economy. By leaving China and not making direct investments, Levi's may be passing up the chance to clothe an increasingly affluent population. (Urban income has doubled since 1985.) Without production facilities in China, Levi's will be hard pressed to compete because of stiff tariffs on all imported apparel. "They're going to lose opportunities in the market that someone else will fill," stated one Asian business consultant (Gull and Zukerman, 1993).

A manufacturing presence could also help Levi's combat the growing counterfeiting problem. In China and other Asian nations the company has been victimized by operations that simply steal Levi's trademark. Although the company will not put a dollar figure on the amount involved, it does concede that the figure is large. However, with Levi's severing much of its relationship with China, the problem is likely to get worse. Evidence exists that the Chinese government condones counterfeiting, particularly in the software and video games industry.

Just as important is the loss of centralized control. Rapid economic change has eroded government power to the point that *The Wall Street Journal* calls the situation in China not free enterprise but a "free-for all." Added to this is the fact that corruption and bribery within the trademark-enforcement system is reportedly widespread.

Although Levi's has stated that it has not totally closed the door on China, the Chinese government could close the door on Levi's. As one observer on the situation put it in speaking of the Chinese leadership, "They don't tend to forget things. They have elephantine memories" (Gull and Zukerman, 1993). Thus, if and when Levi's decides to return to China, the door may be locked.

References

M. Brauchli, "Beijing's Grip Weakens, as Free Enterprise Turns into Free-for-All," *The Wall Street Journal,* August 26, 1993, p. A1.

"Business Partner Terms of Engagement and Guidelines for Country Selection," *Levi Strauss & Co.,* 1994.

J. Carlton, "Ties with China Will Be Curbed by Levi Strauss," *The Wall Street Journal,* May 4, 1993, p. A4.

"Chinese Abuses Unveiled," *Pittsburgh Tribune-Review,* May 19, 1994, p. A12.

B. Dumaine, "Exporting Jobs and Ethics," *Fortune,* 126 (October 5, 1992), pp. 114–116.

S. D. Gull and L. Zukerman, "Levi Strauss, Leaving China Passes Crowd of Firms Going the Other Way," *The Wall Street Journal,* May 5, 1993, p. A18.

R. Howard, "Values Make the Company: An Interview with Robert Haas," *Harvard Business Review,* 68 (September–October, 1990), pp. 133–143.

"Global Sourcing Guidelines Fact Sheet," *Levi Strauss & Co.,* April, 1994.

"In China Factory Hazards Abound," *Pittsburgh Tribune-Review,* April 3, 1994, p. A11.

J. J. Laabs, "HR's Vital Role at Levi Strauss," *Personnel Journal,* December 1992, pp. 34–46.

C. Miller, "Levi's to Sever Link with China: Critics Contend It's Just a PR Move," *Marketing News,* June 7, 1993, p. 10.

Nissan U.K.: A Worker's Paradox?   *Integrative* Case Six

Source: Judith Kenner Thompson and Robert R. Rehder, "Nissan U.K.: A Worker's Paradox?" *Business Horizons,* January–February 1995, pp. 48–58. Copyright © 1995, JAI Press Inc. All rights reserved. Reprinted with permission.

The major Japanese automobile companies have now established a successful beachhead in Europe, located in the United Kingdom. As they have in North America, these Japanese transplants are exemplifying high levels of technology transfer, combined with learning and adaptation that results in globally competitive new hybrid manufacturing organizations. These new organizations combine, in highly creative ways, subsystems of the Fordist and lean systems, with diverse national and European innovations.

In many ways, the Japanese lean system unfroze the traditional Fordist manufacturing paradigm, resulting in not one dominant lean system but many creative and continuously evolving hybrid spinoffs as diverse as the geographic sources from which they emerge. Nissan Motor Manufacturing (UK) Limited, or NMUK, is one exemplar of these emerging new hybrid systems, demonstrating high levels of organizational learning and adaptation as well as sociotechnical problems and paradoxes.

Europe's automobile industry in the early 1990s was no better prepared for the Japanese transplants than was Detroit's Big Three in the early 1980s. However, because of the Japanese learning experience with their transplants' lean system in North America, they are more readily adapting and developing new Japanese-European hybrids, which are already setting new quality and productivity standards. Still, the quality of work life shows little improvement.

As is now widely recognized, the term "lean production system" was coined by the MIT study team in their landmark book, *The Machine That Changed The World* (1990). A more recent study by Martin Kenney and Richard Florida (1993) documents the remarkable breadth of the Japanese lean system's transfer and adaptation within North America and its major role in the continuing global industrial diffusion and transformation. Unlike the MIT study, however, Kenney and Florida provide a more balanced view of both the system's strengths as an innovative, mediated organization and the considerable social and technical tensions and contradictions experienced by the North American transplants.

Like the American research findings, the early studies of the lean system hybrids developing in the U.K. tend to be highly divergent in many of their findings. In his 1987 book *The Road to Nissan*, Peter Wickens, NMUK's director of personnel and information systems, presents an understandably corporate view of the company's practices. Conversely, Garrahan and Stewart (1992) focus on NMUK's less favorable labor and community relations practices and experiences.

The purpose of this article is to provide a more balanced analysis of the emergence of the Japanese lean system as a hybrid in the United Kingdom along with the paradoxes it raises. We will analyze the case of Nissan in the U.K. as an example of technology transfer and organizational adaptation and learning, as well as the comparative stakeholder outcomes.

THE AMERICAN TRANSPLANT EXPERIENCE

The American experience with Japanese transplants has been both highly beneficial and costly. The Japanese lean system has indisputably established new world standards for quality and productivity. Although significantly influenced by the Fordist mass production system, it was shaped in Japan by major social and economic forces and historical events that were quite different from those in the West. The result has been a unique organization and management hybrid system that is catalyzing a new global industrial revolution.

A recent major study by McKinsey's Global Institute (1993) found that the Japanese transplants have played a pivotal role in improving domestic productivity by putting competitive pressure on other domestic producers and transferring knowledge of the best practices through normal personnel transfers. The key elements most widely associated with lean production are:

- ◆ quality as the central corporate philosophy and unifying superordinate goal;
- ◆ suppliers delivering just-in-time (JIT) directly to the assembly line;
- ◆ assembly line teams with team leaders, rather than foremen;
- ◆ a constant training and improvement process known as *kaizen;* and
- ◆ tailoring products and services to customer needs through the cooperative efforts of design, engineering, production, and dealers.

But there is much more, of course. The Japanese generalist's holistic view of the organization as an open sociotechnical system makes cooperation and integration of the subsystems inside and outside it central. Certainly, putting back together what the Fordist system separated is key to the success of the lean system: the mind from the body of the worker; the R&D function from factory and market; management from its workers; suppliers and retailers from the firm; the traditional business functions from one another. Kenney and Florida (1993) point out that at the heart of the Japanese system, which they prefer to call "innovation-mediated production system," lies a fundamental difference from the Fordist system: The former is based on the integration of mental and physical work both on the factory floor and in the R&D laboratory essential to a high-performance learning organization.

Other recent studies underscore the major significance of the Japanese system as a complex of macro- and micro-learning, adaptation, innovation, and diffusion systems. This newer focus emphasizes the complex process by which the Japanese use their interconnected *zaibatsu* foreign direct investments to diffuse technology and develop new hybrid organizations adapted to their varied global environments.

Abo (1994) presents an international transfer model of the Japanese management production system that provides an analytical framework for measuring the degree of direct application of the Japanese system and its adaptation to local conditions or the degree of hybridization. Based on field research on the application-adaptation evaluation ratings of 34 Japanese transplants in North America, ten types of typical Japanese transplants have been identified and analyzed. The findings suggest the following:

> Japanese companies undertaking local production in the United States, where the management environment differs radically from that in Japan, continue to favor the application of the Japanese-style management and production system. However, due to the need for adapting to local conditions in the United States, they implement a type of hybrid system that differs from that of U.S. companies as well as from that of their own parent companies in Japan.

In addition, these studies point out significant elements in the learning and adaptation process, such as the important roles of the expatriate Japanese management personnel.

Norman Coates, while a visiting professor at the International University of Japan, developed a series of propositions about Japanese automobile manufacturing organizations in Japan and the United States as learning systems (1994). Coates stressed the importance of considering global enterprises as a network of alliances that includes joint ventures, partnerships, and other strategic alliances. These allied networks around the world share control of financial resources, markets, management, and technology, blurring individual corporate boundaries. The resultant globalization of knowledge is dramatically changing the concept of organizational learning.

Coates further suggests that the extraordinary competitive success of Japanese companies is partly caused by their capacity for generative learning, which is characterized by systemic change, transformation, and openness. He identifies key characteristics of types of learning organizations. These conceptual and analytical frameworks will provide valuable theoretical references for our analysis of NMUK as a learning and adapting hybrid transplant that has been greatly influenced by the network of alliances within which it is embedded.

NISSAN IN THE UNITED KINGDOM

Nissan made the final decision to locate its first European plant in the United Kingdom in 1984. The decision ended many years of searching and negotiating for the ideal location. In the end, Nissan garnered a total of £112 ($168) million in subsidies from the British government as an incentive to locate the plant in Britain. The initial plans to invest £330 ($495) million to set up a factory that would produce 200,000 cars by 1986 were drastically reduced. Nissan started the plant with an initial investment of £50 ($75) million to produce 24,000 vehicles. However, the company quickly agreed to a major expansion, which boosted production to 100,000 cars and jobs up to 2,700.

The company eventually decided on a location outside of Sunderland, in the northeast region of England. This decision was heavily influenced by three critical factors. First, Nissan was looking for a greenfield site to build on that was large enough to accommodate significant expansion plans in the future. A coalition formed by the local council and development corporation was able to offer Nissan a 930-acre site, the former Sunderland airport, at agricultural land prices, which were £1,800 ($2,700) per acre at the time. Second, the negotiating council acceded to one of Nissan's primary demands—that the plant be a single union plant. This agreement was highly controversial and unprecedented in the U.K. and is discussed in more detail later.

The third reason for choosing the northeast was based on Nissan's (and other Japanese transplants') experience in the United States. In some ways, the northeastern region of England is remarkably similar to the Ohio-Kentucky-Tennessee region of the U.S., where most of the Japanese automobile transplants are located. The similarities include long-standing high unemployment rates, a relatively ethnically homogeneous population, and the availability of government subsidies, in addition to necessary logistical criteria. The latter two reasons for locating in Sunderland provide evidence from the start that Nissan had learned from its experiences in the U.S. and was trying to avoid making the same mistakes while attempting to duplicate the successes, in adapting to the European environment.

NMUK's Production and Management Systems

Established over a decade ago, in 1984, NMUK is already widely recognized as Europe's benchmark automobile assembly and manufacturing plant. NMUK can build a Micra in 10.5 hours and a Primera in 12.5 hours. In 1993, its Nissan Micra was awarded both the European and Japanese Car of the Year awards as well as the coveted Gold Auto Design award for quality of design, construction, and finish.

Another major accomplishment at NMUK has been excellent relations with suppliers. There are currently 132 British companies supplying parts and components to NMUK. Company engineers have worked closely with local companies to specify what is needed and bring quality standards up to those demanded by NMUK. The cross-cultural technology transfer from Nissan's Smyrna, Tennessee plant has been significant. Over ten years, the Smyrna plant has developed a supplier training program and has achieved close working relationships with its U.S. suppliers. Nissan has helped suppliers develop their R&D skills in-house. This has resulted in essential quality improvements and cost reductions in the Nissan manufacturing chain by providing both essential lean system training and long-term contracts that call for step-by-step price reductions and quality improvement. These key lean system tenets, adapted and refined in the U.S., have also served as important building blocks at NMUK.

NMUK is a Mecca for British and European manufacturers who are trying to compete by transforming their outdated Fordist systems into the lean system or hybrid variations of it. About 800 to 1,000 industry people visit this plant each week from all over Europe and the world. Many of these visitors are representatives from Nissan's global alliances. McKinsey Global Institute's *Manufacturing Productivity* (1993) study found that "transplants (foreign direct investment) have been a more powerful way of improving productivity than trade has been, especially in Germany and the U.S. Transplants from leading edge producers: (1) directly contribute to hyper levels of domestic productivity; (2) prove that leading edge productivity can be achieved with local labor and many local inputs; (3) put competitive pressure on other domestic producers; (4) transfer knowledge of best practice to other domestic producers."

Japan's foreign direct investment in North America and Europe provides its automobile corporations with rich cross-cultural learning experience in the triad markets, while Detroit's Big Three and Europe's auto makers have no counterparts in Japan. Further, the Japanese have a highly developed system of industrial intelligence involving listening, observation, copious note taking, mentoring, written and verbal networking in the firm and its extended strategic alliances, and professional and governmental exchanges on a continuing basis. Moreover, Japanese foreign direct investment in 1990 was $310.8 billion in contrast to foreign direct investment in Japan of $18.4 billion. This provides Japanese corporations with a much greater opportunity, given their intelligence system, for cross-cultural learning and technology transfers.

NMUK's Hybrid Organization and Management Systems

NMUK's main Sunderland plant includes an automobile and component manufacturing facility, an engine machining and assembly plant, a foundry, a plastics injection and blow molding plant, and a service parts operation. All are located on one site and are configured as shown in Figure 1.

| **Nissan Motor Manufacturing (UK): Sunderland Plant** | FIGURE 1 ◆ |

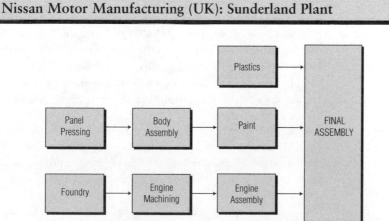

NMUK's key corporate and people principles, listed in Figure 2, were given to the authors by Peter Wickens, director of personnel and information systems at the Sunderland plant. The vast majority of these principles

---

◆   **FIGURE 2**   **Principles of Nissan Motor Manufacturing (UK) Ltd.**

People Principles
All other objectives can only be achieved by people

Selection	Hire the highest caliber people; look for technical capabilities and emphasize attitude
Responsibility	Maximize the responsibility; staff by devolving decision making
Teamwork	Recognize and encourage individual contributions, with everyone working toward the same objectives
Flexibility	Expand the role of the individual: multiskilled, no job description, generic job titles
Kaizen	Continuously seek 100.1 percent improvements; give "ownership of change"
Communications	"Every day, face to face"
Training	Establish individual "continuous" development programs
Supervisors	Regard as "the professionals at managing the production process"; give them much responsibility normally assumed by indirect departments; make them the genuine leaders of their teams
Single Status	Treat everyone as a "first class" citizen; eliminate all illogical differences
Trade Unionism	Establish single union agreement with AEU emphasizing the common objective for a successful enterprise

Key Corporate Principles

Quality	Building profitably the highest quality car sold in Europe
Customers	Achieve target of No. 1 in customer satisfaction in Europe
Volume	Always achieve required volume
New Products	Deliver on time, at required quality, within cost
Suppliers	Establish long-term relationship with single-source suppliers; aim for zero defects and just-in-time delivery; apply Nissan principle to suppliers
Production	Use "most appropriate" technology; develop predictable "best method" of doing job; build in quality
Engineering	Design "quality" and "ease of working" into the product and facilities; establish "simultaneous engineering" to reduce development time

are those most commonly associated with the Japanese transplants' lean system. However, several distinctive people principles emerge. One is the unusual single union arrangement at NMUK, discussed below. Another is the supervisors' professional status and team leadership role.

Wickens characterizes the Nissan Sunderland facility as having six levels of management, including the team leaders and a top-down control process with a bottom-up motivation system. This is certainly not a flat organization; however, the principle of single status is consistent with the single cafeteria and recreational facility, as well as common uniforms and near absence of private offices. At NMUK the use of traditional Japanese open spaces instead of individual offices so characteristic of North American and European corporations greatly enhances the exchange of information so essential in high learning and adaptive organizations. One distinctive aspect of the management system at NMUK has been the ability to use a large number of British managers within the company. With a total of 39 managers and nine directors (including the managing director), NMUK has only two Japanese nationals remaining in senior positions: the deputy managing director and the finance director.

The importation of management from Japan has created many problems in the Japanese transplants in the United States. Among the four industries studied, Kamiyama (1994) found that the automobile industry had the highest ratio of Japanese expatriates, which he concluded resulted from the considerable authority the Japanese parent company reserves for itself regarding decisions affecting the transplant. Conversely, Abo (1994) identified the presence of Japanese expatriate managers as a positive force for the transfer of knowledge. The potential for both the negative and positive effects of Japanese managers has been reduced by the predominance of British managers at NMUK. This may account in part for the hybrid nature of the NMUK organization.

All managers are compensated under the same pay systems, resulting in fewer problems and more harmony within the plant, according to Wickens. The use of predominantly local rather than Japanese management personnel is a change in policy when compared with the majority of other Japanese transplants and is consistent with the thesis of learning and adaptation. However, as in the North American transplants, the team members' voices in decision making are largely limited to quality improvement and have little or no say in quality of work life. This is also the case at NMUK, which has a well-defined hierarchy and a self-described top-down control of process. The latter, combined with a very young, green-grass work force, unusually powerful supervisors, and a weak union, leaves no doubt as to who is in charge.

The Demanding Role of the Supervisor

Supervisors at NMUK are leaders of the team and professionals and are given unusual power and responsibility. They are at the same level as the engineers and controllers. However, they are represented by the same union as the workers, further blurring the line between management and labor. At NMUK, overcoming the infamous British shop steward adversarial culture ("them and us") on the shop floor was particularly critical for the collectivistic Japanese ("just us") lean philosophy and system to succeed.

The importance of this collectivistic principle is seen in the elaborate screening, selection, and training systems for supervisors. It is also given extraordinary attention in all of their published literature, the single union agreement, training methods, and team shift startup meetings as well as company sports, social activities, and the company-wide salary system. *The Road to Nissan* (Wickens 1987) testifies how central this collectivistic philosophy and management system is to NMUK management and the Japanese lean system managers at home and abroad. Though British managers benchmarking NMUK may focus on technology and the production process, teamwork and commitment to a shared philosophy and principles are equally crucial elements of the plant's success. These are largely the responsibility of the supervisors and team leaders to establish and inculcate into the company culture.

Each supervisor manages approximately 20 teams, each with its own team leader. As professional managers of the production process, the supervisors are also responsible for the team budgets, organization and scheduling, the *kaizen* system, hiring and firing, and maintaining fact files on team members, including individual appraisals every two weeks. They motivate their work force and control the production process.

Because incongruities appear to exist between the NMUK philosophy and principles and their actual practices, supervisors must somehow attempt to rationalize them and make everything work. A meeting with supervisor Gary Harris, a six-year veteran with NMUK, left little doubt about the supervisors' high levels of technical and leadership skills. Conversely, this unusually powerful supervisor's role is not congruent with NMUK's "single status" principle, nor with the "self-directed team" often associated with the Japanese lean system. Again, this emphasizes the hybrid nature of NMUK.

Garrahan and Stewart's findings from their field of study of NMUK are very difficult to reconcile with Wickens' description of the "Nissan Way." Although Garrahan and Stewart's study has been highly criticized by some, such as Hanson (1992), it is the only full-scale study that has been done of the NMUK plant. At this writing, the company's management allows few academic researchers access to the plant, and workers are strongly discouraged from speaking to outsiders without the company's permission. Their findings provide insight on organizational learning and adaptations that have resulted in NMUK's particular hybrid form.

Work Stress, Discipline, Management Control of Employees, and the Role of Unions

Based on their field study of NMUK, Garrahan and Stewart conclude that the "Nissan Way" is incongruous. They contend that although the company claims three elements in its tripod of success—flexibility, quality, and teamwork—all tied together by consensus, the reality is more accurately described as an elaborate system of control defined by the iron grip of supervisors and team leaders on production workers and the absence of any effective mechanism for voicing opposition to the company. Their comparisons between the appearances and the realities of the main features of the "Nissan Way" are listed in Figure 3.

One of the claims that NMUK has made in its adaptation of the Japanese lean system is that increased flexibility will develop multi-skilled employees with better career prospects than are found in the Fordist system. However, Garrahan and Stewart argue that the extensive training Nissan employees undergo creates skills that are of value only inside the organization. In their interviews, they found that "what passed for multi-skilling was really knowledge of a number of general and cognate tasks. These are almost entirely company specific."

Appearance and Reality of the Main Features of the "Nissan Way"   FIGURE 3   ◆

Appearance *(As Nissan sees its "tripod," tied together by a fourth element, consensus)*	Reality *(What lies behind the appearance)*
1. Flexibility	1. In practice, only in terms of cognate tasks with the same team.
2. Consensus	2. No mechanism for challenging one-dimensional company views. In this sense, consensus must be seen as imposed.
3. Quality	3. Used to impose consensus via tight Neighbor Check, Visible Management System, and Vehicle Evaluation Score.
4. Teamwork	4. As in number 3, cuts across the potential for solidarity via both individual peer assessment and technical structure (JIT) of hierarchy.

Source: Garrahan and Stewart (1992), p. 109.

Regarding quality and teamwork, Garrahan and Stewart found that the rigid control systems used by NMUK imposed consensus and a high level of fear among employees. The mechanisms for enforcement of quality include several different peer reporting systems (such as Neighbor Check) and a visible management system through which quality data and performance of teams are displayed for all to see. The result of these systems creates an environment of intimidation and stress, in which peer monitoring, evaluating, and reporting on each other is reinforced by machine pacing, close supervision, and individual performance evaluation.

According to NMUK's vision, consensus—the glue that holds the tripod together—is achieved through the team system, in which members of the teams discuss problems and suggest production improvements. But according to Garrahan and Stewart, the company does not allow for voicing of opposition. With no such approved mechanism, it is difficult to imagine a true consensus rather than one that has been imposed. This intolerance to opposition is illustrated most clearly in Nissan's position on the role of unions.

The ability to strike a single union deal was highly important to Nissan from the start of its search for a plant location and most likely was a significant variable in the company's choice to locate in the northeast of England. The single union agreement was controversial from the beginning, and continues to be hotly debated. Nissan's competitors see the single union deal as favoring the Japanese company, because sole negotiating rights do not exist at any other company within the British motor industry. The Ford Motor Company calculated that, along with its other advantages—the greenfield site, maximum government grants, a young work force—Nissan would be able to build a car for "£330 ($445) to £550 ($825) less than an equivalent model from its U.K. rivals" (Gooding and Garnett 1986). One critic claimed that it is "morally wrong" for unions to compete against each other, arguing that employers will shop around for the best deal and leave workers in the lurch. Further, Thompson (1986) argued that foreign companies should not be granted special concessions that are not available for U.K. employers.

Three unions competed for the position of Nissan's single union: the Amalgamated Engineering Union (AEU), the Transport and General Workers Union, and the General, Municipal, Boilermakers and Allied Trades Union. The contract was won by the AEU, which is perceived as the least aggressive and assertive of the three. Although the union did not agree to an outright no-strike clause in the contract, it does include a commitment to resolving problems internally if at all possible. In addition, unresolvable issues are subject to "pendulum" arbitration, which rules either in favor of the company or the workers—a rule that encourages moderate demands.

As of July 1993, approximately 36 percent of NMUK employees were members of the AEU. This low level of union membership exists despite company claims it has made repeated efforts to encourage its employees to join the AEU. The union plays a minimal role in collective bargaining.

Inside the company, all work rules and wage decisions are negotiated and implemented by the company works council. The council consists of 18 members: eight selected by management and ten elected by workers representing different work areas within the company. An employee need not be a member of the union to serve on the council, and no union member has ever been elected to serve. Every Western European country except Britain and Ireland has legally mandated works councils or similar groups for advancing workers' interests. These councils are usually elected by the employees and give them organized collective input into many relevant managerial decisions. NMUK, it would appear, has successfully adapted the European system to meet its needs. It gives workers a symbolic input in decisions while avoiding the potentially powerful role these councils give unions in most European manufacturing firms.

It seems that Nissan actively set out to avoid some of the more glaring pitfalls it encountered in its Smyrna, Tennessee plant. The company actively opposed unionization from the outset in Tennessee, which caused the company numerous confrontations, unfavorable public relations, and ongoing battles with at least some of its employees. The stance in the U.K. has been much less confrontational and probably more effective from the company's perspective. At no time has Nissan expressed anti-union sentiments openly in the United Kingdom. Rather, it has chosen to pursue a single union strategy, which appears to have thrown unionists off balance.

According to Peter Wickens (1987), the company felt it had no choice but to reach an accommodation with the unions, even if it was only minimal. He states that there are more than 2,000 manufacturing companies with 500 employees or more in the U.K., and of this total only about 20 can be described as nonunion. Of these 20 companies, most are in the high-technology sector. If Nissan had chosen the same strategy in England that it pursued in Tennessee, says Wickens, it would have been "interpreted as a declaration of war." Nissan learned from its experience in the U.S. and in Japan with company unions and adapted its strategy to the U.K. environment.

To win on the issue of a single union deal, NMUK promised guaranteed lifetime employment in return for labor peace. Nearly a decade later, in November 1993, the company found itself in a position of rapidly sliding demand because of a severe recession in Europe. The response was a call for voluntary departures from any of the 4,600 employees. Workers were offered the equivalent of about six months' salary as an incentive to quit. Although NMUK held fast to its promise of no forced layoffs, and the managing director reiterated job security as the company's number one priority, the voluntary layoffs with incentives were clearly a departure from the traditional lean system paradigm. This change in human resources management is another example of learning and adaptation. Although Nissan has not attempted such a voluntary layoff policy at its U.S. transplant, it has nonetheless been exposed to and learned from American downsizing policies that favor efficiency over employees' needs.

The single union strategy was a very clever way to diffuse pressure to unionize the plant. On the one hand, Nissan was not opposing the presence of a union within its plant. Conversely, the company retained ultimate authority over its work force, while the union was relegated to play a smaller role in the determination of work rules, wages and benefits, termination policy, disciplinary policy, or any other function than unions normally play in a unionized setting. Although unionists continue to cry foul over what they see as a sham union, the company can still point to the existence of the union and the freedom of its employees to sign on if and when they should desire representation. The company has continually stressed publicly that it wanted a strong union, not a company union.

It is interesting to note the similarity between NMUK's union stance and its minimal use of Japanese managers in the plant—two parallel adaptations that represent cross-cultural learning from its Japanese plants and its U.S. transplant. As noted previously, there are only two Japanese managers at NMUK, the deputy managing director and the finance director. Nissan can point out that it has used an overwhelming majority of British managers at NMUK and thereby avoid the criticism that had characterized Japanese transplants in the United States. At the same time, it is clear that the two key positions held by Japanese managers at NMUK and their critical linkage with corporate management in Japan are crucial to continuous learning and adaptation, as well as to the control of the entire operation. The parallel here with the single union strategy is striking. While appearing to be accommodating to the casual observer, a closer look reveals that far less control has been relinquished than appears.

Employment Discrimination Within NMUK

Although claims of discrimination in employment have been growing against Japanese transplants in the U.S., there have been few such claims in England. Those that have been made have claimed discrimination based on age and gender. Few if any claims have been based on race, which differs from the cases brought forth in the United States. Of course, it must be noted that the northeast region of England is ethnically homogeneous, especially compared to other areas in Britain, such as the greater London area or the Midlands area. Both of these areas have experienced significant levels of racial tensions in the recent past. It could be stipulated that the ethnic homogeneity of the northeast region was one of the factors weighed by the Japanese in their final location decision. By choosing this location, they largely avoided charges of racial discrimination that have been alleged in their American plants.

The average age of production workers at NMUK is 25. Charges of age discrimination have pointed out that jobs created by Nissan are not really available to all qualified applicants in the region. The company received 11,500 applications for the first 250 assembly jobs at the plant. According to the British press, the overwhelming majority of job seekers were wasting their time because Nissan was only interested in hiring workers who already had a job, but who were "still young enough to be molded into the Japanese production philosophy" (Smart 1986). In other words, the Nissan jobs were not intended for the unemployed or for those over 30.

The question of gender discrimination is interesting because NMUK's dismal record in hiring women differs greatly from the American transplant experience. In the U.S., the Japanese auto makers, aware of federal equal employment opportunity regulations, have hired women in all capacities—from the shop floor to supervisory and middle management positions. In the U.K., the lack of female employees, except in clerical and secretarial capacities, is glaring. NMUK claims to have made an effort to recruit women but contends that very few women are interested in applying for the jobs. But because the levels of women in the work force in the U.K. are similar to those in the U.S., this argument is difficult to sustain. Learning from experience at home and abroad to adapt the lean system to various political economies, the company apparently simply took advantage of a severely depressed labor market in northeast England to select the best and brightest young, mostly male workers who have few if any job opportunities in the area at anywhere near Nissan's starting wages.

The hybrid mix of manufacturing and management practices found at NMUK form a unique English blend of the Fordist and lean systems. Examples of these practices include using an integrated quality control system, designing cars for quality and ease of manufacture and assembly, building close working relationships with suppliers necessary for the just-in-time delivery system, reducing setup times, introducing Tayloristic standardized operations into their teams, and using quality control and continuous improvement systems employing small group controls and activities and combining them with "working with pride" concepts and, until recently, job security.

It is apparent that this Japanese-English hybrid has achieved productivity and quality standards comparable to Japanese automobile factories in Japan. Nissan UK can build a Micra in 10.5 hours—almost double the average European autoworker's output. Again, like the experience in the United States, NMUK seems to have had many unfavorable effects on working conditions. These include the repetitive short cycle, machine-pacing of work, and added group social controls and rigid *kaizen* pressures to meet production quotas, coupled with high levels of supervisory controls and less than ideal ergonomic working conditions, including high noise levels, all combined with an ineffective union. In Japan, these working conditions are increasingly seen as unacceptable. Even during the current economic recession, the Japanese are having much more difficulty recruiting automobile workers at home than in the U.K. or the United States.

In the middle of the nineteenth century, Great Britain was leading the world's industrial revolution and was the world's wealthiest nation. Today, manufacturing investment and productivity in Britain lag well behind those in the U.S., Japan, Germany, France, and Italy. Manufacturing companies from abroad and particularly Japan, however, have demonstrated that with significant capital investment and new management knowhow, manufacturing plants in Great Britain, such as NMUK, can again set world standards. A recent British manufacturing audit by the Confederation of British Industry found that in 1988, Britain's foreign-owned plants had 46 percent higher productivity than similar British-owned plants.

As in North America, the three major Japanese manufacturing and assembly transplants in Great Britain—Nissan, Honda, and Toyota—have been joined by a large number of Japanese suppliers. Some of the latter are Japanese green-grass direct investments, others are Japanese joint ventures with British, American, and European companies. With only four automotive suppliers in the north of England in 1984, these new supplier transplants have resulted in a significant increase in direct investment in northeast England, as well as transferring lean system technology and know-how. The Japanese transplants are also having a favorable impact on the U.K.'s exports and trade balance with Europe. The local content of NMUK vehicles in Europe reached 80 percent in 1994. Despite a major recession in Europe, close to 50 percent of its production was exported to Europe in 1993–94. NMUK's current share of the European market is close to 3.9 percent, despite the recession and its failure to break even in 1993. The company has invested $1.43 billion in the U.K. since 1984 and has created thousands of jobs in Britain. NMUK plans to export between 12,000 and 15,000 vehicles to Japan in 1994. The company has also established the Nissan European Technology Center to design and develop new products for Europe in the United Kingdom.

Paradoxically, even as the six big European auto makers recognize their unproductive ways and seek to benchmark NMUK and other Japanese transplants as the new competitive management paradigm, apparent weaknesses are now being exposed by the global recession and excessive automobile production capacity. Japan is experiencing a growing fundamental desire in the 1990s to return to the simple life and away from the highly stressful compulsive materialism that has characterized life in Japan during its miraculous economic boom years.

The financial bubble bursting of the 1990s in Japan has resulted in wide dissatisfaction with business and political scandals, corruption, pollution, and excessive consumption, as well as what many Japanese see as a loss of spiritual satisfaction. The lean system, which was seen as a panacea in the 1970s and 1980s, has been significantly tarnished in Japan in the 1990s as its basic principles are being reexamined, modified, or abandoned. Lifetime employment, always a basic tenet of large firms, is now increasingly seen as another costly luxury both in Japan and in the transplants abroad, as evidenced by the recent Nissan layoffs in Japan and at NMUK. Voluntary retirement is being encouraged much earlier than the previous standard retirement age of 50–55. Women who have always been expected to leave work in their 20s to get married are now under even greater pressure to leave—married or not.

Company loyalty, fostered by the traditional paternalistic management system and drive for materialism, is undergoing significant generational changes, with growing interest in a better balanced life, such as that enjoyed in most Western industrialized countries. Fear of death by overwork (*karooshi*) is a growing concern in the ever more demanding Japanese management system, as is stress from "lone transfers," whereby male managers and workers are sent to other company posts away from families and friends, often for several years.

Long-term single supplier or bank relationships with *keiretsu* members are increasingly being abandoned for foreign suppliers because of severe financial pressure. Consensual management is also increasingly seen as a luxury. Fewer and shorter meetings are being replaced by time and budget management, which is seen as essential to cultivate high value-added management.

Consensus management has also been replaced with more top-down decision making at Honda's American operations. Major Japanese companies, including the largest automobile companies, have become concerned that although their blue-collar productivity is world class, their white-collar productivity is not and is adversely affecting their profits. Japanese-style management, still seen in North America and Europe as a powerful economic force, is increasingly seen in Japan as a demanding engine driving an aging work force that is experiencing a highly stressful work life, and diminishing benefits, including job security.

The Japanese and American long-term experience with the lean system, both good and bad, raises some interesting questions for the U.K. and other European countries as they seek to follow Japan and the U.S. into more competitive lean system hybrids. Some of the relevant questions that need to be addressed are: What does the emerging pattern of learning and adaptation mean for the various stakeholders of the firm? As technology advances and creates significant increases in productivity, to whom do the benefits accrue? How long will it take until the level of worker dissatisfaction reaches the point at which the Japanese will move on from Europe or Japan to a fresh start in a different country?

Stakeholder theory posits that various stakeholder groups have legitimate claims to the resources of corporations. Clearly the learning and adaptive behaviors of Japanese firms that have established transplants in North America and Europe, resulting in multiple hybrids of the lean system, have bestowed rewards on most stakeholder groups—particularly investors, managers, and consumers. But the employees—arguably one of the most important internal stakeholders—have not had an equitable share of this winning equation. Their primary benefit has historically been long-term job security. Today even this is in question.

The Japanese have succeeded in adapting the lean system to its relevant local environment, and the resulting paradigm, according to critical theorists, contains many of the worst of Western employee practices and is abandoning many of the best Japanese practices. For example, we have seen that NMUK has abandoned the practice of lifetime employment. At the same time, very little of the workplace social safety net, so prevalent throughout Western Europe, has been adapted by the Japanese at NMUK. The co-governance structures mandated by most Western European nations are markedly absent from Japanese transplants. The predominant theme for the worker remains one of hierarchy, authority, control, and highly demanding work.

One could argue that for the worker this new hybrid transplant is not a radical departure from the highly controlling Fordist system. Critical philosophers, such as Jacques Ellul (Gandy 1994), envision a continuing technological determinism wherein technology has become a philosophy with efficiency as its god, economists as its priests, and engineers as its servants. The paradox remains as we transfer global technology at an unprecedented rate in the search for greater competitiveness and market share but in this frenzied quest continue to diminish the lives of the very human beings who make it possible.

The challenge for the twenty-first century is to discover methods for the transfer of technology in ways that engage workers as more equal partners and enhance the quality of their lives on and off the job. Today's corporate stakeholder interests, despite the TQM, lean systems, and reengineering phenomena, are still heavily weighted toward the interests of shareholders and other investors, as well as consumers. What continues to receive far less priority are the human interests of the employee stakeholders. The lean system and its global hybrid spinoffs may be portrayed as the technological yellow brick road leading to the Utopian Emerald City. But, for the worker, it may indeed seem to be more smoke and mirrors magic by the technological wizard, only this time it had its origins in Toyota City instead of Detroit.

In his most recent book, Matthew Fox (1994), the philosopher priest, envisions a world in which work life is in balance with personal life—where human values and goals are integrated in both life and livelihood, where there is deep satisfaction beyond monetary rewards that nourishes the human spirit in the workday, rather than the all too common feelings of insecurity, alienation, and a crushing defeat of spirit. Technological progress and transfer without human values offers little promise for the twenty-first century.

References

T. Abo. ed., *Hybrid Factory: The Japanese Production System in the United States* (Oxford: Oxford University Press, 1994).

N. Bray, "Nissan Motor to Urge 4,600 Workers to Quit at U.K. Unit Amid Sales Slump." *Wall Street Journal,* November 15, 1993, p. A7.

"The Britain Audit: Manufacturing the Confederation of British Industry." *The Economist,* August 21, 1993, pp. 46–47.

L. Chappell and M. Gates, "Trade Spat Revives Debate on Transplant Jobs," *Automotive News,* March 14, 1994, p. 4.

N. Coates, "Organizations as Learning Systems: The Case of the Japanese Automobile Manufacturing Organization." *The International Executive, 36,* 2 (1994): 171–187.

R. Cole and D. Deskins, Jr., "Racial Factors inside Locations and Employment Patterns of Japanese Firms in America," *California Management Review,* November 1988, pp. 9–23.

Company Profile 1993 Statistics & Awards, Nissan Motor Manufacturing (UK) Limited, Sunderland, United Kingdom, 1993.

Foreign Investment: Growing Japanese Presence in the U.S. Auto Industry, U.S. General Accounting Office, Washington, D.C., 1988.

M. Fox, *The Reinvention of Work: A New Vision of Livelihood for Our Time* (San Francisco: Harper Collins, 1994).

R. E. Freeman, *Strategic Management: A Stakeholder Approach* (Boston: Pitman, 1984).

"GM's German lessons," *Business Week,* December 20, 1993, p. 68.

O. H. Gandy, "The Information Superhighway as the Yellow Brick Road," *National Forum, 74,* 2 (1994): 24–27.

N. Garnett, "Ground Broken by Union Deal," *Financial Times,* July 1, 1986, p. 18.

P. Garrahan and P. Stewart, *The Nissan Enigma: Flexibility at Work in a Local Economy* (London: Mansell Publishing Ltd., 1992).

D. Gelsanliter, *Jump Start: Japan Comes to the Heartland* (New York: Farrar, Straus, Giroux, 1990).

K. Gooding and N. Garnett, "Facing an Uphill Struggle," *Financial Times,* July 1, 1986, p. 15.

C. Handy, *The Age of Paradox* (Cambridge, MA: Harvard Business School Press, 1994).

C. Hanson, "Cooking the Books Will Not Make 2+2=5," *Newcastle Journal,* August 16, 1992, p. 5.

S. Hori, "Fixing Japan's White Collar Economy," *Harvard Business Review,* November–December 1993, pp. 157–172.

"Losing Its Way: Japanese Industry," *The Economist,* September 18, 1993, pp. 78–79.

M. Kenney and R. Florida, *Beyond Mass Production: The Japanese Lean System and Its Transfer to the U.S.* (Oxford: Oxford University Press, 1993).

K. Kamiyama, "The Typical Japanese Overseas Factory," in T. Abo, ed., *Hybrid Factory: The Japanese Production System in the United States* (Oxford: Oxford University Press, 1994), pp. 58–81.

D. Levin, "The Graying Factory," *New York Times,* February 20, 1994, Section 3, p. F1.

Manufacturing Productivity, McKinsey Global Institute, Washington, D.C., October, 1993.

T. O'Neill, personal interview, Amalgamated Engineering Union, Newcastle, England, July 28, 1993.

"One Union Could Tip Nissan Scale," *Newcastle Evening Chronicle,* March 13, 1984, p. 3.

V. Smart, "Car Factory that Puts Young in the Driving Seat," *London Observer,* April 13, 1986, p. 5.

N. Thompson, "Nissan Deal Attacked," *Newcastle Journal,* January 27, 1986, p. 8.

C. Tighe, "Lines at Nissan," *Newcastle Evening Chronicle,* September 1, 1986, p. 4.

J. Tomany, personal interview, Centre for Urban and Regional Studies, Newcastle University, Newcastle, England, July 30, 1993.

P. D. Wickens, *The Road to Nissan: Flexibility, Quality, Teamwork* (London: Macmillan Press Ltd., 1987).

P. D. Wickens, personal communication to authors, March 15, 1994.

J. P. Womack and D. T. Jones, "From Lean Production to the Lean Enterprise," *Harvard Business Review,* March–April 1994, pp. 93–103.

J. P. Womack, D. T. Jones, and D. Roos, *The Machine That Changed the World: The Story of Lean Production* (New York: Harper Collins, 1990).

Integrative Case Seven   *McDonald's Conquers the World*

Source: Andrew E. Serwer, "McDonald's Conquers the World," *Fortune*, October 17, 1994, pp. 103–116. Copyright © 1994, Time Inc. All rights reserved. Reprinted with permission.

Sometime over the next 24 hours, while the rest of us merely work, eat, and sleep, McDonald's will open three more shiny-new restaurants. One may be out in a fast-growing suburb of Salt Lake City, another in the pristine downtown of Singapore, and the third in the smoggy bustle of Warsaw, where it will soon be flooded by smartly dressed young Poles hungry for a taste of America. Chances are good that within a year's time each of these stores will be grossing about $1.7 million a year and operating well in the black. And tomorrow? Same thing. Three more stores will open.

It wasn't long ago that many predicted McDonald's was doomed to become a lumbering cash cow in a mature industry. As events have turned out, the company has remained the nation's most profitable major retailer over the past ten years, even as the competition has become nimbler. Since 1983, McDonald's profits have more than tripled to almost $1.1 billion on revenues of $7.4 billion and systemwide sales of over $23 billion from over 14,000 stores.

Not that some of those predicted age marks aren't starting to show. Operating profits from the U.S. and same-store sales have climbed only slightly over the past several years, and the highly organized McCulture shows signs of becoming too rigid, too steeped in its own orthodoxy to cook up that all-important break-out-of-the-box, home run innovation. Most analysts believe a new hitwich on the order of the Big Mac or the Quarter Pounder will be required to solve McDonald's so-called "menu problem."

Whatever problems McDonald's may be having at home, however, are more than offset by its spectacular success abroad. Few of those skeptical about McDonald's in the Eighties were able to foresee that the fast-food giant—after stumbling in Holland in the 1970s—would take its act on the road and go global with a vengeance. In 1988 the company had 2,600 foreign stores and $1.8 billion in overseas revenue. Six years later it has 4,700 stores doing $3.4 billion a year. The result: McDonald's today is arguably the most awesome service machine on the planet, and a virtual blueprint for taking a service organization global. While the seers and the management consultant crowd crow that service will become America's next great export, McDonald's is already doing it today, delivering world-standardized food, smiles, value, and cleanliness to every continent except Antarctica.

"We are seizing the global marketplace," says James Cantalupo, the raspy-voiced former accountant who heads McDonald's International.

McDonald's is in the rare and enviable position of possessing a truly global service brand, a name known to hundreds of millions around the world. "Only a few American brands are easy to export," says Caroline Levy of Lehman Brothers. "The recognition level must be very high, and the price point low. That means Coke, Marlboro, Wrigley, and McDonald's."

Note: Of Levy's fab four, only McDonald's sells a service, not a packaged good. And if the packaged-goods purveyors are any model, McDonald's untapped potential remains enormous. The company already sells its burgers in 73 countries and pulls in about 45% of its operating income from foreign operations. But global soft drink behemoth Coca-Cola, for instance, sells to 195 countries and brings home 80% of its income from abroad.

"It's hard for Americans to understand, but McDonald's is almost heaven-sent to these people," says Tim Fenton, the head of McDonald's Poland, as he gestures toward one of his 17 booming stores. "It's some of the best food around. The service is quick, and people smile. You don't have to pay to use the bathroom. There's air conditioning. The place isn't filled with smoke. We tell you what's in the food. And we want you to bring kids."

For all the strength of its brand, what McDonald's really has to export around the globe is that almost intangible, fragile concept—service. How does it do it? The answer: a collection of surprisingly simple strategies, mostly from the Lost Art School of Management. Here's what's on the syllabus:

- Gather your people often for face-to-face meetings to learn from each other.
- Put your employees through arduous and repetitive management training.
- Form paradigm-busting arrangements with suppliers.
- Know a country's culture before you hit the beach.
- Hire locals whenever possible.
- Maximize autonomy.
- Tweak the standard menu only slightly from place to place.
- Keep pricing low to build market share. Profits will follow when economies of scale kick in.

Of course McDonald's also lends incredible marketing support to its brand, blanketing the world with advertising and promotion. A $1.4 billion annual global budget makes McDonald's the most advertised single brand in the world. Kids, minorities, and the handicapped tug at emotional sleeves in dozens of languages, begging potential customers to "get up and get away." Ronald McDonald, according to some in the company, is more recognizable than Santa Claus.

McDonald's slavish devotion to regimentation is also a key, and the company is constantly refining its organization, which is now so complex and far-reaching that one of those James Bond masterminds might envy it.

"Never have I seen a company more focused than McDonald's," says Don Keough, a McDonald's board member and retired president of Coca-Cola, a major supplier. "The company is an army with one objective that has never strayed."

Driving these zealous troops forward in the hamburger crusades is CEO Mike Quinlan, 49, or "Q," as he is called. (Hmm, maybe there is something

How Many McDonald's Can He Build?

Cantalupo's Theorem: If nearly 15,000 McDonald's already sounds like plenty, just wait. James Cantalupo, president of McDonald's International, uses a formula to guesstimate how many stores he can build. He divides a country's population by the number of people per store in the U.S. and adjusts for differences in per capita income. Of course it doesn't account for factors like competition and eating habits. *Fortune* calculated the potential number of McDonald's that could be built worldwide. Answer: 42,000.

$$\frac{\text{Population of Country X}}{\begin{array}{c}\text{No. of People per}\\ \text{McDonald's in U.S.}\\ (25,000)\end{array}} \times \frac{\text{Per Capita Income of Country X}}{\begin{array}{c}\text{Per Capita Income}\\ \text{of U.S.}\\ (\$23,120)\end{array}} = \begin{array}{c}\text{Potential}\\ \text{Penetration}\\ \text{of McDonald's}\\ \text{in Country X}\end{array}$$

McDonald's Biggest Markets			Some Underpenetrated Markets		
	Current number of restaurants	Minimum market potential		Current number of restaurants	Minimum market potential
Japan	1,070	6,100	China	23	784
Canada	694	1,023	Russia	3	685
Britain	550	1,794	Colombia	0	79
Germany	535	3,235	India	0	489
Australia	411	526	Pakistan	0	90
France	314	2,237	South Africa	0	190

to this James Bond thing.) Only the company's third CEO, the carrot-topped Quinlan, who started in the mailroom 31 years ago, wears a mantle passed down from patriarch Ray Kroc and current chairman Fred Turner. While Quinlan is proud of the company's record under his watch, he's more frustrated than anyone by its inability to develop that next big hitwich. So Q has placed a bounty on innovation and is now scouring the globe for winners. "Want to know my definition of insanity?" asks Q. "It's doing the same thing over and over again and expecting different results. If there's anything I try to impart to our people, it's to never be satisfied. That means coming up with new ideas."

While many of the company's greatest successes, such as the Big Mac and the Egg McMuffin, came from rank-and-file U.S. franchisees, other brainstorms—mostly operational—have begun to filter in from overseas. The Dutch created a pre-fab modular store that can be moved over a weekend. The Swedes came up with an enhanced meat freezer. And satellite stores, or low-overhead mini-McDonald's, were invented in high-rent Singapore.

"There used to be resistance to ideas from abroad," says Ed Rensi, the portly chief of McDonald's USA. "No more."

And nowhere is the spirit of this global burgerpreneurism more evident than in Poland. Five years after the fall of communism, the Poles are busy scrubbing four decades of soot off buildings. New, brightly colored commercial signs, including those of Pizza Hut and Burger King, are cropping up like wild mushrooms. Fenton, McDonald's man in Poland, gazes out over Warsaw from a bar atop the new Marriott hotel and reflects on what he's seen. "When I first came here, two years ago, there were practically no lights. Now look," he says gesturing to the buddingly lit city. "I like this view because you can see all four of the city's McDonald's from here."

Nowadays Fenton can take time off to have a Johnnie Walker, a pleasant change from when he faced challenges not covered back home at Hamburger U. When he first arrived in Poland, one local official told him he would have to change "that silly logo with those arches." Say what? After a patient explanation on the power and value of trademarks, the apparatchik finally backed off.

And for all its brand recognition, McDonald's has to walk a fine line between being perceived as global or local and American. "People are more the same than they are different," says International chief Cantalupo, whose charge it is to sow the company's stores like seed around the world. "I don't think our food is seen as American. It's seen as McDonald's." A lot of very intense preparation before entering a market, including the hiring of local managers, helps make this most American of brands seem pretty local too. Before Fenton came to Poland, the company planned for 18 months. Locations, real estate, construction, supply, personnel, legal, and government relations were all worked out in advance. Finally, in June 1992, Fenton charged in with a team of 50 from the U.S., Russia, Germany, and Britain. Since then all except Fenton have been replaced by Poles in what McDonald's calls a sunset program.

Now Poles don't just want to eat at McDonald's; they want to work there too. With the average annual income in Poland around $2,000, counter jobs paying $1.70 an hour—or about 75% above that average—are snapped up. No wonder counter kids appear to hustle harder than in the U.S. Managerial jobs at $900 a month, with a stint at Hamburger University in the U.S., are especially coveted.

Doesn't this high profile rile the locals who don't get jobs? Isn't McDonald's in danger of being seen as some kind of U.S. culinary imperialist? "The only resistance comes from the same people who didn't want political change in the late 1980s," replies Fenton, as he sits in his Western-style open-architecture office in downtown Warsaw, fingering a brochure that teaches the Poles how to use a drive-in.

If the palpable excitement of Fenton's customers is any indication, the hard-liners had better find another capitalist stooge to pick on. It's the first day of school in Warsaw, and kids in new outfits stream into a McDonald's in the shadow of the Ministry of Culture building, a gift from Stalin and an ironic symbol of how quickly change has come to Poland. Fenton, a sturdy meat-and-potatoes guy from upstate New York, beams, frowning only when he uses his Polish to shoo away a ragged gypsy woman who is begging near the store entrance.

Fenton's Polish managers are taking to the McDonald's system with only a few small hitches. "The toughest concept to teach has been negotiation," he says, "because under communism there wasn't any. Also, the first year they came to a barbecue at my house in suits. This year I said, 'Anyone wearing a suit gets sent home.' " He also had to suggest, in Pollyanna-like McDonald's fashion, that customers not bring in vodka to drink with their Big Macs. By year-end, Fenton will be running 22 stores, and his operation should have positive operating income, even with prices 25% below those in the U.S. By 1998, Fenton anticipates Poland will have 100 stores, but by then the sun will have set on him, and at his desk will sit a Pole.

Each country McDonald's enters presents its own problems—or opportunities. German law prohibits special promotions like "buy one, get one free" and advertised discounts. Labor unions in France recently accused the company of cheating workers out of overtime pay. Coping with foot-dragging officials sometimes requires McDonald's to take the offensive. In Germany a recent Chinese food promotion worked so well that the company ran out of spring rolls. "I tried to order more from our supplier in Denmark," explains Hans Griebler, the affable head of purchasing in Germany, "but he told us his company needed permission from the government to work on the weekends. I called the Danish labor minister and got it."

That kind of drive to provide service—which we almost take for granted in the U.S.—is at the core of what McDonald's offers its overseas customers. Listen to Rolf Kreiner, head of marketing at McDonald's 535-store German operation. "The world is becoming a service society. People are hungry for service, but in many countries they don't get any except at McDonald's. That's why our stores are so crowded. That's why we're ahead."

Supplying stores abroad can be a nightmarish exercise in logistics. When McDonald's first enters a country, it often has to import many of its supplies. Then the company tries to source locally as quickly as possible. "Transportation is cheaper when you stay in one country and you don't have to change currency," says vice chairman Jack Greenberg, an easygoing former CPA with Arthur Young and the rare outsider among McDonald's top management (he has only 12 years there). Sometimes the company contracts with local suppliers, with happy results for both parties. A German mustard and mayonnaise company that started with a $100 order some 20 years ago now sells McDonald's $40 million of condiments annually.

More frequently, though, McDonald's encourages its domestic suppliers to follow the company abroad. Chicago-based meat supplier OSI Industries has joint ventures in 17 countries, where it works with local companies making McDonald's hamburgers. One such site, a spotless meat plant in postcard-pretty Guenzburg, Bavaria, cranks out some 2.5 million patties a day. Computers mix ground beef to ensure that fat content meets the McDonald's world standard, 20% or less. Young second-generation Turkish women box patties quick-frozen by liquid nitrogen just as their counterparts would in the U.S. The specs and production demands are exacting, and with monthly evaluations, the pressure for quality is constant. Says OSI International President Douglas Gullang: "Meeting McDonald's standards is a huge challenge. To some it seems insane what we do. But we realize our product isn't just meat; it's service. We've turned a meat plant into a service business."

For McDonald's, finding potential business partners around the globe isn't a problem—rather, the company is swamped with inquiries. Sorting through them is the real challenge. "McDonald's spent years going over dozens of applications before it picked its joint venture partner in Singapore," says Bob Kwan, managing director of the operation in that country. "Of course, I'm happy they chose me." The company prefers partners with connections. One of the heads of its Saudi Arabian operation is a member of the Saudi royal family.

The company also has more than one way of structuring its operations overseas, choosing from several options before it enters a new country. In the European theater, as Q calls it, the company usually runs wholly owned subsidiaries. The thinking is that since these markets resemble the U.S., they can be run in roughly the same way as the domestic business, allowing for some adjustment. Take Holland. (In the early days of overseas expansion, the company would have said, "Please!") "We put stores in the suburbs like in the U.S.," says Michiel Hiemstra, a director of McDonald's Netherlands. "That didn't work because of different eating patterns. We learned to build downtown."

As in the U.S. market, these subsidiaries operate company-owned stores and also license out franchises—about 70% of the company's stores world wide are franchised. Snagging one of these franchises ain't easy. Also as in the U.S., potential franchisees slog through a two-year screening process. They must work at a store and go through training before gaining final approval, all for the right to plunk down $45,000 and sign a 20-year contract that guarantees McDonald's a royalty of 4% of sales, plus another 8.5% or more of sales for rent. Add to that 4% of sales for advertising, or over 16 cents of every dollar taken right off the top. But shed no tears for McDonald's operators, who organize themselves into webs of co-ops and service groups; they wind up taking home about $200,000 a year per store. High-volume stores in locales like Warsaw or Moscow can net three times as much.

In Asian markets, the company prefers joint ventures, such as the 1,000-plus store operation in Japan headed by eccentric billionaire Den Fujita.

These usually fifty-fifty arrangements allow the company to tap into its partner's contacts and local expertise. The company lets such partners negotiate with cumbersome entities such as the Chinese government, which has already allowed McDonald's to open 23 restaurants, with dozens more on the way. McDonald's grabs the standard royalty off the top in these joint ventures, as well as 50% of the bottom line.

In its most exotic markets—Saudi Arabia, for example—the company reduces its risk by putting up no equity capital. It simply licenses the name with strict requirements as to standards and takes an option to buy in later. Repatriating all these earnings and royalties from countries like Oman and New Caledonia is yet another challenge. McDonald's treasury department uses derivatives to hedge in 12 currencies, though in these derivative-phobic days, Greenberg insists it's never to make a trading profit.

While other companies increasingly rely on technology to fill in gaps in communication, McDonald's still believes in the power of the good old face-to-face sit-down. The company that helped pioneer advanced point-of-sale computing has no E-mail system at headquarters, and Q doesn't even have a computer in his office. Ergo, no company gathers together more of its people from more places as often as McDonald's. "We constantly get together by region as well as by discipline, such as purchasing, construction, and accounting" says Kwan from Singapore. "We share successes and failures, and we work together to cut costs." A sampling of a typical month's meetings: an Asian store managers' conference in Sydney, the European purchasing board get-together in London, a worldwide communications conference in Chicago.

McDonald's has also globalized its powerhouse real estate operation. For years a clique of managers saw McDonald's more as a real estate company than a fast-food chain, much to Ray Kroc's chagrin. It's easy to see why. The company owns about 9,000 properties, or about 60% of its store locations, making it the world's largest collector of land parcels, totaling some 36 million square feet of space. Book value: $10 billion. Market value: hard to say. One and a half times as much?

Today, though, real estate is pretty far down on the list of McDonald's priorities. No. 1 worry: that same old frustration at not finding a breakthrough at home—the double-digit-growth menu item. And there's no apparent solution in sight. Even Quinlan, a self-described "glass-is-half-full kind of a guy," calls new-product development "disappointing" and concedes that "new products are basically on the back burner." A long-standing, costly pizza project has been "like rolling a snowball uphill," says U.S. chief Rensi. A tableful of other dinner entrees, from pasta to corn on the cob, has also been coldly Sisyphean. "We're focusing on burgers, chicken, and breakfast. That's why people come to McDonald's," says Quinlan. But in the face of sluggish domestic growth, that focus has begun to look a bit like rationalization. To create a real winner, McDonald's may need to do something incredibly radical in its culture, like buying someone else's concept or hiring outsiders to come up with the next Quarter Pounder.

So far, the closest thing to a Nineties hit has been the Extra Value Meal, a discounted package of burger, fries, and drink that offsets its lower margins with increased volume. But its success just shows what a tough game of nickel and dime the U.S. fast-food market has become. McDonald's now has one store per 25,000 people in the U.S., and the company takes great pains not to cannibalize an existing store's volume when it opens another restaurant stateside, as it did 324 times last year. Grand Metropolitan's Burger King and PepsiCo's Taco Bell, KFC, and Pizza Hut are fierce, moneyed competitors that have all won battles against McDonald's.

So, Mike Quinlan, would you buy McDonald's stock if the company had only domestic operations? "Of course I would, you nut!" But why? Jim Adamson, CEO of Burger King, has an answer: "There are still so many new points of distribution out there—hospitals, sports arenas, and roadways. There's room for double-digit domestic growth in our business."

McDonald's is catching up, especially to Taco Bell, in the search for innovative locations. Examples: a train in Germany, an English Channel ferry, and an ice-skating rink in Wisconsin. It will also open over 500 smaller satellite stores in places like New York City and Brazil this year. Q is adamant: "I'm less concerned about saturation than at any point in my career. We only have a 21% share of the U.S. quick-serve restaurant business. Meanwhile we continue to lower costs, which allows us to penetrate smaller and smaller markets. We're vacuuming our P&L." Example: Standardizing kitchen equipment last year cut about $40,000 from the cost of equipping a restaurant.

One place McDonald's isn't cutting corners is employee training. Every geeky, pimply-faced burger flipper from Taipei to Topeka is put through the paces for two to three days. More than a few of us remember those lessons. The company claims the first job of one out of every 15 Americans was at a McDonald's.

For McDonald's managers the real business of training means matriculating at Hamburger University at company headquarters in Oak Brook, Illinois, just west of Chicago. Once mostly the butt of jokes, Hamburger U. today is—and hold the guffaws—akin to a crash executive MBA program. Procter & Gamble, Amoco, and the Red Cross all have visited recently looking for ways to improve their training. Fourteen times a year, 200 McDonald's managers with two to five years of experience arrive from 72 countries for the intensive two-week program. Simultaneous translation into 20 languages is provided for courses such as Building Market Share and Staffing and Retention II. Team building, just in time, close to your customer, TQM—called MQM here—it's been taught at HU for years. Some HU training borders on axiomatic: "Don't say: 'Juan! Clean up the parking lot!' Ask: 'Juan, would you please sweep up the parking lot?' " Other exercises are more challenging. Students are yanked out of classes and confronted in role-playing scenarios: "Hey, Jack, my hamburger tastes like it was made by Du Pont! What are you going to do about it?" Some 50,000 McDonald's employees, franchisees, and suppliers have received diplomas.

Whoa—suppliers you say? Yes, suppliers. In fact, many of today's cozy-up-to-your-supplier companies, such as Wal-Mart, learned from McDonald's. Why let the guys with the goods in on the system? Because "McDonaldizing" suppliers helps them meet company specs—though McDonald's suppliers are a unique animal to begin with. How about this for different? Many suppliers have open-book relationships in which McDonald's sets their profits. Some of them have McDonald's as their only customer, yet they have no contract with the company.

Though McDonald's does some business with companies like H.J. Heinz, Kraft General Foods, and Coca-Cola (see box), it buys a majority of its food from this shadow industry of formerly small companies whose collective annual sales now total around $3 billion. Meat supplier OSI Industries, distributor Martin Brower, and French-fry king J.R. Simplot Co. have grown from mom and pop operations to $500 million dollar-plus companies mostly based on sales to McDonald's. Kroc didn't like buying from big food companies because they weren't responsive enough. According to John Love, author of *McDonald's: Behind the Arches,* Kraft once had McDonald's entire cheese business but lost three-quarters of it because it wouldn't make a sharper cheddar.

McDonald's gravitated in its earlier days toward small, hungry companies like J.S. Simplot's, then a mere sprout of an Idaho potato company. Simplot, today 85, remembers hooking up with Kroc back in 1967. "I went down to Santa Barbara and visited with Ray. He told me what he needed in a potato plant. I said, 'You got it.' We shook hands, and that was it—no price mentioned. McDonald's doesn't shop for the lowest price; they want service. They prize the relationship."

Don't kid yourself, though. With suppliers or anyone else, McDonald's knows how to throw its weight around. But in the past, McDonald's has learned all too well what it's like to play the bad guy and today works like hell—more than any other large consumer company—to avoid wearing the black hat. The company took it on the chin as a symbol of the system in the Sixties. When it was accused of racism, sexism, anti-environmentalism, it reacted defensively, exacerbating the situation. No more.

"Now we try to be ahead of the curve," says the head of communications, Dick Starmann. Three years ago the company stopped using bleached white bags. "Half the scientific community said nay on white bags, the other half said yea, but customers didn't want them, so we got rid of them," says Starmann. A pilot program in Holland that recycles 100% of the waste at each store may be expanded to other countries.

This year the company banned smoking in company-owned U.S. stores and suggested that franchisees do the same. "There was no immediate pressure from customers, but we could see it coming," says Starmann. The tobacco companies were furious and demanded a sitdown. McDonald's

Things go better with Coke—just ask McDonald's

Talk about corporate love affairs. Ask McDonald's CEO Mike Quinlan about his company's relationship with Coca-Cola Co., and his eyes light up. "Just wonderful," he gushes. "They are our partner." Echoes Don Keough, Coke's former No. 2 guy and now a McDonald's board member: "It's an enormously important strategic alliance. McDonald's is a hallmark customer."

No kidding. Not only is McDonald's the largest fountain-sales customer of Coke, but the two global giants also share a common No. 1 enemy: PepsiCo, which in addition to making Pepsi Cola owns fast-food rivals Pizza Hut, Taco Bell, and KFC.

Like any successful affair of the heart, the two companies enjoy getting together for those special occasions. Every 18 months or so, the top 100 executives from each company meet for a weekend at some locale like Palm Springs or Palm Beach, and they don't scrimp on the speaking fees. In past years, for example, they have given the podium over to Ronald Reagan, Margaret Thatcher, and Henry Kissinger.

The next gathering will be held this February in Phoenix, with an undisclosed heavy hitter scheduled to speak. "The focus of these meetings is on the future of the global marketplace," says Keough. "The companies have much common ground there." For example, the two companies worked together to open up the Russian market earlier this decade.

The relationship has a long history, going back some 40 years to McDonald's infancy. The payoff for Coke has been tremendous. Coca-Cola products are served in all 14,500 or so of McDonald's stores and account for about 5% of its U.S. volume. Not a single restaurant serves Pepsi—although there is no actual company edict that prohibits it. The heresy of that act would be unthinkable to a McDonald's franchisee.

Those of us who aren't invited to these big powwows can certainly speculate that they're a great opportunity to get out on the links. Or plot the total destruction of PepsiCo? Not so, insists Keough. "We really don't get into that," he says, leaving the impression that McDonald's and Coke are too busy looking deeply into each other's eyes and swooning to bother with the competition. Not to mention carving up the world.

said no. The latest charge: using beef from cattle that grazed in pastures cleared from the rain forest. "We don't serve any," says Starmann, who eagerly pulls a policy statement out of his briefcase.

Even the staple McDonald's food is less unhealthy than it was ten years ago. "McDonald's has gotten better," says industry critic Michael Jacobson, executive director of the Center for Science in the Public Interest and co-author of *Fast-Food Guide,* "though much of the improvement is in the addition of healthier foods like cereal, a no-fat bran muffin, salads, carrots, and celery, and low-fat McLean burgers." According to Jacobson's work, McDonald's burgers generally contain fewer calories and less fat and sodium than comparable sandwiches from Burger King or Wendy's. But a steady diet of McDonald's Biscuit with Sausage & Egg might tie up traffic on the aortal highway in short order. Overseas, besides serving localized fast food—like black currant shakes in Poland—McDonald's offers more body-friendly items like salads with shrimp in Germany and veggie burgers in Holland. "Yes, people are interested in healthier food," says Quinlan, who is sensitive about his own double chin, "but they are most interested in taste, convenience, and value." And to those who say McDonald's is simply serving up junk to the world? "I say, 'Wake up, pal, you're not on the playing field.' We're giving customers what they want."

It's true that the more McDonald's globalizes, the more risks the company takes on. Still, it would take a mighty big log to make it stumble. Ultimately McDonald's isn't going to be hurt by a grandmother in Albuquerque suing over hot spilled coffee, nor Green protests in the Czech Republic, nor penny shortfalls in earnings, nor Burger King, nor PepsiCo. Probably only McDonald's could stop McDonald's.

But with all that focus that Don Keough talks about and an army of 840,000 system-wide employees fixated on its operations, McDonald's will in all likelihood still be teaching everyone else a thing or two about service into the next century. The best indication of this probably comes from talking to those throughout the McDonald's system—from Q on down. In those conversations you never get the feeling that there's any sense of victory within McDonald's. These folks are still at war—on all fronts.

GLOSSARY

Adaptable management A firm's management is able to adapt managerial techniques to the unique needs of specific countries.

Adaptive transformative innovations Modify and adjust existing modern technologies (for example, in farming, a modern, more efficient tractor replaces an older, less efficient model).

Badwill What international corporations create when they exploit foreign markets without sharing benefits with locals.

Body language Includes eye-contact, physical distance and touching, hand movements, pointing, and facial expressions.

Cartels Groups of private business agreements to set prices, share markets, and control production.

Circular cultures Believe that since individuals can see what has happened in the past, their past is ahead of them, and since they cannot see into the future, their future is behind them.

Confucianism A system of practical ethics based on a set of pragmatic rules for daily life derived from experience.

Confiscation Occurs when a government seizes foreign-owned assets and does not make prompt, effective, and adequate compensation.

Corporate culture Refers to an organization's practice, such as its symbols, heroes, and rituals, and its values, such as its employees' perception of good/evil, beautiful/ugly, normal/abnormal, and rational/irrational. The practice aspects differs from corporation to corporation within a national culture, and the value aspects varies from country to country.

Countertrade A buyer of a product pays the seller with another product which has the equivalent monetary value.

Cultural shock What expatriates experience after the novelty of living in a new culture wears out.

Culture Comprises an entire set of social norms and responses that condition people's behavior; it is acquired and inculcated, a set of rules and behavior patterns that an individual learns but does not inherit at birth.

Culture-free A theory proposing that managerial behavior is affected by specific situations in all cultures.

Culture-specific A theory proposing that managerial behavior is affected by a nation's culture.

Cultural briefing Educating and orienting the expatriate and his or her family about their temporary foreign home before leaving, including the country's cultural traditions, history, government, economy, living conditions, and so on.

Cultural relativism The belief that no culture's ethics are any better than any other's.

Customization Products are modified to fit the needs of specific markets.

Cybernetic system A system that enables corporations to monitor the activities of its subsidiaries throughout the globe for coordinating purposes.

Diffusion of innovation The process by which innovation is communicated through certain channels over time among members of a social system.

Direct exporting The firm produces at home and creates a division to export to foreign markets.

Domestic enterprises Companies that derive all of their revenues from their home market.

Dual translation Using an interpreter in a country to translate a sender's message into a foreign language and then using an interpreter in the foreign country to translate the message into the sender's language.

Ethnocentric strategy Companies produce unique goods and services which they offer primarily to their domestic market, and when they export, they do not modify the product or service for foreign consumption.

Ethnocentric staffing outlook   Holds that key positions in foreign subsidiaries should be staffed by citizens from the parent company's home country.

Expatriate   A home-country national, usually an employee of the firm, who is sent abroad to manage a foreign subsidiary.

Expropriation   The seizure by a government of foreign-owned assets with prompt, adequate, and effective compensation.

Extortion   An official in a foreign country in a position of power seeking payment from an individual or corporation for an action that the individual or corporation may lawfully be entitled.

Fatalism   A view that individuals cannot control their destiny, that God has predetermined what they are during life.

Five stages of economic development nations go through   A theory proposing that nations advance from an agricultural economy to an advanced industrial economy in five stages.

Foreign Environment   Refers to factors in a country which affect international business, including the country's cultural, legal, political, competitive, economic, and technological systems.

Foreign subsidiary   An international firm's operating unit established in foreign countries which typically has its own management structure.

General Agreement on Tariffs and Trade, now called World Trade Association   A 124-nation organization provides the conditions under which a nation can impose trade barriers, such as tariffs. The new World Trade Organization was created to settle trade disputes.

Geocentric staffing outlook   Holds that nationality should not make any difference in the assignment of key positions anywhere (local subsidiary, regional headquarters, or central headquarters); that competence should be the prime criterion for selecting managerial staff.

Global corporate culture   Corporate core values that cut across all of a firm's subsidiaries located throughout the globe.

Global corporations   International businesses that view the world as their marketplace.

Global manager   An international executive with the ability to manage enterprises in diverse cultures.

Global strategy   A corporation using this strategy uses all of its resources against its competition in a very integrated fashion—all of its foreign subsidiaries and divisions are highly interdependent in both operations and strategy.

Globalization   The notion that in the future more and more companies will have to conduct their business activities in a highly interconnected world, thus presenting their managements the challenge of re-engineering their systems to the extent that they can cope with this new environment.

Goodwill   What international corporations create when they share the benefits derived from the markets they exploit with locals.

Guanxi   A major dynamic of the Chinese society, which refers to special relationships two people have with each other, a relationship where they have agreed to exchange favors.

Hard currencies   Money that is readily acceptable as payment in international business transactions—usually the currencies of industrially advanced countries.

High-context cultures   In the course of business, establish social trust first, value personal relations and goodwill, make agreements on basis of general trust, and like to conduct slow and ritualistic business negotiations.

Host-country national   A resident of the country where the firm's subsidiary is located, or to be located, employed to manage the operations.

I-Ching   A Chinese philosophy which emphasizes that as social beings, people must deal with social responsibilities throughout their lives, and the greatest social welfare is achieved through the joint efforts of individuals creating better social and physical environments in which others can actualize their capacities, and greater value is placed on the ability to lead individuals and groups to cooperative output than on the actualization of one's own individual talent.

Indirect exporting The firm manufactures at home and employs a middle person to export its product(s) to foreign markets.

Individualism Refers to the degree people in a society look primarily after their own interests or belong to and depend on "in-groups."

Inhwa Influences South Korean business behavior, stresses harmony, links people who are unequal in rank, prestige, and power, and stresses loyalty to hierarchical rankings, and superiors being concerned for the well-being of subordinates.

International corporations International businesses that produce products in their home country and export to other countries.

International division A unit established to supervise a firm's exports, foreign distribution agreements, foreign sales forces, foreign sales branches, and foreign subsidiaries.

International environment Refers to groupings of nations (such as the European Union), worldwide bodies (such as the world bank), and organizations of nations by industry (such as the Organization of Petroleum Exporting Countries).

International pricing A managerial decision about what to charge for goods produced in one nation and sold in another.

International product life cycle (IPLC) A theory proposing that many products which are exported to foreign countries are eventually produced abroad, and that foreign producers subsequently obtain a competitive edge over the original producers, forcing them to either create a new product or go out of business.

Jidka A team orientation practiced in Japanese organizations referred to as total quality control (TQC).

Joint-ventures Two or more firms band together to establish operations in foreign markets in order to capitalize on each other's resources and to reduce risk.

Keiretsu Japanese giant industrial groups linked by cross-ownership.

Linear cultures View the past as being behind them and the future in front of them, and view change as being good and attempt to take advantage of business opportunities which they foresee in the future.

Low-context cultures In conduction of business, get down to business quickly, value expertise and performance, like agreement by specific, legalistic contract, and like to conduct business negotiations as efficient as possible.

Lubrication bribes A payment made to an official to facilitate, expedite, and speed up routine government approvals or other actions to which the firm would legally be entitled.

Masculinity Refers to the degree to which people in a society stress material success and assertiveness and assign different roles to males and females.

Master of destiny A view that individuals can substantially influence their future, that they control their destiny, and through hard work they can make things happen.

Monetary barriers Sometimes employed by governments to restrict trade or reduce competition or to encourage certain imports. Monetary barriers occur when governments sell foreign currencies needed to pay for undesired imports at a higher rate than the one charged for currencies needed to pay for desired imports.

Multinational corporations International businesses that establish subsidiaries in foreign markets.

Multidomestic strategy Unlike companies that apply a ethnocentric strategy, firms that apply a multidomestic strategy have a different strategy for each of their foreign markets.

Nationalization Occurs when a government takes over private property—reasonable compensation is usually paid by the government.

Nontariff barriers   Sometimes employed by governments to restrict trade or reduce competition. Nontariff barriers occur when governments impose restrictive and costly administrative and legal requirements on imports.

Normative integration   The headquarters-foreign subsidiary control relationship relies neither on direct headquarters involvement nor on impersonal rules but on the socialization of managers into a set of shared goals, values, and beliefs that then shape their perspectives and behavior.

Overcentralization   Expatriates are unable to establish and maintain an effective relationship with local associates because their authority is constrained by headquarters management overcentralizing decision making.

Polycentric staffing outlook   Holds that key positions in foreign subsidiaries should be staffed by host-country nationals (locals).

Power distance   Refers to the degree people in a society accept centralized power and depend on superiors for structure and direction.

PM theory of leadership   A Japanese leadership theory, the P standing for showing a concern for subordinates experiencing leadership that is oriented toward forming and reaching group goals, and the M standing for leadership that is oriented toward preserving group stability.

Regiocentric staffing outlook   Holds that key positions at the regional headquarters should be staffed by individuals from one of the region's countries.

Regional structure   An international corporate structure wherein regional heads are made responsible for specific territories, usually consisting of multi-countries, such as Europe, Far East, and South America.

Repatriation   Reassigning the expatriate back home.

Reverse cultural shock   What expatriates experience upon returning home after a long assignment in a foreign country.

Ringi   A group-oriented participative decision-making technique used in many Japanese organizations.

Scanning system   A system which enable corporations to monitor the activities taking place in markets throughout the globe for the purpose of responding to changing market needs.

Self-reference criterion   The unconscious reference to one's cultural values.

Sequential oral interpreters   Used by clients involved in cross-language business negotiations and social functions. Unlike simultaneous oral interpreters, they translate both language and culture.

Simultaneous oral interpreters   Used by speakers in formal presentation situations, such as conferences, where the audience and the speaker communicate using a different language.

Social responsibility   The notion that corporations have an obligation to constituent groups in society other than stockholders and beyond that prescribed by law or union contract.

Soft Currencies   Refers to money which is not readily acceptable in international business transactions—usually the currencies of industrially less-advanced countries and of communist countries.

Standardization   Products sold unchanged or only slightly changed in all markets.

Stereotypes   Distinguish a particular culture and its members.

Tariffs and quotas   Often employed by governments to restrict trade or reduce competition. Tariffs are a form of tax imposed on incoming goods, and quotas specify the number of foreign units that can be imported.

Theory T and Theory T+   Complementary theories based on South East Asian assumptions that work is a necessity but not a goal itself, people should find their rightful place, in peace and harmony with their environment, absolute objectives exist only with God, and in the world, persons in authority positions represent God, so their objectives should be followed, and people behave as members of a family and/or group, and those who do not are rejected by society.

Third-country national   A resident of a country other than the home-country or host-country assigned to manage a firm's foreign subsidiary.

Time equals money   The perception of people in some cultures that time is a commodity and an asset, and high importance is placed on it.

Transformative technological innovations Replace traditional technologies (in farming, a tractor replaces the plow).

Uncertainty avoidance   The extent people in a society tolerate uncertainty and ambiguity.

United States Foreign Corrupt Practices (FCPA)   Makes it illegal for U.S. citizens and businesses to practice the act of bribery in the conduction of business not only in the U.S. but in other countries as well, even when it is an acceptable or expected business practice there.

Universalism   A rigid global yardstick by which to measure all moral issues.

Wa   A Japanese concept which necessitates that members of a group, be it in a work team, or a company, or a nation, cooperate with and trust each other.

Whitemail bribery   Payments made to induce an official in a foreign country who is in a position of power to give favorable treatment where such treatment is either illegal or not warranted on an efficiency, economic benefit scale.

Wholly-owned subsidiary   The firm establishes a subsidiary in a foreign country maintaining 100 percent ownership; unlike joint ventures, risks are not shared.

NAME & COMPANY INDEX

SUBJECT INDEX
